BULBS

A COMPLETE HANDBOOK

BULBS

A COMPLETE HANDBOOK
OF BULBS, CORMS AND TUBERS

ROY GENDERS

ROBERT HALE & COMPANY
LONDON

ISBN 0 7091 3156 9

Robert Hale & Company
63 Old Brompton Road
London, S.W.7

PRINTED IN GREAT BRITAIN BY
RICHARD CLAY (THE CHAUCER PRESS), LTD.,
BUNGAY, SUFFOLK

CONTENTS

I HISTORY, CULTURE AND CHARACTERISTICS

Bulbs of the Near East—earliest bulbs grown for their beauty—bulbs of the seventeenth century—decline of the bulb—the modern bulb-growing industry —bulbs of South Africa and of the New World

Description of a bulb—a corm—a tuber—a rhizome—families: Liliaceae— Alliaceae — Amaryllidaceae — Techophylaeaceae — Iridaceae — Ranunculaceae — Fumariaceae — Begoniaceae — Oxalidaceae — Primulaceae — Gesneriaceae

Methods of propagation—growing from seed—lifting and dividing established plants—growing on bulblets and cormlets—growing from bulbils—propagation by scales—propagation by leaf cuttings—propagation by division of tubers— propagation by basal incisions—propagation of tubers by cuttings—propagation of rhizomes

To make a wild garden—plants for a calcareous soil—lilies in the woodland garden—planting and care of the bulbs—trees and bulbs for an acid soil

Bulbs in the lawn—correct planting depths—a chamomile 'lawn'

Plants and bulbs for a calcareous soil—bulbs for a sun-baked soil—shrubs and bulbs for an acid soil—care of the shrubbery

ILLUSTRATIONS

COLOUR

CREDITS

Reproduced by courtesy of Blackmore & Langdon Ltd: 4a, 4b, 4c; Walter
Blom & Son Ltd: 5a, 6, 7a, 7b, 8, 9a, 9b, 11, 10b, 13a, 13b, 14, 17, 18, 21a,
21b, 23a, 23b, 24, 25, 26a, 26b, 29a, 29b, 30c, 32; Garrod & Lofthouse
Ltd: 2a, 2b, 5b, 15, 16a, 16b, 16c, 16d, 19, 20, 22a, 22b, 27, 30a, 30b, 31;
Thompson & Morgan (Ipswich) Ltd: 1, 3, 10a, 28; W. J. Unwin Ltd: 12a,
12b, 12c, 12d.

ILLUSTRATIONS

BLACK AND WHITE

Ruffled miniature gladiolus.

Hymenocallis tubiflora. Bulbs of *Iris reticulata.*

Iris reticulata blooms. *Iris danfordiae. Iris hoogiana.* Dutch iris.

Ismene calathina.

(between pages 464 and 465)

Leucocoryme irioides. Lilium candidum.

Lilium auratum. Lilium regale.

Muscari botryoides album. Muscari tubergenianum.

Narcissus bulbocodium conspiruus. Narcissus telamonius plenus.

Daffodil, Music Hall. *Narcissus triandrus albus.* Narcissus, La Riante. Narcissus Semper Avanti.

Narcissus poetaz. Narcissus tazetta. Trumpet Narcissus. Large-cupped Narcissus.

Bulbs of Ornithogalum species. *Ornithogalum umbellatum* blooms.

Ornithogalum arabicum. Ornithogalum nutans.

Oxalis adenophylla.

Polianthes tuberosa. Puschkinia scilloides.

Scilla tubergeniana. Scilla sibirica.

Planting tulips in fibre. Late double tulip blooms.

Lily-flowered tulip.

Tulipa tarda. Tulipa turkestanica.

Tulipa kaufmanniana. Tulipa biflora.

Springtime colour: tulip beds.

CREDITS

The author wishes to thank the following for providing black and white illustrations: J. E. Downward (Begonias, *Erythronium dens-canis* on the rockery, Miniature ruffled gladiolus); H. Smith (*Polianthes tuberosa*); C. G. Van Tubergen (Anemone, *Camassia, Eucharis amazonica, Freesia refracta, Gladiolus grandis, Hymenocallis, Iris hoogiana, Ismene calathina, Leucocoryme irioides, Lilium regale, Muscari tubergenianum*); and particularly Mr John Gledhill who provided the remaining photographs.

LINE DRAWINGS IN THE TEXT

ACKNOWLEDGEMENTS

I would like to thank all those who have helped me with illustrations. Details of the sources are given in the lists in the preceding pages. Without their co-operation it would have been impossible to convey the range of colour obtainable from bulbs and corms. As with my other books Mr John Gledhill has produced a splendid collection of black and white pictures, many of them taken specially for this book. The line figures were drawn by my son, W. A. C. Genders.

R. G.

TO
MY BROTHER
A. C. GENDERS M.A.
SCHOLAR, SPORTSMAN AND FRIEND

PART I

HISTORY, CULTURE AND CHARACTERISTICS

I

Early History

Bulbs of the Near East—earliest bulbs grown for their beauty—bulbs
of the seventeenth century—decline of the bulb—the modern bulb-
growing industry—bulbs of South Africa and of the New World

More species of bulbs and corms are to be found growing in the Middle East
and south-eastern Europe than in any other part of the world. If a circle be
drawn with Istanbul as the centre and taking in Greece and Bulgaria, Syria and
the Lebanon, Persia and Afghanistan and neighbouring countries, it will be
seen that many of the most popular of flowering bulbs grow within that area.
They were the first bulbs to reach the western world. From Persia and northern
Arabia came *Crocus sativus*, the saffron, which was grown for the product
obtained from the stigma and which had more uses than any other commodity
with the possible exception of flax. Saffron was used to dye garments; it was
used to flavour and colour food; and in a tenth-century Saxon leech-book it is
written 'when he baths, let him smear himself with oil, mingled with saffron'.
No monastic foundation was without it for it was often used instead of gold leaf
in the illumination of missals. Theophilus, writing in the tenth century, gave
these instructions: 'If you wish to decorate your work in some manner, take tin
pure and finely scraped; melt it and wash it and apply it with glue upon letters
you wish to ornament with gold. When you have polished it with a tooth, take
Saffron, moisten with white of egg and when it has stood a night, cover with a
pen those places you wish to gild.'

Saffron bulbs or the finished product may have reached Britain with the
Romans. It was reintroduced in the middle of the fourteenth century by Sir
Thomas Smith, Secretary of State to Edward III, who began its commercial
culture in his native village, now Saffron Walden. This was the time when bulbs
first came to be imported into Britain and western Europe from the Near East,
for it was the beginning of trading contact with that part of the world. It is,
however, possible, that a number of bulbs may have been brought back to
England and France by the returning Crusaders in the twelfth century.

The reign of Edward III saw the beginning of the cloth industry and saffron
was needed for its colouring. Before Edward died, Chaucer had made two visits to
Italy on the King's behalf and he may have brought various bulbs back with him.

The earliest bulbs to be introduced into western Europe were obtained entirely for their food value, for gardens were almost non-existent. A small plot of land grew only a few herbs and some vegetables, and the rest of the householder's requirements was made up from those plants which grew naturally about the countryside. Bulbs and roots were the most prized of all plants because they were easily transported. Hence the value which those of the East placed upon plants with scented roots, like the violet-scented iris of Florence and spikenard, the root of *Valeriana jatamansi*, which could be carried many hundreds of miles without loss of condition. For the same reason was great value put upon aromatic seeds which grew in southern Europe and which reached Britain with the Roman invasion.

Earliest Bulbs Grown for Their Beauty. With the first of the Tudors and the return to more peaceful days after the Wars of the Roses, gardens came to be made by cottager and lord of the manor; and with the stimulation of overseas trading, many new bulbous plants reached Britain, mostly from south-eastern Europe and the Near East. One such introduction was the tulip, a native of northern Persia, which was first observed in 1554 by Busbecq, Ferdinand I's ambassador to Constantinople. He sent bulbs to Vienna and to Prague with the information that the Turks charged large sums for the blooms which greatly resembled the Eastern turban. In 1559 Conrad Gesner reported having seen the tulip growing in Augsburg, in the garden of John Herwart, 'flowering with a single beautiful red flower, large, like a red lily, formed of 8 petals of which 4 were outside, the rest within. It had a very soft, sweet and subtle scent . . .'. Twenty years later it reached England, Thomas Hakluyt stating (1582) that 'within these four years there have been brought into England from Vienna divers kinds of flowers called tulips'. By that time they must have become relatively inexpensive for a bill in the possession of the Marquis of Salisbury at Hatfield House of 'roots, flowers, seeds, trees and plants' purchased by John Tradescant (then his gardener) for the marquis, shows an item 'for tulip roots purchased at Haarlem at 10s. 100'. By the early seventeenth century in France and Holland, however, the demand for tulip bulbs had reached astronomical heights. Ten million pounds was paid for bulbs grown in the city of Haarlem and to this day the city has remained the centre of the Dutch bulb industry. The first named tulip was *Semper Augustus* which was sold by its raiser for 4,600 florins, together with a new carriage and two horses and harness!

Gervase Markham in *The English Husbandman* (1613) described those plants used to decorate knot gardens—soon to be replaced by French-style parterres, really knots of more intricate design. Among these plants was the tulip, and Markham suggested that in every bed should be planted 'flowers of one kind and colour such as . . . several coloured hyacinths, as the red, the blew, and the yellow or several coloured Dulippos [tulips] and many other Italian or French flowers'. He goes on to say that 'as soon as these flowers shall put forth their beauties, if you stand a little remote from the knot, you shall see it appear like a knot made of divers coloured ribbons, most pleasing and most rare'.

The hyacinth was one of the earliest of bulbs to reach England, arriving about 1560, soon after the visit of Anthony Jenkinson to Persia on a trading mission. It may have reached England by way of Russia for Jenkinson obtained the exclusive right to import foreign commodities into Russia, and shortly after Lefechin found it there, bearing purple-blue and yellow flowers.

The oriental hyacinth grew in the Botanic Gardens in Padua, soon after its opening in 1543. It may have been introduced from Persia at about the time of Jenkinson's journey. Gerard, writing in 1597, said that these 'jacints have been brought from beyond the seas . . . from the East, whereof they took their name orientalis'.

Another bulbous plant to reach England at about the same time was the crown imperial. It reached Europe in 1576, sent by Charles de L'Ecluse (Clusius) who was employed by Emperor Maximilian II of Austria for the sole purpose of collecting bulbs from the Near East. Clusius was on friendly terms with Sir Francis Drake to whom he may have sent bulbs, for shortly after Drake had completed his circumnavigation of the globe in 1580, the crown imperial was to be found in several of London's most famous gardens. Gerard said, 'this plant hath been brought from Constantinople, among other bulbous roots and made denizons in our London gardens, whereof I have great plenty'. Chapman, translator of Homer writing in the same year spoke of 'Fair Crown Imperial, Emperor of Flowers'.

Shakespeare may have known the plant growing in Gerard's Holborn garden which he would no doubt often have visited when he lodged in nearby Silver Street only 15 minutes walk away, past the church of St Bartholomew the Great and the City Temple. As Gerard said he had 'plenty', he may have given bulbs to Shakespeare, to plant in the garden of New Place, Stratford-on-Avon, which he had purchased long before his retirement there in 1610. In *A Winter's Tale*, which the playwright wrote shortly after his return to his home town, he mentions his love for the flowers which grew in his garden. Perdita says:

> I would I had some flowers o' the spring. . . .
> . . . bold oxlips and
> the crown imperial; lilies of all kinds,
> The flower-de-luce being one.

Shakespeare rightly observed that the crown imperial bloomed in spring, usually by 18th March, day of St Edward, king and martyr, to whom the flower is dedicated. Writing twenty years later, Parkinson began his *Paradisus* (1629), which he dedicated to Henrietta Maria, queen of Charles I, with a description of this plant, saying that 'for its stately beautifulness, it deserveth the first place in our Garden of Delight'.

Several lilies also reached Britain at the same time and from the same place. Of *Lilium chalcedonicum*, the scarlet turk's cap, Gerard said: '[it] groweth wilde in the fields and mountains, many days journey beyond Constantinople', and he tells that it was first sent to this country 'by Master Harbron, Ambassador there, unto my honourable good lord and master, my Lord Treasurer of England who bestowed them on me for my garden'.

Bulbs of the Seventeenth Century. The asphodel and anthericum also reached England during Elizabethan times, the roots of the former lily being a popular food when boiled. Many bulbs followed early in the seventeenth century. *Crocus aureus* of Greece reached Gerard from Jean Robin, gardener to the King of France, and by Parkinson's time there were 27 species of crocus which he illustrates in the *Paradisus*. The modern gardener knows mostly the large flowering Dutch hybrids, yet those known to Parkinson are available today and extend the flowering season with their beauty. The same may be said of the muscari, the grape hyacinth, native of south-eastern Europe and Asia Minor, several of which were known to Gerard and many more to Parkinson. Gerard described *M. botryoides* 'as consisting of many little bottle-like blew flowers, closely thrust together like a bunch of grapes, of a strong smell yet not unpleasant', and it was to be found in many London gardens, growing with the scillas or starry jacinths, 14 of which were to be found in gardens at the end of the sixteenth century.

A number of bulbs came from Spain early in the seventeenth century. Gerard knew *Narcissus hispanicus*, the Great Spanish daffodil and *N. jonquilla*, the jonquil, the double form of which was known to Parkinson. Like the angel's tears daffodil, *N. triandrus*, they are native of the Pyrenees, home of most of the daffodil species and, like so many of the early introductions, were plants of dwarf, compact habit, ideally suited to the knot gardens of the times.

By the time Parkinson published his great work, flowering bulbs were so popular that he devoted 200 pages to their description, with illustrations of the species. Perhaps the popularity of bulbs was due to their flowering season, for many came into bloom as winter ended and continued during springtime, almost all of them being able to withstand the rigours of the British climate for, though of warmer parts, many came from higher mountainous regions where the bulbs were cold and dry in winter and baked by the summer sunshine, ideal conditions for most bulbous plants.

In 1665 John Rea, a nurseryman of Bewdley in Worcestershire, published the first book setting out designs for garden beds displaying bulbs to the best advantage. In his *Flora, Ceres and Pomona*, the designs fit into the angles of a walled garden. In the corners, he advised planting 'crown imperials, martagon lilies and other tall flowers; in the middle of the squares, great tufts of paeonies, and around them several sorts of cyclamen; the rest to be planted with daffodils, and hyacinths. The straight beds [borders] are fit for the best tulips. Ranunculus and anemones also require particular beds. The rest may be set with ordinary sorts of tulips, fritillaries, bulbous iris and other kinds of good roots.'

Sir Thomas Hanmer, friend of John Evelyn, writing about the same time, gives instructions for the cultivation of tulips: 'Set them in the ground about the full moon in September, about 4 in deep and set the early flowering ones where the sun may come hot on them. Let the earth be mold taken from the fields, or where woodstacks have been, and mix it with a fourth part of sand. Make your beds at least half a yard thick of this mold.' Hanmer also advised planting tulips in beds to themselves, but he added, 'you may put some anemones with them on the outside of the beds'. Rea also advised planting anemones for spring display, a suggestion which could be followed with advantage in the small garden of today for anemones are as hardy as tulips.

By this time, with the restoration of the monarchy and the French influence, which coincided with the era of Vanbrugh, gardens began to take on a new look. Vanbrugh's houses, of vast proportions, demanded gardens of corresponding size as at Blenheim and Castle Howard. Abraham Cowley wrote:

> When lavish art her costly work had done,
> The honour and the prize of bravery
> Was by the garden from the Palace won.

Parterres were made at the front of the house and were formed into beds of the most intricate designs, to be filled with the larger flowering bulbs for spring display. This part of the garden was above the level of the landscaped park from which it was divided by a low terrace wall, permitting one to admire the distant view. William Kent carried this new gardening a stage further, dispensing entirely with walls so that lawns displaced flower beds, harmonising with the parkland and expressing Kent's passion for imitating nature.

Decline of the Bulb. Kent's ideas were followed by those of 'Capability' Brown who, about the middle of the eighteenth century, designed the gardens at Castle Ashby, Blenheim and Croome Court, dispensing almost entirely with flowering plants for garden decoration. The agreement he made with Lord Scarborough in 1774 for the alterations to the gardens and landscape at Roche Abbey contains no mention of any flowering plants apart from trees. Brown had an imitator in Humphrey Repton, who carried the new ideas of landscaping to small villa gardens, a practice condemned by J. C. Loudon in his *Hints on the Formation of Gardens* (1812). At that time cast iron for constructional work was coming to be appreciated, and both Repton and Loudon showed their enthusiasm for its use in the construction of greenhouses. This was first put into practice at Chatsworth, home of the Dukes of Devonshire, by Joseph Paxton, head gardener there, in 1826.

Soon after his arrival at Chatsworth, Paxton was supervising the construction of several glasshouses to accommodate the many exotic plants which were now reaching Britain from all parts of the world. These included orchids and begonias from South America; camellias from Japan and the Phillipines; the gardenia and plumbago from North America; pelargoniums and heaths from the Cape. The plants needed protection and warmth during the winter months in the cooler climate of Britain, but their novelty and brilliance of colour ensured their immediate popularity for summer display in the garden, while for spring, pot-grown azaleas and rhododendrons, brought into bloom under glass, took the place of bulbs and the more familiar spring-flowering plants.

In his book, *Hardy Florist's Flowers*, James Douglas tells how the tulip was saved from extinction by a small band of enthusiasts, members of the Manchester Botanical and Horticultural Society. He tells how 'this gorgeous flower, once held in such esteem both in Britain and in Europe is now but little grown south of the Trent or north of the Tweed yet . . . as late as 1854, Mr Groom of Clapham Rise, catalogued show tulips at enormous prices', a single bulb of Duchess of Cambridge being listed at £100. James Douglas says, 'the following year the whole of Mr Groom's collection (a quarter of a million) was sold at auction at very low prices, and from this the tulip declined in the public favour at a rapid rate, due to the system of bedding-out new and more tender plants'.

The tulips of the Manchester florists were the 'broken' or feathered ones so well described by Francis Thomson:

> Then comes the tulip race, where beauty plays
> Her idle freaks; from family diffused
> To family, as flies the father dust,
> The varied colours run; and while they 'break'
> On the charmed eye, th'exulting florist marks,
> With secret pride, the wonders of his hand.

With the Victorian love for pageantry and ostentation carried through to the garden, most bulbs continued to be neglected until the ending of the Second World War when the high price of labour and of fuel made it difficult for all but the very wealthy to maintain a heated greenhouse filled with those plants which required to be lifted and replanted each year after wintering under glass. It was then that the hardy bulb and those plants which could tolerate adverse climatic conditions took on a new popularity. This popularity meant the advance of the bulb-growing industry in Lincolnshire, commenced by Mr J. T. White during the latter years of the nineteenth century. In 1928 the Royal Horticultural Society conferred on Mr White the Victoria Medal of Honour in recognition of his pioneer work in the building of the British bulb industry.

The Modern Bulb-growing Industry. According to official returns, some 7,000 acres were devoted to the growing of bulbs in England and Wales in 1968, the greater acreage being in Lincolnshire, particularly in the Spalding area where bulb-growing is linked with farming. Though large numbers of hyacinths are cultivated for the dry bulb trade, tulips and daffodils are the most important, for each year large quantities are grown for the cut-flower markets.

The bulb-flower season in the British Isles is usually long. Forced daffodil and tulip bloom begins to arrive at Christmas-time and continues until the end of March. Early in the new year large quantities of outdoor daffodil and anemone bloom begin to arrive from the Scilly Isles and Cornwall with Lincolnshire bloom following early in spring. Each year, the cut-flower crop is worth many millions of pounds.

Bulbs of South Africa. It was not until Kew sent Francis Masson to collect plants in Cape Province in 1772 that this important bulb-growing area came into prominence. If southern Europe was the home of the family Liliaceae, in southern Africa was found most of the families Iridaceae and Amaryllidaceae, among which were many genera previously unknown to European gardeners. Masson arrived at the Cape with Captain Cook and was left there, meeting Carl Thunberg, a pupil of Linnaeus, whom he accompanied on his journeys to the interior. Thunberg, a Swede, remained in southern Africa for three years and is looked upon as the 'father' of South African botany. With him went Dr Spaarmann; and later, Sir John Barrow covered the same ground, as did William Burchell early in the nineteenth century but it was not until the union of the South African states that a full botanical survey of the area was undertaken. South Africa and Rhodesia is amply supplied with flowering bulbs, including 24 genera and 230 species of the genus *Amaryllis*.

First to reach Britain was the vallota or Scarborough lily, discovered by Masson. It is native only of the district between Cape Town and Port Elizabeth, where lie the Outeniqua Mountains, while the equally handsome belladonna lily is to be found growing wild in the western side of Cape Province, where it bears its flowers of delicate pink early in spring. Near Cape Town, Thunberg collected *Crinum longifolium* and *C. moorei*, both plants of the woodlands. Crossed together, they have given us that lovely hybrid, *C. powellii*. Closely related is cyrtanthus, native of the Transvaal where it is known as the fire lily, for it usually appears after large areas of scrubland have been burnt. From late autumn until spring it covers the ground with its drooping scarlet bells on their 12-in (30·5-cm) stems. Hardy only in those parts which enjoy warm climatic conditions, it is a striking plant for a cool greenhouse.

The torch lilies (haemanthus) of the same family and which splash the Drakensbergs with their flowers of red, yellow and orange, grow under similar conditions. In contrast is the blue African lily, *Agapanthus umbellatus*, which inhabits the lower slopes of Table Mountain together with those species of gladioli known as the 'painted ladies'. Like the homerias and moreas, they are of the Iris family, several being included among those first discoveries at the Cape sent back by Masson.

Several of the gladioli species are sweetly scented. Sweetest of all is the blue Afrikander, *Gladiolus recurvus*, which bears flowers of shades of blue and mauve, the lower petals being marked with gold. But of greater importance was the finding of *Gladiolus primulinus* by Frank Fox in 1904. He was supervising the bridging of the Zambesi River at the Victoria Falls when he found in the mist created by the falling water, a flower of pale-yellow colouring, a colour not previously seen in the gladiolus, and its stamens were protected from the wet by an attractive hooded petal. When exhibited at the Royal Horticultural Society in 1906, it caused a sensation and was taken up by breeders in all parts of the world, including James Kelway and W. J. Unwin in Britain. As well as passing on its dainty hooded petal and its small neat flowers, it was soon apparent that *G. primulinus*, so called because its colour so nearly resembled that of the primrose, was to bring an entirely new colour range to gladioli, and varieties soon appeared in shades of orange, flame, pink and orchid-brown. The first *primulinus* of quality was raised in the United States by James Taylor and was named *Zona*. Its deep-pink flowers have a striking yellow throat and it was the forerunner of many lovely varieties.

Among other plants of the same family is the ixia, discovered by Thunberg in the Roode-Land Valley. *Ixia maculata* reached Europe in 1779 and with it came the *Watsonia* and *Sparaxis*. The sweetly scented *Freesia refracta*, which grows wild on the south-eastern tip of Cape Province, reached Britain in 1852, the year Livingstone began his famous journey. It was neglected until the end of the century when Robert Armstrong, after completing his travels in southern Africa, sent to Kew a species bearing a deep-pink flower. *Freesia armstrongii*, as it was named, was crossed with *F. refracta* by F. H. Chapman and G. H. Dalrymple, who introduced a wide range of named hybrids, but it was not until Mr J. C. Eauwens of Offenham took up freesia culture commercially in the mid-1930s that the flower began to achieve the popularity it now enjoys.

Bulbs of the New World. Native plants of South America began to reach Europe towards the end of the eighteenth century. They were tuberous rooted rather than bulbous. One example was the dahlia. In 1789 seed was sent by Cervantes of the Botanical Gardens of Mexico City to the keeper of the Royal Gardens in Madrid and from where it was introduced into England by the Marchioness of Bute. At about the same time, the lily of the Incas, *Alstroemeria caryophyllaceae*, had reached Spain, to be followed in 1830 by the Peruvian lily, *A. aurantiaca*. Like the tigridia which had arrived shortly before, the *Alstroemeria* is of the lower mountainous regions of Chile and Peru and, though of the lily family, has long tuberous roots, like the dahlia and potato.

Known to Europeans in the sixteenth century, the tigridia, called the tiger flower from its numerous spots, was reported in the *Botanical Magazine* (which carried an illustration of it) as having been introduced into Britain in 1801 by a Mr Hodgson of Liverpool. Also from Mexico came *Polianthes tuberosa* with its tuberous-looking bulbs and flowers of outstanding perfume which were in demand for evening wear during Victorian times.

Among the first of the bulbous plants to reach Europe from North America was *Lilium canadense*. It is to be found on the Eastern seaboard of North America, from Nova Scotia, as far south as Georgia where it grows in moist meadows and swamplands. It may have been brought into Europe by John Tradescent. In 1737 John Bartram, the American botanist, sent to the Chelsea Physic Garden *L. philadelphicum* and *L. superbum*, both of which are to be found in deciduous woodlands from Ontario to North Carolina. *L. superbum* was painted by Redouté and quickly established itself in Europe for, growing up to 8 ft tall and enjoying both shade and moisture, it was most suitable for the wild garden as advocated by William Robinson and Gertrude Jekyll in place of the bedding-out schemes which were so popular with the early Victorians.

From North America at an earlier date came the dog's-tooth violet, *Erythronium americanum*, and though Parkinson may have been the first to grow it in Europe, it had evidently not flowered by the time the *Paradisus* appeared. Unlike the European *E. dens-canis*, it bears yellow flowers mottled with purple and inhabits damp woodlands extending from Nova Scotia to Florida, where during springtime it is as common as the primrose in England. It may have been the first of bulbous plants to reach Europe from the New World, since Parkinson says that bulbs came to him from Virginia. *E. origanum* and *E. californicum* of the Pacific West came later as did other plants from the western states of America. In 1827 the camassia was found by David Douglas, a Scotsman who had previously discovered the Douglas fir (named after him) in the same area. Douglas found the camassia near the Columbia River where the Indians made use of its bulbs as a valuable winter food. Shortly after his American discoveries, the young botanist met with a horrible death in the Sandwich Islands, where he had gone plant hunting. Falling into a camouflaged pit prepared for the trapping of wild animals, he was ferociously attacked and killed by a wild bull.

Growing with the camassia along the Pacific West from British Columbia south to Mexico is to be found the calochortus or mariposa lily, which also reached Europe early in the nineteenth century. The plant is prominent in California where the tulip-like flowers of deep yellow, white, purple or scarlet, colour the higher mountainous slopes during summertime as if daubed with paint. With them bloom the 'blue dicks', the brodiaeas, which bear their flowers in loose umbels.

There was, during the seventeenth century and later, a two-way exchange of bulbs between North America and Europe for by the early years of the seventeenth century, the Dutch East India Company was firmly established in Barbados and in North America, where the company's fort at New Amsterdam (now New York) was situated at the mouth of the Hudson River. Among the large volume of Dutch shipping trading between Europe and North America were bulbs, especially the tulip which by that time was greatly in demand throughout the world. By the mid-seventeenth century, Dutch settlers were established on Long Island and in New Jersey, where it is recorded, each possessed 'a patch of cabbages, and a bed of tulips'. Manors, as large estates were called, came to be granted to individuals during the latter half of the seventeenth century and were planted with box trees for privacy and protection and with bulbous plants of all descriptions, including 'tall red lily-like tulips'. At this time, English settlers in Virginia, mostly supporters of the vanquished Stuarts, founded large estates, the gardens of which they planted with all manner of bulbs. These were taken with them out of Britain, for bulbs are the most easily transported of all plants and quickly re-establish themselves almost anywhere.

2

Botanical Characteristics of Bulbs, Corms and Tubers

Description of a bulb—a corm—a tuber—a rhizome—families:
Liliaceae—Alliaceae—Amaryllidaceae—Techophylaeaceae—Iridaceae
— Ranunculaceae — Fumariaceae — Begoniaceae — Oxalidaceae —
Primulaceae—Gesneriaceae

BULBS, corms and tubers contain within themselves a dormant plant, together
with sufficient nutriment to provide sustenance during early stages of growth.
Whether this is so will depend upon the ability of the plant during the previous
year to fortify itself from a balanced diet. This, in turn, is passed down to the
underground bulb or corm to continue the sequence. Though bulbs, corms and
tubers have similar functions, they differ in several ways.

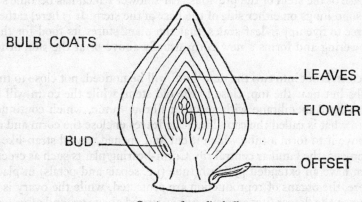

BULB COATS

LEAVES

FLOWER

BUD

OFFSET

Section of a tulip bulb

Description of a Bulb. A bulb is an underground stem surrounded by thick
overlapping scales, really modified leaves, which retain food in the form of
starch and sugar, collected by the leaves and roots of the previous year's growth.
This enables them to support the embryo stem until the plant is able to form
new roots of its own. Many bulbous plants, such as hyacinth, tulip and narcissus,

are provided with a thin outer protective tunic which becomes 'dry' when the bulbs are out of the ground for any length of time. This drying of the tunic will not be harmful to the bulb and the future flower stem if the bulb is stored in a dry, airy place, for the embryo stem is situated near the centre of the bulb, enclosed in layers of leaf scales. With lilies, the outer tunic is absent.

While the tulip dies back after flowering, the narcissus and hyacinth do not, but continue to increase in size each year. They form new bulbs around the base, which also continue to increase in size.

With bulbous plants it is of the utmost importance that the foliage be allowed to die back before it is removed, while the bulbs or corms should not be lifted from the ground for any reason until such time as the foliage has completed its proper functions, otherwise the embryo stem will have insufficient food for its development.

If a bulb is cut into halves from apex to base the embryo stem will be clearly observed almost at the centre. It will be seen to form a continuation of the basal disc from which the roots develop. From this embryo stem is formed the flower and leaves. It will also be noticed that nearer the base and slightly to one side is the embryo 'bud', which in the tulip becomes the new bulb and the embryo stem the following year. Its vigour will depend upon the amount of nutriment the bulb can store from the previous year after it has finished flowering.

A Corm. While bulbs are mostly oval or pear-shaped with an elongated neck, a corm is usually flat both at the top and at the bottom and is really the underground base of the stem of the previous year's flower which has become swollen like two solid lungs on either side of the base of the stem. It is here, rather than in the three to five upper leaf scales, that the plant stores its food for the next year's flowering and forms a new corm usually above or at the side of the old one.

If the corm is cut into two the new 'bud' will be noticed, not close to the base as in bulbs but near the top, close to the old stem, while the corm will be enclosed in a hard membrane with an outer fibrous tunic, which continues upwards into what is called the cap. The scale leaves enclose the corm and appear to rise above it to form a tube which if cut and opened, reveal strap-like leaves with, in crocus, the familiar central rib. Corm-bearing plants such as crocus and colchicum have an extended perianth tube (i.e. sepals and petals) in place of a stem. Here, the organs of reproduction are protected, while the ovary is below ground when the flower first appears, but is carried above ground after fertilisation.

Unlike bulbs, which in most instances continue to increase in size each year, a corm usually withers after flowering. The base of the stem, however, continues to increase in size as it stores up food and moisture to form the new corm in which the young 'bud' will eventually become the flowering stem, while at the base new roots are formed. The procedure continues each year, the vigour of the new corm depending upon the culture given to the plant during its growing season.

With the colchicum, a foot-like appendage at the base of the tuber-like corm is formed, and at the top there is an upper projection with a groove, in the base of which the new bud is formed. Though botanically a corm, the underground portion of the colchicum has a tuber-like appearance, being vertical rather than flattened and round.

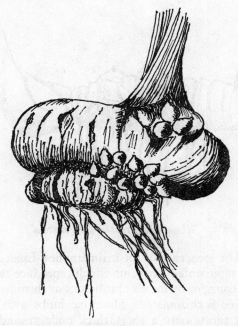

Gladiolus corm showing old and new corm and cormlets

A Tuber. A tuber is the swollen part of an underground stem which may only be an extension of a thick root. Like bulbs and corms, it has leaf scales but these may be almost invisible, while the main body is solid. It is here that the supply of food is stored. It is often difficult to distinguish between a tuber and a corm. *Anemone coronaria* and cyclamen are usually sold as corms, though they are really tubers; while *Erythronium dens-canis*, the dog's-tooth violet, is often described as bulbous, though it, too, forms a tuber.

From the underside of the tubers, roots are formed and search out for a considerable distance for nutriment and moisture with which to fortify the tubers. By means of chlorophyll in the leaves, the food obtained by the roots is converted into food more readily absorbed by the plant and is stored in the scales of a bulb or in the fleshy part of corm and tuber.

A Rhizome. A rhizome is similar to a tuber but differs in one main respect; it spreads by underground stems from which arise above ground new flowering stems as in convallaria, the rootstock forming a few scales. In iris, the leaves are produced from the end of the rhizomes, each leaf sheathing a younger one at the base. In sisyrinchium, the rhizome is short and may be little more than 1 mm in length at the end of which is a bunch of fibrous roots.

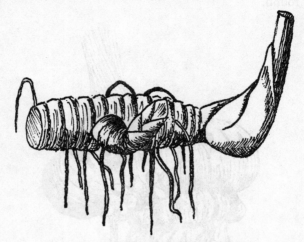

Rhizomatous root of polygonatum

Families. As will be seen, each of the main families, Liliaceae, Amaryllidaceae and Iridaceae are represented by plants which reproduce themselves either by forming a bulb or corm, or by means of tuberous or rhizomatous roots. Thus in Liliaceae, convallaria is rhizomatous, lilium has bulbs with overlapping scales, while anthericum forms only a short thick underground stem, difficult to define.

In Amaryllidaceae, narcissus forms a scaly bulb, alstroemeria is tuberous rooted, while pauridia of southern Africa is one of the smallest of all corm-bearing plants—hence its name from the Greek, *pauridios*, meaning 'very small'.

Of the family Iridaceae, most are either rhizomatous or corm-bearing as in the genus *Iris* (which is also bulbous), while gladiolus and crocus are corm-bearing. Bulb-forming plants in the Iridaceae are, with the exception of *Iris xiphium*, rare though several are of shrubby habit with fibrous roots as in the bobartias of Table Mountain.

Almost all those plants represented by the three main families which store up their food requirements by means of swollen underground roots are not dependent upon sunlight to produce flowers and leaves, though once they have flowered sunlight is necessary for the conversion of the nutrition in the leaves and roots to suitable plant food, to be stored underground during the dormant period. Sunlight is also necessary to ripen the bulb or corm. When once these requirements have been provided, many bulbs will bear flowers without the aid of sunlight, soil or moisture. The colchicum is the obvious example, for if the dried tubers are placed on a window ledge with a northerly aspect, they will, under ordinary room temperatures, begin to bear bloom almost at once. Many species of crocus, too, will come into leaf and bloom in a similar way, though it is more satisfactory if the base of the corm is in contact with water into which it can send out new roots—as is also the case with hyacinths. Special glass containers are obtainable for this purpose, and enable bulbs and corms to be brought into bloom without soil or fibre. After flowering, the plants should be set out in the open ground, or planted in pots or boxes of soil and placed in the open to enable the underground rootstock to be replenished.

Almost all the world's bulb and corm-bearing plants belong to the order Liliflorae comprising six chief families:

  (i) Juncaceae
 (ii) Liliaceae
(iii) Alliaceae (intermediate between (ii) and (iv))
 (iv) Amaryllidaceae
  (v) Tecophilaeaceae
 (vi) Iridaceae.

Of the remainder, the tuberous *Anemone*, *Eranthis* and *Ranunculus* are of the family Ranunculaceae; the *Cyclamen* of the family Primulaceae; the *Begonia* of the family Begoniaceae; while Gesneriaceae is represented by *Achimenes*, *Gloxinia* and *Gesnera*.

Juncaceae, inhabiting the temperate and cooler regions of the world including the Antarctic, are mostly rhizomatous plants of rush-like habit resembling grasses and do not come within the scope of this book.

Liliaceae (genera 250; species about 3,700). One of the largest families of flowering plants, it is distributed throughout the world. Most are perennial herbs growing from a bulb or a rhizome as in polygonatum; convallaria. Occasionally, a genus may produce a tuber or corm, as in colchicum, or reproduction may be from bulbils formed in the axils of the leaves, as in certain lilies. Only rarely do they reproduce themselves by stolons as with *Tulipa sylvestris*. Those forming bulbs reproduce themselves by forming new bulbs in the axils of the bulb scales which replace the old bulb. The leaves are produced in radical tufts or may appear at the end of or along the branches.

The flowers are usually hermaphrodite, borne in a racemose or a cymose (as in allium) inflorescence. In certain genera solitary terminal flowers occur, as in *Tulipa*. The perianth is petaloid consisting of six segments; occasionally

B

sepaloids with the six stamens attached to the base of the segments. The ovary is superior and three-celled. The fruit is a capsule or an indehiscent berry, the seeds containing fleshy endosperm.

Pollination is by insects which come to search for nectar usually secreted from glands situated at the base of the perianth leaves (petals) or in its absence for pollen, as in *Tulipa*. Those in which it is secreted have open flowers in which the honey is readily accessible. They are visited by Diptera (flies) and by other short-tongued insects. Those genera where the flower forms a pendulous bell—e.g. *Fritillaria, Scilla, Convallaria*—rely upon bees for their fertilisation, though these are the most heavily scented members of the family. It would seem that at one time they were adapted to visits from Lepidoptera or have retained their scent to attract pollinators to their woodland habitat. Those which rely mostly upon Lepidoptera for their pollination are those members of the genus *Lilium*, bearing white or pale-yellow flowers.

The plants are mostly of the temperate regions of the world, predominating in North America, Europe and central Asia, where they inhabit deciduous woodlands or short grassy slopes, growing in full sunlight. There are several exceptions to this: *Gloriosa*, which climbs by means of leaf appendages being native of tropical Asia and Africa; and *Aloe*, a succulent plant, native to tropical Africa and Madagascar. Very few genera are to be found in Australia and New Zealand and these are mostly of climbing habit like *Geitonoplesium*, native of Queensland and of several Pacific islands, and *Thysanotus*, both of which have tuberous roots. Only the spring-flowering *Anguillaria*, a genus confined to sub-tropical Australia, is a bulbous herb, and it is rarely seen away from its native land.

The family Liliaceae has been divided (by Engler; later by Bentham and Hooker) into 11 to 12 sub-families, based mostly on their vegetative habit.

(i) Melanthioides. The plants form a corm or rhizome and bear their flowers in a terminal inflorescence. Represented by about 40 genera which inhabit the tropical forests of south-eastern Asia and are also present in the Arctic (*Tofieldia*). *Petrosavia* is a leafless root-parasite, while *Gloriosa* is of climbing habit and is present in tropical Asia and Africa. Only one, *Colchicum*, a tuber-forming plant of some 30 species, has garden value though others will beautify the greenhouse. Native of the Mediterranean region and eastern Asia, *C. autumnale*, the autumn crocus, is present in the British Isles and central Europe where it is to be found growing in meadows and on hilly slopes.

(ii) Herrerioideae. Represented only by the genus *Herreria*, a tuberous-rooted climbing plant, bearing its flowers in short racemes and native of Brazil.

(iii) Asphodeloideae. Rhizomatous plants (rarely tuberous or bulbous) with leafy branched stems and bearing their flowers in a terminal inflorescence with the perianth leaves free or united. The fruit is a capsule, rarely a berry. Represented by 70 genera including *Asphodelus, Hemerocalis* and *Paradisia* of southern

Europe; *Kniphofia* and *Aloe* of southern Africa; *Funkia* (*Hosta*) of China and Japan.

(iv) Allioideae. Bulbous or rhizomatous plants bearing their flowers in a cymose umbel and enclosed by a pair of narrow bracts. This sub-family is represented by 30 genera and 600 species but chiefly by *Allium* with about 450 species, native of central and southern Europe, North America and Mexico and the Near East; *Brodiaea* of Pacific West America; *Agapanthus* of southern Africa. (This sub-family is now usually given separate classification.)

(v) Lilioideae. Bulbous plants with a stem having one or more leaves and bearing their flowers in a terminal inflorescence or raceme (singly in *Tulipa*). Represented by the family including *Lilium* and *Fritillaria* scattered throughout the northern temperate regions of the world and *Tulipa* in central Europe and Asia.

(vi) Scilloideae. Bulbous plants, closely related to Lilioideae except that their flowering stems are leafless. The genera include *Scilla*, *Endymion* and *Ornithogalum*, present in the British Isles and central Europe, the Near East and southern Africa; *Hyacinthus* and *Muscari*, mostly eastern Mediterranean.

(vii) Dracaenoideae. Fibrous-rooted plants with an erect stem crowned with leathery leaves and flowers borne in panicles, the perianth leaves free or united at the base, the fruit a berry or capsule. Represented by yucca, an ornamental garden plant in Central and South America; *Dracaena* and *Cordyline* in tropical Africa and Asia; *Sansevieria* in tropical Africa and India.

(viii) Asparagoideae. Rhizomatous plants, in *Asparagus*, the leaves reduced to scales and represented, in addition to *Asparagus*, by *Convallaria*, *Maianthenum* and *Polygonatum* of northern temperate regions, particularly North America, northern Europe and the British Isles, and which bear their dangling bell-shaped flowers in loose cymes.

(ix) Ophiopoganoideae. Plants with a short rhizomatous or tuberous rootstock and with narrow basal leaves. The flowers are borne in racemes, the perianth leaves being free or united. Represented chiefly by *Ophiopogon*, native of the Himalayas, Japan and south-east Asia.

(x) Aletridoideae. Plants with short rhizomatous roots and bearing narrow radical leaves. Perianth leaves free or united; anthers dehiscing semi-introrsely. Seeds numerous. Represented only by the genus *Aletris* with 25 species distributed throughout eastern Asia and in North America.

(xi) Luzuriagoideae. Shrubs of erect or climbing habit and bearing their flowers in terminal cymes, the perianth whorls usually alike. Fruit a berry. Represented by *Luzuriaga*; *Lapageria*, climbing plants of South America and New Zealand.

(xii) Smilacoideae. Shrubs of climbing habit with net-veined leaves and bearing their flowers in small axillary umbels or in terminal panicles. Represented by *Smilax* with 200 species, mostly tropical. The family Liliaceae is linked to Amaryllidaceae through *Allium*, now a separate family Alliaceae.

TABLE I. *Chief plants of the family Liliaceae*

Genus	Natural distribution	Species
Albuca	South Africa	50
Anthericum	Southern Europe, South Africa	300
Aphyllanthes	Southern Europe, South Africa	1
Arthropodium	Australasia, Madagascar	9
Asparagus	Warmer parts of Old World	300
Asphodeline	Southern Europe	15
Asphodelus	Southern Europe to Himalayas	12
Blandfordia	Eastern Australia	5
Bulbine	Tropical and South Africa	55
Bulbocodium	Southern Europe	1
Calochortus	North-west and central America	60
Camassia	North America	5
Chionodoxa	Crete, Cyprus, Asia Minor	6
Colchicum	Southern Europe, central Asia, India	65
Convallaria	Northern temperate regions	1
Daubenya	South Africa	1
Dichopogon	Australia	2
Dipcadi	Mediterranean, Africa, Madagascar	55
Disporum	Northern temperate Asia and America	20
Drimiopsis	Tropical and South Africa	22
Endymion	Western Europe	10
Eremurus	Western Asia (Himalayas)	50
Eriospermum	Southern Africa	80
Erythronium	Southern Europe, Asia, North America	25
Eucomis	Tropical and southern Africa	14
Fritillaria	Northern temperate regions	85
Galtonia	South Africa	4
Gloriosa	Tropical Africa, Asia	5
Gonioscypha	Western Asia (Himalayas)	2
Hemerocallis	Europe, Asia	20
Hosta	China, Japan	10
Hyacinthus	Southern Europe, Asia Minor, South Africa	30
Ipheion	Mexico, South America	25
Lachenalia	South Africa	65
Lilium	Northern temperate regions	80
Littonia	Tropical and South Africa	8
Lloydia	British Isles	1
Merendera	Asia Minor, Afghanistan	10
Muscari	Southern Europe, western Asia	60

TABLE I—*Continued*

Notholirion	Persia, western Asia, western China	6
Ornithogalum	Temperate regions of Old World	150
Paradisia	Southern Asia, Tibet	2
Polygonatum	Northern temperate regions	50
Puschkinia	Western Asia	2
Sandersonia	South Africa (Natal)	1
Scilla	Europe, Asia, South Africa	80
Trillium	Southern Asia, Japan, North America	30
Urginea	Mediterranean, Africa, India	100
Uvularia	Eastern North America	4
Veltheimia	South Africa	6

Alliaceae (genera 30, species about 600). Perennial bulbous or rhizomatous herbs intermediate between Liliaceae and Amaryllidaceae. They have the superior ovary of Liliaceae and the umbellate inflorescence of Amaryllidaceae. Almost all the genera of this order were at one time classified under Liliaceae.

The largest genus is *Allium*, 450 species, which includes *A. cepa*, the onion (Persia and Asia Minor) and the flowering garlics, distributed throughout the

TABLE II. *Chief plants of the family Alliaceae*

Genus	Natural distribution	Species
Agapanthus	South Africa	5
Allium	Northern Hemisphere	450
Bessera	Southern United States, Mexico	3
Bloomeria	Western United States	3
Brodiaea	Western North America	30
Leucocoryne	South America (Chile)	5
Nothoscordum	North and South America	35

Northern Hemisphere. They are mostly bulbous (rhizomatous as in *Agapanthus*) with linear leaves and bear their flowers in cymose umbels. In a number of genera, bulbils are formed in the axils of the leaves as flower replacements and from which the plant is reproduced. Distribution is cosmopolitan except Australasia but is mostly confined to the northern temperate regions of the world and to South America, as with *Bloomeria, Leucocoryne*. Fertilisation is by bees, sand-wasps, flies and Lepidoptera, the honey as in *Allium ursinum* being secreted by the ovary in the three notches between the carpels.

TABLE III. *Plants of the family Amaryllidaceae*

Genus	Natural distribution	Species
Alstroemeria	South America	50
Amaryllis	South Africa	1
Ammocharis	Tropical and South Africa	5
Anoiganthus	Tropical and South Africa	2
Boophone	South and east Africa	5
Bravoa	Mexico	7
Brunsvigia	Tropical and South Africa	15
Caliphruria	South America	2
Calostemma	Australia	4
Chlidanthus	South America	1
Cooperia	United States, Mexico, Brazil	9
Crinum	Tropics and sub-tropics	100
Cyrthanthus	Tropical and South Africa	47
Eucharis	Tropical and South America	10
Eurycles	Malaysia, north-east Australia	3
Eustephia	South America (Peru)	6
Galanthus	Europe	20
Gethyllis	South Africa	20
Griffinia	South America (Brazil)	7
Habranthus	South America (Brazil)	20
Haemanthus	Tropical and South Africa	50
Hippeastrum	Tropical America	75
Hymenocallis	Sub-tropical America	50
Ixiolirion	Western Asia	3
Leucojum	Southern Europe, northern Africa	12
Lycoris	Himalayas to Japan	10
Narcissus	Europe, western Asia	60
Nerine	South Africa	30
Pancratium	South-eastern Europe, tropical Asia, southern Africa	15
Phaedranassa	Chilean Andes	6
Placea	South America (Chile)	5
Polyanthes	Mexico	1
Sprekelia	Mexico	1
Stenomesson	Tropical America	20
Sternbergia	Asia Minor, Caucasus	8
Urceolina	Chilean Andes	5
Vallota	South Africa	1
Zephyranthes	Tropical America, West Indies	40

Amaryllidaceae (genera 85, species about 1,000). Mostly bulbous perennials, native of the warmer parts of both hemispheres, with radical leaves which appear in spring. The inflorescence is usually borne on a leafless scape with the flowers (one to many) arranged in cymes, subtended by spathe-like bracts. The plants are occasionally rhizomatous rooting and sometimes are shrubs.

The flowers are hermaphrodite, regular or zygomorphic. The perianth is in two similar whorls, the petals usually united to form a long or short tube; the anthers introrse. The stamens usually number six, opposite the perianth segments. The ovary is inferior and three-chambered, each chamber containing two or more ovules. The fruit is a capsule, rarely a berry, the seeds covered in a fleshy endosperm.

White is the dominant colour as in *Galanthus, Leucojum, Narcissus, Eucharis, Pancratium*, members of the sub-family Amaryllidoideae which mostly rely upon night-flying Lepidoptera for their pollination, though bees may visit the flowers at those times when Lepidoptera are not prevalent. Self-fertilisation is also possible in the absence of insects as in *Galanthus, Leucojum*.

The family is represented chiefly by *Narcissus*, native of the British Isles (*N. pseudo-narcissus*) and of the western Mediterranean regions; also by *Galanthus*, native of south-eastern Europe, and *Leucojum*, of the British Isles and central Europe—which differs from *Galanthus* in bearing more than two leaves and numerous flowers. The plants may form new bulbs each year when the fleshy scales of the old bulbs become exhausted of nourishment. With *Narcissus* and with *Crinum* and *Amaryllis*, natives of southern Africa and Australia, the bulbs may reach large proportions, increasing in size each year.

The family is also represented by *Agave*, mostly native of desert lands of North America and Mexico; by *Alstroemeria*, rhizomatous plants native of Chile; and by *Vellozioides*, woody plants of the tropical regions of Brazil, Africa and Madagascar.

Several genera are corm-bearing, e.g. *Spiloxene*, which inhabits damp meadows and marshlands in southern Africa and produces a fleshy conical cone covered in fibrous scales; and *Empodium*, which has a corm with netted scales covered in blunt spines.

Tecophilaeaceae (genera 6, species 22). Somewhat intermediate between Liliaceae, Alliaceae and Iridaceae with characteristics resembling each. Perennial herbs with corms or tubers, distributed throughout Pacific North and

TABLE IV. *Plants of the family Techophylaeaceae*

Genus	Natural distribution	Species
Cyanella	South Africa	7
Tecophilaea	South America (Chile)	2

South America and southern Africa. The leaves are alternate, mostly radical; flowers regular or zygomorphic. Inflorescence racemose as in *Cyanella*; perianth segments six, free; stamens six, perfect or one to three reduced to staminodes. Ovary inferior, usually three-celled, a many-seeded capsule when ripe. Corms fibrous-coated as in *Cyanella*, native of southern Africa and in *Tecophilaea*, native of the Chilean Andes.

Iridaceae (genera 60, species about 800). Perennial herbs, distributed throughout the temperate and warmer regions of the world and reproducing themselves by means of an underground corm or rhizome, rarely a bulb, though several are shrubs. They are distinguished by their sword-like leaves sheathing at the base. They are often two-ranked with the upper also sheathing. The flowers are hermaphrodite, borne in cymes or spikes, or they may be terminal and solitary as in *Crocus, Sisyrinchium*. The perianth segments number six and are arranged in two whorls, free or united at the base to form a tube. The stamens number three and are opposite the outer perianth segments. The ovary is inferior and three-chambered, with the style usually dividing into three (or six) branches which are sometimes petal-like. The fruit is a capsule with the embryo enclosed in a fleshy endosperm.

The family may be subdivided into three main families:

(i) Sisyrinchieae. Here the spathe is solitary flowering with the two perianth whorls sub-equal. The leaves are linear or filiform, arranged in several rows. The genera comprise *Crocus, Romulea*, native chiefly of southern Europe and Asia Minor (*Romulea* of southern Africa), several species of *Crocus* being autumn and winter flowering; while *Sisyrinchium* with about 100 species is native of North America (and the West Indies), being prominent on grassy hillsides from Newfoundland to British Columbia and in the United States of Virginia, Nebraska and Utah. It is also prominent in the Falkland Isles. Here the perianth petals are united at the base to form a tube into which nectar is secreted around the base of the style. Pollination is by Lepidoptera (nocturnal in certain species of *Crocus*) and by Hymenoptera (bees), though in *Crocus* self-pollination is possible as pollen from the anthers falls on the stigmas situated immediately beneath the anthers as they unfold.

(ii) Ixieae. Mostly corm-bearing plants with a terminal leafy stem ending in the inflorescence. The spathe is single-flowered. The leaves are formed in two rows. The principle genus is *Gladiolus* with 150 species, mostly native of southern Africa but extending into Europe with *G. illyricus*, native of the British Isles. *Ixia* and *Freesia*, native of southern Africa, bear heavily scented flowers and are grown commercially for cutting.

(iii) Irideae. Widely distributed plants which grow from a corm, rhizome or bulb and usually produce a leafy stem ending in the inflorescence, the spathes being two- to many-flowered. The leaves are arranged in two rows.

TABLE V. *Plants of the family Iridaceae*

Genus	Natural distribution	Species
Acidanthera	Tropical and South Africa, Madagascar	40
Anapalina	South Africa	7
Anomalesia	South Africa	2
Antholyza	Tropical and South Africa	25
Aristea	Tropical and South Africa, Madagascar	60
Babiana	Tropical and South Africa	60
Bobartia	South Africa	17
Chasmanthe	Tropical and South Africa	7
Crocosmia	Tropical and South Africa	6
Crocus	Europe, Asia Minor	75
Cypella	Mexico, Argentina	15
Engysiphon	South Africa	8
Exohebea	South Africa	13
Ferraria	Tropical and South Africa	2
Freesia	South Africa	20
Galaxia	South Africa	6
Geissorhiza	South Africa, Madagascar	65
Gladiolus	Throughout Old World	300
Herbertia	Southern United States, South America	8
Hesperantha	Tropical and South Africa	50
Hexaglottis	Tropical and South Africa	5
Homeria	Tropical and South Africa	37
Homoglossum	Tropical and South Africa	20
Iris	Northern temperate regions	300
Ixia	South Africa	45
Lapeyrousia	Tropical and South Africa	60
Libertia	New Guinea, Australasia, western South America	10
Micranthus	South Africa	3
Moraea	Tropical and South Africa	100
Rigidella	Mexico, South America (Peru)	4
Romulea	Southern Europe, South Africa	90
Schizostylis	South Africa	2
Sisyrinchium	Southern United States, South America, West Indies	100
Sparaxis	South Africa	4
Streptanthera	South Africa	2
Synnotia	South Africa	5
Syringodea	South Africa	8
Tigridia	Mexico, South America (Chile)	12
Tritonia	Tropical and South Africa	55
Watsonia	South Africa, Madagascar	60

The largest genus is *Iris* with more than 200 species, distributed throughout the northern temperate regions of Europe and Asia and with *Iris versicolor* present in North American marshlands and in damp meadows from Newfoundland and Manitoba, south to Florida. Australia is represented by only two genera, *Patersonia*, a rhizomatous plant limited to tropical parts and the grass-like *Libertia*, present throughout Australasia. *Patersonia* extends north into Indonesia.

Ferraria is present in tropical Africa; *Morea* in the Cape Peninsular with *Tigridia* native of Mexico and South America.

Ranunculaceae (genera 50, species 800). It is of the order Ranales which includes the families Magnoliaceae and Myristicaceae, among the most primitive plants to inhabit the earth, many of which are provided with resinous oil cells in their bark and foliage. Also included is the family Ranunculaceae, among which is included the *Ranunculus*, *Anemone*, *Eranthis* and *Paeonia*, tuberous-rooted plants inhabiting the cooler regions of the world. A family of 50 genera which have a thickened rootstock, tuberous or rhizomatous as in *Anemone*, *Eranthis*, *Paeonia*. The leaves are palmately lobed and there is often present a whorl of three stem leaves beneath the flower. The flowers are borne solitary. Petals and sepals number five and usually have a nectar-forming duct at the base. *Anemone coronaria*, *Eranthis* and *Ranunculus* are native of southern Europe, the Levant and Asia Minor; *Paeonia officinalis* of northern Europe, Asia and Pacific North America.

TABLE VI. *Plants of the family Ranunculaceae*

Genus	Natural distribution	Species
Anemone	Cosmopolitan	150
Eranthis	Europe, Asia	7
Paeonia	Europe, Asia, western North America	33
Ranunculus	Cosmopolitan	400

Fumariaceae (genera 16, species 450). Closely related to the order Ranales in that they have pinnately divided leaves and hypogynous flowers with free petals and stamens. Tuberous-rooted perennials resembling Ranunculaceae in this respect, though in *Corydalis bulbosa* of the family Fumariaceae, the plants form a bulb. *C. cava* has excessively swollen tuberous roots.

Native of the northern temperate regions and of eastern and southern Africa, where they are to be found high up on rocky slopes. They bear their flowers in terminal racemes.

Begoniaceae (genera 5, species about 1,000). Of the order Peponiferae, native of the tropical regions of the Old and New World, plants of the family Begoniaceae are succulent herbs, often of climbing habit. Though the family includes four other genera, it is composed almost entirely of the genus *Begonia*, perennial herbs forming an underground rhizome or tuber. The stems are succulent and brittle. The leaves are arranged alternately in two rows with large stipules which persist after the leaf has fallen. The tubers are often formed in the axils of the leaves.

The flowers are monoecious and are borne in an axillary inflorescence. The anthers are two-chambered and dehisce by slits. The two or three styles are united at the base and forked. The fruit is a horned capsule with the seeds the most minute of all flower seeds.

The family mostly inhabits damp tropical forests of South America, India and the Malayan Archipelago; those with corm-like tuberous roots are native of the higher mountainous regions of the Andes and of southern Africa.

Oxalidaceae (genera 3, species about 900). Included in the order Geraniales are the families Oxalidaceae and Tropaeolaceae, both closely related to the Pelargonium and which form tuberous or bulbous roots. The family Oxalidaceae differs from Geraniaceae in that the stamens are united at the base and in its mode of shedding its fruit. The family contains only three genera of which *Oxalis* is by far the most widely represented with more than 800 species, mainly distributed in southern Africa and South America and with *Oxalis acetosella*, the wood sorrel, native of the British Isles. A number of tuberous-rooted species come within the scope of this book.

Of the family Tropaeolaceae, native of the Chilean and Peruvian Andes, *T. speciosum*, the hardy scarlet flame flower, has tuberous roots.

Primulaceae (genera 20, species about 1,000). Largest family of the order Primulales, which includes the genus *Primula* of about 500 species, distributed over the cooler regions of the earth's surface; also the genus *Cyclamen* with 15 species, present in the Mediterranean region with *C. europeum* distributed as far north as the British Isles. The species form large tubers (corms), *C. neapolitanum* often assuming saucer-size when well-established and forming its roots on the upper surface. Separate species will bloom at different periods of the year and often have attractively mottled or veined leaves, which are heart-shaped and borne on long petioles. The flowers have reflexed petals and are pendent. After fertilisation the stem coils up, forcing the seed receptacle into the ground.

Gesneriaceae (genera 120, species about 2,000). Herbaceous or woody plants mostly of tropical and sub-tropical areas, those of the sub-family Gesnerioideae forming a thick tuberous rhizome. The leaves simple with an entire or serrated margin and often covered in silky hairs. Stipules absent. The showy tubular flowers are borne solitary in the leaf axils, or in a cymose inflorescence. Closely

TABLE VII. *Plants of the family Gesneriaceae*

Genus	Natural distribution	Species
Achimenes	Tropical America	50
Gesneria	Tropical America, West Indies	50
Gloxinia	Tropical America	6
Niphaea	Mexico, West Indies, Cuba	5
Sinningia	South America (Brazil)	20

allied to Scrophulariaceae, those of the sub-family Gesnerioideae include *Achimenes*, native of tropical America; *Sinningia* (*Gloxinia*) of Brazil; and *Gesneria*, native of the West Indies. All require greenhouse culture in the British Isles and northern Europe.

3
Propagation

Methods of propagation—growing from seed—lifting and dividing established plants—growing on bulblets and cormlets—growing from bulbils—propagation by scales—propagation by leaf cuttings—propagation by division of tubers—propagation by basal incisions—propagation of tubers by cuttings—propagation by cutting the rhizomes

---

Methods of Propagation. Bulbs, corms and tuberous-rooted plants may be propagated by one or more of several methods:

(i) By sowing seed. This is done when raising new varieties; and where a stock of plants is to be obtained from those which readily respond to this inexpensive method of propagation, e.g. *Ixia*, *Freesia*.

(ii) By lifting and dividing the roots as with *Asphodelus*, *Alstroemeria*; or by dividing the clumps into numerous offsets (bulbs or cormlets) as with *Scilla*, snowdrop, montbretia (*Crocosmia*). This is necessary not only to increase the stock of named varieties but should be done every three or four years to maintain the vigour of the plants.

(iii) By the removal of the 'spawn'. These are small cormlets which usually form at the base of a corm as in *Gladiolus* and *Crocosmia*; or bulblets as in *Vallota*, *Lily* and *Hippeastrum*. They are removed when lifting the bulb or corm and are detached and grown on, to flower in two years or more.

(iv) By planting bulbils, which in certain species of lily form in the axils of the leaves. Treated like cormlets or bulblets, they will bloom about their fourth year.

(v) By planting scales that occur, for example, in lilies and which are removed from the base of the bulb to be grown on in a cold frame or greenhouse when they will form roots at the base.

(vi) By taking leaf cuttings. The leaves are removed with a short piece of stalk and are rooted in a sandy compost as for *Gesneria* and *Gloxinia*; or with a small piece of tuber attached to the leaf stalk as with *Cyclamen* and *Begonia*.

(vii) By dividing the tuber with a sharp knife into several pieces, each containing an 'eye', which will grow on to form a flowering plant in 12 to 18 months as with *Begonia*, *Anemone*, *Cyclamen*.

(viii) By making incisions at the base of the bulb as with hyacinth. The bulbs are placed on the bench and in six months tiny bulblets will form where the cuts were made.

(ix) By producing cuttings by inserting tuberous roots in a suitable compost in gentle heat.

(x) By cutting the rhizomatous roots into sections as with *Iris*.

Growing from Seed. This is the most inexpensive method of raising a stock of bulbs or corms, and is to be recommended for those plants which will grow readily in this way. Seed may be obtained from specialist growers—e.g. the freesia growers of southern Africa—or from wholesale or retail seedsmen of reliable reputation. In America most seeds are produced in California, where the seed is ripened after long hours of warm sunlight; other producers are in southern Africa, where similar conditions prevail. Almost every bulb or corm raised from seed demands slightly different treatment and this is given with the descriptions of each plant in Part II. There are, however, general lines to be laid down for raising seedlings.

The seed must be ripe when gathered and it must be carefully stored until ready for sowing. This should be done with the minimum of delay, when once the seed has been removed from the capsule. Seed is not fully ripe until the receptacle has turned brown and is hard and dry with the chambers opening. The capsules should then be removed with a pair of scissors and placed on a sheet of clear white paper in a dry, airy room where they remain until all moisture has been dried off. The seeds are then emptied from the capsules and placed in small wooden boxes until ready to sow either in autumn where a warm greenhouse is available, or early in spring, if sowing in a frame or in boxes or pans outdoors. It is not advisable to sow seed until there is sufficient warmth to bring about its germination. The John Innes Sowing Compost is suitable for the germination of almost all seeds. It is made up of

> 2 parts sterilised loam
> 1 part peat or leaf mould
> 1 part coarse sand ⎫per bushel
> 1½ oz of superphosphate of lime
> ¼ oz chalk or ground limestone ⎭

The compost should be freshly prepared for the superphosphate, which promotes vigorous root action, will soon lose its strength, while loam which has been long sterilised may have become recontaminated with weed seeds and disease spores. The chalk or ground limestone is necessary to counteract any acidity of the peat or leaf mould but should be omitted for Gesneriaceae which prefer an acid soil.

Before filling the containers, they should be checked for cleanliness. Pans or pots must be scrubbed clean while the boxes should not previously have been used for sowing seed. Seed pans or boxes require ample drainage before filling with compost. Cover the drainage holes with crocks to prevent the holes being choked with compost. When filling the containers, the compost should be in a friable condition so that it may be made firm after filling the containers to within ½ in of the top. Make the surface quite level so that the small seeds are not covered too deeply in some parts and their germination hindered. Also, if the compost is not made level, moisture will tend to drain to the lower levels, leaving the seeds (or seedlings) on the higher parts deprived of moisture.

Seedlings may be raised in the sunny window of a warm room where the seed may be sown fully a month before the climate is suitable for sowing outdoors. The modern room with its 'picture' windows to ensure maximum warmth and often with central heating also available is a suitable place in which to raise seedlings and to grow the plants. Where large numbers are to be raised from seed, a cold frame will be a necessity. This may occupy a place in the garden or on a veranda or terrace, and may be obtained complete with wooden base and a light ready to use. The frame will be available to accommodate the seed pans or boxes and to grow the seedlings after transplanting, while bulbs or corms may be brought into bloom at all periods of the year. To assist drainage, the pots or pans should be stood on a layer of shingle at the bottom of the frame.

For quick germination of those seeds which have a reputation for being difficult to germinate and for those which require stove temperatures—e.g. Gesneriaceae—an electric propagator to supply the necessary bottom heat will be a necessity. There are several on the market suitable to use inside a greenhouse or garden room where there is insufficient heat to raise many of the bulbs and corms which require higher temperatures to ensure rapid germination. There are also several makes of propagator of a size suitable for use in the window of the home. Highly efficient is the Kwikseed propagator of laminated fibre glass. It may be connected to 200/250 volt AC or DC mains, the element being sealed into the plastic to eliminate any fear of shock. Temperature and ventilation are controlled by glass sheets which slide into position in grooves. A temperature of 70° F (21° C) may be maintained.

The seeds of most bulbs and corms are small, begonia seed being the smallest of all seeds, and care must be taken with their sowing. Place the seeds on a piece of clean white paper, then, using a pencil or smooth piece of wood or bone, scatter the seeds evenly over the surface of the compost. Sow thinly so that the seedlings do not grow weakly and 'drawn' as they compete with each other for moisture and plant food. Each should have space to develop.

Cover the seed with a thin sprinkling of compost, sufficient only to exclude light. Then water lightly, so that the compost is not washed off the seeds and cover with a piece of clean glass or thermo-plastic sheeting to hasten germination. If the direct rays of the sun cause the compost to dry out too rapidly, provide shade by whitening the glass or that of greenhouse or frame but this is usually necessary only in warmer areas.

Keep the surface comfortably damp but not wet, and if in dull weather moisture does not evaporate, give no more water until it does so. For the compost to be kept excessively damp will be to cause the seed to decay before germination or the young seedlings to die back. The compost must be kept in a friable condition so that air may reach the roots of the seedlings.

The most satisfactory way to water is to immerse the base of the container rather than to water from the top. The pan or box should be allowed to stand in the water for several minutes whenever necessary and until such time as the moisture reaches the surface. In this way, neither the seeds nor the compost covering them will be disturbed by water sprinkled from a can. For the same reason, the glass should be removed each day and the moisture drops wiped away before they can fall on to the compost.

Where sowing in a warm greenhouse—and this is necessary where raising hothouse plants in a cool climate—a temperature of 65° to 70° F (18° to 21° C) should be provided during winter and spring. If this is not possible, sowing should be delayed until the natural heat of the sun is able to maintain this temperature. Seed of those plants requiring cooler conditions will germinate readily in a sunny window or frame if sown in spring.

Seedlings should be moved as soon as large enough to handle, either into deeper boxes, spacing them 2 in apart, or to pots where they are planted 1 in apart around the edge. Their transplanting should be done with a smooth stick or cane, gently loosening the compost from about the roots and replanting as quickly as possible into the John Innes Potting Compost. This is made up of

7 parts fibrous sterilised loam
3 parts peat or leaf mould
2 parts coarse sand

to which is added (per bushel) the John Innes Base consisting of:

2 parts hoof and horn meal
2 parts superphosphate of lime
1 part sulphate of potash
¾ oz ground limestone.

The compost should be sterilised before adding the Base and for lilies, cyclamen and Gesneriaceae, leaf mould should be used instead of peat and the limestone omitted.

Do not empty the box of its contents too soon if, after possibly several months, there is no sign of any seeds germinating. Some seeds take as long as a year to germinate, especially if the seed was not fresh and if insufficient warmth was provided. If the seeds are taking an unduly long time, the pans or boxes should be placed in the open for several weeks, completely unprotected and exposed to severe frost, then given a temperature of 70° F (21° C). As with the seeds of certain alpine plants, the shock of moving from excessive cold to warmth will often bring about germination when other methods fail.

When transplanting, the seedlings should be set well down in the compost with their first or lower leaf just above soil level. Make comfortably firm before watering. Water whenever the surface of the compost appears to be drying out but never give more moisture than the action of the roots can utilise or sunlight can take up by evaporation.

After two to three months, the young plants will be ready for moving to individual pots or to open-ground beds which have been prepared in advance. The compost should now be increased in strength. Some decayed (or de-hydrated) cow manure which is supplied in a dry state by most bulb firms may be added to the John Innes Potting Compost, while the Base may be used at double strength to enable the plants to be grown on without any check as to their diet.

A word about ventilation. At no time should the seedlings be kept in unduly humid and stuffy conditions. Most are plants of the lower mountainous slopes of western Asia, southern Europe or southern Africa. They are to be found growing among rocky outcrops and meadowlands where the soil is sparse and drainage is ample and where their flowers are exposed to sunlight and cold air of lower alpine regions. Ample ventilation must be provided, especially for the corm-bearing plants such as freesias and ixias. Being natives of southern Africa and being among those plants more easily raised from seed, they will not tolerate a humid atmosphere once germination has taken place. From that time onwards, the young plants should be given more and more fresh air but pro-tected from draughts.

The seed of a number of bulbs which will germinate easily may be sown in the open ground. The gladiolus and ixia may be raised in this way, while the Dutch growers raise many millions of anemone tubers each year from seed sown in drills in the open. Select a sunny situation and bring the soil to a fine tilth. Humus materials such as hop manure, peat, decayed cow manure or the clearings from ditches should be incorporated and before sowing give a 1 oz per square yard dressing with superphosphate of lime to encourage vigorous root action.

The seed is sown in early spring in shallow drills made only 1 in (2·5 cm) deep and allowing 9 in (23 cm) between the rows to permit regular hoeing after the seed has germinated. Sow thinly, cover with soil and water gently. From this time the soil must not be allowed to dry out or germination will be delayed. When the seed has germinated, move the hoe between the rows to stir up the ground and to prevent the formation of weeds. Then, when the seedlings are large enough to handle, transplant them to beds of prepared soil and to an open, sunny position. Here they will grow on to make pea-size corms or bulbils which are lifted in autumn. They are dried and wintered in a frost-free room until planted out the following spring when several genera may bloom early in summer. Gladioli will take another two years before they bear bloom but anemones and freesias will bloom within 18 months of sowing.

TABLE VIII. *Length of time from sowing to blooming*

These plants will bloom within 12 to 24 months of sowing the seed:

Achimene	Gloriosa
Allium	Gesneria
Anemone	Lapeyrousia
Begonia multiflora	Nomocharis
Cyclamen	Ixia
Freesia	Sparaxis

These plants will bloom within three years of sowing the seed:

Antholyza	Nerine
Brodiaea	Homeria
Bulbocodium	Ixiolirion
Chasmanthe	Ornithogalum
Chionodoxa	Oxalis
Endymion	Ranunculus
Hippeastrum	Watsonia

These plants will bloom within four years of sowing the seed:

Alstroemeria	Gladiolus
Camassia	Hymenocallis
Chlidanthus	Lilium
Colchicum	Muscari
Crocosmia	Puschkinia
Eranthis	Tigridia
Galanthus	Tulipa

These plants take four to five years to come into bloom from seed:

Brunsvigia	Iris reticulata
Calochortus	Leucojum
Crinum	Moraea
Crocus	Narcissus
Erythronium	Pancratium
Eucomis	Sternbergia
Hyacinthus	Scilla

A number of hardly bulbous plants will in certain seasons produce and sow their own seed in the open, no plant being more accommodating in this respect than *Cyclamen europeum*. After fertilisation, the flower stalk coils spirally, drawing the seed receptacle to the ground where it deposits its seed when ripe. The seedlings may be moved to wherever they are required to bloom after the seed has germinated the following year.

Lifting and Dividing Established Plants. It is mostly the bulbous plants and those with tuberous roots, members of the family Liliaceae and Amaryllidaceae, that require lifting and dividing every five to six years for they continue to increase in size, in addition to forming small bulbs at the base which will also increase in size, thus exhausting the soil where overcrowded. If left without attention, the result will be a gradual deterioration of quality of bloom, while those bulbs at the centre of each clump will die back, deprived of nourishment and moisture. Some bulbs resent disturbance and may be left many years without lifting. But *Narcissus* and *Lilium* (especially *L. martagon*), the scillas and ornithogalums in particular, soon become overcrowded and if after five to six years the original plants are lifted, they will be found to have formed clumps as large as a dinner plate in circumference. Snowdrops also increase rapidly under cool conditions.

Where growing in grass, lifting may prove difficult. First, the turf should be removed above the bulbs and this is done during the latter weeks of summer when the foliage has died down.

First, cut out a circle of turf around the bulbs of about 12 in (30·5 cm) diameter. This is done with a sharp spade and to a depth of about 2 in (5 cm) so that the circle of turf can be lifted away, to be replaced later. Then insert a garden fork at the outer edge of the circle and loosen the clump to a depth of about 9 in (23 cm). Lift out, place in a deep box and shake the soil off the bulbs, which may then be gently pulled apart. The often decayed bulbs at the centre should be discarded, the others planted into new ground. Clumps of the smaller flowering bulbs, such as the narcissus species, the scillas, snowdrops and snowflakes, are best lifted and divided before they have finished flowering and the clumps split up into several 'pieces' or clusters, each with a number of small bulbs attached. They should be replanted at once. In this way there will be little or no loss of flowers the following year as there would be if very small individual bulbs are replanted, and which may take several years to reach flowering size.

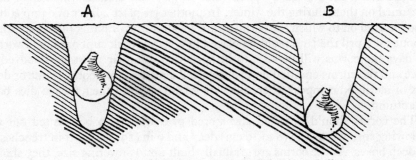

(A) wrong and (B) correct method of planting a bulb

The small clusters are planted by first lifting the turf with a spade and planting to the correct depth before replacing the turf with the foliage of the plants left exposed. Tread firmly to exclude any air pockets.

Very large clumps of bulbs may be divided in the same way as used to divide the old rootstock of herbaceous plants. Two forks are placed back to back in the root or cluster of bulbs and the handles forced apart so that the clump is divided into two, each part of which may be subdivided by 'teasing' apart with the hands.

Growing on Bulblets and Cormlets. When dividing clusters of bulbs and corms—which is necessary for many plants of the family Iridaceae—it will be observed that attached to the bases of the older corms are numerous pea-size cormlets which if grown on for three to four years—as in the case of gladioli—will bear flowers of outstanding quality. Where a stock is grown on in this way, the corms, which are known as 'spawn', will have become acclimatised to the soil of one's garden and will possess a vigour not to be found in imported corms. Growing on the tiny corms and offsets found around tulips and narcissi and at the base of crocuses and montbretia will be an inexpensive method of increasing stock of a new and expensive variety but not all will produce the same number of cormlets. Some will produce few cormlets and where this is so, even the smallest should be saved for growing on.

The offsets attached to *Narcissus* and *Hippeastrum* bulbs may be planted in deep boxes or in a frame, or directly into the open ground, in beds prepared by incorporating drainage materials and some humus such as leaf mould and dehydrated cow manure. They are best planted in rows 8 in (20 cm) apart, spacing them at 3- to 4-in (8- to 10-cm) intervals and planting them 2 in (5 cm) deep. Cormlets may also be grown on in this way, planting them out in spring but will give better results if, after wintering in a dry room, their hard brown outer shell or covering is first made soft. This is done by placing them in a glass jar and covering them with a dilute Lysol solution made by adding a tablespoonful to a quart of water. After 24 hours the corms will be soft and will also be safeguarded from attacks by pests (e.g. thrips) and disease which may have remained on them during the winter. In another jar place a layer of damp cotton wool or sand on to which the cormlets are set after first draining off the solution. About 1st April the jar should be placed in a warm, dark cupboard, and within 14 days the corms will be seen to be sprouting. The jar must be removed at once and the corms emptied on to a tray (to be planted outdoors), frame or deep box of sterilised compost where they are grown on until their foliage dies back in autumn.

The corms should be dried and stored over winter, to be planted out the following spring 3 to 4 in (8 to 10 cm) deep and 6 in (15 cm) apart in trenches or in deep boxes. As the corms are gradually built up to flowering size, they should be fed each week from midsummer with dilute manure water and when lifted in autumn, will have reached a size at which they will be capable of producing flowers the following year.

Growing from Bulbils. A number of species of *Lilium*, notably *L. tigrinum* and *L. bulbiferum*, and several members of the onion family (*Allium*) produce tiny bulbils at the axils of the leaves. If these are removed before the flowers have faded, the bulbils may be planted in outdoor beds or in boxes, 1 in (2·5 cm) deep and 2 in (5 cm) apart, and left there for two years, being fed in their second year as described for cormlets. They may then be planted in their flowering quarters and may bear bloom the following year.

It is possible to have the bulbils at flowering size a year earlier if the flower buds are removed from the parent plant as soon as they form. The bulbils will then increase in size before they ripen and are detached.

Where the bulbils are very small they are best planted or sown in boxes or frames of sterilised soil and leaf mould where they are grown on for a year before being planted out.

Bulbils or bulblets may form near the base of the stems of certain species of lily such as *L. brownii* and *L. henryi* if the stems be earthed up early in the season as they grow. They will form in clusters around the stem and should be detached in autumn, care being taken not to damage their tiny roots. If they are planted out in drills or in boxes and grown on as previously described, they will come into bloom in four years.

Propagation by Scales. By removing the fleshy scales from the base of lilies and rooting them in a suitable compost, it is possible to have them in bloom two or more years sooner than where growing from seed—and in the knowledge that the resulting bulbs will be an exact reproduction of the parent plant.

The scales should be fleshy and wax-like and have a succulent appearance. They must not be too dry when removed from the parent bulb. Each wedge-shaped scale may be encouraged to form a bulblet at the base either by inserting it upright with its base in a compost composed of sterilised loam, sand and leaf mould in equal parts and placed in a warm room or propagator; or by laying it flat on damp sphagnum moss in a jar and covering it lightly with leaf mould, sand and sterilised loam which should be kept just moist. In a temperature of 70° F (21° C), which is readily maintained in an indoor propagator, bulblets will form at the base of the scale in about three months. As soon as they have formed the first roots, remove them to individual pots containing a mixture similar to that recommended for their rooting and leave them there for 12 months.

Propagation by scales may be carried out at almost any time of the year, depending upon available heat, early summer being the most suitable time where one must rely on the warmth of the sun to encourage root formation. Any plants which form large bulbs with fleshy scales may be propagated in this way (the autumn-flowering scillas, for example).

Propagation by Leaf Cuttings. The green leaves of a number of tuberous plants resemble the leaf scales of bulbs and may be propagated in the same way. Like the scales, they should be thick and fleshy and must be fully mature. The leaves of *Gloxinia* and *Gesneria*, also of begonia rex may be propagated in this way as well as several non-bulbous plants such as the African violet (*Saintpaulia*). One method is to remove a leaf which is clean and fresh-looking and to place

Vein cutting for leaf propagation

it 'face' downwards on a sheet of clean paper. Then, with a penknife, short cuts are made across the main veins and at the point where the side veins join the main arteries. About twelve cuts are made on each leaf and it is usual to remove only two or three leaves from each plant so as not to defoliate excessively.

The leaves are then placed cut-side downwards on compost previously prepared and which may be of a mixture of peat and sand in equal parts by bulk. This is made moist and is placed in a seed box or pan to within 1 in (2·5 cm) of the top and made level. Depending upon their size, each container will accommodate two to eight leaves which are held in place by a strip of wire or by small pebbles. Over the top of the box or pan is placed a sheet of clean glass or plastic material to encourage rooting, while a temperature of 60° F (16° C) is maintained. A home propagator will ensure this temperature, which will also be reached in a greenhouse in summer.

The cuts are spaced evenly about the leaf so that when the tiny bulbils form at the points where the veins meet, they will each have room to develop and send out their roots. The compost must always be kept comfortably moist by immersing the base of the container in a pan of water whenever the surface appears to be drying out. In a month or so, the tiny bulbils will have formed and the rest of the leaf will have decayed. When large enough to handle (in about three months), the bulbils are lifted with care and transferred to 3 in (7·5 cm) pots containing a mixture of sterilised loam, leaf mould and sand in equal parts. If the leaves are removed early in summer, the plants will be ready for larger pots by early autumn in which they will remain during winter.

The succulent leaves of gesnerias, begonias and cyclamen may also be rooted by inserting their stalks in a compost of peat and sand in the same way as for leaf scales. The leaves are detached with a small piece of stalk attached and this is inserted up to the base of the leaf and around the side of a large pot or pan with the leaf in an upright position. It is made firm and the compost kept moist.

Leaf propagation

In a temperature of 60° F (16° C) roots will form at the end of the stem in about a month and within three to four months, a small tuber will appear.

Another method is to cut the leaves wedge-shaped with the part terminating the main vein inserted to a depth of about $\frac{3}{4}$ in (2 cm). Roots will form at the main artery and eventually a tuber will develop. While rooting, the leaves must

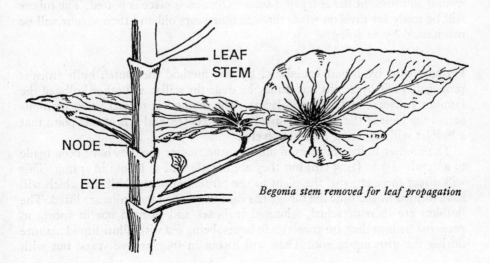

LEAF
STEM

NODE

EYE

Begonia stem removed for leaf propagation

be shaded from strong sunlight which would cause the too rapid evaporation of moisture in the leaf and prevent satisfactory rooting.

Tuberous begonias may also be propagated by stem cuttings. At the axils of the leaves and main stems, side growths are produced, several of which are allowed to grow on to bear bloom, but one or more may be removed for rooting before it can do so. Each will be found to contain an 'eye' or embryo bud formed at the point where the side shoot joins the main stem and this 'eye' must remain on the shoot when detached. This is done with a sharp knife, making a V-cut into the main stem. The cutting is then inserted around the side of a pot, shielded from the direct rays of the sun and kept moist by syringeing. Early July is the best time to take the cuttings and they will root in about six weeks. By early autumn, they will have formed tubers which are slowly dried off and stored during winter.

Propagation by Division of Tubers. Tuberous plants—e.g. begonias, cyclamen and anemones—may be increased by dividing old tubers into several pieces, each of which should contain an 'eye' from which the plant will grow. This is one of the most reliable methods of propagation and is best carried out when the tubers begin to sprout in spring. The tubers are started by placing them flat-side uppermost, in boxes of compost. They should be pressed into the compost with the surface exposed. They are watered in and covered with a sheet of glass or piece of thermo-plastic to help retain moisture and the boxes are placed in a sunny window or cool greenhouse. The tubers will soon start into growth. They are divided by placing on a firm surface and cutting them with a sharp knife into as many pieces as there are 'eyes'. The cut portions should be rubbed with powdered charcoal, flowers of sulphur or hydrated lime to close up the wound and prevent the entry of disease before each piece is potted. The tubers will be ready for division when three to four years old and their vigour will be maintained by so doing.

Propagation by Basal Incisions. By this method the Dutch bulb growers propagate their hyacinths but it may be done for scillas and other bulbs of the families Liliaceae and Amaryllidaceae. The method is to make two incisions across the base of the bulb, crossing near the centre, and it is at this point that a bulblet will form and possibly several.

The mother bulbs are planted out in autumn after the cuts have been made to a depth of $\frac{1}{2}$ in (1·25 cm) but they are not allowed to bloom in spring. This will direct the energy of the plant to the formation of the bulblets which will have formed by the time the foliage has died back when the bulbs are lifted. The bulblets are then detached, wintered in boxes and planted out in spring in prepared beds or they are grown on in boxes, being fed with dilute liquid manure during the growing season. They will bloom in four or five years, but with specialised culture the Dutch growers are able to bring the bulbs to flowering size in three to four years.

Propagation of Tubers by Cuttings. Tuberous-rooted plants may be increased to form cuttings. These are formed at the crown of the plant, at a point where the tubers join the old stem. The roots are planted in deep boxes after lifting from the ground, cleaning and dusting with sulphur. Spread out the roots on a 2 in (5 cm) layer of moist peat and pack peat and sterilised loam around the tubers, leaving the crown exposed. In gentle heat and keeping the roots moist, they will begin to form cuttings in about six to eight weeks and will do so throughout winter and spring. The cuttings are removed with a sharp knife when about 2 in (5 cm) long and will root readily if removed with a small piece of tuber attached to the base. They should be dusted with sulphur and inserted around a pot or be planted in boxes, spaced at 2 in (5 cm) intervals. They will root in eight weeks and should then be transferred to individual pots.

Propagation by Cutting the Rhizomes. Those plants, e.g. certain species of *Iris* which grow from a rhizomatous rootstock, may be increased by dividing the rhizome in much the same way as for dividing a tuber. The plants are lifted early in spring and the rhizome cut into pieces, each of which should contain a leaf and fibrous roots.

4

Bulbs in the Woodland Garden

To make a wild garden—plants for a calcareous soil—lilies in the woodland garden—planting and care of the bulbs—trees and bulbs for an acid soil

The most valuable quality of many bulbs, tubers and rhizomes is that they are happy not only in partial shade but also when growing under the natural conditions of a wild garden. Few are fortunate enough to possess a woodland garden, but even the modern town garden can be provided with the semi-natural conditions enjoyed by many bulbous plants. The wild garden is labour-saving, and once planted will require little attention beyond the clipping of long grass when the bulbs have died back. Suitable bulbs will continue to increase each year.

To make a wild garden is to provide untold pleasure throughout the year from the beauty of the ornamental trees and bulbs, an additional factor being that many bulbous plants which grow best in shade also bear the most sweetly scented flowers. Their pale ethereal beauty and powerful scent attracts the night-flying Lepidoptera so necessary for their survival through pollination.

To Make a Wild Garden. Even the smallest of gardens can be converted to a wild garden. One can also be made in a corner of a large garden or on ground in a northerly position at the side of a house and suitable only for growing hardy trees and bulbs. That part of the garden overshadowed by buildings and where little else will grow may also be used for shade-tolerant trees and bulbs.

A small part of a garden may be converted to a wild garden and made more interesting by enclosing it with interwoven fencing or with white paling to a height of 6 ft (1·8 metres), to provide shelter for the newly planted trees and to give privacy. It may be made separate from the rest of the garden by enclosing it completely, giving access by a small gate. Or a wild garden may be made along one side or at the very end of the garden, using interwoven fencing as a background in place of a hedge which would require constant clipping or pruning. A border some 6 to 8 ft (2 metres) wide may be made there and planted with ornamental trees, beneath which bulbs are set out in groups; hardy ones if the ground is in a cool area, those which prefer warmer temperatures in more favourably placed gardens.

Plants for a Calcareous Soil. Those trees and bulbs which enjoy similar soil conditions should be planted together, and as trees should be free to make rapid growth when once established, those of larger habit should be planted well away from the house.

Trees suitable for a chalk or limestone soil and flowering during winter and spring are the Japanese cherries, one of which, *Prunus subhirtella autumnalis*, bears its semi-double white flowers upon leafless branches intermittently throughout the winter whenever the sun shines on it. A more graceful form is *Prunus yedoensis* (yoshino) which comes into bloom early in spring, bearing almond-scented flowers of purest white along its arching stems. With it blooms *P. amanogawa*, a fastigiate tree resembling a Lombardy poplar in habit and bearing scented flowers of soft shell pink. Later comes *P. hisakura* which during early summer covers itself in hanging clusters of rich rosy-pink blossoms and is followed by the variety Ukon which bears trusses of pale-yellow flowers and has copper-tinted foliage. The leaves of the ornamental cherries take on rich golden tints and remain on the trees until the end of autumn.

Among the loveliest bulbs to plant beneath the cherries are the grape hyacinths which bloom from early March to early summer. *Muscari botryoides* bears its 8 in (20 cm)-long spikes of dark-blue grape-like flowers early in spring and is followed by *M. armeniacum* Cantab, bearing flowers of Cambridge blue. Later into bloom is *M. tubergenianum*, known as the Oxford and Cambridge grape hyacinth. Native of the rocky limestone slopes of the mountainous regions of northern Persia, it grows to 9 in (23 cm) tall. The bulbs are inexpensive and should be planted in drifts beneath the trees, for the muscari will provide a striking contrast to their white and candy-pink blossoms. The most dwarf of the muscari should be reserved for planting in short grass or in the shrubbery.

The robinias, the false acacias, are suitable trees to plant with the cherries for they also flourish in calcareous soils and are splendid for a town garden. *Robinia pseudoacacia frisia* has elegant fern-like foliage which in autumn turns to brilliant golden yellow. *R. luxurians* is also attractive with its pale-pink flowers and pale-green foliage.

The sumachs are small trees which take readily to a chalky soil. Growing to a height of about 10 ft (3 metres) is *Rhus glabra*. It has attractive pinnate leaves which turn brilliant crimson in autumn, while the clusters of red seed vessels are equally conspicuous.

The hardy *Cyclamen neapolitanum* may be planted beneath the robinias and sumachs. It begins to bear its rose-pink flowers early in autumn before forming ivy-shaped leaves mottled with silver which are retained throughout winter. This cyclamen will also flourish in an acid soil, growing beneath conifers. Self-seeding it rapidly makes ground cover.

Another bulbous plant to set below the trees is *Colchicum speciosum*, a native of Persia and the Levant. It is the most vigorous of the colchicums, and though it will flourish in a limestone soil it requires some moisture about its roots. Bearing large tulip-like flowers of carmine-purple it blooms late in autumn to a height of 9 in (23 cm) and so is conspicuous even in quite long grass.

Pyrus nivalis is a small pear tree from Asia Minor. Its pure-white flowers appear early in spring at the same time as the leaves, covered in silvery down, begin to unfold. It grows well on chalk. Beneath it plant the scarlet-flowered tulip from the same part of the world, *Tulipa eichleri*, the combination of red and silver being a most striking sight. This tulip has grey-green leaves like those of the *Pyrus* when fully expanded.

It is not realised how well many of the tulip species perform when growing beneath mature trees and in long grass, but those who have seen *T. eichleri* growing in the long grass beneath the elms leading to the back of Trinity College, Cambridge, will know how showy they can be, for most shade-loving flowers are either white or pale yellow, with the purple-blue flowering scillas and muscari notable exceptions. Another shade-loving tulip to plant as a companion is *T. sylvestris*, native of the English deciduous woodlands and naturalised as far south as northern Africa. It grows 17 to 18 in (42 to 45 cm) tall and spreads rapidly by means of underground stolons. It has long, narrow leaves and bears a flower of yellowish-green. *T. gesneriana* is another red tulip which may be planted in shade.

In bloom at the same time are the flowering crab apples, which possess great charm. At their best in a chalk or limestone soil, one of the loveliest is *Pyrus coronaria flore pleno* which bears violet-scented double flowers of porcelain-pink while its leaves take on rich golden-orange tints in autumn. To accompany it, plant the hybrid Profusion which has coppery-red leaves and bears its scented flowers of rich wine-red in handsome clusters during early springtime. Most attractive planted beneath them and in bloom at the same time are many of the daffodils. The large-cupped all-white daffodils are at their loveliest in the dappled shade cast by the trees, and none excels Castella with its rounded petal segments and well-proportioned cup. Another attractive white is Tresamble, a *Triandrus narcissus* which grows 15 in (38 cm) tall and bears four to six icy-white flowers of dainty form to every stem.

The dogwoods are among the most ornamental of small trees, rarely exceeding a height of 10 ft (3 metres) and happy in a limestone soil. Outstanding is *Cornus contraversa*, native of Japan, its sweeping branches clothed in early summer with clusters of creamy-white flowers followed by small black fruits. Beneath them may be planted members of the scilla family, including the British bluebell, *Endymion non-scriptus*, and the Spanish bluebell, *Endymion hispanicus*, bearing flowers in shades of blue and in bloom at the same time as the *Cornus*.

The erythroniums are suitable for a shaded garden, flourishing in a chalk-laden soil or in one which is slightly acid. They bloom from early spring until the daffodils appear but not all are suitable for the wild garden, for *E. dens-canis* and several other species grow only 6 in tall and would be hidden in long grass. *E. tuolumnense*, which bears reflexed flowers of buttercup yellow on 15-in (38-cm) stems, and *E. oregonum*, which bears drooping flowers of creamy white, both of which are native of north-west America, may be planted in long grass and are among the loveliest of all bulbous plants.

In bloom with the winter flowering cherries are the snowdrops, which in partial shade will prove suitable for a cool calcareous soil. But select those which grow taller than the more common *Galanthus nivalis* which does not exceed a height of 4 to 5 in. *G. byzantinus*, native of the shores of the Bosphorus, is one of the most showy of the snowdrops and distinguished by the green markings on its inner segments. *G. elwesii*, which has large erect leaves and stems, is one of the latest of the snowdrops to bloom.

Delightful for planting in open woodlands in a moist calcareous soil are the fritillaries which are distributed through the world's northern temperate regions. The European *Fritillaria meleagris*, the snake's-head lily or ginny hen flower of the early garden writers, blooms in spring and early summer. The blooms are coloured purple, white or bronzey-green and are covered in tiny black squares. In short grass the flowering stems do not exceed 6 in (15 cm) in height but attain 9 to 10 in (24 cm) in partial shade. Most inexpensive, they should be planted in generous drifts.

Among the finest of all plants for the matured wild garden is the camassia or Californian quamash, which blooms early in summer with the scillas. It is one of those plants which is hardy anywhere. It forms a large globular bulb, from which arise spikes of rich blue star-like flowers on stems 3 ft (90 cm) tall. It is one of the most useful of all for cutting, for the flowers remain fresh in water for several weeks. One of the best is *Camassia cusickii* which has flowers of steely-blue with golden anthers.

The silver birches with their exceptional hardiness and tolerance of calcareous soils should be included in every spinney if only for the brilliant silver of their new bark. One of the most beautiful is *Betula japonica*, the Japanese birch. Another is *B. coerulea-grandis*, which has chalky-white bark and showy catkins. The leaves of the birches turn brilliant golden-yellow before they fall in autumn.

At its finest in damp woodlands is the summer snowflake, *Leucojum aestivum*, which requires a cool, deep soil but is tolerant of calcareous conditions. It grows to a height of 2 ft (60 cm), whereas the spring snowflake grows only 6 in (15 cm) tall and is better when planted in short grass. The summer snowflake bears pendulous white flowers with green-tipped petals and it blooms during the early weeks of summer.

The more vigorous of the alliums are suitable for open woodland planting. To provide a succession of colour throughout the summer months, several species should be planted, beginning with *A. affatumense*, native of northern

Persia, which bears spherical umbels of lilac-purple flowers on a scape 3 ft (90 cm) tall. This is followed by the golden garlic, *A. moly*, which spreads rapidly, grows in any type of soil and bears bright yellow umbels on 15-in (38-cm) stems. To continue the display until the end of summer, *A. giganteum* will bear its huge violet globes on 3-ft (1-metre) stems and so will be conspicuous in the most mature of woodland gardens.

Ornithogalum nutans, the star of Bethlehem, is a delightful plant to use near stone steps leading down to a dell, for its flowers are of silvery white and shine in diffused sunlight. Growing 10 to 12 in (30 cm) tall, they bloom in early summer, and are seen at their loveliest growing in drifts near wild hyacinths (bluebells) and they will increase just as freely.

Lilies in the Woodland Garden. Among the finest of all bulbous plants for the wild garden are the lilies, several of which are capable of flourishing in partial shade and in a calcareous soil. Like all bulbs, they benefit from the cool moist conditions provided by the woodland garden and the continual mulch of leaves which fall from the trees. For this reason, lilies will retain their vigour over a longer period when growing in a woodland garden than elsewhere, and flowering at a height of 3 to 6 ft (1 to 2 metres) will rise above long tufted grass and bracken.

Under these conditions, the martagon lilies in particular are outstanding. Indeed, the Turk's cap lily of Constantinople established itself in English woodlands soon after its introduction early in our history. It is a base-rooting lily and once established will freely increase. It is happy in any soil, bearing its pendulous blooms of purple-pink on 3- to 4-ft (1-metre) stems during midsummer.

Growing to a similar height and flowering during the first weeks of summer is the yellow Turk's cap, *L. pyrenaicum*, native of the Pyrenees. It is also base-rooting and may bear ten or more waxy yellow blooms on each stem. The blooms are spotted with velvet-black.

Another of the martagon-type lilies is *L. hansonii*, native of Korea, which follows *L. martagon* into bloom, producing fragrant flowers of orange-red on a 3- to 4-ft (1-metre) stem. *L. humboldtii* is also a Turk's cap. Native of the Sierra Nevadas, it reaches a height of 6 ft (1·8 metres) and bears on each stem up to a dozen or more orange-scarlet flowers. It makes a fitting companion to the equally tall *L. henryi*, which is also of the martagon type and blooms early in autumn.

Two or three bulbs of each of the lily species should be planted 18 in (45 cm) apart, forming a small group to provide a generous display when in bloom. The martagons will continue to increase each year, forming large clumps which may be left undisturbed for several years needing only a regular mulch of decaying leaves.

Solomon's seal and lilies-of-the-valley should be planted in clearings where bracken has been cut and many of the roots dug out for here the soil will be rich in leaf mould and they will have no competition from long grass.

TABLE IX. *Bulbs suitable for a wild garden with a calcareous soil*

Species	Height	Flowering time
Allium affatumense	3 ft (90 cm)	May–June
Allium giganteum	3 ft (90 cm)	July
Allium moly	15 in (38 cm)	June–July
Camassia cusickii	2 ft (60 cm)	May–June
Colchicum speciosum	9 in (23 cm)	September–October
Cyclamen neapolitanum	6 in (15 cm)	August–September
Endymion hispanicus	16 to 17 in (40 cm)	May–June
Endymion non-scriptus	12 to 15 in (35 cm)	May–June
Erythronium oregonum	12 to 15 in (35 cm)	April–May
Erythronium tuolumense	12 to 15 in (35 cm)	March–April
Fritillaria meleagris	12 in (30 cm)	April–May
Galanthus byzantinus	9 in (23 cm)	February
Galanthus elwesii	8 to 9 in (23 cm)	March
Leucojum aestivum	12 in (30 cm)	May–June
Lilium hansonii	3 ft (90 cm)	June–July
Lilium henryi	6 ft (1·8 metres)	August–September
Lilium humboldtii	3 ft (90 cm)	June–July
Lilium martagon	3 ft (90 cm)	June–July
Lilium pyrenaicum	3 ft (90 cm)	May–June
Muscari armeniacum	8 in (20 cm)	April
Muscari botryoides	8 in (20 cm)	March–April
Muscari tubergenianum	9 in (23 cm)	April–May
Narcissus in variety	12 to 18 in (30 to 45 cm)	April–May
Ornithogalum nutans	12 in (30 cm)	May–June
Tulipa eichleri	15 in (38 cm)	April–May
Tulipa sylvestris	15 in (38 cm)	April–May

Planting and Care of the Bulbs. Where planting bulbs in mature woodlands, the shade cast by trees, ferns and bracken will almost entirely prevent the growth of long grass. Provided the bracken is cut down in late autumn (or it may die back naturally) the more vigorous bulbs can be planted in clearings which the diffused sunlight will penetrate, while bulbs of daintier habit may be planted about the roots of trees or beside paths. Once planted, they will require no further attention for they will obtain a much appreciated yearly mulch from decaying leaves.

Where a wild garden is being newly made, coarse grass and weeds will require cutting down each year, or at least until the trees and bulbs are established when they will tend to obliterate the grass and weeds by the shade they cast. As the bulbs should be allowed to die back completely before the old foliage is removed—so that they will have received their supplies of food and moisture for the development of the embryo bud—the cutting of the grass must be delayed. This means grouping together those bulbs which come into bloom during winter, spring and early summer and which will have died back by the end of July and planting together those which bloom from midsummer until late in autumn. In groups around the boles of trees will be planted *Colchicum speciosum* and *Cyclamen neapolitanum*. It will be advisable to delay the cutting of the grass until such time as the later-flowering plants have made enough growth to be readily detected.

Unsightly banks of rough grass may be made colourful by planting the dwarf bulbs, including miniature daffodils and snowdrops, the crocus species, dwarf muscari and several of the tulip species, almost all of which bloom during the first half of the year. During autumn the grass may then be cut back and the dead foliage of the plants removed. In this way the bank will be neat and tidy for the winter and also during spring and early summer when the bulbs are in bloom. The same bulbs may be used for orchard planting so that the grass beneath the trees can be cut early in autumn; windfall apples are more easily gathered when the grass is short and the trees are better reached for their pruning and spraying in winter.

Trees and Bulbs for an Acid Soil. Where the soil is of an acid nature, one of the most suitable trees to plant is *Arbutus unedo*, the so-called strawberry tree which grows wild among the bracken and heather of Killarney. An evergreen, it has large glossy leaves and is not too large for a small garden. In autumn it bears panicles of white funnel-shaped flowers and strawberry-like, edible fruits. Muscari and scillas look attractive beneath its dark-green leaves.

With Arbutus, plant *Oxyodendron arboreum*, a small tree of North America. Its foliage is a brilliant crimson in autumn, while in August it bears slender racemes of pure-white scented flowers. For companionship, plant *Pieris taiwanensis*, native of Formosa. It is evergreen and early in spring bears elegant clusters of creamy-white flowers held well above the leaves. Spring flowering bulbs of bright blue show up well beneath it.

In a mature woodland several of the gaultherias may be planted in groups. They are tufted shrubs increasing by underground stems and flourish in almost full shade. Probably the best is *G. forrestii* from western China which bears racemes of waxy white fragrant flowers followed by blue berries. Several of those lilies also enjoying an acid soil may be planted about them. The base of the lily stems will be protected by the twiggy growth of the shrubs.

All the shade-loving lilies enjoying acid soil conditions are from North America, where they are to be found growing naturally in open deciduous woodlands. One of the most beautiful is *L. parryi*, native of the lower mountainous woodlands of Arizona and California. Growing 6 ft (1·8 metres) tall, it bears up to 20 funnel-shaped flowers of clear lemon-yellow on each stem. *L. pardalinum*,

(*Above*) Comparative sizes of bulbs

Tulip   Crocus   Snowdrops
Narcissus   Hyacinth

(*Below*) Typical examples of bulbs, corms and tubers

Tubers of ranunculus   Corms of Anemone   Bulbs of *Erythronium dens-canis*
Corms of freesia   Bulbs of *Fritillaria meleagris*

(*Above*) Bulbs of species tulips compared in size with an ordinary 'Dutch' tulip

Tulipa clusiana	Keizerskroon	*Tulipa chrysantha*
Tulipa tarda		*Tulipa sylvestris*

Species tulips (*below left*) are happy planted five to a 5-in. pot. (*Below right*) Tulips occasionally produce bulbils in the leaf axils, above ground level; these may be planted and will flower like a normal bulb.

(*Above*) Bulbs of miniature daffodils compared with a garden hybrid

Hybrid Carlton

Narcissus triandrus albus

Narcissus minimus

Narcissus canaliculatus

(*Below left*) Planting miniature daffodils in a pocket in the rock garden. (*Below right*) *Narcissus minimus*, compared with a standard matchbox.

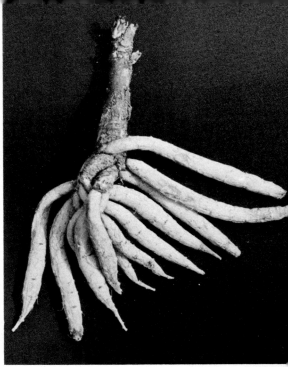

(*Above*) The quaintly shaped tubers of *Hermodactylus tuberosus*, the Shakeshead or Widow Iris. (*Above right*) Tubers of *Incarvillea delavayi*. (*Below*) The corms of *Crocus ancyrensis* have beautifully reticulated tunics.

(*Above*) The corms of gladioli are carefully eased out of the ground with a garden fork.

(*Left*) The plants, tied in small bundles, are hung in an airy shed until dried out.

(*Below*) The stem is severed with a sharp knife 1 in. above the corm.

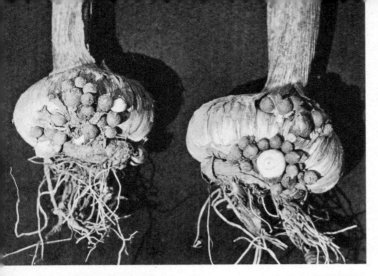

Gladioli corms as lifted at the end of the season showing the clusters of cormlets.

These are gently detached from the parent corm.

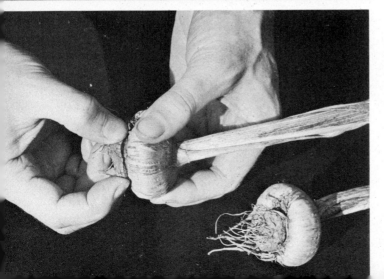

After drying out, the old corm is twisted away from the new corm.

(*Above*) Efficient staking and tying of large flowered gladioli is essential.
(*Below*) Bulbs of *Oxalis adenophylla*.

(*Above left*) Potting hyacinths. In a 6-in. pot two-thirds filled with compost three bulbs are pressed firmly into place. (*Above right*) Compost is pressed firmly around the bulbs, and the surface is made level with the 'noses' of the bulbs just showing. (*Below*) The soil is made firm by gentle 'hammering' with a fairly soft brush.

'Plunging'. (*Left*) Pots of bulbs placed in a trench; they are sunk to the rim and must stand on a layer of sand or ashes to ensure drainage. (*Above*) A 6-in. layer of soil covers the pots. Section shows how pots are completely surrounded and protected.

(*Below*) Where no 'plunge-bed' is available the pots may be sunk in a light garden soil with a few inches of loose soil raked over them. Sand beneath ensures drainage. (*Right*) 'Plunging' in the backyard in a simple wooden frame resting on the brick surface. With sand beneath for drainage, the pots are covered with a 2–3-in. layer of peat.

(*Above*) Forcing bulbs. The bulbs are placed close together on a layer of soil in a seed tray.
(*Below*) Soil is pressed firmly between the bulbs by gentle 'hammering' with a brush.

(*Above left*) A pan of daffodils at the right stage of growth to be brought into daylight. (*Above right*) The strong root growth which must be established before the plants are brought into daylight. (*Below left*) *Vallota speciosa* ready for repotting. Note the new white roots pushing down from the base of the stem. (*Below right*) The plant removed from its pot. Note the two offsets and the mass of roots.

Planting bulbs. *Fritillaria meleagris*: eight bulbs to an 8-in. seedpan.

Iris reticulata: eight bulbs to an 8-in. seedpan.

(*Left*) Crocus species: twelve bulbs to a 6-in. seedpan. (*Below*) Miniature bulbs set out in 6-in. seedpans half-filled with compost.

(*Above*) Gladiolus corms are planted out 6 in. apart on a layer of coarse sand. (*Below*) *Lilium candidum*: plant on a layer of sand with the top of the bulb just below surface of soil.

(*Above*) Miniature bulbs set out beneath a sunny wall.
Whenever possible bulbs should be planted on a layer of coarse sand.
(*Top left*) *Eranthis hyemalis*.
(*Bottom*) Scilla bulbs.

(*Above*) Pans of miniature bulbs bring colour to the alpine house. (*Below*)
Pans of *Crocus chrysanthus* Snow Bunting placed in a sunny window soon
fill a room with delicious fragrance.

(*Above*) Soil-less bulb culture. 'Acorn glasses' may be used for growing snowdrops, grape hyacinths and other miniature bulbs. (*Below*) Bulbs in glasses should be put in a cool dark place until a good root system is formed. At the stage shown here they should be brought into the light.

the panther lily of Californian woodlands, has orange Turk's-cap flowers strikingly spotted with black. It loves a damp soil enriched with peat or leaf mould and, like *L. parryi*, blooms in July with *L. superbum*, which is known as the swamp lily and which bears upwards of 36 blooms of orange-yellow to each 8-ft (2·4-metre) stem. *L. canadense* will be in bloom at the same time. It is native of the shady woodlands of eastern North America and has yellow funnel-shaped flowers gracefully recurving at the tips.

TABLE X. *Bulbs suitable for planting in an acid soil*

Species	Height	Flowering time
Anemone nemorosa	12 in (30 cm)	April–May
Anemone sylvestris	15 in (38 cm)	April–May
Cardiocrinum giganteum	9 ft (2·7 metres)	August–September
Endymion non-scriptus	15 in (38 cm)	April–June
Erythronium tuolumense	12 in (30 cm)	March–May
Lilium canadense	5 to 6 ft (1·5 to 1·8 metres)	July–August
Lilium parryi	5 to 6 ft (1·5 to 1·8 metres)	July
Lilium pardalinum	5 to 6 ft (1·5 to 1·8 metres)	July
Lilium superbum	8 ft (2·4 metres)	July
Narcissus cyclamineus	9 in (23 cm)	March–April
Narcissus pseudo-narcissus	9 in (23 cm)	April–May
Oxalis bowieana	9 in (23 cm)	May–July
Trillium cernuum	18 in (45 cm)	April–May
Trillium grandiflorum	15 in (38 cm)	May
Trillium luteum	15 in (38 cm)	April–May
Zephyranthes candida	9 in (23 cm)	September–October

A magnificent lily from the Himalayas is *L. giganteum*, now usually classed as *Cardiocrinum giganteum*. Unlike those of other lilies, the bulbs have only a few scales and require shallow planting. The bulbs should only just be covered with soil, whereas the lilies of North America should be planted at least 6 in (15 cm) deep. *C. giganteum* blooms during midsummer but produces its large heart-shaped leaves early in spring. In June the flower stem grows up to a height of 9 ft (2·7 metres), at the top of which appear 12 or more funnel-shaped lilies of ivory-white with a purple stripe down each petal. The raceme may measure 3 ft (90 cm) in length. After flowering the bulbs die but the two or three bulblets grow on to bloom in two years time.

To plant in woodlands, the swamp lilies of Central America and the West Indies, the zephyranthes, are most attractive. They bear crocus-like flowers on 12-in (30-cm) stems and bloom early in autumn amidst a forest of rush-like leaves.

c

The trilliums, the American wood lilies, are admirable plants for a slightly acid soil containing liberal quantities of leaf mould and they flourish in partial shade. They bloom early in spring, bearing their handsome white flowers above whorls of decorative leaves. Possibly the best is *T. cernuum*, the nodding trillium, which bears its drooping flowers on 18-in (45-cm) stems. Also lovely is *T. grandiflorum* which has three-petalled flowers of purest white and which measure 3 in (7·5 cm) across.

To plant with the trilliums, wood anemones are most suitable. *Anemone sylvestris*, known as the snowdrop anemone since its buds hang down like those of the snowdrop, is most attractive. The flowers are white with golden stamens and as they open they turn upwards. Held on 15-in (38-cm) stems they have a soft sweet perfume. Plant with them *A. nemerosa*, Royal Blue or the lavender-mauve Robinsoniana, discovered growing in the grounds of Gravetye Manor in Sussex by William Robinson the Victorian advocate of the wild garden. They bloom with the trilliums, early in spring.

Several of the species narcissus flourish in an acid soil in the open conditions of a deciduous woodland, one of the best being *N. cyclamineus* which bears its flowers on 9-in (23-cm) stems and with its reflexed perianth and clear yellow colouring is most enchanting when seen in woodland clearings. The hybrid February Gold with its orange-yellow trumpets borne on 12-in (30-cm) stems is equally lovely, while the Lent lily, *N. pseudo-narcissus*, with its white perianth and pale-yellow trumpet also grows well and increases rapidly in a mature woodland. Dog's-tooth violets are also tolerant of an acid soil.

To maintain the acid condition of the soil, peat should be used as a mulch, preferably in winter when the bulbs have died down. It should be remembered that most bulbs enjoying acid conditions flower during late summer and in autumn and must be allowed to die back naturally. The ground may then be tidied up at the end of winter.

Small bulbs such as winter aconite (*Eranthis*), puschkinia, scilla and crocus may be planted in the bare soil beneath the large branches of mature trees. They may be planted in groups or drifts of between 12 and 100 and will produce a most striking effect in spring, or in autumn and winter.

5

Bulbs in Short Grass

Bulbs in the lawn—correct planting depths—a chamomile 'lawn'

THE dwarf-flowering bulbs may be planted in the short grass of a lawn. They are among the most beautiful and accommodating of all the bulbs, for besides their value for planting in a lawn, they may be used by the side of a path and also about the rock or alpine garden, while they are equally suitable to plant in a trough or window box. They are not seen to advantage in rough grass which would hide their flowers, but in grass which is kept neat and tidy and for planting in bare ground beneath mature trees they are delightful.

An alpine lawn may be made at the side of a wild garden or alongside a path or drive leading to the house, utilising a strip of grass 6 to 7 ft (2 metres) wide which is to be kept short. Or the bulbs may be planted at one side of a lawn which will not need mowing until the foliage of the bulbs has had time to die back after flowering. For this reason, it may be better to plant only spring-flowering bulbs here and to use those which come in summer and autumn either in the wild garden or in the shrubbery where apart from a yearly mulch in winter, they will require no attention.

An Alpine Lawn. A delightful alpine lawn may be made by inserting into the grass large pieces of tufa stone with the flat surface showing above ground. After removing the turf to the necessary dimensions, the stone should be inserted into the ground so that only about 6 in is showing above the level of the surrounding lawn. One part of the stone may be slightly higher than the rest so that there will be a gentle slope. Each stone should be made to slope in the same direction and there should be ample space between each in which to plant the miniature bulbs in groups of six or more. Stones having a large upper surface should be used so as to provide the natural effect as of a mountainous slope. Make the soil quite firm about the sides of the stones and replace the turf right up to them.

The grass around and between the stones in which the bulbs are growing may be kept tidy by clipping with shears after the foliage has died back. The alpine lawn can be treated like a rock garden and planted with bulbs for all seasons.

Bulbs in the Lawn. Bulbs in the lawn should be planted as late in autumn as possible, after the grass has been given its final cut for the year. The shorter the grass, the easier they are to plant. As selective weed killers of the hormone type, based on MCPA potassium salt, are now widely used to keep a lawn free from weeds, their possible ill effects on bulbs must not be overlooked.

The weed killer Verdone may be safely used during autumn, when spring-flowering bulbs are dormant and the foliage has died back and has been removed. Verdone must not, however, be used when the leaves of the bulbs are showing above ground. Autumn is the most effective time for using the selective weed killers, when the ground is warm from the summer sunshine and the autumnal rains cause the weeds to make vigorous growth. One treatment given at this time of the year should be sufficient to keep the lawn free from weeds, and the bulbs should not be harmed.

There are two methods of planting. Either a section of turf is lifted by cutting it out with a sharp spade to the required measurements, or the bulbs are inserted singly, using a special bulb trowel or a bulb-planting tool suitable for small bulbs. It will save time and energy where the garden is large. A bulb trowel is so designed that a small circular piece of turf, and soil to the correct depth, may be cut away with ease. The bulb is then dropped in and the turf replaced and made firm.

Planting bulbs in turf

Where a section of turf is removed with a spade or is rolled back by cutting on three sides, the soil should be stirred and a little peat and sand placed over the surface into which the bulbs will be pressed. Six to eight small bulbs may be planted where about one square foot of turf has been removed. Do not plant in straight lines, and do not remove the turfs with geometric precision; aim at a natural-looking arrangement.

When planting singly, as each opening is made drop in some compost before the bulb is placed in position (the right way up). It is important to ensure that the base of the bulb is in contact with the compost, so that root action may begin promptly. If the bulb is in an air pocket it may not form satisfactory roots. For this reason a pointed tool should never be used for making the hole. It is a good idea to mark out the ground by means of plant labels printed with the name of the bulb before any planting is done. Plan as you would do before planting the herbaceous border, so that the purple-blue grape hyacinths may bloom with the yellow and white-flowered miniature daffodils, and let the spring snowflakes mingle with the scillas.

Bulbs are ideal plants for the labour-saving garden, for even if the garden has been left derelict for any length of time, it will come alive again through its bulbs just as soon as a clearance has been made, even though almost all other plant life will have been choked out of existence.

Correct Planting Depths. Planting depths must not be haphazard, for though certain liberties may be taken with the larger bulbs, the miniatures must be planted with care. Those producing a corm rather than a bulb—e.g. anemone and aconite—should be planted no more than 2 in (5 cm) deep; other depths may vary between 3 and 4 in (7.5–10 cm), depending upon the size of bulb and soil conditions. All bulbs should be planted an inch deeper in sandy than in heavy soil.

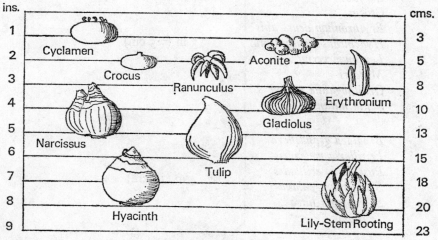

Planting depths outside

Many more of the dwarf bulbs may be grown if one moves away from the traditional grass lawn and plants the creeping bent grass, *Agrostis stolonifera*. As such a 'lawn' will not require cutting until late in June each year, the later-flowering spring bulbs may be planted, those which do not finish flowering until the end of May.

The bulbs are best planted before the 'lawn' is made, so as not to disturb the grass tufts, but if planting later it is not difficult to part the tufts. Always plant in groups where space permits.

TABLE XI. *Suggested planting depths in grass for a loamy soil*

Cyclamen cilicium Cyclamen neapolitanum	1 in (2·5 cm)
Anemone Bulbocodium vernum Chionodoxa Colchicum Eranthis Iris reticulata Narcissus Ranunculus Scilla sibirica	2 in (5 cm)
Allium moly Corydalis Crocus Erythronium dens-canis Hyacinthus amethystinus Leucojum vernum Muscari Ornithogalum nutans Scilla nutans	3 in (7·5 cm)
Brodiaea grandiflora Fritillaria meleagris Puschkinia scilloides Scilla tubergeniana Sternbergia lutea Trillium	4 in (10 cm)
Cyclamen europaeum Galanthus	5 in (12·5 cm)
Lilium Tulipa	6 in (15 cm)

TABLE XII. *Bulbs suitable for planting in a lawn*

Name	Flowering time	Height
Chionodoxa gigantea	March–April	5 in (12 cm)
Chionodoxa luciliae	March	4 in (10 cm)
Chionodoxa sardensis	March	4 in (10 cm)
Crocus balansae	March	2 in (5 cm)
Crocus biflorus	March	3 in (7·5 cm)
Crocus candidus	April	2 in (5 cm)
Crocus chrysanthus	February–April	4 in (10 cm)
Crocus corsicus	March	3 in (7·5 cm)
Crocus fleischeri	February–April	2 in (5 cm)
Crocus imperati	January–March	3 in (7·5 cm)
Crocus laevigatus	December–February	3 in (7·5 cm)
Crocus niveus	December–March	4 in (10 cm)
Crocus sieberi	February–March	3 in (7·5 cm)
Crocus vernus	March	2 in (5 cm)
Eranthis cilicica	February–March	2 in (5 cm)
Eranthis hyemalis	January–March	2 in (5 cm)
Galanthus 'Colesbourne'	February–March	4 in (10 cm)
Galanthus imperati	December–January	6 in (15 cm)
Galanthus latifolius	March–April	3 in (7·5 cm)
Galanthus nivalis	February–March	5 in (12 cm)
Hyacinthus amethystinus	March–April	8 in (20 cm)
Iris bakeriana	January–February	6 in (15 cm)
Iris danfordiae	February	4 in (10 cm)
Iris reticulata	March–April	6 in (15 cm)
Narcissus bulbocodium	March–April	6 in (15 cm)
Narcissus cyclamineus	March	8 in (20 cm)
Narcissus lobularis	February–March	8 in (20 cm)
Narcissus minimus	February–March	4 in (10 cm)
Narcissus minor	March–April	6 in (15 cm)
Narcissus, 'Rip van Winkle'	March	6 in (15 cm)
Puschkinia libanotica	March–April	6 in (15 cm)
Scilla bifolia	February–March	6 in (15 cm)
Scilla sibirica	February–March	8 in (20 cm)
Scilla tubergeniana	February–March	5 in (12 cm)
Tulipa tarda	April	3 in (7·5 cm)
Tulipa urumiensis	April	6 in (15 cm)

A Chamomile 'Lawn'. Miniature bulbs may also be planted among carpeting plants which form a colourful 'lawn' and which will be entirely labour-saving and beautiful almost throughout the year.

The plants will grow in an outward direction rather than upright, and will quickly cover the ground, if planted about 9 in apart. They will require trimming only once or twice each summer. This may be done either with shears or with a mower which has the blades raised as high as possible. It was Falstaff who said of such a lawn, 'the more it is trodden upon, the faster it grows', and if the herb lawn is not walked upon at all often, it should be rolled as frequently as possible. The drier the soil the more fragrant will the plants be, and there are few more agreeable couches than a dry, sweet-smelling herb lawn on a hot day in summer.

6

Bulbs in the Shrubbery

Plants and bulbs for a calcareous soil—bulbs for a sun-baked soil—
shrubs and bulbs for an acid soil—care of the shrubbery

FLOWERING trees and shrubs have usually a short-flowering season, so that for long periods they offer little of beauty but their foliage, yet bulbs planted beneath them will provide a carpet of colour all the year. Here may be grown many of those less hardy bulbs and corms which in the company of low-growing shrubs and heathers will receive the protection they require in the more exposed gardens.

The shrubbery may be an alternative to the semi-wild garden; though whereas in the woodland garden the bulbs will be shaded, and the soil be moist and leafy, the soil of most shrubberies is entirely without humus. Ornamental trees may be used to give privacy and they should be planted at the back of the shrubbery. To the front, evergreen and deciduous shrubs combine to provide as long a period of colour as possible, whether of flowers, berries or foliage. In front of the shrubs, groups of heathers may be planted in suitable soils, and among these the less hardy bulbs. Winter-flowering heathers will give ground colour to a shrubbery from Christmas until early spring, at the same time protecting from cold winds those bulbs which will come into bloom in spring and early summer.

Those bulbs which will grow under dry and poor soil conditions should be planted as well as those whose foliage tends to become coarse and untidy after flowering (e.g. the colchicums and narcissi), and which will benefit from being hidden by low-growing shrubs.

As the shrubbery will be left undisturbed for several years, the soil should be cleaned of all perennial weeds and enriched with humus before any planting is done, for it must be remembered that both shrubs and bulbs will be expected to bloom with but little attention for some considerable time. As they become established the bulbs will increase rapidly and will quickly cover the ground, choking out any weeds, but at the same time making it difficult to work the soil.

The soil of a town garden will often be of an acid nature due to constant deposits of soot and sulphur, and where lime is not naturally present, this should be incorporated before planting.

Plants and Bulbs for a Calcareous Soil. A number of bulbs will tolerate a calcareous soil but among those plants suitable for ground cover among which are the heathers, only varieties of *Erica carnea* will prove lime-tolerant. These are the winter-flowering heathers which come into bloom in November and it is possible, by planting several varieties, to have colour until May. They grow 9 in (23 cm) tall and will quickly make clumps 18 in (45 cm) in diameter. Outstanding is the variety Eileen Porter, which begins to bloom towards the end of October and continues to bear its rich carmine flowers until mid-April. It remains in bloom longer than other heathers. For colour during the midwinter months, *E. praecox rubra* has dark-green foliage and flowering spikes of crimson; Queen Mary has bright pink flowers and prefers lime in its diet. *Calluna vulgaris aurea*, with its golden foliage and bright, deep-pink flowers, is also attractive. For spring flowering, plant *E. vivellii*, which has bronze leaves and carmine-red flower spikes, and the Springwoods, white and pink, of almost prostrate habit.

In a chalky soil may be grown the philadelphus or mock orange, the flowering currants, the forsythia and flowering quince, buddleias, weigelias and lilacs. Here, too, may be planted (with the winter-flowering heathers to provide ground cover) the rock roses and dwarf barberries. Like plants tolerant of lime, they also flourish in a dry, sun-baked soil. Like the heather, they are evergreen, provide valuable protection for the bulbs and will hide their dying foliage.

Of the dwarf rock roses, *Cistus corbariensis* is one of the hardiest, growing 2 ft tall and bearing pure-white flowers in summer. Of the barberries, *Berberis chrysophaera* makes a low, broad bush 18 in (45 cm) high and has dark, shiny leaves and lemon-yellow flowers. Growing to a similar height is *B. buxifolia nana*, which forms a graceful little bush with dark, box-like foliage.

The closely related *Mahonia nervosa* makes a prostrate plant 12 in (30 cm) tall with long glossy leaves which provide protection for early flowering bulbs.

The shrubby potentillas also provide ground cover, one of the best being *P. fruticosa manshurica* which forms a spreading mat of grey-green and in summer bears greyish-white flowers in long succession. The hybrid Primrose Beauty is of similar habit but bears flowers of moonlight yellow.

Of those bulbs and corms suitable to plant in a limestone soil which is exposed to full sunlight, outstanding are the brodiaeas, natives of California, which bloom from the end of May until mid-July. First into bloom is *B. bridgesi*, which bears pale-lilac flowers on 18-in (45-cm) stems and is followed by *B. laxa* with its umbels of deepest purple-blue. Then blooms one of the most exciting of all plants, *B. coccinea*, the Californian fire-cracker, which revels in sunlight and a dry soil containing lime. It bears pendulous flowers of crimson-red tipped with green and blooms after the leaves have died back.

In bloom at the same time is *Ornithogalum arabicum*, native of northern and southern Africa and which is satisfactory only in a well-drained sun-baked soil. It bears umbels of glistening white flowers on 20-in (50-cm) stems and may be wintered outdoors only where the climate is almost frost-free.

For blooming early in spring, the Fosteriana tulips are remarkable in their diversity of colours. Known as the Bokhara tulips and native of the mountainous desertlands, none is more striking than Red Emperor with its blooms of vermilion-scarlet. To provide contrast there is Golden Eagle, its orange-yellow flowers having jet-black anthers.

Among the most suitable bulbs for a lime-laden soil are the anemones: not only the poppy anemones, grown in large numbers for cutting, but several species which quickly form a carpet of rich colouring and are cheap enough to buy in quantity. They are not really bulbs but tubers, and though their name is derived from the Greek *anemos*, meaning wind (flower), they are intolerant of strong winds and are happiest in the shelter of low shrubs. Plant them in drifts beneath the golden bells of the forsythia, which will be in bloom at the same time and which will act as a foil for the brilliant blue flowers of *A. blanda* and *A. apennina*. With them plant miniature daffodils of taller habit such as the golden-flowered W. P. Milner, for which the anemones will in their turn provide a carpet of blue.

As soon as the snow has melted, *Anemone apennina* shows its fern-like foliage; later, in early April, appear its bright-blue flowers with their golden centres. Equally fine is the Grecian windflower, *A. blanda*, which will flourish in a chalk hollow beneath young trees and is most effective planted at the foot of silver birch trees. It bears flowers of deepest blue on 4-in (10-cm) stems in early spring.

Best confined to the wild garden or shrubbery is the golden garlic, *Allium moly*, which bears bright yellow heads on 12-in (30-cm) stems early in summer; it provides a welcome glow of colour in the shadowy nooks of a shrubbery. It will grow almost anywhere and in any type of soil, especially one containing lime. Parkinson tells us that John Tradescant, who achieved fame at the beginning of the seventeenth century as a collector of new plants for the Duke of Buckingham, grew this *Allium* in his own garden; and adds, 'It was he (Parkinson) who sent me a root to plant in my garden' (now Long Acre, London). The two great gardeners must have been firm friends for in the year of the publication of the *Paradisus*, 1629, Parkinson was appointed botanist to Charles I and Tradescant head gardener to the King. Gerard called the *Moly* a 'stately' plant.

With *A. moly* plant *A. coeruleum*, which grows to a height of 2 ft (60 cm) and bears handsome heads of purple and blue flowers in June and July. There are many other choice flowering garlics for the shrubbery, such as *A. flavum* and *A. pulchellum*, the latter with violet-pink flowers in August. They should be included where space permits, since they are extremely hardy and are among the most inexpensive of bulbs.

Where the soil is dry and sun-baked and has a high lime content, the dwarf irises should not be omitted. *Iris reticulata* in its numerous forms may be planted, but, though it is expensive, do not omit *I. bakeriana*, hardier even than *I. reticulata* and coming into bloom early in the year. The standards are shot with mauve, and the violet fall petals have a large white blotch, studded with black spots. It is similar to *Iris histrioides*, which blooms at the same time.

The miniature daffodils will also grow in a lime-laden soil, though not for choice. They are suitable plants for a shrubbery, where their foliage may be left undisturbed to die back completely, hidden by low-growing shrubs. Plant in clumps or circles of half a dozen bulbs, preferably near the irises and anemones for colour contrast.

TABLE XIII. *Bulbs for shrubbery planting in a soil containing lime*

Species	Flowering time	Height
Allium anceps	August–September	6 in (15 cm)
Allium coeruleum	June–July	2 ft (60 cm)
Allium karataviense	May–June	10 in (25 cm)
Allium moly	June–July	12 in (30 cm)
Anemone apennina	March–April	6 in (15 cm)
Anemone blanda	March–April	6 in (15 cm)
Brodiaea bridgesi	May–June	18 in (45 cm)
Brodiaea coccinea	July–August	18 in (45 cm)
Brodiaea laxa	June–July	20 in (50 cm)
Cyclamen libanoticum	March–April	6 in (15 cm)
Cyclamen repandum	April–May	6 in (15 cm)
Iris bakeriana	January–March	6 in (15 cm)
Iris histrioides	February–March	6 in (15 cm)
Iris reticulata	March–April	7 in (18 cm)
Narcissus cernuus	April–May	9 in (23 cm)
Narcissus in variety	April–May	12 to 15 in (30 to 37·5 cm)
Narcissus juncifolius	April–May	6 in (15 cm)
Nerine bowdenii	September–October	2 ft (60 cm)
Ornithogalum arabicum	May–June	20 in (50 cm)
Sternbergia lutea	September–October	9 in (23 cm)
Tulipa fosteriana	March–April	18 in (45 cm)

N. juncifolius, the miniature rush-leaf daffodil, is most tolerant of lime. It bears fragrant flowers like those of the jonquil and should be planted near the front of a shrubbery. *N. cernuus*, with its nodding flowers of silvery white, grows to a height of 10 in (25 cm). It is delightful near evergreens, as is Queen Anne's double daffodil, *N. capax plenus*. All will appreciate some leaf mould packed around the bulbs at planting time.

The chionodoxa, puschkinia and galanthus species will also grow well in a soil containing lime, but, like the narcissus, they will grow better in a neutral soil and in a soil enriched with humus.

To provide autumn colour, *Sternbergia lutea* is outstanding. Though native of the barren hillsides of the Middle East, it is hardy in all but the most exposed gardens and enjoys a limestone soil and sun-baked conditions. It has large, deep-green, strap-like leaves which require hiding and so their planting should be confined to a shrubbery in full sun. Its shining golden crocus-like flowers appear early in autumn and remain colourful until the end of October.

The South African nerines will be in bloom at the same time and are among the most beautiful plants for a sunny border or shrubbery where their large bulbs will appreciate winter protection provided by the ground-cover plants. They grow 2 ft tall and form their leaves with the flowers in autumn, the leaves persisting until late in the following summer when they die back and are replaced. The hardiest and most free-flowering form is *Nerine bowdenii* which bears umbels of soft pink flowers.

Bulbs for a Sun-baked Soil. In a shrubbery where the toil tends to be dry and sun-baked but is neither too acid nor too alkaline, plant the grape hyacinths. The botanical name, *Muscari*, is derived from its old name, *Hyacinthus moschatum*, the musk hyacinth, its dingy yellowish-purple blooms having the pronounced perfume of musk. Though natives of Mediterranean shores, all the *Muscari* are extremely hardy; the smaller are suitable for the rockery, and all are attractive for growing in small pots. They increase rapidly from seed and by means of offsets, so do not plant too close.

Interesting rather than beautiful is the plume hyacinth, *Muscari comosum monstrosum*, which bears its flowers on 12-in stems. The lower flowers, which are fertile, are of greenish-purple, and above these the brilliant blue filaments which are infertile 'flowers' produce a plume-like effect. It is excellent for cutting, for mixing with late spring flowers and it blooms in May. Of recent introduction, in bloom in April is *M. tubergenianum*, the Oxford and Cambridge hyacinth, its 'grapes' opening pale blue, changing to dark blue with age. But for massing there are no more striking flowers than those wonderful hybrids Cantab and Heavenly Blue, both of which are fragrant, their dainty spikes made up of numerous tiny globular bells lasting throughout April and into May and acting as a charming contrast to the miniature daffodils. Their prostrate leaves cover the ground and thus protect the flower spikes from soil splashing. *M. neglectum* is also excellent for a shrubbery. Free flowering, its spikes of blue-black 'grapes' appear above pale-green foliage.

For a sunny border, the spring meadow saffron, *Bulbocodium vernum*, is a delightful plant. It bears its colchicum-like blooms on 4-in stems in early spring before the leaves. The flowers are lavender-pink, and appear star-like as they open. It likes sun and a dry soil, so plant it to the front of a shrubbery where its rather coarse leaves, as they die back, will be hidden by dwarf shrubby plants.

With foliage of the same coarse habit, the colchicums or autumn crocuses should join the *Bulbocodium* and *Sternbergia* in the shrubbery, for they are not suitable to grow elsewhere. The new hybrids have flowers like those of the Dutch spring-flowering crocuses and bloom from early autumn until December, long after their coarse strap-like foliage has disappeared. Naked ladies is their country name. The most striking species is *C. bornmüelleri*, the first to bloom, its huge lilac-rose flowers having a silvery centre. Plant for succession, so that the shrubbery will remain bright with their colour through autumn. The last in bloom is *C. autumnale* (purple) and its pure-white counterpart, *album*. Planted with them, the autumn-flowering crocus will provide additional colour during dull November days.

TABLE XIV. *Bulbs for a sun-baked soil*

Name	Flowering time	Height
Bulbocodium vernum	March	3 in (7·5 cm)
Calochortus albus	May–June	12 in (30 cm)
Calochortus pulchellus	May–June	12 in (30 cm)
Colchicum agrippinum	September–October	4 to 5 in (10 to 12 cm)
Colchicum autumnale	October–November	6 in (15 cm)
Colchicum bornmüelleri	August–September	8 in (20 cm)
Colchicum byzantinum	August–October	6 in (15 cm)
Colchicum callicymbium	September–October	6 in (15 cm)
Colchicum luteum	April	3 in (7·5 cm)
Colchicum speciosum	August–November	9 in (23 cm)
Crocus species	September–April	2 to 4 in (6 to 10 cm)
Muscari comosum	April–May	12 in (30 cm)
Muscari conicum	April	8 in (20 cm)
Muscari moschatum	March–April	6 in (15 cm)
Muscari neglectum	April–May	6 in (15 cm)
Muscari plumosum	May	9 in (23 cm)
Muscari tubergenianum	April–June	9 in (23 cm)

In a sheltered shrubbery in full sun, and where the hardy heathers are used to give protection, most of the less-hardy bulbs, chiefly those native to South Africa, may be grown. *Tritonia*, the *Sparaxis* and the closely related *Streptanthera* will survive if given winter protection, but as they are so striking, they merit cool-house culture where this can be provided. If used about the shrubbery, they should be kept away from those bulbs of more vigorous habit. As most of the bulbous plants from warm climates bear their flowers on thin, wiry stems, they will receive support from the heathers as they grow up through them in the same way as freesias.

The *Calochortus*, the mariposa lily of western America, may be planted in a dry, sun-baked border but it is often difficult to bring into bloom away from its native haunts. The bulbs are best planted in spring so that they grow away without having to endure several months of damp weather which may cause them to decay. One of the best is *Calochortus albus* which bears its drooping flowers of waxy-white on 12-in (30-cm) stems, like fairy lanterns. A reliable species to accompany it is *C. pulchellus* which bears fragrant golden lanterns during May and June.

Shrubs and Bulbs for an Acid Soil. An acid soil may be brought into a neutral condition by the addition of lime rubble, but there are numerous plants and bulbs which will grow well in an acid soil. The most important are those of the rhododendron group, which includes the azaleas.

For early-spring blooming, the Japanese azaleas, with their neat box-like foliage, growing only 18 in (45 cm) tall, are most suitable for small garden planting. Slightly taller are the *A. malvatica* hybrids, also evergreen, their foliage later taking on brilliant autumnal hues. One of the loveliest is Fedora, with its dusky-pink flowers, while Blaauws Pink bears hose-in-hose flowers of rich salmon-pink. The *A. mollis* hybrids bloom in May. They are not evergreen and grow tall and bushy.

Next in importance are the heathers, which, with the exception of *E. carnea*, enjoy a peaty soil. *E. cinerea atro-rubens* is summer-flowering and has ruby-red flowers on stems only 6 in (15 cm) tall. It should be planted to the front of a shrubbery, and for contrast plant the variety *alba* for its abundance of white flowers.

The Dorset heath, *E. ciliaris*, makes a compact plant 2 ft high, and in summer bears spikes of clearest pink; Mrs C. H. Gill has cerise flowers and dark-green foliage. For contrast, plant *Calluna aurea* with its golden leaves.

Varieties of *Calluna* (*Erica*) *vulgaris* will bloom throughout autumn and among the best are *aurea*, with purple flowers and golden foliage which turns bronze in winter; and *cuprea*, its copper-coloured foliage later turning to crimson. There are many more lovely heathers; a whole border could be planted with them to give colour the whole year round with bulbs growing through them.

The daphnes will also grow well in a peaty soil, as will the pieris or lily-of-the-valley bush, and the kalmias. Of the more vigorous shrubs both the arbutus and magnolia flourish under such conditions.

For planting in the shade of tall trees as well as in the shrubbery, *A. nemorosa*, the wood anemone, is an exquisite plant. Like *A. vernalis*, it will not tolerate lime. It is native to our shady woodlands and if used in the shrubbery should be planted in pockets of peat or leaf mould. The best form is Robinsoniana, with large flowers of pale lavender and with golden anthers. Of this variety, the Reverend Harpur Crewe said, 'All fade before its simple and innocent loveliness.' The variety Royal Blue should also be planted for its deep-blue flowers. There is also a double white form, *flore pleno*.

A. sylvestris, the snowdrop anemone, also likes a peaty soil. Its nodding snow-white flowers bloom in June with the later flowering scillas, which also do well in an acid soil. The variety Amethystina bears large spikes of clearest blue on 6-in (15-cm) stems.

For their beauty as well as for the earliness of their blooms, the winter aconites are deserving of a prime place in our gardens. They like a moist, peaty soil, but will grow well almost anywhere. Most know *Eranthis hyemalis*, the old winter aconite, which covers the ground with its bright emerald-green foliage long after its yellow cups have died away. Few know *E. cilicica*, from Asia Minor. It is more expensive but its flowers are larger, and the foliage, more delicately cut, is tinted with bronze. Both should be grown, for *E. cilicica* comes into bloom when *E. hyemalis* has finished flowering. They hold their blooms full face to the winter sunshine and even a fall of snow will have little effect on their hardiness; the flowers will be shining bright as soon as they emerge from their winter covering.

A bulbous plant which will grow in a peaty soil is the corydalis. It used to be grown on a sunny rockery with complete lack of success until it was discovered that the plants were native of the woodlands of Russia and northern Europe, and though liking a well-drained soil, do best in partial shade. Not all are bulbous plants. *C. cava* (for the shrubbery), so called because of its curiously hollow bulb, is a charming plant, bearing, during April and May, pale-lilac blooms on 9-in stems above attractive grey foliage. Of similar habit and in bloom at the same time is *C. angustifolia*, which bears loose sprays of pale-pink flowers. Its dwarf counterpart, *C. solida*, seems to be easier to grow.

TABLE XV. *Bulbs, suitable for a shrubbery, on a high acid soil*

Name	Flowering time	Height
Anemone nemorosa	April–June	6 in (15 cm)
Anemone sylvestris	May–June	12 in (30 cm)
Corydalis cava	April–May	8 in (20 cm)
Corydalis decipiens	May	9 in (23 cm)
Corydalis densiflora	March–April	6 in (15 cm)
Corydalis wilsonii	April–May	8 in (20 cm)
Eranthis cilicica	February–March	2 in (5 cm)
Eranthis hyemalis	January–February	2 in (5 cm)
Scilla amethystina	May–June	8 in (20 cm)
Scilla pratensis	May–June	8 in (18 cm)

Care of the Shrubbery. Before planting the bulbs, the ground should be brought into suitable condition. Ground which has been planted with shrubs for some time will be exhausted, and humus must be worked in. Material from the garden compost heap, old mushroom bed compost, peat and leaf mould, bark fibre and hops are all suitable for digging into the soil around the shrubs,

which will also obtain considerable benefit from their new diet. Sour soil will
benefit from a dressing of lime or lime rubble.

If the shrubbery has been long established, a number of the plants may have
made excessive growth, causing overcrowding and depriving nearby plants and
the ground beneath them of sunlight and moisture. They should be cut back at
the appropriate time, taking into consideration the natural habit of the plants.
To prevent overcrowding, remove one or two of the most vigorous plants, possibly replacing them by those of more compact habit.

The bulbs should be planted in generous groups with those of taller habit
behind the low-growing shrubs. Space out the plantings so that there will be
splashes of colour all the year.

If the ground has been prepared before planting, all that will be necessary
will be to give a liberal mulching when the dead foliage of the bulbs is removed
in autumn and when the shrubs are trimmed, any dead or decayed wood being
removed at the same time. There will be no need to fork over the ground, for
this would cause disturbance and perhaps damage to the bulbs. A regular mulch
will enable the shrubs to form plenty of vigorous new wood and will also keep
the bulbs supplied with valuable humus and plant food. They will multiply
rapidly and yet remain free-flowering for many years without lifting, dividing
and replanting.

7

Spring Bedding

Suitable schemes—bulbs to accompany primroses—bedding tulips—
hyacinths for bedding—shape of the beds—soils and their treatment
—making a flower bed—preparation of the soil

OF all garden plants, none will provide a better springtime display than bulbs.
They may be used for bedding in two ways: (*a*) For permanent planting between spring and summer flowering perennials, to bloom each year and thus
require the minimum of attention; or (*b*) they may be planted in autumn, either
by themselves or with other spring-flowering plants which replace the summer
bedding plants, in turn to be removed from the beds when they have ceased to
be colourful. Many bulbous plants are suitable only for planting in the wild
garden or in the shrub border for either they grow tall and have a loose informal
habit which disqualifies them for bedding, or they may take a year or more to
become established. Thus they would not be suitable for bedding schemes
unless set out in pots in which they have had time to establish themselves. Also,
those bulbs which prefer partial shade will be unsuited to an open, often windswept situation. Yet there is a wide variety from which to choose, either for
permanent planting or to occupy the beds only during winter and spring.

Suitable Bedding Schemes. To be inexpensive and as colourful as possible,
inter-planting should be done, using spring bulbs with other spring-flowering
plants and possibly also those plants which will continue the display through
summer and autumn. These will be plants of perennial habit which will require
no attention for several years, when they may be lifted with the bulbs and
divided and replanted into freshly cleared beds.

Use bulbs of dwarf habit with spring-flowering plants of similar habit so that
they will not hide each other when in bloom. If plants to provide later bloom—
e.g. dwarf chrysanthemums—are to be used in the same bed this need cause no
difficulty, for the chrysanthemums will make little growth until the spring
display has ended.

One of the most colourful displays for small beds and for cool climatic conditions is provided by winter pansies which bear flowers of yellow, white or pale
blue. They may be readily raised from seed, sown in boxes or in shallow drills.

By sowing in spring and transplanting the seedlings to beds of prepared soil, the plants will be ready to move to their flowering quarters early in autumn. If planted 8 in apart they will soon carpet the ground and will come into bloom almost at once, continuing without a break for several years if the soil has been enriched with leaf mould and decayed manure (or hop manure) before planting.

Tulips may be planted in the spaces between, and a contrast to white or yellow-flowering pansies is *T. eichleri* which will remain healthy and vigorous for several years. It bears its lily-like flowers of brilliant red above foliage of battleship grey and will bloom from mid-March until early May. The Fosteriana tulips will also retain their vigour, and for planting with the white or yellow pansies there is the variety Cantata which bears flowers of vermilion red above glossy dark-green leaves. Like *T. eichleri*, it blooms on a 10-in (25-cm) stem. With blue pansies, use the tulip Yellow Emperor with its elegant blooms of buttercup yellow.

Several of the crocus species will give colour all the year, beginning with *C. imperati* which will open its violet goblets early in the year whenever the sun shines down upon it and after the snows have melted. *C. sieberi* Firefly, with its tubes of lavender-blue, and *C. susianus*, bearing cups of brilliant orange, will follow, and then the Dutch hybrids, the purple-and-silver-striped Pickwick and Queen of the Blues, rich in colour and lasting in bloom. For autumn, plant *C. speciosus* with its goblets of bright purple-blue and the sky-blue Conqueror, to be followed by *C. ochroleucus*, its cups of creamy-white being almost transparent and which will extend the season until *C. imperati* is in bloom again.

Obtain a dozen or more of each species (depending on the size of the bed) and mix them together in a bag, planting them just as they are taken out. In this way there will be colour over most of the bed throughout the year.

Once planted, the bed should not be disturbed apart from the removal of dead flower heads, while some finely riddled leaf mould or peat should be worked around the plants as a mulch.

A pleasing way to grow the crocuses and also the dwarf *Iris reticulata* is to plant the corms beneath the spreading mats of those hardy garden pinks of prostrate habit which retain their silvery green foliage throughout the year. Each of these plants requires a soil containing liberal quantities of lime, best provided in the form of lime rubble or mortar and each has leaves which so much resemble each other that it is difficult to single out one from another. Slim and dainty, the foliage of the dwarf irises and the crocuses will be as pleasing as that of the pinks. *Iris reticulata* will bloom during early spring. The crocus species will bloom the year round and will be much enhanced by the matted ground covering of the pinks which will suffocate all annual weeds.

Other dwarf bulbs may be planted beneath the clumps of pinks such as chionodoxa and muscari, both of which will grow well where lime is present.

Only those pinks of low, spreading habit should be selected. One of the most suitable is Grace Mather which bears a succession of salmon-pink flowers in summer. Excellent too is Pike's Pink, while Keith bears double flowers of richest crimson. When out of bloom, colour will be provided by the bulbs pushing up through the grass-like foliage of the pinks, which should be planted 12 in apart.

The cushion saxifrages of the Kabschia section may be substituted for the pinks and here one of the finest is the white flowered *S. burseriana* Gloria and also the pale-yellow sulphurea, both of which bear their flowers on reddish stems 3 in (7·5 cm) tall above bright-green foliage.

The dwarf periwinkles, *Vinca minor alba* and the double blue-flowered *flore plena azurea* which are evergreen and make spreading mats in sunshine or shade, may also be underplanted with dwarf bulbs for which the rich green foliage of the vincas makes an admirable foil.

For a position of full sun such as at the top of a wall or by the side of a path, small bulbs may be planted beneath mats of spring flowering aubrietias which retain their foliage all the year. Purple muscari and blue chionodoxas are most attractive in bloom among mats of crimson aubrietia, Mrs Rodewald or Belisha Beacon.

Bulbs to Accompany Primroses. A colourful display may be enjoyed by planting Juliae primroses or polyanthuses. One of the finest of all is Barrowby Gem—described by Miss Sinclair Rohde as 'a real treasure'—which bears heads of pale yellow, shaded with green on 6-in stems. It diffuses an almond-like perfume whenever the sun shines upon it. During a mild winter it will bloom continuously and is lovely when growing among blue winter pansies, accompanied by *Crocus imperati* and *C. sieberi*.

Yellow-flowering polyanthuses will give a striking spring and early summer display if inter-planted with red or purple tulips or with blue-flowered hyacinths. The April-flowering scarlet single tulip, Dr Plesman, or the deep-blood-red Cassini, both of which bloom on 15-in stems well above the polyanthuses, are most striking. Or plant blue polyanthuses and with them the yellow tulip Bellona, which, like Dr Plesman, is scented and blooms at the same time.

The season will be extended by later varieties which should be planted with them, using those which grow to a similar height such as the carmine and white Garden Party, one of the finest of all bedding tulips, and Apricot Beauty of unique colouring.

Yellow polyanthuses are equally pleasing where inter-planted with purple tulips such as Reliance, a Darwin which bears huge globes of shining royal purple, or Queen of the Night with its flowers of darkest maroon. Both are at their loveliest when planted with the polyanthus-primrose Enchantress which bears trusses of dusky-pink flowers above foliage of darkest green.

Sutton's Brilliancy strain, with flowers in exciting shades of rust, terra-cotta, scarlet and bronze, may be used with the May-flowering water-lily tulip, Queen of Sheba, with its long tapering flowers of orange-scarlet, its reflexed petals

being edged with gold; or with Arcadia, which also has reflexed petals of
deepest golden yellow and is exquisitely beautiful.

To plant between the yellow woodland primroses or the Buckland Variety
with its bronze foliage and trusses of ivory-white flowers, are the Greigii
tulips, unsurpassed with their handsome leaves mottled with brown and which
are an admirable complement for the bronze foliage of the polyanthus. Outstanding is Red Riding Hood with its flowers of velvet-red borne on 9-in (23-cm)
stems.

Bedding Tulips. Both the Greigii and Kaufmanniana tulips are most suitable
to plant in small beds to themselves for both grow to a similar height of about
10 in (25 cm) and have attractive broad leaves which almost cover the ground,
thus providing a carpet for the beds and displaying the handsome blooms to
advantage while preventing the blooms from being splashed by soil during
heavy rain. One of the most striking is *T. greigii* Plaisir, the carmine-red colouring shading into the buff-yellow edging of the petals. It could accompany Cape
Cod, whose flowers of apricot, yellow and bronze have bases of jet tinted with
red. Plant with them *T. kaufmanniana* Shakespeare, bearing flowers of apricot,
salmon and orange, shaded with red on the inside.

Beds made up of double early-flowering tulips, interplanted with later-
flowering Cottage or Darwin tulips, will provide colour from early April until
well into June. They may be planted where the beds are to be cleared after they
have flowered, to be replaced by begonias or geraniums. Or they may be under-
planted with wallflowers which will bloom at the same time. To plant with wallflowers use the multi-flowering tulips which grow 2 ft (60 cm) tall and on each
stem bear four or five large blooms. Georgette is lovely, with its clear-yellow
flowers edged with red; while the variety Wallflower has blooms of rich
wallflower-red with yellow shading at the base.

Among the finest of the wallflower strains are Golden Bedder and the dazzling
Scarlet Bedder, which grow only 9 to 10 in (23 to 25 cm) tall and make bushy
plants which retain their compact habit when in bloom.

Though the forget-me-not, *Myosotis sylvestris*, grows naturally in moist
woodlands, it will give a good account when used for spring bedding if provided
with some humus about its roots. Early June is the best time to sow the seed,
which germinates quickly. When large enough to handle, the seedlings should
be thinned in the rows, and they will make sturdy plants to set out in autumn.
Among the best strains is Blue Ball, which makes a compact plant 6 to 8 in
(15 to 18 cm) tall, and Royal Blue, both of which are at their loveliest at the
same time as Darwin tulip Jewel of Spring, which, with its refined flowers of
sulphur yellow, is seen at its loveliest in beds carpeted with forget-me-nots. The
lemon-yellow Niphetos is equally fine; likewise Magier, which bears a bloom of
unrivalled charm, the milky-white flowers being shaded and edged with rosy-
purple.

The Siberian wallflower, and especially the variety Orange Bedder which blooms with the last of the cottage tulips, make a striking display together. They extend the spring bedding programme until the end of June when the geraniums and begonias take over. Easter Queen is a handsome tulip to grow with Siberian wallflowers. The flowers are of deepest orange, shaded with gold at the base. The parrot tulip, Merriment, in bloom at the same time, is also arresting with its frilled and lacinated petals of golden yellow, edged and feathered carmine-red. Or use Nizza, a double late-flowering tulip, the blooms being striped scarlet and gold. Each of these tulips grows 2 ft (60 cm) tall, the blooms being held nicely above the Siberian wallflowers which bloom at a height of 18 in (42 cm).

Beds planted with both early and late double tulips (paeony-flowered) will give colour from early April until midsummer when they make way for summer plants. Scarlet Cardinal and the blood-red Dante will be first into bloom and with them Marechal Niel, canary-yellow tinted with orange. Then as the flowers begin to fade, the later varieties come into bloom. With Nizza, plant Orange Triumph, which bears paeony-like flowers of deepest orange, over-laid with brown. Or for contrast, plant the refined Mt Tacoma with its flowers of glistening white.

A striking display may be obtained by using tulips to provide colour from early April until summer by planting them in a large circular bed, raised at the centre. The bed could be 8 ft (2·5 metres) or more in diameter and be made as the centrepiece for a large lawn or courtyard when the display, seen from all angles, will be one of brilliance.

At the centre may be planted two or three dozen bulbs of the Cottage tulip, Bond Street, with its flowers of brilliant yellow, and surround with a double circle of the orange-scarlet, Beverley. Both flower at a height of 2 ft (60 cm). Then plant the salmon-rose Darwin, Perry Como and Insurpassable with its rich lilac flowers of great substance.

To follow, the mid-season tulips bloom two weeks earlier than the Cottage and Darwin tulips, and do not grow so tall. Dutch Princess bears flowers of glowing orange and gold and around it plant a circle of Apricot Beauty which grows only 15 in (37·5 cm) tall and blooms at the same time. Its salmon-pink blooms are flushed with apricot.

Then come the early double-flowering varieties such as the orange-and-yellow Wilhelm Kordes and the fiery-red Vuurbaak, both April-flowering on 12-in (30-cm) stems. They may be surrounded with the single early Ibis, its globular flowers being of a unique shade of flamingo pink. To edge the bed, plant *T. kaufmanniana*, Jeantine, its buff-rose flowers with their creamy white base held on only 6-in (15-cm) stems. It is one of the first to bloom, showing colour before the end of March and is followed by the others in rapid succession, ending at the centre of the bed with the Cottage and Darwin varieties which will continue the season until June.

Hyacinths for Bedding. The oriental hyacinths are among the finest of all bulbous plants for spring bedding but as they are more expensive than tulips and other bulbs, they should, for economy, be planted with less expensive bulbs. For a small bed of the size 6 ft (1·8 metres) by 4 ft (1·2 metres) a charming display is obtained by using 10 or 12 bulbs of the hyacinth Scarlet Perfection amidst a bed of the myosotis, Marina, its dainty sprays of brightest blue off-setting the stiffer, more formal habit of the hyacinths. The colour combination is exquisite for Scarlet Perfection is a double 'sport' of the best of all the single red hyacinths, Madame du Barry, and bears spikes of mulberry red which retain their beauty for weeks. For contrast, the double Ben Nevis could be used. It bears wax-like bells of pure glistening white. L'Innocence is its single counterpart. Orange Charm, its buff-coloured blooms being flushed with orange, and the cream-coloured Yellow Hammer are also lovely planted in a bed of forget-me-nots.

For a small bed, a charming effect may be obtained by planting the fairy hyacinths with forget-me-nots. They resemble the Roman hyacinths in that they produce from each bulb sprays of fairy-like daintiness. They come into bloom early in spring and remain colourful over a long period. To plant with blue forget-me-nots, use the charming Rosalie with its sprays of brightest pink and with rose-pink forget-me-nots, plant the bright blue hyacinth, Vanguard. The fairy hyacinths are also lovely for a tub or window box and for planting among Juliae primroses such as Snow-Cushion—the plants being studded with white star-like blossoms throughout spring—or with the purple-flowering Jill, which will quickly cover a large area with its brilliant green heart-shaped leaves and purple stems. This primrose is also valuable to plant on a sunless bank with dwarf daffodils growing among them and which will bear their white or yellow blooms above mats of purple and green.

Hyacinths are also right to grow with double Brompton stocks, which bear flowers of pale blue or deep rose pink. With the former, plant red, yellow or white hyacinths, and with the latter use Ostara with its spikes of brilliant blue or Myosotis, which bears flowers of silvery blue.

The balsam-like scent of the hyacinths, combining with the clove perfume of the stocks, will give additional pleasure during the calm days of early summer.

Arabis makes a charming foil for the oriental hyacinths and also for the later flowering tulips, for with its feathery habit it will reduce the somewhat stiffness of form of the hyacinths and the tulips. *A. albida flore plena* is the double white form, while *A. coccinea* bears masses of deep rosy-red flowers throughout early summer.

The perennial *Alyssum saxatile*, the 'gold dust' of cottage gardens, is a plant usually confined to the rock garden; but planted by the side of a path or in narrow beds, it will give brilliant colour from early spring until midsummer and will be enhanced by the company of *Tulipa praestans*, Fusilier, when pushing its orange-scarlet flowers up through the mass of brilliant gold. Or plant the alyssum, Lemon Queen, which bears soft yellow flowers and with it *T. kolpa-kowskiana*, whose cherry-red flowers provides a charming contrast to the glowing yellow alyssum. After flowering, the foliage of the tulips may be tucked inside the clumps of alyssum to die back.

Double Daisies, *Bellis perennis*, are effective and inexpensive plants to use in small beds for spring and early summer. During mild weather, whey will bloom through winter and will provide colour, while the bulbs are pushing through the ground. The best of many strains is Pomponette, pink or red. The tiny button-like flowers with their quilled petals appear with freedom and the plants always retain their compact habit. Of similar dainty habit to plant among them are the Siberian squills. They grow 6 in (15 cm) tall and with their tiny bells of Prussian blue and their extreme hardiness, will bloom for months from the end of winter, unmindful of the weather. The variety Spring Beauty has large flowers and, being sterile, remains longer in bloom.

If planting summer-flowering annuals between the double daisies when the Siberian squills have finished flowering, the squills may be grown in small pots, three or four bulbs to each and are planted in their pots between the double daisies. The pots should be inserted so that the rim is just covered with soil. This is also the best way in which to grow the narcissus species to use in beds for they resent disturbance and so may be dried off and retained in their pots after flowering, while the foliage of most species takes several weeks to die back and looks anything but pleasing in the beds. For this reason daffodils are best confined to the wild garden or shrubbery unless they can be grown in pots. Used in this way, several of the Angel's Tears narcissi and the *N. cyclamineus* hybrids are attractive when planted among hardy auriculas with their velvet-like blooms of crimson, blue and yellow, colours with which the seventeenth-century Dutch flower artists loved to beautify their paintings. Liberty Bells is a *N. triandrus* hybrid of richest colouring, capable of matching that of the auriculas. It bears three or four dainty blooms of deep old gold on a slender stem 12 in (30 cm) long. Another attractive bulb is the *N. cyclamineus* hybrid, Peeping Tom, with its reflexed perianth and long elegant trumpet.

Shape of the Beds. Before planting, thought must be given to the size and type of beds which will be most suitable for one's garden. For example, a bold display will always prove more suitable in a small garden than will one provided by numerous small beds. Contrary to popular belief, it is the larger garden that can best accommodate a series of small beds. As William Robinson advocated in his wisdom, let the plants themselves make up the pattern rather than make the beds of too intricate design. Wherever possible, it is a good idea to allow the beds to follow the shape of the garden. The gentle curving or sloping of a bed will add interest and informality, for nothing is more monotonous than that the beds should give the appearance of having been made to a geometrical plan, while it must be remembered that many bulbs used for bedding have a habit which is stiffer and formal, more suited to the parterres and terraces of nineteenth-century gardens than to those of modern times. Hence the value of using with them the more informal ground cover plants. Every advantage should be taken of curves and undulations in the garden, always bearing in mind aspect so that the display may be seen from the home. The more brilliantly coloured flowers such as those of the tulips are effective where seen against a wall of weathered stone, while yellow tulips are most attractive against a background of red brick. For the same reason they provide a striking display where beds are surrounded with paving stones or where they are made alongside a path made of stone or brick. They are also right when seen against a background of dark evergreens.

Soils and their Treatment. If the soil is friable and not lacking in humus and plant foods, bulbs will give a good account of themselves in almost all soils and in most gardens, though the less tender plants should be confined to those more favourably situated. Unhappily not all gardens measure up to these requirements. There is the soil of a heavy clay nature and that containing an excessive amount of sand, both requiring care to bring them into suitable condition. Most often encountered is the acid soil of town gardens, the result of an accumulation of sulphur and soot deposits which is so often the cause of a disappointing display. There is also the naturally acid soil into which plants requiring acid conditions should be planted, and its counterpart, the lime-laden soil which should be planted with lime-loving plants. But first consider the making up of a bed of a simple design which will most probably be cut from a lawn.

Making a Flower Bed. A circular bed is marked out by placing a stake at the centre of the chosen site. Then a piece of strong twine fastened to the centre stake and of the length of half the required diameter is taken in an arc, stakes being placed at short intervals to form the circumference of the circle. A sharp stainless-steel spade should be used to make the cut round the circumference. To remove the outer ring of turf cleanly, an inner circumference should be made to the width of a spade. This should also be marked with stakes and the cut made. The turf will then be easily lifted. If the bed is made on a lawn mellowed with age, the turf will be valuable and should be carefully removed for use elsewhere. Where the turf is of little value, it may be dug in and a raised bed more easily made by digging first round the circumference and working towards the centre.

A rectangular bed will present no difficulty. The correct width should be marked out and the turf removed as described, the digging being continued from one end of the bed to the other. More ornamental beds will call for more accuracy, but if the design is not too complicated, it will prove charming for a small courtyard or to occupy the centrepiece of a small town garden with the pathways made either of grass or of paving stone. A design like that used to make up the parterre at Longford Castle in Wiltshire has great charm without being too ornamental. Such a design filled with bulbous plants of formal habit would provide the maximum of colour from but a small piece of ground. Remember when making up a rectangular bed to give it ample width, for unless planted against a wall or interwoven fencing for a background, it will be difficult to provide a pleasing effect if too long and narrow.

Preparation of the Soil. A bed well made will remain free from trouble for many years, and this is why some time should be taken in its preparation. To skimp the work will be to evoke disappointment, and where expensive plants are being used this cannot be tolerated. The first consideration is to provide thorough drainage, and this will depend upon soil and situation. A garden on high ground or with a pronounced slope will drain itself, so will one where the soil is of a sandy nature. Frequently, and this is especially noticeable where a garden to a newly built house is being made, the soil will contain too much clay, often brought to the surface when taking out the foundations of the house. To make a satisfactory bed with a clay soil or one of a heavy loam, drainage must be provided for bulbs will not grow in a waterlogged soil. This is done by 'double digging'. Soil from the first two 'spits' or trenches are removed entirely and carried to a place where the soil remains until required for filling in the last 'spit'. Into the first trench, approximately 15 in (38 cm) deep, a layer of crushed brick, stone or gravel is placed and over this is turned one 'spit' of soil. A layer of compost is then added. This is important in helping to break up the soil and to provide humus and aeration. The compost may be cow manure, stable manure, straw broken down with an activator and to which pig or poultry manure in the dry state is added, or hop manure, seaweed, wool shoddy, or any nitrogenous manure which will decompose and open up the soil. Peat is an excellent and cheap form of humus, as is poplar tree bark, obtainable in bulk, which should be spread on the bed as it is being prepared.

When the compost has been added and another 'spit' placed over it, the procedure is continued until completion. The bed should be allowed a week to settle down before planting, when it will be found to be raised just sufficiently to give help with drainage and to display the plants to advantage. For dwarf plants, the bed may be raised at the centre by throwing up some of the soil from the outer perimeter.

The value of dressing a clay soil with caustic lime must not be overlooked. This will not only correct acidity in the soil, which is often of a high ratio in a heavy soil, but will help to break up the clay particles as it generates heat, in the same way as decomposing manure. Caustic lime worked into the soil before preparing the bed will help to bring the soil into a fine tilth. The soil should be left for ten days after working in the lime before its preparation begins.

Soil of a fibrous loam will require the minimum of attention. It may be necessary to provide a slow fertiliser and this may be given as bone meal, steamed bone flour or hop manure, in small quantities. This is forked into the soil, together with a small quantity of peat.

A light sandy soil will present no difficulties as far as drainage is concerned, rather will it be necessary to provide a moisture-retaining medium. Even after a heavy shower moisture will have left the soil in a few hours. Much may be done to prevent this by incorporating all manner of humus-forming materials, wool shoddy in particular being invaluable, and farmyard manure. It will depend upon where one is situated and the materials available. Those close to deposits of peat will use this in quantity. Those gardening in coastal districts will find seaweed an excellent form of humus. Those in the country will be able to obtain animal manures, while the northern town gardener will have wool shoddy readily available. Old mushroom-bed compost is ideal for opening up a heavy soil and has also a valuable nitrogen content, while grit will assist with drainage.

The soil of a town garden, often of an acid nature, should first be treated with hydrated lime forked well in a fortnight before the beds are prepared. Spent hops obtainable from a brewery, peat, decayed leaves and shoddy, all readily and cheaply obtainable, are excellent materials for enlivening a town soil.

It is important to strike a balance between soil and plant. A too rich soil and one kept continually moist will mean that a plant will give an abundance of leaf and few flowers over a long period. A too dry soil, starved of both food and moisture-holding material, will produce an abundance of bloom, but only over a short period. Somewhere between the two extremes will be the happy medium, which is to bring all types of soil as far as possible to this condition, though never forgetting that each plant should be given its individual needs.

However carefully the flower beds may have been made up, it must be remembered that a bed which for a number of years has grown but one variety of plant may tend to become 'sick' and the display will gradually deteriorate. It was Lord Kanes, in the *Gentleman Farmer*, who, as long ago as 1788, first drew attention to the possible discharge from plants that would eventually become so concentrated that in time the ground would become 'sick' of a particular species, but only recently has the question of soil sickness become widely understood. It is not advisable to grow certain plants in a bed for more than three or four years.

8

Summer Bedding

Multiflora begonias—anemones for bedding—the gladiolus for
summer display—lilies for bedding—summer-flowering plants of
southern Africa and South America

WHERE climatic conditions permit, the sparaxis with its harlequin-painted
flowers is a striking plant to bloom late spring and early summer, bridging the
gap between the spring and summer flowering bulbs. In most parts of the
British Isles and in those parts of America which experience winter frosts, the
sparaxis should be grown indoors in pots to bloom in May but where frost is
rare, the corms may be left permanently in the ground or they may be planted
in autumn each year and removed after flowering. In southern Africa they
bloom from August until October, bearing several flowers to each stem. The
flowers are flaming red or yellow with a black blotch at the base of each petal.
They require an open sunny situation and a light gritty soil. In all but the most
favourable districts, the corms should be planted 3 in (7·5 cm) deep and be
given a 2-in (5-cm) covering of boiler ash to protect them against frost. The
flowers, which are borne on 18-in (45-cm) stems, have a light, airy habit, being
in no way stiff and formal.

The ixias require the same cultural conditions, for they too are native of
southern Africa and will be harmed by frost. Like the sparaxis, the flowers open
only in sunlight and, growing to a height of about 15 in (38 cm) bear several
blooms of the most brilliant colourings to each stem. Before they open, the buds
resemble ears of corn, hence their name, corn lily. There are a number of
varieties including the distinctive Afterglow, the orange-buff flowers being
shaded with rose on the outside and Vulcan, its crimson flowers being flushed
with orange.

Streptanthera, also native of southern Africa and in bloom at the same time
as ixia and sparaxis, requires similar treatment. *S. cuprea coccinea* bears flowers
of six petals of glowing orange with a striking black centre, while Zwanenburg
has crimson flowers with a yellow centre. Plant with them Glory of the Sun,
Leucocoryne ixioides odorata, which bears richly scented flowers of clearest blue
on wiry 15-in stems.

For a garden enjoying a mild winter climate, the Cape cowslips, the lachenalias, are ideal bedding plants with thick shining strap-like leaves often mottled with purple. The pendulous tubular flowers appear as if waxed and, flowering in spring, are long lasting. Recently several beautiful garden hybrids which are hardier and more free flowering have been introduced. *L. nelsonii* bears tubes of golden yellow and *pearsonii* yellow flowers edged with claret. Possibly the former is the best for bedding for it makes a bushy plant only 9 in (23 cm) tall. Both are derivatives of *L. aloides* (*L. tricolor*) and bloom during spring and early summer. Another outstanding bedding plant for growing in a frost-free garden is *Synnotia metelerkampiae*, which blooms early in summer and bears deep violet-purple flowers with a brilliant orange flake on each petal. In less favourable parts, these natives of southern Africa are best grown in a cool greenhouse or frame and planted out in pots, though where they can be given protection from frost by planting beneath ground-cover plants, they should take little harm. They must, however, be given an open situation in full sun for, unlike the hardy bulbs of the Near East, the flowers will usually fail to open in dull weather or in shade. They are sun lovers.

When we consider those plants suitable for summer display we invariably think of the half-hardy geraniums and calceolarias and annuals such as antirrhinums and nemesia, alyssum and lobelia, sold in boxes each year by their millions hardened for planting out. Rarely are bulbs and corms used, though the begonia is at last receiving the attention it deserves. This is because it is inexpensive and easy, but of greater importance is its ability to flower in dull wet weather, whereas the geranium gives of its best only in sunshine and dry conditions.

Multiflora Begonias. Outstanding among summer bedding plants is the multiflora begonia, introduced by Lemoine of France in 1907 by crossing *B. octopetala* with a tuberous hybrid of unknown origin. *B. pearcei* was another species used in the hybridising. The first hybrid to become popular was named in honour of Count Zeppelin and, like all the multifloras, it bears masses of small flowers on a bushy plant, growing no more than 6 in (15 cm) tall. By the end of summer, however, it will cover the ground with its foliage and flowers for at least a square foot. From June until the end of October, it bears its brilliant flowers, an inch across. Perhaps no other plant will bear as many blooms during the season, and especially in dull, wet weather when the geranium and most other summer bedding plants will sometimes be devoid of colour. In addition, the wiry stems and the way the foliage almost hugs the ground ensure the blooms are untroubled by strong winds. Consequently they may be planted in exposed situations. When introduced into France they quickly became favourite plants for parterre bedding, and their popularity spread throughout northern Europe and the British Isles since their brilliance of colour and ideal bedding habit made them well suited to the temperament of those prosperous times and to climatic conditions.

Though usually started into growth by planting the small tubers in boxes of moist peat or leaf mould in a warm greenhouse, they may be brought into growth in pots (or boxes) in the sunny window of the home or garden room. They should be started into growth early in spring and planted out when fear of frost has vanished for their parents are natives of South America and the islands of the West Indies. The first begonia species, *B. rotundifolia*, was discovered there in 1690 by a Franciscan monk, Fr Plumier, who named it after his patron, Michel Begon, French Governor of Santo Domingo. As many of the begonia species are native of the tropical rain-forests of the New World, their hybrids are tolerant of damp conditions and, contrary to popular belief, are able to flourish in dappled shade. They enjoy protection from the midday sun even in the British Isles, which is rarely troubled by an excess of summer sunshine.

Multiflora begonias may be used in the smallest of beds, for the plants are of a neat, compact habit. The beds may be made circular or rectangular, possibly using one variety to provide the main display at the centre and surrounding it with a more dwarf variety of contrasting colour. Outstanding is Jewel, which has foliage almost black-green in colour to enhance the double blooms of brilliant apricot and gold which are borne in generous trusses. It could be planted with Amy Bard, its double blooms of peach-pink being flushed with apricot, or with William Eysser, which bears blooms of warm salmon-pink.

Lovely together are Evelyn Tavanet with its flowers of bright salmon-rose and Madelon, its double blooms of satin-pink being enhanced by the dark foliage. For contrast, Flamboyant, with its smaller leaves and flowers of brilliant scarlet, and the yellow Helen Harms are striking when in bloom together. Also lovely is Princess Beatrice, which bears shell-pink flowers above leaves of palest green.

After flowering, the tubers are lifted, dried and stored over winter, to be started into growth again early in spring when the larger tubers may be divided.

Tubers of the large-flowering begonias, descended from *B. boliviensis* with its handsome tapering leaves and flowers of brilliant orange-scarlet, may also be used for summer bedding and are started into growth in the same way. Large tubers may be cut into two or more pieces (each with an 'eye') as soon as they begin to sprout. They are then replanted and grown on until ready to set out early in summer. Being of more upright habit and with thicker stems which are more brittle than those of the multifloras, they are more liable to wind damage but will find protection from suitable companion plants which may be used with them to enhance the display. One is the purple heliotrope or cherry pie, a half-hardy plant which will be ready to plant out with the begonias. The informal habit and grey-green foliage acts as a pleasing contrast to the begonias. Perhaps the best form is Madame Bruant, the deep-purple flowers being edged with white. Lovely, too, is White Lady when used as a contrast to scarlet begonias, likewise *Cineraria maritima* with its fern-like foliage of silvery grey which seems to pick out to advantage the orange and scarlet colours of the begonias and will provide an exotic appearance to a bed even in a small town garden.

Another excellent 'mixing' plant is *Leucophyta brownei*, which forms a twiggy bush of the same height as the begonias. It appears as if covered in silver paint, while the stems are rubbery to the touch. It is striking when used with scarlet or pink begonias.

Also to provide contrast is the coleus with its variegated foliage and it is a plant which enjoys the same damp conditions and a humus laden soil. *C. verschaffelti* (and its hybrids) is the best bedding form. Cuttings from it may be rooted round the sides of a pot and grown on in gentle heat during winter. The plant should be transferred to small pots when rooted.

Celosia cristata, the cockscomb, a half-hardy plant which bears its brilliant scarlet 'combs' on 12-in (30-cm) stems, is striking when planted among white- or yellow-flowering begonias. Or use the slightly dwarfer Empress which has red-tinted foliage and bears 'combs' of deepest crimson. It may be used with crimson begonias to produce a symphony in red and especially colourful is the crimson Fimbriata begonia which has blooms like large red carnations. Nor should the golden Featherfew, *Chrysanthemum parthenium*, be forgotten for its dainty habit and contrast of colour. It will remain colourful all summer.

Anemones for Bedding. One of the finest plants for spring and summer bed- ding is the anemone, yet only rarely is it used in this way. *Anemone tenuifolia*, parent of the Caen anemones of northern France, was illustrated in Parkinson's *Paradisus* as early as 1629 and he described 30 kinds, some of which differ but little from the modern strains. There are also those descended from *A. latifolium*, which are called the garland or St Brigid anemones. M'Intosh in *The Flower Garden* (1838) lists 130 varieties of the double anemone, the St Brigid, and tells that 'one hundred fine named sorts may be purchased from 3–5 guineas per hundred'. Today, the corms (really tubers) cost considerably less and will bloom throughout spring and summer. In a warm, sheltered garden they will bear some bloom throughout almost the whole year.

Anemones may be used in beds to themselves or as carpeting plants for other spring- and summer-flowering bulbs. In a circular bed, raised at the centre they are seen to advantage and especially where several varieties are planted in circles of various colours. If possible, plant them where they may be seen from above, from the upper rooms of a house, for the corms will quickly cover the ground with bright green lace-like foliage above which the flowers are borne on 9-in (23-cm) stems.

If planted in autumn, after the summer annuals have ended their display, the corms would come into bloom early in spring and continue until the end of summer. If planted in March, after the snows have melted, they will begin to bloom in May. They are particularly attractive when used as ground cover for Cottage and Darwin tulips, in bloom during May and early June. Plant contrasting colours, using white tulips above red anemones or yellow tulips above purple anemones. The anemones will continue the display long after the tulips have finished flowering and have been gently removed from the ground. Both may be planted together during October. Because the anemone is mostly grown in the more sheltered parts for early cut bloom, it is believed to be less hardy than it is. It will grow as far north as the Shetland Isles and in Norway and Canada, where, if planted 3 in (7·5 cm) deep, it will endure many degrees of frost and come into bloom as soon as the sun begins to raise the air temperature in spring.

Oriental hyacinths with their stiff formality and the upright habit of the leaves will also be enhanced by a carpet of anemones, planting together those bearing flowers of pink and pale blue. Crimson hyacinths could be used with a ground cover of white anemones. The anemone foliage will act as a brilliant green carpet for the hyacinths. The anemone is a lime lover and, though requiring some humus in the soil, will grow well in a calcareous soil.

The corms may also be planted alongside a path or at the front of a shrubbery, together with the species *A. apennina* and *A. blanda*, and with them also the Dutch hybrid crocuses. Both these anemones bear flowers of sky-blue and, though flowering only in springtime, come into bloom so early that their presence in the garden is very welcome. They are also inexpensive and easy to grow.

Closely related to the anemone is the ranunculus, native of Turkey and Persia. This is less hardy, the corms being lifted in autumn after the foliage has died back, though this is not so necessary in those gardens enjoying a mild winter climate. Because the ranunculus is somewhat tender and in bloom only during the early weeks of summer, it has been neglected by modern gardeners though its popularity with the florists of the eighteenth and early nineteenth centuries has never been equalled by any other flower. Maddock writing in 1792 claimed to have had over 800 varieties growing in his garden. These ranged in colour from 'black' to white and through all shades of red, yellow and bronze— also striped or spotted.

The root is made up of a series of tuber-like claws which are formed around the 'eye' and which are planted downwards with the 'eye' about 3 in (7·5 cm) below the surface. Early spring is the best time to plant in all but the most favourably situated gardens, but the roots may be stored in winter exactly like those bulbs and corms requiring half-hardy treatment, keeping them away from frost in boxes of sawdust or sand.

The Gladiolus for Summer Display. It is rarely that the gladiolus is used for bedding. It is usually grown in the border in groups or in the kitchen garden to provide cut bloom for the home. But by planting the early and mid-season varieties in beds and using various other plants for ground cover, they may be expected to provide brilliance of colour towards the end of summer and throughout autumn. That the large spikes will require staking should not be detrimental to their planting. The primulinus hybrids with their delicate pastel shades will require little or no support and may be planted more closely together to support each other and provide more colour.

The graceful upright habit of the gladiolus will do much to relieve the often flat appearance of a large bed. The display will be particularly arresting if they are planted with dwarf-flowering dahlias which will put forth their maximum brilliance exactly when the gladioli is coming into bloom. If the sprouting tubers of the dahlias are planted between the gladioli early in June, the dahlias will begin to bloom in July and will have reached a crescendo of colour when the gladioli buds begin to unfurl.

The dwarf cactus and decorative dahlias grow about 20 in (50 cm) tall, and among the best are Downham, with its lemon-yellow flowers; New Fun, coral with a soft-rose centre; Arnhem, cardinal red; and Rocquencourt, which has bronze foliage and bears flowers of vivid marigold-orange. The latter grows less than 18 in (45 cm) tall. Or use the dwarf single-flowering Coltness types, which do not exceed 12 in (30 cm) in height. Summer Beauty bears flowers of soft phlox-pink and with it plant Princess Marie José, its large flowers being of a unique shade of soft lilac. Also plant gladiolus Fledermaus with its flowers of cream, yellow and lilac, or Misty Eyes, shell pink and plum, both of which bloom early in August. To plant with Downham and also a gladiolus of early-flowering qualities is the steel-blue and grey Firmament, or for striking contrast there is Oscar, its ruby-red blooms having jet-black anthers. The white-flowered Maria Garetti provides contrast to dahlia Arnhem or the single-flowering Red Sparks with its blooms of tomato colouring.

The most dwarf of the dahlias may accompany the miniature butterfly gladioli which grow only 2 ft (60 cm) tall and bear dainty florets, often with frilly edges to the petals and with 'butterfly' markings in the throat. To plant with the dahlia Summer Beauty, Blue Goddess has considerable attraction, while the green and tangerine Chinatown is delightful with the lemon-yellow Bush Coltness.

Gladioli may also be accompanied by annual plants such as antirrhinum Malmaison with its flowers of rosy-pink and gladiolus Peter Pears, which bears blooms of coral and pink; or use gladiolus Wedgwood, its lavender-pink flowers with their cream throats combining most attractively with the pink antirrhinums. Plant white or yellow gladioli with flame-coloured petunias which are also at their best late in summer. Likewise the asters, especially the pompones with their bushy branching habit. Most colourful is Pirette, which bears button-like flowers of vivid cerise and should be planted in a bed of yellow gladioli. Plant the dwarf marigold Lemondrop, which bears its large globular heads of lemon yellow on 6-in (15-cm) stems with the miniature gladiolus Alicide. It is of primulinus form, bearing flowers of fiery red at a height of 2 ft (60 cm).

A pleasing summer display may be obtained by planting gladioli in a bed of violas or pansies. Bright-red gladioli are most striking in bloom above pansy, Coronation Gold, with its large flowers of purest yellow, while yellow gladioli

D

are lovely above a carpet of blue pansies such as Ullswater with its flowers of inky-blue. If the dead pansy blooms are removed as they form and any straggling shoots cut back, they will remain colourful through summer and autumn.

Where using half-hardy annuals, it will be possible to arrange the grouping between the gladioli to best advantage, for they will not be set out until early summer, by which time the gladioli shoots will have appeared above the surface of the soil to make planting between them all the easier. Gladioli require a soil capable of retaining the maximum amount of moisture and this is especially necessary for the large-flowering types. Where the garden is untroubled by strong winds, the bronze- and green-leaved cannas are most striking used for summer bedding. Potted in March and kept in a sunny greenhouse or garden room, they will be ready to plant out early in June and are arresting where used in a bed of begonias or gladioli, giving an exotic appearance to the garden.

Lilies for Bedding. Several of the hybrid lilies may be used for summer bedding provided one does not mind staking them. The Mid-century hybrids, which grow less than 3 ft (90 cm) tall, are ideal for this purpose, though flowering only during the weeks of midsummer, they should be planted with late summer-flowering plants to extend the season. They may be used with bedding dahlias which will not have made any considerable growth before the lilies come into bloom—the dahlias will continue the display until late autumn. By planting with dahlias, staking may not be necessary unless the garden is exposed. Bred from the tiger lily, the Mid-century hybrids have the same robust constitution and will grow anywhere in a soil enriched with humus, for although requiring a well-drained soil in winter, the bulbs must not be allowed to dry out in summer. The heavy growth of the dahlias when the lilies are coming into bloom will help to prevent soil evaporation.

Among the best of the lilies for bedding is Cavalier, its bright-yellow blooms having broad overlapping petals; and Paprika, its crimson-red flowers being borne almost horizontally on stiff pedicels. Also suitable is Valencia, bearing large flat heads of richest orange, and Brandywine, its apricot-yellow flowers, almost brandy coloured, being spotted with black. None of these lilies exceed a height of 30 in (75 cm).

To extend the flowering season of the lilies, *L. amabile luteum*, which grows to a similar height and which bears Turk's cap flowers of saffron yellow, could be planted for it blooms in August and September. Also suitable for bedding is *L. tenuifolium pumilum* which has narrow grasslike leaves and in June bears bright-scarlet flowers with ruffled petals; and its yellow-flowering counterpart Golden Gleam, both of which grow less than 2 ft (60 cm) tall.

Summer-Flowering Plants of Southern Africa and South America. The Mexican tiger flower, *Tigridia pavonia*, may be used for summer bedding. A hundred corms will be sufficient to plant a bed 6 ft (1·8 metres) by 5 ft (1·5 metres), spacing them about 6 in (15 cm) apart. If planted in early spring they will begin to bloom in June and continue until summer ends. The flowers, in shape like three-bladed ship's propellors and of dazzlingly brilliant colours spotted with red or black at the centre, last only for a day or so, but continue to appear in long succession, each bud 'firing a burst' of great brilliance. The buds will not open except in the sun and during dull weather remain closed, so are best confined to those gardens which receive more than their normal share of sunshine and where late frosts are unknown. In those favourably situated gardens, the corms may be left undisturbed, to increase each year and they will not need lifting when flowering has ended as they will do in most parts of the British Isles. As the flowers are borne on 20-in (50-cm) stems, a few twigs placed about the bed as they come into bloom will enable them to grow upright so that their full beauty may be enjoyed.

Native of tropical South America and resembling the Tigridia is the exotic-looking *Cypella herbertii*. It requires an open situation, and where the winter climate is mild the corms may be left in the ground. Like *Tigridia* it has three widely spreading petals which are waved or twisted. They are of rich golden yellow, spotted with purple at the centre. The flowers are borne during July and August on 15-in (38-cm) stems and their branching habit makes it an ideal bedding plant for a warm garden.

The homeria, native of southern Africa, may be treated in the same way. *H. collina* will, if planted out in spring, come into bloom early in summer and continue until the end. It produces a single spathe-like leaf from the fold of which arises a spray of orange, salmon or yellow cup-shaped flowers, borne on a 2-ft (60-cm) stem. The corms are inexpensive and, if a sunny situation can be provided, this is an interesting summer-flowering plant to use either by itself, with *Tigridia* or with the primulinus gladioli to extend the season until autumn.

To give those plants which are sparse with their foliage suitable ground cover, they may be under-planted with *Phlox drummondii* or the trailing verbenas, delightful plants in their own right, which cover themselves in bloom in July and August. Alternatively the dwarf petunias may be used. Provided the ground is enriched with humas, they too will be happiest in full sun.

Small beds may be made in a sheltered part of the garden, possibly beneath a wall in a southerly situation. Here freesias specially 'prepared' for outdoor culture may be grown in those parts which enjoy climatic conditions approaching those of their native southern Africa. If planted 2 in (5 cm) deep and about 2 in (5 cm) apart late in spring, they will begin to bloom towards the end of summer and continue until autumn. They are best planted among low-growing perennials which enjoy similar conditions and will extend the flowering season, in addition to giving support to the stems.

9

A Border of Bulbs

Planning the border—a border of miniature bulbs

WHILE the shrubbery and the herbaceous border consisting of hardy perennials is a common feature of modern gardens, it is only rarely that a bulb border is to be seen. Yet it has the same degree of permanency and will be just as colourful. By the judicious selection of species and varieties and attention to correct planting depths, a bulb border will provide colour the whole year round and be as permanent and labour saving as a border of shrubs, roses or herbaceous plants. The bulbs will continue to increase each year, providing more and more colour, and only those less hardy plants which in northern regions will require lifting after flowering, to be kept over winter in a frost-proof room, will demand additional care in their culture. They may be omitted from the planting scheme if it is required that those bulbs are to remain permanently.

Many bulbs may be planted in the partial shade of trees and in a cold northerly aspect where few other plants would be expected to flourish. Here again, those plants requiring an open, sunny situation would be omitted, the selection being determined by the position of the border, where in the partial shade cast by overhanging trees or by nearby buildings, bulbs alone will prove suitable, possibly accompanied by paeonies which make their foliage early and provide the early bulbs with protection from the cold winds of spring.

A bulb border is made in the same way as a herbaceous border, planting at the back those bulbs of taller habit with the dwarf bulbs to the front. So that the border will be colourful throughout with no unduly large areas devoid of blossom for long periods, thought must be given to the flowering time of each species or variety. The summer-flowering bulbs should be planted near those which will bloom in spring or in autumn so that when one group begins to die back, another will take its place and hide any unsightly foliage. The bulbs should not be planted too formally or their natural charm will be lost. They should be set out in groups of ten or so, though the larger-flowering lilies and crown imperials are best planted in threes. Other bulbs may be planted in large circles or in drifts between them so that there will be few empty spaces, with the border taking on something of the appearance of an alpine 'lawn' without the grass. The most dwarf species should be excluded from the border and instead should be used in the trough or alpine garden, or planted in drifts beneath trees. There are those—such as the winter aconite and *Crocus speciosus*—however, which are so inexpensive that they may be planted in generous drifts about the border for one will bloom early in the year, the other towards its close and they will provide colour at a time when it will be absent. With *Crocus speciosus* may be planted *C. longiflorus*, its sweetly scented violet tubes adorning the garden on dull November days.

Planning the Border. Before planting, a plan of the border should be made. When the bulbs arrive and the ground is ready for them, the plan is transferred to the border, marking out the places where the bulbs are to be set by lines made of sawdust or sand. Make each section large enough for a generous planting. Do not plant too closely for it must be remembered that the border may be undisturbed for several years during which time the original plantings of lilies and crown imperials will have grown into large clumps.

At the back plant the taller-growing lilies and the alliums, the tuberous-rooted eremurus and the asphodelus, selecting the best from many species. They will reach a height of 5 to 6 ft (1·5 to 1·8 metres) and may require staking, though this may not be necessary if they are protected by a windbreak of interwoven fencing. Among the finest of the lilies for a border made in dappled shade and in a cool climate are the trumpet hybrids of *Lilium regale* type. Pink Perfection grows 6 ft (1·8 metres) tall and bears at the end of its sturdy stem 12 or more graceful trumpets of deep fuchsia pink which open from pale-green buds. To grow near it, plant the fragrant Limelight, with its flowers of rich chartreuse green measuring 8 to 9 in (20 to 23 cm) across when open and revealing striking orange anthers. Elsewhere at the back, plant *L. regale*, its glistening white flowers being marked with purple on the outside; and with it, Black Dragon, its trumpets of white-shaded purple brown on the outside. Each is scented and will bloom in July and August.

Also late-summer flowering is *L. henryi*, a lily of extreme hardiness and vigour, bearing on each stem as many as 30 nodding flowers of deepest orange with prominent green stamens; and *L. davidii*, its flowers of cinnabar red having attractive reflexed petals. All are late-summer flowering and stem rooting; they should be planted 4 in (10 cm) deep and 12 in (30 cm) apart, in groups of three.

With them plant several groups of *Galtonia candicans*, native of mountainous slopes of Cape Province and Natal. Planted 5 in (12·5 cm) deep, it is perfectly hardy in the northern temperate regions, and late in summer bears its drooping bells of white tinted with green on 4- to 5-ft (1·2- to 1·5-metre) stems.

At the back of the border, the giant foxtail lilies may be planted and will grow up to 8 ft (2·4 metres) in height so they should be used only where the border can be protected from wind. Native of Turkestan and the western Himalayas, they bloom from early summer until autumn, *Eremurus elvesianus* being the earliest to bloom. Growing 8 to 9 ft (2·4 to 2·7 metres) tall, the elegant spikes of soft shell pink may measure more than 4 ft (1·2 metres) in length. The variety *albus* bears flowers of glistening white.

The taller growing alliums, the flowering onions, could also be used at the back of the border. Especially handsome is *A. giganteum*, native of the Himalayas. It will bloom with the later-flowering lilies, towards the end of summer, bearing enormous globes of violet-blue on 4- to 5-ft (1·2- to 1·5-metre) stems. The bulbs are expensive but three or four planted between the lilies will give flowers of a different colouring.

To plant in front, *A. karataviense* is early summer flowering and bears its violet umbels above tulip-shaped leaves on 3-ft (1-metre) stems. Near it plant *A. elatum* which bears flowers of soft lilac pink at a similar height, while to the front *A. moly*, the golden garlic, should be allowed to spread and will produce its loose umbels of brightest yellow early in summer. It is delightful when planted with the Spanish bluebells, especially the deep blue Excelsior which bears its bold spikes at the same time. It should be said that once established the bulbs of both plants will be difficult to eradicate. Plant them about 2 ft (60 cm) from the front of the border so that drifts of the early flowering scillas, muscari and crocuses can be set in front of them.

With the scillas and flowering garlics may be planted *Ornithogalum nutans* which blooms several weeks earlier, bearing its umbels of greenish-white flowers on 9-in (23-cm) stems. It, too, will spread about the border if undisturbed.

For the middle of the border, a place should be found for *L. candidum*, the Madonna Lily, the purest white of all lilies, which will diffuse its sweet honey scent about the garden on the warm days of midsummer. But whereas the other lilies should be planted 4 to 5 in (10 to 12 cm) deep, the Madonna Lily requires no more than 1 in (2·5 cm) of soil over its bulb but some lime rubble should be packed around it at planting time.

With these lilies, plant two or three groups of the crown imperial in shades of lemon yellow and orange. Both were well known to Elizabethan gardeners and, being native of Persia, Afghanistan and the western Himalayas, are hardy wherever they are planted. They grow 3 to 4 ft (1 metre) tall and bloom in spring when the back of the border is devoid of colour. Near them may be planted, in groups of six or more, some of the taller-growing mid-season tulips which bloom late in spring on 30-in (76-cm) stems. Outstanding is First Lady, with its flowers of warm violet-mauve, and Nova, its rosy-lilac flowers having a silvery sheen with rosy shading on the outside. The well-named Sulphur Glory and Orange Sun, both bearing blooms of great size, could also be used and would bring a splash of brilliant colour before this part of the border comes to life. Shortly after come the lily-flowered tulips, Queen of Sheba being one of the most exciting in this section, the long reflexed petals being margined with gold. With it plant the Cottage and Darwin tulips such as Bond Street and Easter Queen and the Multiflowered Georgette.

To the front, the April-flowering single early tulips such as Brilliant Star and Bellona, deepest yellow will be the first of the border tulips to bloom and will be followed shortly after by *T. fosteriana*, Red Emperor, bearing blooms of vivid crimson-scarlet, which for contrast should be planted with White Emperor. These tulips grow about 18 in (45 cm) tall and should be planted 6 in (15 cm) deep. They would not be as permanent as other plants of the border but in good soil could be left undisturbed for two years while the other plants are becoming established when they may be removed and replaced by plantings of other bulbs.

In place of the hybrid tulips could be planted the more permanent *T. marjoletti* which bears on 18-in (45-cm) stems dainty yellow flowers marked with purple, and *T. eichleri*, with its striking scarlet flowers and handsome grey foliage.

Here could be planted the yellow asphodel from southern Europe which loves a sunny situation and from a tuft of grass-like leaves bears, in early summer, spikes of starry yellow sweetly scented flowers, on a 3-ft (90-cm) stem.

Also plant *Alstroemeria*, the Peruvian lily, which, like *Eremurus* and *Asphodelus*, forms tuberous roots with a conspicuous crown. It should be planted over a mound of sand where the soil is heavy, spreading around the finger-like tubers. They are sun lovers and will not do well in shade. Once established, the *Alstroemeria* spreads rapidly but it should be planted 6 in (15 cm) deep or the roots may be damaged by frost. *A. aurantiaca* bears orange-bronze lily-like flowers on stems 2 to 3 ft (60 to 90 cm) in length and blooms during July and August.

Several species of lily may be planted near the front of the border. One is *L. rubellum*, native of Japan, which bears two to four dainty trumpets of softest pink on 18-in (45-cm) stems and they carry a soft sweet perfume. More compact is *L. × maculatum*, which bears its flowers of fiery scarlet on only 12- to 15-in (30- to 36-cm) stems; and *L. pumilum*, Golden Gleam, with its Turk's cap blooms of golden orange. Flowering in May, it is the earliest of the hardy lilies to come into bloom. A lily of slender habit is *L. cernuum*, which blooms a little later, its flowers of soft lilac-purple having delicious perfume.

The crocosmias (montbretias) may be planted towards the front for they bear their flowers on 18-in (45-cm) stems and will bloom during the latter weeks of summer and in autumn. The corms are planted in March, 4 in (10 cm) deep so space must be reserved for them. Half a dozen corms should be set out in groups, spacing them about 4 in (10 cm) apart, for they will quickly form large clumps and will need dividing in four to five years. Bearing a dozen or more star-like flowers on long wiry stems, they are long-lasting in the border and also when cut. Among the best is Emily McKenzie, which bears large star-like flowers of deepest orange, flaked with brown at the centre; and Lady Wilson, which bears flowers of rich orange-yellow on rigid stems. Striking, too, is Jessy, its large carmine-red flowers having a distinctive cream centre, while most unusual in its colouring is Lady Oxford, its pale-yellow flowers being shaded with peach.

Rhinegold is also lovely and bears large flowers of deep golden yellow with petals of velvet-like texture.

The large trumpet-flowering daffodils will be a permanent feature of the border and will bloom during spring and early summer. One of the earliest to bloom is Fine Gold, bearing flowers of purest gold with broad overlapping perianth petals and a beautifully shaped trumpet. Also early is Rembrandt with its refined trumpet of richest yellow. To follow are two yellows of outstanding beauty, Dutch Master and Unsurpassable, while Spellbinder adds distinction to any part of the garden. Its colour is greenish-sulphur yellow with a perianth of gold and a trumpet edged with golden-yellow.

The white daffodils will also enhance the border, one of the finest being the crystal-clear Beersheba, one of the purest of all white daffodils, while Silver Wedding with its elegant straight-sided trumpet is a beauty. The large-cupped narcissus Missouri, with its perianth of shining gold and scarlet cup, is outstanding; likewise Eddy Canzony which has a white perianth and orange corona. The double flowered Texas is a delightful combination of gold and orange, and Golden Ducat, a double form of the most popular of all daffodils, King Alfred, should also be grown.

To the front may be planted the *N. cyclamineus* hybrids, February Gold and Peeping Tom, which, with their elegant slim trumpets and reflexed petals, come into bloom early in spring and are at their best with the dwarf scillas.

The camassia, which grows about 20 in (50 cm) tall, is a valuable plant to set between the taller flowering daffodils, for they quickly form clumps. Planted 3 in (7·5 cm) deep and 6 in (15 cm) apart, *C. esculenta* bears showy spikes of steely blue above its graceful linear leaves. And for planting towards the back of the border, *C. leichtlinii atrocoerulea* bears spikes of clear mauve-blue on 3- to 4-ft (90-cm to 1·2-metre) stems.

The taller-growing muscari may be planted to the front for they bear their bloom on stems 10 in (25 cm) tall, and by planting several species there will be bloom from early spring until the daffodils have finished flowering. They will increase through the years and many will seed themselves. *M. latifolium* grows 10 in (25 cm) tall and is distinct. It forms a single broad leaf from which arises a large spike, the top half of which is pale blue, the lower half being dark blue. It comes late in spring and is followed by *M. comosum*, the tassel hyacinth which will remain in bloom until late in June. Its small greenish-purple flowers appear in clusters at the top of 12-in (30-cm) stems. The form *M. comosum plumosum*, the feather hyacinth, has sterile flowers converted into feathery plumes of violet filaments. It lasts well when in the garden or when cut and in water. To the front plant *M. tubergenianum*, native of western Persia and known as the Oxford and Cambridge grape hyacinth for the turquoise buds open to 'grapes' of darkest blue.

With the muscari, plant groups of the spring and summer snowflakes, *Leucojum vernum* and *L. aestivum*, which bear a succession of drooping bells

from early spring until late summer. Valuable for the border is *L. aestivum*
Gravetye, discovered by William Robinson in the garden of Gravetye Manor his
home. It bears drooping bells of purest white tipped with green and on 18-in
(45-cm) stems. With them plant the snowdrop and most suitable for a border is
Galanthus nivalis, Arnott's Variety. Though expensive, it increases rapidly and
bears a flower of beauty, the petals being more than 1 in (2·5 cm) long, the
inner segments having brilliant green margins and a delicious scent. They
bloom on 12-in (30-cm) stems.

A Border of Miniature Bulbs. A small area of ground may be made colourful
by planting the small flowering or miniature bulbs, beginning with those which
grow no more than 18 in (46 cm) tall and graduating the heights down to the
most dwarf, which will be planted to the front. Not always, however, will a
border of bulbs be made against a background of a wall or fence. Permanent beds
planted with bulbs may be made in a lawn, removing the turf in circles or to the
contours of the ground, making the beds kidney-shaped or oval, and here the
taller-growing bulbs will be planted at the centre, with those of dwarfer habit
grouped around them. Lilies and daffodils and all those bulbs described as being
suitable for the large border may also be used in this way, the size and height of
the plants to be used depending upon the size of garden.

By planting later-flowering bulbs near those which bloom early, the fresh
foliage of the one will help to hide the foliage of those which have died back.

Annual plants which grow only a few inches tall may be sown around the
bulbs as they come into growth in spring. The annuals will cover any bare
spaces and will help to hide the dying foliage and will remain green and colourful
through summer. The rock pimpernel, *Anagallis linifolia philipsii*, will quickly
cover the ground and has flowers of gentian-blue, while equally useful is *Linaria*
maroccana, Fairy Bouquet, which bears richly coloured flowers like tiny antirrhinums on 4-in (10-cm) stems. *Phacelia campanularia* will also quickly form a
green carpet spangled with bells of navy blue.

Among the most colourful plants for a miniature border will be the tulip
species. They will be more permanent than the large-flowering hybrids, while
they possess a daintiness of habit to be found in few other plants. *T. acuminata*,
possibly a variety of the old *T. gesneriana*, grows 15 in (38 cm) tall and has long
spider-like petals of greenish-yellow streaked with red. It could be planted
with *T. whittallii*, a native of Smyrna, which also blooms in April and grows to a
similar height. Its orange-bronze flowers with their black centre are most
striking. In front, plant *T. chrysantha*, its flowers of deepest gold being shaded
with cherry on the outside, and *T. batalinii* with its dainty goblets of primrose
yellow. Also suitable is *T. orphanidea*, which bears its flowers of buff-orange,
shaded with green and bronze, on 9-in (23-cm) stems. Each of these tulips will
continue to increase each year if growing in a well-drained soil.

Groups of the miniature daffodils, so valuable for growing in small pots and on grassy banks, may also be planted about a border, but the tiniest, such as *Narcissus minimus* and *N. minor*, should be reserved for alpine house and rockery. Several hybrids, for example the fragrant Lintie and February Gold, grow rather too tall for a miniature border; but there are many others of great charm, such as *N. cernuus*, a daffodil known to gardeners of Stuart times. It bears its nodding flowers of silvery white on 9-in (23-cm) stems above blue-green foliage. A hybrid worthy of growing is W. P. Milner, with its elegant cream-coloured trumpet.

For the centre of the border the new Hawera, a cross between *N. jonquilla* and *N. triandrus* is delightful, bearing four blooms to each 8-in (20-cm) stem. Another is Beryl, a *N. cyclamineus* hybrid, bearing globular cups of orange. It should be said that the miniature daffodils may take two years to become fully established before they come into bloom.

The bulbous irises should not be omitted, for they are quite untroubled by the severest of weather. Though *I. danfordiae* is best planted on a rockery, a group of two or three at the front of a border will add a touch of brilliant gold during February. Use as liberally as possible the violet-scented *I. reticulata*, which blooms on 9-in (23-cm) stems during March and April. The purple flowers have an orange blotch on the fall petals.

Where there is grass for naturalising, the bulb border might be kept for the more select bulbs such as *Erythronium tuolumnense*, a species of the dog's-tooth violet. Most free-flowering, it has dark-green glossy leaves above which, on 12-in (30-cm) stems, cyclamen-like flowers of brilliant golden yellow appear during April. There is also *E. californicum*, White Beauty, which has rich mottled foliage and large creamy-white flowers with a distinctive chocolate zone at the centre.

In small pockets plant, as liberally as possible, the winter aconite, its golden cups nestling among emerald-green leaves will be seen with the first warm rays of February sunshine.

There are many more charming little bulbous plants for use in the miniature border. One may add to the original plantings as the years pass by, until the border has become the most interesting part of the garden. For the more sheltered gardens, a number of the less hardy bulbs may be grown. Here the lovely tritonia and the brilliantly coloured sparaxis would be happy in well-drained soil if given a thick mulch before winter. These bulbs, natives of the Southern Hemisphere, will be happier with the protection of low shrubby plants such as dwarf heathers and veronicas. But try to plan for colour through-out the year rather than a profuse display in springtime. Plant the dwarf *Allium ostrowskianum* which grows less than 6 in (15 cm) tall and in midsummer bears large heads of purple-pink; and *Oxalis adenophylla*, which bears its attractive cups of lilac-pink at the same time—though in exposed gardens it will require winter protection. The same may be said for *Gladiolus nanus*, which bears its dainty spikes on 12-in (30-cm) stems in July. During winter the corms should be covered with weathered ash or peat but left undisturbed so that they will continue to increase in size.

For autumn-flowering, several of the crocus species are delightful in the small border. *C. zonatus* will open its pale-lilac cups early in September together with *C. nudiflorus*, its purple flowers appearing before the leaves. Then follows *C. speciosus*, which opens its mauve and violet tubes in the October sunshine as if by magic. Being inexpensive, the corms should be planted freely. The corms should be mixed with those of *C. zonatus* and *C. nudiflorus* so that there will always be some colour during autumn.

To follow is *C. longiflorus*, native of Malta, which brings the sunshine of the Mediterranean to the dull November days of North European gardens. The lavender tubes with their soft sweet perfume open to show a brilliant vermilion stigmata. It blooms with *C. asturicus*, which bears its violet flowers until mid-December.

10

Bulbs for the Alpine Garden

Value of bulbs in the alpine garden—making the garden—
suitable bulbs for the alpine garden—bulbs for crazy paving

Value of Bulbs in the Alpine Garden. It is in the alpine garden that the
miniature bulbs are most effective, for they find conditions similar to those of
their native haunts where, at 10,000 ft above sea level, they are to be found
snuggling among large boulders, seeking protection from the cold winds of
spring. They are, however, subjected to low winter temperatures and baking
heat in summer. Away from their natural habitat they will remain healthy and
vigorous and will bloom year after year if planted in pockets between stones in
a well-drained soil. They grow naturally in a sandy loam overlying rubble,
where sufficient moisture will be retained in summer and the excess will drain
away in winter. Under such conditions the plants remain healthy almost in-
definitely. Dwarf conifers may be used to provide winter colour and a background for the bulbs when in bloom.

Plant liberally. Most of the dwarf bulbs are admirable in that their foliage is
neat and tidy and dies back without any unsightly appearance. In a town garden
where perennial plants are often troubled by deposits of soot, the fact that the
foliage of the bulbs dies down after flowering is greatly in their favour. In this
respect the compact Juliae primroses are similar, and for several weeks in winter
they lose their foliage entirely. They should be planted with dwarf bulbs to
provide pleasing ground cover.

The miniature bulbs need less attention than many other alpine plants, such
as those of vigorous, trailing habit which tend to over-run their neighbours. But
in those gardens not troubled by soot deposits, the best of the evergreen carpeting plants will make admirable ground cover for the bulbs, providing conceal-
ment for their foliage as it dies back, while preventing the blooms from being
splashed by heavy rain. They will also suppress weeds and keep the bulbs cool
and moist during dry weather. A number of carpeting plants suggested for use
in a trough garden (Chapter 11) may also be used in the alpine garden. There
are others, however, none of them coarse, of rather too vigorous habit for a
trough. These include the alpine phloxes, particularly *P. douglasii*, May Snow,
bearing sheets of purest white during May and early June. Beneath its foliage

should be planted *Muscari armeniacum*, Cantab; and with *Phlox douglasii*, Violet Queen, plant the pure white *Muscari argaei album*, which also blooms in May and June.

The early-flowering kabschia or cushion saxifrages are excellent for planting with miniature bulbs, forming hummocks of silvery green and blooming from March until mid-May. With *Saxifraga jenkinsae*, with its blooms of clearest pink, plant the tiny Dalmatian hyacinth, for the azure blue spikes will flower at the same time. Plant *Iris reticulata* and *Iris histrioides* (both purple) among the Burseriana saxifrages with their large white and yellow flowers.

The dainty double daisy, Dresden China, with its buttons of palest pink, looks quite enchanting alongside *Crocus chrysanthus*, Blue Pearl, while for later in the year, *Nierembergia rivularis*, which forms mats of darkest green on which sit stemless white cups in early autumn, acts as a pleasing foil to the lavender flowers of *Crocus nudiflorus*, whose blooms appear before the leaves.

Another pleasing combination is to plant the little perennial candytuft, *Iberis jordani*, which forms a mat of glistening white flowers in May, with the Persian tulip, which bears several orange and yellow blooms to each 4-in (10-cm) stem. Another lovely alpine tulip is *T. pulchella* which grows 4 in (10 cm) tall and bears star-like flowers of pinky-lilac during March. Plant it in a pocket of leaf mould and sand with the tiny *Primula clarkei*, which in March bears almost stemless flowers of glowing pink. For May and June, another delightful combination is *Fritillaria citrina*, with its bright lemon-yellow flowers, to accompany *Viola gracilis major*, its purple, violet-like blooms being held on short stems above pale-green foliage. In flower at the same time is the prostrate *Veronica rupestris*, Mauve Queen, which bears dainty spikes of rich purple.

Colourful plants for a dry, sunny situation include *Anomatheca cruenta*, with the creeping, aromatic thymes; *T. serphyllum coccineus*, with its mats of brilliant crimson flowers, and Snowdrift, with its white flowers, in bloom together.

As an alternative to carpeting plants, limestone chippings placed around and over the bulbs during winter will provide protection for the less hardy bulbs, suppress annual weeds and prevent soil from splashing on to the flowers.

Where miniature bulbs and such accommodating plants as the saxifrages and sempervivums and other shade-lovers are to be used, a colourful rockery can be made in partial shade, possibly against the wall of an outbuilding, or near tall trees—though not too close, since drip from trees may cause waterlogging or 'panning' of the soil.

An alpine garden may also be made at the end of a garden, or used to divide one part of the garden from another. Here, raised above ground level, the plants are seen to advantage. A small rock garden may be made as an alternative to a low grassy bank. Any ground having a pronounced slope may be made interesting by the use of suitable stones and miniature bulbs.

An alpine garden may be made on either side of stone steps leading down to a dell, with the overhanging branches of trees providing a grotto-like appearance.

Throughout the year the garden can be alive with the rich colour of shade-loving plants, the hardy cyclamen and dog's-tooth violets, the chionodoxas and dwarf hyacinths. Snowdrops and winter aconites may carpet the ground in winter and, as the trees come into leaf, the filtered sunlight will shine down on the brilliant blues of the scillas and the golden daffodils, to produce a most striking effect beneath the pale-green foliage of the trees.

Making the Garden. An alpine garden should look as though it were a part of the mountainous landscape where the plants are to be found growing naturally and not be merely a jumble of rocks which have the appearance of being tipped from a lorry. Made on the flat it may be constructed to represent a level outcrop where the rock has weathered into gentle undulations and fragments of rock have gathered. Here the plants begin to build up humus and so are able to flourish between the harder rocks that have resisted wind and weather.

Whatever the type of rock, it should look as though it were an outcrop from a solid mass below the soil. Limestone and sandstone are laid down in layers and these layers should slope in the same direction so that the maximum effect is obtained by creating a gentle slope which the stones follow.

Westmorland limestone is the best of all stone to use for its layers show clearly, while it has many crevices to take plants such as sedums and sempervivums. It is also frost-resistant and its grey colour contrasts beautifully with the small and brilliant corollas of dwarf bulbs. Sandstone is effective too and is often cheaper, but it will look red and raw for a considerable time, while frost often causes it to flake. Westmorland limestone may be obtained from alpine garden contractors, who will usually have small quantities for disposal and will often deliver it for a small extra cost. The correct use of stone will be observed by those visiting the premier flower shows when the specialist alpine garden contractors compete for various awards.

When making a small alpine garden, it is better to use stones of average size and as near as possible to the same size throughout. Avoid the use of numerous small pieces, as it is not easy to arrange these in a natural-looking 'outcrop'. A quantity of fresh loamy soil, preferably sterilised, will probably be obtainable from a local nurseryman, and with this should be incorporated some grit to encourage drainage and a small proportion of peat to help to retain summer moisture. A quantity of boiler ash or similar material should be available for drainage at the base of the rockery, and this may be collected and stored until required.

Once the stone is on the site, the making of the alpine garden should proceed slowly. It is generally believed that the more haphazard the stone is set, the better will be the effect. This is far from being so, for many things need to be considered beyond mere casualness of disposal.

A rock garden on the flat should face south if possible, but if this is away from the view of the house it can face in any direction without detriment to the plants. Dig out the soil 4 in (10 cm) deep, keeping the upper layer to make brought-in loam and peat go farther, and taking great care to remove all perennial weed roots, especially those of couch-grass and convolvulus. If it can be built up a little towards the back, the appearance will be further improved because the plants and rock at the back will be better displayed.

Where the base has been excavated, half fill with a 2-in (5-cm) layer of small clinker or boiler ash sifted to remove the dust, for you do not want a solid mass but an efficient means of drainage. Then consider the stone, which for a flat site should be constructed of long flat pieces—a bank or a steep rock garden requires stone with tall 'faces', a flat garden needs less face and more top.

The 'face' of limestone is the surface showing the layers, those that are softer having been eroded away by the rain driving against the front of the rock. The 'top' is where the rain beats down on it, or where standing water has worn it away, and this will have rounded holes in it and good crevices for planting, while the underside will be jagged or flat where it was broken off the solid rock.

A stone may be 'two-faced', i.e. where one side was exposed to weather; but a face should always look to the front with the tops upward.

A flat site may be built downwards, upwards or sideways, bedding the rocks into the drainage layer so that they look like hard parts sticking up, with soil in between. Here, the bulbs will grow in the depressions.

Make each rock higher at the face than at the back, so that it has a slant away from the angle of the slope. This is because when rock slopes the other way it will neither show its face nor trap soil in the pockets—rain will sweep everything clear. Only a little difference in height is necessary but it should be roughly the same for every stone.

Instead of dotting the stones about, concentrate them, so that they fit together one behind the other, like the sides of a ravine. Place a few across the mouth of the ravine, face forward, with a flat planting space behind them as if it were a waterfall over the 2-in (5-cm)-high cliff. Use long rocks, pointing the way the 'stream' would flow, but always face forward with the top upwards.

Because the site is flat, the strata lines on the faces also need to be flat, but if there is a slope two ways, follow this, with the strata lines parallel with the slopes. Always think of the rock garden as one big rock with parts of it showing through the soil.

Put on the soil, 3 to 4 in (8 to 10 cm) deep, ramming it firmly round the rocks. They need to be firm enough to be immovable when treading about them for weeding and planting. In the spaces between, plant the bulbs. If there are any rocks with good tall faces, have them fairly high on the slope. Plant low-growing bulbs in front of them, so that yellow or bright-blue flowers show against the grey stone.

To make an alpine garden on a low bank, insert the stone into the bank after removing the grass. Aim at giving the completed rockery as natural an appearance as possible by following the suggestions already made. The stones should again be placed with their flat surface uppermost and each slope gently in the same direction. It may not, however, be possible to build up the stones as gradually as desired (for the more gradual the slope, the more natural the appearance) since the slope must be determined by the fall of the ground. It may be possible to make an extension by adding soil at the base, thus lessening the acuteness of the angle where the bank is unduly steep.

An alpine garden at the foot of a wall or in a corner should be built up by degrees, and it will first be necessary to provide a foundation. The core of the garden may be of material which will have little value for use elsewhere and indeed most new gardens contain quantities of stone, broken bricks and mortar and all manner of unwanted material left behind by the builder. An old property, too, generally abounds in broken pots and glass and other refuse which will need to be removed and which, with boiler ash and clinker, will be ideal for making a base for an alpine garden. Where no rubbish is available, a load of broken brick from a building site will be necessary. This will make for efficient drainage and help to raise the garden. Over this fresh loam is tipped, then the stones are placed as previously described. Do not attempt to make the garden too high, and do not use too much stone or pieces that are too long.

Plant the bulbs in the pockets formed by the stones, setting those bulbs forming upright grass-like leaves in groups of four or five, and plants of low, bushy habit (e.g. *Erythronium dens-canis*) in groups of two or three. Plant in June and July those bulbs which come into bloom in autumn and early winter; plant in autumn, which is the most suitable time for making up the alpine garden, those that bloom in spring. Observe the correct planting depths, though where the alpine garden affords a certain amount of protection and the soil is well-drained, greater liberties may be taken in this respect.

Suitable Bulbs for the Alpine Garden. Among the most charming bulbs for the alpine garden, where they may be given that little extra attention they would not otherwise receive, are the smallest of the miniature daffodils. Like snow-drops, they are best taken up and planted soon after they have flowered, being divided while in leaf and replanted with the minimum of delay.

Narcissus minimus, which grows less than 3 in (7.5 cm) tall, is a plant of charming delicacy. It is the first of the miniature daffodils to bloom, bearing its tiny golden trumpets before the end of February. Parkinson tells us that the first bulbs were brought to this country at the beginning of the seventeenth century by a Frenchman, Francis le Veau, 'the honestest root gatherer that ever came over to us'. *N. juncifolius*, the miniature rush-leaf daffodil with flattish little blooms on 4-in (10-cm) stems is also 'at home' in the alpine garden. The flowers are fragrant, as are those of *N. canaliculatus*, a charming polyanthus narcissus, which has four blooms to each stem, their white perianths enhanced by tiny golden cups. *N. minor* is also right. Early into bloom, its twisted perianth and lobed trumpet are of deepest yellow. The Hoop Petticoat daffodils are also

elegant. They bear their flowers on 6-in (15-cm) stems, the first to bloom being
N. bulbocodium romieuxii. Then follows the lemon-yellow form, *citrinus*, and
later, *conspicuus*, with its conical trumpets of brilliant gold. Natives of southern
France and Spain, these lovely miniature daffodils require a well-drained sandy
soil containing some peat. There are others, and early to bloom is *N. lobularis*,
which has a sulphur perianth and yellow trumpet, likewise the new hybrid
Wee Bee, with its golden flowers. A rare and extremely beautiful species from
Morocco, *N. watieri*, bears a tiny pure-white flower of 'crystalline texture' and
is a gem for the rock garden or for pans in the alpine house. It is late to bloom.
The lovely *N. rupicola*, which will seed itself when established, should also be
planted. It has bright yellow flowers with six-lobed coronas on 4-in (10-cm)
stems. The cyclamen-flowered narcissus, *N. cyclamineus*, with its reflexed
perianth, should also be included, though it is happiest in a damp situation near
a pond or stream.

The chionodoxas should be planted close to the daffodils for they will be in
bloom at the same time, the brilliant blue enamel colouring of their flowers
providing exquisite contrast. They are valuable little flowers in that they are
quite unresentful of the cold winds and sleet showers of early spring, and, unlike
the crocus, they refuse to close their flowers to protect themselves from the
elements. Their delicate-looking blooms deceive with their appearance, for they
are among the toughest of all flowers and can be seen from afar. The rockery
will suit the Glory of the Snow, for it enjoys a more open, sunny situation than
most of the miniature-flowering bulbs, and it likes a well-drained soil. The
blooms are of such distinctive, and rather harsh, colouring that they should be
kept quite separate. Unlike the crocuses, the blooms are rarely troubled by
birds nor do the bulbs prove an attraction for mice.

First into bloom, early in March, is *C. sardensis*, bearing flowers of rich
gentian blue with a glistening white centre. Then follows *C. luciliae*, the vivid
blue flowers with their striking white eye borne in dainty sprays at a height of
4 in (10 cm). There is also an attractive pale-pink form, *rosea*. *C. gigantea* is at
its best throughout April. It is taller growing than the others, and bears soft
lavender-blue flowers on 6-in (15-cm) stems. It seeds itself freely.

The most dwarf of the crocus species are ideal plants for the alpine garden
and they may be seen in bloom from September, when *C. zonatus* comes into
flower, until the following May, finishing with the sapphire-blue *C. tomasinianus*. For October flowering, the lovely *C. pulchellus*, with its lavender
flowers and white anthers, and *C. medius*, with its rich violet blooms and orange
stigmas, should be included in every rockery. For November, the sweetly
scented *C. longiflorus* should be planted. Then follows the delicately perfumed *C. imperati*, its outer petals being fawn coloured feathered with violet,
while *C. ancyrensis* is always at its loveliest where given the protection of
stone. It comes into bloom with the first warm Febraury sunshine, its tiny tubes
of burnt-orange providing a welcome appearance.

To give a splash of brilliant colour, the tulip species stand supreme and it is difficult to understand just why they are not more widely planted for this purpose. They are right for planting in groups of three or four with the grey tufa stone for a background. *T. pulchella* is one of the first to bloom, and with *P. persica* it is one of the smallest. It is in bloom by early March, its urn-shaped flowers of pale mauve borne on 4-in (10-cm) stems opening flat in the sun to reveal a bright-yellow centre. Then follows *T. biflora* from the Caucasus, each 6-in (15-cm) stem being terminated with three starry white flowers, and in early April comes *T. batalini*, expensive but charming. Its creamy-yellow blooms are held on 6-in (15-cm) stems above unique grey foliage. With it plant *T. chrysantha*. It has dainty yellow blooms shaded cherry-red on the outside. And include the unusual *T. dasystemon*, which bears several pale-yellow flowers shaded with grey and green on the exterior.

For early summer, *Brodiaea grandiflora* offers its umbels of deep blue during June when the garden will be devoid of the brilliant colouring of spring, though there will be many summer-flowering alpine plants in bloom. Plant with it the equally pleasing *B. crocea*, with umbels of lemon-yellow flowers on 6-in (15-cm) stems during May and June. Though a native of California, it is perfectly hardy and will prove to be long living in a well-drained soil and sunny situation.

The smallest of the flowering garlics, *Allium ostrowskianum*, is a most attractive plant for the rock garden and, like the brodiaeas, bears its heads of deep rosy-red on 6-in (15-cm) stems during June. More difficult to obtain is *A. cyaneum*, native of China. It has glossy leaves, and the flowers of vivid blue have an attractive green eye.

To maintain the bulbs and plants in a healthy condition, provide them with a mulch of peat or leaf mould augmented with a small amount of decayed cow manure or used hops. This is worked into the soil around the plants and over the bulbs where they are not covered with carpeting plants. The foliage of the bulbs may be partially hidden by pressing it beneath nearby plants or by pinning it to the soil as it dies back. It may also be hidden, as described earlier, by using plants of shrubby habit which grow about 6 in (15 cm) tall. If the spring- and early summer-flowering plants are planted in the same group as those that bloom later in summer and early autumn, this will help to hide the dying foliage of the early-flowering bulbs, which must not be entirely removed until they have had time to die right back.

Cloches may also be used to bring various plants, including bulbs, into bloom before their natural time. But remember that alpine plants are used to cold regions, and at all times fresh air must be admitted. The use of an open-ended cloche will help to bring the bulbs into bloom a little earlier than normally and will protect the more tender winter-flowering plants from fog and soot deposits and excessive moisture. Cloches are also useful for giving any newly planted alpines protection from cold drying winds of springtime until they are established. If no glass is available, twigs and small branches of evergreens inserted into the soil around the plants will provide protection.

It is advisable to remove from the rockery all leaves which may have fallen from nearby trees in late autumn. These become saturated, and may cause nearby plants and bulbs to decay should the winter be unduly wet.

Provided both plants and bulbs are given care in their culture they should remain vigorous and free-flowering for many years without the need to lift and divide. Overcrowding must, however, be guarded against and where this occurs, the bulbs may be thinned by lifting a number from each clump so as to allow more room for those left in the ground. Those which have been lifted may be divided and replanted elsewhere.

Bulbs for Crazy Paving. Where space is limited, bulbs may be used in pockets of soil about a path of crazy paving stone, two or three bulbs of the smallest species and varieties being planted in each pocket.

When laying a path of crazy paving, begin by marking out the necessary length and width, then remove several inches of soil, depending on (a) the depth of stone and (b) whether it is proposed to lay the stone on a thin bed of concrete.

The question of the concrete bed is all-important, for not only will it provide a firmer foundation which will prevent various stones from falling below the original level, which in time they will do, but it will prevent the appearance of grass and weeds between the stones. The concreting will add slightly to the cost and will mean more labour, but will be more than worth while. Pockets between the stones may be left free of concrete at irregular intervals to take the bulbs, but do not overdo this; a few look better than too many. The still wet concrete can be removed from the pockets after sections of the path are laid.

First select the stones before the work is to begin and if possible place them into something like order by the side of the path. A better job can be made of a terrace where either flags or crazy paving stone is being used, if first a solid foundation of clinker or crushed brick or stone is made. This means taking out an extra 2 in (5 cm) or 3 in (7·5 cm) of soil, but a clinker foundation will make a better base over which to place the concrete. Even where no concrete is used, a clinker base will prove of value in providing additional drainage, especially if the path is at all low-lying. The soil may be used to fill up the pockets, but a prepared compost would be better.

Apart from a good spade, the only tool needed will be a spirit level which will ensure a neater and more professional job, with stones laid level. Obtain a builder's level large enough to span across the path so that the top of the stone may be kept level with the sides of the bed. Make use of the level from the time the clinker base is put down, for this will ensure that the concrete will also be level and will make the final laying of the stone so much easier. Be sure to have the flattest surface of the stone to the top and keep the sides as near straight as possible. A neat job can be done by laying a row of bricks in cement down each side of the path, placing them on their sides and just above the level of the stones. The contrast in colour of brick and stone adds to the finished effect and the bricks will help to prevent the soil from falling on to the concrete while this is being placed in position.

Remember to set the stones as close to each other as possible, for if too much concrete is used to point the path on completion, it will spoil the effect. If the stone can be laid close, no pointing need be done beyond the filling-up of those pockets into which there is no intention of setting a plant. Plant as the work proceeds. First make a satisfactory base which is quite level, then lay the stone in possibly 6-ft (1·8-metre) lengths, completely finishing the stretch in every way before continuing with the next 6 ft (1·8 metres). Concrete should be removed while still wet from pockets intended for bulbs and the hole left behind filled up with compost.

The compost mixture should be of leaf mould, soil, decayed manure and sand in equal parts and should be placed between the stones to a depth of at least 4 in (10 cm), otherwise there will not be a sufficient root run for the bulbs. Before the compost is added, a few pieces of crushed brick or mortar should be put in to encourage drainage. Firm the compost. Two or three bulbs should be planted in each pocket, the most suitable being the winter aconites, snowdrops, the smallest of the crocus miniatures, *Bulbocodium vernum*, *Muscari argaei album*, *Hyacinthus dalmaticus*, *Oxalis adenophyla* and *Scilla verna*. If several of the carpeting plants are also used, the sedums and thymes being outstanding in this respect, the crazy paving will be colourful for long periods. The following bulbs will be suitable for the alpine garden. All are of dwarf, dainty habit and have neat, tidy foliage:

TABLE XVI. *Bulbs for an alpine garden*

Species	Flowering time	Height
Allium cyaneum	July–August	4 in (10 cm)
Anomatheca cruenta	July–August	5 to 6 in (12·5 to 15 cm)
Brodiaea crocea	May–June	5 to 6 in (12·5 to 15 cm)
Brodiaea minor	June	5 to 6 in (12·5 to 15 cm)
Bulbocodium vernum	March	3 in (7·5 cm)
Chionodoxa lucilae	March–April	4 in (10 cm)
Chionodoxa sardensis	March	4 in (10 cm)
Chionodoxa tmoli	April	4 in (10 cm)
Crocus ancyrensis	February–March	2 in (5 cm)
Crocus balansae	March	1½ in (3 cm)
Crocus fleischeri	February–April	2 in (5 cm)
Crocus korolkowi	January–March	1½ in (3 cm)
Crocus laevigatus	December–February	3 in (7·5 cm)

TABLE XVI—*Continued*

Species	Flowering time	Height
Crocus medius	October	3 in (7·5 cm)
Crocus minimus	March–April	1½ in (3 cm)
Crocus nudiflorus	October–November	3 in (7·5 cm)
Crocus ochroleucus	November–December	2 in (5 cm)
Crocus olivieri	April–May	2 in (5 cm)
Crocus sativus	October	2 in (5 cm)
Crocus vernus	March	2 in (5 cm)
Cyclamen orbiculatum	December–February	3 in (7·5 cm)
Cyclamen atkinsii	December–March	3 to 4 in (7·5 to 10 cm)
Cyclamen cilicium	September–November	3 in (7·5 cm)
Cyclamen graecum	July–September	4 in (10 cm)
Eranthis cilicica	February–March	2 in (5 cm)
Eranthis hyemalis	January–February	2 in (5 cm)
Erythronium dens-canis	March–April	6 in (15 cm)
Erythronium hendersonii	April	4 in (10 cm)
Fritillaria citrina	April–May	5 to 6 in (12·5 to 15 cm)
Fritillaria pudica	April–May	4 in (10 cm)
Galanthus allenii	April	3 in (7·5 cm)
Galanthus byzantinus	December–January	4 in (10 cm)
Galanthus latifolius	March–April	3 in (7·5 cm)
Galanthus nivalis	February–March	5 in (12·5 cm)
Hyacinthus azureus	April	5 in (12·5 cm)
Hyacinthus dalmaticus	April	4 in (10 cm)
Iris bakeriana	January–February	6 in (15 cm)
Iris danfordiae	February	4 in (10 cm)
Iris histrioides	March	6 in (15 cm)
Iris reticulata	March–April	6 in (15 cm)
Muscari argaei album	May–June	4 in (10 cm)
Muscari armeniacum	April–May	6 in (15 cm)
Muscari polyanthus album	April–May	5 to 6 in (12·5 to 15 cm)
Narcissus bulbocodium	March–April	6 in (15 cm)
Narcissus canaliculatus	April	6 in (15 cm)
Narcissus capax plenus	April	6 in (15 cm)
Narcissus juncifolius	April	4 in (10 cm)
Narcissus minimus	February–March	4 in (10 cm)
Narcissus nanus	March–April	6 in (15 cm)
Narcissus rupicola	April	4 in (10 cm)
Narcissus triandrus	April–May	6 in (15 cm)
Narcissus watieri	May	4 in (10 cm)

TABLE XVI—*Continued*

Species	Flowering time	Height
Puschkinia scilloides	March–May	4 in (10 cm)
Scilla bifolia	February–March	6 in (15 cm)
Scilla tubergeniana	February–March	5 in (12·5 cm)
Scilla verna	April	4 in (10 cm)
Tulipa australis	April	6 in (15 cm)
Tulipa batalini	April	4 in (10 cm)
Tulipa biflora	March–April	5 in (12·5 cm)
Tulipa dasystemon	April–May	6 in (15 cm)
Tulipa linifolia	May	6 in (15 cm)
Tulipa maximowiczii	April	6 in (15 cm)
Tulipa persica	May	3 in (7·5 cm)
Tulipa pulchella	March–April	4 in (10 cm)
Tulipa wilsoniana	May	6 in (15 cm)

11

Bulbs for Trough Garden and Window Box

Advantage of a trough garden—construction of a trough—suitable plants for a trough—indispensable bulbs—carpeting plants—preparing the box—the sink garden—the window box

---

The Advantage of a Trough Garden. A delightful garden in miniature may be formed where there is only sufficient space on which to stand a trough. This may be placed almost anywhere so long as overhead moisture from a roof or trees cannot drip on to it. Under the overhanging eaves of a house, a trough may be placed directly against a wall, possibly beneath a window, from which the beauty of the bulbs may be enjoyed whatever the weather, in much the same way as a window box. A trough may be placed against the walls of a paved court-yard, on a terrace or veranda, or on a flat roof. Here, the miniature garden may be planted to give colour throughout the year and may be enjoyed during all weathers.

Though there is nothing quite comparable to weathered stone for the trough garden, concrete will prove suitable where a stone trough cannot be obtained. Concrete has the advantage of being porous, so the soil will keep sweet for much longer and the plants remain healthier.

Of whatever material the trough is to be constructed, it must be provided with a drainage hole, but where the stone is thick, and this is not possible, ample drainage materials should be placed at the bottom before the trough is filled with compost.

Construction of a Trough. The most satisfactory way of constructing a concrete trough is to make two boxes of timber which has been planed, making one about 1½ in (3 cm) smaller in all dimensions. The smaller box will fit inside the other. For the base and walls of the trough, mix 2 parts of sand to 1 part of cement, adding sufficient water to make it into a paste that will 'pour', yet not letting it become too 'sloppy'. The cement should be poured inside the larger box to a depth of 1½ in (3 cm), two large corks being held in position at the base to provide the drainage holes. To reinforce the base and sides, a length of wire netting should be pressed into the cement mixture just before it begins to set, and this must extend almost to the top of the sides. A second piece of netting should be pressed into the mixture so that it extends up the other two sides in a similar way. Use 2-in (5-cm)-mesh netting, cutting the pieces to the exact measurements of the mould. Thus for a box 2 in (5 cm) long by 18 in (45 cm) wide by 6 in (15 cm) deep, the two pieces of netting will measure 42 in (1·1 metres) and 30 in (75 cm). The smaller box does not require a base. Make the four sides and hold them together by small pieces of wood nailed across each corner and long enough to stretch across the corners of the first box to prevent it pressing into the concrete base. The cement is then poured between the two boxes. Insert a piece of stick to hold the netting away from the mould and this will prevent it showing when the concrete has finally set hard, which it will do in about 24 hours if not made too thin. Just before the cement has set completely, the sides of the boxes are carefully removed, the inner mould being left in position until the cement is thoroughly hardened. The wooden base and the corks are then pressed out.

Troughs are heavy, so, of whatever material they are constructed, they should be in their permanent sites before they are prepared for the plants. Make certain that they are made firm on the single or double pedestal, using wedges where necessary. Over the drainage holes place several large crocks, or pieces of brick or stone, then cover the base with a layer of small stones or crocks to a depth of 6 in (15 cm). Over this place old turves upside down and then fill to the top with the prepared soil mixture, pressing it down round the sides. This should be composed of:

2 parts fresh loam, sterilised if possible

1 part top-grade peat, which is superior to leaf mould because it contains no weed seeds

1 part coarse sand and grit.

Add a sprinkling of superphosphate to encourage root action, some lime to keep it sweet, a little bone meal, a slow-acting fertiliser; and mix together. If one has no garden, sterilised loam, peat and sand may be obtained from a local nursery; and as a general guide, a barrowful of compost will be required for a sink of approximately 36 in (90 cm) by 18 in (45 cm) by 6 in (15 cm). Most stone troughs are several inches deeper, but rarely more than 24 to 26 in (60 to 65 cm) in length, so that compost requirements will be much the same. Some troughs have no drainage holes and so should be given a greater depth of material to assist in their drainage, while some broken charcoal should be mixed with the compost to maintain its sweetness.

Suitable Plants for a Trough. Where more than one trough can be made up, it will be possible to confine to one those plants which enjoy lime in their diet, such as the dwarf alpine pinks and a number of the saxifrages and sempervivums. *Androsace sempervivoides*, which bears umbels of pink flowers during

April, loves lime and will often be in bloom at the same time as those other lime lovers, *Iris reticulata*, *Cyclamen coum* and *C. repandum*. *Aethionema iberideum*, the Persian candytuft, also likes a dry, chalky soil, its ash-grey foliage and white flowers acting as a pleasing foil to the April-flowering crocuses and irises. There are also later-flowering forms of these delightful alpine plants to extend the season. Another trough may be made up with those plants enjoying a moist, peaty soil such as the extremely dwarf Juliae primroses, F. Ashby, with its tiny blooms of claret red and Snow Cushion. The tiny heather, Mrs Ronald Gray, which forms a small prostrate clump 1 in (2·5 cm) high and is covered with deep purple bells in September; and Mrs Pat, which blooms in spring, are suitable for a peaty soil. Besides being good to look at, they will prevent the tiny blooms of the bulbs from being splashed. The lovely *Cassiope lycopodioides*, a shrublet of the heather family, which bears masses of tiny white bells during May, is also suitable. Bulbs for planting in a trough containing a peaty soil, and where situated in partial shade should include the dog's-tooth violets, with their pretty mottled foliage and dainty rosy-mauve blooms. The snowdrops and winter aconites will also do well in such a soil.

Where the trough is in full sun, suitable plants will be the androsace, aubrietia, *Asperula gussoni*, *Helianthemum alpestre* and *Veronica halleri*. Each of these plants, with the exception of the aubrietia, which is useful for planting to trail over the sides, is of dwarf, shrubby habit, thereby affording protection to the miniature bulbs as they come into bloom. For a sun-baked position, some of the most suitable bulbs are the irises—*Anomatheca cruenta*, which bears its salmon-orange flowers on 4-in (10-cm) stems during July and August, *Brodiaea minor*, with its tiny umbels of deepest blue—and the crocuses. Also, where the trough is in a sheltered, sunny position, do not omit *Rhodohypoxis baurii*, with pink flowers borne on 2-in (5-cm) stems and attractive grey leaves.

Bulbs for a trough garden should be of dwarf habit; and those which tend to increase rapidly, whether from seed or by the formation of bulblets, should be omitted, for they will crowd out their neighbours. The bulbs should not grow more than 6 in (15 cm) tall, and their foliage should remain neat and tidy after flowering. This rule will exclude a number of the dwarf tulips, the colchicums and dwarf alliums which would be suitable in all other respects.

The best effect will be obtained by making the trough into a tiny alpine garden complete with tufa stone and miniature trees. Two or three pieces of stone should be used, placed well down in the soil in the same way as recommended for the alpine garden so as to give the stone a natural appearance, the grain at a slight slope and in the same direction for each piece of stone. About the stones one or possibly two miniature trees should be planted to give the trough a garden-like appearance, and none is more suitable than the dwarf Norway spruce, *Picea excelsa nana compacta*, which grows broader than it grows tall, rarely exceeding 5 in (13 cm) in height. Add a few dwarf alpine plants to provide protection for the bulbs and to give colour over as long a period as possible, often when the bulbs will not be in bloom. Between these, the bulbs will be planted in groups of two or three.

Indispensable Bulbs. Indispensable bulbs for a trough garden are the chiono-doxas—not *C. gigantea*, which is rather too robust, but *C. luciliae* (brilliant blue) and *rosea* (delicate pink). There is also a white form, *alba*.

The daintiest of the crocuses are suitable, three bulbs being planted together, almost touching, for best effect. To flower in October: *C. asturicus*, pale mauve; and for November: *C. ochroleucus*, creamy white. For February there is *C. fleischeri* and *C. ancyrensis*. The hardy cyclamen, which blooms in autumn, is also an excellent plant for trough culture. Its pale-pink flowers, which look like moths, hover above the small rounded leaves. The foliage is enhanced by an attractive silver zone. The spring-flowering *C. coum* and *C. repandum* may also be used.

The most slender of the grape hyacinths, *Muscari azureum*, with its spikes of pale-blue 'grapes', also its white counterpart, *alba*, do well in a trough; also the little *Scilla bifolia*, in its dark-blue and shell-pink form.

No trough garden will be complete without at least one of the tulip species, though with most the foliage tends to grow rather too large for a trough. Suitable is the shining scarlet *T. maximowiczii*, and *T. dasystemon*, which has several yellow flowers to each stem. Both flower in April, while for May *T. persica*, with its tiny yellow and bronze blooms held on only 3-in (7·5-cm) stems, is indispensable.

Of the miniature daffodils, *Narcissus minimus* and *N. minor*, the fragrant *N. juncifolius* and the dainty double-flowered Wee Bee, are all suitable for a trough, but will not usually bloom in their first season.

A rare little bulbous plant of great beauty is the Pyrenean meadow saffron, *Merendera sobolifera*. Its fragile cups of palest pink borne on 3-in (7·5-cm) stems begin to appear early in April, and these are followed by dark-green leaves which are so neat as to make this plant one which may be recommended for trough garden and rockery.

Another gem, in bloom throughout spring and equally at home on the rockery, is *Fritillaria pudica*. A native of North America, it is hardy and enjoys a sunny position. It is best planted in a pocket of sand, for the bulbs will decay with an excess of winter moisture. On a 5-in (12·5-cm) stem it bears four or five nodding bells of purest gold, which are most enchanting in the spring sunshine.

When the leaves begin to die down after the bulbs have flowered, those bulbs with upright, grass-like leaves will never be too conspicuous as they turn brown. If carpeting plants are used as freely as space permits, the leaves will be even less noticeable, as they grow through the carpeters.

Carpeting Plants. The bulbs should be planted so that as they spread, they may grow up through the carpeting plants, obtaining support, shelter and protection from soil splashing. This last, however, may also be prevented by covering the soil around the plants with spare chippings, which will set off the flowers to perfection and will also suppress weeds until they have covered the trough.

TABLE XVII. *Carpeting plants for a trough garden*

Name	Foliage	Flowers
Acaena buchanani	Glaucous green	—
Acaena intermis	Purple-bronze	—
Arenaria caespitosa aurea	Golden	White
Armeria caespitosa	Green	Pink
Asperula lilaciflora	Emerald green	Pink
Campanula E. H. Frost	Bright green	White
Campanula pulla lilacina	Bright green	Lilac rose
Cotula species	Purple-green	—
Draba bryoides imbricata	Grey-green	Yellow
Draba pyrenaica	Dark green	Mauve
Frankenia thymaefolia	Grey-green	Pink
Globularia bellidifolia	Bottle green	Blue
Hippocrepis E. R. Janes	Bottle green	Lemon
Houstonia coerulea	Bottle green	Blue
Linaria aequitriloba	Dark green	Mauve
Lippia repens	Grey-green	Pink
Nierembergia rivularis	Dark green	White
Raoulia australis	Silver	Yellow
Raoulia lutescens	Grey	Golden
Saxifraga oppositifolia splendens	Emerald	Crimson
Sedum acre minor	Bronze	Yellow
Sedum dasyphyllum	Glaucous green	White
Sedum hispanicum aureum	Gold	White
Sedum lydium	Green, turning scarlet	Yellow
Silene acaulis saxatilis	Emerald	Pink
Thymus nieciffii	Silver-grey	Cerise
Thymus serpyllum minus	Grey-green	Pink
Wahlenbergia serpyllifolia	Dark green	Purple

So valuable are carpeting plants for use with miniature bulbs, not only in the trough garden but also about the alpine garden, that a list of suitable plants may prove helpful.

As the alpine plants will be pot-grown, they may be set out at almost any time except when the soil is frozen or excessively wet. The best time to make up a trough, however, will be in the early weeks of autumn, when the spring- and

TABLE XVIII. *Bulbs suitable for a trough garden*

Name	Flowering time	Height
Anomatheca cruenta	July–August	4 to 5 in (12 cm)
Chionodoxa lucilae	March–April	4 in (10 cm)
Chionodoxa sardensis	March–April	4 in (10 cm)
Crocus ancyrensis	February–March	2 in (5 cm)
Crocus asturicus	October–November	4 in (10 cm)
Crocus candidus	April	2 in (5 cm)
Crocus korolkowi	September–October	1½ in (3 cm)
Crocus laevigatus	December–February	3 in (7.5 cm)
Crocus minimus	March–April	1½ in (3 cm)
Crocus ochroleucus	November–December	2 in (5 cm)
Crocus olivieri	April–May	2 in (5 cm)
Crocus sativus	October–November	2 in (5 cm)
Crocus zonatus	September–October	4 in (10 cm)
Cyclamen alpinum	December–February	3 in (7.5 cm)
Cyclamen coum	January–April	3 in (7.5 cm)
Erythronium dens-canis	March–April	5 to 6 in (12.5 to 15 cm)
Erythronium hendersonii	March–April	4 in (10 cm)
Fritillaria pudica	April–May	4 in (10 cm)
Hyacinthus dalmaticus	April–May	4 in (10 cm)
Iris danfordiae	February	3 to 4 in (7.5 to 10 cm)
Iris reticulata	March–April	5 to 6 in (12.5 to 15 cm)
Merendera sobolifera	April–May	3 in (7.5 cm)
Narcissus juncifolius	April	4 in (10 cm)
Narcissus minimus	February–March	4 in (10 cm)
Narcissus watieri	May	4 in (10 cm)
Narcissus Wee Bee	April	4 in (10 cm)
Puschkinia scilloides	March–May	4 in (10 cm)
Rhodohypoxis baurii	May–June	3 in (7.5 cm)
Romulea sabulosa	May–July	3 in (7.5 cm)
Scilla verna	March–April	4 in (10 cm)
Tulipa batalini	March–April	4 in (10 cm)
Tulipa biflora	March–April	5 in (12.5 cm)
Tulipa dasystemon	April–May	6 in (15 cm)
Tulipa persica	May	3 in (7.5 cm)
Tulipa pulchella	March–April	4 in (10 cm)
Tulipa wilsoniana	May	3 in (7.5 cm)

summer-flowering bulbs should be planted. First plant the dwarf trees and any suitable alpine plants which will serve to prevent an over-flat appearance. Then plant the carpeters and those plants that are to trail over the sides, finally inserting the bulbs in small groups almost anywhere. Let them push up through the carpeters and other plants, but do plant so that they will produce colour the whole year round. Also, leave a few spaces for the autumn- and winter-flowering bulbs which can be planted during June, setting them close to those bulbs which will have bloomed early so as to hide the dead foliage. The trough garden will take fully 12 months to become established but afterwards there will be a continuous display for the minimum of trouble.

During dry weather, the plants will require watering, sometimes as often as twice a day, while they will appreciate an occasional syringeing with cold, clean water. Do not water while the sun remains on the plants for fear of scorching the foliage. Nightfall is the best time. Make sure that the soil is thoroughly soaked or the roots will turn to the surface in search of moisture. Town-grown plants often end the winter coated with grime from fogs. This may be removed by spraying with tepid water into which a pinch of Wetting Compound has been mixed: the compound enables the water to remain on the foliage to do its work of cleaning. Warm and gentle spring rains will soon give a new look to the trough garden, and as the sun gathers strength, more and more bulbs will begin to flower.

At the end of each winter stir up the surface soil as gently as possible, adding a little decayed manure which has been finely screened. At the same time, remove the dead foliage of those plants which have flowered in autumn and press soil around the roots of those plants made loose by hard frost.

Both the carpeting plants and the bulbs will need cutting back or dividing after a time, and so that the display will be maintained, a few clumps of bulbs should be lifted and divided each year. As soon as possible after the foliage has died down, lift with care and wash away the soil, then divide and replant.

To maintain vigour, remove all faded blooms without delay, but retain the foliage until it has become brown. This will not be unsightly if later-flowering bulbs and alpine plants are there to hide it.

The Sink Garden. Almost all those miniature bulbs which are suitable for a trough garden may be grown in a sink. An old kitchen sink may be brought into suitable condition by first removing some of the glaze so that the plant's roots are able to anchor themselves to the surface. Drainage will usually be limited to the plug-hole, and to ensure that it functions correctly, a ball of wire netting should be pressed inside before the drainage materials are added. If the sink is so wedged on to its pedestal that there is a slight fall towards the plug end, surplus moisture caused by heavy rain will drain away.

To assist with the drainage, a layer of broken crocks should be placed over the base, on top of which should lie some shingle. Then add a layer of turf loam and fill up the sink with compost as recommended for a trough garden. As there will not be so great a depth of compost in a sink, this should be as rich as possible.

The Window Box. Dwarf bulbs are ideal for window boxes, as they are not only low-growing, which makes them able to withstand strong winds when exposed, but they are also inexpensive and colourful.

A suggestion which will greatly prolong the display will be to have additional boxes planted with dwarf bulbs at the same time as the original box, or in spring for bulbs to bloom in autumn. If the boxes have been so constructed that they will fit inside the permanent window box, the display may be extended for many weeks. The permanent box may be planted with bulbs and plants which may be expected to bloom during the latter part of winter and early spring, using the crocus species, *Iris reticulata*, the chionodoxas and winter aconites, the early-flowering polyanthus Barrowby Gem, and the winter-flowering pansies. When the fixed box is planted in November, prepare also an additional box (or boxes) to act as replacements for when the early bulbs and plants have finished flowering at the end of April.

After the boxes containing the earliest-flowering bulbs have been removed, the replacement boxes are put into position, then, in turn, after their bulbs have finished flowering early in June, the boxes are removed to a shaded corner (or to the cellar or attic) where the bulbs are allowed to die down gradually, just as they would if growing in pots or the open ground. They should not be disturbed in any way, though the foliage will be removed later in the year. Where the boxes have been kept under cover, they should be exposed to the elements again, at the approach of autumn. At the same time, the boxes may be topped up with fresh compost and covered with ashes. The bulbs will come into growth again early the following spring and the flower buds will have formed by the time the boxes are ready for replacement in April.

A well-prepared compost in the first instance, and watering with dilute liquid manure for several weeks immediately after the bulbs have flowered, will maintain them in condition for several years without removal from the box or the replacement of the soil. Geraniums and salvias, or other half-hardy summer plants, could follow in a second replacement box in June. The plants will be thoroughly established when introduced to the fixture box and will come into bloom without delay.

If the provision of boxes for succession is not practicable, bulbs which are dying back may be replaced by later-flowering bulbs, grown separately in small pots. They should be planted in autumn, and must be allowed several months in the plunge bed, or in a cellar or darkened room, to enable them to form a strong rooting system. They are then moved to a cool place where the light is partly diffused and where they will continue to make growth. The pots are transferred to the window box at the appropriate time as replacements for the early flowering bulbs as these die down. The pots should be inserted so that the rims are just covered with soil. At the end of May the pots are removed together with any other bulbs of the original planting, so that the boxes may be replanted for the summer display. It will not be necessary to remove the bulbs from the pots each year and with those bulbs which resent disturbance, i.e. the dwarf daffodils, it should not be attempted.

Preparing the Box. Before placing any compost in the boxes it will be necessary to ensure thorough drainage. First the drainage holes in the base must be made, and in order to prevent wastage of soil, lay a piece of fine-mesh wire netting over the base. Then add a layer of crocks to a depth of about 1 in (2·5 cm) to ensure efficient drainage during winter. Over the crocks, a layer of turves placed grass downwards will occupy another 1½ in (3·5 cm) of the box. The remaining space is filled with prepared compost.

TABLE XIX. *Bulbs suitable for a window box*

Name	Flowering time	Height
Begonia multiflora	June–October	6 to 8 in (15 to 20 cm)
Brodiaea crocea	May–June	6 in (15 cm)
Chionodoxa gigantea	April	5 in (12·5 cm)
Crocus chrysanthus	February–April	4 in (10 cm)
Crocus, Dutch Hybrids	March–April	5 in (12·5 cm)
Crocus imperati	January–March	3 in (7·5 cm)
Crocus karduchorum	September–October	4 in (10 cm)
Crocus niveus	December–March	4 in (10 cm)
Galanthus elwesii	March–April	8 in (20 cm)
Galanthus nivalis	February–March	5 in (12·5 cm)
Hyacinthus amethystinus	March–April	8 in (20 cm)
Hyacinthus azureus	April	5 in (12·5 cm)
Iris reticulata	March–April	6 in (15 cm)
Muscari, Heavenly Blue	March–April	6 in (15 cm)
Muscari tubergenianum	April–May	9 in (23 cm)
Narcissus cyclamineus	March–April	9 in (22·5 cm)
Narcissus odorus	May	8 in (20 cm)
Narcissus Rip van Winkle	March	6 in (15 cm)
Narcissus tenuior	May–June	9 in (23 cm)
Scilla sibirica	February–April	8 in (20 cm)
Tulipa eichleri	April	10 in (25 cm)
Tulipa fosteriana Princeps	April–May	8 in (20 cm)
Tulipa griegii	April	9 in (22·5 cm)
Tulipa hageri	April	9 in (22·5 cm)
Tulipa kaufmanniana	March–April	8 to 10 in (20 to 25 cm)
Tulipa tubergeniana	May	10 in (25 cm)

The soil in the compost mixture should preferably be taken from pasture, or be a good-quality loam from a country garden not troubled by deposits of soot and sulphur. Soil taken from a town garden will generally be acid and full of weed seeds. A satisfactory compost will be made up by mixing:

3 parts loam
1 part peat
1 part grit or coarse sand (by weight).

Allow 2 lb of ground limestone or lime rubble to a box 3 ft (90 cm) long and 6 in (15 cm) deep; 4 oz of bone meal (a slow-acting fertiliser) and a sprinkling of superphosphate which encourages vigorous root action. Or as an alternative, the John Innes Compost may be used.

The compost should be allowed a few days to settle down before planting and to prevent compost being scattered over the sides when the boxes are watered, or during periods of heavy rain, allow about ¾ in (2 cm) space between the top of the compost and the top of the box. Always water with care so as not to cause splashing; and when the compost appears to be dry on the surface, the roots of the plants need not come up in search of it.

The bulbs should be planted at depths approximating to those in the open ground, but closer together, with no more than 1 in (2·5 cm) between them. They should be planted in groups of three or four rather than as odd bulbs placed here and there about the box.

To keep the boxes tidy, the flowers should be removed as they fade; since replacement boxes are to be used, the unsightliness of dying-back foliage will not cause trouble.

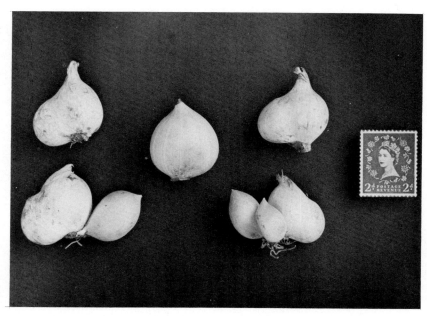

(*Above*) Bulbs of *Allium moly*, the Golden Garlic. (*Below left*) *Allium moly* bears clusters of golden blooms on strong stems, with foliage of an attractive green-blue colour. (*Below right*) *Allium cepa proliferum*, the Tree Onion, a striking border plant and useful in the kitchen garden. The small onion bulbs are on 2-ft. stems.

(*Above*) Anemone corms
(*Below*) Anemone de Caen

Begonias on the greenhouse bench

(*Left*) Camassia. (*Bottom left*) *Chionodoxa luciliae*, Glory of the Snow. (*Bottom right*) *Colchicum autumnale*, the Meadow Saffron.

Clivia miniata

Crocus susianus, Cloth of Gold Crocus, cultivated since 1587. Orange, its outer petals are veined with bronze.

Crocus medius

Crocus sieberi, Hubert Edelstan

Crocus ancyrensis, Golden Bunch – each corm produces numerous blooms of shining gold-orange.

Crocus dalmaticus – silvery lavender-blue flowers with bright orange stamens, for pots or outdoors.

Crocus chrysanthus, Snow Bunting – fragrant creamy white blooms with golden centres.

(*Above left*) *Eucharis amazonica*. (*Above right*) *Erythronium dens-canis*,
Dog's Tooth Violet – pink, white or red blooms, the foliage attractively
mottled. (*Below*) *Erythronium dens-canis roseum* on the rockery.

Freesia refracta

(*Above left*) Corms of *Freesia refracta*. (*Above right*) Bulbs of *Fritillaria meleagris*. (*Below left*) *Fritillaria meleagris*, Snakeshead Fritillary or Chequered Daffodil. (*Below right*) *Fritillaria citrina* – a dainty species bearing one or two bell-shaped flowers on each stem.

Galanthus nivalis, Arnott's
Seedling

Two blooms of *Galanthus
ikariae* compared for size
with an ordinary snowdrop
bloom (right)

Gladiolus grandis

Ruffled miniature gladiolus Bo-Peep

(*Above*) *Hymenocallis
tubiflora*. (*Left*) Bulbs
of *Iris reticulata*

(*Above left*) *Iris reticulata*, Cantab. (*Above right*) *Iris danfordiae* – an attractive miniature iris, its canary yellow blooms having delicate green spots in the throat. (*Below left*) *Iris hoogiana*. (*Below right*) Dutch Iris, Wedgwood.

Ismene calathina, Advance

12

Bulbs for Alpine House and Frame

Advantages of indoor bulbs—housing the bulbs—planting and care
of the bulbs

The Advantages of Indoor Bulbs. A most inexpensive structure may be
used to give protection for a wide variety of half-hardy bulbs. In addition,
miniature bulbs which are suitable for a rockery, or trough garden, may also be
grown under cover so that they may be brought into bloom several weeks early.
No heat will be required, apart from the natural warmth of the sun's rays, for
the miniature bulbs will, with but one or two exceptions, be intolerant of forcing
conditions. Even bulbs of South African origin will give a better account of
themselves where grown in a cool house, for all the bulbs require is protection
from excessive winter moisture, and protection from cold winds when in bloom
in spring. Bulbs given glass protection will come into bloom fully a month
earlier than those growing in the open ground, and the blooms, free from deposits
of soot and from soil particles, will have a luminous quality about them.

Flowers which are attractive to birds will also benefit from protection, and
mice will rarely attack bulbs or corms growing under glass, as they so often do
bulbs growing in the open. The more choice and expensive bulbs, those
described as being 'difficult', should be grown under glass. A number of the
lovely fritillarias and erythroniums should be protected in this way—not because
of their tenderness but because only in this way will the full beauty of their
flowers be observed in detail when at eye level.

A cold frame, constructed of secondhand bricks or breeze blocks deep
enough to allow those plants with stems of anything up to 12 in (30 cm) in
length ample room to develop, will prove suitable to house a large number of
species; while a structure in which the bulbs may be grown and flowered on
benches will be useful, for here, even where there is no heat, many winter- and
spring-flowering plants may be brought into bloom at a time when the garden
may be covered with frost and snow.

Where there is no garden, a small structure may be erected on a veranda—
where it may also serve as a sun-room—or in a small courtyard—where tubs or
troughs may be the only alternative means of exhibiting one's skill with bulbs.
The bulbs may spend the whole of their life in such a structure for they may

E

be started into growth beneath the benches, in pots or pans covered with ashes, until they have built up a strong rooting system. They may then be gradually introduced to the light by placing them on the benches. Where no heat is available, the half-hardy bulbs should not be placed on the benches until the spring sun gathers strength, or they may suffer damage if hard frost prevails at night. The most hardy bulbs, such as the crocuses, snowdrops, chionodoxas and iris species, all delightful subjects for pot culture, may be set on the benches just as soon as they have become well rooted, though where growing throughout under cold conditions there is not so great a necessity for the bulbs to build up a strong root system before they are brought into bloom. In a cold greenhouse, the bulbs will continue to form roots even when exposed to full light, though the stronger the rooting system, the better they will bloom.

Housing the Bulbs. A simple house may be erected by using stout timber (for the upright supports) with tongue and grooved weatherboarding to enclose the lower part of the structure to a height of 3 ft (90 cm) from the ground. It may be built over a concrete surface or one of soil covered with ashes and made quite firm. The upper part of the structure need not be of glass, which would add to the expense, but may be enclosed with polythene sheeting or Windolite, both of which will prove extremely durable and will admit the essential light rays and exclude unpleasant weather. The roof should have a slope of about 12 in (30 cm) from the back to the front, to allow snow and rainwater to drain away. The roofing material may be of Windolite, made secure by nailing to the crossbars which will prevent the roof from collapsing under the weight of snow. Nothing elaborate is called for, just something that is strong and weatherproof. The door, possibly obtained for little expense from a government department property auction, may be fixed to the back of the structure. The benches should be erected by fixing the woodwork at the top of the weatherboarding. They must be quite secure, for when filled with pots their weight will be considerable. Flat or corrugated-iron sheeting should be used to cover the benches and this should be covered to a depth of 1 in (2·5 cm) with washed gravel on which the pots will stand. The ground beneath the benches should be covered with ashes, for here the pots will be placed while the bulbs are forming their roots and again after flowering, while they die back. Bulbs to be grown in the house may also be placed under the bench both before and after flowering or they may, of course, be placed beneath a bed of ashes outdoors while they form roots. Winter- and spring-flowering bulbs will fit in with a cold-house tomato crop, the tomato plants being set out in pots or boxes on the benches early in May and trained over the roof of the house. Summer-flowering annuals, such as the hybrid petunias, may also be grown in pots, the plants being obtained in the seedling stage after having been hardened.

Where bulbs are placed beneath the benches to form roots, canvas or sacking should be fixed to the front of the benches to exclude light; and where bulbs are being grown in a frame, the lights, which may be made either of Windolite or glass, should also be covered while rooting is taking place. The same canvas may also be used to protect the plants from the midday sun during April and May when in full bloom, for this will enable the blooms to remain fresh for a longer period. A lean-to 'glasshouse' may be constructed even more reasonably and for bulbs, auriculas and most other winter- and spring-flowering plants, a northerly situation will prove suitable.

Planting and Care of the Bulbs. Bulbs to be grown in a cold greenhouse should be grown in either pots or pans, complete with a drainage hole. Pans made of earthenware and about 6 in (15 cm) deep will provide a more generous display, for a dozen small bulbs may be planted in each pan. Where the bulbs bear their bloom on stems almost 12 in (30 cm) tall, they should be supported by placing thin sticks or canes around the sides of the pots to which green twine is fastened to prevent the foliage and bloom from becoming untidy; or twigs may be inserted among the foliage. Coloured bulb bowls should not be used for cold-house culture for they will often be without drainage holes, and bulbs planted in such containers will rarely prove successful.

The pots or pans should be well crocked before adding the compost, which should be of 2 parts friable turf loam; 1 part peat, leaf mould or old mushroom bed compost; and 1 part coarse sand or grit, to which should be added a sprinkling of bone meal and some lime rubble where suitable. Do not obtain soil from the garden, for where situated in or near a town this may be in an inert condition through constant lack of attention, or may be of too acid a nature. Garden soil will also contain numerous weed seeds which will germinate and prove troublesome when the bulbs are coming into bloom. Fresh, friable loam from pastureland will prove ideal for bulbs, and the compost should be well mixed and stored under cover until ready for use.

To plant the bulbs, first place the compost in the pans to the necessary depth, which will be about two-thirds of the depth of the container. Into the compost the bulbs are pressed with the broader and more rounded end downwards, as this is the rooting end. Space out the bulbs evenly, allowing about 2 in (5 cm) between each, or about half that distance where the bulbs are very small. They should then be carefully covered with the compost to a depth of $\frac{1}{2}$ in (1 cm) or slightly more and so that the surface of the compost is just below the rim of the pan. The label bearing the name of the species or variety should be inserted at the side of the pot, which will then be ready for covering to exclude light so that the bulbs will not come prematurely into growth. Certain bulbs will not, however, require a period in darkness.

Those which require a period of darkness should be placed either beneath the benches or in a sheltered corner in the open where they should be covered with ashes or sand to a depth of 6 in (15 cm). If placed beneath the greenhouse bench the bulbs should first be given a thorough watering, which may be sufficient to keep the compost moist until the pots are lifted on to the bench when they are brought into bloom. The bulbs will be kept in the dark either by covering with ashes or by hanging canvas from the front of the bench. Those which are to bloom during autumn and early winter should be potted in August; and, so that they are kept cool until they have formed their roots, they are best placed in a dark corner outdoors until they are removed to the greenhouse in late September. Those which will bloom during the latter weeks of winter and early spring, should be potted in October and may be brought into the light towards the end of November. Many of the half-hardy bulbs are best potted in October and will be placed on the bench while rooting. They should be watered sparingly during the winter months.

Those which are to be brought into bloom indoors, after a period in total darkness, should be introduced to the light by degrees, first removing the canvas where the bulbs are being rooted. Where they have been grown outdoors beneath ashes, when first introduced to the house they should be placed under the benches for several days without the canvas being fixed to the sides. After about a week the pots may be placed on the bench in full light.

There will be need for little ventilation during the winter months; in fact, plants growing in a cold house will require none at all; but as the sun gathers strength in spring, more fresh air should be admitted either by leaving the door open or by opening the ventilators of a properly constructed greenhouse. During periods of strong sunlight brown paper should be tacked on to the inside of the structure to provide shading, or canvas may be used on the sunny side.

Little moisture will be required by the growing bulbs during autumn and winter, for after a thorough watering at planting time they will usually obtain all the moisture necessary from the atmosphere. As conditions become warmer, the compost should be watered whenever it begins to dry out, and on all sunny days both foliage and blooms will benefit from spraying with clean water at around midday.

Care should be taken with watering so as not to splash the compost on to the flowers, for many alpine house plants bloom on very short stems. To prevent splashing, the compost may be covered with shingle or with a layer of fresh moss, held in place by hair-pins. Both will enhance the beauty of the blooms and foliage and will keep them clean.

After flowering, the pots should be placed on their sides beneath the benches and all water should be withheld. When the foliage has died down it may be removed with care and at the same time the bulbs should be shaken from the pots, cleaned of all soil and stored in boxes of dry peat until ready for potting again. Or they may be left in the pots and stood outside during summer, to be top-dressed and brought indoors again in autumn.

13

Bulbs in the Home

Causes of failure—suitable composts—planting indoor bulbs—lifting outdoor bulbs—soil-less bulb culture—bulbs in a warm greenhouse.

Causes of Failure. Perhaps more bulbs are grown indoors, in the shelter and privacy of the home and garden room than anywhere else. Of all flowering plants none respond better to indoor culture. However their ease of cultivation is all too often the cause of their failure, for it encourages that lack of attention to detail in their culture which results in a mediocre display rather than one of great beauty. The chief causes of failure are:

(i) The incorrect use of the growing medium, mostly of fibre which is usually maintained in a too dry condition, so that the bulbs are unable to obtain sufficient moisture for their growth.

(ii) Insufficient time allowed in total darkness to enable the bulbs to form a satisfactory rooting system to support the growing plant.

(iii) Excessively high temperatures, of which many bulbs are intolerant, and poor ventilation.

(iv) The use of unsuitable containers, such as plastic bowls which may have no drainage holes and which are unable to ensure the gentle evaporation of moisture from the compost. The result is that the bulbs remain in a too damp condition which causes them to decay. Though they may be somewhat unsightly about the house (though not in the garden room), porous earthenware pots or bowls are the best of all containers in which to grow bulbs.

To discuss each in turn. Most important for successful bulb growing indoors is the medium in which the bulbs will grow. Those with no garden and no means of providing a suitable plunge bed where the bulbs may be kept until they have formed their roots, must rely on artificial methods throughout, but the bulbs will need to form a heavy rooting system all the same, and this means they will need a compost which can be maintained in a cool, moist condition throughout the life of the bulb. This is made more difficult in the dry atmosphere of a centrally heated house where a temperature of 70° F (21° C) is often maintained. These are almost forcing (stove) conditions, very different to those provided in homes heated only by a coal or small gas-fire and where the bulbs have to rely to a limited extent on the warmth of the winter sunlight to bring them into bloom a month or so before they would bloom outdoors.

Where the atmosphere is dry and warm, care will be necessary to ensure that the compost is retentive of moisture and that the bulbs may be kept as cool as possible, at least until they have formed their roots. Lack of moisture during their growing period and an inadequate rooting system will cause stunting of growth; the blooms will be borne on a short stem, which will greatly detract from the display. Also, coming into bloom before they have formed their roots, the display will be over before the bulbs achieve their full beauty for bulbs that have no roots will be unable to make use of the moisture provided. In certain cases it may be that where the bulbs are introduced to a warm room without their forming an efficient rooting system, they will be 'blind' and will form nothing more than a few leaves. Bulbs cannot be hurried into bloom and even where planted late, they must be given time to develop before being introduced to light and warmth.

Suitable Composts. Most bulb composts consist of coconut fibre to which has been added a quantity of peat. It is always difficult to add sufficient moisture to such a fibre, while it will also rapidly dry out in the warmth of the home. A more suitable compost is to be obtained from a good-quality peat moss such as 'Eclipse', which is a humus peat and is more readily able to absorb moisture and retain it for long periods. To maintain it in a 'sweet' condition, the peat should be mixed with a small quantity ($\frac{1}{2}$ oz per bowl) of crushed oyster shell (or egg shell) or pieces of charcoal. Before placing the compost in the containers, it should be made thoroughly damp, for it is not possible to add sufficient moisture once the bulbs have been planted. The fibre should be made pleasantly moist and friable before placing it in the bowls. It ought to bind together when tightly squeezed.

Better results may be expected from adding to the fibre a small amount of pasture loam or sterilised soil. This will give additional 'body' to the growing medium and will enable it to be more retentive of moisture. Old town garden soil, often of an acid nature through the accumulation of deposits of soot and sulphur should not be used. The compost should be clean of weeds and it must be sweet and friable. A little soil in the compost will also enable staking to be done more efficiently—which is rarely possible in a fibre which lacks body.

Bulbs most enjoy an earthenware container. They love to form their roots around the rough side of the container, and an unglazed earthenware bowl will be porous, permitting air to reach the bulbs and moisture to evaporate slowly from the compost. In this way it will remain 'sweet'. These are the conditions under which bulbs will grow well, though bulbs in an earthenware pot will require more moisture than those growing in a glazed or plastic container.

Watering is all-important, especially where the bowl is not equipped with drainage holes. Lack of moisture will cause 'stunted' growth, while excess will cause decaying of the base of the bulb and its roots, when the foliage will turn yellow and may collapse.

Those with a small garden or courtyard may root their bulbs outdoors in a plunge bed, provided the containers have drainage holes, for they will be exposed to the elements unless covered by garden lights. The use of an outdoor plunge bed in which to place the bulbs for several weeks will ensure that they receive sufficient moisture and will provide them with cool dark conditions in which to form their roots. Where there is no garden but only a courtyard or veranda, a plunge bed may be made from lengths of timber, cut to the size of a garden light and fastened at the corners. If earthenware containers are being used, it is not necessary to cover the bowls to exclude rain. They should be placed closely together in the frame and covered with weathered ashes, sand or peat to a depth of about 8 in (20 cm). If a garden is available, a plunge bed may be made by digging out the soil to a width of 3 ft (90 cm) and a depth of about 12 in (30 cm). At the bottom place a layer of ash or sand to exclude light. If you are using a frame, this will not be necessary for sacking or canvas may be fastened to the inside of the light. Here, all that is necessary is to keep the bowls covered and ensure that the fibre remains in a moist condition. Those bulbs in a plunge bed formed in the ground, may be left entirely exposed to the elements, for excess moisture will drain away from the containers and from the ash base on which the containers rest.

A cellar or outhouse will also provide the cool conditions so necessary for the bulbs to form their roots before making top growth. The containers may also be placed beneath the bench of an unheated greenhouse, light being excluded by hanging canvas or sacking down the side of the bench. Moisture and cool conditions while the bulbs are forming their roots is essential to a satisfactory display, and those who live in a flat which will have neither cellar nor garden should select as dark and as cool a place as possible. This may be beneath the kitchen sink or in a cupboard on the landing or beneath the stairs, and here the containers should be covered with plastic bags or with several layers of newspapers which should be kept moist. This will exclude light and will help to prevent the undue evaporation of moisture from the compost. Where space is strictly limited, light may be excluded by enclosing each container in a black plastic bag which will also help to retain moisture in the compost. Another method is to place the containers in a deep box and to pack over and around them moist peat, which is kept damp until the bowls are removed and introduced to the light. The peat being clean and light to handle, the box may be placed almost anywhere.

Householders will find that a simple method of rooting the bulbs will be to place the pots or bowls at the base of an outside wall facing due north. Here, peat or sand may be packed between and over the pots and here they may remain until the roots have formed. This will normally take about eight weeks and if the bulbs are planted early in autumn, the long white roots will be seen growing out from the drainage holes before winter frosts can be expected. The containers will then be ready to move indoors or if growing on in a frame, light should be admitted. This must be done gradually.

When removing indoors, it will be necessary to knock away the covering of ash or peat from the top of the containers, taking care not to damage the blanched shoots of the bulbs which will be seen beneath the covering of ash. The containers should then be introduced to the light and warmth gradually, first placing them in a half-lighted cupboard or on the window-sill of a cool room, away from the sunlight and the warmth of a radiator. After about a week, more light and warmth can be given but many bulbs will not tolerate excessive heat and these include the snowdrops, the dwarf irises, the chionodoxas, muscari and most narcissi, while if introduced too quickly to the light, the foliage will turn brown and there may be stunted growth.

As they make top growth, more moisture may be given and if the atmosphere is dry as is usual in a room heated by a gas-fire or central heating, it will be advisable to stand the pots or bowls in an earthenware 'saucer' glazed on the inside and which is kept filled with water. The roots will take up moisture through the drainage holes, while the water will also create a more humid atmosphere in the room.

There is no 'rule of thumb' as to the moisture requirements of bulbs, for so much depends upon atmospheric conditions and the amount of sunlight the bulbs receive and upon which the moisture evaporation of the compost will depend. Some bulbs such as hyacinths require more moisture than others, as do those growing under stove conditions. But do not conclude that the bulbs require moisture just because the surface of the compost appears dry. First, give the container a tap with a piece of wood and if there is a dull 'thud', water should be withheld until next day when further tapping of the pot produces a 'ringing' sound. Then give water around the side of the container, taking care not to splash the foliage and blooms. To prevent plant growth from being drawn to the light, it is advisable to turn the pots each day so that all parts of the plant receives its share of sunlight. This will encourage foliage and flower stems to grow straight and sturdy.

Planting Indoor Bulbs. While all bulbs require slightly different cultural treatment there are certain details applicable to all bulbs which are to be grown indoors. The finest of all containers are the earthenware bowls which have drainage holes at the base and which are also porous. After using, they should be scrubbed clean with soap and water and stored with care until ready to use again in autumn. Excellent too, are the Vencel-ware containers of marble-like finish and which are provided with drainage holes. They are light to use, yet are durable and encourage healthy root growth. Highly glazed containers which cannot breathe and do not allow the steady evaporation of moisture are not to be recommended. Wherever possible, use a container with drainage holes, over which should be placed pieces of broken 'crocks' to prevent the holes being clogged with compost.

When ordering compost, it may be calculated that a bushel will be sufficient for about 18 containers, each of 8 in (20 cm) diameter and 6 in (15 cm) deep. In each bowl put several pieces of charcoal to absorb the gases and then add a 2-in (5-cm) layer of compost, which should have been made moist. The amount of moisture should be sufficient for the compost to bind when tightly squeezed. On to this layer of compost the bulbs are planted, spacing them out evenly so that each will have room to develop and will make its contribution to a pleasing display. About 1 in (2·5 cm) should be allowed between each bulb so that a bowl of 8 in (20 cm) diameter will accommodate four hyacinths, six tulips or a dozen of the smaller bulbs.

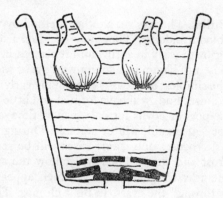

Planting in pots

The bulbs should be pressed into the compost and additional compost should then be firmed around them so that when the planting is complete, the nose of the bulbs should be level with the top of the compost and just beneath the rim of the pot or bowl to allow for watering.

Plant the bulbs at the correct time. All too often planting is delayed and then, wishing to have the bulbs in bloom by Christmas or at an early date, insufficient time is allowed for them to form their roots before introducing them to warmth and light. Narcissus, with one or two exceptions, will require at least 12 weeks to form their roots and hyacinths 10 weeks, and if they are hurried into bloom, stunting may result. Most bulbs will require a minimum of 8 weeks to form a rooting system without which they will not bloom well. During this time, all they will require will be to keep them cool and moist. A number of the South African Iridaceae require no time in the dark for rooting.

Where growing bulbs indoors, top-size bulbs should be obtained. This will ensure that they will give the best possible display given correct cultural care. Top-size bulbs cost a little more than 'seconds', which may be suitable for planting outdoors and for naturalising but which may take a year or more before they produce flowers. Indoors, small-sized bulbs will bear few flowers and they will be of inferior quality though taking the same amount of time and attention in their growing.

The narcissus and the taller-growing tulips may need support and this should be provided as the plant makes growth, by inserting several thin green-painted stakes of split bamboo and tying to each, lengths of green twine to support the foliage and (later) the bloom. Hyacinths are usually supported by short lengths of strong wire inserted near the bulb and looped round the flower stem. The Christmas-flowering Duc van Thol tulips, which will have been heavily forced, are also supported in this way. Small ferns may be planted among the hyacinths and tulips to hide the wires almost completely. But unless they have been grown in heat, most indoor bulbs will bloom without the need for support.

Lifting Outdoor Bulbs. There is yet another method by which bulbs may be brought early into bloom indoors. They may be lifted from the open ground when showing new growth early in spring and replanted in pots or bowls when they will come quickly into bloom in a sunny window or warm room. For those with a garden, it is the simplest of all ways of enjoying early bloom, for when the plants are lifted, the flower buds will have formed and little can go wrong. Since the bulbs occupy the pots or bowls for only a short time, any friable compost, such as moist peat or leaf mould, will be suitable. During the first days of the new year snowdrops, crocuses and dwarf irises will be seen pushing through ground free from frost and snow. Then will follow the scillas and miniature daffodils, grape hyacinths and chionodoxas which appear beneath the dead leaves of autumn or through the grass, in tight clumps. They should be lifted with a small garden fork, taking care to reach well down beneath the bulbs, otherwise the sheathing leaves will break away. Transfer them to the pots, pack compost around them, water and place in a warm (though not hot) room. With regular watering the bulbs will come into bloom within two to three weeks after lifting.

After flowering, the bulbs should be replanted in the same positions from which they were lifted, though this may be a suitable time to divide the clumps before replanting. All bulbs in pots after flowering indoors should be placed in a cellar or outhouse, beneath the greenhouse bench or in a shady corner and laid on their side so that the foliage may be dried off and the bulbs planted out in autumn. Those bulbs, e.g. the miniature narcissus, which resent root disturbance should be retained in the pots and slowly dried off during summer, to be started into growth again during autumn when they will come into bloom early in the new year. They will benefit from an occasional application of dilute manure water.

Soil-less Bulb Culture. A number of bulbs lend themselves to the method of water culture. Storing in their scales the nutrition necessary for the development of the flower the following year, they require only moisture to attain their fullness of beauty and will bloom without soil or fibre. It should, however, be said that bulbs and corms brought into bloom in water cannot store up the necessary plant food to enable them to bear bloom the following year and will require a year in the open ground before they will bloom again. For those who would wish to dispense with soil and fibre, water culture is a clean and easily manageable method of bulb-growing with particular appeal to children. Among the most suitable bulbs to grow by water culture are hyacinths (both the Fairy or Roman types and the large-flowering Dutch hybrids), dwarf early-flowering tulips, snowdrops, muscari, and the Dutch crocuses. Several species of narcissus may be grown in pebbles which provide an anchorage for the bulbs and which will have their bases submerged in water. From an autumn planting in the glass containers, each of these bulbs may be expected to come into bloom by Christmas or early in the new year.

Hyacinths and other bulbs have been grown in water-containers since the bulbs were introduced into Europe towards the end of the sixteenth century. Early in the eighteenth century, pewter bulb pots were made with cup-shaped holders at the top to accommodate four or six bulbs, and these were filled with water to the base of the bulbs. Towards the end of the century they came to be replaced by jasper stoneware, introduced by Wedgwood and other Staffordshire potters. These early bulb containers are now eagerly sought after by antique collectors.

Glass containers of all sizes are obtainable at most glass and sundries stores and are inexpensive. The bulb is placed in the cup and the roots grow through the aperture into the water below. Rainwater is preferable to chlorinated tap-water and the glass container is filled so that the base of the bulb is almost in contact with the water. Before adding the water, a few pieces of charcoal should be placed at the bottom of the jar for it will keep the water clean and sweet.

Top-size bulbs should be used, for only bulbs of this quality will have stored up sufficient plant food to produce a display of maximum beauty.

Place the containers in a cool dark room until the roots have formed and the bulbs have begun to sprout. They must be frequently inspected for water evaporation and topped up with rainwater should the roots lose contact. When growth is 2 in (5 cm) high, the bulbs should be gradually introduced to light and warmth when they will soon come into bloom. Hyacinths specially prepared for early flowering and the Duc van Thol tulips are excellent subjects for glass culture, while for snowdrops and grape hyacinths 'acorn' glasses should be used. These are glasses used by country children for sprouting acorns. Slightly taller than a matchbox, they are attractively tinted in shades of blue, green or amber and several may be placed in a sunny window or on a table or desk and are most attractive when in bloom. Larger glasses are obtainable for crocuses.

With the culture of all bulbs in glass containers, it is important that they are not rushed into bloom. They need early planting and several weeks in a cool, dark cupboard or cellar to form a vigorous rooting system. The scillas, snow-drops, grape hyacinths and crocuses will in no way tolerate a warm, stuffy atmosphere, for they are native of cooler mountainous regions. To have bloom in early autumn, the species colchicum will flourish in glass containers, especially C. *byzantinum* which bears its star-shaped blooms of rosy-mauve during August and September. The late Mr E. A. Bowles in his *Handbook of the Crocus and Colchicum* has told of having seen bulbs of this plant in full bloom in the window of a Cornish cottage, growing entirely without soil or water. The C. *bornmüelleri* hybrids, such as Lilac Wonder and The Giant which bloom early in August, are particularly suitable for glass culture. After flowering, the bulbs and corms should be planted in the open ground.

TABLE XX. *Bulbs to grow in the Home*

Species	Flowering time	When to plant
Amaryllis	December–February	September–October
Chionodoxa	January–March	September–October
Chlidanthus	May–June	March–April
Colchicum	October–December	August–September
Crocus	December–March	August–October
Galanthus	January–March	September–October
Habranthus	August–November	May–June
Haemanthus	May–June	March–April
Hyacinthus	December–March	August–September
Iris	January–March	September–October
Lilium	February–April	October–November
Muscari	March–April	September–October
Narcissus	January–April	August–September
Nerine	October–January	March–April
Pancratium	July–September	April–May
Scilla	December–March	September–October
Sprekelia	May–June	February–March
Sternbergia	December–February	September–October
Tulip	December–March	September–October
Vallota	August–September	May–June
Veltheimia	December–April	August–September

The taller-flowering narcissus are usually grown in bowls of clean pebbles which are submerged in rainwater. The water should reach up only to the base of the bulbs, as many as eight or nine top-size bulbs being planted in a shallow bowl covered with pebbles almost to their necks. They should go through exactly the same procedure as for bulbs growing in fibre or in water-containers being placed in a cool dark place until the roots have formed, and gradually introduced to light and warmth. The roots will become entwined about the pebbles and will form a suitable anchorage for the tall-growing plants. It is important to maintain the level of water throughout the growing and flowering period. The Tazettas, for example Cheerfulness, Cragford and Silver Chimes respond admirably to pebble culture, also the Paperwhite grandiflora types in white and yellow which may be grown throughout in a sunny window and in a warm room without going through the usual period in darkness to form their roots. The plants may need support which is provided by means of split bamboo canes inserted into the pebbles.

All forms of the hyacinth may be grown in open bowls of pebbles and water, the pebbles providing a pleasing base. They may also be grown, in black plastic pots fitted with a holder to accommodate three bulbs. This fits over the rim of the pot which is filled with rainwater to the base of the holder on which the bulb rests.

Bulbs in a Warm Greenhouse. Bulbs and corms to grow in a warm greenhouse require a more humid atmosphere than is provided in the home, higher temperatures and more light. Begonias rarely do well in the home, for, with insufficient light and humidity, they will drop their flowers before reaching perfection and often in the bud stage. They may, like many other plants raised in a warm greenhouse, be moved to the home when in full bloom and may be enjoyed for several weeks in a sunny window. The Gesneriaceae family, native of tropical South America are also happiest in the warm humidity of a greenhouse or sun-room where the plants may be given all the light they need. A sun-room, heated by the central-heating system of the home and constructed with a glass roof to admit the maximum amount of light, will prove an ideal alternative to a greenhouse, for around the sides the plants may be grown on shelves of plate glass or formica which may be readily kept clean. Alternatively, a small lean-to greenhouse may be erected against the wall of a small courtyard, where it will receive its fair share of sunlight and if it may be connected to the home from which it may be heated, there will be many advantages—not least being the economical use of heating. A small greenhouse or sun-room may be erected on a veranda or terrace and entered from the house by means of a French window. Only the minimum amount of space will be needed so that with the efficient use of shelving very many plants may be grown throughout the year and may be managed through all their stages of growth, an attractive occupation for those who are no longer able to cut grass, trim hedges or dig the ground.

To enable the maximum amount of sunlight to reach a greenhouse which may have to be erected along a wall of a yard which enjoys only a limited amount of sunlight, the three-quarters span lean-to should be used. It should be of such a height that a portion of the roof is above the top of the wall. In this way every beam of sunlight will be utilised to the full.

The all-glass greenhouse of the lean-to type is now most favoured. Here, the plants may be grown on narrow shelves arranged in tiers along the back wall in addition to shelves fixed around the glass, and this enables the largest possible number of plants to receive the maximum amount of light. Also while the watering of the plants may occupy rather more of one's time when housed in this manner, the display will be greatly enhanced.

The older-style greenhouse will require a base about 4 ft (1·2 metres) high, which may be built of brick, concrete blocks or wood with glass above, the plants usually being grown on benches fixed at the same height as the base. To facilitate the most economic use of the greenhouse the benches would need to be 3 ft (90 cm) wide and 2 ft (60 cm) in width on either side of a 2-ft (60-cm)-wide door. When using shelves arranged in tiers, it should, however, be possible to fix three shelves along the side of an all-glass lean-to of similar width and at least four shelves along the back wall, so that maximum use may be made of the structure.

14

Scent in Bulbs

Bulbs bearing scented flowers—classification of flower
scents—essential oil of a flower

In addition to the durability of many bulbs, corms and tuberous rooted plants
there is the exotic scent of their flowers. At least 50 genera which come under
the scope of this book and comprise a great many species and varieties, possess
perfume which must be among the most potent of all flower scents. Jason Hill
has written of the additional dimensions to be enjoyed in a garden of scented
flowers: 'by thinking in terms of our sense of smell . . . the scent of flowers is
no small part of their beauty and by giving a little attention to it, we can have a
garden within a garden, an invisible garden, not much less rich and various than
the other which appeals to the eye'.

Lawson in *The Countrie Housewife* said that 'the garden should be divided
into two parts. The one shall contain those flowers used to make nosegaies and
garlands, such as March violets, Provence gillyflowers, purple gilly flowers,
small paunces [pansies], double daisies, marigolds, lily convally, daffodils . . .
lilies and suchlike as may be called the nosegay garden. . . . Also Tulippes,
Narcissus, Hyacinthes . . . pleasant and delectable to behold.' Lawson suggests
that the other part of the garden be filled with sweet-smelling herbs, for, as
Bullein said in his *Bulwarks of Defense* (1562): 'Man only doth smell and take
delight in the odours of flowers or sweet things.'

Francis Bacon in his 'Essay of Gardens' suggested planting sweet-smelling
flowers for each month of the year, and in his list he includes a number of
bulbs grown in England at the time. 'For January and February, Crocus vernus,
the yellow and the grey; the early tulip and Hyacinth orientalis. For March,
come violets . . . and the early daffodil. In April, fleur-de-luces and lilies of all
natures. . . . In June, lily-of-the-valley. . . .'

In Bacon's time all the early-flowering crocuses were called 'Crocus vernus'
and those he alluded to as being early-flowering would most likely be *C. aureus*
(yellow) and *C. versicolor*, also known as *C. fragrans*. Both of these are native of
the alpine regions of southern Europe and are in bloom at the same time. With
them blooms *C. imperati*, native of Italy, its purple elongated petals opening
starlike to the sun to reveal brilliant orange anthers. It is sweetly scented, as is

C. vernus, also native of southern Italy and cultivated by the Romans for its rich perfume. The petals were dried and used for filling cushions and pillows, while Roman women used its fragrant water in their toilet preparations. *C. chrysanthus* also has a sweet scent resembling that of the primrose with undertones of honey, like a softer version of the double primrose Marie Crousse with its honeysuckle scent.

Bulbs bearing Scented Flowers. Several of the autumn- and winter-flowering species also bear scented flowers *C. sativus* opens its purple flowers early in October to reveal the scarlet stigmas which when dry yield saffron, one of the most important of all products during medieval times. In bloom at the same time is *C. longiflorus*, also known as *C. odorus*, which is the most sweetly scented of all the crocus species. Native of Italy, Sicily and Malta, it resembles *C. imperati* and has a long elegant tube of deepest violet which opens to reveal an orange stigma.

C. laevigatus, which blooms during midwinter whenever the sun shines down upon it, is also scented. Its white tubular flowers are veined and feathered with mauve and brown, and it has pure white anthers. Its perfume resembles that of the cowslip.

A large number of bulbs and corms which bloom during autumn and winter have scented flowers with which they attract for the purpose of pollination the few insects about at this time. In bloom in autumn is the hardy *Cyclamen neapolitanum*, its heart-shaped leaves attractively marbled with white, whose pinkish-red flowers are sweetly scented. Closely related is *C. autumnale*, a native of the oakwoods of northern Africa, which blooms later. Both species come into bloom, after *C. europeum*, during the latter weeks of summer and early in autumn. This too has heart-shaped leaves marbled with white and bears purple-red flowers which emit a musk-like perfume.

C. libanoticum which blooms in April has heart-shaped leaves which are attractively waved at the margins and bears rosy-red flowers of outstanding perfume. To extend the season until *C. europeum* is ready to come into bloom, there is *C. repandum* from the mountains of Corsica, its scented flowers of blush-white marked with purple at the base.

The spring-flowering snowflake, *Leucojum vernum*, bears sweetly scented flowers, while those of the summer-flowering species have no scent at all, since it flowers in May and June it does not need pronounced scent to attract pollinators. The spring snowflake has broad strap-like leaves and bears its white bells, tipped with green on 6-in (15-cm) stems. Its scent has been likened to that of the hawthorn or violet, hence its old name of 'white violet', the Greek being *leucoion*. Gerard classed it with the clove-scented plants, naming it the bulbous stock gillyflower.

Several of the reticulate irises are winter and early spring-flowering and all bear scented flowers which have the violet perfume. *Iris bakeriana* blooms during February and March and has sky-blue standards and erect white fall petals. Varieties of *I. reticulata* are among the most beautiful plants of the garden. All bear scented flowers, especially the species with its blooms of darkest purple.

In bloom throughout the winter following a warm, dry summer is *I. stylosa*. It has a rhizomatous rootstock of finger thickness and bears sky-blue flowers which are powerfully scented. They appear amidst tufts of pointed leaves from October until April. To see them at their best, set them beneath a sunny wall where they will be protected from the cold winds of winter. Use a soil devoid of humus, but one containing some lime rubble and plenty of grit. The Florentine iris, which blooms in May and June, and many of the flag irises, varieties of *I. germanica*, are also scented.

All members of the genus, the snowdrop family, emit the soft fragrance of mossy woodlands when in quantity, but one in particular has pronounced scent. This is Arnott's Variety, a *G. nivalis* seedling which bears large globular blooms on 10-in (25-cm) stems. Gerard mentions growing a dozen different daffodils in his Holborn garden, one being the short-cupped Tazetta, 'the narcissus good in scent' mentioned in the nineteenth idyll of Theocritus. This was Homer's bunch-flowered narcissus, 'at the fragrant odour thereof, all the broad heaven above and all the earth laughed . . .'. So powerful is their scent in the warmth of their native land that Pliny has told of the plant being named narcissus from *narce*, to 'dull the senses' from which is derived our modern word 'narcotic'. Burbidge has said that in a warm room, so heavy is their smell as to be injurious to those of delicate health.

Possibly the most powerfully scented of all flowers in comparison to its size is *N. minimus*, the Spanish daffodil, which is illustrated in the *Paradisus*. It is also one of the earliest to bloom, being at its loveliest in the alpine garden or in pans in the alpine house. *N. canaliculatus* follows shortly after. It is from Sicily and is like a tazetta in miniature, growing only 6 in (15 cm) tall with a white reflexed perianth and a tiny cup of orange. Of ravishing scent, it bears three or four blooms to each stem above blue-green, grass-like foliage. In bloom with it is *N. cernuus*, originally known as *N. moschatus* on account of its musk-like scent. Then follows the campernelle with bright-yellow flowers borne on 10-in (25-cm) stems; the flowers embalm the air with their sweet perfume. It is perhaps a natural hybrid of *N. jonquilla*, the jonquil of southern Europe and Algeria, which carries the same rich perfume. Last to bloom is *N. gracilis*, which bears, in June, sulphur-yellow flowers of intoxicating scent.

In several of the most heavily scented narcissi, as in lilies, indol is present. It is this substance that gives rise to the unpleasant smell experienced where the most heavily scented narcissi and lilies are used in quantity for decoration and where, in the warm stuffy atmosphere of a badly ventilated room, they cause mental disturbance among those present. Especially is this noticeable when the flowers begin to fade, for as flowers die, the sweetly scented compounds become broken down into more simple substances which (as the case may be) have either a pleasant or an unpleasant smell. The same substance indol, is present in the putrefaction of animal tissue and is present as methyl indol, in the glandular excreta of the civet cat, a substance which is used as a fixative in perfumery. It was the poet Cowper who said he was unable to speak with civet in a room and it is on record that people have been completely overcome by a concentration of lilies or narcissi. James Thomson wrote of the 'jonquil of potent fragrance' and Gerard said, 'the scent is too sweet, troubling the head in a strange manner'.

The tuberose may also be grouped with the lily and narcissus, though benzyl benzoate gives it a lightness; in lily-of-the-valley, the scent is made so pleasing by its lemony quality.

Closely allied to the heavily scented narcissi is the oriental hyacinth, but this has a refreshing balsamic undertone in the scent of its flowers, resembling the perfume of a field bean. The aromatic undertone is due to the presence of cinnamic alcohol which is also present in Balsam of Peru and is the connecting link between the spices of the East and the flower attars.

Writing in 1559 of the first tulip seen growing in Europe, at Augsburg and named after himself, Conrad Gesner said, '. . . it was like a red lily, with a pleasant smell, soothing and delicate'. The first tulips were acclaimed entirely for their scent and were popular with ladies at the French Court during the seventeenth century for evening wear. Both *T. gesneriana* (Gesner's tulip) and *T. suaveolens*, native of the Caucasus, bear scarlet flowers and are rose-scented. It was from these species that the first of the early-flowering single tulips were evolved. Among those most heavily scented is Prince of Austria, its orange-scarlet flowers having the scent of orange blossom. For contrast and to plant with it is Bellona, the best of the golden-yellow flowered early tulips with the clove perfume of carnations. Both grow 16 in (40 cm) tall and they come into bloom early in April. They are ideal bedding varieties and in addition to their brilliance of colour will scent the air around. The single Duc van Thol tulips, including the vermilion Fred Moore, are also sweetly scented. Several of the double early tulips, especially Tearose, which bears pale-yellow flowers flushed with pink and which have a pleasing honey perfume. The paeony-flowered Murillo and its numerous 'sports' are scented. Outstanding is Schoonoord, a pure white of great beauty and David Teniers which bears large full blooms of rich violet-mauve. They may be grown with the double primrose Marie Crousse which bears deep purple flowers with the scent of honeysuckle. Another Murillo sport with outstanding scent is Marquette, its rich crimson flowers being edged with gold.

Of the Breeder tulips, which with their purple and bronze shadings are so popular for indoor decoration, none is lovelier than Cherbourg, its golden-bronze flowers being flushed with purple and during May and June will diffuse its lily-of-the-valley scent about the garden.

Several of the parrot tulips with their fringed or scalloped petals, which first appeared in 1665 are scented, none more so than Black Parrot which bears glossy maroon-black flowers and is the darkest of all tulips. Of interest is that it is a 'sport' from Darwin tulip, Philippe de Commines, which is one of the few in its section with perfume. It may be planted with the pale yellow cottage tulip, Mrs Moon, which bears large globular blooms with the scent of almonds or with the sweetly scented parrot, Orange Favourite, its orange-coloured blooms being feathered with green and rose. Other Darwins with scent include the violet Demeter, which has an aromatic clove-like perfume, and Golden Age, which has the unusual aroma of an amontilado sherry. White Victory has something of the scent of white jasmine in its equally thick petals.

Besides those earliest of known species, several other tulip species bear scented flowers, one of the loveliest for alpine house or rock garden being *T. aucheriana*, native of Teheran. Its pale-mauve flowers, flushed with orange, like old brocade, open flat, like stars, and diffuse a soft sweet scent for several weeks. The flowers are borne on 4-in (10-cm) stems above tapering grey-green leaves. Hardy and extremely perennial, it is perhaps the finest of all the tulip species. Equally dwarf and alluring is the Persian tulip, *T. persica*, which bears its fragrant flowers late in May, several to a stem. They are brilliant gold, shaded with bronze on the outside and the foliage, twisted and corrugated and marked with bronze, is equally attractive.

The wild tulip of southern Europe, *T. sylvestris*, naturalised in coppice and meadow of southern England bears scented flowers. They are borne on 15-in (37·5-cm) stems and are of softest yellow, opening in April. The buds dangle downwards, but as they open turn to the sky, diffusing a deliciously sweet scent. Increasing by stolons, it should be planted in the wild garden or orchard where it is allowed to increase and be left undisturbed.

Classification of Flower Scents. No recognised classification of scent has ever been made for the simple reason that, due to several factors, there is so great a variation in perfumes. To one person, a flower may have a pleasant smell, to another it is less so. This is due to the type of pigment of the olfactory mucous membrane. Again, perfumes change with dilution, being pleasing and suggesting a particular scent from a distance, whereas inhaled close to or in greater concentration, the same perfume may seem most unpleasant.

It was not until 1893 that an attempt was made to classify perfumes. This was done by Count von Marilaun, who arranged flower scents into groups according to the chemical substance that predominated in their essential oil. He classified flower perfumes into six main groups—indoloid, aminoid, benzoloid, terpenoid, paraffinoid and the honey group. Several however were unsatisfactory, as with those of the terpenoid group, which comprise the lemon-scented flowers, for it was apparent that the terpenes make no contribution to the perfume and it was changed to the lemon group. It was also thought necessary to divide the benzoloids into three groups so that there are now ten groups of classified flower scents. The flowers of each group have their special pollinators and are of a colour which is most attractive to those insects upon which they rely for their reproduction.

Indoloid Group. Here, indol is present in concentration, giving the flowers the foetid smell of badly decayed meat. The flowers are usually pale-brown or chrome-yellow in colour and blotched with purple to resemble carrion. The unpleasant smell and appearance attracts bluebottles, dung flies and midges. Included in the group are the aroids and several members of the lily family, such as *Smilax herbacea*, known as the carrion flower; and *Trillium erectum* (*T. foetidum*), the purple flowers resembling decaying meat and with an unpleasant smell.

Aminoid Group. Here, the flowers are mostly dingy white or cream-coloured and are borne in clusters with their nectar readily accessible to the flies which pollinate them. The flowers have a fishy smell due to the presence of trimethylamine, which occurs in the early stages of putrefaction and also in herring brine. Included in this group are the *Sorbus* and *Pyracantha* but no bulbous plants.

Heavy Group. Indol is present but in less concentration than in the indoloid group. Included here is the lily and narcissus, the tuberose and eucharis, plants with white flowers which are highly scented at night and rely on moths for their pollination. They have thick petals which help to retain their scent for a considerable time. The flowers have a sickly perfume and are unpleasant to smell at close range, the exceptions being lily-of-the-valley (which is lightened with undertones of lemon) and *Cyclamen europeum*, both being woodland plants and which have much in common with the night-scented flowers.

Aromatic Group. Those flowers with a balsamic scent are included here and members of the Leguminosae family, the laburnum and sweet pea which have vanilla-scented flowers with lemon undertones. Those with a balsamic scent, due to the presence of cinnamic alcohol and which are familiar are the hyacinth and bluebell (*Endymion non-scriptus*), the scent being powerful but not unpleasant even in concentration. The clove-scented flowers may also be mentioned here, the carnation and pink and *Gladiolus tristis*, which at night (but not by day) releases the same aromatic smell of pinks, due to the presence of eugenol.

Violet Group. Here, the essential oil is due to ketones of the ionone type and the violet is the outstanding example. Its scent quickly tires the nerves so that after a few moments the scent is lost. Shakespeare knew of this soporific effect when he wrote that its scent was

> Sweet, not lasting
> The perfume and suppliance of a minute.

Of bulbous plants, *Iris reticulata* and *I. bakeriana*, also *Leucojum vernum* and *Triteleia uniflora*, most nearly resemble the violet in the perfume of their flowers. It is present also in flowers of mignonette and of the vine. It is a scent similar to that of freshly cut cucumber or of woodland moss with sweeter undertones. The violet fragrance is pronounced in the dried rhizomes of *Iris florentina* and in *I. pallida*, the flower of which has the vanilla perfume usually associated with flowers of the legumes.

Rose Group. Flowers of this group resemble those of certain roses and their scent, though sweet, is usually combined with a refreshing fruity scent described by Parkinson in his notes on the Damask rose: 'It is neither heady nor too strong nor stuffing nor unpleasantly sweet.' *Tulipa gesneriana*, the first to reach Europe, and *Iris hoogiana* have the rose perfume. Several varieties of the herbaceous paeony have the perfume of the tea rose, like that of the plywood chests from which china tea has been emptied.

Lemon Group. The lily-of-the-valley may be included here, for its blooms possess refreshing lemon undertones, likewise those of *Cyanella odoratissima*. The scent is closely allied to the rose group, for its main component, citral, is the first oxidation product of geraniol which predominates in the rose.

Fruit-scented Group. Included here are all those flowers with fruity scents, other than lemon. For example, the Japanese rambler rose has the smell of green apples and *Rosa dupontii* smells of ripe bananas. In bulbous plants the most obvious example is the freesia, whose flowers have the refreshing smell of ripe plums, one of the most satisfying of all flower scents. *Muscari racemosum* and *Crocus lengiflorus* have a similar smell.

Animal Group. This group is allied to the fruit-scented group through the esters (compounds formed by the combination of an acid and an alcohol) of fatty acids, some of which produce a fruity scent and some the smell of animal fur. The hypericum smells both of goats and of ripe apples and the early purple orchid smells of vanilla from a distance but has a cat-like smell when inhaled close to. In bulbs the obvious example is the crown imperial which when fully open has a foxy smell, while *Ferraria undulata* has the smell of dead rats. In this group could be included the musk scent which is the connecting link between this and the honey group.

Honey Group. The musk scent closely resembles that of honey, depending upon degree of intensity, examples being the flowers of the buddleia and the sweet scabious and, in bulbs, the musk hyacinth, *Muscari moschatum* which has given its name to the genus. The musk rose, *Rosa moschata*, and the musk-scented *Delphinium brunonianum* as well as *Muscari moschatum* are native of the Himalaya regions extending from Afghanistan to western China where the musk deer is to be found grazing. Tonquin musk is found in a 'pod' beneath the belly of the male musk deer and it takes the animal four years to produce one ounce. Tonquin musk is used as a fixative in the perfume industry.

Essential Oil of a Flower. The essential oil of a flower is secreted in minute drops into the epidermal cells (or sepals), which evaporate on exposure to the air to release a sweet- (or unpleasant)-smelling vapour which is most noticeable when the air is warm and calm. Thus, those bulbs which bloom outdoors during winter and spring are more fragrant when indoors in the warmth of the home. Scent is most pronounced in those flowers which have thick petals or where the petals are numerous because of doubling. The essential oil is present in the unopened flower bud in an inert form. It is stored as a glucoside which is a combination of sugar and essential oil and which is released only by the action of a ferment which is present in the living cells. The decomposition of the glucoside is a reversible action; it ceases when the oil accumulates in quantity such as when the flower is closed, the opening and closing being governed by temperature.

The scent of a flower is the waste product of the plant and those substances that are present in essential oils such as indol and trimethylamine are present also in the decomposition of animal tissue in which the first products are usually pleasantly sweet but as putrefaction proceeds, the same sweet-smelling compounds are broken down into more simple substances which are mostly of unpleasant scent. In the same way that scent is an excretory product of a plant so is methyl indol an excretory product of the civet cat and Tonquin musk a similar product of the male deer. They are used as fixatives, to 'hold' a scent after its extraction from the flower in the same way that its rapid release from the flower by evaporation is prevented by reason of the waxy coating which covers the petals.

The most highly scented flowers are white, next come those which are pale-yellow and pale pink (blush) and the greater the amount of pigment in a flower the less likely it is to be scented. Red (scarlet) and blue flowers rarely have perfume for they are mostly pollinated by humming-birds or bees which search by sight rather than by smell. The most heavily scented flowers are pollinated by butterflies and moths which themselves are also scented, possibly like the flowers they visit. Butterflies by day and moths mostly by night may also be guided to the flowers by their pale evanescent quality.

15
Diseases and Pests of Bulbs and Corms

DISEASES

Basal Rot (*Fusarium bulbigenum*). It attacks narcissi bulbs and freesia corms (also the gladiolus, in a slightly different form), causing yellowing of the foliage and finally total decay. It begins at the base of bulb or corm and when the dry outer scales are removed, blackish-brown colouring is seen around the base. Upon removal of the outer scales, pink spores are seen, while upon gentle pressure, the bulb (or corm) appears soft.

F. bulbigenum is a soil fungus which may enter the bulb through damage to the roots or through abrasions made in the bulb upon lifting and it may be undetected during storage, the yellowing of the leaves and unopened flower buds observed soon after replanting being the first indication. Imported bulbs should be carefully inspected and stored in a dry frost-free room but in a temperature not exceeding 60° F (16° C) Narcissus King Alfred and Sir Watkin and their progeny are rarely troubled by the disease. Dipping bulbs and corms in a 0·5 per cent solution of formalin will give control.

Black Disease (*Sclerotium denigrans*). It attacks lily-of-the-valley and is prevalent in Germany and Denmark. It is unknown in Britain, though it may occur on roots sent over from Europe for forcing. The covering scales of the buds become black, and later the buds fall off, while the blackening extends to all parts of the plant first as small grey spots on the leaves, later turning black and also occurring on the roots and underground stems. A careful watch should be kept on imported roots when being forced and should the disease be noticed, the plants may be removed and destroyed. After forcing, burn the plants so as not to introduce the disease to outdoor beds. If older plants are lifted and divided outdoors, they should be replanted into freshly prepared ground.

Botrytis (*Botrytis gladiorum* and species). *B. gladiorum* is one of several forms of botrytis which attacks many bulbous plants and is mostly troublesome on gladioli growing in areas of heavy rainfall and high humidity. As it attacks both foliage and corm it may prove troublesome where the corms are planted in a badly drained soil or if lifting is too long delayed after flowering has ended. Its presence is observed by small greyish-brown spots which appear on the foliage of gladioli and also on the flowers, making them unsuitable for sale or for exhibition. Red-flowering varieties may be troubled more than others and as spores are released in the wind or washed off by rain, the infected bloom and foliage must be removed and destroyed as soon as observed. Too-close planting will encourage the disease to spread.

Infected corms will decay during storage. The disease may take the form of a dry brown rot which penetrates down the neck to the centre of the corm. Or the corms may decay from the base upwards, while small black swellings may appear on the outside of the corms. Dusting the corms with flowers of sulphur or Botrilex when placing in storage will help to control the trouble. Commercial growers have found that dipping the corms for two hours in a 0·1 per cent solution of mercuric chloride solution has given protection to the corms. Keeping them after lifting and cleaning in a temperature of 84° F (29° C) for 10 days to bring about the rapid healing of wounds caused in lifting has ensured almost trouble-free stock.

Corms infected by *Botrytis gladiorum* may fail to grow or the young growth will turn yellow, then brown and will die back at an early stage.

Botrytis, known as grey mould disease, attacks *Anemone coronaria* and other species of anemone, making the stems decay at ground level. It may be caused by careless removal of the bloom during periods of humidity, thus allowing the fungus to gain entry. Too close planting, where growing under cloches or in frames, and insufficient ventilation may encourage an outbreak. Where growing under glass, the routine dusting of the foliage with the non-poisonous salicyl-anilide emulsified with Agral or in its proprietary form Shirlan AG will prevent a serious outbreak.

The grey mould disease of the galanthus, *Botrytis galanthina*, may appear following alternating periods of frost and warmer weather. As soon as the shoots appear above ground they become covered with a grey mould which extends down to the bulb. Affected plants should be immediately dug up and destroyed, and others dusted with flowers of sulphur.

The disease, in the form of *Botrytis cinerea*, is one of the most troublesome of cyclamen diseases, especially of the indoor Persian cyclamen. It will attack seedling plants, also the new leaves and flower stems of older plants, covering them with a grey mould and causing rapid collapse. It may also spread to the corm itself. It is caused by excessive warmth and humidity and careless watering. Ample ventilation is essential for the health of this plant. An over-rich soil may cause the appearance of the mould. Routine spraying with Shirlan AG (1 oz to 2 gal of water) has given encouraging results.

Botrytis hyacinthi is a troublesome disease of the hyacinth; in Holland it often spreads through plantations at an alarming rate, especially during a cold, wet spring. The tips of the leaves first become affected, but the fungus quickly spreads downwards and the leaves become brown and decay near the base. The flowers may also be attacked with the familiar grey mould of botrytis which does not, however, attack the bulbs. Spraying with Shirlan AG will give control.

The disease appears on irises as *Botrytis convoluta* and is especially common to those species—e.g. *I. pallida*, and *I. germanica*—which form a rhizomatous root. Its presence may be detected by the leaves turning yellow as they appear in spring. Upon close inspection, the rhizomes will be seen to be covered with the purple mycelium of *B. convoluta* and to have become shrivelled. When this happens they should be destroyed. Where only a part of the root is attacked, it may be lifted and the diseased area cut away, treating the cut healthy part with a weak Lysol solution before replanting. Too-deep planting of the rhizomes may encourage an outbreak, as will damage to the rhizomes when clearing the beds.

As *Botrytis elliptica*, the disease attacks lilies, especially *L. auratum*, and its hybrids, and, to a lesser degree, *L. candidum*, covering the leaves and buds with grey mould. Later deep spots may be observed on the stems, though the bulbs are rarely attacked. Plants growing in badly drained soil will be those mostly troubled. Spraying with a weak solution of Bordeaux Mixture will be a safeguard.

Botrytis tulipae is the most troublesome of tulip diseases, attacking all parts of the plant above ground and appearing on the leaves and stems as greyish-yellow spots. After a few days, the leaves and stems fall over, while the bulb will also be affected in the form of black pits which are deeply embedded in the outer scales. During damp weather the disease will make rapid headway, causing complete disintegration of the bulb. The disease may originate in the soil or the spores may be carried by air currents or spread by splashing during rain. The Murillo tulips are most susceptible.

Shirlan AG, used as advised for *Anemone coronaria* will give control. The plants should be sprayed early in spring and at fortnightly intervals until the foliage begins to die back.

Brown Root Rot (*Thielaviopsis basicola*). It is a disease of the roots of tuberous begonias causing them to turn brown and decay, while it may extend to the tuber. It may also attack cyclamen. The foliage turns pale yellow and dies back. It is a fungus of the soil and is common in leaf mould, so it is better to use the almost sterile peat for indoor plants. Outdoor plants that have become affected should be destroyed and the ground given a rest from begonias for two years.

Cluster Cup (*Puccinia pruni-spinosae*). This fungus occurs on plum leaves as well as on the leaves of *Anemone coronaria* and *A. fulgens*, infecting the underside with clusters of bright orange cups, while tiny black dots appear on the upper surface. Diseased plants seldom flower and should be dug up and destroyed. It is not advisable to plant anemones beneath or near plum trees as there is no known cure for the disease.

Rust may appear as *Puccinia iridis* on the foliage of *Iris pallida* (and *I. germanica*) and as *Puccinia sessilis* on polygonatum, herb paris and lily-of-the-valley, first as orange or yellow cluster cups which later turn brown. Their host is *Berberis vulgaris* and its hybrids, from which they attack cereals and grasses; these in turn affect the above-mentioned bulbous plants. There is no known cure.

Copper Web (*Rhizoctonia crocorum*). It mostly attacks crocus corms and is a rare soil fungus. Strands of purple mycelium cover the dry scales surrounding the corm and later grow into the corm causing rapid decay. It attacks many vegetable crops and is a serious disease of sugar beet. There is no known cure and long rotational cropping must be practised if it appears.

Crown Rot (*Sclerotium delphinii*). It is a disease which may attack *Anemone coronaria* and the bulbous irises, especially during periods of excessive rain or where planted in badly drained soil. It attacks the leaf bases or flower stems, also the upper part of bulb or tuber with white mycelium. The routine dusting of bulbs and corms with Lindex at planting time and with flowers of sulphur upon lifting will usually prevent an outbreak.

Damping Off (*Corticium solani*). It is one of the worst diseases affecting young seedlings. It forms a mycelium web over the bulbous plants and causes rapid collapse. It mostly affects cyclamen, begonias, lilies and is prevented by watering the compost before sowing (also the box or pan) with Cheshunt Compound. It is a disease of the soil. When raising plants from seed, sterilised soil and peat instead of leaf mould should be used, and cleanliness should be the order. Cheshunt compound is made by mixing together 11 parts of ammonium carbonate and 2 parts of copper sulphate, which should be crushed and kept in an air tight drum until required. Dissolve a half ounce of the compound in a gallon of water and the compost should be given a thorough soaking several days before the seed is sown, again after sowing and covering the seed.

Dry Rot (*Sclerotinia gladioli*). It is one of the most troublesome of gladiolus diseases, accounting for many losses, especially during storage. The first symptom is the yellowing of the leaves which decay near the base of the sheath before they fall away. Upon lifting, the new corm will reveal brown markings which may also be seen on the leaf sheaths. On the corm the markings later turn black and become sunken. The disease begins inside the corm and works up into the foliage and as soon as yellowing is observed, the plant must be dug up and burnt. Upon inspection, the corm will confirm the presence of the disease.

The fungus is unable to live in the soil, only in the corm, so that when lifting in autumn it is important to clean the corms before inspecting each one separately. One badly infected corm may contaminate several hundred while in storage. It is also important when lifting to clear the ground of all dead foliage and stems upon which the fungus may remain during winter to contaminate the next year's crop, or better, allow the ground to have a year growing another crop before planting again with gladioli.

The disease was first recorded in the United States in 1909 and its presence was confirmed in Europe 20 years later. It also attacks the crocus, freesia and montbretia, indeed almost all corm-bearing plants.

Planting in well-drained land free from rank manure will do much to keep the trouble at bay, while correct storage is all-important, for under damp or excessively warm conditions the smallest outbreak will quickly assume dangerous proportions. It is also important to obtain clean stock, while dipping the corms in a 0·1 per cent mercuric chloride solution before planting has given complete control. Mercuric chloride however, is a poison and must be used with care. The disease will also attack freesias, causing the foliage to turn yellow and the corms to shrivel and die. They should be treated in a similar way.

Fire Disease (*Sclerotinia polyblastis*). The disease is so called because of the rapidity with which it spreads, appearing on the foliage of narcissi as yellowish-brown spots which quickly cover the whole leaf. It may also appear on the flowers as greyish spots. The disease will not attack the bulbs. The removal of all dead foliage after flowering, and spraying the young foliage in spring and early summer with Bordeaux Mixture (before and after flowering) will give control. The disease may also affect muscari and hyacinths, reducing the plants to a black slimy mass.

Freesia Mosaic. It attacks freesias and is caused by a virus, for affected plants show no sign of fungus activity. About a month after planting, when they have developed three leaves, large brown circles appear, causing them to wither. There is no known cure and affected plants should be dug up and destroyed.

Fusarium Yellows (*Fusarium oxysporum*). Known also as 'premature yellowing', it is one of the most troublesome of gladiolus diseases. Though infection enters the corm while in the ground, it is during storage that the disease is noticeable. It mostly attacks the lavender and purple-flowering varieties, while Picardy and its offspring possess marked resistance. The disease is detected by the yellowing of the leaves between the veins, as if showing potassium deficiency, but the veins remain green, giving a striped appearance.

The disease enters the corm through the roots, first causing decay at the base. It then attacks the centre, causing it to turn dark brown. The fungus may remain in the soil for as long as seven years, during which time it is not advisable to plant gladioli in the same ground. To plant in the same place year after year will be an invitation to the building up of the disease, for which there is no known cure.

Severely infected corms may not reveal the disease until some time after they have been in storage when they may have been reduced to black mummy-like objects, and upon handling the corm will disintegrate. To prevent infected corms reaching this stage, inspect them frequently, removing any that show the first signs of disease. The fungus may attack crocus corms in a similar way.

Grey Bulb Rot (*Sclerotium tuliparum*). It is a common disease of indoor tulips and Spanish iris and often shows itself immediately the boxes are taken indoors for forcing. Where present, the bulbs fail to sprout and upon inspection the tip will be seen to be brown. The disease extends inside the bulb, causing the formation of grey patches and decaying of the bulb. It was first discovered in Holland by Wakker in 1884. It may also attack *Iris reticulata*, *Scilla sibirica* and *Fritillaria imperialis*, causing destruction of the bulb. It is a soil fungus and, where it is present, the ground should be soaked with a 2 per cent formalin solution at least two months before making fresh plantings, while boxes in which tulips are to be forced should be subjected to the same treatment.

Hard Rot (*Septoria gladioli*). It is also known as leaf spot, for on the foliage of gladioli and freesias and occasionally crocuses, the fungus appears as small circular purple-brown spots, while similar spots may be observed on the corms when the scales are removed. Later they turn black, sink into the flesh and become hard and woody. The fungus is similar to dry rot in that it winters in the corms and on the leaves, so that all dead foliage must be cleared from the ground and burnt, while the corms must be inspected before storing. The disease is most troublesome during a cold, wet summer, and rarely affects freesias or gladioli grown under cloches or in a warm greenhouse. Where the bulbs are growing in the open, it is usually mid-July before the first signs of hard rot appear on the foliage. The plants should then be removed and burnt. The disease is carried from one plant to another by splashing during heavy rain or by artificial watering. Too-close planting should be avoided in districts of heavy rainfall.

Routine spraying with Bordeaux mixture from mid summer onwards will usually prevent a serious outbreak. The mixture is prepared by adding $\frac{1}{2}$ lb copper sulphate and $\frac{1}{2}$ lb hydrated lime to 6 gal of water, which is sprayed on the plants during a showery day. Repeat the treatment every fortnight. Note that a metal container should not be used for Bordeaux Mixture. Dipping the corms into a 0·1 per cent mercuric chloride solution before planting will control the disease which appears to attack *Primulinus* gladioli more so than the large-flowered type. Planting in clean ground in alternate years will also do much to prevent an outbreak.

Ink Disease (*Mystrosporium adustum*). It attacks the bulbous irises, causing black ink-like markings to appear on the outer scales of the bulbs. Later, it will penetrate into the flesh, causing the bulb to mummify. It will disintegrate upon touching into a cloud of dust. The fungus may also appear on the leaves. It will attack the leaves and corms of montbretia and tritonia, and the leaves and bulbs of lachenalia, causing brown spots to appear on the leaves. There is no known cure, and where it is observed the plants should be destroyed.

Iris Mosaic. This virus disease is rare on all but bulbous irises. It first appeared in England in 1928 and in North America six years later. It is carried to the leaves by aphides and is controlled by their extermination. The leaves become mottled or striped with pale green or yellow and dark spots may appear on the flowers. There is no cure and affected plants should be removed and destroyed.

Leaf Scorch (*Stanonospora curtisii*). It often happens that during a cold wet spring, the edges and tips of narcissus leaves become brown soon after they show. Later, brown circles appear on the foliage and upon microscopic observation reveal the presence of brown dots. The flower stems may also be attacked. The disease does not infect the bulbs and it may be prevented by spraying the foliage with weak Bordeaux Mixture when the leaves are about 6 in (15 cm) tall and thereafter every fortnight until they begin to die back in June.

Leaf Spot (*Didymellina macrospora*). It may attack the foliage of narcissus, gladiolus, freesia, hemerocallis and the rhizomatous irises, appearing on the leaves as small brown markings with grey dots at the centre, which are the spores of the fungus. The disfigured leaves should be removed at once, and as routine, spraying with Bordeaux Mixture to which a wetting agent has been added, will give control.

Lily Mosaic. It is similar to iris mosaic and affects most species of lilium causing spotting and streaking of the foliage and stunting of the flower stem. The virus is introduced by aphides which puncture the leaves to feed on the sap so that their extermination is the best prevention. There is no cure for diseased plants, which should be destroyed.

Lily-of-Valley Leaf Spot (*Dendrophoma convallariae*). This disease of lily-of-the-valley has proved troublesome in Europe but not in the British Isles. Dark-brown spots appear on the leaves and may eventually cover the whole of the leaf surface, causing entire defoliation. Spraying with a copper fungicide will usually prevent an outbreak.

Root Rot (*Cylindrocarpan radicicola*). A disease of the soil, affecting plants of narcissi and lilium, which may appear stunted, while the foliage turns pale green. Upon lifting, the roots will be seen to be brown instead of white, especially near the tips, and upon further inspection, the fungus may be seen to have attacked the basal plate. Formalin treatment as for basal bulb rot will give some immunity but it is essential to plant new bulbs into ground which has not previously grown narcissi and lilies, while the soil must be well drained.

Scab (*Bacterium marginatum*). The disease attacks gladioli and may be observed first on the leaves as tiny reddish spots which gradually become large and circular and raised at the edges. In a severe attack the spots join together to cause decaying of the leaf tissues near the base when the leaves may fall away entirely. The corm will already be infected, for on the corm the disease usually appears 4uring storage as brown saucer-shaped spots which may be removed with a knife point to leave behind a clean cavity.

Routine spraying of the foliage with Bordeaux Mixture and dipping the corms in a 0·1 per cent solution of Mercuric chloride before planting will give control.

Shanking (*Phytophthora cryptogaea*). Like *Pythium ultimum*, it is a water mould which enters the bulb through the roots and attacks the base of the flower stem, preventing the shoot from developing. The flowering stem will decay or it may grow, but will bear no bloom, a characteristic known to professional cut-flower growers as 'shanking'. It is a disease of the soil on which Cheshunt compound has no effect. Growing in sterilised soil or where the soil has been treated by disinfectant or a 2 per cent formalin solution will prevent an outbreak.

The closely related *Phytophthora cactorum*, prevalent in North America, attacks the base of the stems of tulips in wet, humid weather, causing them to fall over as the blooms open, a condition known as 'topple'.

Smoulder (*Botrytis narcissicola*). This is one of the most troublesome of narcissus diseases, attacking the foliage as it shows above ground in spring and causing it to decay at the neck. The fungus also occurs on the bulb, reducing it to a black slimy mass. The fungus will affect the foliage from the bulb which will reveal its presence by numerous black spots beneath the outer skin. Where detected in the ground, bulbs should be dug up and burned, while those bulbs in storage found to be unsound must be destroyed.

Smut (*Urocystis anemones, U. gladiolicola, U. colchici*). It attacks members of the Ranunculus family, including the common buttercup but also may be troublesome on *Anemone coronaria* and *A. eranthis*. In a slightly different form, it is also a disease of the gladiolus and snowdrop. On the leaves appear irregular grey blisters which burst during strong winds, releasing a powder of black spores. There is no known cure and infected plants should be removed with care and destroyed before the black spores are released.

In Holland the fungus is also known to attack the corms of the meadow saffron, *Colchicum autumnale*, especially the hybrids of *C. bornmüelleri*. It forms a brownish-black blister containing black spores on the outer skin of the corm. There is no known cure.

Soft Rot (*Bacterium carotovorum*). Closely related to *B. phytophthorum*, the dreaded leg rot of potatoes, it is often present in turnips and carrots and other vegetable crops as well as in hyacinth and cyclamen. With hyacinths, it usually attacks the fleshy neck of the bulb, but it may attack all parts, secreting poison into healthy cells.

The disease enters through wounds in the bulbs and attacks the lamella which binds the plant cells together. Soon the whole bulb becomes a decaying mass and emits a most unpleasant smell. It is a soil fungus and so rotational cropping is essential with the hyacinth. It is also important to scrub down the trays or boxes in which hyacinths are stored with a 1 per cent formalin solution a month before storing and again immediately afterwards. Hyacinths should not be grown near carrots or other vegetable crops.

The disease occasionally attacks the rhizomatous iris and is detected by the tips of the leaves turning yellow, then brown and finally becoming a slimy mass at the base before falling away. The rhizome will also be affected, becoming a wet mass of evil-smelling bacteria. The diseased portion should be cut away at once and the healthy part, where cut, treated with a 1 per cent Lysol solution. It has been found that plants given a light dressing with superphosphate of lime each year will rarely become affected.

Storage Rot (*Rhizopus necans*). Lilies and narcissi suffer from the rotting of their bulbs during storage though *L. speciosum* and *L. longiflorum* are highly resistant. The disease enters through wounds and forms dark spots on the scales, later working its way down to the base and causing it to decay. The bulb emits an unpleasant smell. Care should be taken in lifting and transporting lilies especially, also during their planting, for their scales are brittle and easily damaged.

During the late 1930s O'Leary and Guterman discovered that *Rhizopus necans* could be controlled by mixing bleaching powder with the lily potting compost or in the garden soil before planting, at the rate of 1 oz to every 14 lb of compost. It also gave control against bulb mite (*Rizoglyphus echinopus*). The disease in a slightly different form also attacks the corms of the gladiolus in storage. For this there is no known cure.

Stump Rot (*Phytaphthara parasitica*). It attacks the centre part of the rosette of leaves formed by *Lilium longiflorum* and *L. giganteum* and is caused by soil splashing over the rosette during heavy rain where growing outdoors, or by careless watering where growing indoors. It will also attack the leaves of sinningia (gloxinia), spreading down to the corm. It may be controlled by watering with Cheshunt Compound, while 'topping' the pots with a layer of sand will help to prevent an outbreak.

Tulip Root Rot (*Pythium ultimum*). It is a water mould introduced by the soil and causing grey areas at the base of the bulbs. The shoots fail to grow more than an inch or two and may be pulled from the bulb with gentle pressure. Sometimes the disease attacks only the roots through which it gains entry and the flower may appear normal before the fungus attacks the bulb. There is no known cure and diseased bulbs should be destroyed, but as the disease attacks while the bulbs are rooting (in the dark), the use of clean compost or sterilised soil will prevent its appearance.

White Mould (*Ramularia vallisumbrosae*). It attacks narcissus and is most prevalent in the moister, warmer parts, appearing on the leaves as small grey spots. They gradually grow larger, become covered with a white powder and kill the foliage before its time. The fungus is unable to survive a severe winter in the ground, while its appearance may be prevented by routine spraying of the foliage from early spring until it begins to die back with weak Bordeaux Mixture.

Winter Browning. It is a common trouble with *Anemone coronaria* and is, caused by the plants receiving little or no protection from cold winds. It may wipe out an entire crop. Treading of the soil during wet weather and lack of potash will bring it about. The undue treading of the ground in tending or picking the crop, thus causing consolidation of the soil and depriving the corms of the necessary oxygen will encourage the trouble. It is kept in check by regular hoeing between the rows and by watering the foliage once every fort-night with dilute Cheshunt Compound. Vigorous young 'pea'-size corms rarely suffer from the trouble and should be planted in preference to old 'jumbo'-sized corms which have lost vigour.

Yellow Disease (*Xanthomonas hyacinthi*). A disease of the hyacinth, prevalent only in Holland, though it may be spread elsewhere by imported bulbs. The disease may enter the bulb through the foliage or flower stem and is difficult to detect during storage, for it is present as tiny pale-yellow spots between the scales. If, however, a bulb is cut open, yellow slime exudes from between the scales. Stripping of the leaves may reveal its presence. Diseased bulbs should be dug up and destroyed and the surrounding ground treated with a 5 per cent formalin solution. The use of fresh manure or of artificials of high nitrogen content, causing the bulbs to become 'soft' may cause an attack for which there is no known cure.

TABLE XXI. *Plants and diseases*

Plant	Disease	Treatment
Anemone	*Botrytis cinerea*	Dust foliage with Shirlan AG
	Puccinia pruni-spinosae	No known cure
	Sclerotium delphinii	Dust corms with Lindex
	Urocystis anemones	No known cure
	Winter browning	No known cure
Begonia	*Botrytis cinerea*	Dust with Shirlan AG
	Corticium solani	Water with Cheshunt Compound
	Thielaviopsis basicola	No known cure
Colchicum	*Urocystis colchici*	No known cure
Crocus	*Fusarium oxysporum*	No known cure
	Rhizoctonia crocorum	No known cure
Cyclamen	*Bacterium carotovorum*	No known cure
	Botrytis cinerea	Spray foliage with Shirlan AG
	Corticium solani	Water with Cheshunt Compound
	Thielaviopsis basicola	No known cure
Freesia	*Didymellina macrospora*	Spray foliage with Bordeaux Mixture
	Fusarium bulbigenum	Dip corms in o·5 per cent formalin
	Mosaic	No known cure
	Sclerotinia gladioli	Dip corms in o·1 mercuric chloride solution
	Septoria gladioli	Spray foliage with Bordeaux Mixture
Fritillaria	*Sclerotium tuliparum*	Treat soil with 2 per cent formalin solution
Galanthus	*Botrytis galanthina*	Dust foliage with flowers of sulphur
	Urocystis galanthi	No known cure
Gladiolus	*Bacterium marginatum*	Spray foliage with Bordeaux Mixture
	Botrytis gladiorum	Spray foliage with Bordeaux Mixture
	Fusarium bulbigenum	Dip corms in o·5 per cent formalin
	Fusarium oxysporum	Dip corms in o·5 per cent formalin
	Rhizopus necans	No known cure
	Sclerotinia gladioli	Dip corms in o·1 per cent mercuric chloride solution
	Septoria gladioli	Spray foliage with Bordeaux Mixture
	Urocystis gladiolica	No known cure
Hemerocallis	*Didymellina macrospora*	Spray foliage with Bordeaux Mixture
Hyacinthus	*Bacterium carotovorum*	No known cure
	Botrytis hyacinthi	Spray foliage with Shirlan AG

TABLE XXI—*Continued*

Plant	Disease	Treatment
Hyacinthus —contd.	Sclerotinia polyblastis	Spray foliage with weak Bordeaux Mixture
	Xanthomonas hyacinthi	No known cure
Iris	Bacterium carotovorum	No known cure
	Botrytis convoluta	Spray foliage with Shirlan AG
	Didymellina macrospora	Spray foliage with Bordeaux Mixture
	Mosaic	No known cure
	Mystrosporium adustum	No known cure
	Puccinia iridis	No known cure
	Sclerotium tuliparum	Treat soil with 2 per cent formalin solution
Lachenalia	Mystrosporium adustum	No known cure
Lily	Botrytis elliptica	Spray foliage with Bordeaux Mixture
	Corticium solani	Water with Cheshunt Compound
	Cylindrocarpon radicicola	Dip bulbs in a 0·5 per cent formalin solution
	Mosaic	No known cure
	Phytophthora parasitica	Water with Cheshunt Compound
	Rhizopus necans	Add bleaching powder to potting compost
Lily-of-the-valley	Dendrophoma convallariae	Spray foliage with copper fungicide
	Puccinia sessilis	No known cure
	Sclerotium denigrans	No known cure
Narcissus	Botrytis narcissicola	Dip bulbs in 0·5 per cent formalin solution
	Cylindrocarpon radicicola	Dip bulbs in 0·5 per cent formalin solution
	Didymellina macrospora	Spray foliage with Bordeaux Mixture
	Fusarium bulbigenum	Dip bulbs in 0·5 per cent formalin solution
	Ramularia vallisumbrosae	Spray foliage with Bordeaux Mixture
	Sclerotinia polyblastis	Spray foliage with Bordeaux Mixture
	Stagonospora curtisii	Spray foliage with Bordeaux Mixture
Montbretia	Mystrosporium adustum	No known cure
	Sclerotinia gladioli	Dip corms in 0·1 per cent mercuric chloride solution

TABLE XXI—*Continued*

Plant	Disease	Treatment
Scilla	*Sclerotium tuliparum*	Treat soil with 2 per cent formalin solution
Sinningia	*Phytophthora parasitica*	Water with Cheshunt Compound
Tulip	*Botrytis tulipae*	Spray or dust foliage with Shirlan AG
	Phytaphthora cryptogaea	Treat soil with 2 per cent formalin solution
	Pythium ultimum	No known cure
	Sclerotium tuliparum	Treat soil with 2 per cent formalin solution

PESTS

Aphides. Greenfly is one of the most troublesome of the pests which attack anemones, and heavy infestations may occur when the pests cling to the underside of the petals, causing disfigurement of the blooms and possibly virus entry by their sucking at the buds and stems, thereby weakening the plant. The best method of control is to spray regularly with Lindex, used at the rate of half a fluid ounce to 2 gal of water. Or use Lindex dust, making sure that it reaches to all parts of the foliage. Heavy infestations may be controlled by using $\frac{1}{4}$ oz of 98 per cent strength nicotine dissolved in 4 gal of water, to which a wetting agent has been added. It is sprayed on to the plants after the flush of bloom has been removed. Nicotine is a poison, to be kept under lock and key and used with the utmost care.

Bulb Mite (*Rhizoglyphus echinopus*). This microscopic pest mostly attacks tulips and lilies but occasionally narcissi bulbs, entering where the bulbs have become damaged during lifting. It is usually during storage that the pest is destructive, moving from one bulb to another. The hot-water treatment may be given to narcissi in early August but not to other bulbs, from which eradication proves difficult as the mites collect in large colonies on the underside of the scales. With tulips, the outer scales should be removed and the bulbs washed before planting in a solution of 1 oz of sulphide of potassium in 3 gal of water.

Under a microscope the mites will be seen to have pinkish-white oval bodies and eight hairy legs. Their presence may be detected by small red markings on the outer skin of the bulbs.

Caterpillar. It is the caterpillar of the angle shades moth which proves troublesome to anemones and gladioli, not only causing damage to the stems, flowers

and foliage, but by so doing providing an entrance for virus diseases which may
be the cause of winter browning of anemone foliage. An efficient deterrent is to
dust the foliage at fortnightly intervals with Lindex dust using 1 oz for 20 sq yd
of ground, for it is in the soil that the moth lays its eggs. The plants as well as
the soil should be treated.

Eelworm (*Tylenchus devastratix*). At one time this pest was so troublesome that
it almost wiped out commercial narcissus growing in the Fenlands of England
and in Holland. Bulbs so affected become distorted, while the leaves become
swollen and turn yellow almost as soon as they appear above ground. If
opened, the bulbs reveal brown areas which are soft to the touch, and it is
here that the eelworms exist. The blooms will be stunted and will fail completely.

Eelworms appear in bulbs which have been grown in humus-laden ground,
and when growing narcissus rank manure should be avoided. The worms
(nematodes) are almost colourless and so tiny that they can be seen only through
a microscope. They are pointed and able to enter the leaves or base of the bulb
by piercing a minute hole. After pairing, the females lay their eggs in large
numbers and quickly destroy the living plant cells upon which they feed. If
bulbs show symptoms of their presence, those growing in that particular area
should be dug up, for it is impossible to eradicate the pests while the bulbs are
still in the ground. Damaged bulbs should be destroyed. The others should be
placed in clean sacks and immersed for three hours in a tank of water kept at a
constant temperature of 110° F (40° C). Only narcissi will withstand so high
a temperature for so long.

After treating the bulbs they should be dried and replanted in clean ground
which has not grown narcissi for some years. Where growing on a commercial
scale, either for the production of bulbs or for the bloom, plantings into fresh
ground should be made every three years. Should the attack have been on a large
scale, the ground should be left vacant for as long as possible and treated in
spring and again in autumn, with a steriliser such as formalin or a proprietory
disinfectant, at a strength of two tablespoons to each gallon of water. Besides
attacking narcissus, bulbous irises, hyacinths and tulips, eelworm can also
prove troublesome to chrysanthemums, tomatoes and potatoes.

Large Narcissus Fly (*Merodon narcissi*). It lays its eggs during May on the
necks of the bulbs and may attack several members of the Amaryllidaceae
family in addition to the narcissus. The fly is large with a hairy body and is
black with a yellow ring around the base of the head at the end of its body. It
resembles a small bee but has only two wings. The eggs are white and hatch
out pale-yellow grubs, which work their way down into the bulb, eventually
devouring the whole of the inside—or only a part of it when the new leaves will
grow up yellow and stunted. So active is the pest that growers of high-quality

varieties lift and treat the bulbs during early August as a matter of course, subjecting them to the hot-water treatment recommended for eelworms.

For the amateur, Plant Protection Ltd. have devised a most effective method of control by dipping the bulbs when dormant in August, into a solution of 4 pt liquid BHC and 1 pt of spreader (Agral LN), dissolved in 100 gal of water, or its equivalent where growing on a small scale. The bulbs should be placed in clean sacks, immersed for three hours and afterwards spread out to dry.

Leather Jacket Grub. This is the larva of the daddy long legs, which feeds on bulbs, corms and tubers. It has a blackish-grey body, no legs and measures about 1 in in length. It may be controlled by treating the soil as for wireworm several weeks before planting or by moistening 1 oz of Paris Green with 2 lb of bran and scattering it among the growing plants.

Mealy Bug. It confines its activities to bulbs and other plants which grow in warm greenhouses. It is a wingless insect with an oval 'flour-dusted' body, and it attacks the foliage of plants by piercing and sucking the sap, quickly reducing their vitality. It is difficult to eradicate, for it makes its home at the base of the leaf stalks. Sponging the foliage with Lindex solution or with Jeyes Fluid as for thrip will act as a deterrent, while the pest may be eradicated by dusting with Lindex.

Mice. Mice are frequently troublesome to winter crocuses and to anemones, when they uncover the soil from shallowly planted corms and nibble through them, often causing considerable damage in one night. They may also devour the young buds of cloche-grown anemones, causing loss of bloom when flowers are scarce. Commercial growers place baited traps along the rows and may even have to surround the beds with small-mesh netting buried 6 in (15 cm) into the ground. The netting will also give protection against cold winds.

Where mice have proved troublesome, the corms may be sprinkled with red lead before planting, but red lead is poisonous and should be used with care, especially where there are children and animals about. An ounce of red lead will treat 100 corms of crocus or anemone.

Millepedes. They differ from wireworm in their dark-grey colour and have legs all along their body. They occasionally attack bulbs and corms and may be killed by treating the ground before planting as for wireworm. Watering the soil around the plants with a dilute solution of common salt will prove helpful.

Slug (*Arion hortensis*). This pest may cause damage to the young shoots of summer-flowering bulbs. They will rarely attack during cold weather or prey on those plants growing in a dry, climate. The succulent stems of summer bedding begonias are always an attraction and the stems of anemones and hyacinths. They attack the base of the stems and may devour large numbers during any warm, wet night.

As a deterrent it is advisable to water the ground with liquid Slugit as soon as the young shoots appear above ground. One ounce of Slugit dissolved in 1 gal of water will treat 10 sq yd of ground. The treatment should be repeated a month later, for besides causing damage to the flower stems, the slugs lay their eggs beneath the new corms, where they hatch out and cause untold damage.

Small Narcissus Fly (*Eumerus strigatus*). A small edition of *Merodon narcissi*, being about ¼ in in length and likewise it is black with two wings. It makes its appearance about two weeks later than *M. narcissi* and lays its eggs near the base of the leaves. The grubs feed on the tissue at the top of the bulbs and as many as 20 or more may be present at the same time, causing damage to the bulb. The bulbs should be treated as for large narcissus fly where the presence of the pest can be detected, or given preventive treatment.

Thrip (*Taeniothrips gladioli*). It is a tiny black thread-like insect, about one-twentieth of an inch in length which was first discovered on a batch of gladioli corms in Ohio in 1930. Since then it has continued to attack the gladiolus in all parts of the world, feeding on the buds, stems, foliage and corms and causing damage in all stages of growth. The larvae and pupae, which are pale-yellow, are often to be found both in the leaf sheaths and in the buds, while the eggs are laid on all parts of the plant.

Taking only 12 days for the adult stage to be reached, the pests will continue to feed on the corms while in storage, attacking the root initials and the buds, the most succulent parts, and covering them with a brown transparent film. It is rarely that the hard-shelled cormlets are attacked.

When the corms have been planted, the insects come above ground with the foliage, feeding on the leaves, stems and flowers, while the buds will turn brown and become shrivelled. The pests are difficult to reach during daylight when they spend their time hiding in the leaf sheaths and laying their eggs in the leaf tissues. Where growing expensive new varieties or planning for exhibition, it is advisable to treat each leaf separately, by soaking a piece of cloth in a solution of Jeyes Fluid, 1 teaspoonful dissolved in ½ gal of water and applying it by wiping both sides of each leaf in an upwards direction.

From early June the foliage should be given routine treatment with a spray or powder. Lindex applied once every 10 days should keep the plants free from attack. An alternative is to use Sybol, spraying the foliage every 10 days. Another method is to make up a solution of 2 oz of Tartar emetic and 8 oz of brown sugar dissolved in 3 gal of water and to apply to the foliage as soon as growth commences, for should the pests enter the flower buds they will prove impossible to eradicate. Spraying should be discontinued as soon as the buds show colour.

An extra precaution against thrip is to dip the corms after lifting and cleaning and again prior to planting, in a solution of Lysol or Jeyes Fluid (1 tablespoonful to 1 gal of water). The corms should be immersed for two hours and may be planted while still damp. Treatment of the corms before planting is especially desirable where planting into the same ground for several years in succession for the pests are able to withstand normal winter conditions.

When lifting the corms, dust with Lindex, then string them up to enable them to receive a free circulation of air. Later, after removing the foliage, shake up the corms in bags containing naphthalene flakes, 1 oz to every 100 corms. Naphthalene flakes are harmless both to the corms and to humans. Cormlets should be given the same treatment.

TABLE XXII. *Plants and pests*

Plant	Pest	Treatment
Anemone	Aphides	Spray or dust with Lindex
	Caterpillar	Dust foliage with Lindex
	Slug	Water with Slugit
	White centipede	Treat soil with Aldrin
Begonia	Mealy Bug	Spray or dust foliage with Lindex
Crocus	Leather jacket grub	Treat soil with Aldrin
	Mice	Sprinkle corms with red lead
Cyclamen	Weevil	Include Gammexane in compost
Gladioli	Caterpillar	Dust foliage with Lindex
	Thrip	Dust with Lindex or spray with Sybol
	White centipede	Treat soil with Aldrin
	Wireworm	Treat soil with Aldrin or Abol wireworm dust
Hyacinthus	Eelworm	No known cure
	Slug	Water with Slugit
Iris	Eelworm	No known cure
	Leather jacket grub	Treat soil with Aldrin dust
Lilium	Bulb mite	Dip bulbs in sulphide of potassium solution
Narcissus	Bulb mite	Hot-water treatment
	Eelworm	Hot-water treatment
	Large narcissus fly	Immerse bulbs in liquid BHC
	Small narcissus fly	Immerse bulbs in liquid BHC
Tulip	Bulb mite	Wash bulbs in sulphide of potassium solution
	Eelworm	No known cure
	Millepedes	Treat soil with Aldrin or Abol wireworm dust

Weevil. The grubs are white, fat and legless and may be introduced to green-house plants in unsterilised compost or in unclean pots. They are partial to the corms of cyclamen and may be seen congregating around the base. Cleanliness of the house and utensils, the use of freshly sterilised soil and giving the compost a dusting with Gammexane will prevent their appearance.

White Centipede. The pest attacks below soil level, burrowing into bulbs and corms and into the stems of the flowers. The pests are most troublesome to anemones and gladioli and are controlled by treating the ground with Aldrin dust at the rate of 1 oz per square yard, raking it well into the soil just before planting the corms. Or water the ground with Lindex solution, 1 fl oz dissolved into 3 gal of water, before planting. Both preparations will also control wireworm.

Wireworm. It is the larvae of the click beetle. It is orange-coloured, of wire-like appearance and attacks corm-bearing plants such as crocus and gladioli, severing the roots from the base of the corm and causing the plant to collapse. Corms treated with naphthalene will prove almost immune to attack, but as a further safeguard treat the soil with Aldrin or Abol wireworm dust before planting, using 1 oz per square yard of ground. Naphthalene may be used as an alternative but at double the strength. The preparations should be worked in at a depth of 6 in (15 cm) when the soil is friable.

PART II

ALPHABETICAL GUIDE

A

ACHIMENES (Gesneraceae)

Named from *a-cheimaino*, to suffer from cold, it is a genus of about fifty species, native of tropical America, especially Mexico and Brazil. It has scaly rhizomatous roots, opposite leaves and bears its flowers solitary or in panicles. The leaves are fleshy and wrinkled and without stipules, while the flowers are tubular or bell-shaped with a five-lobed corolla and with four or two stamens. Greenhouse perennials in the British Isles and northern Europe, they require a temperature of 60° F (16° C) when starting into growth in spring. In warmer climes, they may be grown in the open without protection and are suitable for summer bedding and window boxes.

Culture. For indoor culture they require a compost composed of turf loam, sand and peat in equal parts by bulk, and if planted at monthly intervals, with the first planting made early in February, there will be a succession of bloom through summer and early autumn. Pans or pots may be used, filling them with compost to within 2 in (5 cm) of the rim. The scaly tubers which should be firm when planted are placed 2 in (5 cm) apart, five or six to each container, and are covered with a 1-in (2·5 cm) layer of compost. Soak with clean water and place in a sunny window or on the greenhouse bench and provide a night temperature of 60° F (16° C), keeping the compost moist. As they come into growth, give more moisture according to conditions. During summer they will need shielding from the sun by whitening the glass or by moving the plants to a more northerly aspect.

They will come into bloom from an early February planting before the end of May, and as they are held on succulent stems which are brittle, support them by inserting a few twigs into the compost. They will grow 15 in (37·5 cm) tall. To keep the foliage free from red spider, syringe daily during warm weather.

A pleasing display may be enjoyed by inserting small split canes at an angle around the rim of the pot to which the stems are tied. The effect will be increased if the pot is placed over an upturned pot of similar size and the shoots are allowed to grow beyond the end of the canes to give a cascade effect. Enjoying partial shade, the plants are suitable for home culture but should be sprayed often and watered by immersing the base of the pot for several hours. Plants may also be allowed to trail over the side of a hanging basket in the garden room or in a sheltered corner outdoors.

Those plants which grow in pots and are to be kept low and bushy, should have the tips of the main shoots removed to encourage the formation of side shoots. This should not be done to plants in hanging baskets. Keeping pot plants dwarf will remove the need for support.

For hanging baskets, achimenes are best started into growth in small pots containing two or three rhizomes. Remove from the pots when the soil ball is filled with fibrous roots and plant around the side of the basket. If required for outside display, the baskets should not be put out until there is no fear of frost damage. The plants will respond to an occasional watering with dilute liquid manure.

After flowering, they should be treated like begonias and allowed to die back gradually, withholding moisture by degrees. After the flower stems have been removed and the leaves have begun to turn brown, place the pots on their sides beneath the bench or in a shaded room where they remain during winter in a minimum temperature of 40° F (4° C). Alternatively the rhizomes may be removed from the compost and stored in boxes of dry sand or peat until required for starting into growth again in fresh compost.

Achimenes may be grown entirely without heat, though the display will be limited to the warmer days. The rhizomes are started into growth early in April in a greenhouse or sunny window when they will come into bloom before the end of June and will remain colourful for two months. A second planting a month later will ensure a colourful display from late June until the end of September.

Propagation. Increase by cutting up the rhizomes when repotting as for begonias, each piece having an 'eye' or sprout. Alternatively, the young shoots may be removed like dahlia shoots when about 2 in (5 cm) tall and inserted around the side of a pot in a compost of peat and sand. Shade until rooted. Named varieties may also be increased by removing mature leaves and inserting the stalks in compost to the base of the leaf blade.

Where raising plants from seed, sow in May in the John Innes sowing compost, scattering the seed evenly over the surface and lightly covering with sand. They require a temperature of 65° F (18° C) to germinate and should be large enough for transplanting to small pots in six to eight weeks.

Species and Varieties. *Achimenes antirrhina.* A Mexican species, it is distinct and unusual. It is tall growing, attaining a height of 3 ft (90 cm), with large dark-green leaves and bearing elegant trumpets of brilliant orange, speckled with yellow in the throat.

Achimenes bella. Native of Brazil, it grows 2 ft (60 cm) tall, with large leaves. Its tubular flowers of mid-blue have dark-blue markings in the throat.

Achimenes coccinea (Syn. *A. pulchella*). Its home is Jamaica. It is a plant of compact habit and is free flowering, bearing over a long period numerous medium-sized flowers of brilliant red, enhanced by the dark-green leaves.

Achimenes escheriana. It makes a plant of compact habit growing 12 in (30 cm) tall and bears masses of tubular blooms of deep violet-pink, speckled red in the throat.

Achimenes flava. Similar to *A. coccinea* in habit, it bears masses of small flowers of palest yellow.

Achimenes ghiesbreghti. Native of Mexico, it grows 12 in (30 cm) tall with large leaves and bears large tubular flowers of deep velvety red.

Achimenes grandiflora. Native of Mexico, it grows 18 in (45 cm) tall, its oval leaves having toothed edges, while it bears tubular flowers of deep purple blue.

Achimenes harveyi (Syn. *A. hybrida Shirley Fireglow*). Received the Award of Merit from the Royal Horticultural Society in 1961. It is a plant of dwarf, compact habit, covering itself for several weeks, in masses of medium-sized blooms of brilliant orange-scarlet.

Achimenes hirsuta. Native of Guatemala, it grows 2½ ft (75 cm) tall and has heart-shaped leaves which are deeply toothed and, like the stems, are covered in hairs. The rose-coloured flowers are shaded yellow at the centre.

Achimenes hybrida, Little Beauty. A hybrid of distinction and most suitable for pots. It grows less than 12 in (30 cm) tall and is bushy, with a short sturdy stem. It commands attention with its blooms of vivid cerise-pink. If the plants are being marketed, they should be wrapped in white paper to accentuate the beauty of the flowers and to guard against draught during transit.

Achimenes hybrida, Paul Arnold. Named after the achimenes specialist of Binghampton, New York, who has done so much to identify the species and to introduce new hybrids of merit. Like Little Beauty, it makes a valuable pot plant, for it has a compact habit and bears a profusion of small tubular blooms of crimson-red held on long pedicels.

Achimenes joureguia maxima. Native of tropical Central America, it is a rare and beautiful plant growing 12 in (30 cm) tall, its large white flowers being veined with purple in the throat.

Achimenes longiflora major. Native of Guatemala its leaves are borne in circles of threes, while it bears the largest flowers of all, nearly 3 in (7·5 cm) across and of rich aniline blue. Of compact habit. The form *margaritae* bears pure white flowers of equal beauty.

Achimenes, Michelssen hybrids. Of this important new strain, several varieties introduced in 1970, will bring additional popularity to this flower on account of their compact bushy habit and unusual colour range. Growing less than 6 in (15 cm) tall, the plants may be grown in small pots and will cover themselves in bloom from April until October. Viola Michelssen bears flowers 2 in (5 cm) across and of bright rosy-orange. Johanna Michelssen is deep salmon, and Tarantella is brilliant scarlet.

Achimenes patens major. Native of Mexico, it grows 15 in (37·5 cm) tall. Its purple flowers have throats of white and are held on short sturdy stems.

Achimenes pedunculata. It grows 2½ feet (75 cm) tall and comes into bloom later than other species. It bears handsome orange flowers shaded with yellow and speckled with red in the throat, while they are held on long pedicles. It is native of Mexico.

Achimenes tubiflora (syn. *Gloxinia tubiflora*). Found in the hills around Buenos Aires, it grows 18 in (45 cm) tall, its leaves being oblong and pointed, while its flowers are purest white with a tube 4 in long. They are deliciously scented, relying on perfume rather than colour to attract pollinators.

ACIDANTHERA (Iridaceae)

A genus of 40 species, native of tropical and South Africa, with smooth- or fibrous-coated corms and taking their name from *akis*, a point, and *anthera*, an anther, a reference to the pointed pollen sac. Closely related to the gladiolus and babiana but of more tender habit, with erect stems and flat linear leaves, only one species *A. bicolor* and its variety, *murielae*, is hardy in the British Isles and northern Europe—and then only in the more sheltered gardens, for they require a night temperature of not less than 50° F (10° C). For this reason, in a cold climate they are best grown in a cool greenhouse, planting them in April—a month earlier if gentle heat is available.

Culture. If growing outdoors, the corms should not be planted until the end of April, though in warmer parts they may be left in the ground to multiply like montbretias. The corms are about 1 in (2·5 cm) thick. They should be slightly rounded at the crown and quite firm when pressed. They should be planted 4 in (10 cm) deep and 6 in (15 cm) apart. They require a position of full sun and a light, well-drained soil which will quickly become warmed by the early spring sunshine, while if the corms are to be long-lasting in the ground, the soil should be such that winter moisture will drain away. A heavy soil may be lightened by incorporating some peat, old mushroom bed compost, leaf mould, shingle and clearings from ditches. The corms take some time to grow and will not bloom from a mid-April planting until early September in northern Europe. They need all the help possible and ample supplies of water during summer.

Where growing under glass, the corms may be planted about 1st April or a month earlier if in gentle warmth. Plant them in boxes or pots, 2 in (5 cm) deep and 3 in (7·5 cm) apart and in an 'open' compost fortified by some decayed manure. Gentle bottom heat will bring them quickly into growth and they will come into bloom in July. They may be taken outdoors when the flower spike has formed.

After flowering, allow the foliage to die back before lifting the corms and cleaning and drying as for gladioli. One of the secrets of success with their keeping is to winter them in a temperature of not less than 60° F (16° C), close to the central-heating boiler and in boxes of dry sand.

Propagation. The acidantheras are increased by the spawn or offsets which, as with gladioli, form around the basal plate. Detach them when the corms are lifted in late October, and place in a glass jar. Cover with sand and winter in a temperature of 60° F (16° C). They are planted in shallow boxes of sandy compost in spring and grown on to flowering size as for gladioli.

Species and Varieties. *Acidanthera aequinoctialis.* Of the mountainous regions of Sierra Leone, it was discovered in 1892 and described in the *Gardener's Chronicle* the following year. It grows 3 ft (90 cm) tall with sword-like leaves and bears flowers which measure 4 in (10 cm) across. They are white with a crimson blotch at the base of each petal and are sweetly scented.

Acidanthera bicolor. Native of the highlands of Ethiopia, with corms about 1 in (2·5 cm) thick, it grows 18 in (45 cm) tall and is suitable for a sheltered garden; also for pot culture. It bears its scented creamy-white flowers blotched with chocolate at the end of graceful arching stems, each of which bears 8 to 12 flowers. Their pointed segments give them a star-like quality when fully open.

Its variety *murielae*, native of western Ethiopia grows 3 ft (90 cm) tall, its white flowers with the crimson blotch at the base of each segment measuring 3 in (7·5 cm) across. They, too, are sweetly scented.

Acidanthera candida. Native of the steppelands of the Altai Plains of eastern Africa, it has narrow pointed leaves and bears its sweetly scented pure-white flowers with their long cylindrical tube on 18 in (45 cm) stems. A tender species, it requires warm climatic conditions to bloom outdoors.

Acidanthera tubergenii. A hybrid, raised by van Tubergens at Haarlem from *A. murielae* and *A. bicolor*, its chief merit being that it blooms about three weeks earlier than either parent. It has thus greater value for the cut-flower grower and for those who garden in cooler regions. The blotches at the base of the segments are larger than those on the flowers of its parents, while the inner segments are tinted with pink.

AGAPANTHUS (Alliaceae)

A genus of five species of evergreen perenniels, native of southern Africa and taking their name from *agape*, love, and *anthos*, a flower. The plant forms a short rhizome and has thick fleshy roots, resembling those of Alstroemeria. The strap-like leaves are of brilliant green and about 2 ft (60 cm) long, while the flowers are borne in umbels on erect scapes. With deep planting, it is hardy in all but the coldest parts of North America and northern Europe. In such areas plant in large tubs and move before winter to the shelter of a garage or outhouse.

The flower is funnel-shaped, with six equal segments and six stamens attached to the base of the tube. It blooms during the latter weeks of summer and in autumn.

Culture. In the open ground it appreciates the protection of a wall or of the overhanging eaves of a house and requires a position of full sunlight. It may also be grown in large pots in a cool greenhouse or garden room, where, apart from the occasional topping up of the compost, it will require no other attention for years. It is attractive planted in groups by the side of a lake or pond.

For planting in tubs it requires a compost made up of turf loam (2 parts) and decayed manure and grit (1 part each). The tub or pot should be provided with adequate drainage, especially where it is to be placed in the open. Plant in April, at a depth 8 in (20 cm), spreading out the roots. Three may be planted in a large tub; one in a small tub or pot. Provide with ample moisture, for it is a copious drinker and will remain so until flowering has ended. Water should then be withheld gradually but not entirely for the plants are evergreen. If they can be removed to the shelter of a cellar or garage at the beginning of winter they may be taken outside again in late spring and started into growth. Where growing outdoors they may be protected by placing around the crowns some grit or ash. This is preferable to straw which tends to harbour slugs and other harmful pests which may attack the leaves. Alternatively, the plants may be lifted and removed to a cellar or outhouse, their roots wrapped in sacking.

Propagation. Plants may be raised from seed though by this method it will take at least five years for them to reach flowering size. Seed is sown in pots of sterilised loam, peat and sand (in equal parts by bulk) in April, and germination may take six months. It is essential to use fresh, well-ripened seed and never to allow the young plants to suffer from cold or lack of moisture. The seedlings will be ready to transplant to small pots the following spring. During summer, they may be grown on outdoors in an open frame, and by the end of summer will be ready to move to larger pots.

To increase the stock by vegetative methods, it is usual to lift and divide in spring, each plant yielding several pieces, each with a crown and a number of fleshy roots. They should be repotted or planted out immediately after dividing so that the roots will not lose too much moisture.

Species. *Agapanthus pendulinus.* It is a less hardy form, bearing its flowers of thundercloud blue on 5-ft (1·5-metre) scapes and in large umbels. It is almost deciduous, the leaves dying back during winter, but it requires protection from cold like *A. umbellatus.*

Agapanthus umbellatus. The most common and hardiest form, it is known as the blue African lily and is one of the loveliest attractions of Table Mountain where it blooms from December until February. It has leathery strap-like leaves 2 ft (60 cm) long and 2 in (5 cm) wide. To keep them healthy, they should regularly be wiped with soap and water. The flowers are borne on erect scapes 2 ft (60 cm) tall, while the umbels may be of 12 in (30 cm) diameter, the flowers being of deep hyacinth blue. They will bloom from July until October. There is a double form, *flore pleno,* and a pure white of great beauty, *albus.* Weillighi bears drooping umbels of deepest blue. In their native land they are followed by attractive flat seed vessels containing black seeds.

ALBUCA (Liliaceae)

A genus of 50 species of white-flowering plants, native of southern Africa, closely related to Galtonia. They take their name from *albus*, white, and have tunicated bulbs and linear leaves. Their flowers, borne in loose racemes, have three spreading outer segments and three shorter inner segments enclosing six stamens.

Culture. In the British Isles, northern Europe and North America, except in the most sheltered gardens of the south-west Pacific coast, the plants should be confined to a warm greenhouse, though *A. nelsonii* is sufficiently hardy to be grown under glass where no heat is available and if frost is excluded. It is also the most reliable species for outdoor culture where it should be grown in a light, well-drained soil and in full sun. Plant the bulbs 5 in (12·5 cm) deep in September for them to come into bloom early in summer.

For indoors plant three bulbs to a large pot and into a mixture of turf loam, sand and peat in equal parts. Plant early in October and keep in a shaded frame until the end of November, during which time they should receive little water. Before frost, move indoors and bring on in gentle heat, giving more moisture as the plants make growth. They will bloom under glass early in summer and after flowering should be taken outside and placed on their sides to die back. They should be repotted and started into growth again early in autumn.

Propagation. Around the base of the bulbs when removed from the pots will be found numerous small bulblets. These should be detached and grown on in boxes of sterilised loam and sand, to be transplanted the following summer into small pots in which they grow on to flowering size.

They may also be raised from seed sown in John Innes compost in spring, the seedlings being moved to small pots when large enough to handle. They will take four years to bloom.

Species. *Albuca elwesii* (syn. *A. wakefieldii*). Native of tropical eastern Africa, it is a delightful plant for a warm greenhouse, where it will grow only 12 in (30 cm) tall from small oval bulbs and will come into bloom early in spring. It has long pale-green leaves and flowers of similar colouring, which are borne in loose racemes.

Albuca nelsonii. Native of Natal, it is perhaps the finest of all the species and is a valuable plant to decorate a garden room. It grows 4 to 5 ft (1·2 to 1·5 metres) tall with long, narrow leaves of similar length and about 2 in (5 cm) wide. The flowers appear early in May and are borne in loose racemes. They are white with a red stripe down the centre of each segment on the outside, while they are sweetly scented. They will remain in bloom for six weeks.

ALLIUM (Alliaceae)

A genus of about 350 species of bulbous plants, native of the Northern Hemisphere, mostly of Europe. Their name is from the Celtic *all*, hot, a reference to the burning qualities of many of them. They have tunicated bulbs, linear leaves and bear their flowers in cymose umbels on the top of a sturdy scape. The perianth is of six segments, free or scarcely united at the base, spreading or bell-shaped with a single stamen. They are among the most useful of all plants for naturalising in the woodland garden or shrubbery, for they are happy in partial shade and in all soils and once established, quickly spread into large colonies. They are valuable for a poor dry soil while several species are attractive in the rock garden or for growing in pans in the alpine house. Almost all are hardy, but those few exceptions, e.g. *A. neapolitanum*, should be confined to those gardens enjoying a favourable climate or to the alpine house. The first of the species to bloom, *A. affatunense*, bears its umbels of lilac-mauve early in May on a 3-ft (90-cm) stem and is a valuable cut flower, for, like all the alliums, it remains fresh in water or on the plant for several weeks. With it blooms *A. karataviense* which grows 12 in (30 cm) tall, and with its handsome foliage is an excellent pot plant for a cold house. Then follows *A. moly*, the golden garlic, and the dainty *A. ostrowskianum*, a delightful species for the alpine garden. Last to bloom is *A. cyaneum*, the blue allium of Kansu, which flowers in August and is a most attractive species for the rock garden. The various species planted in numerous places about the garden will produce handsome splashes of colour throughout summer. They are unmindful of adverse weather. Several have foliage which is unpleasantly smelling, but, apart from the native *A. ursinum*, they will not usually release their smell unless trodden upon.

Culture. When planting outdoors, set the bulbs in wide circular groups of a single species, or as inner and outer circles, using species of contrasting colour. *A. moly*, with its golden flowers, and *A. coeruleum*, bearing umbels of sky-blue, are attractive together. Both bloom at a similar height and at the same time. Do not plant alliums too closely for they spread rapidly.

Propagation. This is by the small bulblets which form at the base of mature bulbs. They are detached when the plants are lifted and divided in autumn and are planted 1 in (2·5 cm) apart in boxes of sterilised loam and sand where they are grown until reaching flowering size, when they are planted out. Alternatively, they may be raised from seed and may be expected to come reasonably true. Seed is sown in the John Innes compost early in spring and the seedlings transplanted to pots or boxes when they have formed their seed leaf. They will bloom two to three years after sowing.

Species. *Allium affatunense*. Native of northern Iran, it comes into bloom early in May, bearing rich lilac-mauve flowers in dense spherical umbels and on 3-ft (90-cm) stems.

Allium albopilosum. With its decorative foliage, the leaves being covered at the margins in white hairs, and bearing flower heads 10 in (25 cm) in diameter during June, it is one of the best of the alliums for cutting. Its flowers, which measure 2 in (5 cm) across, are lilac-pink and star-like, the flower heads being held on 2-ft (60-cm) stems. It is native of Iran.

Allium accuminatum. It was discovered in western North America during Dr Vancouver's expeditionary voyage and bears small heads of lilac-pink flowers on 12-in (30-cm) stems during July and August.

Allium album (syn. *A. cowanii*). The finest of the white-flowering alliums and hardier than *A. neapolitanum*. It bears ball-shaped heads of purest white on 18-in (45-cm) stems and blooms during midsummer.

Allium amabile. Native of Yunnan, where it was found by George Forrest, it grows 6 in (15 cm) tall and during July and August bears graceful umbels of rosy-red. A plant for the alpine house or scree.

Allium beesianum. One of Mr Forrest's discoveries in north-western China, it has immense beauty, bearing its brilliant blue flowers in drooping umbels during July and August from a clump of linear leaves. It is suitable for the rock garden or for edging, for it grows only 9 in (22·5 cm) tall.

Allium coeruleum (syn. *A. azureum*). Native of Siberia, it is a plant of distinction bearing, during June and July, small compact heads of rich cornflower blue on 2-ft (60-cm) stems. As the bulbs are so inexpensive, this species is worth growing as a commercial cut flower.

Allium elatum. A rare species from central Asia with broad, glossy, bright-green leaves and bearing in May, on 3 ft (90 cm) stems, umbels of rosy-lilac.

Allium flavum. Native of southern Europe, it forms tight clumps of linear leaves from which arise, on 12-in (30-cm) stems, umbels of buff-tinted urn-shaped flowers. July-flowering.

Allium giganteum. This rare and splendid species, native of Siberia, bears globular heads of richest lilac, which measure 6 in (14 cm) across and are held on 3-ft (90-cm) stems. Flowering in June and July, it is a valuable plant for the back of the border, and is long-lasting as a cut flower.

Allium kansuense. Native of Kansu, it is a blue-flowered garlic of charm, bearing its flowers in large umbels on 6-in (15-cm) stems during August. Suitable for the alpine house or rock garden.

Allium karataviense. Native of Turkestan, it has crimson-tinted glaucous leaves which spread over the ground, and it bears the largest flowers of all the species, sometimes measuring 12 in (30 cm) across and of lilac or pinkish-grey. Held on a 12-in (30-cm) stem, it is in bloom early in summer and makes an admirable pot plant.

Allium moly. Native of southern Europe, they were grown by Elizabethan gardeners who knew them as 'mollies'. They may have been introduced by the Romans, for Pliny considered them to be among the most precious of all plants. Gerard in his *Herbal* (1597), called *A. moly* a 'stately plant', and it was one of fourteen species grown by Parkinson, botanist to Charles I. *A. moly* is valuable for a poor sun-baked soil or for a shrubbery or spinney. It blooms in May and June, bearing star-like flowers in loose umbels on 12-in (30-cm) stems—they are of a lovely shade of bright golden yellow, hence its name, golden garlic. It will withstand gentle forcing when grown for the spring pot-plant trade.

Allium narcissiflorum. Native of the Italian Alps, it is difficult to establish in cultivation and increases slowly. It requires a warm position and shielding from excessive winter moisture. It blooms in midsummer, its bell-shaped flowers of glowing ruby-red appearing from between a pair of strap-like leaves. It grows 6 in (15 cm) tall.

Allium neapolitanum grandiflorum. Native of southern Italy, it is the only garlic with flowers of pleasing scent. It bears its pure-white flowers with their green stamens in loose umbels on 12-in (30-cm) stems in May and June. Slightly tender, it should be confined to warm gardens and planted 5 in (12·5 cm) deep.

Allium oreophilum (syn. *A. ostrowskianum*). Native of Turkestan, it is a delightful treasure for the alpine garden, growing 6 in (15 cm) tall and it increases rapidly. It bears dainty heads of carmine-pink in June. The variety Zwanenburg bears flowers of rich ruby-red.

Allium pulchellum. Native of southern Europe, it is one of the best for naturalising and blooms during early summer. It bears its violet-pink blooms on 2-ft (60-cm) stems and their beauty is enhanced by their long pointed buds.

Allium rosenbachianum. Native of central Asia, it has orange-coloured bulbs from which large ball-shaped flowers of deep purple arise at the end of 3-ft (90-cm) stems. In bloom May and June.

Allium roseum. Native of the Mediterranean coastline, it is less hardy than most but, given a warm situation, will increase rapidly bearing its pretty bright-pink flowers in loose umbels on 9-in (22·5-cm) stems. June-flowering.

Allium schubertii. A rare native of the mountainous regions of Israel, it requires a warm corner and a well-drained soil. It blooms in June and grows 2 ft (60 cm) tall, bearing rosy-red flowers in loose umbels and on long pedicels. Plant 4 in (10 cm) deep.

Allium triquetrum. Native of southern Europe, it is similar in habit and in its flowering to *A. ursinum*, being happiest in the partial shade of the woodland garden where it spreads rapidly. It blooms in May, bearing pendulous flowers of green and white at the end of a three-sided stalk 12 in (30 cm) long.

Allium tibeticum. Native of the lower mountainous regions of Tibet, it grows only 6 in (15 cm) tall and is suitable for the alpine house or rock garden, where, in June, it will bear tiny umbels of deepest blue.

Allium ursinum. A British native plant known as rampions, its presence in deciduous woodlands being detectable from a distance because of its powerful garlic smell. It is valuable for naturalising, for when in bloom in May its white hairy leaves and snow-white flowers have an appearance of snow-in-summer.

ALSTROEMERIA (Liliaceae)

Named in honour of Baron Alströemer, the Swedish botanist, it is a genus of 50 species, native of South America and is unusual in that the narrow stem leaves twist at the base with the result that the underside of the leaf faces uppermost. It has thick tuberous roots, like long fingers, which radiate from the crown, and the plants are usually sold for commercial planting by the bushel, like mint. Known as the Peruvian lily, it is one of the few plants better known by its botanical name, and though several species possess reliable hardiness and are among the finest of all garden plants, they remain almost unknown to modern gardeners.

When established, they will send up numerous flowering stems 2 ft (60 cm) high at the end of which are 9 to 12 funnel-shaped flowers composed of six segments formed in two circles. The lower segment of the inner circle is distinct. In bloom June and July.

Culture. Alstroemerias may be planted in the border, in bold groups and the best method is to make a circle 3 ft (90 cm) in diameter, which will accommodate six roots. Soil to a depth of 8 in (20 cm) is removed and some decayed manure or hop manure mixed into the soil before it is replaced. The roots should be spread out around the crown which must be raised up on a small mound of sand to improve drainage, as when planting asparagus. Fill in the soil around the roots, pressing it down gently to prevent air pockets. After completing the operation, mark out the ground with canes and twine so that it is not disturbed by later plantings. Plant in clean ground for it will be almost impossible to clean afterwards when roots will have spread out and intermingled, throwing up multitudes of flowering stems—so that to the cut-flower grower, this is one of the most profitable of all plants to grow.

The stems are sufficiently sturdy to support themselves and all that the plants require to remain in a healthy and vigorous condition for 10 or more years is occasional watering with liquid manure and a thick mulch when the flowering stems have died down in autumn. The mulch may consist of decayed manure, peat or leaf mould, used hops or mushroom bed compost and it should be applied to a depth of at least 6 in (15 cm). This will not only provide the plants with valuable food but will protect them from frost damage.

Propagation. The plants are readily increased either by lifting and separating the roots—and it is necessary to dig right down into the soil with a garden fork—or by sowing seed. Seed is sown in April in pans or boxes of gritty compost in a greenhouse or frame. Sow thinly and, when large enough to handle, transplant into pots or boxes, or directly into a frame. Two years after sowing, the young plants will be ready to move to their flowering beds outside. Care must be taken not to injure the brittle roots nor to expose them for too long to sun or wind. They will bloom in two years time.

Another method is to obtain freshly harvested seed and to sow in October in the open ground where the plants are to remain. The seed will germinate in spring and within three to four years, the plants will begin to flower. Mark out the place where the seeds have been sown and make sure that the ground is clean. A circle of about 2 ft (60 cm) in diameter should be drawn and the seed scattered within it.

Species and Varieties. *Alstroemeria aurantiaca.* Native of the lower slopes of the Chilean Andes and of Peru, it is a vigorous species growing 3 ft (90 cm) tall with lance-shaped leaves. At the end of the stems it bears 9 to 12 funnel-shaped blooms of yellowish-orange, the inner petals being marked with red. It is one of the longest lasting of all flowers when cut and in water, and it does not drop its petals. The variety Moerheim Orange is an improvement on the type, the flowers being larger and of deepest orange.

Alstroemeria brasiliensis. Native of tropical Brazil, it is tender in gardens of the Northern Hemisphere, where it should be grown under glass in large pots or in deep boxes. Growing 3 ft (90 cm) tall, it has lance-shaped leaves and bears reddish-bronze flowers, the inner segments being spotted with brown.

Alstroemeria caryophyllaceae. Native of Brazil, it is winter-flowering in the Northern Hemisphere, but is too tender to be grown outdoors. It should be planted in pots or pans and brought into bloom in a temperature of 60° F (16° C) when it will bloom in February. It grows only 9 in (22·5 cm) tall and bears scarlet flowers of great beauty which are deliciously clove-scented. During autumn and early winter, the plant should be rested and brought into growth again at the turn of the year.

Alstroemeria chilensis. Native of Chile, it is a species of reasonable hardiness and blooms during the latter weeks of summer and in autumn. It grows 3 ft (90 cm) tall with spoon-shaped leaves, and it bears red or pink flowers, the two upper inner segments being shaded with gold.

Alstroemeria haemantha. Native of Chile, it grows 3 ft (90 cm) tall and has glaucous lance-shaped leaves. It bears its flowers in compound umbels, the outer segments being of scarlet tipped with green with inner segments of burnt orange, spotted with purple. Though rare in cultivation, it is hardy and easy.

Alstroemeria ligtu (syn. *A. pulchra*). A species of outstanding beauty, bearing flowers in various shades of pink, apricot, red and white, the latter possessing the pleasing clove scent of *A. caryophyllaceae*. The flowers are borne on 2-ft (60-cm) stems throughout summer. Though native of Chile, it has the same hardiness as *A. aurantiaca*.

Alstroemeria pelegrina. Native of Peru, it is the famous lily of the Incas and grows 12 in (30 cm) tall. It has lance-shaped leaves 2 in (5 cm) long and bears pale-lilac flowers, the inner segments being spotted with purple. It may be grown outdoors in a sunny sheltered corner, and is a most attractive subject for a cool greenhouse or garden room.

Alstroemeria pulchella. Native of Brazil it is of similar hardiness to *A. pelegrina.* It grows 3 ft (90 cm) tall with scattered lance-shaped leaves, and it bears clusters of wine-red flowers tipped with green, each petal being spotted with brown on the inside.

AMARYLLIS (Amaryllidaceae)

A genus of a single species, though its name is generally used also for the genus *Hippeastrum. Amaryllis belladonna* or belladonna lily (*Brunsvigia rosea* in America) is native of South Africa and was introduced into cultivation in 1712. The ovoid bulbs measure about 4 in (10 cm) through, and from them arises in autumn a solid scape some 20 in (50 cm) tall, at the end of which are 6 to 10 funnel-shaped flowers 3 in (7·5 cm) in length and resembling the trumpets of old-fashioned gramophones. They are of a lovely shade of soft rose-pink with golden anthers and emit a sweet perfume. The eight to nine strap-like leaves follow the flowers.

Culture. The bulbs may be planted outdoors, or in large pots for flowering in a cold or slightly warmed greenhouse, but wherever they are to be grown, the secret of success with this plant is the correct ripening of the bulbs each year, without which they will not bloom. If planting outdoors, and this should be done only in those gardens with a favourable climate, select a position of full sun, protected from cold winds. The foot of a wall is suitable or, as with the agapanthus, plant in a tub and lift indoors early in November, after flowering.

For outdoor planting, provide a well-drained soil fortified by some decayed manure (old mushroom bed compost is ideal) and peat or leaf mould. Plant the bulbs on a bed of shingle or crushed brick with the nose 6 in (15 cm) below soil level. Plant early in May, 18 in (45 cm) apart, and throughout summer feed regularly with dilute manure water. After the flower stems have died back in late autumn (and the plants may not bloom the first year), heap ashes or sand around the crowns for winter protection. Do not disturb the bulbs.

For the successful culture of the bulbs indoors, plant in a rich compost, made firm. Select a large pot, and over the crocks used for drainage place a layer of decayed turf. Then fill the pot with a mixture of loam, decayed manure and sand in equal parts and up to about 4 in (10 cm) from the top. Make the compost firm, then press down the bulb and around it pack in more compost so that when the operation is complete, the nose of the bulb should be just above the top of the compost (as for hyacinths) and just below the level of the rim of the pot to allow for watering.

During the potting, make the compost firm by constant pressing, either with the fingers or by using a piece of wood rounded at one end. The compost should be in a friable condition, neither too dry nor too moist, and the time to pot is March while the bulbs are still dormant. The plants may be grown in a sitting-room window or in a garden room, or they may be kept in a frame or at the base of a wall until the flower spike can be seen to be pushing through the wall of the bulb.

Throughout summer, they must not lack moisture and in July and August require copious amounts, even flooding those growing in the open ground or in tubs for the flower stem will not form correctly if the bulbs are dry.

After flowering, plunge the pots in ashes outdoors until growth and ripening is complete at the end of autumn, then remove the pots to a frost-free room withholding water until towards the end of winter, or the pots may be placed on their side beneath the greenhouse bench and covered with straw if the house is unheated. Do not repot for about five years for the plants resent disturbance. Instead, continue to feed both before and after flowering with dilute manure water and early in spring when starting into growth again, top-dress the pots and tubs with a mixture of turf loam and decayed manure. If correctly fed and well ripened, the bulbs will remain healthy and vigorous for years without the need for repotting.

Propagation. When repotting it will be seen that well-ripened bulbs will have produced around the base a number of offsets. These should be detached with care and planted in small pots, then into a larger size, to grow on to the flowering stage. They require a compost similar to that described.

The hippeastrum may also be raised from seed sown in April in the John Innes compost and in a temperature of 65° F (18° C) to hasten germination. When large enough to handle, transplant the seedlings to small pots containing a richer compost and to larger pots the following year. They may reach flowering size in eight years but may take longer.

Species and Varieties. *Amaryllis belladonna.* Native of Cape Province, it forms a large oval bulb and in September produces a leafless scape with 6 to 10 funnel-shaped flowers of deep pink arranged around the top. The flower stem is followed by eight to nine strap-like leaves 18 in (45 cm) long and 1 in (2·5 cm) wide.

The variety purpurea major has flowers of a deeper shade of rose-pink and stems nearly 3 ft tall, while Jagersfontein bears large pink flowers shaded yellow in the throat. Also of outstanding beauty is Windhoek, the rosy-pink flowers having an attractive white throat. The Royal Dutch hybrids are also obtainable in scarlet, orange, striped and pure white. Another of beauty is Elata, the pale pink flowers having a central stripe of red, while Parker's Variety (*parkeri*), raised in Australia by crossing the belladonna lily with *Brunsvigia josephinae*, bears flowers of deepest pink, shaded yellow in the throat and with as many as 12 blooms to each stem.

AMMOCHARIS (Amaryllidaceae)

A genus of five species, native of tropical and South Africa and taking its name from *ammos*, sand and *charis*, loving, a reference to the natural conditions under which the plant grows. It was at one time identified with crinum and amaryllis and, like them, bears its flowers before the leaves. In its natural habitat, it blooms during February and March, while the leaves are formed in May. In the British Isles and northern temperate regions it blooms under glass in autumn and early winter and the leaves form during spring and early summer. The bulb is ovoid, the leaves two-ranked and strap-like, one to two new leaves appearing each year. The flowers are borne in umbels of up to 30 or more and are tubular with widely spreading segments, the stamens being united to the tube. They are creamy-pink with a powerful scent.

Culture. In warm parts it may be grown outdoors in a sunny corner and in a well-drained sandy loam, but as it is winter-flowering it is best confined to a cool greenhouse or garden room where its beauty and perfume is appreciated. The ovoid bulbs of up to 12 cm in diameter should be planted one to a 7-in (18-cm) pot and into a compost made up of turf loam, decayed manure and coarse sand in equal parts. Plant early in summer with the neck of the bulb exposed as for amaryllis. In summer the bulbs will form their leaves and should be liberally supplied with water until the appearance of their flowers. Until early autumn they may be grown on outdoors, but should then be lifted inside to bloom. Feeding with dilute liquid manure will maintain their vigour for many years.

Propagation. Like amaryllis, it is increased by removal of offsets which will have formed after several years in the pot and they may have almost reached flowering size before being removed. They are grown on in small pots in a similar compost, as for mature bulbs.

Species. *Ammocharis falcata.* Native of South Africa where it is to be found on Lion's Head and on the Karbonkalberg, it is known as the malagas lily. It sends up its flowering stem to a height of 18 in (45 cm) and bears sweetly scented flowers of creamy-pink or rose-red in umbels of 20 to 30. They are followed by narrow strap-like leaves which attain 2 ft (60 cm) or more in length. The bulbs are ovoid, up to 6 in (15 cm) through and are covered in brown tunics.

ANEMONE (Ranunculaceae)

A genus of about 150 cosmopolitan plants, taking their name from *anemos*, the wind, hence their name, windflower. They are plants with tuberous or rhizomatous roots and with radical leaves, divided and lobed like those of each genus of the family. They bear their flowers solitary or in cymes. *A. nemorosa* is native of the woodlands of the British Isles and northern Europe but most inhabit the dry mountainous slopes of southern Europe where their tubers may be ripened by the sun. These are the conditions most species enjoy, a light well-drained soil and plenty of summer sunshine and on lower mountainous slopes, the poppy anemone (*A. coronaria*) and the star anemone (*A. stellata*) will, in spring, set the landscape ablaze with their brilliance and which only a few days before appeared barren and lifeless. Contrary to its name, the flower does not like cold wind and though Pliny has said that 'the flower hath the propertie to open when the wind doth blow' it does so only in the gentle breezes of the Mediterranean. It was around the Caen and Bayeux districts of northern France that the anemone first came to be grown commercially early in the eighteenth century, a time when so much was done to improve the size of bloom and length of stem that *A. coronaria* came to be known as the Caen anemone. A letter from a nurseryman of Paris dated 8th September 1881, tells that 'the anemone as a florist's flower in France is of ancient date, the finest strains coming from Caen more than a hundred years ago'. By 1800 it had become recognised as a florist's flower in England. Because it was possible to obtain the plants in bloom during the winter and early spring months with little or no protection when the rest of the country was covered in snow, the Cornish growers took advantage of the commercial possibilities of the flower. The anemone, however, can be grown in almost all parts of the world, as far north as Hudson's Bay and the Shetland Isles but here they will not come into bloom until the weather becomes warmer in spring.

Culture. The tuberous anemones are lovers of a limestone- or chalk-laden soil in which they grow in their native lands and where lime is absent a quantity should be incorporated before planting the corms or tubers. For a succession of bloom, the corms should be planted in early autumn to come into flower early in spring, while another planting should be made in April to provide bloom throughout summer. Yet another planting may be made in June to provide flowers for autumn. Though rarely used for the purpose, anemones make inexpensive and colourful plants for spring and summer bedding, providing a succession of bloom from April until the end of summer.

They should be planted in a friable sandy soil as the tubers will decay if moisture cannot drain away. If the soil is heavy, incorporate some decayed manure (old mushroom bed compost is ideal) or used hops and crushed brick or grit. Do not omit the dressing of hydrated lime. Only *A. nemorosa*, the Wood Anemone, is intolerant of lime. William Robinson, in *The English Flower Garden* suggests that the soil for anemones be prepared to a depth of 18 in (45 cm) for they are deeply rooting. In this way the soil will provide fertility over a long period, while the humus materials will help the soil to retain moisture during the dry summer months.

Prepare the soil a fortnight before planting the corms (tubers) to allow it time to settle down, for anemones do not like a loose soil. Just before planting, rake in $\frac{1}{2}$ oz per square yard of sulphate of potash which will help the plants through a cold winter and do much to prevent 'winter browning'. It will also accentuate the colour of the blooms. It is not advisable to use peat for anemones, for unless of the highest quality it will be too acid.

Anemone corms as they are incorrectly called for they are really tubers, may be obtained as 'dust', so small that they are sown along the rows like seeds. 'Dust' or 1- to 2-cm size corms, known as 'peas' are used by the Cornish growers, for not only are they the least expensive but they are also the most vigorous. Commercial growers also use the 2- to 3-cm size but none larger, for what are known as 'jumbo' corms are too old, having become acclimatised to the soil in which they have been grown for years. The anemone is the only tuberous plant which loses vigour as it increases in size and amateur growers should guard against planting anything larger than a 3- to 4-cm corm. This is the most suitable size to plant where the garden is in any way exposed and is the best size to withstand the winter away from the warmer parts. Corms up to 4 cm will produce flowers with longer stems and of better quality than corms of a larger size.

Correct planting is also important. The corms may be planted in drills, like peas, or in shallow trenches but do not plant closer than 4 in (10 cm) apart however small the corms may be, for the roots need room to develop. They should also be planted 1 to 2 in (4 cm) deep. To plant too deeply will often prevent the corms from making correct growth. 'The tubers,' wrote William Robinson, 'are formed of irregular fleshy bunches each having a number of small crowns. These tiny crowns are obtuse points, often a darker colour than the surrounding skin. They are usually in clusters near the centre . . .' M'Intosh said that 'the eye should be planted uppermost'.

It is important to store the corms in a dry, airy place, for if damp they quickly deteriorate, and while it is sometimes suggested that the corms will grow away more quickly after planting if first soaked in warm water, this is not necessary and is a dangerous practice if the soil is heavy and badly drained. Plant when the soil is friable and under normal conditions fresh green growth, like parsley leaves, will be seen in about 16 days. If the ground is dry, give a thorough soaking once each week, while the plants will benefit from an occasional watering with dilute liquid manure when once the buds have begun to form.

Though perennial, anemones are so inexpensive that after a prolonged period of flowering they are usually dug up and destroyed and the beds made ready possibly for some other plant, for the ground may become 'anemone sick' if growing anemones continuously.

Propagation. Anemones may be readily raised from seed though since early times this method of reproduction has been practised only in Holland and Belgium. Parkinson writing in 1629 said, 'in raising them from seed lyeth a pretty art not yet well known to our Nation, although frequent in the Low Countries' and the writer goes on to give a description of the method followed in collecting and germinating seed of the poppy anemone: 'The seed must be carefully gathered, but not before it be thoroughly ripe which you shall know by the head; for when the seed with the woolliness beginneth to rise a little of itself at the lower end, it must be quickly gathered lest the wind carrieth it away. After, it must be left to dry for a week or more, which then being carefully rubbed with a little dry sand will cause the seed to be better separated, although not thoroughly from the downe that encompasseth it.' Parkinson also advises that the seed be sown within a month of its harvesting. M'Intosh said, 'rub the seed with dry sand until separated' and the most up-to-date method suggested by the Gulval Experimental Station in Cornwall is to incubate the seed in damp sand for 10 days before sowing, after first rubbing with dry sand to separate them. The seed is incubated in a temperature of 60° to 65° F (16° to 18° C). It is sown early in spring in pans or boxes of John Innes compost, or outdoors in drills made 1 in (2·5 cm) deep with the back of a rake. It should be mixed with silver sand to facilitate sowing but shaking up the seed with dry sand not only hastens germination by removing the downy coating but ensures more even distribution. It is estimated that the cost of planting an acre with Caen tubers is about £60 and from seed which has been incubated, the cost is reduced to one-third that sum.

Where growing on a small commercial scale, seed may be sown broadcast in a prepared bed beneath the trees of an orchard and here the plants may be grown on to flowering time. Sow thinly and where there is overcrowding, thin to 4 in apart. Like the polyanthus, anemones will grow well in dappled sunlight and if seed is sown in July, the plants will begin to bloom early in spring before the trees come into foliage. The seedlings should be protected from cold winds and must never be allowed to lack moisture.

Where raising plants in pans or boxes, prick out to a frame or to outdoor beds when large enough to handle though as they resent moving, it is usually better to allow them to die back and to save the corms. The young plants should be sheltered from cold winds and protected from the rays of the mid-day sun.

Where growing for corm production, the seed is sown in July and in April the plants are brought to rest by artificial methods. Moisture is withheld by placing lights over the bed and the foliage when dry, is burnt off with a blow-lamp or flame-gun. The top 2 in (5 cm) of soil is then passed through riddles of 1- to 2-cm and 2- to 3-cm gauge to grade the corms and if the seed was sown in July, the corms (tubers) may have reached 3 to 4 cm in size. They may be stored in boxes of dry silver sand until ready to plant.

Anemones may also be propagated by division of the older corms but unless it is required to perpetuate a special variety this is rarely done, as new corms are inexpensive to obtain and possess exceptional vigour. Divide the tubers after the foliage has died back. They should first be washed clean of soil and must be divided before they harden. Even the smallest pieces will produce 'eyes' from which there will be new growth and after cutting with a sharp knife, the pieces must be shaken up in a box of sulphur to guard against fungus entering the wounds and they should then be stored in dry peat or sand until ready to plant.

Species and Varieties. *Anemone apennina.* Native of southern Europe, it has long black tuberous roots, and stem leaves borne in whorls of three with blunt ended lobes. It grows 6 in (15 cm) tall and blooms in March, its flowers being of a lovely shade of sky blue, while there is a white form, *alba*, and a mauve-pink, *purpurea*. Liking a limestone soil and being tolerant of shade, it may be planted in generous drifts in the wild garden where the spring sunshine may reach it, and in the shrubbery or orchard. It enjoys a light sandy soil.

Anemone biflora. Native of Kashmir, it is a rare and beautiful tuberous anemone, bearing in twos its lilac flowers, shaded blue on 6-in (15-cm) stems and it blooms in spring.

Anemone blanda. Native of the mountainous slopes of southern Greece and producing a large oval tuber, it resembles *A. apennina* in habit, growing 6 in (15 cm) tall and in its three-partite leaves but it is earlier-flowering. The rich blue flowers which measure 2 in (5 cm) across appear early in the new year, depending on situation and climate. It is at its best on grassy banks in full sun but it also does well beneath thinly planted conifers, for like *A. nemorosa* it is tolerant of an acid soil. The form *atrocoerulea* bears flowers of deepest violet blue, while *synthinica*, native of Kurdistan bears flowers of brilliant blue on the outside, white on the inside. Of recent introductions, Radar bears bright-red flowers with a white centre, and for contrast, Bridesmaid and White Splendour both bear flowers of purest white, like silver goblets when in bud.

Anemone coronaria. Native of southern Europe it has given rise to the single Poppy or Caen anemone, grown by commercial growers. It grows 8 to 12 in (20 to 30 cm) tall and has deeply cut leaves with narrow segments, while the flowers have six to eight rounded sepals and are obtainable in shades of red, purple, blue and white as named varieties:

GERTRUDE. Originally named Lady Seton, the flowers are of a unique shade of strawberry-pink with a black central boss.

HIS EXCELLENCY. The flowers of rich velvet-red have a striking white ring around the centre boss.

HOLLANDIA. The brilliant scarlet flowers are borne on long stems and are shy blooming during cold weather.

MR FOKKER. Most prolific of all anemones in cold weather, the deep purple-blue flowers shade off to paler blue at the centre.

SYLPHIDE. The flowers are of a lovely shade of rose magenta with a black centre.

THE BRIDE. The flowers are purest white accentuated by its central boss of black. The blooms should be handled with care as they are prone to bruising.

Anemone fulgens. The scarlet windflower of the Pyrenees and of the vineyards of southern Europe, its dazzling scarlet flowers held on 10-in (25-cm) stems and its readiness to bloom during a mild winter, making it valuable for cutting. It has bright-green three-lobed leaves and bears solitary flowers which measure 2 in (5 cm) across. The variety *annulata grandiflora* bears scarlet flowers which have a striking ring of gold around the central boss of black anthers. *Multipetala* is without the golden ring but has a double row of petals.

Anemone nemorosa. The wood anemone, native of the British Isles, northern Europe and North America, where it enjoys the slightly acid soil and dappled shade of deciduous woodlands. It grows 6 in (15 cm) tall, its leaves thrice divided into narrow segments and covered with silky hairs. The flowers are white, occasionally mauve and measure 1 to 2 in (2·5 to 5 cm) across. They bloom during April and May, and into June in cooler climes. The plant forms a cylindrical rhizomatous root which should not remain out of the ground for any length of time. The variety Robinsoniana, found by William Robinson in the grounds of Gravetye Manor in Sussex is an outstanding form bearing pale lavender-blue flowers with golden anthers, while Royal Blue bears flowers of rich clear blue. The form *allenii*, raised by Mr Allen in Somerset bears flowers of an exquisite shade of lavender-blue, while *flore plena* is a double white. Plant in autumn in bold drifts beneath trees or about the shrubbery, setting the tubers 12 in (30 cm) apart and 3 in (7·5 cm) deep. They like a soil containing plenty of leaf mould or peat.

Anemone palmata. A tuberous-rooted species, native of southern France with heart-shaped leaves 3- to 5-lobed and slightly hairy. It bears large flowers of polished golden-yellow, like those of the closely related *Ranunculus pedatus*. They open in early summer but only in full sunlight, though it grows best in a damp soil. There is a double form *flore plena* and a handsome white variety, *alba*, which bears shining flowers of satin-white on 6-in (15-cm) stems, like a large celandine. They are increased by division of the rootstock in autumn.

Anemone ranunculoides. The Yellow Anemone, native of the mountainous slopes of south-eastern Europe where it covers the ground with its fern-like foliage and its dainty flowers of golden-yellow which appear early in spring from a slender rhizomatous root. It grows 6 in (15 cm) tall and enjoys an open sunny situation and a limestone soil. The variety superba has bronze foliage and bears flowers of deeper yellow.

Anemone stellata (syn. *A. hortensis*). It is to be found growing naturally from Spain across southern Europe and into Asia Minor and bears star-like flowers of lilac-pink on 12-in (30-cm) stems. Possibly from a crossing with *A. fulgens multipetala*, it produced the St Brigid anemones which are semi-double with pointed petals:

LORD LIEUTENANT. The blooms are large and of deep navy-blue with a velvet-like sheen.

MOUNT EVEREST. The large double blooms are of glistening white with a striking red ring midway between the colossal boss and petal tips.

QUEEN OF BRILLIANCE. A rare variety, its cherry-red blooms having an inner ring of deeper red.

ST BAVO. A strain derived from *A. fulgens annulata grandiflora* and *A. fulgens multipetala*. The large star-like flowers appear in shades of red, pink, cherry, carmine, salmon and blue. It is valuable for cloche or frame culture, for it is less tolerant of cold winds than the Caen and St Brigid strains.

Plants may be brought into bloom early in the year in a warm greenhouse. Pot the tubers in autumn and place outdoors or in a frame, moving indoors at monthly intervals from early December. The foliage will be kept healthy by regular syringing with lukewarm water.

THE ADMIRAL. It bears large double blooms of rich violet-mauve.

THE GOVERNOR. Like *R. fulgens multipetala*, the semi-double blooms are of brilliant scarlet.

ANTHERICUM (Liliaceae)

A genus of about 300 species, mostly native of tropical and southern Africa with *A. liliago* of southern Europe. They are herbaceous perennials few of which have value as garden plants. They have fleshy tuberous roots, like the dahlia and radical, linear leaves. The flowers are borne on tall leafless scapes, the perianth twisted with three- to five-nerved segments and six stamens. Those species native of southern Europe are valuable plants for the herbaceous border.

Culture. They form their roots in long tuberous fingers like *alstroemeria* and require a light but rich well-drained soil and an open sunny situation. As they come into bloom early in summer, they should be planted in March or in September if the soil is sandy, spreading out the roots around the crown which should be raised on a small heap of sand. Plant 6 in (15 cm) deep and 18 in (45 cm) apart and near the front of the border as the plants grow about 20 in (50 cm) tall. Their value lies in their long-flowering period, being in bloom from mid–May until the end of summer, during which time there will be few days when the plant will be without flowers.

Propagation. Plants may be raised from seed sown in April in pans or in a frame. Transplant the seedlings to another part of the frame or to an outdoor bed where they are grown on until ready to move to their flowering quarters. They will come into bloom within three years. Or lift the roots early in spring (or in autumn in a mild locality) and divide by 'teasing' apart the crowns, taking care not to break the roots away. They should be replanted almost immediately, packing about them some peat or leaf mould.

Species. *Anthericum liliago.* St Bernard's lily, it has been cultivated for at least four centuries. It forms numerous crowns from which arise tufts of narrow recurving leaves 15 in (37·5 cm) long and on 2-ft (60-cm) stems, sweetly scented pure white trumpets with striking golden anthers.

Anthericum ramosum. Like *A. liliago* it is native of the alpine meadows of southern Europe and is a plant of similar habit with flat rush-like leaves and bearing trusses of white star-like flowers on 20-in (50-cm) stems. It blooms through summer and does well in the partial shade of a woodland garden.

ANTHOLYZA (Iridaceae)

A genus of a single species, those previously classified now being included under *chasmanthe*. It is native of southern Africa and takes its name from *anthos*, flower and *lussa*, rage a reference to the open flower resembling the open mouth of a roaring lion. The corm is globose with a tunic of brown fibres, the leaves being about 20 cm long, pleated and acuminate.

Culture. It is only half hardy in the Northern Hemisphere where it may be grown outdoors only in the most sheltered gardens and in a position of full sun. Elsewhere it should be grown in pots or deep boxes in the greenhouse or garden room where it will bloom in May and June without heat. Plant the corms in autumn 6 in (15 cm) deep where growing outdoors and they may be prevented from frost damage by giving a thick covering of leaves. Indoors, plant early in the year 2 in (5 cm) deep in a compost composed of loam, decayed manure and sand in equal parts. They must be watered with care until coming into growth and as the sun increases in strength, when extra moisture should be given.

Propagation. Upon lifting established plants, small cormlets will be seen to be clustered about the base. These may be detached and grown on in boxes of sandy compost as for most Iridaceae.

Species. *Antholyza ringens*. It forms long sword-like leaves and on 18-in (45-cm) stems bears scarlet and yellow flowers, the perianth tube being curved and funnel-shaped, the uppermost lobe erect, with the five lower lobes forming a projecting lip with the stamens and style longer than the upper lobe.

ARTHROPODIUM (Liliaceae)

A genus of nine species, all with but a single exception being native of Australasia. They are herbaceous plants with thick rhizomatous or bulbous roots and they take their name from the Greek meaning jointed-foot, a reference to the long pedicels. They have narrow strap-like leaves and bear white flowers in showy panicles. The perianth is composed of six segments and there are six stamens.

Culture. Resembling the anthericum, they are plants for a warm border or they may be grown in pots in a cool greenhouse, in a compost made up of turf loam, peat or leaf mould and coarse sand in equal parts. Outdoors they should be planted in March and will bloom during mid-summer, November to February in their native land, where they are known as the rock lilies. In exposed gardens and in cooler climes the plants should be potted in autumn and after wintering in a plunge bed, they are taken indoors early in spring when they will come into bloom in about three months.

Acindanthera murielae

Alstroemeria Moerheim Orange

Alstroemeria ligtu

Propagation. They may be increased by division of the roots in spring or by removing offsets which form around the main root. They may also be raised from seed sown in April in a cool greenhouse or frame. The young plants may be moved to small pots when large enough to handle or to a frame where they remain during their first winter and are then moved to the open ground.

Species. *Arthropodium candidum.* Known as the White Arthropodium, it grows only 6 in (15 cm) tall and should be confined to a warm rock garden or to the alpine house. It makes a tufted plant with grass-like leaves and bears its pure-white flowers on slender stems. The flowers measure ½ in (1·25 cm) across and have swept-back petals resembling those of the dog's-tooth violet. Found about rocky outcrops, it blooms from January to March in its native land.

Arthropodium cirrhatum. A handsome plant growing 3 ft (90 cm) tall with narrow glossy leaves 12 in (30 cm) long and bearing white star-like flowers 1 in (2·5 cm) across. When seen under a magnifying glass, the stamens appear like tiny brushes of pink or orange bristles. In its native New Zealand it is to be found growing about rocks and cliffs on North Island where it is in bloom during December.

ASPARAGUS (Liliaceae)

A genus of about 300 species mostly confined to the warm dry parts of the Old World and taking their name from the Greek *sparasso*, to tear, a reference to the prickles on several species. Many have thick tuberous roots, including *A. officinalis* the culinary asparagus. The leaves which are reduced to leaf-like bodies are borne in the axils of climbing or decumbent stems, while the flowers are greenish-white and minute. Two species *A. plumosus* and *A. sprengeri*, both native of southern Africa and with ovoid tuberous roots are widely grown for their cut foliage ('fern') in warm greenhouses in the British Isles and northern Europe, and in the United States.

Culture. The two mentioned species require to be grown in pots or in a border. Both are deeply rooting and require a well-prepared soil composed of 3 parts turf loam and 1 part each of decayed manure, leaf mould and sand or grit. Where growing in a bed made up on the floor of a greenhouse, soil should be removed to a depth of 6 in (15 cm) and the trench filled in with compost. Plants from 6-in (15-cm) pots are set 9 in (23 cm) apart and made quite firm, or the same plants may be moved to larger pots containing a similar compost and in which they are grown on. They may occupy the pots or bed from 6 to 10 years during which time they will produce a profitable amount of fronds used in floristry.

A day temperature of 56° F (13° C) should be maintained and this may be reduced to 48° F (9° C) at night. As the plants make growth they will require careful watering and will absorb liberal quantities from the compost during

G

summer when the glass should be shaded. An even temperature and care with watering will ensure the formation of those bright green sprays which are so attractive to those who make up bouquets and buttonholes. Large numbers of plants are raised from seed and grown on in thumb-size pots to use in bowls of early tulips and hyacinths for Christmas.

Where grown for cutting, plants are trained up wires stretched across the roof of the greenhouse but it is usual to start them up twine stretched from the pot to the first wire. The sprays are cut when as long as possible and made into fan-shaped bunches of 6 or 12 sprays, depending upon size. They are graded 'long', 'medium' or 'short' and demand progressively lower prices as the size diminishes.

Propagation. As they are so readily raised from seed which has been freshly harvested, this is the sole method of propagation. Seed is sown in October in a temperature of 65° F (18° C), a propagating frame being necessary. Keep the compost comfortably moist when the seed will germinate in 16 to 18 days. Early December, the seedlings are moved to 3-in (7·5-cm) pots containing a mixture of 4 parts sterilised loam and 2 parts each leaf mould and sand. It is usual to plant two seedlings to each pot. They should be kept steadily growing and will be ready to plant into their permanent quarters by mid-April. The plants will appreciate regular syringing with clean water during the summer months.

Species. *Asparagus plumosus.* Native of southern Africa, it forms long tuberous roots arranged symmetrically around the crown from which arises long slender stems to a height of 18 ft (5 metres) furnished with fronds of glossy green pointed leaves (cladodes).

Asparagus sprengeri. Native of Natal, it has large ovoid tuberous roots and stems which grow to 6/7 ft (2 metres) in length, furnished with fronds of bright glossy green leaves (cladodes). It may be grown in pots placed on a shelf at the end of a greenhouse or garden room 6 ft (2 metres) above ground and the fronds allowed to trail down. It may also be used in hanging baskets in the garden room, with trailing begonias and achimenes.

ASPHODELUS (Liliaceae)

A genus of 15 species of herbaceous plants native of south-eastern Europe with clusters of short rhizomatous roots and taking their name from *a*, not and *sphello*, to supplant, an allusion to the beauty of their flowers. Their country name is Asphodel. They have narrow straplike leaves, somewhat three-sided and formed in a tuft from which arises a dense raceme of star-like flowers.

Culture. The plants require a well-drained sandy soil from which winter moisture may readily drain, otherwise the tuberous roots will decay. They are also heavy feeders and require some well-decayed manure or used hops in their diet. Plant in spring, 6 in (15 cm) deep, spacing out the fleshy roots around a small heap of sand and packing peat or leaf mould around them before covering with soil.

Propagation. They are readily increased by root division in spring, 'teasing' apart the crowns and fleshy roots. Established plants, however, resent disturbance and should not be moved for at least five years.

Species. *Asphodelus luteus.* Native of south-eastern Europe it grows 3 ft (90 cm) tall with three-furrowed stem leaves and bears its sweetly scented starry yellow flowers in a straight raceme. Each flower arises from a buff-coloured bract. There is a rare double form, *flore pleno*. It blooms from early June until late August.

Asphodelus ramosus. Native of southern Europe, it is the Giant Asphodel growing 4 to 5 ft (1 to 2 metres) tall and blooms from mid-June until August. It forms dense tufts of grey grass-like leaves and bears large dense spikes of starry white flowers, each segment being marked by a purple stripe down the centre. Once established, the asphodels are free-flowering.

ASPIDISTRA (Liliaceae)

A genus of six species, native of south-eastern Asia and taking their name from the Greek *aspidiseon*, a little shield, an allusion to the flat shield-like style which covers the aperture formed by the six perianth-leaves. They are herbaceous plants with thick creeping rhizomatous roots from which arise smooth glossy dark green leaves about 15 in long with long stalks. The flowers appear just above the surface of the soil and are bell-shaped, purple or yellow in colour. The plants are not frost-hardy but where grown indoors they will remain healthy for many years in the dry atmosphere of a sitting-room, provided the temperature does not fall to freezing point. For a shaded room or for a window facing north, they are without equal in their tolerance of such conditions.

Culture. They behave best when their roots are restricted and should be given a 7-in (18-cm) pot. This will cause the roots to send up a succession of new leaves. The plants require a compost made up of 2 parts fibrous loam and 1 part each leaf mould and sand. Plant 2 in (5 cm) deep and make firm. During summer the plants are copious drinkers, but in winter give only sufficient moisture to keep them alive. If given too much water at this time the foliage will turn yellow. Each year top-dress with a mixture of fresh loam and decayed manure which will do much to maintain the continual appearance of fresh leaves which will benefit from regularly wiping clean with lukewarm water. This will also prevent the appearance of red spider.

Species and Varieties. *Aspidistra lurida.* Native of China and Japan, it was grown in most Victorian homes and made famous in a song of Miss Gracie Fields. It has thick rhizomatous roots from which arise lance-shaped leaves of dark glossy green 12 to 20 in (30 to 50 cm) long. The form *variegata* has silver streaks running from base to apex and a well-grown plant gives an appearance of great beauty. An occasional watering with dilute liquid manure will enhance the colouring of the leaves.

B

BABIANA (Iridaceae)

A genus of 60 species, native of tropical and South Africa, being common north of Cape Town. They take their name from the Dutch for little baboon for the creatures have a liking for the fibrous-coated corms. The leaves are long and narrow and are plaited, while they are also covered in small hairs. The flowers are funnel-shaped and appear in a dense spike. They may be grown outdoors in a sunny border in the most favourable parts of the British Isles, Europe and North America, planting them 6 in (15 cm) deep but they are not frost-hardy and if left in the ground during winter, should be covered with a mulch to a depth of 6 in (15 cm). Elsewhere, they are best grown in pots in a frame or greenhouse when they will bloom throughout summer.

Culture. They should be planted five to six to a 4-in (10-cm) pot or pan, using a compost composed of 2 parts fibrous loam and 1 part each leaf mould and coarse sand. Planting is best done in October and the pots plunged in a bed of ashes or sand in a frame where they remain until the year end and given no water. They should then be taken indoors and grown on in a temperature of not less than 45° F (7° C) giving additional moisture as the sun gathers strength and the plants make growth. They are dried off after flowering and the pots are again placed in the frame and given no water until started into growth again. During the warmer months, the pots may be stood out on a balcony or veranda, and where no greenhouse is available may occupy the frame until such time as the weather permits them to be moved outdoors.

Propagation. At the base of the corms when lifted will be numerous cormlets which are detached and if dried and kept in jars over winter, may be grown on in boxes or frames as for gladioli and other Iridaceae.

Species and Varieties. *Babiana bainsii* (syn. *B. hypogaea*). A rare species of the Cape, it is a most striking plant bearing sweetly scented bright-blue flowers, like miniature gladioli and on 6-in (15-cm) stems. Autumn-flowering in southern Africa; spring-flowering in the British Isles and North America.

Babiana disticha. It has broad, spreading lanceolate leaves and bears its pale-blue flowers on a branched stem 12 in (30 cm) high. They are pale yellow in the throat and have attractively recurved segments. They have a powerful balsamic scent and remain long in bloom.

Babiana hyemalis. The Winter Flowering Babiana, native of mountainous slopes around Cape Town with prostrate leaves and it bears its flowers in a three- to seven-flowered spike. The flowers are pale blue with a white star in the centre, while the tube is long and narrow. It grows 6 in (15 cm) tall.

Babiana plicata. It grows only 4 in (10 cm) tall, with spreading leaves, and bears sweetly scented violet-blue flowers with the two lower side lobes cream-coloured and with purple markings at the base. It is charming in the alpine house.

Babiana stricta. The finest and most popular species of which there are a number of varieties and from which several hybrids have been raised. It has erect, spreading leaves and sends up its flower stem to a height of 10 in (25 cm). The flowers are pale blue, violet or crimson, borne in a lax spike. They have a long perianth tube and when open are cup-shaped with a soft sweet perfume. The variety *rubro-cyanea* bears sky-blue flowers shaded crimson at the centre, while of several lovely hybrids, Tubergen's Blue bears soft blue flowers on a tall erect stem. White King bears pure white flowers with unusual bright-blue anthers. Zwanenburg Glory has the segments alternating blue and white.

Babiana tubiflora. Native of Cape Province where it is usually found in sandy flats near the coast, it has leaves 12-in (30-cm) long, with the flower stem shorter than the leaves. In its natural haunts it blooms in September; in the British Isles and northern Europe, in May. The flowers are creamy-white with a long slender perianth tube and they are sweetly scented.

BEGONIA (Begoniaceae)

A genus of more than 900 species, mostly native to sub-tropical South America and taking the name of that of Michel Begon, a patron of botany, and one time French governor of Santo Domingo. They are herbs or undershrubs of perennial habit, some with a tuberous rootstock; leaves lobed or parted, irregularly toothed with long stipules. One side of the leaf is longer than the other, hence their name Elephant's Ears. The flowers are monoecious, the males consisting of two outer and two smaller inner segments, the stamens free or united into a single bundle. The female has two to ten segments, the two outer being larger; ovary inferior; styles two to four, free or united at the base with branched stigmas. The fibrous-rooted species are not considered here and are mostly suitable only for under glass culture in the British Isles and northern Europe. The tuberous-rooted garden varieties now share with the zonal pelargonium, first place for summer bedding display and being more tolerant of rain, are gaining in popularity each year for their flowering period extends from mid-June until mid-October. Indoors, they are easily managed and will provide a display of great brilliance in a cool or warm greenhouse, though will not give a good account of themselves in the home where conditions are usually

too dry, being plants of the rain-forests of Bolivia and Peru. The rhizomatous
B. rex is however most adaptable to room conditions. Though the begonia (*B.
rotundifolia*) was first discovered in 1690 by a Franciscan monk, Fr Plumier, it
was not developed until a century later, and for this credit must be given to
James Veitch. Born at Exeter in 1792, son of a Scottish gardener, he started his
own small nursery there in 1835. This was the time when Joseph Paxton was
supervising the building of the first greenhouse for the Duke of Devonshire at
Chatsworth and the vogue for hot-house plants had begun. Prices the wealthy
were prepared to pay were high, and by 1853 Veitch had done so well that he
moved to King's Road, Chelsea, with his son, also James, in charge. So great
had the demand for exotic greenhouse plants become that the firm had Charles
Maries collecting plants in Japan, John Veitch in America and Richard Pearce
in Peru and Bolivia. It was Pearce whom begonia lovers should remember with
gratitude, for he introduced (though did not actually discover) *B. boliviensis*,
which was to lay the foundation of the large-flowered tuberous begonia. The
plant had glossy dark-green leaves, tapering to a point, and bore single blooms
of vivid orange-scarlet, the blooms being suspended on long drooping stems,
being more like a fuchsia in appearance and habit.

Pearce also sent to his firm *B. rosaeflora*, which has the familiar red begonia
stems and bears a large round flower, and *B. pearcei*, a truly beautiful plant
which has velvet-green leaves and bears a large yellow bloom. He also introduced *B. veitchii*, which bears large rounded flowers of brilliant vermilion-rust.
Here then was something to work on.

The first crosses were made at Exeter but soon died out without being used
further, but at Chelsea, John Seden, Veitch's foreman and a brilliant hybridiser,
crossed *B. boliviensis* with *B. rosaeflora* to produce a plant having the qualities of
both parents and which was named *B. sedeni*. This was in 1868 and was the first
step in the raising of the modern large-flowered begonia.

Two of the greatest enthusiasts were J. B. Blackmore of Bath and the
Reverend Lascelles of the same city, who had as his gardener Charles Langdon.
The two worked together and were so successful that they were able to market
thousands of their seedlings each year and in 1901 founded the firm bearing
their name.

Ten years after the first Veitch collections had been made by Richard Pearce,
another Veitch collector, Walter Davis, discovered in the same locality a plant
which now bears his name and which has become as famous as those discovered
by Pearce. It was of tufted, compact habit, had dark glossy green foliage and
bore numerous small scarlet blooms. Crossed, in 1882, with a tuberous hybrid
of the earliest species, it gave the scarlet-flowered hybrid Miss Constance
Veitch, a plant possessing all the characteristics of the modern multiflora
begonia. It is said that *B. davisii* also passed its intense scarlet colouring to the
large-flowered hybrids.

The basket or weeping begonias, amazingly beautiful plants with their cascading habit, were raised in France at the same time, *B. boliviensis* being a parent. They were introduced into America by Frank Lloyd and have since become known as *B. lloydii*. More recently, the interesting *B. baumanni*, also found in the Andes, has been used to give its delicate perfume to the new pendulous hybrids. It was discovered by a Dr Sacc and introduced by Lemoine. It gave its fragrance to John White, a pale-pink double, and recently to Yellow Sweetie and Orange Sweetie, raised by Leslie Woodriff at the Fairyland Gardens, Oregon, U.S.A., and now obtainable in Britain. They are superb plants for a hanging basket. Also used in their raising and passing on its fragrant qualities was *B. micranthera fimbriata*, discovered as recently as 1937 by Dr Goodspeed of the University of California, which may later be used to give perfume to the large-flowered begonias.

If the first double-flowered tuberous begonias made big money, the foliage begonias, *B. rex*, were an even greater success. The plant was first seen growing in northern India in 1856, and the following year John Simons brought the original plant to London with a collection of orchids to be sold at Stevens' Auction Room.

For the hybridist there was already a 'cross' which was to transform *B. rex*, for in 1853 Roezl had crossed *B. xanthina* with the silver-spotted *B. rubro-venia* to produce a plant of beautiful silvery foliage which he named *B. xanthina pictafolia*. This was used by Linden for crossing with *B. rex* to lay the foundation of the *B. rex* hybrids we know today. The first exhibition of Rex begonias was arranged at the Royal Horticultural Society gardens at Chiswick in 1884, and received a first-class certificate. This gave the plants a new popularity and prices were soon within the reach of the average gardener.

Later *B. evansiana*, with its upright habit and hardy constitution, and *B. diadema*, with its many-lobed leaves, were utilised for crossing, but it was not until 1895 that the red-leaved *B. decora* was used. This brought a new interest to the *B. rex*, the new hybrids taking on the most attractive rich shades of bronze, red, violet and pink. The best was Glory of St Albans, one of the most striking foliage plants ever introduced. Though now rare, it is still obtainable.

In 1903 the raisers, Messrs Sanders of St Albans, Hertfordshire, went a step further by introducing *B. cathayana* with its velvety leaf texture, a characteristic which it imparted to the new hybrids. At that time the Rex begonias were being widely used for formal bedding, for planting with the vividly coloured multi-floras and large-flowered varieties, and they were almost always wintered in a warm greenhouse. Rarely were they found in the home for which purpose they are ideally suited, for, unlike the large-flowered tuberous varieties which desire humidity, the Rex begonias are tolerant of dry conditions and shade.

The Tuberous Begonia. You may require to have an early display, either indoors or in the open. Some form of heating will be necessary by which tubers may be started into growth early in March; but, where relying on the natural warmth of the sun, too early starting of the tubers should not be attempted, for if dormant for a long period in a moist compost they may decay.

Two-year tubers may be obtained from specialist growers when starting a collection. To commence with, the less expensive varieties should be obtained, and when one has gained knowledge of their culture, others may be obtained. A young tuber will be quite firm at the top or flat part when pressed, for it is here that the sprouts or shoots appear and any softness or decay will mean that the tubers have been badly stored. This is why it is important to obtain a stock from specialist growers with a reputation to uphold, for exhibition begonias are always expensive.

When starting one's own tubers into growth, the boxes should be made ready in plenty of time. Boxes about 2 in (5 cm) deep will be suitable, the tubers, which will vary in size from $1\frac{1}{2}$ in (3·5 cm) to 3 in (7·5 cm) in diameter, being placed $1\frac{1}{2}$ in (3·5 cm) apart. While it is quite permissible to plant into peat made firm and level, some sterilised loam and a sprinkling of coarse sand mixed with the peat will ensure more satisfactory growth. Where planting in peat which is devoid of food value it will be necessary to move the tubers to pots containing prepared compost as soon as the shoots are 1 in (2·5 cm) high, for they will be supported only on the food stored in the tuber. Bedding begonias which are to remain in the boxes for a longer period before being planted outdoors straight from the boxes should be given a richer starting compost, one made up of sterilised loam, peat or leaf mould and old mushroom bed manure in equal parts. To the compost should be mixed a small amount of sand. Such a compost will provide the necessary food and will maintain sturdy growth should there be delay in setting out the plants due to late frosts.

It is essential to moisten the peat before use, and it is surprising the quantity of water dry peat will absorb.

Press the tubers firmly into the surface so that the rounded part of the tuber is in contact with the compost with the top of the tuber level with the compost. Water in and keep the compost comfortably moist, though the plants will require more moisture as the season and plant growth advances and the sun gathers strength. A sheet of polythene placed over the tubers will encourage rapid growth by maintaining humidity without causing the roots to decay through maintaining the compost in too damp a condition.

Whether the tubers are started in boxes or pots, no food should be given apart from a little decayed manure for at this stage the plant should be grown 'hard'. An excess of plant food will only cause the sprouts to grow 'soft', when they will be unable to support their large blooms and foliage without support. To encourage vigorous root action, it is necessary for the fibrous roots to have to search for whatever food and moisture they can find. It should therefore not be made too easy for them. Again, tuberous begonias root horizontally and will take time to reach the compost in the lower parts of a pot. The result is that not only is there a waste of compost but it will become sour, and begonias are never happy under such conditions. For this reason, begonias, like show auriculas, should never be over-potted, a condition which occurs where the pots are too large. The begonia likes to send out its roots around the sides of a pot. For the first potting, a 60-size pot will be adequate, and though repotting to a 48-size pot will be necessary when growing plants of exhibition quality, better results will be obtained by potting in stages than by making the first planting into too large a pot.

The tubers will be ready for potting when the shoots are about 2 in (5 cm) high. It is, however, more important to encourage the tubers to form a heavy rooting system rather than excessive top growth. This is obtained by keeping the compost on the dry side, yet maintaining humidity. Bottom heat is also a help in achieving a heavy rooting system, and where a length of electric tubular heating, a row of hot-water pipes, or a fumeless oil-convector stove can be placed beneath the boxed tubers, they will receive valuable stimulation to form roots. Tuberous begonias are very like bulbs; attention should be given to their rooting before making top growth, and a tuber which makes top growth before it has had time to build up a strong root run will never be a success.

Tuberous begonias grown for exhibition or greenhouse display should not be asked to bear too many shoots. Each tuber should be limited to two or three shoots, perhaps only a single shoot where a variety lacks vigour. The number of shoots must depend upon the vigour of the plant, any weak shoots being removed when the tubers receive their first potting. It will not be possible to determine the quality of the shoots to enable any to be removed earlier.

The compost for the first potting should consist of friable turf loam made porous by the addition of a little peat and sand and a small amount of plant food. A too-rich diet with begonias should be avoided or growth will be too soft. Artificial fertilisers should not be used, not even in small quantities, as sometimes advocated. It is important to obtain a good-quality loam for the potting composts, for this will form the basis of the plant's requirements. Do not use soil from the garden, for this will be a mass of weed seeds, and where the garden is situated in an industrial area the soil will be sour. The loam should have been taken from pastureland, or turf should be removed to a depth of 4 in (10 cm) and stacked for several months until it has become a mass of fibrous roots. Quantities may be taken as required and rubbed through a riddle to remove unwanted vegetation and stones. Soil from old pastureland, and where constantly grazed over a long period will be enriched by the washing in of animal manures. This is the secret of success of Kettering loam when used for the potting of almost every plant.

The potting soil should be friable when used and be protected from heavy rain. A good-quality loam taken from land which has been grazed will supply almost the entire food requirements of the plant, and the potting compost

should be made up according to the quality of the loam. Where of good quality
the compost may consist of:

    Fibrous turf loam, 5½ parts
    Decayed cow or old mushroom bed manure, 1 part
    Horticultural peat, 1 part
    Coarse sand or grit, ½ part.

Into each barrowful of the compost, mix two handfuls of steamed bone flour. It
is essential that the cow manure be thoroughly decayed and in a dry condition.
If the loam is not of the best quality, then increase the manure, using 5 parts
of soil to 1½ parts decayed manure. There is a tendency to use an excess of peat
for potting, but, apart from providing drainage and aeration, this will make
little contribution to the culture of the plant and should not be overdone. For
successful begonia culture in pots, a balance must be held between materials
which will provide the necessary drainage and the food requirements of the
plant. The pot should be well crocked and then three parts filled with the
compost, which is shaken down by tapping the base. The sprouted tuber is
placed gently on the compost. The tubers are removed from their boxes with
care, for by 1st May, when the first potting is done, they will have become
heavily rooted. Take care not to break off or damage the shoots, which will be
succulent and brittle, and do not knock off more compost than necessary for fear
of injuring the roots. A small, pointed trowel will be ideal for lifting the tubers.
Not all the tubers will be ready for moving at the same time, some varieties take
longer to come into growth than others, so that those remaining in the boxes
should be disturbed as little as possible. Those most backward will be ready for
moving about a week or 10 days later.

The tubers are pressed lightly into the compost in the pots, additional compost being pressed around and over them so that the first leaves appear just
above soil level. After potting, the plants should be watered, which will leave the
compost about ½ in (1 cm) below the rim of the pot. As the sun gathers strength
and the plants make more growth, ventilation should be given during the daytime. Do not over-water the plants for the first 10 days after transplanting. They
will more quickly form new roots if kept on the dry side, though they will
appreciate a daily syringeing. Excessive humidity and too high a temperature
should be avoided, and during the first week or so in their pots it will be better
to damp down the house rather than give the plants too-frequent waterings. A
day temperature of 55° F (13° C) will be ideal and ventilation should be
regulated accordingly. This temperature will be suitable for the plants until they
are in bloom, but generally during July and August higher temperatures prevail
and it is necessary to provide shading.

Little new growth will be made during the first week after the plants have
been moved to their pots. As the new roots form in a horizontal direction new
growth will be observed, and if after about four weeks a plant is carefully shaken

from the pot, the roots will be seen to have reached the sides. This denotes that it is time to move to a larger pot in which the plants will bloom. While in their first pots, the compost should not be kept too moist and any tendency towards saturation must be avoided. A humid atmosphere and a compost which is comfortably moist will promote healthy plant growth. A saturated compost will cause the roots to decay. The heaviest rooting will take place in the upper part of the compost, hence the importance of not using too large a pot.

For larger pots a similar compost may be used, though the plants will benefit from a little more decayed manure, preferably cow manure or old mushroom bed compost. The roots of the plant must not be disturbed when moved; merely crock the pots, place at the bottom a few small pieces of fibrous turf, then add some fresh compost. The plant is then transferred to the larger pot.

As the plants make growth in their new pots, the main stems should be given support as the buds form. This will be towards the end of June. Not all lateral shoots should be allowed to bear bloom. Those formed at the base may have been removed for rooting, but most should be removed in any case, leaving only one or two side shoots on each stem, to bear bloom along with that formed on the main stems.

To support the plants use a small cane or wooden stick with a wire looped at the top to go round the stem. It should be inserted into the compost, away from the tuber to avoid damage and in such a way that it is almost hidden by the stems and foliage. As the side growths, which are to bear bloom, form, smaller stakes should be inserted to provide these shoots with support also. Wide raffia should be used for tying, for any material that is too thin may cut into the stems and cause damage. Being brittle, handle the stems with care, for the breaking of a' stem at this stage will affect both flowers and the future vigour of the tuber. Do not tie the raffia too tightly because the stems will continue to swell until the plant has finished flowering. The plants should be inspected periodically, when new and additional ties may be made.

After the buds are first observed, they will take between three and four weeks to open fully.

On each flower stem or shoot, three buds will have formed: a centre bud, flanked on short separate stems by two others which are larger and flatter. The centre bud is the male, which is allowed to bloom, while the two side buds should be removed as soon as they are large enough to handle. These are the females or seed bearers, which are single blooms comprised of four petals and have a bulbous base, which is the seed pod. Though these female flowers are produced on all types of begonias, it is only from the large-flowering tuberous form that they are removed. They enhance the display of the small-flowering types, but not of the large-flowering begonias, where the male flowers attain such beauty of form that they should have no distractions. The female flowers in this case, while adding nothing to the display, make use of valuable plant food which should be concentrated into the male bloom. The two female or side buds are pinched off as soon as they may readily be distinguished from the male, and this should be done with all flowering stems as they come into bud. It is advisable to remove all flower buds until the plants are thoroughly established in their final pots.

The most common cause for disappointment with large-flowered begonias is that if growing conditions are not entirely satisfactory, the male buds may themselves fall, even as they are beginning to show colour.

Bud dropping is caused by either under- or over-watering, by too-heavy feeding, by excessive humidity or by too-dry conditions. It is therefore necessary to pay particular attention to the watering and feeding of the plants and to greenhouse temperatures from the time of disbudding until the plants are in full bloom.

The watering of the plants at this stage calls for care. At the height of summer there will be considerable soil evaporation if humidity of the greenhouse is not maintained. This does not mean that a stagnant atmosphere should be allowed; as the buds begin to open, conditions should be cool and airy. Even so, begonias are always happiest in a moist heat and will appreciate regular syringeing of the foliage until the buds show colour and begin to open, after which humidity may be provided by damping down the floor. The plants will also benefit from being allowed to stand on a bed of moist peat on the greenhouse bench. If the peat is kept moist, it will help to reduce the need for excessive watering of the compost. With all pot plants, the less watering the compost is given the better. Heavy watering will cause plant food to be washed from the compost, while it will also make it sour. The roots, however, must not dry out or bud dropping will result, as it will if the roots are kept in a saturated condition.

As the plants come into bloom they may require shading by stretching a piece of canvas along the inside of the roof or down the side of the greenhouse, or the inside of the roof may be whitened. Where only one or two plants are showing their blooms too soon, these may be shielded individually. A stake may be placed in the compost at the side of the pot and to the top a piece of cardboard is fixed.

The blooms should be supported on wires placed immediately beneath the bloom before it is fully open. The supports are necessary for the blooms to reveal their full beauty and to give help to the stems, which may not be able to support the blooms unaided.

By mid-September the plants will have finished flowering and should be slowly dried off. It will be advisable to continue with their feeding until the end of August, for this will not only help to produce finer bloom but will contribute to the building up of a strong tuber for next season's flowering. When flowering has finished water should be gradually withheld. The drying off should be gradual and it is wrong to withhold all moisture from the time the blooms die.

As moisture is decreased, ventilation should be increased, leaving the ventilators open day and night. This drying off may be done between the time the begonias finish blooming and late October when the house is required for chrysanthemums.

As the plant is dried off, first the bloom stems, then the leaf stems will fall away until only the main stem is left. This must not be forcibly removed or the tuber will be harmed. Never cut away the main stem, however long it takes to die back, for the tuber is continually receiving or storing up valuable foods from the stems as the drying continues. During this time the roots of the tuber should not be completely dry, for they are still playing a part in the health of the tuber.

The tubers may be left in their pots until the year end, when the compost is removed and the tubers shaken out.

The soil will now be set quite hard and care must be taken to remove the tuber without breaking the skin covering and so permitting disease to enter during storage. Most of the roots will have died back, but those left should not be removed. See that the labels are removed with each tuber and placed with them in storage. After uncovering, the tubers should be inspected for decay, which must be cut away and powdered sulphur rubbed into the wound.

Store the tubers in boxes of dry sand. The tubers should be covered to a depth of several inches and placed in a cool, frost-proof room. Tubers of one variety should be stored together. Keep them away from warmth of any description, or shrivelling will occur. A temperature of 45° F (7° C) is ideal for storage.

These begonias are suitable for exhibition:

A. L. BERRY. One of the finest yellow begonias, the large, solid blooms being of a lovely shade of primrose, while it forms a plant of compact habit.

BEAUTY. A vigorous variety, first class in every way, the large amber-coloured blooms being held on strong stems.

BLACK KNIGHT. The beautifully shaped medium-sized blooms are of deepest crimson.

BLAZE. Of compact habit, the enormous blooms are noted for their long-keeping qualities. The colour is rich crimson-scarlet.

CHARM. A most attractive variety and, though the blooms are not large, they are of exquisite shape and of a lovely Jersey cream colour.

CHARMAIN. It comes early into bloom and is of robust habit. The blooms, which are extremely large, are of pure pink and of perfect form.

CLARISSA HUTCHINSON. The blooms are of beautiful shape and extremely full and are of a lovely shade of salmon-pink.

DIANA WYNYARD. The finest white begonia yet raised. The blooms have great solidity, the petals being pure white and of great substance. Measuring nearly 12 in (30 cm) across they are held on sturdy stems.

EL ALAMEIN. A superb variety, the large velvety-crimson blooms are held on sturdy stems above dark-green foliage.

ELIZABETH WOOLMAN. Outstanding, the large, beautifully shaped blooms are of deepest amber with an apricot sheen.

EVEREST. An excellent white, the huge circular blooms have great substance, the petals being attractively frilled.

F. J. BEDSON. The blooms are of enormous size, and of brightest salmon-scarlet, freely produced.

FLAMBEAU. It bears flowers of brilliant orange-scarlet, probably the brightest of all begonia blooms. The habit is excellent, while the blooms are large and of perfect shape.

HERCULES. A magnificent new introduction and winner of numerous awards. The blooms are enormous and of a rich shade of salmon-orange.

PAMELA SIMPSON. The large, well-shaped blooms are yellow, being somewhere in colour between A. L. Berry and Yellow Hammer. The habit is vigorous and free-flowering.

PERCY SYMONS. Forming one of the most beautifully shaped blooms of all begonias and possessing great substance. The colour is brilliant orange-scarlet.

PRISCILLA LEWIN. An old favourite, the medium-sized blooms being freely produced and of a rich apricot, suffused with amber and yellow.

REBECCA. The blooms are of rose shape and excellent form, the colour being pale candy pink.

RHAPSODY. No variety bears a more circular bloom nor one of more solidity. The flowers, which are of a lovely shade of soft salmon-pink, retain their beauty for a long period.

SAM PHILLIPS. A yellow of great substance and outstanding form. A fine exhibitor's variety.

T. B. TOOP. An old favourite of exhibition form, the blooms are of pure orange-scarlet, freely produced. Named after the curator of the Ballarat Botanic Gardens.

TOSCA. Probably the best of its colour, the enormous blooms being of a pure rose-pink, free from any shading.

WAYNE PARKER. A magnificent variety with flowers of an attractive shade of blush-pink.

W. H. MILNER. A fine variety; the huge blooms of exquisite form are of a bright salmon-pink colour.

YELLOW HAMMER. An excellent deep yellow, the bloom being refined and having attractively frilled petals.

Begonias Outdoors. In the garden tuberous begonias provide a most exotic appearance, and have a robustness which belies their appearance. They give as good an account of themselves on the cold north-east coast of England as they do in the favourable moist warmth of the south-west. The same may be said of the small-flowering hybrid multifloras, which are also tuberous-rooted and which may be expected to flower from a sowing of seed made the same year.

Begonias flourish in partial shade, which is contrary to popular belief, for being natives of those countries with a warm, sunny climate it is thought that they must have a position of full sun and dry conditions. The opposite is the case for, besides their liking for shade, they flourish in cool, moist conditions.

They like a soil which retains moisture and are always happiest in a wet summer.

Purchase begonias for bedding from a reputable grower, who will offer tubers which are not too old and will not have lost vitality. The tubers will be smaller than those sold for indoor exhibition bloom, but should be as plump, thus revealing that they have been grown and stored with care. They will be seedling tubers two years old, varying in size from 4 to 6 cm. Tubers less than 4 cm will give only a small bloom. Named varieties which are propagated only by vegetative methods are always more expensive than those raised from seed, which in Britain cost about 50p per dozen tubers. The multifloras, which breed reasonably true from seed, are generally propagated in this way or from cuttings.

Tubers for outdoor planting should be started into growth about 1st April. A cold greenhouse or frame will be suitable, the tubers being given additional moisture as the sun becomes warmer. By keeping the frame or greenhouse closed and the tubers moist, a humid atmosphere is obtained and growth will soon commence. By mid-May the tubers will have made leaf and stem growth and will be ready for hardening, the frames being gradually opened by day, then by night, until the lights are removed altogether.

The plants are removed from the boxes with care so that neither the roots nor the brittle stems will be damaged. They should be planted without delay, before the roots begin to dry. The large-flowered types should be planted 12 in (30 cm) apart, with the crown or upper part of the tuber about 1 in (2·5 cm) below soil level.

Plant during wet weather, or immediately following rain, to enable them to get a good start. This, however, is not always possible during early June, and if the ground is dry give a thorough soaking before planting and afterwards. At this stage the plants must not lack moisture, and during dry weather frequent watering will be necessary until they are established. At this time the plants will appreciate syringeing their foliage at nightfall which will give them a pleasing freshness, while they will greatly benefit from a mulch of peat or leaf mould given at the end of June, working the material right up to the stem of the plants. This mulch will suppress annual weeds while it will help to conserve moisture in the ground.

Tuberous begonias are surface-rooting, new roots being continually formed from the base of the stem and around the crown of the tuber. Therefore, more than most plants, they will benefit from a mulch which should be worked around the stems. This will keep the new roots moist as well as providing a valuable rooting medium.

As the large-flowered begonias make growth they will appreciate some support. A few twigs placed about the stems will prevent them breaking, due possibly to strong winds, as they come into bloom.

Begonias should never suffer from lack of moisture. This will cause the buds to fall. The soil must be kept moist, but, rather than give light waterings to the surface, give a thorough soaking when necessary, preferably in the evening. A soil containing ample humus, and where a mulch has been given, should retain moisture for long periods and so reduce the labour of constant watering. The plants will also benefit from an occasional application of dilute manure water. This will enhance the colour and quality of the bloom and in the case of the multiflora begonias will greatly extend the flowering season. So will the removal of all dead blooms and seed pods. Generally, with the large-flowered types, the male flower will fall away when it begins to die back, leaving the two side or female flowers to form seed. If allowed to set seed, the flowering period of the plants will come to a premature end. As soon as the male has died back, remove the stem with a pair of scissors. It is advisable to look over beds of the large-flowering begonias every week, removing unwanted blooms and damaged or decayed foliage. Spraying the foliage with clean water will keep the plants fresh and in full bloom until lifted late in autumn.

A small garden fork should be used for lifting and care must be taken not to damage the tubers. Carefully shake away surplus soil and place each plant, with its stems intact, into a deep box. Lifting should be done before the soil becomes wet, for if the tubers are long in drying they may decay. The plants should be set out on paper on the shed bench or on the floor of a dry room, turning them each week so that air will reach to all parts. The stems will die back slowly and will eventually fall away altogether. All soil is then shaken from the tubers, which should be dusted with flowers of sulphur and placed in boxes of peat for storing in a frost-free room.

Although the multifloras are usually grown for outdoor bedding, they also make charming pot plants for summer display in the greenhouse. The small tubers are started in boxes any time between mid-March and early May, and when the shoots are about 2 in (5 cm) high they are transplanted to 60-size pots in which they will bloom. The compost should be of friable turf loam to which has been incorporated some peat, a little decayed manure, some sand and a small quantity of bone meal. The plants will benefit from frequent syringing during warm weather.

In 1907 Messrs Lemoine's introduced a number of multiflora hybrids by crossing *B. octopetala* with a tuberous hybrid of unknown origin. Each had bronzy-red foliage and bore its double flowers mostly in early autumn. Rouget de l'Isle bears blooms of intense scarlet; Lafayette, deep crimson; and Gambetta, a bloom of an attractive coral-salmon colour. Many lovely hybrids followed which bloom throughout summer and autumn:

COUNT ZEPPELIN. A fine variety now rarely seen and bearing a profusion of fully double flowers of deep crimson-red.

EVELYN TAVANET. A beautiful variety having dark-green foliage and bearing masses of bright salmon-pink flowers.

HOMELAND. It bears single salmon-orange blooms in great profusion.

TASCO. A fine variety, the large double blooms being fiery scarlet with dark-green foliage, shaded bronze.

WILLIAM EYSSER. Outstanding, the blooms being double and of a lovely warm shade of deep salmon.

AMI BARD. A striking variety having deep-green foliage and bearing double blooms of peach-pink, flushed with apricot.

COMMANDER FELIX. A lovely variety, the large semi-double blooms being of an attractive shade of soft rose-pink.

FLAMBOYANT. The blooms are larger than any in this section and have the familiar double centre. They are of brilliant scarlet. Though the blooms are larger, the leaves are smaller than most varieties, deeply veined and of a dull, bottle-green colour making it excellent for small beds.

HELEN HARMS. The blooms are semi-double and held above their leaves, which are dull pale-green in colour and heavily veined. The blooms are yellow, flushed with salmon and pink and are borne with profusion.

HIS EXCELLENCY. One of the few multifloras introduced during the last quarter of a century. Like Flamboyant, it is of compact habit and bears very large fully double blooms of orange-scarlet.

JEWEL. A superb bedding plant, having pointed, almost black-green, foliage and bearing a fully double bloom of brilliant apricot which stands up to all weather conditions.

MADELON. An exquisite variety, its dark foliage being offset by double blooms of dark satiny pink.

MME RICHARD GALLE. Its buff-salmon blooms are borne in great profusion above its medium-green leaves.

PETIT HENRI. Its blooms are double and of a lovely shade of rosy-orange held well above the dark-green foliage.

Basket Begonias. The pendula, weeping or basket begonias *B. lloydii*, which are tuberous rooted, are among the most beautiful of all plants and may be grown in hanging baskets, large pots or vases in a greenhouse or glass porch, or in the open so long as they are protected from cold winds. The blooms, which are double, are held in clusters on gracefully drooping stems, a well-grown plant covering itself in a mass of colour which persists through summer and early autumn.

The weeping begonias may be grown in large pots and placed on a shelf high up in the greenhouse or garden house, where they will trail over the sides of the pot and shelf, almost entirely covering them. For weeks they will bear their blooms in cascading fashion, and no plant is more attractive for decorating the garden house. The pots may also be placed on the edge of a low wall, such as a terrace—where they may be protected from strong winds—or tubs may be arranged round a small courtyard or on a veranda or terrace. The plants look charming in ornamental vases, used as a centrepiece to a circular bed of multi-flora begonias, or at the sides of an entrance.

Planted in hanging baskets suspended from the roof of greenhouse or garden room, where the full beauty of their cascading bloom may be appreciated, they are seen at their best. Hanging baskets may be suspended from strong iron brackets placed 6 to 7 ft (about 2 metres) above ground level on the walls of a courtyard, where the plants will provide rich colour under the most drab conditions. Or they may be suspended by stout hooks from the eaves of a bungalow or low-built house. Where used around the walls of a yard, a more pleasing effect may be obtained by washing the walls with a cement wash. This will not only permit the flowers to reveal their full beauty but also will give more light to a dark wall. Here, sheltered from the direct rays of the sun and strong winds, baskets, vases and small tubs may be used to advantage. The baskets should be placed where they may be reached by standing on a strong box or an old chair, for watering. Regular attention is necessary if the baskets are to be a success, and they must not be fixed so high up as to make watering too difficult. The tubers may be started in the sunny window of a garden house or in the home, or a miniature frame may be made by inserting the box of tubers into a larger and deeper wooden box and placing a sheet of clean glass over the top. Placed outdoors in early April in a sunny position, they will soon commence growing. Undue forcing must not take place, the tubers should be brought on slowly— thus permitting them to form a sturdy rooting system—or they will bloom themselves to death and the display will soon end. Keep the tubers comfortably moist, and by the end of April they will be ready for their first move. The multifloras used for pot and vase culture may be grown in the same way.

When using hanging baskets, do not obtain them too large. One of 14-in (35-cm) diameter is large enough to accommodate three or four plants from 5-in (12·5-cm) pots. The weeping begonias make such vigorous growth and bear such a profusion of bloom that they are better grown on their own. To see them at their best, each basket should be made up to a separate colour or variety. Where obtaining unnamed tubers see that they are not less than 4 cm in diameter. They may be obtained in all the usual begonia colours and no plants will provide more bloom over so long a period—from early July until late autumn.

The baskets, which may be obtained from most sundries stores or nurserymen are made of strong galvanised wire closely welded together and will last many years. The baskets should first be lined with fresh green sphagnum moss to a depth of nearly 1 in (2·5 cm). This will greatly improve the appearance of the basket, prevent the compost falling through the wires and also absorb excess moisture, thus helping to keep the compost moist, which is all-important.

Over the moss, pieces of turf should be placed with the soil to the inside. This will act as an additional means of maintaining moisture and preventing the soil from falling. Both the moss and the turves should be moulded to the shape of the basket, and when this has been done the basket should be filled with prepared compost to within 1 in (2·5 cm) of the top. The compost for begonias must contain liberal quantities of humus, for it must be able to retain moisture when on occasions the baskets may have to be left untended for several days at the height of summer. Decayed turf loam to which has been added some peat, leaf mould or used hops, a small quantity of decayed manure and a sprinkling of bone meal, will be suitable. When mixed, it should be friable and have the appearance and smell of rich mould. A dusting with lime will also prove beneficial, or mix in some crushed charcoal to maintain sweetness.

If the basket is placed in a box or on top of a pot, the work may be more easily done, and after filling allow the basket to stand for 24 hours to allow the compost to consolidate, before planting. By the end of May, the plants will have formed several stems which will be almost upright and show little signs of their weeping habit, except that they will be more slender than with other begonias. The plants must be watered the day previous to 'knocking' them from their pots and planting in the baskets. Plant firmly and in an upright position, for as soon as the plants come into bloom they will assume a weeping habit without any 'stopping' or artificial methods being employed.

After planting give the baskets a thorough soaking. When the surplus moisture has drained away, suspend the baskets where they are to bloom. For the first fortnight or so all flower buds should be removed to allow the plants to devote their energy to making growth.

Where the baskets are suspended outdoors beneath the eaves of a house or from a wall they will receive only a small amount of water, even in a prolonged period of rain. It is, therefore, important to press a finger or a piece of cane into the compost to ascertain its moisture content. Never allow the plants to show signs of exhaustion before giving water, for if they dry out they will drop their buds.

The baskets should be given a thorough soaking rather than a gentle spraying at the surface, for it is important that the moisture reaches down to the roots. Give the plants a daily syringeing preferably in the evening whenever the weather is warm and dry, in addition to the watering of the compost. Eventually the shoots will reach 3 to 4 ft (90 cm to 1·2 metres) in length, while the blooms will be so numerous as to completely hide the basket.

After flowering has ended, outdoor baskets may be taken inside the greenhouse or garden room in October to continue blooming for several weeks. The plants are then dried off and the tubers stored in a dry, frost-free room until the spring. Propagation is the same as for other tuberous begonias.

The weeping begonias may also be grown in large pots which, placed on a shelf in a greenhouse or garden room or along a low wall, will provide a cascade of colour throughout summer. Started tubers may be obtained ready for planting or they may be started in a box covered with glass, by placing them in a sunny window.

The compost for pot-grown plants should be well-enriched with humus and prepared exactly as for the hanging baskets, and the plants should be given the same culture.

A pleasing way of growing weeping begonias in pots is to fix several pots to the walls of a courtyard by means of wrought-iron holders and a bracket, using them in the same way as for wall plants indoors. If fresh moss can be packed around the outside of the pots and kept moist, it will help to prevent too rapid moisture evaporation of the compost and hide the pots until the plants make growth.

Small tubs, placed on a brick or wooden base, will be most attractive planted with weeping begonias, using three or four plants round the sides of the tub. They will look particularly pleasing around a courtyard, or on a veranda or terrace. They may be used in a garden room, though like all begonias they must not be deprived of light and moisture.

Varieties of the weeping begonia:

ALICE MANNING. The best yellow variety, the blooms being very richly coloured and borne with great profusion.

ANDY PANE. The blooms are of a lovely warm crimson-red colour and are produced over a long period.

DAWN. The blooms are of a lovely shade of buff-yellow and are produced with freedom.

EUNICE. A plant in full bloom is quite enchanting, bearing showers of apple-blossom pink flowers.

FLAMING TORCH. The first weeping begonia to bear flowers of a brilliant orange-flame colour, which it does with great freedom.

JOAN. With its coral-pink flowers, a plant in full bloom is a most arresting sight.

JULIA. The blooms are borne over a long period and are of a lovely shade of rose-cerise.

MOLLIE. An unusual variety, bearing blooms of a pleasing shade of blush-white.

MRS BILKEY. An outstanding variety, bearing masses of bloom of brilliant orange.

NIAGARA. A new introduction and most free-flowering. The blooms are white, shaded green, a plant in full bloom having the appearance of a waterfall.

ROBERTA. A superb variety, the blooms are of deepest crimson-red and are produced in abundance over a long period.

SHIRLEY DESIRE. A lovely variety, bearing blooms of a soft shade of rose-pink.

SUNSET. One of the finest of all, the blooms being of a rich shade of salmon, flushed with orange.

YELLOW SWEETIE. A new introduction of great beauty. The blooms are of a pale primrose-yellow and possess a delicate perfume.

Rhizomatous Begonias. The coloured-foliage begonias, the evergreen hybrids of *B. rex*, native of Assam, are among the most adaptable of all pot plants. They will withstand what may be described as violent temperature fluctuations, for they grow well in a cold entrance hall in a winter temperature between 40° and 45° F (4° and 7° C). The *Begonia rex* (and other species noted for their richly coloured foliage) is another instance of a member of the begonia family remaining neglected because of the general belief that the plants are tender. Their exotic appearance belies their robust constitution, and of all indoor plants they are the most successful. Not only do they withstand wide variations in temperature, but should the plants become dry at the roots during one's absence from home, they will quickly respond to an hour's immersion in cold water. The plants may also be grown in positions which other house and greenhouse plants would find intolerable. The foliage begonias are as happy in shade—almost full shade—as they are when in sunshine. In fact, while shade will accentuate the delicate markings and colours of their foliage, too strong sunshine will tend to cause fading.

A greenhouse is not necessary for their culture, nor for their propagation, for the plants may spend their whole life in the home in all manner of situations, demanding the minimum of attention.

All they ask for is protection from frost during winter and from the direct rays of the summer sun. For this reason, the plants are appreciative of dwelling-house conditions, where in October they may be transferred from the greenhouse or they may be grown in the home throughout their life. It is, however, during wintertime that the foliage begonias are most appreciated, the brilliant silver colouring of their leaves brightening the dullest corners of the home. They will be happy in a cool room or in a room where there is a coal or gas fire, but will require more moisture in the latter. In a room where there is central heating the plants should be stood in a dish containing moist sand. The warmer and drier the conditions, the more moisture will the plants require, but they seem to be at their best in cooler temperatures. They are also tolerant of draughts. So long as frost is excluded, the plants will be almost foolproof, the easiest of all indoor plants for the beginner.

The Rex begonia presents no difficulties in any way with its culture. It forms a rhizome, which may be likened to both a stem and a fleshy root. Propagation is usually from leaf cuttings.

Three or four mature leaves may be removed from each plant every summer without causing unsightly defoliation, and from a dozen or so plants these may be expected to grow into several hundred ready for disposal within 15 to 18 months from their propagation. The rooted plants should be transferred to small pots as soon as large enough to handle, using the John Innes compost obtainable already made up. The plants should be grown on in a warm greenhouse, living-room or frame, until November, when watering is reduced so that the compost is just comfortably moist. They should then be removed to a frost-free room to winter in the home if a warm greenhouse is not available. In April the plants are repotted in 4-in pots.

The final potting compost should consist of:

    3 parts fibrous turf loam
    1 part decayed manure
    1 part peat or leaf mould
    1 part coarse sand or grit.

The most important ingredient is the loam, which should be fresh, clean and sweet as from old pastureland. Soil of a town garden must be avoided. A barrowful of prepared compost will be sufficient to pot two dozen plants, and to maintain soil sweetness, add a sprinkling of lime or crushed charcoal and mix well in. The compost should be friable and 'open' so that drainage will be efficient, while the plants love a gritty compost in which to get their roots.

Pot firmly. During summer the plants will require regular attention as to watering; give them a soaking when the compost begins to dry out. The cooler the position the less moisture will the plants require, and in winter they may be several weeks in a cool room without attention. Indeed, heavy watering in winter must be avoided. Feeding is not necessary, but the plants will appreciate a daily syringeing of the foliage when grown in a greenhouse during summer, while those plants grown in the home will benefit from being placed outdoors in their pots during a period of showery weather.

The Rex begonias will provide a display of rich colour when planted out in shady beds, and so long as the soil is enriched with humus and does not easily dry out, the plants may be grown in the open from early June until early October, when they are repotted and taken indoors to give of their beauty through winter and spring. It should be said that where *B. rex* and all coloured foliage begonias are being grown in a greenhouse during summer, they should be given ample ventilation both during daytime and by night. A too warm and humid atmosphere will cause the leaves to turn brown.

The plants will continue to form fleshy rhizomatous roots from which the leaf stems are produced, and those leaves which have become old and are beginning to fade and curl at the edges should be removed together with their stems. In this way the beauty of the plants will be retained throughout their life. Where the plants have been grown outside during summer, damaged or soiled leaves should be removed when the plants are lifted and repotted.

Those plants grown entirely indoors will benefit from being stood in the kitchen sink on occasions and immersed in water long enough to provide them with a copious drink. At the same time remove any decaying leaves. The plants will soon take on a new lease of life, the rich colours of their foliage being greatly accentuated. Varieties of *Begonia rex*:

CHICAGO. A striking variety, the silver leaves being margined and blotched with carmine-red.

COTSWOLD. Of compact habit, the silver leaves have deep-green markings.

EBFORD. The bottle-green leaves have contrasting mauve and silver veins.

ETNA. Of compact habit, the leaves being crimson-brown splashed with silver and pink.

EVEREST. A variety of extreme beauty, the leaves being of brilliant silver with deep-green central veins.

FIREFLUSH. Striking in that the bright-green leaves have darker edges over which grow red hairs giving the foliage a crimson sheen.

FRENCH FAVOURITE. Of robust habit, the large leaves are crimson at the centre, shading out to pale silvery green and with a margin of maroon.

GLADE. A vigorous grower, the rich bright-green leaves are shaded with bottle-green.

GLOIRE DES ARDENNES. A vigorous large-leaved variety which is bright crimson-red throughout.

GLORY OF ST ALBANS. Found as a chance seedling at Sanders' Nursery, St Albans. The leaves are of vivid rose-red, margined with olive-green.

GREENSLEEVES. The sage-green leaves are attractively dotted with dark green.

GREEN VELVET. A lovely plant, the deeply indented leaves are of dark green with black markings.

HALDON. Striking in that the leaves alternate between dark and light green in wide bands.

HELEN LEWIS. A striking American variety of robust habit, with large crimson and white leaves.

HIMALAYA. Of vigorous habit, the large green leaves are heavily splashed with silver.

ICELAND. One of the most vigorous varieties, the large silver leaves with their deep-green veins being tinted with purple.

LA MARQUISE. The pale-green foliage with its deep green veins is spotted with silver and pink.

LA PERIE DE MORTEFONTAIN. A striking variety, having bright reddish-pink leaves, mottled dark crimson at the edges.

LYMPSTONE. An attractive variety of medium habit, the bright silver leaves having deep green veins.

MOUNTAIN STREAM. A lovely variety of compact habit with glittering leaves of silver, pink and green.

MRS HATCHER. Of vigorous habit, the large leaves are crimson-red with darker veins.

PRINCESS CHARLES OF DENMARK. A lovely variety, the bright-silver leaves with their dark veining being flushed with pink.

PURPLE RAY. A striking variety, the elegantly pointed leaves being of purple and silver.

QUEEN ALEXANDRA. A fine old variety. Between the centre and green edge is a broad zone of silver.

REMILLY. Of medium vigour, the silver leaves are beautifully tinted or flushed pale-mauve.

Propagating Begonias from Seed. Tuberous begonias may be brought into bloom within 18 months of sowing the seed, but it is important to obtain fresh seed. Fresh seed will germinate rapidly and evenly, in a temperature of 65° F (18° C), taking about 15 days for the first seedlings to appear; and germination should be complete within a month. If a temperature of 60° F (16° C) cannot be maintained, sowing should take place only during summer or in spring, with the aid of a hot-bed or frame.

Fresh seed is reddish-brown in colour, like grains of sand, and it requires handling with care. So that sowing may be more even, mix the seed with a small amount of dry silver sand. Shaking it up will also help the seed to germinate more readily. A clean wooden box or earthenware pan will be a suitable container. It must be scrubbed clean.

Use the John Innes compost pressed lightly down and made level. This is most important for if the surface is not level, the seed will tend to be washed to the lower level when the compost is watered, while any seed remaining on the higher parts may receive insufficient moisture for successful germination.

Before sowing, the containers with their compost should be placed in a temperature in which sowing and germination are to take place, and the compost should be watered before the seed is sown.

Until the seed has germinated, the pans may be wrapped in polythene, again to encourage humidity and lessen the need to water the compost, while the floor of the greenhouse should be constantly made damp. When germination has taken place, humidity should be reduced to prevent damping off.

Where there is only limited warmth in a greenhouse—sufficient possibly to winter the Rex begonias, which require a temperature of 50° to 55° F (10° to 13° C)—seedlings may be raised in an electric propagator or indoor frame. A propagator may be worked where there is an electricity supply in the greenhouse. The seed is sown by taking a pinch between finger and thumb and scattering it as evenly as possible over the surface of the compost. If the seed is sown too closely together there will be every chance that the seedlings will damp off before they are transplanted.

After sowing, do not cover the seed. Place a sheet of glass over the container and over that provide a sheet of brown paper to exclude light until germination has taken place. Remember to place the container in a level position so that all the seed receives the same amount of moisture. A temperature of 60° F (16° C) must be maintained, whatever the weather, for a full month until germination is complete. The amount of watering will depend upon the degree of humidity but whenever the glass is removed and wiped dry, the compost should be inspected as to its moisture content. If it is necessary to water, do so from a fine spray and ensure that it reaches every part of the compost. Or water by immersing the base of the containers for several minutes so that the compost will be able to take in sufficient moisture. This method will ensure that the tiny seeds do not become buried as may happen when watering from above. Adding Cheshunt Compound to the water will prevent the seedlings damping off, which may be as troublesome with begonias as it is with stocks and asters.

Guard against draughts and give no ventilation until the seedlings are ready for transplanting. If using a cold frame, make sure that it is kept closed. After 10 to 12 days, if the correct humidity and warmth has been maintained, the first seedlings will appear and the paper must be removed, otherwise the tiny plants will become 'drawn'.

The glass should be partially removed during daytime and must be kept free of moisture, which would cause damping off. The seeds will not all germinate together and it may take as long as a month before germination is complete.

When transplanting the seedlings, never handle directly with the fingers or they will bruise. Obtain a piece of thin cane rounded at one end or a small pastry fork. They will be useful for loosening the roots and should be held in the right hand. In the left hand hold a thin wooden label, as used for naming pot plants, with a narrow *V* cut at one end. This is placed beneath the leaf and with it the seedlings are transferred to new quarters. At the same time a small hole to take the roots should be made with the dibber. After a little practice the procedure can be carried out with the greatest of ease. This tip on transplanting came from an old grower of exhibition begonias who raised many hundreds of seedling plants each year and never touched them with his fingers.

After making up a box or pan, water in. This will firm the compost about the roots. The seedlings remaining in the sowing pans should also be watered so that the roots may be covered with compost if they were disturbed. They may then be allowed to grow on for a week before being transferred to another box.

After transplanting, the boxes should be placed close to the glass so that the young plants will grow sturdy. Where sowing and raising plants in summer this may cause scorching of the foliage if the plants are not shaded from the sunlight, which is done by whitening the glass.

The young plants will continue to make rapid growth in a temperature of between 56° and 60° F (13° and 16° C), and as the sun's rays increase in strength during March and April heating may be gradually reduced until, at the end of April, heating is used only at night. During daytime ventilation will be necessary to encourage a buoyant atmosphere, though draughts must be guarded against. Where growing in a frame, the frame light may be lifted when the weather is calm and the sun is shining.

By the middle of May the plants will be sturdy and ready for hardening before planting out early in June. When first moved to the frames, they should be kept closed at night and covered with sacking to guard against frost. Gradually more fresh air should be admitted by day, until towards the month end the lights may be left off altogether, and during the last days of May they may also be removed at night. During this period the plants will make rapid growth and will require copious amounts of water except during periods of rain.

Vegetative Propagation. Propagating the large-flowered tuberous-rooted begonias by means of cuttings is done during summer as the plants make growth. Cuttings are severed close to the main stem, at a point where the axils of the leaves join the stem of the plant where each will contain an 'eye' or embryo bud which will later form the tuber. The shoot is removed with a sharp knife when 3 in (7·5 cm) long. It should be taken from the main stem by means of a *V*-cut. It is then inserted, as described for the winter-flowering begonias, around the sides of a pot. Keep moist by syringeing and shade from the sun until rooting has taken place, which will be in three to four weeks. As a precaution against mildew, the cuttings should be dusted with flowers of sulphur after inserting in the pots. In the natural summer temperatures of a greenhouse, rooting should present no difficulty, and when this has taken place the plants are potted individually and grown on to come into bloom the following summer. From mid-June to mid-July is the best time to take the cuttings. It will be found that the wound on the main stem will quickly heal.

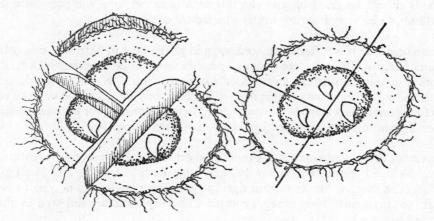

Dividing a begonia tuber

Division of the tubers is another method of propagation. The tubers may be cut into two or more pieces with a sharp knife, but each piece must have an 'eye' or shoot, without which it cannot bear bloom. Into the cut portion, ground charcoal, lime or flowers of sulphur should be rubbed to prevent disease from entering the wound. Each portion should then be potted separately, using the same compost as described for potting cuttings.

There will be little loss of bloom during the summer that division takes place; indeed, with no other shoots to compete for the food in the compost, the single shoot will grow on and bear a bloom of outstanding quality. It will receive exactly the same cultural treatment as for undivided tubers. The tuber may be dried off in autumn in the usual way and stored through winter when the process may be repeated the following spring.

BELAMCANDA (Iridaceae)

A genus of a single species, native of south-eastern Asia and introduced into Europe from China in 1759. It was originally classed with ixia but is known as the leopard flower for it resembles tigridia. In its native land it is the blackberry lily, for its flowers are followed by large black seeds.

Culture. Only half-hardy, the stolon-bearing rhizomes may be planted in a sunny border in those gardens which enjoy a favourable climate, setting them 8 in (20 cm) apart. They may be planted early in spring—as they bloom during July in the British Isles and northern Europe—or in autumn. They may be grown in frames or in pots under glass, planting in March when they will bloom during early summer. They require a well-drained sandy soil and very little moisture for about a month after planting, but the moisture content of the soil should be increased as soon as plant growth appears. After flowering, the plants should be dried off and the rhizomes removed from the pots early in autumn, to be stored during winter in a frost-free room.

Propagation. It is raised from seed sown in gentle heat in March or in a cold frame in April. The seeds are large and pea-like and are best sown singly in small pots containing a mixture of sterilised loam and sand. The young plants are later moved to larger pots containing a richer compost. They will bloom in three to four years. They may also be propagated by root division, for they are stolon forming and may be increased by this method after flowering.

Species. *Belamcanda chinensis.* From the short rhizomatous root arises tufts of sword-shaped leaves about 12 in (30 cm) long, each leaf being 1 in (2·5 cm) wide. The flowers, like miniature tigridias are borne in clusters of 4 to 12 on 3 ft (90 cm) stems. They are red, spotted with purple and are followed by the large black seeds.

BESSERA (Alliaceae)

A genus of three species, native of the southern United States and Mexico, closely resembling the flowering garlics. The flowers are like orange (or purple) snowdrops, hence their name of coral drops. They have tunicated bulbs from which arise narrow grass-like leaves, and drooping bell-shaped flowers borne at the end of a 2 ft (60 cm) stem.

Culture. The globose bulbs may be grown outdoors in those gardens which are untroubled by frost, for they are only half-hardy. They should be planted in a light sandy soil and in a position where they are baked by the summer sun, such as at the foot of a wall where the tall flowering stems may be protected from wind. Plant in spring, 4 in (10 cm) deep and 8 in (20 cm) apart, and as they make growth water copiously. They will bloom from early July until autumn, having a longer flowering period than most bulbs. After flowering, withhold moisture while the bulbs die back.

They may also be grown under glass in large pots, planting three or four bulbs to each and using a compost composed of fibrous loam, leaf mould and sand in equal parts. Plant in March, just covering the bulbs and giving little moisture until they begin to make growth. Then increase the watering

until the plants have finished flowering. They should then be dried off. Allow
the bulbs to remain in the pots, when they may be started into growth again
in spring.

Propagation. Older bulbs will form numerous offsets, which may be detached
upon lifting to be grown on in boxes of sandy loam in a frame, or in prepared
outdoor beds where climate permits.

Species. *Bessera elegans*. Native of Mexico, it bears elegant drooping bell-
shaped flowers in loose umbels. They are of deep orange-red with creamy
stripes down the segments and are held on 2-ft (60-cm) stems. In bloom June
to September.

BLOOMERIA (Alliaceae)

A genus of three species, native of southern California and named after H. G.
Bloomer, curator of the Academy of Natural Science. They are closely related to
bessera and allium and have tunicated bulbs, and long linear leaves. They
bear bright-yellow flowers in an umbel on a scape 12 in (30 cm) tall.

Culture. They require similar treatment to bessera—i.e. a well-drained soil
and a warm, sunny situation. The bulbs may be planted in spring, 4 in (10 cm)
deep and 6 in (15 cm) apart and they resent disturbance. Or they may be
planted in pots or pans for flowering under glass. They are also valuable for the
rock garden for they enjoy the protection of the stones and especially like to
send down their roots into moisture-retaining tufa stone.

Propagation. They are increased by offsets like allium, bessera, etc.

Species. *Bloomeria aurea* (syn. *Nothoscordum aureum*). Native of California, it
has long linear leaves and bears bright-yellow flowers in umbels at the end of a
12-in (30 cm) scape. The flowers have six spreading segments and six stamens.

BOBARTIA (Iridaceae).

A genus of 17 species, native of South Africa and named in honour of Jacob
Bobart, Professor of Botany at Oxford University in the seventeenth century.
They produce a corm like a woody rhizome and have basal leaves only, which
are sword-like and flat, like those of the gladiolus. The flowers are borne in
terminal clusters on a leafless stem 2 ft (60 cm) tall and are borne solitary or
several in a compact head. They are yellow, opening in succession from green
spaths, the perianth segments being joined at the base.

Culture. In their native land the plants grow on mountainous slopes in an open
situation and in a well-drained soil, where they bloom from August until

December. In the British Isles and northern Europe, and in North America, they bloom early in summer and, as they are only half-hardy, are best grown under glass in all but those gardens enjoying a favourable climate and where the corms or rhizomes may occupy the ground during winter. They require a sandy soil, enriched with some decayed manure and should be planted 4 in (10 cm) deep. Cover them with some litter in winter to protect them from the cold. Where growing indoors, plant in autumn, three or four to a large pot and place in a frame until early in spring, when they should be removed to a cool greenhouse or placed in gentle heat. They should not be watered during winter but must be given ample supplies as they make growth in spring. After flowering, they are dried off and should remain in the pots in which they are brought into growth again in spring.

Propagation. The plants are increased by division of their rhizomatous roots after flowering.

Species. *Bobartia filiformis.* It makes a small corm-like root from which arise three or four flattened leaves, shorter than the 18-in (45-cm) long flower stem, which is also flattened. The yellow flowers appear in small clusters and are marked with reddish-brown at the base, the inner perianth segments being slightly shorter than the outer segments.

Bobartia gladiata. It inhabits the slopes of Table Mountain, where it grows 2 ft (60 cm) tall with long sword-shaped leaves and bears its flowers in large clusters at the end of flattened stems. With the variety *major* the flowers are borne in more numerous clusters, the yellow perianth segments being spotted with brown at the base.

Bobartia indica (syn. *Bobartia spathacea*). It grows 20 in (50 cm) tall with cylindrical rush-like leaves (used for basket making) and attractive lemon-yellow flowers borne in a dense head. The outer segments are long and narrow. The variety *minor* is a plant of less vigorous habit and like all the bobartias appears in greater vigour following the destruction of vegetation by fire. The species is present from the Cape to Natal.

BOMAREA (Amaryllidaceae).

A genus of about 150 species, native of South America and the West Indies. Most are of trailing or climbing habit. Named after Valmont de Bomare, they are closely related to *alstroemeria* and *lapageria*, but are of more tender habit and in the Northern Hemisphere require the protection of glass and a night temperature of not less than 48° F (9° C). They have slender tuberous roots which in several species are edible, while the leaves, oblong and pointed, are held on long stalks. The flowers are funnel-shaped and are borne in large drooping umbels. With their climbing habit, the plants may be grown up the rafters of a warm greenhouse or garden room.

Culture. Plant one to each large pot, using a compost made up of sterilised loam, decayed manure, leaf mould and grit in equal parts. The crown is planted just below soil level, which should be 1 in (2·5 cm) below the rim of the pot to allow for watering. Plant in spring. As the plant makes growth it will require ample supplies of moisture at the roots and regular syringeing during warm weather, for the plants are native of the tropical rain-forests. They will bloom in summer and are among the most beautiful flowers in cultivation.

Propagation. This is by division of the crowns in spring, 'teasing' apart the fleshy roots; or by sowing the ripe seed in a propagator in a temperature of 65° F (18° C) in a mixture of sterilised loam, sand and leaf mould. Until the end of their second year, the seedlings require a close, moist atmosphere with regular syringeing. They should be moved to small pots when large enough to handle and to larger pots when the first pots have become too small to accommodate the large fleshy roots. At all times, they demand plenty of light.

Species. *Bomarea caldasiana.* Native of Ecuador, where it is found at altitudes of up to 10,000 ft, twining about the trees and shrubs. It has long leaves and equally long stalks and bears its tubular flowers of yellow and brown in drooping umbels of up to 20 or more.

Bomarea carderi. Native of the Colombian Andes, it has leaves 6 in (15 cm) long and bears umbels of soft shell-pink tubular flowers, spotted with brown at the tips.

Bomarea edulis. It is to be found throughout tropical South America and in Cuba, the tuberous roots being eaten as a substitute for potatoes. The flowers are borne in large umbels and are pale pink, tipped with green and spotted with brown on the inside. The variety *chontalensis* has inner segments of palest yellow.

Bomarea frondea. Resembling *B. caldasiana*, it is also native of the Andes of Colombia, has oblong leaves and bears large umbels of crimson-brown tubular flowers with spotted inner segments of brilliant yellow.

Bomarea patacocensis. Native of Ecuador and Colombia it is one of the most striking plants in cultivation, bearing enormous dangling clusters of brilliant red with the inner segments spotted with yellow.

BRAVOA (Amaryllidaceae).

A genus of seven species, native of Mexico and named after the botanist Max Bravo. They have tuberous roots and narrow leaves 6 to 12 in (15 to 30 cm) long and bear red or white flowers, usually in pairs with a short, cylindrical perianth tube and oblong segments. The flowers are held on stems 18 to 24 in (45 to 60 cm) tall and appear in summer.

Culture. They are only half-hardy and in the British Isles, northern Europe and North America should be planted in those gardens enjoying a favourable winter temperature and a light, well-drained soil. Otherwise they should be grown in pots or boxes in a greenhouse from which frost is excluded. Plant the tubers in autumn and keep them dry until they begin to make growth in spring, from which time they will need increased supplies of moisture as the sun gathers strength. Two or three tubers should be planted in each large pot.

Propagation. Offsets will form around the old tubers and may be detached when they are repotted to be grown on in boxes in a frame or greenhouse or, under suitable conditions, in a prepared bed outdoors. They will bloom in three years.

Species. *Bravoa bulbiana*. It has ovoid tuberous roots, about 1 in (2·5 cm) through and covered in a fibrous tunic. The leaves are brilliant green, about 6 in (15 cm) long and 1 in (2·5 cm) wide, while the almost stalkless white flowers are borne in pairs on 2 ft (60 cm) stems.

Bravoa geminiflora. The globose tubers are almost 2 in (5 cm) in diameter with fibrous tunics, and the strap-like leaves measure up to 18 in (45 cm) long. It grows in high altitudes in Mexico and is the hardiest species. It is also the most attractive, the coral-red flowers hanging in pairs of 20 or more on 18-in (45-cm) stems.

BRODIAEA (Alliaceae)

A genus of about 30 species, closely related to allium and resembling it in the manner in which it bears its flowers. Native of North America, especially California, where the plants take the place of allium of the British Isles and Europe, inhabiting deciduous woodlands and bearing their flowers of purple, blue, yellow and scarlet in generous drifts. Named after J. J. Brodie, the Scottish cryptogamist, the nomenclature of the genus has given rise to much confusion, several species now being classified as *Brevoortia, Triteleia, Hookera, Dichelostemma*. Botanists have reached agreement in that those species with three fertile stamens should be classified as *Brodiaea*. These plants have tunicated bulbs almost corm-like, and narrow grass-like leaves, while their flowers are borne in umbels at the end of a simple scape. The perianth is bell-shaped with six equal lobes.

Culture. They require a warm, sunny situation such as clearings in woodlands, and in the more exposed parts of North America and Europe they should survive all but the most severe winter. They require a light, sandy soil but, as they are deep rooting, one which has been prepared to a depth of at least 12 in (30 cm) and enriched with decayed manure. They bloom during midsummer and may be planted in autumn or in spring. Set the bulbs on a layer of sand, 6 in (15 cm) deep and 6 in (15 cm) apart. Close planting may be recommended, for the linear leaves die back before the flowers appear. Several species are

Babiana stricta

Begonia: Allan Langdon

Begonia: Wedding Day

Begonia: Judy Langdon

suitable for growing in the rock garden, while in the most exposed parts the bulbs may be planted in pots or deep boxes which are wintered in a frame and placed in the open early in summer, when they will bloom in their containers. *Brodiaea crocea*, which comes into bloom early in May, is a delightful subject for the alpine house when grown in pots or pans. It may be placed in the open after flowering and remain there during summer and autumn, to be taken indoors again before the frosts.

Propagation. Seed, freshly gathered is sown in pots or pans in a frame or greenhouse, the seedlings being transplanted to deep boxes in spring. They require a compost made up of sterilised loam, sand and peat in equal parts and they should be watered with care, for the young plants are liable to damp off. They will bloom in about three years.

The bulblets may also be separated from the parent and grown on in boxes of sandy loam when they will come into bloom within two years.

Species. *Brodiaea bridgesii*. Native of Oregon and California, it forms a tuft of grass-like leaves and bears lilac-pink flowers in umbels of 12 to 20. The flowers have blue anthers inserted in a single row. The blooms open star-like and are borne on 18-in (45-cm) stems during June and July.

Brodiaea californica. It grows 18 in (45 cm) tall and bears its rosy-mauve tubular flowers in loose umbels of 12 to 20 during midsummer. The beauty of the flower is enhanced by its long perianth segments.

Brodiaea coccinea. The Californian firecracker, also the crimson satin flower. It is a plant of arresting beauty but difficult to grow away from its native California. Unlike the other species, it requires a heavy loam and, unless given a warm sunny situation so that the bulbs ripen well, it will produce few flowers. It is a plant of tufted habit with narrow leaves and it bears its drooping crimson-red flowers, tipped with green on 2-ft (60-cm) stems during midsummer.

Brodiaea congesta (syn. *Dichelostemma congestum*). It has round rush-like leaves, and in June bears dense umbels of amethyst-blue flowers on scapes up to 3 to 4 ft (90 cm to 1·2 metres) tall.

Brodiaea crocea. Native of California, it comes into bloom in May, bearing pale-yellow tubular flowers on slender stalks 8 in (20 cm) tall. It has dainty narrow leaves and requires a soil which is well supplied with grit.

Brodiaea grandiflora (syn. *Brodiaea coronaria*). Native of British Columbia and and Oregon, it was discovered in 1808, being the first of the Brodiaeas to be introduced to gardens. It has long linear leaves and bears violet-blue flowers in umbels of 3 to 12 on a 6-in (15-cm) scape. The perianth tube is long, with spreading segments. It is a valuable species for the alpine garden.

Brodiaea hyacinthina (syn. *B. lactea*). The Missouri hyacinth, a dainty species with narrow linear leaves and bearing on an 18-in (45-cm) scape umbels

H

of 20 to 30 or more violet flowers. The variety *lactea* bears pure-white flowers, and *lilacina* white flowers suffused with mauve.

Brodiaea ixioides. Known as pretty face or golden star in its native California, it has narrow fleshy leaves and on an 18-in (45-cm) scape bears umbels of 10 to 20 deep golden star-like flowers with dark brown rays on the exterior of the perianth. *Splendens* is an earlier flowering form. This is the most frost-tender species.

Brodiaea laxa. One of the most attractive species, with rush-like leaves and bearing on a 2-ft (60-cm) stem, umbels of 30 to 50 pale violet-mauve flowers with the segments shorter than the tube. Like *B. bridgesii*, the flowers have steel-blue anthers.

Brodiaea minor. It resembles *B. grandiflora* and bears flowers of deep purple-blue, which are held on 3-in (7·5-cm) stems. A most attractive species for the rock garden or alpine house.

Brodiaea multiflora (syn *B. parviflora*). It grows nearly 3 ft (90 cm) tall and bears large compact umbels of pale-blue flowers late in summer.

Brodiaea peduncularis. Its long-stemmed flowers of porcelain-white, some-times shaded with pink and with white anthers are borne in large loose umbels and on a 20-in (50-cm) scape. This species is valuable for naturalising, enjoying partial shade and a moist soil. By crossing this species with *B. laxa*, Messrs van Tubergen raised a hybrid of outstanding beauty, *B. tubergenii*, its pale-blue flowers, deeper blue on the exterior, being borne in large compact umbels. It blooms during June and July and may be planted about deciduous woodlands through which the sun's rays may penetrate.

Brodiaea pulchella (syn. *B. capitata*). Known as the wild hyacinth in north-western America, it comes early into bloom, sometimes in April, and bears large umbels of violet-blue flowers on slender 15-in (37·5-cm) stems.

Brodiaea rosea. A rare Californian for the rock garden for it grows 4 to 5 in (10 to 12·5 cm) tall with small rounded leaves and it bears its rosy-red flowers in a dainty umbel of five or six.

BRUNSVIGIA (Amaryllidaceae)

A genus of 13 species, native of tropical and South Africa, and named in honour of the House of Brunswick. It differs from crinum and *Amaryllis belladonna* in its irregular flowers. The bulbs are large, often measuring 8 in (20 cm) in diameter, and they are tender, requiring, in the British Isles and northern Europe, the protection of a warm greenhouse or garden room during winter. The tunicated bulbs have strap-like leaves which appear after the flowers. These are funnel-shaped and are borne in large umbels on a 15-in (37·5-cm) scape. The umbel is comprised of 12 to 50 flowers arranged evenly around the scape on long pedicels.

Culture. To bloom in July, they should be potted in spring, one 4-in (10-cm) bulb to a 5-in (12·5-cm) pot, using a mixture of fibrous loam, decayed manure, leaf mould and coarse sand in equal parts. They require firm planting with the neck and shoulder just above the level of the compost. They should be given a temperature of 55° F (13° C) to start them into growth, and as the sun increases in strength they will require more moisture. The pots should be well 'crocked' before planting, and to keep the compost sweet it is advisable to add a few small pieces of charcoal. The pots should be sufficiently large to allow a space of about half an inch (1·25 cm) between the side and the bulb. Do not plant too deeply as water may enter the neck and cause decay.

About six weeks after planting, the buds will be seen pushing up through the wall of the bulb, and possibly two stems will be produced in a season depending upon size of bulb. It will be advisable to turn the pots each day so that the stems grow up straight and, though the plants will require ample supplies of moisture, the compost must not become stagnant or the roots will decay. They will require a sunny window until showing colour, when they should be moved to a position of partial shade. After flowering, the bulbs continue to make growth and watering should continue until they begin to die back in winter. They are then given almost no water until brought into bloom again in spring.

After flowering, remove the dead blooms and place the pots outdoors, if possible beneath the eaves of a house and in a position of full sun for the bulbs to ripen, without which they will not bloom the following year. For the bulbs to form roots and bear flowers at the same time, they require all the help possible and will benefit from a weekly application of dilute manure water until the leaves begin to wither.

If well cared for, the bulbs will last 20 years or more but should be repotted every four years, taking care to disturb the roots as little as possible.

In the warmer parts, the bulbs may be planted outdoors in a sunny position, preferably at the base of a wall. They are planted 4 in (10 cm) deep and should be protected during winter by a mulch of decayed manure and leaves, which will also provide valuable plant food. Or they may be covered with frame lights in autumn which may be reared against a wall. They may be inexpensively constructed from laths and Windowlite or plastic material for all that is necessary is to keep off the winter rains and to provide some protection from frost. The lights may be used to cover *Amaryllis belladonna* and agapanthus growing in the open beneath a wall.

Propagation. *Brunsvigia josephinae* and most other species rarely produce off-sets and propagation is usually by sowing seed in a sandy compost and in a propagator. They will, however, take 12 to 15 years to bear flowers.

Species. *Brunsvigia gigantea* (syn. *B. orientalis*). The bulb may grow to 6 in (15 cm) across, and from it arises a 12-in (30-cm) scape at the top of which is formed a circular umbel of 20 to 30 funnel-shaped flowers held on long pedicels. The umbel may measure up to 20 in (50 cm) across, while the flowers are brilliant red. They bloom in spring in their native Cape Peninsular, and in August and September in the British Isles, Europe and North America. The plant has leaves 12 in (30 cm) long and 3 to 4 in (7·5 to 10 cm) wide.

Brunsvigia josephinae. Introduced in 1814, it is the most free-flowering species. It has grey-green, strap-like leaves 2 ft (60 cm) long and 2 in (5 cm) wide, and it blooms during July and August, bearing on an 18-in (45-cm) scape, a large circular umbel of about 30 scarlet blooms (sometimes twice that number). The funnel-shaped blooms are about 3 in (7·5 cm) long. The form minor grows only 9 in (22·5 cm) tall and bears 20 to 40 smaller pale-red blooms in a symmetrical umbel.

BULBINE (Liliaceae)

A genus of about 50 species, native of tropical and South Africa and taking their name from *bulbos*, a bulb, though many have merely fleshy or tuberous roots. The basal leaves are lance-shaped or linear, sometimes fleshy; the flowers are usually yellow (occasionally white) and sweetly scented. They are borne in few or many-flowered racemes. The flowers have a narrow green stripe down each segment, similar to the anthericum, to which the plant is closely related. The perianth segments are free, the stamens bearded. The seeds are black and winged.

Culture. The plants are readily managed in well-drained soil, but as they are only half-hardy they require a garden enjoying a warm winter climate and should be given an open, sunny situation. Plant the roots 6 in (15 cm) deep in spring and mulch in autumn.

Propagation. The plants are increased by offsets, removed and planted in spring.

Species. *Bulbine alooides.* Common on lower mountainous slopes in Cape Province, it forms three to six fleshy pale-green leaves which come before the flowers, which are star-like and deep yellow in colour.

Bulbine asphodelioides. It has a small tuberous rootstock and leaves which are formed in a spiral rosette. They are dark green with serrated margins. The pale-yellow flowers are borne in a dense inflorescence with conspicuous bracts.

Bulbine favosa. It is a common plant of mountainous slopes of Cape Province, where it blooms from April to July, the two or three leaves appearing after the flowers, which are yellow and borne in a lax raceme followed by rough, sharply angled seeds.

BULBINELLA (Liliaceae)

A genus of 15 species of herbs with bulbous roots, native of South Africa and New Zealand. The leaves are basal, strap-like and narrow, while the yellow flowers are borne in a dense raceme with six perianth segments and six stamens, with the filaments bearded.

Culture. The plants require similar conditions to *bulbine* and *anthericum* to which they are closely related. They often reach a height of 3 to 4 ft (90 cm to 1·2 metres) and should be planted towards the back of a warm border, in a well-drained soil.

Propagation. They are increased by offsets removed in spring which is the best time for planting. Plant 20 in (50 cm) apart.

Species. *Bulbinella floribunda.* It is found on the lower slopes of Table Mountain, where it usually blooms after a fire. It grows 3 ft (90 cm) tall, its strap-like leaves sheathing at the base. The flowers are borne in a dense conical raceme and are creamy-white, appearing in August and September, in May in the British Isles and Europe.

Bulbinella hookeri. Frequent in both North and South Islands of New Zealand, it is known as the Maori onion. It grows 20 in (50 cm) tall and inhabits mountainous slopes which in October become a sheet of brilliant gold. The flowers measure about 1 in (2·5 cm) across and appear in dense racemes.

Bulbinella rossii. It is present in the Auckland and Campbell Islands of New Zealand, where it grows to a height of 3 to 4 ft (90 cm to 1·2 metres), with a thick stem and long recurved leaves. The flowers are yellow and star-like, resembling those of the asphodel.

BULBOCODIUM (Liliaceae)

A genus of a single species, it is the spring meadow saffron and is closely related to colchicum. It takes its name from the Greek *bulbos*, a bulb, and *kodion*, a woolly covering, the reference being to the strange woolly covering of the tuberous roots or bulbs. It resembles the crocus in appearance but differs in that it has a superior instead of an inferior ovary and six stamens instead of three. It blooms with the winter aconite and the snowdrop during February and March and is a suitable subject for the alpine house and rock garden. Like *colchicum*, it blooms before the leaves appear.

Culture. It is a plant of extreme hardiness but is intolerant of excess winter moisture so must be given a dry, well-drained soil and a sunny situation. Plant 3 in (7·5 cm) deep in autumn and 4 in (10 cm) apart. For the alpine house, plant four to five tubers or bulbs to each pot or pan, using a compost made up of 2 parts sterilised loam and 1 part each leaf mould and coarse sand. Plant in autumn and keep in a shaded frame until towards the year end, when the pots should be removed to a cool room or to the alpine house as that they will come into bloom early in the new year. The plants require the minimum of compost—sufficient only to support the bulbs.

Propagation. This is one of those bulbous plants which will benefit from lifting and replanting every two or three years. This should be done early in autumn, when the offsets are removed and replanted.

Species. *Bulbocodium vernum* (syn. *Colchicum vernum*). Native of the European Alps, the bulbs are about 1 in (2·5 cm) through and are black, the flower being produced from a side appendage before the strap-like leaves appear. The rosy-mauve funnel-shaped flowers are about 4 in (10 cm) long, with narrow petals resembling those of the crocus. They open star-like and are most attractive.

C

CALIPHRURIA (Amaryllidaceae)
A genus of two species, native of the Andes of Bogata and closely related to *eucharis*. They take their name from *kallos*, beauty, and *phroura*, prison, a reference to the flowers being enclosed by the spathe.

Culture. They require the protection of a warm greenhouse in the northern temperate regions and a compost made up of fibrous loam, leaf mould and sand in equal parts. The bulbs are planted in autumn, two or three to a pot, and during winter the night temperatures should not be allowed to fall below 50° F (10° C). They require little moisture until they begin to make growth early in the year. They will bloom during May and June. After flowering the pots are taken outdoors and placed in a sunny situation, where the bulbs will ripen. They may then be taken indoors again and brought into bloom the following year.

Propagation. The plants produce stolons, which are detached and potted as the mother bulbs are shaken from the pots and repotted every three or four years.

Species. *Caliphruria hartwegii*. It was introduced in 1843 and is the only species in cultivation. The small ovoid bulbs, covered in brown tunics like the tulip, produce brilliant green leaves about 6 in (15 cm) long and 2 in (5 cm) broad. The flowers are white and funnel-shaped and are borne in umbels of six or eight on a stem 12 in (30 cm) long.

CALLIPSYCHE (Eucrosia) (Amaryllidaceae)
A genus of four species, native of the Peruvian Andes and taking their name from *kallos*, beauty, and *psyche*, a butterfly. The species are now grouped under a single genus, *Callipsyche*. They have tunicated bulbs and produce broad blunt leaves with long stalks. They appear after the flowers, which are produced early in summer. The flowers are pendant, grouped around the end of the tall scape and are remarkable for the length of their filaments, which protrude 6 in (15 cm) beyond the short perianth tube.

Culture. The plants require light and warmth and may be grown in a greenhouse or garden room with a minimum winter temperature of 50° F (10°C) by night. They like a compost made up of fibrous loam, leaf mould and sand in equal parts and are planted singly in 4-in (10-cm) pots or two or three bulbs to a larger pot. Plant in autumn and give little water until they begin to grow early in the year when moisture should be increased. Like *eucharis*, to which they are closely related, the plants will bloom early in summer and after a rest may be brought into bloom again at Christmas. Water should then be withheld, while the plants are rested, after which with additional watering they will bloom again in summer. They will benefit from an occasional application of dilute manure water and a top-dressing of dehydrated cow manure.

Propagation. The older bulbs will form offsets, which are detached and grown on in small pots.

Species. *Callipsyche aurantiaca*. It has ovoid bulbs of about 2 in (5 cm) diameter and it has heart-shaped leaves 4 in (10 cm) broad at the widest part. The flowers are borne six to eight in an umbel on a 2-ft (60-cm) stem and are brilliant yellow with the stamens protruding 3 in (7·5 cm) beyond the perianth segments. It blooms in February and March and again towards the end of summer.

Callipsyche bicolor (syn. *Eucrosia bicolor*). Introduced into cultivation in 1817, it has ovoid bulbs 1 in (2·5 cm) through and lance-shaped leaves 6 in (15 cm) long and 1 in (2·5 cm) wide with long stalks. The beautiful orange flowers are veined with green, while the stamens protrude 4 in (10 cm) beyond the petal segments. The flowers are produced in loose umbels on 12-in (30-cm) stems and appear in spring.

Callipsyche eucrosioides. Its rounded bulbs are about 2 in (5 cm) in diameter and large leaves, 12 in (30 cm) long and 4 in (10 cm) wide. The flowers are pale yellow, shaded with green and are borne eight to an umbel on a 2-ft (60-cm) stem. The stamens protrude 4 in (10 cm) beyond the segments. In bloom early May and again towards the year end.

Callipsyche mirabilis. It was described in *Gardener's Chronicle* for 31st March 1900 and is one of the most arresting plants in cultivation. It blooms in mid-summer and again at the year end and has bulbs of 2 in (5 cm) diameter and broad oblong leaves 12 in (30 cm) long and 6 in (15 cm) wide. The yellow flowers are borne 20 to 30 to an umbel and are symmetrically arranged around the end of a 3-ft (90-cm) scape. The white stamens protrude 5 in (12·5 cm) below the perianth segments, like miniature waterfalls painted in Chinese white.

CALOSTEMMA (Amaryllidaceae)

A genus of four species, native of the coastline of eastern Australia and taking their name from *kallos*, beauty, and *stemma*, a crown, the flowers being formed in a circle at the end of the 18-in (45-cm) stem. Known as the Australian daffodil, it resembles *caliphruria* and *callipsyche* except that its stamens do not project beyond the perianth segments. The bulbs require similar cultural conditions.

Culture. In those gardens free from winter frosts, the bulbs may be planted in a sunny situation and in a light, sandy soil. Plant 6 in (15 cm) deep and 12 in (30 cm) apart in spring, and there will be no need to disturb the bulbs for several years. In less favourable parts, it is advisable to lift the bulbs each year in autumn and winter them in a frost-free room. It is an admirable plant for either a cool or a warm greenhouse or garden room, when it will bloom towards the end of summer. Several bulbs should be planted to a 6-in (15-cm) pot using a compost made up of fibrous loam, peat and coarse sand in equal parts and planting the bulbs 2 in (5 cm) deep. Plant early in the year and increase supplies of moisture as there is an increase in natural warmth.

Propagation. Usually by offsets which form around the base of bulbs which are several years old. They are detached when the bulbs are repotted and grown on in boxes of sandy loam.

Species. *Calostemma album.* It is more tender than the other species and has almost round leaves, borne on long stalks. Its flowers are white, each being about 1 in (2·5 cm) long, and are borne in umbels of 10 to 20 on an 18-in (45-cm) stem.
   Calostemma luteum. Native of Queensland and New South Wales, it has long linear leaves which appear after the flowers. The blooms are bright yellow, resembling those of the crocus when open to reveal the golden stamens. They are borne in an umbel at the end of a 15-in (35-cm) scape.
   Calostemma purpureum. The most widely grown species, it is native of southern Australia and New South Wales and, like *C. luteum*, has long linear leaves produced after the flowers. The blooms are rosy-purple, arranged in an umbel of 12 to 20 around the end of the slender 20-in (50-cm) stem, and they remain in fresh condition for several weeks.

CALOCHORTUS (Liliaceae)
   A genus of about 50 species, native of the desert-lands and lower mountainous slopes of north-western and Central America and Mexico and taking their name from *kallos*, beauty, and *chortus*, grass, an allusion to their slender grass-like leaves. In its native lands it is known as the mariposa or star lily. It has a tunicated bulb and bears white or yellow flowers on branched stems. The perianth consists of six segments bearded on the inside, each with a central honey gland, the three outer segments being sepal-like and smaller than the inner segments. Stamens six, slightly adhering to the base of the segments.

Culture. One of the most difficult of all Liliaceae to establish away from its natural habitat, requiring an open, sunny situation and a well-drained soil. So important is the matter of drainage that where the soil is heavy, the bulbs should be planted in raised beds and into a soil which has been made porous by incorporating some shingle or crushed brick, and humus-forming materials

such as clearings from ditches and old mushroom bed compost, dug in to a depth
of at least 12 in (30 cm).

Plant the bulbs in October or November, 4 in (10 cm) deep and 4 in (10 cm)
apart, the method being to remove 3 in (7·5 cm) of top soil and to plant on a
layer of sand before covering the bulbs. To guard against the heavy rains of
winter, cover the beds with wattle hurdles or fronds of bracken to a depth of
8 in (20 cm), removing these early in spring. After the flower stems have died
down, it is recommended that frame lights be placed over the beds to keep the
bulbs dry while ripening. They require moisture only when beginning to grow
in spring and until they have finished flowering. Given this treatment, they will
be long-lasting and will bloom each year in profusion.

Propagation. The bulbs should be undisturbed for at least four or five years,
when, upon lifting, offsets will be found clustering around the base. They are
detached and grown on in boxes of sandy loam in a frame or greenhouse. They
should be kept dry during winter and protected from frost and will be ready to
plant out into prepared beds in two years. It should be said that if the soil is
heavy, it is better to grow the later summer-flowering species and to treat as
half-hardy, planting them early in spring and lifting the bulbs each year in
autumn after ripening. They are, however, more free-flowering when left undisturbed.

With certain species, small bulbils are often produced in the axils of the leaves
on the upper part of the stem. These are detached when ripe and planted on the
surface of a sandy compost in boxes or pans, to be grown on in a frame or
greenhouse.

Seeds may also be sown in August when ripe, or in spring, in boxes containing
a sandy compost. Sow thinly for the seedlings should not be disturbed for two
years. They are then moved to small pots in which they are grown on for two
more years before being planted into prepared beds. They must be kept dry
during winter and free from frost. They will bloom five to six years after sowing,
but this may be reduced by about a year if the seeds are germinated in heat.
Where left undisturbed, most species will seed themselves following a warm
sunny summer and in a well-drained soil will quickly establish themselves.

Species. *Calochortus albus* (syn. *Cyclobothra alba*). Native of California, it grows
18 in (45 cm) tall, and in early summer bears on each stem up to 20 nodding
blooms of pinkish-white with a purple blotch at the base of each segment. The
petals are also fringed with small hairs.

Calochortus amabilis (syn. *C. pulchellus*). Known as golden lanterns in its
native California, it is with *C. albus* and *C. benthamii* the most reliable of the
species under cultivation. It bears on a 12-in (30-cm) stem, four to six nodding
flowers of golden yellow which are scented.

Calochortus benthamii (syn. *C. elegans luteus*). One of the easier Californian species, at one time considered a variety of *C. elegans* but now classified as a separate species. It is valuable in that it blooms very late in summer, prolonging the season. It has long linear leaves and bears upright flowers of pale citron yellow, two to four to a 6-in (15-cm) stem. It is at its best in the alpine garden.

Calochortus clavatus. The most vigorous Californian species, it grows 3 ft (90 cm) tall and blooms during midsummer. The large flowers are yellow veined with brown and are borne four to six to a much-branched stem.

Calochortus coeruleus. A dwarf species of the mountainous slopes of Sierra Nevada, it grows 4 in (10 cm) tall and bears in July, dainty flowers of pale blue, fringed with blue hairs, while the outer segments are spotted with pale blue.

Calochortus elegans. A most attractive Californian, in bloom during mid-summer and producing on a 6-in (15-cm) stem, three to five greenish-white flowers tinted with violet at the base. *Amoenus* has pink flowers, the surface of which is covered in silky hairs.

Calochortus leichtlinii. It is native of the mountainous ranges of northern California, where it grows from 20 in (50 cm) tall and in midsummer bears large cup-shaped flowers two to four to a stem. The outer segments are green with crimson stripes, the inner segments being cream-coloured with a purple blotch at the base.

Calochortus lilacinus (syn. *C. uniflorus*). It bears pale-lilac flowers which are scented and beautiful, 6 to 10 appearing on a 6-in (15-cm) stem. A single plant may throw up 10 or more flowering spikes during summer. It requires copious amounts of water while making growth, then dry conditions until it begins to grow again.

Calochortus luteus. Not to be confused with *C. elegans luteus*, it grows 18 in (45 cm) tall, and in July bears large cup-shaped flowers 3 in (7·5 cm) across of deepest yellow with the inner segments fringed with violet hairs.

Calochortus macrocarpus. It is to be found from British Columbia to southern California and it blooms late, during July and August, bearing cup-shaped violet flowers striped with green which measure 4 in (10 cm) across. The flowers are borne singly on a 15-in (37·5-cm) stem.

Calochortus mauveanus (syn. *C. tolmiei*). It bears large cups of creamy-yellow, the surface of the petals being covered in lavender-blue hairs. From the Sierra Nevadas, it grows 5 to 6 in (12·5 to 15 cm) tall and blooms in July.

Calochortus nitidus. August flowering, it grows 18 in (45 cm) tall, each stem bearing 6 to 10 white flowers, the three inner segments having a purple blotch at the base.

Calochortus purdyi. It was discovered in California in 1898 by Mr Carl Purdy of Uriah, the foremost authority on this genus, and it is rare in cultivation. In June it bears white flowers 2 in (5 cm) across, four to six to a 12-in (30-cm) stem, the round inner segments being densely covered with white hairs and blotched with violet at the base.

Calochortus splendens. It blooms early in summer, bearing large lilac-mauve flowers on 12-in (30-cm) stems, the inner segments being marked with purple.

Calochortus venustus. It is hardy and of vigorous habit, growing 18 in (45 cm) tall and bearing in threes or fours, large white cup-shaped flowers 3 in (7·5 cm) across. The inner segments are stained with yellow and purple at the base, where hairs are also present. The variety *citrinus* bears lemon-yellow flowers; *albus* is pure white; while *oculatus* has purple buds which open to large cups with a black centre surrounding the yellow base. This is the only species to flourish in a heavy soil.

Calochortus weedii (syn. *Cyclobothra weedii*). A tender species of desert mountainous slopes of southern California, it bears three to four flat golden-yellow flowers to each 18-in (45-cm) stem. The outer segments are narrow and tapering, the inner broad and wedge-shaped, and covered with long hairs.

CAMASSIA (Liliaceae)

A genus of five species, native of North America and taking their name from quamash, the name given to the plant by the North American Indians who at one time used the bulbs as food. Closely related to *scilla*, it is the American counterpart of the bluebell of Britain. The bulbs are tunicated, the leaves strap-like, while the purple-blue flowers are borne in loose racemes. The perianth consists of six equal segments. Tolerant of partial shade (like the bluebell) they inhabit the sparse forests of the Rocky and Blue Mountains, and meadowlands where they bloom during the early weeks of summer.

Culture. They require a soil which is retentive of moisture during spring and summer but from which excess winter moisture can drain; a soil containing humus in the form of peat or leaf mould and which is light and sandy. The bulbs will decay in a heavy, badly drained soil. They do well in an orchard or spinney and planted in groups in the flower border for they grow from 18 to 36 in (45 to 90 cm) tall. Plant 3 in (7·5 cm) deep and 6 in (15 cm) apart early in autumn, to enable the bulbs to become established before winter. If planting in circular groups, remove the soil to the required depth and over an area sufficient to accommodate a dozen bulb. Plant on a layer of sand. The bulbs are extremely hardy and may be grown almost anywhere.

Propagation. They increase by offsets which will have formed around the mother bulb after several years, or they may seed themselves. They are readily raised from seed sown in a frame or in boxes of sandy loam in spring or summer and will bloom within three to four years of their sowing. Fresh seed will ensure rapid germination and the seedlings will be ready to transplant before the end of summer, to deeper boxes or to a frame where they remain until the following spring.

Species. *Camassia cusickii.* Native of the Blue Mountains of Oregon, it bears asphodel-like flowers of steel-blue in a loose spike on 3-ft (90-cm) stems above rosettes of broad grey-green leaves. The flowers, which measure 2 in (5 cm) across, appear early in summer and are enhanced by the golden anthers. There is a handsome white form, *alba*, which occurs only in localised places in northern California.

Camassia esculenta. Native of British Columbia and Oregon, it comes into bloom in June. It has large white ovoid bulbs and linear leaves 12 in (30 cm) long from which arises the 3-ft (90-cm) tall flower scape. The flowers measure 2 in (5 cm) across and from 12 to 20 appear in a loose raceme. They are of mid-blue with veins of deeper blue, while one segment is separated from the other five. This is the species mostly used by the Indians for the valuable culinary qualities of its bulbs which are baked like potatoes, being floury and of excellent flavour. It is possibly a variety of *C. quamash.*

Camassia fraseri (syn. *C. scillioides*). Native of eastern North America, it has narrow pointed leaves and in midsummer bears 12 to 30 blooms in a loose raceme on a stem 18 in (45 cm) tall. The flowers measure 1 in (2·5 cm) across and are of clearest blue.

Camassia leichtlinii. A vigorous native of British Columbia and Oregon, it grows 3 ft (90 cm) tall and bears large flowers of creamy-white in an elegant raceme. The variety *semi-plena*, introduced by van Tubergen, bears double flowers, while *atroviolacea* bears flowers of deepest mauve, formed in an elegant spike. In bloom midsummer.

CARDIOCRINUM (Liliaceae)

A genus of three species, native of the Himalayas and eastern Asia, which at one time were included in the genus Lilium. They differ in that their bulbs have few scales, while the seed capsules are toothed. They are plants of dense woodlands of Assam and Yunnan, where the rainfall is the highest in the world and they grow best in shade and in a moist humus-laden soil. The basal leaves are cordate, bright-green and glossy; the flowers trumpet-like with reflexed segments. They are borne in umbels of 10 to 20 on stems 10 to 12 ft (3 to 3·6 metres) tall. In their native land they are to be found growing with magnolias and rhododendrons.

Culture. The bulbs are dark green and as large as a hockey ball. Plant 2 ft (60 cm) apart early in spring, away from a frost pocket and with the top part exposed. Three bulbs planted together in a spinney or in a woodland clearing will present a magnificent sight when in bloom. They require protection from the heat of summer and a cool root run; they are also gross feeders so the soil should be well-enriched with decayed manure and should contain a large amount of peat or leaf mould. The bulbs will begin to grow in the warmth of spring, and by early June the flower stems will have attained a height of 8 ft

(2·4 metres) or more and will be bright green with a few scattered leaves. The basal leaves will measure 10 in (25 cm) wide, like those of the arum. The flowers appear in July and last only a few days to be replaced by attractive large seed pods, while the handsome basal leaves remain green until the autumn. The flower stems are hollow.

Propagation. After flowering and the dying back of the leaves, the bulb also dies. Early in November it should be dug up, when it will be seen that three to five small bulbs are clustered around it. These are replanted 2 ft (60 cm) apart with the nose exposed and into soil that has been deeply worked and enriched with leaf mould and decayed manure. They will take two years to bear bloom, but if several are planted each year there will always be some at the flowering stage. To protect them from frost, the newly planted bulbs should be given a deep mulch either of decayed leaves or peat shortly after planting, while additional protection may be given by placing fronds of bracken or hurdles over the mulch.

Plants may be raised from seed sown in a frame in a sandy compost or in boxes in a greenhouse. If the seed is sown in September when harvested, it will germinate in April. In autumn the seedlings will be ready to transplant into a frame or into boxes, spacing them 3 in (7·5 cm) apart. They need moisture while growing but very little during winter when dormant. In June they will be ready to move to their flowering quarters such as a clearing in a woodland where the ground has been cleaned of perennial weeds and fortified with humus and plant food. Plant 2 ft (60 cm) apart and protect the young plants until established with low boards erected around them. They will bloom in about eight years from sowing time.

Species. *Cardiocrinum cathayanum.* Native of western and central China, it will grow 3 to 4 ft (90 cm to 1·2 metres) tall and halfway up the stem produces a cluster of oblong leaves. The funnel-shaped flowers are borne three to five to each stem and appear in an umbel at the top. They are white or cream, shaded with green and spotted with brown and appear early in July. The plant requires similar conditions to *C. giganteum* and behaves in like manner.

Cardiocrinum cordatum. Native of Japan, it resembles *C. giganteum* with its heart-shaped basal leaves, which grow from the scales of the greenish-white bulb and which, like those of the paeony (with which it may be planted), first appear bronzey-red before turning green. The flowers are produced horizontally in sixes or eights at the end of a 6-ft (1·8-metre) stem and are ivory-white shaded green on the outside, yellow in the throat and spotted with purple. They are deliciously scented.

Cardiocrinum giganteum. Native of Assam and the eastern Himalayas where it was found by Dr Wallich in 1816 in the rain-saturated forests. It was first raised from seed and distributed by the Botanical Gardens of Dublin, and first flowered in the British Isles at Edinburgh in 1852. Under conditions it enjoys, it will send up its hollow green stems (which continue to grow until autumn) to a height of 10 to 12 ft (3 to 3·6 metres), each with as many as 10 to 20 or more funnel-shaped blooms 6 in (15 cm) long. The flowers are white, shaded green on the outside and reddish-purple in the throat. Their scent is such that when the air is calm the plants may be detected from a distance of 100 yd. Especially is their fragrance most pronounced at night. The flowers droop downwards and are at their best during July and August. The large basal leaves which surround the base of the stem are heart-shaped and short-stalked.

CHASMANTHE (Iridaceae)

A genus of six or seven species, native of tropical and southern Africa and allied to antholyza, with the same flattened corm covered in a fibrous tunic. They take their name from the Greek *chasme*, gaping, and *anthos*, flower, in allusion to the widely opening blooms. The lower leaves are narrow and two-ranked, while the flowers of scarlet or orange are borne in a short terminal spike. The perianth tube is curved, the upper part being cylindrical with the segments unequal, the upper segment arched, the others being shorter and spreading. The stamens and style are also arched and protected by the upper perianth lobe. Native of equatorial and southern Africa, *C. aethiopica*, flowering late in summer in the British Isles northern Europe and North America, may be grown out-doors, while *C. floribunda*, being earlier into bloom, is best grown in a cool greenhouse or frame.

Culture. The corms of *C. aethiopica* should be planted outside in an open, sunny situation, early in May—a month earlier in those gardens enjoying a warm spring climate. Plant in a friable well-drained soil fortified with some decayed manure and set the corms 4 in (10 cm) deep and 8 in (20 cm) apart. After flowering and when the foliage has begun to die down, lift and string up in an airy, frost-free room for the foliage to complete its functions. After about a month the foliage is cut away just above the top of the corms, which are then placed in boxes of dry sand or peat for the winter. They may be left in the ground only in those gardens where winter frosts are excluded.

Where growing indoors, plant the corms early in the year in pots or boxes containing a compost made up of fibrous loam, peat and sand. Set the corms 2 in (5 cm) deep and 2 in (5 cm) apart and give no water until growth commences in spring. After flowering, dry off the corms, removing the foliage when it has died back and store the new corms in boxes of sand until ready to plant again in January.

Propagation. At the base of the old corm a new one will have formed as for gladiolus. This is detached when the foliage is removed and is stored during winter in a frost-free room. Where the plants are to occupy the ground all the year, the clumps should be lifted and divided, as for montbretia and tritelia, every four to five years.

Plants may also be raised from seed sown early in the year, in gentle heat, in boxes containing a sandy compost or in spring in a frame.

Prick off the seedlings in August and grow on for 12 months, giving the minimum of water during winter, when the plants will have formed small corms. These should be dried off and stored during winter and replanted in outdoor beds in spring.

Species. *Chasmanthe aethiopica.* Native of Cape Province, eastern Africa and Ethiopia, where it is usually found about rocks and beneath trees or shrubs, producing its one-sided seven-flowered spike at a height of 3 ft (90 cm). The flowers are scarlet and orange with a long perianth tube, twisted at the base and shortly pouched. The top segment protrudes beyond the others, thus protecting the stamens and style. In northern Europe and North America it blooms during July and August.

Chasmanthe floribunda. Native of Cape Province, where it blooms in July and August. It blooms in May and June in the British Isles and northern Europe, grows 2 ft (60 cm) high and bears 20 to 25 flowers in a two-ranked spike. The flowers are orange or yellow with a long perianth tube, the upper part tapering into the lower part, which is twisted at the base as with *C. aethiopica*.

CHIONODOXA (Liliaceae)

A genus of six species closely related to the squills and taking their name glory of the snow from *chion*, snow, and *doxa*, glory. They are native of the higher mountainous regions of Turkey, Crete and Asia Minor, appearing in spring with the melting snow. They are at their loveliest in short grass or in the shrubbery, beneath forsythias and azaleas with their flowers of golden yellow. They also bloom with the snowdrops and scillas and like them possess extreme hardiness. They are also suitable for a trough or alpine garden, also for growing in pans indoors or in the alpine house. The American gardener, Louise Wilder, in *Adventures in my Garden*, describes the chionodoxas as being 'like exquisite bits of enamel-work'. They will increase more rapidly than any bulb and, unlike the crocus and other flowers of early spring, the blooms do not resent the cold winds and sleet showers by closing up to protect themselves. Introduced in 1877 by Mr George Maw who discovered a drift of *C. luciliae* in Turkey at 7,000 ft, it first flowered in England in the next year, though some years before the French botanist, Boissier, had found it in Asia Minor at a similar elevation. The chionodoxas have small fleshy ovoid bulbs from which arise linear leaves 2 in (5 cm) long, while the flowers are borne in tiny racemes or umbels on one or more stem 4 to 9 in (10 to 22.5 cm) tall. They differ from *scilla* in that the perianth segments are joined at the base.

Culture. Chionodoxas should be planted in September in clusters, setting the bulbs no more than 2 in (5 cm) deep. It is not so tolerant of damp, shady conditions as the snowdrop or winter aconite, so reserve the more shady corners for these flowers. The chionodoxa enjoys a soil with plenty of leaf mould or peat, but above all it must be given some of the sharp sand or grit in which it grows naturally. As the bulbs quickly reproduce themselves both from offsets and self-sown seed, a light mulch during midwinter will help them to retain vigour as well as providing protection which will encourage them to come into bloom when most appreciated, in March. A mixture of decayed manure and peat or leaf mould would be ideal.

Indoors, plant half a dozen bulbs of several species and varieties in a large seed pan. When taken indoors early in the year they will come into bloom late in January. Starting with *C. sardensis*, the various species bloom, in turn, through the later winter and early spring months. Cover the outside of the pan with a piece of black material, and the effect will cause astonishment. Alternatively, the bulbs may be planted in a large shallow glass or painted pottery bowl. Place some broken crocks at the bottom before filling with compost and mix into the compost a small handful of crushed charcoal which will keep the soil sweet over a long period.

Propagation. Reproduction is by offsets, which form around the older bulbs and by self-sown seed. Or they are raised from seed sown in June when ripe, either in a frame or in boxes of sandy compost. Seed may also be sown in the shrubbery or in ground devoid of grass as beneath mature trees. Sow thinly, just covering the seed with sand and keep moist during their first summer and autumn.

Species. *Chionodoxa cretica.* Native of northern Crete, it blooms in April and bears in ones or twos, white or palest blue flowers on 9-in (23-cm) stems. The flowers measure half an inch (1·25 cm) across.

Chionodoxa gigantea. Native of Turkey and Asia Minor, it bears clear-blue flowers which are larger than those of other species. It is also later to bloom, being at its best in April. There is a white form, *alba*, of glistening beauty. Both bloom on 6-in (15-cm) stems and are like tiny lilies.

Chionodoxa luciliae. Native of Turkey and Asia Minor. From the greenish-white pear-shaped bulbs arise spikes of 6 to 10 flowers, each measuring about 1 in (2·5 cm) across, of vivid or pale blue with a large white contrasting centre. They bloom on 6-in (15-cm) stems. There is a white form, *alba*, like a tiny spray of white orchids, while pink giant bears elegant sprays of soft clear pink on 8-in (20-cm) stems and is valuable for cutting for small vases.

Chionodoxa nana. Native of the mountainous regions of Crete, it is the most dwarf species, with short linear leaves and grows only 3 in (7·5 cm) tall. Its flowers are white or pale blue, less than 2 in (1·25 cm) across and borne in umbels of three or four early in spring.

Chionodoxa sardensis. Native of the mountains of Sardinia, it bears its dainty sprays of six to eight blooms on 4-in (10-cm) stems very early in spring. The flowers are of brilliant gentian blue, free of any white at the centre, which intensifies their beauty.

CHLIDANTHUS (Amaryllidaceae)

A genus of a single species, native of South America and Mexico and closely related to hippeastrum. It takes its name from the Greek *clideios*, delicate, and *anthos*, a flower, and was at one time classed with *pancratium*.

Culture. Native of the Andes of Chile and Peru and of the Argentine, it requires the protection of a greenhouse in the more exposed parts—though where winter frosts are absent the bulbs may be planted at the foot of a sunny wall to be left undisturbed for several years. Lift the bulbs in autumn and winter in a frost-free room, to replant again late in April when they will bloom in July and August. Covering the bulbs with ashes or leaves during winter will give protection where the bulbs are to be left in the ground.

They require a well-drained sandy loam into which has been incorporated some peat or leaf mould and dehydrated cow manure, obtainable from most bulb suppliers. Plant with the nose just exposed and 18 in (45 cm) apart. After flowering, cover the bulbs with lights to exclude the rain until lifted at the end of autumn—or until spring where the bulbs are left in the ground.

Where growing indoors, plant three bulbs to a 6-in (15-cm) pot or five to a larger pot, leaving the nose exposed. They require a compost made up of fibrous loam, leaf mould, dehydrated cow manure and coarse sand in equal parts. Plant early in spring (March), bringing on the plants by increasing their moisture requirements as growth commences and the sun increases in strength. After flowering, dry off gradually by placing the pots on their side, then remove the bulbs, clean and store in boxes of sand or peat until required to be started into growth again the following spring.

Propagation. Around the base of mature bulbs will be found the offsets which are detached and grown on in boxes of sandy compost. They will reach flowering size in three years. Alternatively seed may be sown in spring in boxes containing a sandy compost in a greenhouse or frame. The seedlings are transplanted to 3-in (7·5-cm) pots and grown on for a year before being moved to larger pots. It will take four to five years until they bloom.

Species. *Chlidanthus fragrans* (syn. *Pancratium luteum*). It has large ovoid bulbs, in size like a large single-nosed daffodil, and grey-green strap-like leaves which appear at the same time as the flowers. These are borne on a 12-in (30-cm) scape and are funnel-shaped and erect. They appear in an umbel of three or four and are 4 in (10 cm) long. They are bright yellow with a delicious lily-like scent. The petals are attractively reflexed.

The variety *chrenbergi*, native of Mexico, grows 15 in (37·5 cm) tall and has horizontal flowers, the three outer segments of which are wider than the inner segments. The flowers are of similar colouring and are scented. Both the species and the variety bloom early in July outdoors in the British Isles and northern Europe, a month earlier indoors.

CLIVIA (Amaryllidaceae)

A genus of three species, native of Natal and the Transvaal and named in honour of the Clive family (Clive of India). They have imperfect bulbs consisting of leaf bases but with strong fibrous roots, while the strap-like leaves are arranged in two rows. They are deep green and leathery. The flowers are borne in umbels of 10 to 20 from December until March, or early in summer.

Culture. Clivias require the same culture as the agapanthus. They are not fully hardy in the British Isles and North America but may be grown in tubs or in large pots in the greenhouse or garden room, in a minimum winter temperature of 50° F (10° C). High temperatures are not essential, though the plants may be forced into early flowering in a temperature of 65° F (18° C). When the buds show colour, the temperature should be lowered to 55° F (13° C).

The plants require a compost made up of fibrous loam, dehydrated manure, leaf mould or peat and coarse sand or grit in equal parts. They are gross feeders but, like the *hippeastrum* and *crinum*, resent disturbance and should be allowed to remain in the pot or tub for a number of years before lifting and dividing. In this way, they will bloom better each year. To maintain their vigour, the plants should be given a top-dressing after flowering.

As the plants make growth they will require copious amounts of water, but after flowering only enough to keep them alive. Older plants form large clumps, filling a tub of 2 to 3 ft (60 to 90 cm) diameter and for this reason have lost popularity with modern gardening in restricted spaces.

Propagation. The time to divide the clumps is when the plants begin to make new growth in autumn or in spring, depending upon species and flowering time. Remove the plant from tub or pot, wash off the old compost and pull apart the offsets or cut them with a sharp knife, replanting each portion in pots containing the previously suggested compost. They will quickly become re-established if placed in a temperature of 60° F (16° C) and frequently syringed.

Clivias may also be raised from seed. So that the seed is maintained in the correct condition for rapid germination, Messrs Thompson and Morgan of Ipswich offer the white seeds of *C. miniata* in airtight polythene containers so that quick germination is assured. The seeds cost about 5p each and should not be removed from the container until ready to sow. Use a 2½-in pot for each seed and the John Innes compost. After inserting the seed just below the surface, water well and place the pot in a propagator or greenhouse so that a humid atmosphere and a temperature of 70° F (21° C) can be provided until germination. Under these conditions, the seed will germinate in six to eight weeks and the plants will come into bloom within two years from sowing time. The seedlings should be removed from the propagator and grown on in a temperature of 60° F (16° C) when they have formed their seed leaf. Later, they should be repotted into 3-in (7·5-cm) pots and to flowering-size pots in about 12 months' time.

Species. *Clivia gardeni*. Native of Natal it is named after Captain Garden, who discovered it in 1855. The rich green leaves are 2 ft (60 cm) long and the reddish-orange flowers are tipped with green. They are borne in umbels of 10 to 20 on an 18-in (45-cm) scape and appear from early January until March.

Clivia miniata. Native of Natal, it has leaves of brightest green and blooms during May and June. The brilliant scarlet flowers have a striking yellow throat and are borne in umbels of 10 to 20 on a two-edged scape 18 in (45 cm) tall. The variety citrina bears lemon-yellow flowers.

Clivia nobilis. It was discovered in southern Africa in 1828 and has strap-like leaves 15 in (38 cm) long. It blooms during May and June. The bright-scarlet flowers, yellow in the throat, are tipped with green and are borne in umbels of 50 to 60 on a scape 12 in (30 cm) tall.

COLCHICUM (*Liliaceae*)

A genus of 65 species, native of the British Isles, Europe, the Mediterranean region and central Asia and taking its name from the Armenian city of Colchis, celebrated as the birthplace of Medea and also for its poisonous plants. Horace, in the thirteenth ode of his second book wrote of

> '. . . every baleful juice
> which poisonous Colchian globes produce.'

C. autumnale, the meadow saffron, is native of the British Isles; northern Europe and the Near East, and from its large elongated tuber or corm, the poisonous drug colchicine known to the ancient Egyptians as a cure for gout is obtained. In Britain the plants were confined to orchards, and though their natural habitat was damp meadowlands they were, on account of their poisonous properties, kept away from grazing animals. Modern apothecaries have found a new use for the plant for it has the ability to increase the number of chromosomes in other plants, so that those hybrids which are sterile may be made fertile.

Generally referred to as the autumn crocus, to which it is not even botanically related and from which it is distinguished by its six anthers (the autumn crocus has only three), the plant is also confused with the saffron crocus, *C. sativus*, for the colchicum is known as meadow saffron by country folk. The colchicums bloom in autumn, also in winter and spring. They bear their flowers before the leaves appear in spring, hence their name of naked ladies; and, whereas the leaves of the crocus always remain neat and tidy, those of the colchicum are long and strap-like, resembling daffodil leaves. For this reason they are usually planted in orchards or in groups in the shrub border or on banks by the side of a lake or pond where their foliage is hidden by other plants. They may be planted with saxifrages for ground covering and at the base of an old wall. The saxifrages, with their bright foliage, will act as a pleasing compliment to the naked blooms and will prevent them from being splashed by heavy rain. Or plant the yellow-flowering spring colchicum *C. luteum* among a bed of *Primula juliae* Romeo with its pansy-purple blooms which will be colourful at the same time. The foliage of the colchicums begins to die back early in June when, like that of the daffodil, it turns an unsightly yellow colour then brown, until towards the end of July it has died right back and may be removed. The bulbs are then dormant for only about two weeks.

The blooms are funnel-shaped with a long slender tube and six oblong segments, erect or spreading, which extend down to the bulb. The six stamens are attached at the base. The ovary is three-celled and three-ribbed, though superior (whereas the crocus is inferior), and it pushes itself from beneath the ground to the surface.

Culture. A flowering-size tuber or corm should be of 20 to 22 cm size though the corms are irregular in shape. If less than 20 cm they may not bloom in their first year. The tuber or corm is covered with a brown fibrous tunic and at 20 cm in diameter may be 4 in (10 cm) long. If the tunic is removed, the corm will be hard and white and will be seen to have a groove running down it. At the base of the groove the new flowering bud is formed.

The tunic enclosing the corm forms a tube at the top which reaches up to soil level and through which the bud pushes its way upwards.

The colchicum requires a soil which is retentive of summer moisture, one enriched with decayed manure and containing peat or leaf mould. They will also benefit from an annual top-dressing given before they begin to bloom in autumn. The bulbs are planted during July for by then the foliage will have died down and this is the most suitable time to lift and divide. They will then re-establish themselves before coming into bloom early in autumn. Plant 3 in (7·5 cm) deep and 6 in (15 cm) apart, for, although they are naked when they bloom, the leaves which come later grow large and untidy and if planted too closely will exhaust the soil.

The corms may be grown in pans to bloom in a window in autumn and may be planted into the open ground after flowering. Or they may be placed in a sunny window without soil or moisture, when they will come into bloom within a few weeks. The flowers will remain fresh for several days entirely without moisture.

Propagation. Every third year the clumps should be lifted in July and replanted, separating the small bulbs from those of larger size so that they may be planted separately. Those of 20- to 22-cm size will bear bloom, while those of smaller size will bloom in their second year. After flowering, the old corm dies back in gladiolus-like manner, those corms growing around it bearing bloom the following year.

Colchicums may be raised from seed sown in a frame, or in pots or boxes indoors or in an outside bed brought to a fine tilth. Sow as soon as the seed is ripe, in spring, then in July each year cover the seedlings (which by then will have died back) with a 1-in (2·5-cm) layer of compost until their fourth year when they should be lifted and replanted in July into their flowering quarters. They will bloom the following autumn and will increase rapidly if given a yearly mulch of decayed manure.

Species and Varieties. *Colchicum agrippinum* (syn. *C. tessellatum*). It is included in the tessellated group, wherein the segments are covered in rectangular markings caused by the presence of deeply coloured veins. Parkinson said that some show 'a chequer on the outside', resembling the chequered daffodil, *Fritillaria meleagris. C. agrippinum* is to be distinguished from other tessellated species by the tapering of the segments to a point. Native of the Levant it grows only 4 in (10 cm) tall and is one of the first to bloom, several flowers arising from each corm towards the end of August. An easy species to establish, the lilac-mauve flowers are chequered with purple.

Colchicum alpinum. It grows in profusion in the Swiss and Italian Alps, being the first species to bloom, its small rosy-lilac flowers appearing early in August. In spring it forms two narrow leaves. It requires similar cultural conditions to those it enjoys in its native habitat and does better under cold conditions, where after flowering it may expect a long rest beneath the snow. If grown in the alpine house, the pans should be placed outdoors and exposed to the elements during winter and spring.

Colchicum atropurpureum. Parkinson described and illustrated it in his *Paradisus* and at one time it was classed as a variety of *C. autumnale.* Its origin is unknown, while it differs from *C. autumnale* only in its shorter tube. Its colouring of deep magenta-purple gives it a particularly warm appearance on a dull autumnal day.

Colchicum autumnale. Native of parts of East Anglia, Wiltshire and Somerset, also of the European Alps, it produces a corm in size and shape like a bantam's egg from which appear, in long succession from early autumn until December, pale mauve-pink flowers about 2 in (5 cm) tall. The segments are narrow and open star-like to reveal white styles. The variety *album* bears white flowers, while the double form *album plenum* bears double flowers of great beauty. Its lilac counterpart, *pleniflorum*, is equally fine. Both doubles have at least 20 segments and they retain their form for several weeks if the weather is kind. The flowers are followed by lance-shaped leaves 8 in (20 cm) long. *C. autumnale* and its varieties will bloom in a sunny window entirely without moisture, while it makes an admirable alpine garden plant.

Colchicum bornmüelleri. Native of Greece and the Levant, it was discovered by Joseph Bornmüller in 1889 and is now classed as a variety of *C. speciosum* from which it differs only in the green perianth tube of the rosy-mauve flowers.

Colchicum bowlesianum. Named in honour of the late Mr E. A. Bowles whose book *The Crocus and Colchicum* has remained the standard work since 1924. The species was discovered in Salonica and first named *C. sibthorpii*, thus adding to the confusion in the nomenclature of the genus. The flower is globular with pointed segments and is lilac-pink, handsomely chequered with purple. The corms are large and bear up to 12 flowers early in winter, while they produce a greater number of leaves than any other species. They grow erect, about 12 in (30 cm) long and are 1 in (2·5 cm) wide.

Colchicum byzantinum. This name was given by Clusius in his *Plantarum Historia* of 1601, since the plant had been sent from Constantinople in 1588 to two ladies living in Vienna. The corms are large and knobbly, about 4 in (10 cm) in diameter and produce 12 to 18 globular flowers of lilac-pink, which appear in succession from early August and throughout autumn. It differs from *C. cilicicum* in that the stamens are tipped with crimson, while the filaments are only half the length of the perianth segments and are dull yellow, those of *C. cilicicum* being bright yellow. The leaves appear in spring and are 12 in (30 cm) long and 6 in (15 cm) wide. They are ribbed or corrugated. This is the finest species for growing in a window, for the corms have a flat base and produce a succession of blooms during autumn entirely without moisture.

Colchicum catacuzenium. It was first collected on Mount Parnes near Athens by von Heldreich and is a hardy species. It bears globular lilac-pink flowers with broad segments and, like *C. luteum*, they appear just above soil level. It is the last of the species to bloom (in March and April) and terminates the sequence begun by *C. alpinum* in August. It requires a well-drained soil but one enriched with humus. Its flowers are followed by several narrow leaves.

Colchicum cilicicum. It was collected by G. P. Baker in Asia Minor. It resembles *C. byzantinum* and like that species will do well in all soils and under all conditions, producing in autumn a succession of large deep-purple flowers. The flowers are enhanced by the brilliant golden filaments.

Colchicum decaisnei. Native of Syria and the Lebanon, there are two forms both growing in the same area, one having small hairs in the throat and with broad segments, the other with narrower segments which open star-like. It is winter-flowering, at its best in November and December, the blooms being of palest pink, almost white, and opening 1 in (2·5 cm) above soil level. In northern Europe the flowers have difficulty in overcoming adverse weather.

Colchicum doerfleri. Native of Macedonia, it requires the protection of an alpine house or a frame, for it blooms in February in northern Europe. The flower grows 2 in (5 cm) above the soil and is pale lilac-rose, its narrow tapering petals opening star-like to reveal white filaments. It forms only two leaves, which are borne after it has finished flowering. It requires a gritty, well-drained compost.

Colchicum giganteum. It was first described by Samuel Arnott of Dumfries in the *Gardener's Chronicle* of December 1902, wherein he told of having received it from the plant collector Max Leichtlin of Baden-Baden the previous year. It is later-flowering than *C. speciosum* and *C. bornmüelleri*, its rosy-purple flowers being borne on strong, erect tubes which are tolerant of the most adverse weather. The blooms shade out to white at the base. In spring it forms large leaves similar to those of *C. speciosum*, to which it is closely related, though the flower is larger.

Colchicum luteum. Native of the Himalayas and northern India, where it is to be found growing up to 6,000 ft, it is late winter- and early spring-flowering, being one of the latest species to come into bloom. It is at its best in the alpine garden, in a soil made porous by incorporating quantities of humus and drainage materials. It is also liable to be devoured by slugs and precautions should be taken. It is a dainty colourful species, brightening the alpine garden during the last days of winter. It enjoys the protection of winter-flowering heathers, which will also hide the foliage when it dies back in summer. The flowers grow only 1 in (2·5 cm) above the ground, with narrow petals which open star-like and are of rich glowing yellow. Several flowers are borne in each spathe.

Colchicum macrophyllum. It was discovered in Crete and is winter-flowering, the first blooms appearing in November. They are funnel-shaped with long narrow segments which open star-like and are of palest lilac, almost white, faintly chequered with darker lilac. The leaves are large, about 12 in (30 cm) long and 6 in (15 cm) wide and are corrugated. They appear in spring and are an attraction to the shrub border at this time of year but will flourish only in a garden where frost is excluded. There is a form, native only of the island of Rhodes, which is smaller in all respects.

Colchicum sibthorpii. It was discovered on Mount Parnes and was originally known as *C. latifolium* because of its broad leaves. It blooms in mid-autumn, its lilac flowers with their broad segments being faintly chequered. The leaves, which appear in spring, are 2 in (5 cm) wide and 6 in (15 cm) long and are blue-green with waved edges.

Colchicum speciosum. Farrer wrote that it was 'one of the most noble and beautiful plants in the world'. The flowers appear in September and are globular with broad segments of deep crimson-purple with a white tube often 12 in (30 cm) long. In spring it bears leaves 12 in (30 cm) long and 3 in (7·5 cm) wide. It requires a rich, moist soil and liberal feeding when the leaves have died back, for both the species and its varieties form a large tuber.

The variety *C. speciosum bornmüelleri magnificum* bears even larger flowers than the type and has a green tube with the white throat higher in the tube than in *C. speciosum bornmüelleri*; while *C. speciosum album* bears flowers of purest white. The blooms will remain fresh for up to 10 days indoors, either with or without water.

In 1900 Messrs Zocher and Co. of Haarlem succeeded in raising the wonderful double-flowered variety, Waterlily, by dusting pollen from *C. autumnale album* on to *C. speciosum album*. It is the most distinctive of all the hybrids and is well named for its multi-petalled flowers of brightest lilac resemble giant water-lilies as they open in the sun.

Using *C. speciosum bornmüelleri*, *C. giganteum* and *C. bowlesianum*, which has passed on its handsome chequering, Messrs Zocher also raised several other fine hybrids, among which was Lilac Wonder, Violet Queen and The Giant. Each of these are autumn-flowering and combine the better qualities of each parent. Lilac Wonder bears its violet-purple flowers, like magnolia blossoms, in long succession. It has narrow segments which reveal only slight traces of chequering, while the flowers have weak tubes and tend to fall over after two days. Violet Queen bears flowers of deepest purple, handsomely chequered and opening to reveal a striking white centre. The most outstanding is The Giant, which blooms later in autumn, the rich lilac flowers having a contrasting white base and a long elegant tube. Here the chequering is almost indistinct on the outer surface, in this respect resembling Lilac Wonder. A vigorous variety, it is most suitable for planting in a shrub border or in an orchard, but it needs the sun to show off its beauty.

Colchicum stevenii. Native of Palestine and Arabia, it was named after the Finnish botanist von Steven and in the British Isles and northern Europe needs the protection of a frame. It is winter-flowering. The 9 to 12 narrow leaves appear with the pale rosy-mauve flowers which have narrow segments and open star-like.

Colchicum tenorii. Native of southern Italy, it is rare in cultivation. It blooms late in autumn, the flowers resembling those of *C. autumnale* in their size and form and are of rosy-mauve lightly chequered with purple. The leaves appear in spring.

Colchicum triphyllum. Native of Morocco, from where it was introduced by Mr Bowles in 1936, receiving an award of merit from the Royal Horticultural Society in February of the next year. It is found in sun-baked screes up to 10,000 ft and these are the conditions it requires. It resembles *C. catacuzenium* in that it forms a tiny globe of rosy-lilac with broad petals, the flowers being followed by three narrow leaves. It blooms during February and March.

Colchicum troodii. Native only to Cyprus, where its home is the Troodos Range, it grows into a large clump which is crowded with flowers. It is found below deciduous trees, growing in partial shade and in pure leaf mould, where it sends up its pale-lilac flowers towards the end of autumn.

Colchicum variegatum. Native of Greece and the islands of the Aegean, it is winter-flowering and in the British Isles and northern Europe is not completely hardy. It forms large egg-shaped tubers and in December appear the rosy-lilac blooms chequered with purple. The flowers have a tuber only 2 in (10 cm) long, so that they seem to sit on the soil.

CONVALLARIA (Liliaceae)

A genus of a single species, native of the British Isles, northern Europe and North America, where it blooms during May and June. It takes its name from *convallis*, a valley, denoting its natural habitat. It has a scaly rhizomatous rootstock from which arise shoots bearing two glossy dark-green, lance-shaped leaves with angular stalks 9 in (22·5 cm) tall, on which are borne 12 to 20 dangling bells of purest white. The blooms are enhanced by the six short recurved lobes and by their deliciously refreshing perfume. They are mostly to be found in deciduous woodlands, enjoying the half light and with their roots in moist leaf mould. Sir Walter Scott wrote:

> Sweet May Lilies richest odours shed
> Down the valley's shady bed.

The flower was also known as Our Lady's tears, the tiny dangling bells appearing like tear-drops from a distance. The flowers are followed late in summer by large fleshy crimson-red berries containing the seeds.

Culture. It requires shade as afforded by a spinney or shrubbery and a soil enriched with humus by way of peat or leaf mould, together with some decayed manure. Old mushroom-bed compost is suitable for this plant, also applied as a top-dressing in November. All too often the plants are to be seen growing in the poor soil of a town garden, where they bear little bloom and receive little attention year after year. They will grow well planted in a narrow bed facing east or north—perhaps beneath the eaves of a house—provided they are kept moist about the roots. Planted near a window which may be opened during their time of flowering, they will scent a large room with their perfume.

The time for planting the 'crowns' or the rootstock is in October, and only fat well-nourished 'crowns' will bloom the following spring; smaller 'crowns' in 18 months. Plant them 6 in (15 cm) apart and 3 in (7·5 cm) below the surface. Too close planting will result in the bed becoming overcrowded in a few years, when the plants should be at their best.

Early bloom may be obtained by making up the beds to the width of a frame. Around the beds boards are fixed in March and frame lights placed across. The lights should be 15 in (38 cm) above soil level so that the blooms are clear of the glass. Beds of lily-of-the-valley in bloom before the end of April and early in may will prove a valuable source of income for sale in small bunches, backed by a fresh green leaf, to high-class florists. Flowers grown under glass will be free of rain splashings and command top prices. Care must be taken in picking the sprays which are gently tugged from the rootstock, while no more than one leaf should be removed from each 'crown', otherwise the plants will bear less bloom the following year.

Specialist growers produce the blossom from early November until May by using retarded 'crowns', usually obtained from Germany. Here, growers keep the crowns during summer and early autumn under refrigerated conditions, in a temperature of just below freezing. The plants are dug up in March, before coming into growth, and are prevented from flowering until placed in a warm greenhouse. Upon receipt of the 'crowns' in autumn, pack them into strong wooden boxes, sterilised compost being placed around them so that they are just covered. Place in a frame or outdoors and cover with 6 in (15 cm) of ashes. There they remain for four weeks to form roots. They are then taken to a darkened greenhouse or shed, where the atmosphere is kept moist and where a temperature of 80° F (27° C) is maintained day and night for two weeks. Pale-yellow shoots will then appear. The plants are thereafter allowed more light each day so that the leaves and stems will have turned a bright-green colour by flowering time. This will be from three to four weeks after taking the plants indoors so that batches may be taken inside at monthly intervals. After flowering, forced 'crowns' are of no further value. It should be said that the plants will need large quantities of moisture during the forcing period.

Where a warm greenhouse is available, outdoor 'crowns' may be lifted early in March, to be planted into large pots containing a mixture of sandy loam and peat and if given a temperature of 50° F (10° C) and kept comfortably moist, they will come into bloom early in April. After flowering, replant the roots without delay.

Propagation. Division of the 'crowns' is the usual method. This is done in October when the largest will bloom the following spring. Plants may be raised from seed sown under glass in August. The seedlings are transplanted in 12 months' time into a frame containing a sandy compost. If planted out in spring, they will begin to bloom the following year.

Species and Varieties. *Convallaria majalis.* Native of the northern temperate regions, it has rhizomatous roots from which arise twin leaves and sprays of dangling bells. It comes into bloom early in May. The variety Fontins Giant blooms three to four weeks later, early in June, and has glaucous leaves and larger bells. *Rosea*, bearing bells of palest pink, is attractive, as is the double-flowered *flore plena*.

COOPERIA (Amaryllidaceae)

A genus of eight species, native of the southern United States and Mexico, with one species also of Brazil. They are bulbous plants, closely related to *Sternbergia* and with the habit of *Zephyranthes*, from which it is to be distinguished by its long cylindrical tube. The flowers, which are borne solitary, are funnel-shaped with spreading segments to give them a star-like appearance. The linear leaves appear with the flowers.

Culture. In the cooler parts, they are best grown under glass, protected from frost. Pot the bulbs three or four to a 6-in (15-cm) pot or pan early in the year, February being a suitable month, and use a compost composed of fibrous loam, leaf mould and coarse sand in equal parts. They may be placed in a frame until mid-April, when they are removed to the greenhouse or garden room or to the sunny window of the home and given ample supplies of moisture until they have finished flowering. Water should be withheld while the leaves are dying back. The bulbs should be removed from the pots in autumn and stored in dry sand during winter, to be started into growth again in February.

If growing in the open, select a sunny, sheltered situation such as at the base of a warm wall and plant the bulbs early in April 4 in (10 cm) deep and 6 in (15 cm) apart, interplanting in two or three rows for maximum effect. They require ample supplies of moisture until flowering ends in July, when they should be dried off by covering with frame lights or cloches. The bulbs are lifted for storing early in autumn and replanted in spring.

Propagation. Around the base of the bulbs will grow the small bulblets. These are detached when the bulbs are lifted and are kept in boxes or jars of silver sand until spring, when they are planted 3 in (7.5 cm) apart in boxes of sandy soil and grown on to flowering size.

Species. *Cooperia drummondii* (syn. *Zephyranthes drummondii*). It is native of Texas and northern Mexico and has rounded bulbs 2 to 3 cm in diameter from which arise narrow leaves 12 in (30 cm) long. The flowers appear early in summer and are white, tinted red on the outside and borne on slender stems 9 in (23 cm) tall. The blooms are at their loveliest in the evening when they diffuse a delicious perfume.

Cooperia pedunculata. The bulbs are larger than those of *C. drummondii*, with longer necks, while the leaves are broader and the flower stems 12 in (30 cm) long. The flowers have tubes nearly 2 in (5 cm) long and are white, flushed on the outside with orange.

CRINUM (Amaryllidaceae)

A genus of about 100 species of evergreen plants, native of tropical Asia, South America, Africa and Australasia. The bulbs are large, rounded at the base and with either a short or long neck and broad strap-like leaves, which are untidy in the garden. The flowers are funnel-shaped and are borne in an umbel of 50 or more. The stalk is thick and fleshy. The flowers open in long succession from a large spathe and appear during summer and autumn. The plant takes its name from the Greek *krinon*, a lily, since it has the appearance of one.

Culture. Several species may be grown outdoors in those gardens with a frost-free winter climate and where they may be planted at the base of a wall which is warmed by the summer sunshine. The hybrid *Crinum × powellii* is capable of surviving several degrees of frost if protected by a covering of dry leaves, bracken or dead fern fronds. If planted against a wall, frame lights may be reared up over the bulbs after they have finished flowering in autumn.

Plant the bulbs early in May with the neck at soil level and space them 12 in (30 cm) apart, possibly in a double row. They require a well-drained soil but one rich in organic food such as dehydrated cow manure or old mushroom-bed compost, for they are gross feeders and will increase rapidly by offsets. If left undisturbed for several years, they will bloom in greater profusion as they become crowded in their pot or in the open ground. The plants should be given a top-dressing each autumn. They will also benefit from an occasional watering with diluted liquid manure (Liquinure) during summer. Though requiring the minimum of moisture during the dormant period, the bulbs need copious amounts of water as they begin to make growth early in summer. The flowers open in long succession rather than all at one time, thus extending the display over several weeks.

Crinum × powellii is suitable for tub culture, to plant with *agapanthus*, for it blooms at the same time. Two or three bulbs may be planted in a tub of about 2-ft (60-cm) diameter and they should be set with their necks just above soil level. Provide a compost similar to that suggested for open-ground culture. They may be grown in cooler climes if the tubs can be removed to a greenhouse, shed or garage at the approach of winter, to be taken outdoors again in April. Where the tubs are placed on a balcony or veranda and they cannot be removed indoors, protection may be given by tying sacking around the tubs and fixing polythene material over them.

For pot culture, use a pot 1 in (2·5 cm) larger all round than the bulb and, once planted, do not disturb for five years. The pot must be well-drained and the compost made up of fibrous loam, leaf mould, dehydrated cow manure and sand in equal parts. Plant the bulbs with the neck above soil level, which should be just below the rim to allow for watering and for top-dressing to be done each year after flowering. Plant in March and start into growth in gentle warmth, giving additional water as the plants make growth. After flowering, withhold water during winter—but not entirely, for most are evergreen and must not be completely dried off. Throughout their life, the handsome leaves will benefit from an occasional wiping with clean water, while syringeing twice a day during summer will keep the foliage fresh and healthy. The plants will also appreciate an occasional syringeing during their rest period though will require little moisture at the roots during this time.

Propagation. After several years, the bulbs will have produced numerous off-sets, the crinum being most liberal in this respect. The offsets are detached when the bulbs are repotted and are grown on in boxes of sandy compost or in a frame for three years until they reach flowering size. The crinum also grows readily from seed and will come into bloom within three to four years of sowing. The large fleshy seeds (fruits) are merely pressed into the surface of a sandy compost in a box or pot which is covered with glass. If they are sown in October in gentle heat and the compost is kept moist, a radicle will appear within two to three months. It then begins to grow roots and in summer produces its first green leaves. The plants should then be moved to a 6-in (15-cm) pot in which they remain until reaching flowering size in two years. They are the most rewarding of the 'exotic' bulbs to raise from seed.

Species and Hybrids. *Crinum amabile* (syn. *C. superbum*). Native of Sumatra, it has a bulb of 2- to 3-in (5- to 7·5-cm) diameter, with a neck 10 in (25 cm) long, from which appear green strap-like leaves 3 ft (90 cm) in length and 4 in (10 cm) wide. It bears 20 to 30 bright-red flowers at the end of a 2-ft (60-cm) stem during November and December. The perianth tube is held erect, the segments being 4 in (10 cm) long and sweetly scented, this being one of the few red flowers with perfume.

Crinum americanum. Native of the southern United States, it has bulbs of 4-in (10-cm) diameter and arching leaves 3 ft (90 cm) long. It bears four to six pure white flowers on a 2-ft (60-cm) stem, the richly scented blooms being cylindrical with narrow segments 4 in (10 cm) long.

Crinum asiaticum. Though native of south-eastern Asia, it may be grown in sheltered gardens of western Europe. It produces a bulb 6 in (15 cm) in diameter with a neck 8 in (20 cm) long, from which arise thin tapering leaves 3 to 4 ft (90 cm to 1·2 metres) in length. The flowers appear in July and are greenish-white, shaded pink on the outside, and have a lily-like perfume. The narrow segments are 4 in (10 cm) long and are recurved to reveal attractive pink stamens. The bulbs are reputed to be poisonous.

Crinum bracteatum (syn. *C. brevifolium*). Native of the Seychelles, with ovoid bulbs 4-in (10-cm) diameter and leaves 18 in (45 cm) long, waved at the margins. The white sweetly scented flowers are borne 12 to 20 on a 12-in (30-cm) stem, their slender tubes being 3 in (7·5 cm) long.

Crinum latifolium. It is to be found throughout tropical Asia and forms a round bulb of 8-in (20-cm) diameter. Its leaves are 3 ft (90 cm) long and 4 in (10 cm) wide, while its flowers are borne during May and June in umbels of 10 to 20 on 18-in (45-cm) stems. They are greenish-white flushed with pink, with a curved perianth tube.

Crinum longifolium (syn. *C. bulbispermum*). Native of Natal and the Transvaal, it was discovered in 1750 and is happy in sheltered gardens of western Britain. The ovoid bulbs have a long cylindrical neck from which arise grey-green leaves 3 ft (90 cm) long. It blooms early in summer (in September in southern Africa) and bears 6 to 12 fragrant white flowers flushed pink on the outside and held on a 12-in (30-cm) stem. Crossed with *C. moorei*, it produced the outstanding hybrid *C.* × *powellii*.

Crinum macowani. Native of Natal it is similar to *C. latifolium*, forming a large round bulb 8 in (20 cm) in diameter and has thin leaves 3 in (7·5 cm) wide. The pale lilac-pink flowers are funnel-shaped and are borne in an umbel of 10 to 15 on a 2-ft (60-cm) stem.

Crinum moorei. Native of Natal it is not as hardy as *C. longifolium* or its hybrid *C.* × *powellii* and in northern Europe should be grown under glass. It makes a large ovoid bulb and bears six to eight rose-pink slightly drooping flowers, which are 6 in (15 cm) or more across. The flowers are held on a 2-ft (60-cm) stem and appear during July.

Crinum pedunculatum. Native of Queensland, it is one of only two genera of the family Amaryllidaceae, native to Australia. It forms a bulb of 4 in (10 cm) diameter with a 6-in (15-cm) neck and has glaucous leaves 3 to 4 ft (90 cm to 1·2 metres) long. The greenish-white flowers are borne during midsummer in umbels of 30 or more on a 3-ft (90-cm) stem, several of which appear from each bulb.

Crinum × *powellii*. A hybrid, it is the finest form for British gardens and those of northern Europe and North America, blooming from July until September. It forms a large bulb of 5 to 6 in (12·5 to 15 cm) diameter and bears lily-like blooms of rose-pink in umbels of 6 to 10, held on a 2-ft (60-cm) stem and opening in long succession. They are sweetly scented. The form *album* bears pure-white flowers, and *krelagei* has blooms of deeper pink.

CROCOSMIA (MONTBRETIA) (Iridaceae)

A genus of six species, native of tropical and South Africa and taking its name from *crocos*, saffron, and *osme*, smell, for the dried flowers when immersed in warm water release the sweet scent of saffron. Though native of warmer climes, the plants are hardy in all but the most exposed gardens, where, in a well-drained soil, they will increase rapidly and from July until early October bear their yellow, orange or red flowers in a horizontal spike. They remain fresh in water for 10 days and are valuable for cutting.

Culture. The corms require a light well-drained soil and an open sunny situation, where they may be left undisturbed for several years. They are heavy feeders and before planting the corms 4 to 5 in (10 to 12·5 cm) deep and 12 in

(30 cm) apart early in May, the soil should be enriched with dehydrated cow manure or old mushroom-bed compost, together with some leaf mould. They may be planted in the herbaceous border or in a narrow border to themselves, where they may be left undisturbed for several years, until they have formed large clumps capable of producing numerous flowering spikes in long succession. By mid-autumn, the leaves will have begun to die back and, after removing in November, ashes should be heaped over the plants as protection against frost.

Crocosmias may be grown under glass, planting in deep boxes or three corms to a 5-in (12·5-cm) pot. They should be planted 1 in (2·5 cm) deep in a compost made up of fibrous loam, dehydrated manure, leaf mould and sand in equal parts. Plant in autumn and allow them to remain in a frame or frost-free shed until new growth appears early in spring. During winter give no water. They should then be moved to a greenhouse or garden room and brought on by giving increasing amounts of water as the summer temperature increases. They will require supporting as the flower stems form, and this is done by inserting around the pot (or box) thin stakes painted green, around which green twine is fastened. After flowering, the plants are dried off and may be allowed to remain in the pots to bloom again the following year.

Propagation. After four to five years in the open ground, the clumps will have grown 12 in (30 cm) across and the quality of bloom will deteriorate if not split up and replanted into newly prepared ground. This is done in spring when the plants begin to make fresh growth and when they will quickly re-establish themselves. Each of the small cormlets may be replanted and will come into bloom in two years.

Crocosmias may also be raised from seed sown in spring, in boxes or pans of sandy compost, in which they remain for 12 months, being planted out after hardening, early the following summer.

Species. *Crocosmia aurea* (syn. *Tritonia aurea*; *Montbretia aurea*). It has a fibrous-coated corm and narrow sword-like leaves 12 in (30 cm) long. The flowers are golden-orange with a long cylindrical perianth tube and are borne in slender panicles of 10 to 15 on winged stems 2 ft (30 cm) tall. It blooms from July until September. The variety *imperialis* has fiery red flowers 1 in (2·5 cm) across.

From *C. aurea* and *C. pottsii*, Lemoine raised the Montbretia hybrids (*Montbretia crocos-miiflora*), which bloom late in summer and in autumn, bearing their star-like flowers 10 to 20 to a panicle on graceful arching stems 3 ft (90 cm) tall. Citronella bears large flowers of clear lemon-yellow; Rhinegold is deeper yellow; and Prometheus, golden bronze with a maroon centre. Vesuvius bears flowers of brilliant scarlet; and Lady Oxford, flowers of pale yellow, shaded with peach pink, a most attractive variety. Outstanding too is Emily McKenzie, the large flat blooms being of orange-red with crimson-brown flakings.

Narcissus cyclamineus Beryl with *Muscari azureum* and
Chionodoxa gigantea

Crocus scene

Crocus chrysanthus: Snow Bunting and Blue Pearl

Crocosmia masonorum. Native of Natal it has a tunicated corm and sword-like leaves. It blooms during July and August, bearing 12 to 30 orange-red flowers arranged in a double row in an arching raceme on stems 3 ft (90 cm) tall.

Crocosmia pottsii. It blooms during August and September, bearing its orange-yellow flowers flushed with red on the outside, on a slender arching stem 3 ft (90 cm) tall.

CROCUS (Iridaceae)

A genus of about 75 species, native of the Mediterranean regions and given their name, the Chaldean name for saffron, by Theophrastus. The corm is covered by several scaly leaves and from them arise buds which form the new corm on top of the old one. The channelled leaves arise erect and usually appear before the flowers, which have a long, slender tube replacing the stalk. They appear above the ground wrapped in one or two shielding spathes. They have three stamens and a stigma divided into three stigmata, coloured white, yellow or red. The flowers are borne singly, occasionally in cymes and have three inner and three outer segments which give them a globular appearance when closed—they are star-like when open. They remain closed during dull weather and at night, thus protecting the nectar for visiting butterflies and bees on sunny days. Usually the exterior surface of the outer segments is duller than the inner surface and it is often feathered or stippled, possibly for camouflage effect. The ovary is situated at the base of the perianth tube, where it is protected from adverse weather.

The flowering season is autumn, winter and spring, thus it is possible to enjoy their beauty from August until May. The autumn- and early winter-flowering species are mostly native of Spain and northern Africa, where they bloom before or at the same time as the leaves.

The first species to be grown in northern Europe and the British Isles was *Crocus aureus* followed by *C. vernus*, *C. sativus* and *C. nudiflorus*, each of which was known to Gerard. He mentions in his *Herbal* that *C. aureus* 'with flowers of a most perfect shining yellow colour, from afar like a hot glowing cole of fire' was sent to him by Jean Robin, gardener to the kings of France towards the end of the sixteenth century.

Culture. The crocus may be divided into two main groups: (*a*) autumn- and early winter-flowering and (*b*) late winter- and spring-flowering. Corms of the former should be planted early in July. The corms vary in size with each species but usually a 7- or 8-cm corm will bear bloom the first season and is a suitable size for outdoor planting; a 9- or 10-cm corm is used for indoor flowering. Outdoors, the corms may be planted in generous drifts beneath trees about the shrubbery or as an edging to a flower border. They are admirable subjects for an alpine garden—where they are rarely to be found 'yet nothing in the world is better suited there', wrote Reginald Farrer. Their dainty chalices of purple

I

and gold are among the foremost glories of the alpine garden. They may also be planted between stones of crazy paving. Plant the corms 3 in (7·5 cm) deep, planting too deeply often being the cause of crocuses failing to bloom, while they will not readily increase when planted deeply, unless the soil is especially light. They require a well-drained sandy loam into which is incorporated some decayed manure and an open, sunny situation, for the flowers close up in shade, while the corms need the warmth of the summer sunshine to bake them, so that they will be free-flowering. Plant 3 to 4 in (7·5 to 10 cm) apart, preferably on a layer of sand if the soil is heavy and the ground is not well-drained.

Every fourth year the corms should be lifted and divided, replanting into fresh ground. This should be done in July for the autumn- and early winter-flowering species, and early in September for the spring-flowering crocuses, though they may be planted up to mid-November. When lifting, wash away the soil and remove any old and decayed corms before replanting almost anywhere in the garden—as long as the sun can reach them, for with their neat foliage they never become unsightly as do colchicums and daffodils, nor is there any need to knot the leaves after flowering. Usually, the grass-like leaves will die back unnoticed.

The early writers have said that the crocus enjoys 'some manure', which may be taken to mean humus-forming materials such as scrapings from around a stack, or hop manure. Old mushroom-bed compost is suitable, together with peat or leaf mould. Rather than a too rich soil, they enjoy one supplied with humus and thrive on potash. Where planting in short grass—and the earlier-flowering species are most suitable for a lawn, for they die back before it is time to mow the grass—cut the turf on three sides in 12-in (30-cm) squares and roll it over on the side which has been left un-cut, like a box-lid on hinges. Soil to a depth of 4 in (10 cm) is removed. At the bottom place a 1-in (2·5-cm) layer of decayed humus covered with a sprinkling of sulphate of potash, or wood ash which has been stored dry. Then plant the corms flat part downwards, covering them with more humus before replacing the turf and treading it firmly to exclude air pockets. Ten to twelve corms may be planted to each section and a more pleasing display may be had if the turves are removed unevenly.

The less robust species, e.g. *C. ocholeucrus*, which may be cut down by cold winds when at their best, should be confined to a sheltered nook of the alpine garden or rockery where cold winds will pass over them. Here, in the winter sunshine, they will bloom untroubled by the elements. Several of the yellow-flowering species may be troubled by birds which find the nectar much to their liking during winter and early spring. They will be kept away by black thread fastened to small twigs above the flowers as the buds begin to show colour. Birds will rarely attack purple-flowering species but in a severe winter may destroy dozens of yellow flowers in the matter of a few hours. Mice, too, may scrape away the soil from the corms and eat them, so dust the corms with a deterrent before planting.

The crocus species make admirable pot plants and none more so than the winter-flowering species which may be seen in their full beauty where given the protection of glass. The pots or pans may be placed in a frame or in the open until the first species begin to bloom early in autumn when moved indoors. They are admirable subjects for the alpine house to provide a succession of bloom from August until May, when the pans are placed outdoors in a sunny situation for the corms to ripen. Or the pans may be removed to a plunge bed and covered with a mixture of decayed manure and leaf mould (or peat) which will prove a valuable top-dressing.

Use a compost made up of sterilised loam, peat or leaf mould, dehydrated manure and coarse sand in equal parts and plant the corms 1 in (2·5 cm) deep and 2 in (5 cm) apart. Plant the autumn-flowering species in July, the spring-flowering species in September. They should be given four to five weeks in the frame or plunge bed covered with an inch of fibre to form their roots. Six to eight corms may be planted to a pan. They will require only the minimum amount of moisture until growth commences and after flowering, they should be dried off.

Propagation. *Crocus nudiflorus* is increased by stolons, which it sends out for some distance from the parent, the roots often pushing up to the surface and having the appearance of long white grubs. They are detached and replanted. Other species are lifted and divided every five to six years when the newly formed corms are detached from those which have decayed. From above the old corms appear one or more new corms which will have formed a clump of a dozen or more and to maintain vigour, they should be split up into single corms for replanting into fresh ground. Division is done as soon as the foliage has died back, replanting the autumn- and early winter-flowering species immediately, while those which bloom in spring may be stored in sand until autumn.

Except the Dutch yellow crocus, which is sterile, most species and varieties are readily raised from seed. Many will seed themselves, especially *C. tomasinianus*, possibly the best of all crocuses to naturalise in short grass or in the shrub border. Seed is saved from the large capsules which, by mid-May for the autumn-flowering species, will have pushed up above soil level. Time should be allowed for the seed to ripen before harvesting. Seed of the spring-flowering species will be ready to remove early in July, before the capsule splits and the seeds scatter, to be carried away by birds and ants. *C. korolkowii* is difficult to harvest for it does not push its capsule above the ground.

Seed is sown during July or August, sowing in pans or boxes containing the John Innes compost. Only lightly cover with sand. After sowing, stand the containers outdoors or in a frame; or on the greenhouse bench. The seed will germinate the following spring, but the young plants should not be disturbed for two years when the cormlets will have attained pea size. They may be removed from the compost by drying off. Then empty the containers on to a large sheet of brown paper. The cormlets are planted out 2 in (5 cm) deep and 2 to 3 in (5 to 7·5 cm) apart where they are to flower in three or four years, that is four to five years after the seed has been sown.

Species and Varieties. *Crocus aërius.* Closely related to *C. biflorus* and *C. chrysanthus*, with which it grows in Asia Minor, it comes later into bloom, the bright lilac-blue flowers with their yellow throats appearing early in March. The globular blooms have the outer segments shaded with crimson, while in the form *majus* the blooms are twice as large as the type. Though it soon dies out, it seeds in profusion, so that once planted there is usually some in bloom each year.

Crocus aleppicus. Native of the hillsides of Damascus, it has small white flowers, feathered externally with pale lilac and has white anthers. Rare in cultivation, it blooms in midwinter, is difficult to establish outdoors and is best confined to the alpine house.

Crocus ancyrensis. Known as the Ankara crocus it is native of Turkey and is a late winter-flowering species, the tiny orange flowers appearing in January. The flowers have blunt segments of which the outer may be feathered with bronze. Its flowers are long-lasting, provided they can be given a sunny pocket in the rock garden, protected from cold winds. The leaves appear with the flowers.

Crocus asturicus. Native of the mountains of Asturias in northern Spain, it bears deep violet-purple flowers 4 in (10 cm) long with orange stamens, and blooms throughout October and November, being one of the most reliable species for flowering at this time of year. The leaves, which grow 12 in (30 cm) long, appear with the flowers but become more developed afterwards. Less vigorous than *C. nudiflorus*, it should be confined to the rock garden or to short grass, while it is at its best in pans under glass.

Crocus aureus. Grown in Elizabethan gardens, it was the first yellow crocus to be cultivated and from it the (sterile) Dutch Yellow Crocus has been raised, though it sets seed freely itself. Native of south-eastern Europe and Asia Minor, the orange flowers appear in February, set like tiny cups of brass amidst tufts of dark-green leaves. Gerard's description of the flowers being like 'a hot glowing cole of fire' is accurate. There is a variety, *sulphureus*, which bears pale-yellow flowers.

Crocus balansae. A member of the *C. aureus* group, it is native of Smyrna and was named after the French botanist Benedict Balansa. It blooms with *C. aureus* and remains colourful for fully four weeks, bearing flowers of brilliant orange with deep orange stigmata. The variety Zwanenburg has flowers of reddish-orange with the outer segments beautifully stippled with bronze.

Crocus biflorus. Naturalised in parts of Scotland as a garden escape, it is known as the Scottish crocus but more familiarly cloth of silver. Its silvery-mauve flowers resemble those of Our Lady's smock, having a metallic sheen due to the mauve stippling on the outside of the segments. Native of south-eastern Europe, it is one of the annulate group, the lower portion of the corm tunic appearing in numerous overlapping circles. It was so named, by Philip Miller, because it bears, in March, twin flowers in each spathe and is a species of hardiness and vigour. The variety *alexandri*, native of the Levant and the most expensive crocus, bears flowers of pure white with a dark glossy purple exterior, while *argenteus*, native of the hills around Florence, has pale-lilac flowers feathered with mauve. The form *weldenii* has white flowers feathered with pearly grey, while the narrow leaves have a prominent mid-rib. White Lady is also outstanding, bearing flowers of purest white in March.

Crocus boryi. It is to be found growing with *C. niveus*, the two distinct species at one time being classed as *C. marathonisius*, a name no longer applicable. *C. boryi* is also present in the islands of the Greek archipelago and is to be distinguished by the narrow leaves and prominent central white stripe. The white flowers are smaller than those of *C. niveus* and are less robust. It is therefore best grown in pans under glass.

Crocus byzantinus (syn. *C. iridiflorus*). Native of Hungary. Its outer segments are twice as long as the inner ones. When the flower opens, the pale-lilac inner segments remain in an upright position and are narrow and pointed while the deep purple outer segments are broad and blunt and fold back. The unique lilac stigmata provide additional interest to the blooms as they open in September.

Crocus cambessedesii. Named after the French botanist Jacques Cambessedes, it is native only of Majorca and Minorca and is one of the smallest crocuses, growing less than 1 in (2·5 cm) tall. Also, unlike other species with the exception of *C. laevigatus*, it blooms from early autumn until the end of spring, its pale-lilac flowers being feathered with purple and enhanced by scarlet stigmata. Away from its native haunts it is best grown in pans under glass.

Crocus cancellatus. Native of Greece and Bulgaria and throughout the Near East, it is variable as to its colouring, the blooms being white with silver-grey shading on the exterior or pale lilac, shaded on the outside with purple. It blooms during autumn and is distinguished by its branched yellow stigmata. The flowers appear before the leaves but only just so, as the leaves will be showing before the last flowers have died.

Crocus candidus. Native of the mountains of Crete and the Levant, it blooms during April, in shades of cream, pale yellow and orange, the outer segments stippled with brown. A few corms will rapidly increase to form a large colony. The broad leaves appear before the flowers.

Crocus carpetanus. Native only of western Spain and Portugal, where it is to be found on mountain ranges, its corm has a netted tunic covered in silky hairs, while the leaves are like those of *Narcissus juncifolius*, being rush-like. The flowers are among the smallest of all the crocuses, being less than 1 in (2·5 cm) tall and pale lilac with grey veins and shading on the exterior. The stigmata are of the same lilac-grey colouring.

Crocus caspius. It was discovered in 1838 by the shores of the Caspian Sea, where it grows among shrubby vegetation, flowering from October until early spring, its white flowers having orange anthers and stigmata. A hardy species, it is tolerant of most soils.

Crocus chrysanthus. It was discovered in Bulgaria and closely resembles *C. biflorus* in the shape of its flowers and in bearing more than one flower from each spathe. It also resembles *C. biflorus* in the formation of the corm tunic and in its flowering time but differs in that the anthers have black markings. It is the most variable species as to the colour and markings of its flowers, while there are more named varieties than of any other species. *C. chrysanthus* is widespread in Greece and Asia Minor and in the Balkan countries, where its oval-shaped blooms appear on high ground early in the year, this being the most reliable of the winter-flowering species. The type bears a flower of deep orange-yellow, two to five blooms appearing from each of the usual three sets of sheathing leaves, to give a succession of flowers from mid-January until late March. From the pale-yellow pallidus, the late Mr John Hoog in Holland raised a number of outstanding varieties with larger flowers than the species, each of which has received wide aclaim:

BLUE PEARL. Its flowers, of silvery blue on the inside, have a bronze base and are shaded dark blue on the outside.

BLUE PETER. The flowers are of soft clear blue on the inside with a golden throat, purple blue on the outside.

BUTTERCUP. A 1969 introduction of uniform deep yellow, free of any markings.

CREAM BEAUTY. The flowers are large and globular and of a lovely rich Jersey cream colour.

E. A. BOWLES. Named in honour of the world's foremost expert of the genus *crocus*, it has flowers of buttery-yellow, tinted and marked with greyish-brown on the exterior.

E. P. BOWLES. The blooms are of richest yellow, the outer segments being feathered with purple.

GOLDILOCKS. The orange-yellow flowers with their rounded petals have purple-brown shading at the base.

LADYKILLER. The flowers are arresting in their beauty, being of deep purple with the segments edged white and with a glistening white exterior.

MOONLIGHT. Raised by the late E. A. Bowles, the segments are sulphur yellow, shading to pale cream at the tips.

NANETTE. The large flowers are creamy yellow inside with violet-purple stippling on the outside.

PRINCESS BEATRIX. A beautiful variety, the large refined blooms being of soft lobelia blue with a golden base.

SNOW BUNTING. The scented flowers are glistening white with a golden throat, the exterior being feathered with purple.

WARLEY WHITE. Raised by the late John Hoog it is the first to open, coming into bloom before the end of January, its creamy-white flowers being shaded on the exterior with purple-blue.

ZWANENBURG BRONZE. The deep golden-yellow flowers are shaded dark bronze on the exterior.

Crocus clusii. Native of the Atlantic coastline of Portugal and western Spain, where it grows in the shade and shelter of woodlands. It blooms in October, after the formation of its elongated leaves, the flowers being of rich deep purple. It is best grown in pans under glass.

Crocus corsicus. One of the Imperati group, native of southern Italy, Sardinia and Corsica and which are among the finest of all the species, distinguished by their two-coloured blossoms. *C. corsicus* is native of mountainous regions and under cultivation is difficult to establish. The flowers are large and of rich cream colouring, feathered with purple and with scarlet stigmata. The outer segments are usually shaded buff or straw. In bloom March–April.

Crocus cvijicii. Native of Albania and Yugoslavia, where it blooms at 5,000 ft when the snow begins to melt. In the British Isles and North America it blooms in March. It forms a small corm and increases by self-sown seed. The flowers are of soft lemon yellow.

Crocus dalmaticus. Native of the Adriatic coast, it resembles those of the Imperati group. It blooms from mid-February to mid-March and increases rapidly, the medium-sized blooms with their pointed petals being of soft lavender-grey with a buff exterior. It has unique pear-shaped corms.

Crocus danfordiae. It was named after Mrs Danford, who first collected it in Asia Minor, and it has the smallest flower of all, differing from *C. chrysanthus* only in its size and in its short stigmata. The flowers vary in colour from white to pale yellow and orange, also lilac.

Crocus etruscus. Native of the coast of Tuscany, it has a heavily netted corm tunic and bears a large flower of greyish-mauve. The form Zwanenburg bears flowers of pale blue and like the type is in bloom in March and April.

Crocus fleischeri. Native of Asia Minor, it has a yellow corm interwoven with a tunic of silky fibres. Its leaves appear in January and are followed by small narrow white flowers, the outer segments being veined with purple. Against the winter sun, the scarlet stigmata may be seen through the almost transparent petals which open star-like. Though hardy and tolerant of adverse weather, it is to be seen at its best under glass.

Crocus goulimyi. A recently discovered species, it is native of southern Greece and is a handsome crocus, the large globular blooms of soft lilac having a long elegant tube. It flowers in October before the leaves appear.

Crocus graveolens. George Maw in his *Monograph of the Genus Crocus* (1886) treated it as a variety of *C. vitellinus*, with which it is to be found growing. It differs, however, in several respects, having narrow leaves which spread over the soil, while its flowers are smaller and more heavily marked with brown on the exterior. They emit a most unpleasant beetle-like smell, so powerful that their presence may be detected from a distance. It comes late into bloom, towards the end of February.

Crocus hartmannianus. One of the annulate group represented by *C. biflorus* and *C. chrysanthus*, it was discovered in Cyprus early in the century and named after the German botanist Ernst Hartmann. It has long narrow leaves with a prominent central white rib, while its urn-shaped flowers are of pale lilac with purple shading down the centre of the outer petals. It blooms in February.

Crocus hyemalis. Its starry white flowers, shaded with purple at the base, cover the hillsides around Bethlehem and Jericho at Christmas-time and they are delicately scented. In the British Isles and northern Europe it is best grown in pans under glass for it is not tolerant of excessive winter moisture.

Crocus imperati. One of the most handsome of all the crocus species, it is a familiar plant of the mountains around Naples and was named in honour of Ferrante Imperato, the Italian botanist. If the weather is kind, it will come into bloom during the first days of January, its open flowers measuring 4 in (10 cm) across. They are of a lovely shade of lilac-mauve, the outer segments being tinted with buff on the exterior and stippled with purple. They are scented and are enhanced by the orange stigmata. Two white forms exist, *montanus* and *albus*, both found in the same area. *C. imperati* makes a magnificent pot plant and will usually bloom at Christmas.

Crocus karduchorum. Discovered in Kurdistan in 1859, it is unique in that its grass-like leaves, which grow 2 in (5 cm) tall, persist until new leaves have formed with the flowers the following autumn. The flowers have a long perianth tube and lilac-blue or lilac-pink segments veined with purple. The anthers and stigmata are creamy white.

Crocus korolkowi. A distinct and charming species from Turkestan, where it was discovered by the Russian General, Korolkov. It is also native of Persia and Afghanistan and has the largest corms of any species. The flowers appear in March and are of greenish-yellow shaded on the outside with brown. They open star-like in the sun.

Crocus laevigatus. A tiny Christmas-flowering crocus of astonishing hardiness and beauty, native of Greece and the Cyclades, its corms being covered in a hard woody tunic. The flowers are white with an orange throat, the outer segments being feathered with purple. With *C. suaveolens* and *C. imperati*, it is the most sweetly scented species and shares with *C. cambessedesii* the honour of remaining longer in bloom than any other, from October until March, being indispensable in providing winter colour in sunny pockets of the alpine garden, whilst indoors it will scent a large room with its fragrance. The variety *fontenayi* bears flowers of a lovely shade of rosy-lilac feathered with brown.

Crocus leichtlinii. It was collected in Asia Minor by Max Leichtlin as a variety of *C. biflorus*, but it is distinct from this in several respects, the corm tunic being free of basal rings while the basal spathe is absent. The flowers are small and of an unusual shade of pale yellowish-green with the anthers of similar colouring. It blooms early in February and is sweetly scented.

Crocus longiflorus (syn. *C. odorus*). It is native of southern Italy, Sicily and Malta and it blooms at the same time as the leaves appear, in October, being colourful until the end of November. The tube is long and elegant, while the globular blooms are of deep violet which open to display scarlet anthers. The scent is powerful, like that of ripe plums. It should be given a sunny position, sheltered from wind.

Crocus luteus. The yellow-flowering crocus. Though it would appear to be of garden origin, it is believed to be derived from *C. aureus* and may be John Rea's 'great yellow crocus' which he described in his *Flora, Ceres and Pomona* (1665). It blooms before any other and makes a brilliantly coloured carpet beneath tall trees, or planted in pockets about the alpine garden.

Crocus minimus. 'A wee jewel from Corsica' was how Farrer described it. It bears its purple chalices during March and April, the outer segments being shaded with buff and veined with purple. It is also found in Sardinia, where it blooms from January until the end of spring. The blooms grow 1 in (2·5 cm) tall and are most attractive in pans under glass, though outdoors thay are able to survive periods of the most adverse weather.

Crocus niveus. It is one of the most rare and beautiful species, native of the mountains of south-western Greece. It blooms in November, its large white globular flowers having yellow shading in the throat and pale-yellow anthers, which distinguish it from *C. boryi*. The scarlet stigmata enhances its beauty.

Crocus nudiflorus. It is to be found north and south of the Pyrenees and increases by means of underground stolons, coming into bloom in the second year. Once established it will prove difficult to remove, but flowering as it does, in late autumn and early winter, it is a most welcome member of the bulb garden. The large deep-purple flowers have a bright-orange stigma and appear before the coarse leaves. It is Parkinson's purple crocus of the Pyrenees.

Crocus ochroleucus. Its home is Syria and the Lebanon and it is also found near the shores of Lake Galilee, the creamy-white flowers appearing just before the leaves. The narrow segments open star-like to reveal the white anthers and yellow stigmata. It blooms during September and October, providing a pleasing contrast to the lavender-blue flowers of *C. speciosus*. It does, however, require a well-drained soil and warmth to give of its best, and where the garden is exposed, grow it in pans under glass. It increases rapidly from cormlets.

Crocus olivieri. Native of Greece and Bulgaria and of several islands of the Aegean, it resembles *C. aureus* in the intensity of its brilliant-orange flowers, which appear in March and are entirely free of shading or markings. The leaves are broader than those of any other crocus and grow horizontally, like those of the colchicum. It was named after Antoine Olivier, the French botanist, who discovered it on Chios.

Crocus pulchellus. It is present on the hills around Istanbul, more especially on

Mount Olympus, and is closely allied to *C. speciosus*, though it blooms later, in November. The blooms are pale lavender, shaded orange in the throat and with white anthers. The variety Zephyr bears white flowers shaded grey on the outside.

Crocus salzmannii. Though native of Gibraltar and Tangiers, it is a strong grower and is hardy in the British Isles and northern Europe, its large corm 5 cm across being covered in a soft-brown tunic. The leaves are borne with the pale-lilac flowers, in October. It enjoys a dry, sunny situation.

Crocus sativus. With maize and flax it is one of the oldest of cultivated plants and is thought to be the 'Karkom' of the *Song of Solomon*. Its uses were legion and it came to be grown throughout the civilised world. Native of the eastern Mediterranean, it produces its narrow grey-green leaves before the flowers appear in October. The blooms are of deep purple-red, veined with darker purple in the throat and enhanced by the large scarlet stigma. They open flat and do not close up again, not even at night, hence they are frequently spoiled by rain as soon as they open. The corms require a thorough baking in a hot summer to be free-flowering, for which reason they grow well only in the dry East Anglia region of Britain. They require frequent division and a rich soil.

The variety *Cartwrightianus* was named by Dean Herbert after the British Consul at Constantinople. It grows naturally in that area, also in the Balkans, where it is to be found in pinewoods in sandy soil. It is a handsome variety, as is the pure-white form, *albus*, which has a striking scarlet stigma.

Crocus scharojani. Native only of the Caucasus and of the basin of the Black Sea, where it was first collected in 1865. Its leaves are unusual in that they are grooved at the sides and appear so late in spring that they are usually green when the deep-orange flowers appear early in August, this being one of the earliest crocuses to bloom. It requires different conditions from other species: partial shade from the midsummer sun and a low-lying moist situation.

Crocus sieberi. Native of the White Mountains of Crete, it is one of the most beautiful of all species, though its slight tenderness excludes it from exposed gardens. Its blooms of many colours are so striking that it makes an admirable pot plant, flowering from early January until March. The globular blooms are of bright lilac with an orange throat and are tipped and striped with purple-maroon, a colour to be found in no other crocus. The blooms are enhanced by the orange stamens and scarlet stigmata. The variety Hubert Edelstan, which received an award of merit in 1924, has an area of white between the maroon-shaded tips of the petals and the basal markings, while Firefly has outer petals of palest lilac and inner petals of violet-pink. Bowles's White, raised by the late E. A. Bowles and also the receiver of an award of merit, is one of the best of all-white crocuses.

Crocus speciosus. One of the best of the autumn crocuses, it is found in central and southern Europe, to the Caucasus and as far south as Persia, where in September it brightens the ground with its large globular flowers of bright lavender-blue. Like *C. ochroleucus* it increases rapidly by means of numerous cormlets which congregate around the large parent corm. The flowers appear before the leaves and often show colour before the last days of summer. The variety Oxonion is dark blue, and *albus*, white. Others include *Aitchisonii*, pale blue; and Cassiope which is later-flowering, the blooms of rich aniline-blue having a striking yellow base. Another of high quality is Pollux, the enormous globes of violet-blue having a silvery-blue exterior.

Crocus suaveolens. It is the Roman crocus, to be found in the hills south of Rome, where it blooms early in March. It is like a small and less conspicuous *C. imperati*, being of similar colouring but with distinct purple stripes down the outside of the segments, while its scent is even more pronounced, being the most distinct of all.

Crocus susianus. Native of the Crimea, it is known as the cloth of gold crocus, for in February its small flowers of deepest orange striped with purple or brown on the outside open star-like and with their golden anthers present a picture of brilliance. It is described by Clusius in his *Rariorum Plantarum Historia*, where he tells of having received it in 1587; and by Parkinson, who mentions it in the *Paradisus* (1629). It is at its best planted in drifts beneath tall trees or in pockets in the rock garden protected from cold winds. The variety *minor* is even more dainty and is more free-flowering.

Crocus suterianus. It so nearly resembles *C. olivieri* that it has been taken either for that species or classed as a variety of it, but it grows naturally only in one small colony in Asia Minor, where it was discovered by Henry Suter, Vice-consul at Kayseri. It blooms in March, bearing yellowish-orange flowers and is free-flowering. It increases rapidly and needs regular division.

Crocus tomasinianus. Native of the eastern Adriatic coastline, it comes into bloom early in February, its long slender cups of pale lavender-blue being shaded on the outside with silvery-grey. It is one of the hardiest species and increases rapidly both from seed and cormlets in all soils, an original planting of a dozen corms soon becoming a sheet of colour. One of the best for naturalising, it was named by Dean Herbert in honour of the botanist Muzio de Tommasini of Trieste and received an award of merit. Of several lovely varieties, Ruby Giant bears large blooms of deep ruby-purple, while Barr's Purple bears flowers of soft lilac-mauve.

Crocus tournefortii. It is to be found with *C. boryi* on the Greek islands and blooms with it, in November and December, forming a delightful companion with its flowers of bright rosy-lilac, white anthers and scarlet stigmata. Like *boryi*, it is somewhat tender and is best grown under glass.

Crocus veluchensis. Native of the mountains of Greece and Turkey, it is related to *C. sieberi*, though it has a smaller corm and increases by self-sown seed. The flowers are pale lilac, shaded on the exterior with purple and differ from *C. sieberi* by the absence of orange shading in the throat, while the segments are longer and more pointed.

Crocus vernus. Native of the higher alpine regions of Europe, inhabiting the

Pyrenees, Alps and Carpathians, where its blooms of purple or white often appear as late as June with the departing of the snows. Under garden cultivation, they appear in March before the leaves. Its name has given rise to much confusion in the past, for the early writers used it to describe all spring-flowering crocuses, and not until the publication of Miller's *Gardener's Dictionary* in 1752 was the name used to describe it as a definite species. The white form, *albus*, is desirable to use as a contrast for the purple hybrid Haarlem Gem.

Crocus versicolor. Its home is southern France and northern Italy and, in the slight buff colouring of the exterior segments, it may be classed with *C. imperati* and those other species of Italian ancestry. It may be Parkinson's 'Party-coloured' crocus. The blooms are pale mauve (or white), the inner segments veined with purple on the outside and sometimes shaded with buff. It flowers in February and like the other Italian species, its flowers are scented.

Crocus vitellinus. It is one of the yellow-flowered species of the aureus group, native of Syria and the Lebanon and it is winter flowering, the blooms appearing early in December. They are deep golden-yellow with narrow pointed segments and it is scented. The outer petals are usually feathered with bronze.

Crocus zonatus (syn. *C. kotschyanus*). Its natural habit extends from southern Europe to Syria and it blooms early in autumn from a large corm. Its bright rosy-lilac flowers and creamy-white anthers resemble in colour those of *C. tournefortii*, but it is readily distinguished from this by the orange spots which form a zone at the base of each segment. It readily increases from small corms which form around the base. There is a pure white form, *albus*.

Dutch Hybrids. They are mostly offspring of *C. vernus* and are sold in their thousands each year for outdoor planting in short grass and for growing in pots indoors. They possess extreme hardiness, while the large globular blooms are most colourful during springtime.

Among many fine varieties, Early Perfection is the first to bloom, and bears large flowers of deep purple with a darker edge of violet; Kathleen Parlow is pure white; Paulus Potter, ruby-purple with a silvery grape-like 'bloom'; and Queen of the Blues is soft bluish-mauve. The best of the striped varieties is Mr Pickwick, the large blooms of silvery lilac being striped with purple.

CYCLAMEN (Primulaceae)

A genus of 15 species, native of Europe, extending as far east as the Lebanon and taking their name from the Greek *kyclos*, circular, a reference to the flower stalk which twists spirally after fertilisation, drawing the ripened seed into the ground. They form large corm-like tubers from which arise heart- or kidney-shaped leaves, borne on long stalks. The flowers resemble moths in flight with their reflexed petals and are held on slender scapes above the foliage. The calyx is five-parted with ovate lance-shaped segments, the corolla hypogynous, with a small round tube. The ovary is superior, the capsule many-seeded.

The plant reached England early in her history, the corms being much in demand to assist in child-birth. It is possible that both *C. hederaefolium*, the ivy-leaf cyclamen and *C. europeum*, the common sowbread, native to most European countries, were also British native plants, for Gerard says that *C. hederaefolium* 'groweth upon the mountains of Wales and upon the hills of Lincolnshire and Somerset', while *C. europeum* is to be found naturalised in parts of Kent and Sussex, where it grows about limestone formations in coniferous woodlands. Both species were planted in the knot gardens of Elizabethan times.

Hardy cyclamen (not all are hardy) may be grown beneath mature trees or among flowering shrubs, where they will seed themselves and increase rapidly, while they are delightful plants for the alpine garden and for a trough. They are one of the few bulbous plants to grow well beneath conifers. They may also be grown where there is no garden, by planting the tubers in deep boxes containing a compost made up of loam, leaf mould and decayed manure in equal parts. The boxes may be placed on a veranda or on the shaded side of a courtyard for, like all members of the family Primulaceae, they enjoy dappled shade and are never happy where growing in an exposed position in full sun. Only *C. persicum* and *C. africanum* are really tender and should be grown under glass in gentle heat, though the hardy species are also delightful for growing under glass, either in a frame or in an unheated greenhouse.

Like crocuses, they may be planted for a succession of bloom from early August, through autumn and winter. The flowers of several species are deliciously scented.

TABLE XXIII. *Flowering times of garden cyclamen*

Cyclamen pseudo-ibericum	January–March
Cyclamen libanoticum	March–April
Cyclamen repandum	March–May
* *Cyclamen creticum*	April–May
Cyclamen europeum	July–October
* *Cyclamen cyprium*	August–October
Cyclamen neapolitanum	August–October
Cyclamen graecum	September–October
Cyclamen rohlfsianum	September–October
* *Cyclamen africanum*	September–November
Cyclamen cilicium	September–November
Cyclamen orbiculatum	December–March
var. *coum*	December–March
var. *atkinsii*	December–March

* These species are too tender to be grown outside in the more exposed gardens of the British Isles and North America.

Culture. Corms of the hardy species should be planted from July until October, planting the early autumn- and winter-flowering species in July and those which bloom in spring, during October. They require a soil containing leaf mould and some decayed manure such as old mushroom-bed compost or dehydrated cow manure. Peat should not be used unless in small quantities for cyclamen are happier (like irises) in an alkaline soil and appreciate some limestone chips or mortar from old walls, mixed into the top 3 in (7·5 cm). There is no need to prepare the soil deeply.

Plant the corms with the uppermost surface just beneath soil level, scattering around them a small amount of leaf mould. An exception to the rule of shallow planting is *C. europeum*, the common sowbread, which requires to be planted 6 in (15 cm) deep where the soil is light and friable. This species should also be planted earlier than others for it comes into bloom during the first days of August (sometimes in July) and must be in the ground before the end of May. Plant the rounded or smooth side of the corm downwards on to a layer of sand, and if the soil is dry give regular artificial waterings until established. Most species will not bloom during their first season, due to the woody 'arms' at the top of the corm being damaged in transit or at planting time, but they will more than compensate for this by their beautifully mottled foliage, that of *C. europeum* being evergreen and acting as a foil for the blue-flowering squills and chionodoxas of winter and springtime. After flowering, the corms should be given a top-dressing of leaf mould and decayed manure, for they will eventually grow to a large size and are heavy feeders. Also, forming their roots around the upper surface, an annual top-dressing will be of greater value than enriching the soil at planting time. The corms will push themselves up from their original planting so that they will keep themselves near the surface in spite of a yearly mulch. This should be given with care so as not to damage, at the top of the corm, the woody 'arms' or branches from which the flowers are produced the following year.

Propagation. Hardy cyclamen produce their seed freely and increase by self-sown seed. Or seed may be saved and sown as soon as possible either into a frame containing sterilised loam and sand in equal amounts or into boxes or pans containing a similar compost.

The seeds are large and may be spaced 1 in (2·5 cm) apart. If sown in June, the seed will germinate rapidly, but it is advisable to grow on the seedlings for another 12 months before transplanting to a frame or to the open ground. They will come into bloom three or four years after the seed is sown. They may also be increased by division of the tuber.

Greenhouse or Persian cyclamen, hybrids of *C. persicum* (syn. *C. latifolium*), may be brought into bloom (provided reliable seed is obtained) within 15 or 16 months from a sowing made in July, spacing the seeds 1 in (2·5 cm) apart to allow the seedlings room to develop. The compost should be made up of 2 parts sterilised loam, 1 part leaf mould, 1 part sand, to which is added (per bushel) 1 oz of superphosphate of lime. Cover the seed to a depth of ½ in (1·25 cm) and keep the soil comfortably moist. The seed pans may be kept in a closed frame for about four weeks after which they should be placed in a temperature of 60° F (16° C) when the seed will soon germinate. The temperature should then be lowered to around 55° F (17° C), at which it is maintained during winter, taking care not to over-water, and shielding the seedlings from the sun. By late spring, they will be ready to transplant to small pots, having formed their second leaf, and they will be ready for their final pots towards the end of summer.

To perpetuate a variety, or for those who would wish to grow on their indoor cyclamen for another year, the foliage is allowed to die back gradually by with-holding water. The tubers remain in the old soil, the pots being placed beneath the greenhouse bench or in a frame; or they may be plunged to their rim in a bed of ashes. This will prevent the corms from shrivelling. New growth will appear towards the end of summer, when the corms are repotted into freshly prepared compost and placed in a frame or greenhouse in a minimum night temperature of 50° F (10° C) to be brought into bloom. During warm weather, the plants will benefit from a syringeing with clean water. They may be taken into the home as soon as the flower buds have formed, at the end of October. They must be kept away from draughts and watered with care, preferably around the side of the pot, never giving more than the plants can take up in reasonable time which will depend upon the room temperature. This should be between 50 and 55° F (10 and 13° C) when the plants will give of their flowers in long succession throughout the winter months, the blooms being enhanced by the dark-green fleshy leaves. The dead flowers should be carefully pulled from the tuber as they form.

Species and Varieties. *Cyclamen africanum* (syn. *C. autumnale*). Native of the coastal woodlands of northern Africa, especially of Algeria, it bears a large irregular tuber which may be 9 in (22·5 cm) across when long-established. It comes into bloom early in autumn, bearing sweetly scented white or rosy-red flowers which have a purple spot at the base of each petal and yellow anthers. The broad handsome leaves, toothed at the margins and marbled with white, are borne on long stalks. Not completely hardy in the British Isles, northern Europe and North America, it is best grown under glass unless the garden is in a warm part.

Cyclamen cilicium. Native of the Cilician Mountains and the pine forests of the Lebanon, it blooms from early September until mid-November and is a hardy and dainty species. The rounded leaves of dark green have a heart-shaped zone of silver and appear after the first flowers have unfolded. The blooms with their gracefully twisting petals are powerfully scented and are pale pink, touched with crimson at the base. They hover above the foliage on 3-in (7·5-cm) stems, to make this a most suitable species for planting in a pocket in the alpine garden or in a trough.

Cyclamen creticum. It inhabits the mountains of Crete, where it blooms during May and June with the melting of the snows. The flowers, with their attractively waved petals, are white and diffuse a carnation-like perfume. In the British Isles and northern Europe they bloom during March and April and with their dark-green heart-shaped leaves are most attractive beneath conifers.

Cyclamen cyprium. Native of Cyprus it differs from *C. neapolitanum* in its unlobed leaves and narrow petals. It makes a small round tuber, from which arise at the same time dainty leaves and small pink moth-like flowers with twisted petals, each being marked with a crimson spot. The flowers are vanilla-scented and appear before the end of August. It is not a plant for more exposed gardens and is best grown under glass.

Cyclamen europeum (syn. *C. odoratum*). The common sowbread, native of the wooded slopes of central and southern Europe and of the British Isles. It bears scented flowers of deep carmine-pink, which appear in July and continue until the beginning of winter, though they are most prolific in August and September. The leaves appear with the flowers and are heart-shaped, with silver markings on the upper surface and purple on the underside. They are almost evergreen, dying back only during midsummer to come again fresh in July, with the flowers. When fully established and growing under the shady conditions it enjoys, a plant will bear upwards of 100 flowers in a season.

Cyclamen graecum. Native of Greece and of the islands of Crete and Rhodes, it forms a large, irregular reddish-brown tuber and blooms during September. The flowers are of a lovely shade of deep lilac-pink, blotched with purple at the base of each petal and are slightly scented. The large heart-shaped leaves have a rough horny margin and appear after the flowers.

Cyclamen libanoticum. Native of Mount Lebanon, where it grows to an altitude of 3,000 ft, it has heart-shaped leaves, waved at the margins and with a distinctive zone of yellow. The large flowers appear early in spring, towards the end of March, and are bright salmon-pink with a carmine-purple blotch at the base of each petal. They are scented.

Cyclamen neapolitanum. Native of southern Italy and Greece, it is the finest of all the hardy species, forming a tuber which will eventually measure more than 12 in (30 cm) across after 50 years growing undisturbed. Its dainty fairy-like flowers of mauve-pink appear in July, before the leaves and a large tuber will produce 100 or more blooms before flowering ends in October. By then the beautiful ivy-shaped leaves, mottled with silver, will have appeared and, like those of *C. europeum*, will remain effective until summer. The large globular seed pods will have formed by early May when they may be removed for sowing in July, or they may be left for the plant itself to scatter and the young seedlings moved to their permanent quarters in about 12 months.

The rare white-flowered form, *album*, has white flowers, which in the half-light of evening have the appearance of white moths as they hover above the leaves on 6-in (15-cm) stems. This species grows well beneath conifers and among young plantations of silver birch. Plant the corms 2-in deep.

Cyclamen orbiculatum (syn. *C. ibericum*, *C. vernum*). Under this species are now included the varieties *C. coum* and *C. atkinsii*, believed to be natural hybrids of *C. orbiculatum*, which is native of the Caucasus. It is hardy and free-flowering, in bloom from early December until the end of March, where the tubers can be planted in a sheltered part of the garden. It will multiply by self-sown seedlings. The ovate leaves have a distinctive zone of silver and above them are borne, on 3-in (7·5-cm) stems, scentless flowers of a warm shade of reddish-purple.

Var. *C. coum*. It is present in Greece and Turkey, making a round flattened tuber and bearing dark-green leaves, which are free of markings but are tinted purple on the underside. The flowers of rosy-red are scentless, while there is also a pure white-flowered variety, *album*. At one time *C. coum* was classed as a separate species.

Var. *C. atkinsii*. It has leaves which are marbled with white and bears flowers of a lovely shade of crimson-purple. There is a contrasting white-flowered variety, *album*.

Cyclamen persicum (syn. *C. latifolium*). It differs from others in that its flower stem remains straight when ripening its seed. It is native of the Lebanon and Syria and of the islands of Cyprus, Crete and Rhodes and has ivy-shaped leaves, above which it bears, in March and April, blush-white flowers on 6-in (15-cm) stems. The blossoms have narrow petals which are waved. From this species has been evolved the strains of the large-flowered Persian or greenhouse cyclamen, sold in ever-increasing numbers by specialist growers for Christmas- and winter-flowering.

Cyclamen pseudo-ibericum. Believed to be a natural hybrid, it was first observed in Turkey and is a cyclamen of outstanding beauty with obcordate leaves of darkest green and scented flowers of deepest violet. The first flowers appear during the first sunny days of the new year and reach a crescendo of beauty by mid-March.

Cyclamen repandum (syn. *C. vernale*). Native of Corsica and southern Italy and closely related to *C. neapolitanum*, though making a smaller tuber. The leaves, ivy-shaped at the base, are mottled with silvery-white, while the rosy-lilac flowers, which are pleasantly scented, are borne from March until May. It is one of the most free-flowering species, an established tuber bearing upwards of 200 flowers over a period of 10 weeks. Plant the corms 2 in deep.

Cyclamen rohlfsianum. It is to be found growing with *C. africanum*, in the the pinewoods of the North African coast and, like that species, is less hardy than others. In northern Europe and North America it requires glass protection during winter, when it will come into bloom in September, the flowers of deepest red appearing with the kidney-shaped leaves. It bears a large rough tuber.

CYPELLA (Iridaceae)

A genus of 15 species, native of Mexico and South America and taking their name from the Greek *kypellon*, a goblet, a reference to the shape of the flowers. Closely related to tigridia, they form a bulb rather than a corm and have linear, plaited leaves. The flowers last only for a day, when they are replaced by others in succession during July and August. The perianth consists of six free segments, the outer three being widely spreading and attractively twisted, like a propellor blade, while the three inner segments are recurved at the apex. The blooms are mostly spotted and are brilliantly coloured.

Culture. Mostly native of the warmest parts of South America they will be permanent members of the border only in the warmest gardens of the British Isles, North America and northern Europe, where they may be left down to increase like narcissi and will form large clumps. Elsewhere, the bulbs should be planted 6 in (15 cm) apart and 4 in (10 cm) deep in a sunny border early in May and should be lifted in October when the foliage has died back. After drying, the bulbs are stored over winter in a frost-free room. Where making permanent plantings, set the bulbs 12 in (30 cm) apart, planting *C. plumbea*, which grows 3 ft (90 cm) tall, towards the back of the border.

Cypellas require a light, well-drained soil, for the bulbs will be killed if the ground is waterlogged during the dormant winter period. If the soil is heavy, work in peat or decayed humus and some grit, and if the bulbs are to remain in the ground during winter, cover with a heavy mulch of leaves or bracken. Permanent clumps may be protected from winter rains by covering with a cloche. They will do well if planted in full sun beneath the eaves of a house, where they will be protected from heavy winter rains, though in summer, while making growth and in bloom, they require copious amounts of moisture.

Propagation. They increase rapidly from the numerous offsets formed at the base of the corm. These are detached upon lifting in October and are grown on in boxes of sandy soil or in outdoor beds the following year. They will attain flowering size in two or three years.

Cypellas are not easily raised from seed, which is slow to germinate, and it will be five or six years before the bulbs will be in bloom. Sow in April, in boxes or pans containing the John Innes compost which should be moist. If the seed is sown thinly, it will not be necessary to transplant the seedlings until they have formed pea-size bulbs in two years.

Species and Varieties. *Cypella gracilis.* Native of the Argentine, it grows 2 ft (60 cm) tall with sword-like leaves, while its bright-yellow flowers are tinted with lilac.

Cypella herbertii. Native of Brazil it grows 18 in (45 cm) tall and will come into bloom towards the end of June, the orange-yellow flowers with their twisted petals being spotted with purple at the centre. It has lance-shaped leaves.

Cypella peruviana. Native of the Peruvian Andes, it has thin plaited leaves and bears its bright-yellow flowers spotted with brown at the centre, on branched stems. The yellow stigma is of petal-like appearance.

Cypella plumbea. Native of Mexico and so named for the colour of its flowers —a dull shade of grey-blue, resembling lead. It has plaited sword-like leaves and grows 3 ft (90 cm) tall. It bears its flowers late July and in August. The variety *platensis* bears flowers of clear sky blue.

CYRTANTHUS (Amaryllidaceae)

A genus of about 50 species of bulbous plants, native of tropical eastern and southern Africa, the name being a reference to the curved perianth tube by which the plant is distinguished from crinum. They form large tunicated bulbs, from which arise narrow strap-like leaves and drooping funnel-shaped flowers, borne in umbels on hollow scapes. The perianth tube to which the stamens are attached is longer than the segments. The seed capsule is oblong and contains a number of flat black seeds.

Culture. They require cool greenhouse or garden room culture away from the warmer parts, planting in March three to four bulbs to a large pot. There are several evergreen species which should not be dried off after flowering as is necessary for those of deciduous habit. Provide a compost made up of fibrous loam, leaf mould, decayed cow manure and sand in equal parts and plant 3 in (7·5 cm) deep. They bloom from mid-March until the end of summer.

After planting, stand the pots in a plunge bed outside or on a veranda in boxes and cover with ashes, also with a sheet of glass to retain the warmth of the spring sunshine. Then, towards the end of April move to a greenhouse, giving copious waterings as they make growth and while they are in bloom, gradually drying off the deciduous varieties after flowering. They are wintered where frost is excluded, though in a sunny sheltered garden they may be flowered outdoors during summer. The plants will benefit from a weekly application of dilute manure water and a top-dressing after flowering.

In a sunny, sheltered garden, the plants may be grown outdoors. Plant the bulbs 4 in (10 cm) deep and 9 in (22·5 cm) apart at the foot of a wall and lift them after flowering, drying off and keeping them in a frost-free room, to be planted out again the following April. The later-flowering varieties are more suitable for outside culture.

Propagation. When lifting or repotting the bulbs, numerous bulblets will be seen clustering round the base. These are detached and grown on in boxes of sandy compost for 12 to 18 months, when they are potted and will reach flowering size in two years.

Species. *Cyrtanthus angustifolius* (syn. *C. ventricosus*). It makes a small ovoid bulb with a long tapering neck and it forms one to three narrow leaves 16 to 18 in (40 to 45 cm) long. In its native southern Africa it blooms from December until April; in July and August in northern Europe and North America, bearing its bright orange-red drooping flowers in umbels of 4 to 10 on a 12-in (30-cm) scape. The flowers are about 2 in (5 cm) long with spreading segments and the style longer than the stamens.

Cyrtanthus collinus. From the small ovoid bulbs appear two or three linear leaves 6 to 9 in (15 to 22·5 cm) long and it bears on a slender 12-in (30-cm) scape, 6 to 10 bright-red flowers 2 in (5 cm) long.

Cyrtanthus huttoni. Native of Cape Province it is an attractive species with broad strap-like leaves and bearing in May and June in a stout umbel six to eight funnel- or bell-shaped flowers of pale red with reflexing pointed segments.

Cyrtanthus lutescens. A dainty species with small round bulbs of 1-in (2·5-cm) diameter, from which arise two to four pale-green leaves 12 in (30 cm) long and, on a slender 15-in (37·5-cm) scape, two or three pale-yellow flowers. The variety *cooperi* bears three or four larger flowers of pale yellow to a scape and is sweetly scented.

Cyrtanthus mackenii. Native of mountainous parts of Natal, it is the first to bloom in March where growing in gentle heat. It forms two to six long linear leaves and on a slender 10-in (25-cm) scape bears waxy-white tubular flowers formed horizontally in umbels of 6 to 10. Varieties are also obtainable bearing flowers in shades of pink and apricot.

Cyrtanthus obliquus. The oldest species, known from 1774 when it was discovered in Cape Province. It forms a large bulb 4 in (10 cm) across and it has 10 to 12 strap-like leaves arranged in two rows and produced after the flowers. In May and June it bears on a 2-ft (60-cm) stem an umbel of 10 to 12 bright-red drooping flowers, shaded yellow at the base and measuring 3 in (7·5 cm) long.

Cyrtanthus o'brienii. Closely related to *C. angustifolius*, it is native of the highlands of Natal and has linear leaves 12 in (30 cm) long which appear before the flowers in June. They are of brilliant scarlet, about 2 in (5 cm) long and are borne in umbels of 8 to 10.

Cyrtanthus odorus. It is one of the few plants to bear flowers of brightest scarlet which are powerfully scented. They are tubular, about 2 in (5 cm) long and appear in July in umbels of four to eight. The linear leaves are about 15 in (37·5 cm) long.

Cyrtanthus sanguineus. Native of Natal, it is possibly the most striking species, forming a large ovoid bulb 2 in (5 cm) in diameter from which are borne three or four bright green lance-shaped leaves, unusual in that they are stalked. The funnel-shaped flowers of brightest cherry-red are 4 in (10 cm) long and are borne horizontally in small umbels of two to four on a 9-in (22·5-cm) scape. The variety *glaucophyllus* bears orange-red flowers and has handsome grey-green leaves. It blooms in July.

Cyrtanthus spiralis. It is rare in Cape Province and eastern Africa and has ovoid bulbs 2 in (5 cm) in diameter and two or three linear blue-green leaves 9 in (23 cm) long and spirally twisted. The slender scape is also blue-green, about 12 in (30 cm) long. In October four to eight bright-red funnel-shaped flowers 2 in (5 cm) long appear. It is the latest to bloom.

Cyrtanthus tuckii. Native of eastern South Africa, where it grows at an altitude of 6,000 ft, it has narrow linear leaves 18 in (45 cm) long and, on a blue-green scape of similar length, bears, in July, drooping flowers of scarlet-orange in umbels of 10 or more, on a 12-in (30-cm) scape.

D

DIERAMA (Iridaceae)

A genus of 25 species, native of tropical and South Africa and taking their name from the Greek for funnel, the reference being to the shape of the dangling flowers, which are bell-shaped. The plant forms a fibrous-coated root-stock, swollen to resemble a corm from which arises a long slender wand-like stem at the end of which small dangling bells are borne on wiry footstalks. The perianth consists of six equal spreading segments, the stamens being attached to the base of the tube. The ovary is three-celled. Dieramas or Wand-flowers are herbaceous perennials and though native of warmer parts, several will prove reliable in the more sheltered gardens of the British Isles and North America, though they require a well-drained soil. The plants are valuable in that they bring colour to the border during August and September.

Culture. The fibrous rooted corm-like roots should be planted in April at the back of the border and in a position of full sun. They require a light, friable soil enriched with decayed manure into which some peat has been incorporated. Plant 3 in (7·5 cm) deep and 18 in (45 cm) apart, and once established do not disturb for several years. After planting, the evergreen foliage will die back and will not be renewed for several months, until the plant becomes established. This will be late in summer and it will bloom the following autumn. To protect against frost, cover the plants with bracken after the flowering stems have died back in November. The bracken should be removed early in spring. Established plants will benefit from an occasional mulch of peat and decayed cow manure given after flowering.

Propagation. Plants may be increased by dividing in April into numerous corm-shaped pieces. They may also be propagated from seed saved from the ripe capsule in early October. Or obtain seed of a reliable strain which has been saved from plants grown for the purpose in their native lands. If sown in spring, it will bear flowers in the autumn of the following year. Sow the seed in the John Innes compost, lightly covering it and place in a frame, or cover with a sheet of glass and stand outdoors. Alternatively, seed may be sown directly into a frame. Fresh seed will germinate quickly, and the seedlings be ready to transplant by July and to their flowering quarters the following spring. Seedlings growing in a frame may be left until the following spring when they are moved to the border where they are to bloom.

Species and Varieties. *Dierama pulcherrima.* This is the only species to be in general cultivation, for it is the hardiest and possesses all the qualities of a first-class border plant. Closely related to Sparaxis, it has sword-like leaves and sends up its flowering stem to a height of 5 to 6 ft (1·5 to 1·8 metres). In spite of their wiry appearance, the stems are tough; the bell-shaped flowers of blood-red dangle on thread-like footstalks untroubled by autumnal winds. They bloom from early August until mid-October.

Of a number of named varieties, Peregrine bears large bells of fuchsia-purple; Plover, funnel-shaped blooms of lilac-pink; and Heatherbell, flowers of strawberry-pink flushed with rosy-red. These are tall-flowering, but for the front of a border the Sleive Donard Nurseries of County Down, Northern Ireland, have raised a number of hybrid varieties which grow to only half the normal height. Of these, Iris bears flowers of deep 'in memoriam' purple; Titania, blooms of neyron-rose, and Ceres has flowers of a unique shade of cobalt-blue.

DIPCADI (Liliaceae)

A genus of about 50 species of bulbous plants closely related to *Galtonia* and *Scilla* and native of South Africa, Madagascar and the Mediterranean. They have tunicated bulbs and thick strap-like leaves which appear with the flowers in August and September. The flowers are mostly greenish-brown or greenish-blue and are borne on scapes 3 ft (90 cm) tall.

Culture. Rare away from their native lands, they are not hardy in the British Isles and North America, except in the warmer parts where they may be left undisturbed after flowering and covered with bracken to protect them from frost. Plant early in spring 12 in (30 cm) apart and in a light, sandy loam into which has been incorporated some humus. Plant in groups of five or six, placing the bulbs on a layer of sand to assist drainage. In more exposed gardens, the bulbs may be lifted after flowering and dried and kept in an airy frost-free room until ready to plant out again in April. The bulbs may also be grown in pots indoors and after flowering are dried off gradually and wintered away from frost.

Propagation. Plants may be raised from seed sown in spring in gentle heat, the seedlings being transplanted to deep boxes when large enough to handle. Alternatively, the offsets may be detached from the base of the mother bulb when lifting and grown on to flowering size, which will be reached in two years time.

Species. *Dipcadi hyacinthiflora.* It is present on the slopes of Signal Hill in Cape Province, has grass-like basal leaves and bears its greenish-brown flowers in a lax raceme, the segments darkening towards the tips. The bulb is covered in a grey tunic.

Dipcadi longifolium. Native of Mozambique, it grows 3 ft (90 cm) tall with long linear leaves and bears its large racemes of greenish purple-blue flowers in August.

Dipcadi serotinum. Native of southern Spain, it was formally classed with the scillas and is the hardiest species, its greenish-brown flowers borne on a 9-in (22·5-cm) scape appearing early in August.

DISPORUM (Liliaceae)

A genus of 25 species, native of deciduous woodlands of North-west America and of northern Asia. They are mostly hardy herbaceous plants, increasing by underground rhizomes resembling those of the Solomon's seal. The leaves are alternate, lance-shaped and shortly stalked; the flowers bell-shaped, borne solitary or in clusters. They appear in May and are followed by bright-red berries. This is a delightful plant for a woodland garden in the less exposed parts of Britain and North America. Plant with Solomon's seal and lily-of-the-valley as they enjoy similar conditions.

Culture. Plant the rhizomatous roots in October, 3 in (7·5 cm) deep and 15 in (37·5 cm) apart, for they will spread rapidly. They require a soil containing plenty of peat or leaf mould into which some decayed manure has been incorporated.

Propagation. Increase by division of the roots or by seed sown in July when ripe, either in a frame or in pans or boxes covered with glass. The seed will germinate within three months. In spring, the seedlings are transferred to a frame or to a shaded bed outdoors, containing some peat or leaf mould. Plant the seedlings 3 in (7·5 cm) apart and keep them moist throughout summer. They will be ready to move to their permanent quarters in 18 months.

Species. *Disporum hookeri.* Native of northern California, it grows 12 in (30 cm) tall with heart-shaped leaves, above which it bears greenish bell-shaped flowers in May.

Disporum lanuginosum. It is present in deciduous woodlands of South Carolina, where it grows 12 in (30 cm) tall and blooms in May and June, its bell-shaped flowers being greenish-yellow. Its lance-shaped leaves are net-veined and downy on the underside.

Disporum menziesii. Native of California, it grows 2 ft (60 cm) tall and has lance-shaped leaves, pointed at the apex, which are woolly on the underside. The greenish-white bell-shaped flowers are borne in June.

DRIMIA (Liliaceae)

A genus of 45 species, native of tropical and South Africa and taking their name from *drimys*, acrid, a reference to the acrid juice of the bulbs. Scilla-like plants, they make a large bulb with crimson-purple flesh and form three to five strap-like basal leaves, which in most cases wither before the flowers appear. The flowers are bell-shaped, greenish-white and borne in an unbranched inflorescence. The perianth segments are united for half their length, the free part reflexing. Growing 18 in (45 cm) tall, the plants are only half-hardy and, except in the most sheltered gardens, should be grown under glass. They bloom early in the new year in their native land, early in autumn in the British Isles and northern Europe.

Culture. Outdoors, they should be given a sunny situation and a light, well-drained soil containing plenty of grit and some humus. Plant the late summer-flowering species in April 8 in (20 cm) apart and 4 in (10 cm) deep, placing the bulbs on a layer of sand. During summer they will require plenty of moisture, but after flowering the bulbs should be dried off and wintered in a frost-free place.

For indoor flowering, plant three or four bulbs to a 5-in (12·5-cm) pot containing a compost made up of 2 parts sterilised loam and 1 part each coarse sand and leaf mould. Plant in March, plunging the pots in a frame until the plants begin to make growth, when they should be moved to a greenhouse. Alternatively, if the frame has sufficient depth they may be allowed to bloom there, giving them plenty of moisture and ample ventilation in summer. The plants are dried off in their pots after flowering and wintered indoors, to be brought into bloom again the following summer. Repot in spring.

Propagation. Small bulblets will form around the mother bulb. These should be detached and grown on in boxes of sandy compost for two years, when they are potted and will bloom within three years of removing them from the parent. It will take five years before plants grown from seed come into bloom.

Species. *Drimia elata.* It is present in sand dunes and on gravelly hills around the Cape Peninsular, where it grows to a height of 18 in (45 cm) and blooms in February. The glaucous leaves appear in May but wither before the appearance of the blooms, which are silvery-green and borne in a dense raceme. All parts of the plant are irritant.

Drimia pusilla. Present on Lion's Head, of the Cape Peninsular, it grows to only half the height of *D. elata*, its three to six leaves, which wither before the flowers appear, being covered in brown hairs. New leaves are formed shortly after the flowers appear, borne in an elegant raceme. They are green, shaded brown on the outside.

E

ENDYMION (Liliaceae)

A genus of perhaps 10 species, native of western Europe, and including the English and Spanish bluebell, previously included under *scilla* and *hyacinthus*. To cause additional confusion, during Elizabethan times the native bluebell was known as the 'harebell'. It is Milton's 'sanguine flower inscribed with woe', also the flower referred to by Shakespeare in Cymbeline:

> Thou shalt not lack
> The flower that's like thy face, pale primrose, nor
> The azured harebell like thy veins.

In Scotland, the flower known as the harebell in England, *Campanula rotundifolia*, is called the bluebell! Gerard said that the bluebell 'grew wilde in woods, copses and in the borders of fields everywhere through England', and he added 'the roots being beaten and applied with white wine, hinder or keep back the growth of hairs'. Gerard called the flower the English jacinth or hyacinth, and at the time the white bulbs were known as Sea Onions and eaten by sailors who would string them up on board ship in the manner of onions, to be used when required.

Culture. Plants of moist deciduous woodlands, of hedgerows and of meadows bordering woods and copses, which they beautify during May and June with their purple-blue flowers and rich balsamic perfume, they are happiest beneath mature trees where they enjoy partial shade and a damp humus-laden soil. They will also flourish and multiply about the outside of coniferous woodlands or where there is a not too heavy concentration of trees. They revel in the acid soil built up over the years by cones and needles. Here, bluebells may be grown with yellow-flowering azaleas, which will bloom at the same time. They are plants for acid soils and exposed positions in the garden, where few other bulbs will give so good an account of themselves. They are also suitable to plant in an orchard, in circular groups of 20 to 30, and in the shrubbery, where the bright-green strap-like foliage will provide pleasing ground cover long before and after the flowers have appeared and died. Plant the English and Spanish bluebells together, for they bloom at the same time, and near them plant the Siberian squills (*Scilla sibirica*), which bloom early in March and during April. Plant in autumn 3 in (7·5 cm) deep and 6 in (15 cm) apart, and where the soil is heavy, work in some humus, setting the bulbs on a layer of sand.

Propagation. Increase by lifting established clumps in autumn and dividing up the bulbs for immediate replanting. Indeed, it will be difficult to lift all the multitudes of small bulblets which cluster around the base of the older bulbs and which will soon attain flowering size and prove difficult to eradicate.

Bluebells will also seed themselves, while a stock may readily be obtained from seed saved when ripe in July. Sow in boxes or frames, into a compost containing 2 parts sterilised loam and 1 part each sand and peat. They will quickly germinate but should be left undisturbed for 12 to 15 months, until the seedlings have formed small bulblets and are ready to plant in their flowering quarters when they will bloom in 18 months. Seed may also be sown in July in the shrubbery or beneath mature trees where the grass has died back. Sow thinly and rake into the ground, or cover with a mixture of finely riddled soil, peat and sand.

Species and Varieties. *Endymion hispanica* (syn. *Scilla hispanica, S. campanulata*). Native of the Pyrenees and Iberian Peninsular, it has strap-shaped leaves, narrower than those of the English bluebell, while its flowers are borne in an upright scape 18 in (45 cm) tall which does not arch like that of the English bluebell. The bell-shaped flowers of soft purple-blue remain horizontal or upright. The bulbs are covered with layers of fibres to form a rough outer skin. There are a number of named varieties:

BLUE BIRD. Early-flowering, it bears its deep purple-blue bells in long elegant spikes and is a valuable cut flower.

BLUE GIANT. It bears its large hyacinth-like bells of deepest blue on 18-in (45-cm) stems.

BLUE QUEEN. Free-flowering, the large spikes bear bells of porcelain blue.

DAINTY MAID. The blooms are of a lovely shade of deep rose-pink, flowering early.

EXCELSIOR. It bears the largest bells of any and in long elegant spikes. They are of deep purple-blue.

MYOSOTIS. Early-flowering, the large bells are of bright forget-me-not blue.

QUEEN OF THE PINKS. The spikes are long and elegant, the bells being of a lovely shade of soft clear pink.

SKYBLUE. Valuable in that it is late-flowering, its bells being of dark purple-blue.

WHITE TRIUMPHATOR. The finest white variety, the large bells of virginal whiteness being enhanced by the dark stems.

Endymion non-scriptus (syn. *Scilla non-scripta, S. nutans, S. festalis, Hyacinthus nutans*). The English bluebell or wood hyacinth, which bears its purple-blue bells on graceful arching stems 18 in (45 cm) tall above glossy strap-like leaves during May and June. The variety *rosea* bears pink flowers, and *alba*, white. Considerable damage is done to bluebell plantations by the careless removal of the flower spikes. These should be cut or snapped off near their base and not pulled from the bulb. The stems and bulbs exude a sticky sap which was used in Elizabethan times to 'starch' the ruffs worn by ladies and gentlemen of standing, while it was also used in place of glue to stick the pages of books. The bulbs will lose vigour if an excess of the exudation is lost by careless removal of the stems.

ERANTHIS (Ranunculaceae)

A genus of six species, native of northern temperate regions, especially northern Europe. Like other members of the family, they are tuberous-rooted perennials, one additional tuber being formed each year. From this arises a flower. The plants come into bloom early in the new year and continue until early May, depending upon species and lateness of season. They bear their golden chalices before the leaves as the snow melts from around them. The flowers are backed by an attractive bright-green ruff of leafy bracts:

> . . . winter aconite
> It's buttercup-like flowers which shut at night,
> With green leaf furling round its cup of gold.

It takes its name from *er*, spring, and *anthos*, flower, while from earliest times it was known as the winter aconite because, said Parkinson (1629), 'it groweth upon bare and naked rocks which the Greeks call Aconas'. Lyte in his *New Herbal* called it the little yellow wolfsbane and wrote, 'it seemeth to be well that aconitum the which Theophrastus hath spoken of and is now called A. hyemale because . . . in the winter it flowereth'. Gerard said that 'it bloweth in January . . . the colder the weather and deeper the snow, the fairer and larger is the flower'. The plants have attractive palmately cut foliage and bear solitary globular flowers composed of six petal-like sepals. It is suitable for planting in generous drifts in bare ground beneath trees and shrubs, when it will quickly form a carpet of golden-yellow. It is most attractive growing with early-flowering squills and with *Iris reticulata* and enjoys similar soil conditions.

Culture. It requires a soil made friable by grit and humus, which is well-drained in winter but retentive of summer moisture, hence its liking for a shady situation in summer, where the direct rays of the sun will not dry out the soil. Plant the tubers 3 in (7·5 cm) deep and 6 in (15 cm) apart, in October. They may not bloom the first winter but will do so the following year, increasing the display as the tubers increase in size.

Propagation. The tubers should not be disturbed for several years, until they have become large and knobbly, when a number may be lifted and divided into several pieces. Select one or two here and there, so that the display will not be harmed and repeat the procedure each year. Plants may also be raised from seed but it will be four years before they bloom. Seed is sown in the John Innes compost in July, covering with a sheet of glass to hasten germination or placing the container in a frame. Seed will usually take up to eight or nine months to germinate, and in March or April small growths may be seen. It will remain green only for about three weeks, when it will die back. Do not lift the tiny tubers until the following year, when they again make new growth, and this is the time to move them, transplanting to boxes containing a sandy compost. Here they remain for another year or 18 months when they may be planted out.

Species and Varieties. *Eranthis cilicica*. Native of Greece and Turkey, it has handsomely cut foliage tinted with bronze and bears, during February, March and April, globular flowers of deepest yellow.

Eranthis hyemalis. Widely distributed throughout western Europe, it comes into bloom mid-January, its pale-yellow chalices, like large buttercups, saluting the new year. The blooms appear on 3-in (7·5-cm) stems and come before the leaves, which are bright green and deeply lobed. It increases rapidly.

Eranthis pinnatifida. Native of northern Japan, it blooms during February and March, the small white globes almost sitting on the soil. It may take several years to become established.

Eranthis tubergenii. The result of a cross between *E. hyemalis* and *E. cilicica*, it is a hybrid of great beauty combining the best qualities of both parents. It comes into bloom in February and, as the flowers are sterile, they last until the end of March. They are larger than those of either parent and are of shining golden-yellow, like those of the kingcup.

Of similar parentage, the variety Glory bears large lemon-yellow flowers, while Guinea Gold is the finest of all, the leaves being tinted with bronze while the flowers are of deepest guinea gold and sweetly scented.

ERYTHRONIUM (Liliaceae)

A genus of 25 species, native of Europe, northern Asia and North America, and taking its name from the Greek *erythros*, red, a reference to the leaves being marbled with crimson. The plant was introduced to English gardens during the sixteenth century by the Dutch botanist, de L'Obel, after whom the lobelia is named. He was superintendent of Lord Zouch's botanical garden in Hackney during the time Gerard had his garden in Holborn. De L'obel was later appointed botanist to King James I. Another Dutchman, Clusius, first named the plant *dentali*, and in the *Paradisus* Parkinson called it *Denscaninus* or dog's-tooth violet. It was so named because of the long white shiny tuberous root which resembles canine teeth, while at the time 'violet' was a name used for all those plants bearing small purple flowers.

E. dens-canis is native of woody mountainous slopes of Switzerland and northern Italy, extending eastwards into Siberia and northern Japan. Like *eranthis*, it is tolerant of extreme cold. It is also a handsome plant both in flower and foliage, suitable for naturalising in short grass or beneath trees and equally at home in the rock garden and alpine house. The flowers of *E. dens-canis* are most striking against the silver bark of birch trees. The plant produces a new tuberous root (bulb) each year, usually at the base of the old one. The stem leaves are unequal, one being narrower than the other though a plant may produce up to four leaves. They are dark green and beautifully mottled and blotched with crimson-purple, but the markings vary on almost every leaf. The nodding flowers are borne solitary or in pairs and have reflexed perianth leaves and protruding anthers, which almost unite to form a cone. The erythronium, like the hardy cyclamen, grows well in a limestone soil provided it is generously supplied with humus.

Culture. The plant enjoys protection from the heat of the summer sun and requires a cool humus-laden soil, enriched with leaf mould or peat and decayed cow manure. Old mushroom-bed compost is also suitable. It also enjoys a gritty loam, so some lime rubble or shingle should be given, to enable winter moisture to drain away as quickly as possible when the roots are dormant. The plant, however, requires a soil which is retentive of summer moisture and will benefit from an annual mulch given after the foliage has died back in autumn.

When planting the bulbous roots, note that they will shrivel if too long exposed to sunlight or drying winds. They are usually sent out in bags of peat or sawdust to prevent bruising and here they should remain until planting time. Plant in October, 3 in (7·5 cm) deep and with the 'tooth'-shaped bulb in a layer of sand. Plant 6 in (15 cm) apart and do not disturb for several years.

When growing indoors, plant in pots or pans containing a compost composed of 2 parts loam and 1 part each leaf mould and coarse sand. Set the bulbs 2 in (5 cm) deep and 3 in (7·5 cm) apart, planting three or four to each pot or pan. Place in a plunge bed for six weeks or in a darkened room or cupboard while the roots are forming, then move to a window or cool greenhouse. Like snowdrops, the plants will not tolerate a warm, stuffy atmosphere or a temperature exceeding 50° F (10° C). The leaves are produced first, then the bloom, the first species to bloom being *E. dens-canis*, early in February. After flowering, the bulbs may be kept in the pans and dried off as the leaves fade, or they may be planted out when the leaves have faded. Like the cyclamen, the leaves persist and retain their beauty for several months after the flowers have died.

Propagation. Erythroniums should be moved as little as possible, being left to increase by offshoots and by self-sown seed. If it is required to propagate a variety of merit, the time to do so is in May after flowering, before the leaves die back. If the weather is dry, water until the plants are re-established.

Plants are readily raised from seed sown in July when ripe, either in a frame containing a sandy compost, or in boxes or pans containing the John Innes compost. Do not cover the seed. Maintain the compost in a moist condition, shading from the direct rays of the sun, and do not transplant the seedlings until their second year. They may be planted out in their third year and will come into bloom four or five years after sowing.

Species and Varieties. *Erythronium albidum.* Native of the damp pastures of Pennsylvania, its lance-shaped leaves are mottled with silvery-green. The drooping white flowers, shaded yellow at the base, are borne on 9-in (22·5-cm) stems during April and May, this being one of the latest species to bloom. It is rare in cultivation and also in the wild and increases by stolons.

Erythronium americanum. It is present in damp woodlands of eastern Canada and the United States, from Nova Scotia to as far south as Florida, where the stolon-bearing bulbs are found at a depth of 6 in (15 cm) or more. On the stem

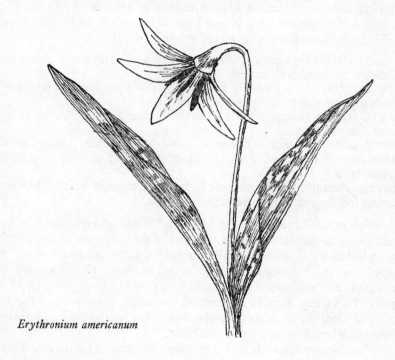

Erythronium americanum

9 in (22·5 cm) long is to be found two leaves of dark glossy green splashed with brown and narrowing into clasping petioles. The nodding flowers are borne singly and are pale yellow, occasionally tinted with purple and with reflexed segments 2 in (5 cm) long. It blooms with *E. albidum,* in late spring. In America it is known as the Yellow Adder's-tongue.

Erythronium californicum. Native of California, where it is found at altitudes

of up to 10,000 ft, it is a species of charm, its dark-green leaves being mottled with dull purple, while its large creamy-white bell-shaped flowers, often 3 in (7·5 cm) across and shaded orange at the base, are borne one to six or more on a 12-in (30-cm) stem. The flowers appear in March and have pure-white anthers. The form *helenae* has white flowers lined with deep yellow.

Erythronium citrinum. Native of the Deer Creek Mountains of Oregon, it has lance-shaped leaves richly mottled with brown, and bears its creamy-yellow flowers in twos or threes on a 6-in (15-cm) stem. The broad segments are strongly recurved and are sometimes tipped with pink. It blooms in March and April.

Erythronium dens-canis. Native of Central Europe, Siberia and northern Japan, its long cylindrical bulbs more nearly resemble the tooth of a dog than those of other species. It has handsome lance-shaped glaucous leaves, splashed with dull crimson-purple and it blooms during March and April, bearing a solitary flower of purple on a 6-in (15-cm) purple stem. The six anthers are also purple. There are several varieties of outstanding beauty:

CHARMER. Its leaves are beautifully marbled with crimson, while it bears white flowers shaded with mauve.

LILAC WONDER. The blooms are large and of a rich shade of imperial purple with a brown spot at the base of each segment.

PINK PERFECTION. Early-flowering, the large refined blooms are of a delicate shade of clear pink.

PURPLE KING. It bears a flower of outstanding beauty, being of rich cyclamen-mauve edged with white, the centre being spotted and striped chocolate-brown.

WHITE SPLENDOUR. The blooms are large and of clearest white. They act as a pleasing foil for the purple-flowering varieties.

Erythronium grandiflorum. Native of Idaho and Washington, where it is found on mountainous slopes, flowering as soon as the snow departs in spring. The dark-green leaves are unmottled, while the bright golden-yellow flowers open star-shaped and are enhanced by the crimson stamens. They measure 3 in (7·5 cm) across and are borne two or three to a 9-in (22·5-cm) stem in March and April. The variety *parviflorum* (syn. *E. nuttallii*), discovered in the Blue Mountains of Oregon, is similar, except that it has cream-coloured anthers. *Albiflorum* has white flowers tinted with green.

Erythronium hartwegii (syn. *E. multiscapoideum*). Native of California, it forms a small ovoid bulb and has lance-shaped leaves of darkest green, waved at the edges and with distinct purple markings. It bears in March creamy-yellow flowers shaded orange at the base and held on a 6-in (15-cm) stem. The flowers are borne singly and open star-like.

Erythronium hendersonii. Native of the Blue Mountains of Oregon, it has dark-green, lance-shaped leaves slightly mottled with brown, and in March bears drooping lavender-mauve flowers with their strongly reflexed segments in twos

Crocus: Gypsy Girl

Crocus: Remembrance

Crocus: Striped Beauty

Erythronium: Lilac Wonder

Erythronium: White Beauty

Eucomis bicolor

Fritillaria meleagris and *Narcissus jonquilla*

and threes on a 6-in (15-cm) stem. The flowers have maroon markings at the base of the segments. It quickly becomes established in the alpine garden.

Erythronium montanum. Native of mountainous slopes of Oregon and Washington, where it comes into bloom with the melting of the snow, it is the most difficult species to establish under garden conditions. It requires a cold, dry winter followed by a hot, dry summer to bloom well. Its leaves are but slightly mottled, while its creamy-white flowers are shaded with pink at the base. It has yellow anthers.

Erythronium oregonum. Native of Oregon and British Columbia, it is the most vigorous of the species, bearing large flowers of creamy-white on stems 2 ft (60 cm) tall. The flowers, which measure 3 in (7·5 cm) across, are shaded with orange at the base of the segments and appear in March.

Erythronium purpurascens. Native of the mountains of Montana, it has small ovoid bulbs from which arise narrow lance-shaped leaves tinted with brown, while it bears as many as seven or eight flowers to a 6-in (15-cm) stem. The blooms are of lemon yellow tinted with purple and shaded deep orange at the base of the segments.

Erythronium revolutum. Native of the woodlands of northern California, it is known as the trout lily for its blooms are of a unique shade of brownish-pink, while the deep-green leaves are mottled with brown and white. The flowers, which measure 3 in (7·5 cm) across, are borne in twos and are held well above the foliage on 6-in (15-cm) stems. The variety Pink Beauty bears flowers of clear pink with extremely reflexed or rolled-back petals and it blooms during April and May. In shade and a soil containing plenty of humus it is readily established.

The variety White Beauty is one of the most attractive of spring flowers, the reflexed segments of ice-white revealing a crimson-brown centre and pale-yellow anthers. It received an award of merit from the Royal Horticultural Society in 1964. This variety has been crossed with *E. tuolumnense*, another Californian species, and resulted in the raising of two hybrids of great merit. Kondo bears three to five large flowers of sulphur yellow, shaded brown at the centre, on a 12-in (30-cm) stem; and Pagoda, which has leaves mottled with bronze, bears flowers of pale yellow with the same brown centre. Both possess great vigour but should be planted where they will not be troubled by March winds.

Erythronium tuolumnense. When not in bloom it is readily distinguished by its yellowy-green leaves, free from any mottling. It comes into bloom in April, bearing its rich golden-yellow flowers in twos and threes on a slender stem 10 in (25 cm) long. With *E. dens-canis* it is the easiest of the species to establish and will quickly form a large plant. It enjoys more moisture than other species.

EUCHARIS (Amaryllidaceae)

A genus of 10 species, native of tropical South America, especially the Colombian Andes and taking their name from *eucharis*, pleasant or agreeable,

K

the reference being to the sweet scent of the flowers. They have large tunicated bulbs like those of narcissus but with a longer neck. The leaves are broad and strap-like, bright glossy-green in colour, while the narcissus-like flowers of pure white are borne in loose umbels at the end of a fleshy scape. They are mostly winter-flowering. The perianth tube is cylindrical with six widely spreading segments. The six stamens unite to form a short corona, often reflexing to resemble a daffodil.

Culture. It requires stove conditions—i.e. a minimum winter temperature of 65° F (18° C)—though *E. grandiflora* will bloom where the temperature does not fall below 60° F (16° C). As the eucharis also requires a damp, humid atmosphere, a greenhouse is essential for its culture. The bulbs, which measure 3 in (7·5 cm) across, may be planted one to a 5-in (12·5-cm) pot or three to a larger pot; or they may be planted in a greenhouse border, allowing 4 in (10 cm) between each bulb. A suitable compost consists of 2 parts turf loam, 1 part each peat or leaf mould and dehydrated cow manure, to which is added a sprinkling of sand.

Plant the bulbs early in March, pressing the compost firmly around them and so that the top of the neck is above the level of the compost, which should be just below the rim of the pot. The pots are placed into deep boxes, and soil or peat is packed around them. Water sparingly until growth begins, but provide a temperature of 60° F (16° C) day and night and increase to 70° F (21° C) when growth commences. Watering must now be increased. Give copious amounts and syringe the foliage at least twice daily. The pots should now be lifted from the plunge bed, but as the flower buds appear they must be shaded from the late summer sunshine by whitening the glass. The flowers are induced to appear by lowering the temperature to 60° F (16° C) again and withholding water for two or three weeks, until the leaves begin to drop. The temperature is then increased and more water given, and it may be necessary to repeat the procedure several times so that it will be several months or more before the flower buds appear in autumn. It is then time to feed the plants, giving dilute manure water each week, for the eucharis is a gross feeder. Maintain a humid atmosphere by regularly damping the floor of the house.

Flowering will continue throughout autumn and winter when moisture should be withheld (not entirely as the plants are evergreen) until the leaves begin to droop and, after a partial rest period, the plants may again be brought into bloom. By regulating moisture and temperature and providing periodical rests, the plants may be made to bloom (on and off) almost the whole year. Where growing for market, it will be necessary to have two lots of plants so that one lot may be brought into bloom while the others are resting. There is always a demand for the bloom by high-class florists, especially in winter.

After a prolonged period of flowering, the plants are given a longer than usual rest period and are top-dressed with fresh loam and decayed manure. At this time, provide a drier than usual atmosphere but never completely withhold moisture. After resting for two or three months, the plants may again be brought into bloom and allowed to occupy their pots for several years before re-potting in fresh compost.

Propagation. After several years in the pots, small bulbs will form around the mother bulb. These are detached when repotting and planted into their own pots, in which they remain for two or three years until reaching flowering size, when they are brought into bloom as described.

Species and Varieties. *Eucharis amazonica* (syn. *E. grandiflora*). It was dis-covered in the Colombian Andes in 1853 and has since remained the most widely grown species. It forms a round bulb of about 3-in (7·5-cm) diameter and sends out broad ovate leaves, waved at the margins. It bears its greatest number of flowers from November until April, five or six pure-white flowers appearing at the end of a 2-ft (60-cm) scape. Each bloom measures 4 in (10 cm) across, with the united stamens forming a 'cup' or corona. They emit a powerful scent. The variety *moorei* bears slightly smaller flowers, while the outside of the corona is striped with yellow.

Eucharis candida. It has been in cultivation longer than any species and has stolon-bearing bulbs 2 in (5 cm) in diameter from which arise long-stalked bright-green leaves. Winter-flowering, it bears 6 to 10 drooping white flowers on an 18-in (45-cm) scape. The blooms measure 3 in (7·5 cm) across and have a neat staminal 'cup'.

Eucharis mastersi. It has small bulbs, 2 in (5 cm) in diameter, and bright-green oblong leaves. The snow-white flowers measure 3 in (7·5 cm) across and are borne two or three to a 12-in (30-cm) scape.

Eucharis sanderi. It is a dainty species with bright-green leaves cordate at the base and bearing five or six pure-white flowers in a compact umbel. The flowers have broad segments terminating in a point and are free of any staminal 'cup'. The variety *multiflora* bears smaller flowers, the segments being striped with green.

EUCOMIS (Liliaceae)

A genus of 14 species, native of tropical and southern Africa and which takes its name from the Greek *eucomis*, beautiful-haired, an allusion to the small tuft of hair-like growths (bracts) to be seen at the top of the flower spike. They have conical tunicated bulbs and lanceolate leaves often 2 ft (60 cm) in length and with wavy margins. The flowers are borne 50 or more in a dense raceme on a stout stem 1 to 5 ft (30 cm to 1·50 metres) tall and are surmounted by the tuft of leafy bracts. The flowers resemble those of *eremurus*, having an exotic appear-ance, though the plants are hardy in the warmer parts of the British Isles and northern Europe, where they may be grown outside as well as indoors. Planted in groups of three or four in the border they look striking when in bloom during July and August.

Culture. When grown outdoors, the plants require a position sheltered from cold winds but where the maximum amount of sunshine can reach them. They also require a rich well-drained loam into which has been incorporated some decayed manure. As the plants bloom late in summer, there is little chance of the new season's growth being harmed by frost. Plant the bulbs 8 in (20 cm) deep so that there will be at least 5 in (12·5 cm) of soil over the top and plant 12 in (30 cm) apart. To assist drainage, plant the bulbs on a layer of sand. Early April is the best time to plant, for then growth will not appear above ground until spring frosts have ended.

The plants should be left undisturbed for several years, giving them a heavy mulch of leaf mould and decayed manure each year in November, when the flowers and foliage have died back. Frost may be excluded by covering the ground with bracken or ashes after mulching.

Where growing indoors, a cold greenhouse will prove suitable, the bulbs being planted early in March, one to a 5-in (12·5-cm) pot and in a compost made up of 2 parts fibrous loam and 1 part each leaf mould and decayed manure with a sprinkling of grit. Give almost no moisture until growth commences, then water freely until the plants have finished flowering. They are slowly dried off and remain in their pots over winter, removing to a frost-free room until it is time to start them into growth again in spring. They will benefit from a weekly application of dilute manure water when once the flower buds have formed and they should be given a top-dressing in spring. The bulbs may be repotted every fifth year.

Propagation. When the bulbs are lifted, offsets will be seen clustering around them. These are detached and grown on in boxes of sandy compost until they reach flowering size, when they are moved to individual pots in which they will bloom.

Plants may be raised from seed sown in boxes of gritty compost in spring and covered with glass, or the boxes or pans may be placed in the greenhouse. The seed will germinate by the end of summer, but the seedlings should not be transplanted until the following year. During winter the seedlings are kept in a temperature of 50° F (10° C) and given only sufficient moisture to keep them alive. Transplant to $2\frac{1}{2}$-in (6-cm) pots containing a similar compost and in which they are grown on for two more years, when they will be ready to move to larger pots, in which they will bloom five or six years from the time of sowing.

Species and Varieties. *Eucomis bicolor.* Native of Natal, it has a large oval bulb and three or four dark-green leaves, waved at the margins. It sends up its flower spike to a height of 16 in (40 cm) early in August, the flowers being borne in a dense raceme resembling a pineapple, hence its name Pineapple Flower. They are greenish-white with a purple edge or rim.

Eucomis nana. It is the most compact species, with lance-shaped acute leaves and bearing brownish-green flowers on a 9-in (23-cm) scape. The variety *purpureocaulis* has purple-red stems.

Eucomis pole-evansii. Native of the Transvaal, it is more tender than other cultivated species and requires a warm greenhouse. It is also the most vigorous, with large spotted leaves and making a flower stem 5 or 6 ft (1·5 to 1·8 metres) tall with the greenish-yellow florets forming a cylindrical spike 2 ft (60 cm) in length.

Eucomis punctata (syn. *E. comosa*). Native of Natal, it has large leaves, re-curving at the tips and of deepest green, spotted with purple on the underside. The creamy-white star-shaped flowers are sweetly scented and appear in July in a cylindrical raceme on a 20-in (50-cm) stem. At the top is a tuft of red-tinted leaves (bracts).

Eucomis undulata (syn. *E. autumnalis*). Native of Natal and Cape Province, it has broad ovate leaves, waved at the margins and in August bears a dense raceme of greenish-cream flowers with a tuft of green bracts at the top.

EUCROSIA (Amaryllidaceae)

A genus of four species, native of the Andes of Ecuador and introduced into cultivation early in the nineteenth century. It takes its name from *eu*, beautiful, and *krossos*, a fringe, an allusion to the unusual fringe forming the stamens. Only one species, *E. bicolor*, is cultivated and requires greenhouse treatment with a winter temperature of 50° F (10° C).

Culture. The small tunicated bulbs should be planted in autumn, three or four to a large pot containing a compost made up of 2 parts loam and 1 part each peat and coarse sand. Just cover the bulbs and place in a plunge bed or in a frame for two months while they form roots. Then remove to a warm greenhouse or garden room to bring on the plants, increasing moisture as they form their lance-shaped leaves. They will bloom early in spring and into summer. After flowering, water should be gradually (but not entirely) withheld while the plants rest.

Propagation. The bulbs may occupy the pots for several years, but when it is necessary to repot, shake from the soil and remove the offsets, which are grown on in boxes of sandy compost until reaching flowering size. They are then potted and brought into bloom.

Species. *Eucrosia bicolor*. It has fibrous-coated ovoid bulbs of about 1-in (2·5-cm) diameter and lance-shaped leaves 6 in (15 cm) long and 2 in (5 cm) wide, with short stalks. The flowers are funnel-shaped and are of deepest yellow, the segments being striped with green. They are borne in spring, in loose umbels on a 12-in (30-cm) stem. The flowers are conspicuous by their stamens which protrude far beyond the perianth tube.

EURYCLES (Amaryllidaceae)

A genus of three species, native of the Malay Peninsula, the Philippines and northern Australia and taking their name from *eurys*, broad, a reference to the broad leaves which are held on long footstalks. The flowers are white and borne in dense umbels, resembling allium with their cylindrical perianth tube and oblong segments. There are six stamens which unite to form a cup. The plants require stove conditions—i.e. a temperature of not less than 65° F (18° C)—though this may be reduced when the bulbs are resting.

Culture. The bulbs measure about 4 in (10 cm) in diameter and should be potted singly, using a 4-in (10-cm) pot for the smaller *E. cunninghami* and a 5-in (12·5-cm) pot for *E. sylvestris*. Provide a compost made up of fibrous loam, leaf mould and decayed manure in equal parts, to which is added a liberal sprinkling of sand. Plant in October, just covering the bulb with compost. Give little moisture until the end of winter, but maintain a temperature of not less than 60° F (16° C), which should be raised to 70° F (21° C) when growth commences and watering is increased. The plants will bloom during summer and benefit from an occasional application of dilute manure water. They are evergreen and must not be completely dried off after flowering but given only sufficient moisture to keep them alive during the winter rest period.

Propagation. After occupying the pots for five years, the bulbs should be re-potted and the offsets detached. They are grown on in small pots containing a sandy compost until they reach flowering size, when they are moved to a 4-in (10-cm) pot.

Species. *Eurycles cunninghami.* Native of Queensland it makes a small bulb of 2-in (5-cm) diameter and has oblong-acute leaves 9 in (23 cm) long. It bears its pure-white flowers in umbels of 12 to 18 on a slender 12-in (30-cm) scape.

Eurycles sylvestris. At one time classed with pancratium, amaryllis and crinum, it is native of south-eastern Asia and northern Australia and forms a large round bulb of 4-in (10-cm) diameter. The leaves are 12 in (30 cm) wide and terminate in a point. There are 15 veins on each side of the midrib. The pure-white flowers are borne in umbels of 20 to 30, to form almost a ball at the end of a 15-in (37·5-cm) scape.

EUSTEPHIA (PHAEDRANASSA) (Amaryllidaceae)

A genus of two or three species, native of the Andes of Peru and, though introduced early in the nineteenth century, it is rare in cultivation, requiring warm greenhouse culture. It takes its name from *eu*, beautiful, and *stephos*, a crown, an allusion to the striking arrangement of the stamens.

Culture. The bulbs are small and several may be planted in a 5-in (12·5-cm) pot using a compost made up of fibrous loam, peat and decayed manure with a liberal sprinkling of sand. Cover the bulbs with 1 in (2·5 cm) of compost and plant in October, standing the pots beneath the greenhouse bench for about six weeks and giving little water until growth commences. They may then be given full light and a winter temperature of 55° to 60° F (13° to 16° C). Moisture may be increased as the plants come into bloom in spring.

Propagation. When the plants are repotted in autumn or early in the year, detach the offsets growing around the bulbs and plant into boxes of sandy compost, then after two years, move to their flowering pots.

Species. *Eustephia coccinea* (syn. *Phaedranassa rubro-viridis*). Native of Peru, it forms a small ovoid brown tunicated bulb 1 in (2·5 cm) in diameter and has bright-green leaves 12 in (30 cm) long, which appear immediately after the flowers. It blooms in April and May, six to eight drooping flowers appearing at the end of a 16-in (40-cm) scape. They are crimson-red, shaded green at the base, while the segments are also tipped with green, making it one of the most handsome flowers in cultivation.

EXOHEBEA (Iridaceae)

A genus of 12 or 13 species, native of South Africa and taking its name from Hebe, goddess of youth. Corm-bearing plants closely related to gladiolus, the corms are covered in reddish-brown fibres which extend up the elongated neck. It has one to four linear basal leaves and a short spike around which the flowers are spirally arranged. They are mostly cream coloured, marked with maroon and emitting a spicy perfume. The short perianth tube widens at the top, the lobes being longer than the tube, the stamens arching.

Culture. Rare in cultivation, the corms bloom late in summer and in autumn and should be treated like the gladiolus, planting in April into a friable soil. Plant 3 in (7·5 cm) deep and 6 in (15 cm) apart. After flowering they are lifted and the new corms stored during winter in a frost-free room.

Propagation. Upon lifting, cormlets will be seen clustering around the base of the old corm. These are detached and wintered in jars, to be planted early in spring in boxes of sandy soil, in which they will grow for two years until they reach flowering size.

Species. *Exohebea fraterna* (syn. *Gladiolus fraternus*). The two-veined leaves grow to about 12 in (30 cm) long, while the cream-coloured flowers are produced 6 to 16 in number on a spike 18 in (45 cm) tall. The three lower lobes of the flower are tinted with pink. It blooms with *E. parviflora*.

Exohebea parviflora. Present about sandy, rocky ground of the Cape Peninsula, it forms short sword-like leaves and a many-flowered spike 12 in (30 cm) long. The flowers are yellow and maroon with a perianth tube about 1 in (2·5 cm) long. In their native haunts, they bloom from November to January; in the British Isles and northern Europe from July to September.

F

FERRARIA (Iridaceae)

Native of southern Africa, it is a genus of only one or two species, for most have now been classed with *morea* or *tigridia*. They bear irregular flattened corms without tunics and spathe-like leaves incurved at the tips. The flowers, borne on a branched stem, are short-lived and have an unpleasant sweet smell. They are usually given cool greenhouse treatment in the British Isles and northern Europe, for they are tender and bloom early in summer—towards the end of April indoors and about six weeks later in the open, where they may be planted only in those gardens situated in warmer parts. The genus is named after the Italian botanist, J. B. Ferrari.

Culture. Indoors, the small corms should be planted early in the new year, three or four to a 5-in (12·5-cm) pot and in a sandy compost containing some peat and a little dehydrated cow manure. Cover with 1 in (2·5 cm) of compost and give little water until growth begins, when increased supplies are given. A winter temperature of 45° to 50° F (7° to 10° C) should be maintained, artificial warmth being replaced by the sunlight as the plants come into bloom at the end of April. After flowering, the foliage will die back gradually when water must be withheld. The pots are then placed under the greenhouse bench or in an attic or cellar, where they remain, free from frost, until started into growth again early in the new year.

Where planting outdoors, set the corms 3 in (7·5 cm) deep on a layer of sand and 6 in (15 cm) apart. Plant early in spring, in a light sandy soil and in an open, sunny situation. The plants will bloom early in June and should be lifted and stored away from frost, as soon as the foliage has died back in autumn.

In the mildest parts, the corms may remain in the ground all year but should be protected from excess winter moisture by covering with cloches which are removed when fresh growth begins.

Propagation. When the corms are lifted, tiny cormlets or spawn found clustering around the base are removed and stored during winter in boxes or jars as for gladioli. They are planted early in spring into boxes of sandy compost and grown on for two years, after which they are dried off and replanted in spring in the pots where they are to bloom.

Species. *Ferraria undulenta* (syn. *Tigridia undulata*). Native of Cape Province it has been in cultivation for 200 years. It grows among rocks on Table Mountain and on Lion's Head, and these are the conditions it enjoys, a well-drained gritty soil where the sun can bake the bulbs in summer. It will then bear bloom in abundance. The sword-like leaves have a prominent mid-rib, while the flowers are borne on branching stems 15 in (37·5 cm) tall. The iris-like flowers appear in succession over about six weeks and are of brownish-purple, like decaying meat, being blotched and spotted with purple-maroon and striped with black. Both the colour and unpleasant smell attract dung flies for its pollination.

FREESIA (Iridaceae)

A genus of 20 species, native of South Africa, with fibrous-coated bulbous corms and flat, narrow leaves. The flowers are bell-shaped and are borne on wiry stems. Several species are sufficiently hardy to be grown outdoors in the British Isles but only in those gardens situated in warmer parts; otherwise, grow in gentle heat. *F. refracta* and its hybrid varieties is the only species in general cultivation and it is grown commercially for its cut bloom. Corms of *F. refracta* reached England about 1850, but it was not until Mr W. Armstrong introduced a variety bearing white and pink flowers 50 years later that any real interest was taken in the flower. It was crossed with *F. refracta alba*, first by Mr F. H. Chapman of Rye in Sussex, then by Mr G. H. Dalrymple and soon a number of varieties were selected and named. They had a wide colour range, one of the earliest being the variety *champmanii*, with its large flowers of soft yellow. By 1950, a century after the introduction of *F. refracta*, several million blooms annually were being produced for the high-class florist trade by specialist growers, the most important being Mr J. C. Eauwens of Offenham, who produces over a million blooms in an all-year-round supply.

Culture. Freesias may be grown indoors entirely without heat, though they give better results where grown in an even temperature of 45° to 48° F (7° to 8° C). A large airy greenhouse will prove most suitable, for, though native of southern Africa, freesias require the same airy conditions as the carnation where grown indoors. It is also one of the few plants that may be brought into bloom directly from a sowing of seed and without transplanting. Seed germinates as readily as mustard and cress seed and may be sown into deep boxes filled with sterilised loam, peat and coarse sand in equal parts. Or the seed may be sown directly into ground beds made up to a similar formula. Freesias are lovers of peat, but no manure should be used, for this will result in weak stems. A quarter of a pound of seed will produce upwards of 10,000 plants. The amateur, wishing to raise a few boxes of plants to provide bloom for the home, will find that a small packet of seed will give several hundred plants. Sow early May, about 30 seeds to each square foot of compost, and cover with a sprinkling of sand. Place the boxes in a frame or cover with a sheet of glass, which should be whitened to exclude the sun. The compost should be watered only when it shows dry patches. Grow on through summer, then early in autumn transfer several boxes to a greenhouse which should have a night temperature of about 45° F (7° C). Then begin to water with dilute liquid manure, which will enhance the colour of the blooms, and fix over the boxes lengths of wire netting to support the flower stems. Again, water only occasionally, giving sufficient to keep the plants alive, for under similar dry conditions they grow and bloom in their natural state. By late November the first buds will be formed, and a day and night temperature of 48° F (9° C) should be maintained. The plants will bloom throughout winter, and if another batch is taken indoors before the winter frosts, these will begin to bloom early in March and continue until May. Where growing for shop sale, the blooms should be cut with the flowers just open and given a drink lasting two hours before dispatching.

Those who have no facilities for raising plants from seed may enjoy a winter crop of bloom from 5-cm-size corms. Plant mid-August, six corms to a 5-in (12·5-cm) pot, placing them 1 in (2·5 cm) below the level of the compost. Stand in a cold frame or beneath the eaves of a house for six weeks, until they make root growth, but do not cover with ashes to exclude light. They require a compost similar to that suggested for raising plants from seed. The compost should also be kept as dry as possible throughout. Before the frosts, remove to a warm greenhouse or garden room, remembering that freesias require the maximum amount of light especially for winter-flowering, while they should be given only sufficient moisture to prevent them from flagging. Also, grow quite cool, never allowing the temperature to rise above 50° F (10° C).

As the leaves and flower stems make growth, insert small green stakes around the pot and to them fasten green twine to prevent the flower stems falling over, but remember that the cooler the plants are grown the sturdier will be their stems. After flowering, remove the dead heads and gradually withhold moisture while the foliage dies back. Then stand the pots on a shelf in the greenhouse or in a frame so that the corms will ripen during summer. They may be brought into bloom again in winter, feeding with dilute manure water as the plants make growth.

Freesias may also be brought into bloom outdoors by covering with barn-type cloches. Corms of the Paradise strain, which have been kept under refrigeration, are planted in April, in shallow trenches made to the width of the cloches. Plant 2 in (5 cm) deep and 2 in (5 cm) apart in rows, and when the plants have made sufficient growth insert among them strong twigs to keep the stems upright. Water sparingly and cover with cloches as soon as the corms have been planted. They will come into bloom by mid-August and continue until early October, when the foliage will die back. The corms may then be lifted and stored indoors or, if in a sheltered garden, they may remain in the ground, covered with the cloches.

In gardens where frost is absent, corms may be planted in the open in April.

If planted among heathers, the twiggy branches will keep the freesia stems upright as they grow. Plant 2 in (5 cm) deep in a well-drained sandy soil. They require an open sunny situation and protection from strong winds. The corms may be left down or lifted after the foliage has died back.

Propagation. Growing from seed is the usual method, for fresh seed will germinate more quickly than that of any other plant and will bloom within nine months of sowing under correct conditions.

Where it is required to propagate a variety which may have produced a bloom of quality or of a new colour, it will be necessary to detach the tiny cormlets which cluster about the base of the mother corm. These are stored in winter in a box or jar and planted in spring in pots in which they will grow on to flowering size by the end of summer.

Species and Varieties. *Freesia refracta*. This is the only species in general cultivation. Native of South Africa, it has oval bulbous-like corms covered in a thick netted tunic from which arise five or six thin linear leaves and a slender flower stem 18 in (45 cm) long, the end of which bends over. It bears six to nine upright funnel-shaped blooms, which carry the most pleasing of all flower perfumes. The blooms open bell-shaped and are of almost every known flower colour, in addition to the creamy-white flowers of the type.

FRITILLARIA (Liliaceae)

A genus of about 84 species, mostly native of northern temperate regions and taking their name from *fritillas*, a chess-board, for the blooms of many species are chequered on the outside. The bulbs are fleshy and should be handled with care, for the scales are readily damaged and if out of the ground for any length of time become shrivelled. The leaves are borne opposite, along the succulent stems at the end of which appear drooping bell-shaped flowers composed of six segments, each of which has a large nectar-bearing cavity at the base. They are suitable for naturalising in short grass and for planting in the rock garden and in the alpine house, where the beauty of the flowers at eye level can be appreciated.

Culture. They require a well-drained loam, enriched with a small amount of decayed manure, into which is incorporated leaf mould and grit, and while several species are happiest in the partial shade of a woodland garden, there are those which require an open, sunny situation in which the bulbs can ripen in summer. Most, however, present no problems. They bloom during March, April and May and should be planted in October 4 in (10 cm) deep. Where planting in grass space them 6 in (15 cm) apart, though, as the species vary considerably in habit, some growing 6 in (15 cm) tall, others 3 or 4 ft (90 cm or 1·2 metres), each species must be treated accordingly. Remember to leave the grass uncut until late July when the foliage will have died down.

Those species of dwarf habit which are to be grown in the alpine house or frame should be planted in October, four to six bulbs to a pot or pan and spacing them about 2 in (5 cm) apart. They require a gritty loam containing some peat or leaf mould and are placed in the open, covered with sand or ashes for several weeks, to form roots before being removed to a cold greenhouse or frame early in December. They will bloom under glass during March and April and may require little or no water until the spring sunshine brings them into growth. After flowering, dry off the bulbs gradually and stand the pots outdoors during summer, to be started into growth again in December. They are hardy and have no shortcomings apart from those one or two species introduced from warmer parts.

Propagation. They are readily increased by means of offsets detached from the base of the mother bulb when they are lifted for division in autumn. They should be replanted immediately into a well-drained soil and will come into bloom in 18 months.

Plants may be raised from seed sown in August when ripe. Use the John Innes compost and sow either in a frame, or in boxes in a frame or greenhouse. Sow thinly and grow on the seedlings for 18 months before transplanting into a compost made up of sterilised loam, peat and sand in equal parts. Here, the plants remain for 12 months, after which they are transplanted again and grown on until they bloom. The bulbs are then dried off and planted out in autumn to come into bloom the following spring, about four years after the seed is sown.

Species and Varieties. *Fritillaria acmopetala.* Native of the Levant, it will grow well in the shade of a dell garden, where it will begin to flower before the end of March. Its translucent bells of bronzey-green, with their recurved pointed tips, shade to yellowish-green at the base and have green nectaries. They are borne one to three on only 6-in (15-cm) stems—which are slightly longer where growing in grass. The scaly bulbs should be planted 4 in (10 cm) deep.

Fritillaria armena. Native of Turkey and northern Persia, it has small scaly bulbs and requires a well-drained gritty soil and exposure to sunlight. The bell-shaped flowers of dull yellow shaded maroon appear in April on 9-in (22·5-cm) stems, and when established form large clumps.

Fritillaria askabadensis. Native of the Caucasus, it resembles *F. imperialis* in that it bears five to eight dangling bell-shaped flowers on a leafy stem 3 ft (90 cm) tall, surmounted by a tuft of pale-green leaves. The glossy leaves are borne in whorls while the blooms of greenish-yellow appear in April.

Fritillaria aurea (syn. *F. latifolia*). Like so many of the species, it is native of south-eastern Europe, especially the Caucasus. It grows only 4 in (10 cm) tall, with two upright stem leaves and bears a single flower of bright yellow chequered with brown. It blooms with *F. meleagris*, which it resembles, during April and May.

Fritillaria camschatcensis. It is present in northern China, Japan, Alaska and north-western America and is a hardy and easily established species, bearing purple bell-shaped flowers on 12-in (30-cm) stems. It blooms late, often flowering well into June in a late season and is usually at its best in the half-shade of a woodland garden.

Fritillaria caucasica. From the Caucasus, it resembles *F. camschatcensis* in its mahogany-purple bell-shaped blooms, borne on 12-in (10-cm) stems, and with its narrow glaucous leaves, though it comes into bloom at least a month earlier. It is a plant of extreme hardiness.

Fritillaria cirrhosa. Native of the Himalayas, it is late into bloom, being at its best during May, its dangling bells of deepest purple, shaded with green and chequered on the inside, appearing in twos and threes on 2-ft (60-cm) stems which are clothed in whorls of linear leaves.

Fritillaria citrina (syn. *F. bithynica*). Native of Greece and Asia Minor, it is rare both in the wild and in cultivation. It bears on a 6-in (15-cm) stem, one to three nodding tubular bell-shaped flowers of lemon-yellow, shaded with green. The flowers, which are covered with a glaucous 'bloom', appear late in April.

Fritillaria crassifolia. Native of Syria and the Lebanon, it bears long elegant bells of deep purple, overlaid with green, and is heavily chequered. It blooms in May, usually in twos on a 15-in (38-cm) stem.

Fritillaria delphinensis (syn. *F. tubiformis*). Native of the Maritime Alps of southern France and northern Italy, it bears solitary bells of grape-purple, chequered with black. The flowers often measure nearly 2 in (5 cm) across and are held on stems 6 in (15 cm) tall. The variety *burnettii* has plum-purple flowers chequered with green, while *moggridgei* bears yellow flowers chequered with crimson, the blooms being cylindrical in shape.

Fritillaria discolor. Native of Turkey and Bulgaria, it has leafy stems along which are borne whorls of lance-shaped leaves and, at the top, flowers of golden-yellow with recurving segments.

Fritillaria gracilis. Native of the eastern shores of the Adriatic, where it grows in woodlands and meadows and bears in May elegant bells of greenish-yellow chequered with crimson on a 12-in (30-cm) stem. The nectaries are jade green, the leaves long and narrow.

Fritillaria graeca. It is present in pinewoods in Greece and Asia Minor, where it blooms in April. It has glaucous lance-shaped leaves and bears one or two nodding bells of olive-green shaded with purple-brown on a 6-in (16-cm) stem. The bells have long segments, recurved at the tips, and down the keel of each segment is a green stripe.

Fritillaria imperialis. Native of Turkey and Persia, where it grows in deciduous woodlands, it was introduced into Europe by Charles de l'Ecluse (Clusius) in 1576, reaching England soon after. Clusius was on friendly terms

with Sir Francis Drake, who sent him plants collected in America, and the
crown imperial lily may have been sent to Drake in exchange, for in 1580 he
had returned, in the *Golden Hind*, from the circumnavigation of the world. It
blooms in April, with the daffodils, and has shiny bright-green stem leaves,
waved at the margins. On a 3-ft (90-cm) stem bears a circular cluster of yellow
or orange flowers which hang down with the stigmas protruding below the rim,
resembling church bells. The flower head is crowned by a tuft of bright-green
lance-shaped leaves, which protect the flowers from rain, in the same way that
nature has bestowed on it the pendulous position of the corollas to protect the
organs of reproduction until fertilisation has taken place. As with all fritillaries,
at the base of each petal is a drop of liquid (nectar) which forms in a tiny cavity
and defies the laws of gravity. Gerard compared it to a 'pearl of the Orient', and
wrote that 'if you do take it away, there do immediately re-appear the like'. He
continues, 'they will never fall away (on their own), no not if you strike the plant
until it is broken'.

Suitable for planting about the shrubbery and herbaceous border, also to
naturalise in an orchard or dell garden where it enjoys the shade in summer,
established plants will prove permanent and will grow to 12 in (30 cm) in diameter, forming a mass of bulbs and sending up numerous flower stems each
year, while the blooms are long-lasting.

The plants require a deeply dug soil enriched with peat or leaf mould and
some decayed manure. They like a soil which retains moisture in summer, while
they are heavy feeders and will benefit from a thick mulch of the same materials
given each year, early in autumn. To keep the plants long-living, remove the
dead flower heads before they set seed, though the seed pods, which are divided
into six projecting grooves or compartments, are most handsome and may be
used for indoor decoration.

Plant a bulb of 18- to 20-cm diameter, placing it slightly on its side so that
water is able to drain away from the hollow at the top. Plant in spring on a layer
of sand to assist drainage. Plant 12 in (30 cm) apart, in groups of three, and 6 in
(15 cm) deep, packing peat about the bulbs before filling in with soil. Parkinson,
who began the *Paradisus* with a description of the plant, said that if undisturbed
'the root doth grow sometimes to be as great as a childes head'. If growing in an
exposed position, the flower stems may require staking, though this is not
necessary where growing in a walled garden or where naturalised in grass.
Remember that if in grass, it should not be cut near the plants until the stems
have completely died back.

It is readily increased by offsets which form around the mother bulb but
which is best left undisturbed for six years or more.

The crown imperial has changed little since Shakespeare mentioned it. The
variety *lutea* bears lemon-yellow flowers, while *lutea maxima* bears flowers of
larger size. Orange Brilliant is clear orange; Aurora, orange-scarlet; and *rubra*
has flowers of bright red.

Fritillaria involucrata. Native of the Maritime Alpine meadows of southern France, it grows 12 in (30 cm) tall and bears its narrow lance-shaped leaves in whorls of three. Its flowers are borne in twos and threes during May and are wine-red shaded with green and slightly marked or tessellated.

Fritillaria liliacea. Native of northern California, where it is found on low-lying land, it blooms in May, bearing its creamy-green bells on a 9-in (23-cm) stem which arises from a rosette of basal leaves.

Fritillaria meleagris. It is native of the British Isles (or it may have been introduced) and of western Europe, especially France, where it grows in low-lying meadows, about the sides of woodlands and on river banks. From Gerard we learn that he received bulbs from Jean Robin, herbalist of Paris, in 1575, but the plant was discovered by one Noël Caperon, an apothecary of Orleans, who perished shortly afterwards in the Massacre of St Bartholomew. Robin may have introduced it into England but from about the end of the sixteenth century it has been seen in Christchurch meadows at Oxford, where it blooms during April and May, bearing its solitary drooping bells on 12-in (30-cm) stems. The flowers are pale mauve, marked with squares of dark purple, 'like the board at which men do play at chesse', wrote Gerard, hence its name of chequered daffodil or ginny hen flower, for at a distance it resembles the guinea fowl, 'surpassing the curiousest paintings that art can set down'. It was also known as the chequered lily and the snake's head daffodil, for before it opens, the flower with its broadly based bud resembles the head of a snake with its markings of purple, green and brown. It is at its best naturalised in short grass beneath mature trees, such as an orchard or shady bank, for like so many of the species it enjoys partial shade in summer. It also requires a soil containing plenty of peat or leaf mould but if it is planted in grass, the grass must not be cut above it until late in summer when the stems have died back.

Plant the bulbs in autumn 3 in (7·5 cm) deep and 6 in (15 cm) apart. It is also delightful in pots and pans in the cold greenhouse. Where it is happy it will increase from offsets and by self-sown seed.

There are a number of named varieties:

ALBA. It bears a flower of purest white without markings and is believed to have been found on the battlefield of Poitiers in France.

APHRODITE. A refined form, bearing large blooms of pure white on sturdy stems.

ARTEMIS. The flowers are of an unusual shade of grey-mauve, chequered with purple.

CHARON. It resembles the old form *nigra* (now a separate species), and bears flowers of purple-black with a dull sheen.

CONTORTA. An interesting form, native of southern Europe and at one time classed as a separate species. It has narrow leaves 6 in (15 cm) long and bears long white drooping flowers mottled with bronze. It is unusual in that the perianth segments are joined at the base.

EMPEROR. An old favourite rediscovered. It grows 15 in (38 cm) tall, the greyish-mauve flowers being heavily marked with purple.

POMONA. Tall-growing and striking, the large white flowers are chequered with violet-mauve.

POSEIDON. The finest variety, the large dangling bells, borne on 6-in (15-cm) stems, are of an unusual shade of pinkish-purple chequered with brown.

SATURNUS. The large flowers are of bright pinkish-purple.

Fritillaria olivieri. Native of the higher mountainous regions of Persia, where it blooms in June. It requires a soil containing plenty of grit and an open sunny situation when it will bloom in profusion and on a 12-in (30-cm) stem, bearing a solitary dangling bell of brilliant green, shaded maroon at the tips of the recurving segments.

Fritillaria oranensis. Native of the deciduous woodlands of north-western Africa, it has broad glaucous green leaves and bears flowers of bright purple, shaded green on the inside and devoid of tessellation. It requires a well-drained soil in winter but one fortified by leaf mould and decayed manure to withhold summer moisture. It also requires a warm garden and some shade.

Fritillaria pallidiflora. Native of Russia and Siberia, where it is found at altitudes of up to 10,000 ft, it has large glaucous leaves, and on a 9-in (22·5-cm) stem bears two or three nodding tulip-shaped flowers of creamy-yellow, chequered with rosy-purple on the inside.

Fritillaria persica. It is found throughout Syria, Persia and Iraq, growing to a height of 3 ft (90 cm) and bearing on each stem, small bells of deepest violet on long footstalks, in appearance resembling the Solomon's seal. From 12 to 30 flowers make up the loose raceme, and they are sweetly scented. It was introduced into English gardens about the same time as *F. imperialis* and, though now rare, is easy to grow.

Fritillaria pinardii. Native of the mountains of northern Turkey, it is a plant of dainty habit but should be confined to a warm garden or to the alpine house, for it is intolerant of excessive winter moisture. The long tubular blooms are of deep purple, olive-green on the inside with the segments recurved at the ends. It has the darkest green leaves of all the species and blooms in May on a 9-in (22·5-cm) stem.

Fritillaria pontica. Present throughout the Balkans and as far east as eastern Turkey, where it blooms in April on 18-in (45-cm) stems and has glaucous leaves. It bears one to three nodding bells of greenish-yellow flushed with rosy-purple on the outside and on the inside glowing green with black nectaries which are visible through the petals.

Fritillaria pudica. The American counterpart of *F. citrina*, though it is rare both in the wild and in cultivation. William Robinson described it as 'one of the most charming of hardy bulbs' and being native of the Rocky Mountains, it is completely hardy. It bears one or two drooping flowers of brightest yellow on a sturdy 6-in (15-cm) stem, from which arise three or four upright lance-shaped leaves. It blooms in April and May and requires a gritty soil to permit winter moisture to drain away, otherwise it is best grown under glass. In the variety *lutescens*, the outer segments are striped with green.

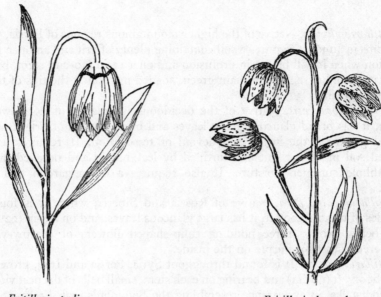

Fritillaria pudica   *Fritillaria lanceolata*

Fritillaria pyrenaica. Native of the Pyrenees, it is one of the taller-growing species, attaining a height of about 20 in (50 cm) and flowering in April. It has glaucous leaves and stems, at the end of which it bears one or two large dangling bells of brownish-purple, chequered with deeper purple. Usually the inside of the flowers is greenish-yellow.

Fritillaria recurva. It is native of Oregon and northern California, where it is found about hilly pastureland. It is remarkable for its orange-scarlet flowers, which are borne in umbels of 2 to 20 on slender stems 2 ft (60 cm) tall. The blooms are yellow on the inside, blotched with purple, while the segments curl back at the end. The leaves are formed in whorls at irregular intervals along the whole length of the stem. This species requires a gritty well-drained soil and an open sunny situation where the bulbs may ripen in the summer sunshine. In bloom April and May.

Fritillaria ruthenica. A rare native of the Black Sea region, coming into bloom early in spring. Its wine-purple flowers, almost black on the outside and slightly tessellated, are amber-green on the inside and borne on a leafy 2-ft (60-cm) stem.

Fritillaria sibthorpiana. Native of Greece and Bulgaria, it is recommended for alpine house culture, where heavy rains will not trouble it. It has small narrow leaves and bears a solitary bright-yellow bell on a 6-in (15-cm) stem. It blooms in April, mid-March indoors.

Fritillaria thunbergii. Native of northern China and Japan it is closely related to *F. verticillata*, its narrow leaves ending in a tendril-like curl, and from the axils appear drooping bell-shaped flowers of creamy-yellow striped with green.

Fritillaria verticillata. Native of the Altai Mountains and of northern China and Japan, where it is found on mountainous slopes to a height of 10,000 ft. It has glaucous leaves arranged in whorls, and in May bears umbels of drooping bells on a 2-ft (60-cm) stem. The flowers are creamy-white, tinted with green at the base and spotted with purple inside.

G

GALANTHUS (Amaryllidiceae)

A genus of 20 species, native of Europe, extending from the British Isles as far east as the Caucasus and from northern Russia and Denmark to as far south as the islands of the Greek archipelago, mostly inhabiting deciduous woodlands. A plant of extreme hardiness, in northern Europe appearing through the melting snow. In France it is called *pierce neige*. Elsewhere it is known as milkflower from the Greek words *gala* and *anthos*. To Gerard it was known as the early-flowering bulbous violet, but in the edition of the *Herbal* (1633) revised by Johnson, it is written 'some call them also snowdrops', which is the first occasion in which the now familiar name was used. It is derived from the German *schneetroppen*, a snowdrop, denoting the almost globular shape of the half-open blooms. To William Wordsworth it was the

> Chaste snowdrop, venturous harbinger of spring,
> And pensive monitor of fleeting years.

It is a plant which enjoys cool conditions. It will not tolerate any degree of heat, whether growing in the open or indoors. For this reason it does better in northern England and in Scotland, especially near the east coast; also in Canada and near the Atlantic coast of the United States. It is the finest of all bulbous plants for a cold, bleak garden, and so that it will be protected from summer sunshine, it is best planted beneath trees or shrubs, in short grass or in a border, planting in drifts, for most species are easy to establish and will increase rapidly by division of the clumps. By planting various species, bloom may be enjoyed from early January until the end of April, the flowers being enhanced by the grey-green strap-like leaves. The buds stand erect but the flowers open drooping and are held on short wiry footstalks. The three outer segments are oblong, milky-white, with the inner segments obovate, notched at the centre and marked with a bright-green crescent-shaped groove from which honey is secreted. They are visited by bees, and with few about at this time of year the flowers remain open for several weeks to allow ample time for their pollination. The tunicated bulbs are about 1 in (2·5 cm) through and are globular or slightly pear-shaped.

The species are at their best planted with groups of winter aconites and chionodoxas, the brilliant blue of the latter providing striking contrast to the icy whiteness of the snowdrops.

Culture. It enjoys a cool, moist soil, enriched with some decayed manure and made moisture-holding by the addition of humus in the form of hop manure, peat or leaf mould. Snowdrops are deep rooting and the ground needs good cultivation.

As they bloom early in the year, the bulbs should be planted during September, setting them on a layer of sand to assist drainage. Plant 4-cm-size bulbs (anything smaller will not bloom the first year) 4 in (10 cm) deep and 4 in (10 cm) apart, preferably in groups of six. Snowdrops resent shallow planting. They will benefit from a yearly dressing of decayed manure and leaf mould given in autumn.

Snowdrops in small pots never fail to give pleasure at Christmas-time, while the market grower will find them a profitable crop.

They may be brought into bloom by one of several methods. Established plants may be lifted in April after flowering and divided into sections or 'pieces' to fill a 3-in (7·5-cm) pot. A mixture of loam, peat and sand is pressed about them and they are stood out in the shade throughout summer, keeping them moist and placing them in a cold frame or cold greenhouse in October, when they will be in bloom for Christmas. Or clumps may be lifted in midwinter, weather permitting, to be replanted in pots which are placed in a cool room indoors. They will come into bloom early in the new year but will not tolerate a temperature above 50° F (10° C). No attempt should be made to force them into bloom.

Plants may also be brought early into bloom from bulbs planted three or four to a small pot in August. Use a 5-cm bulb for indoor flowering and place the pots in a plunge bed until the bulbs are well rooted. They may be taken indoors in November to bloom in January.

Propagation. The usual method is to lift and divide four- or five-year-old clumps immediately after flowering, usually in April or before the foliage begins to die back late in May. The plants are lifted with a border fork, which is inserted deeply into the ground. So that the bulbs are not kept out of the ground longer than necessary, shake away the soil and divide and replant without delay. Each plant should be split up into sections containing three or four bulbs and will give a pleasing display the following year. Planting when the foliage is still green and is readily to be seen in long grass will also facilitate the propagation of the plants and enable them to be planted where required to bloom.

Snowdrops readily increase from seed, which should be sown in June when harvested. Sow in boxes or pans containing a compost made up of sterilised loam, leaf mould (or peat) and sand in equal parts and sow thinly, just covering the seed and keeping it moist. The seedlings should be left for 12 months before transplanting 2 in (5 cm) apart in a prepared bed outdoors and shaded from the midsummer sun. Seedlings should be kept cool and moist about the roots. In 12 months they will have formed small bulblets, which will be ready to move to their flowering quarters. They will bloom in about four years from sowing.

Species. *Galanthus allenii.* Believed to be a garden hybrid of *G. caucasicus*, it has broad recurving leaves of glaucous green and bears a flower larger than those of any other snowdrop. It is without green markings on the inner segments, apart from those on either side of the notch.

Galanthus byzantinus. Native of western Turkey and the Black Sea regions, it comes into bloom early in the new year and is a valuable garden species, flourishing under all conditions. The bulbs are large, while the leaves are broad and glaucous. The flowers have spoon-shaped outer segments and inner segments of bright green.

Galanthus caucasicus. Native of the Caucasus, it is a species of extreme hardiness which comes into bloom early in January. It has broad glaucous leaves 9 in (22·5 cm) long and is distinguished from *G. ikariae* by its large globular flowers which are free from green markings.

Galanthus corcyrensis. Native of Sicily, it blooms in December, before the leaves begin to push up through the ground. The flowers are large with a distinct green band around the notch of the inner segments.

Galanthus elwesii. It is present in western Turkey and on the island of Samos and is one of the latest species to bloom. It is also one of the best, with broad glaucous green leaves, deeply channelled, and bearing large egg-shaped flowers on 6-in (15-cm) stems. It is distinguished by the broad jade-green shading which almost covers the inner segments. The variety *globosus* has broad outer segments, while Colesborne, discovered by Mr Elwes after whom the species is named, has inner segments which are entirely covered in green. It grows only 4 in (10 cm) tall and makes a large bulb up to 8 cm (20 cm) in diameter.

Galanthus fosteri. Native of the Lebanon, it is the tallest snowdrop, flowering on a 12-in (30-cm) stem and having broad blunt-ended leaves of brilliant green. It bears large flowers with the base of the inner segments broadly marked with jade and with twin green marks on either side of the notch. The least hardy species, it requires a sheltered garden in cooler parts.

Galanthus graecus. Native of northern Greece, it is late into bloom, appearing in mid-April and continuing until mid-May. It has narrow leaves and bears small egg-shaped flowers with narrow outer segments and with wide green markings on the short inner segments.

Galanthus ikariae. It is native only of the island of Nikaria, situated near the coast of Asia Minor and is closely related to *G. elwesii* from which it is distinguished by its broad recurving leaves which are dark green. The flowers have large tear-shaped outer segments and inner segments entirely covered with green. It grows 6 in (15 cm) tall, the flowers having a distinct sweet mossy perfume.

The sub-species *latifolius*, native of the Caucasus, has leaves 1 in (2·5 cm) broad, similarly recurving and bears flowers which are smaller in size but with the same green shading on the inner segments.

Galanthus nivalis. The common snowdrop of the British Isles and northern Europe, to be found as far west as the Caucasus. It makes a small ovoid bulb from which arise narrow strap-like leaves 6 in (15 cm) long. It blooms from January until March, bearing its solitary drooping flower on a flattened 4-in (10-cm) scape. It is pure white except for the green crescent around the notch of the inner segments. The bulbs do not exceed 6 in (15 cm) in diameter.

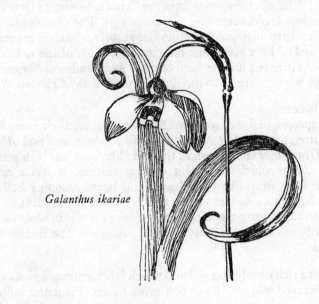

Galanthus ikariae

There are several forms of outstanding beauty; *viride-apice* has outer segments tipped with green, while *lutescens* has inner segments which are marked with yellow instead of green. Outstanding is Arnott's Seedling, which grows 10 in (25 cm) tall, its pure-white outer segments being 1 in (2·5 cm) long, while the inner segments have a distinct crescent of apple green. The flowers are sweetly scented. Increasing rapidly when naturalised, it is possibly the finest of all snowdrops.

An early-flowering form is *atkinsii* which bears a large globular bloom on a 9-in (22·5-cm) stem, while Straffan bears flowers which are almost as large and which is one of the latest to bloom. *Scharlockii* is interesting in that it usually bears twin blooms, the spathes of which stand erect. Its outer segments are tipped with green. It was discovered in Germany in 1850.

There is also a double form *plenus*, a variety of which, Ophelia, bears large flowers filled with green-tipped segments, to give an appearance of great beauty.

The sub-species *cilicicus*, native of Turkey, and *reginae-olgae*, native of eastern Greece, are both autumn-flowering, usually bearing their flowers (like those of *G. nivalis*) before the glaucous leaves. Their planting will extend the flowering season from October until early May in a late spring. They require a more open situation and a light sandy soil to enable the bulbs to be as dry and sun-baked as possible during summer, which is essential to their freedom of flowering. Occasionally *reginae-olgae* is found without the green markings of the inner segments.

Galanthus plicatus. A handsome species from the Crimea, forming a large bulb and with broad glaucous leaves recurving at the margins. The globular flowers appear in February and are distinguished from *G. byzantinus* by their inner segments, which are marked by a green line only on either side of the notch but have the edge white. There is a double form of merit and handsome varieties in Warham and Omega which were introduced at the time of the Crimean War.

GALTONIA (Liliaceae)

A genus of three species, native of southern Africa and taking their name from that of Francis Galton, author of *A Narrative of an Explorer in South Africa*. Closely related to *Hyacinthus* and known as the spire lily, only one is in general cultivation—*G. candicans* which is a plant of easy culture. It has a round tunicated bulb and long strap-like basal leaves and bears drooping bells on leafless scapes which reach up to four or five feet in height. It is a plant for the back of the border to accompany the michaelmas daisies for it is in bloom at the same time. It is hardy in all but the most exposed gardens of the British Isles and North America.

Culture. It requires a rich deeply dug soil into which is incorporated peat or leaf mould and some decayed manure, for it is a gross feeder. Plant the bulbs in April, in groups of six, 12 in (30 cm) apart and 6 in (15 cm) deep, placing them on a layer of sand to assist with drainage. If an 18- to 20-cm bulb is used, it will bloom the first year. After flowering, allow the stems to die back, then cover the bulbs with a thick layer of peat or leaf mould as a protection against frost, for the bulbs are better left in the ground where they will increase each year.

Propagation. If the bulbs are lifted after several years, it will be found that small offsets cluster about the older bulbs. These are detached and replanted again when they will bloom in two or three years, depending upon size. For continuity of bloom, one or two clumps should be lifted and divided in April each year.

Galtonias may be raised from seed sown in boxes or pans containing the John Innes compost and either covered with glass or placed in a frame. Sow in April, transplanting the seedlings to pots or boxes the following year. It will take three years for the bulbs to reach flowering size if planted out about two years after sowing.

Species. *Galtonia candicans* (syn. *Hyacinthus candicans*). Native of Natal and Cape Province, it forms a large round bulb, somewhat irregular in shape, from which arises several long-tapering leaves and a succulent leafless scape 5 ft (2·5 metres) tall. The dangling bell-shaped flowers are borne on footstalks about 1 in (2·5 cm) long, the flowers being white tinted with green. They are scented and are produced in a loose raceme of 20 or more. When cut they remain fresh in water for more than a week.

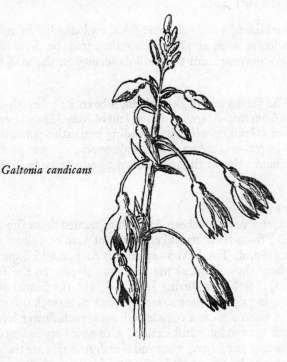

Galtonia candicans

Galtonia clavata. Native of Natal, it differs from *G. candicans* in its smaller flowers, while the stamens have lance-shaped filaments. It bears 10 to 12 creamy-white bell-shaped flowers on a leafless scape 3 ft (90 cm) tall. It is not as hardy as *G. candicans* and the bulbs will often decay in winter.

Galtonia princeps. Native of the same parts as *G. candicans*, it forms a stem 3 ft (90 cm) tall, at the end of which it bears a broad raceme of greenish-white flowers with spreading segments. It also blooms during late summer and early autumn.

GAGEA (Liliaceae)
A genus of about 70 species, native of northern Europe and Asia, few having garden value. The genus is named after Sir Thomas Gage, the British botanist

who gave his name to the greengage. One species, *G. lutea*, native of copses and hedgerows of the British Isles, especially of the North of England where it is known as the yellow star of Bethlehem, is valuable for naturalising in short grass. It spreads by bulbils formed in the axils of the leaves or by offsets.

Culture. A position of semi-shade and ordinary soil which is retentive of summer moisture is suitable. Plant the small, round bulbs in October, 3 in (7·5 cm) deep and 4 in (10 cm) apart.

Propagation. Long-established plants may be lifted and divided in autumn, replanting the small bulbs as soon as possible, or they may be divided after flowering. They will also increase from tiny bulbils formed in the axils of the leaves.

Species. *Gagea lutea.* The yellow star of Bethlehem, it bears its greenish-yellow flowers in small clusters from mid-March until the end of May. They open star-like, resembling the lesser celandine with six spreading perianth segments. The flowers are borne on 8-in (20-cm) stems amidst pale-green, narrow, strap-like leaves with three prominent veins at the back and with two leafy bracts at the base of the umbel.

GALAXIA (Iridaceae)

A genus of six species, native of southern Africa and named from the Greek *galaxias*, the Milky Way, from their star-like flowers of lilac or yellow which open almost flat on the ground. The blooms appear in August and September in their native land, where they frequent mountainous slopes. In the British Isles and North America, they bloom during June and July, the funnel-shaped flowers borne singly on 1-in (2·5-cm) stems, fading quickly, though others take their places. The flowers open amidst a rosette of leaves, each flower having a leafy bract. The perianth tube is long and slender with equal-spreading lobes.

Only in the warmer parts of the British Isles and North America are the plants hardy; elsewhere they should be grown under glass to bloom early in summer. They should be planted in an open sunny position, either alongside a path or on the top of a low wall, in full sun and where the soil is well drained.

Culture. A sandy soil is necessary if the small tunicated corms are to be permanent and this is possible only where hard frost is unknown. Elsewhere the corms should be lifted in autumn and replanted in spring. Plant 4 in (10 cm) deep and 4 in (10 cm) apart.

When growing indoors, plant in March three or four corms to a large pot or pan containing a mixture of fibrous loam, peat and sand in equal parts. Give no water until growth appears, then small quantities, giving more as the sun increases in strength. The corms should be gradually dried off after flowering and all moisture withheld in winter.

Propagation. They spread by underground cormlets, also by cormlets which form in the leaf axils and detach themselves when ripe. Cormlets of pot plants may be detached and repotted when the plants have died back.

Species. *Galaxia graminea* (syn. *G. fugacissima*). Native of Cape Province, where it is common on Signal Hill, it reached Britain in 1800. It forms a rosette of short linear leaves at the centre of which is borne an almost stemless head of yellow or cream flowers which open to about 1 in (2·5 cm) in diameter.

Galaxia ovata. Prominent on Signal Hill, its corm tunic is composed of numerous hard woody ridges. The small linear leaves are deeply channelled and are formed in rosettes, at the centre of which is borne an almost stemless head of yellow or lilac-pink flowers.

GEISSORRHIZA (Iridaceae)

A genus of about 65 species, native of southern Africa and Madagascar and taking their name from *geisson*, a tile, a reference to the overlapping tile-like scales of the corms. Closely related to ixia and gladiolus, the leaves are sword-like, partly sheathing, while the flowers are funnel-shaped with six equal segments. Only in the warmer parts of the British Isles and North America will the plants be sufficiently hardy to remain in the open ground during winter. Otherwise they must be grown indoors in pots. Outdoors they may be grown in a sunny border or at the base of a sunny wall, where the corms can ripen well enough to bear flowers the following year. They bloom between August and October in their native land, between June and July in North America and northern Europe.

Culture. The corms require a sandy loam, well-drained in winter and they are planted out in April, 4 in (10 cm) deep and 6 in (15 cm) apart. The corms may be lifted in autumn and wintered in a frost-free room, to be planted out again in spring. If left in the ground they should be covered with peat to a depth of 4 in (10 cm). Where growing under glass, plant four corms to a 6-in (15-cm) pot, containing a mixture of fibrous loam, peat and sand in equal parts. Plant in March, 2 in (5 cm) deep and give no water until foliage appears, then increase supplies as the plants make growth.

Propagation. When the corms are lifted, the cormlets are detached and, after storing over winter in a box of sand, they are planted in spring in boxes of sandy compost in which they are grown on until attaining flowering size, when they may be planted out.

Species. *Geissorrhiza humilis.* Found on wet sandy flats, it has small spiny corms and three awl-shaped leaves, sticky to the touch and with prominent margins. The bracts are also sticky. The flowers are of bright yellow, the outer lobes often being shaded red, and they are borne in a loose two- to eight-flowered spike on a 10-in (25-cm) glabrous stem.

Geissorrhiza inflexa (syn. *G. vaginata*). It has curving sword-shaped leaves and bears yellow flowers of outstanding beauty, each segment having a dark purple blotch at the base. They are borne on 18-in (45-cm) stems in a three- to six-flowered spike.

Geissorrhiza juncea. Frequent on mountainous slopes of Cape Province, it has narrow grass-like leaves, one of which stands erect and is as long as the 18-in (45-cm) flower stem. The flowers, which are borne in a 4- to 12-flowered spike, are creamy-white, the outer segments shaded pink on the underside and carrying a delicate sweet scent.

Geissorrhiza ovata (syn. *G. excisa*). Frequent on Signal Hill and in the mountains above Simonstown, its small corms are covered in bright-red tunics. It has three short leaves spotted with black and bears a two- to five-flowered spike on an 8-in (20-cm) stem. The flowers, with their short cylindrical perianth tube, are creamy-white, each segment having a crimson basal mark.

Geissorrhiza secunda. Common about rocky slopes in Cape Province, its corm is covered in dark-brown overlapping 'tiles'. It has four or five sword-shaped leaves 12 in (30 cm) long and bears its purple-blue flowers in a four- to eight-flowered spike on a 9-in (22·5-cm)-tall pubescent stem.

Geissorrhiza setacea. A rare native of the rocky outcrops of Table Mountain, where it blooms during January, in early autumn in the British Isles. Its four or five linear leaves have prominent margins, while its ivory-white or pale-yellow flowers are striped on the outside with crimson. The species is distinguished by its long perianth tube.

GESNERIA (Gesneriaceae)

A genus of 50 species, native of tropical America and the West Indies and named after the sixteenth-century Swiss botanist Conrad Gesner. They are hairy plants growing from a tuberous root, with simple opposite leaves, and bear their flowers in terminal cymes. The flowers are tubular, brilliantly coloured with abundant nectar and are adapted for pollination by humming birds. They have no perfume.

Mostly native of Mexico and Brazil, the plants require warm conditions in cooler climes, i.e. a minimum night temperature of 60° F (16° C). By potting the tubers at regular intervals, they may be brought into bloom throughout the year.

Culture. Gesnerias are lovers of peat and slightly acid conditions and should be given a compost made up of 2 parts peat, 1 part fibrous loam and 1 part decayed manure with a liberal sprinkling of sand. By potting in April, it will be possible in a warm summer to bring the plants into bloom during August and September without artificial heat, but to have bloom all the year, warmth is necessary and a planting may be made early in March, followed by one in May and another in

September to bloom during winter. Planting is regulated by the heat available. Plant one tuber to a 4-in (10-cm) pot so that the top of the tuber is level with the compost, which should be just below the rim of the pot. Make the compost firm and, after watering, stand the pots as near to the light as possible so that growth will be sturdy. The tubers may be sprouted (like begonias) in boxes of peat and loam, to be transferred to the pots as soon as growth begins. A temperature of 60° to 65° F (16° to 18° C) should be provided to start the tubers into growth, and as soon as they begin to form their leaves, they will benefit from a daily syringe and should be shaded from strong sunlight. Syringeing should be discontinued once the flower buds show colour. The plants, however, must not be allowed to lack moisture—which is given around the side of the pot—while an occasional application of dilute manure water will enhance the colour of the flowers.

After flowering, gradually withhold moisture while the leaves are dying back, then stand the pots on their side beneath the greenhouse bench or in a frost-free place until they have rested and are ready for repotting into fresh compost.

Propagation. As with begonias, the most satisfactory method is to divide the tubers as they form sprouts, each piece having one or more buds or shoots. The cut portion should be rubbed in sulphur before it is planted into a small pot and brought into bloom.

Named varieties may also be increased by cuttings. This is done by starting old tubers into growth in a temperature of 65° F (18° C) and giving ample supplies of moisture to encourage them to form shoots. Again, as for begonias, the shoots are removed with a sharp knife, either just below a leaf joint or with a small piece of tuber attached. They will readily root if inserted into a sandy compost at the side of a pot. Insert the stems 1 in (2·5 cm) deep and 2 in (5 cm) apart. Shield from strong sunlight and give a daily syringe to prevent excessive evaporation of moisture from the leaves. The shoots will root in three or four weeks when they are moved to 3-in (7·5-cm) pots and grown on. The tubers will increase in size each year, and the size of pot should be gradually increased.

Species. *Gesneria blassii.* Native of Brazil, it has heart-shaped leaves with prominent red veins on the underside, while the flowers of cinnabar-red are borne in drooping panicles on 6-in (15-cm) stems.

Gesneria donkelaari. Native of Peru, it has handsome heart-shaped leaves tinted with crimson and purple and bears flowers of vivid red.

Gesneria douglasi (syn. *G. maculata*). It bears its ovate-toothed leaves in whorls of four and bears drooping bright-red flowers from the axils of the upper leaves.

Gesneria lindleyi. Native of Brazil, it has broad leaves of deep velvety green, shaded crimson on the underside and, on 6-in (15-cm) stems, bears tubular flowers of bright pink spotted with red.

Gesneria macrantha. Native of Brazil, it will eventually form a tuber of 6-in (15-cm) diameter and has large oval leaves, sharply toothed. The long tubular flowers of brilliant cardinal red are borne in a terminal cluster.

Gesneria naegelioides. A hybrid with large oval leaves, coarsely toothed, it bears large tubular flowers of brightest pink with a yellow throat. There are numerous forms bearing flowers of lilac, crimson, violet and white, each with the yellow throat.

Gesneria pendulina. Native of Mexico, it grows 2 ft (60 cm) tall, with ovate leaves borne in whorls of three, from the axils of which it bears drooping cylindrical flowers of glowing scarlet.

Gesneria tuberosa. It has rhizomatous roots like those of the achemene, and from the scaly joints the stems arise. The leaves are heart-shaped and toothed, while the bright-red flowers are covered in short hairs.

GETHYLLIS (Amaryllidaceae)

A genus of 20 species, native of southern Africa and taking its name from the Greek *gethreon*, a leek, an allusion to the long leek-like neck of the bulb. From the tunicated bulb arise narrow leaves which develop after the crocus-like flowers. They are white and salver-shaped with a long perianth tube and with six to many stamens arranged in six groups and inserted in the mouth of the tube. The flowers are scented.

Culture. It requires greenhouse protection in North America and northern Europe, the bulbs being planted in pots in April so that they begin to bloom in August. Where a favourable spring climate is enjoyed, they may be planted 4 in (10 cm) deep in the rock garden and lifted in autumn, to be stored in a frost-free room during winter.

They require a compost made up of loam, peat and sand in equal parts, the bulbs being planted 1 in (2·5 cm) below the surface. Give little moisture until growth begins, then increase supplies as the temperature rises. After flowering, the bulbs are dried off and the pots placed on their side in a frost-free room during winter.

Propagation. Upon lifting the bulbs for repotting in spring, offsets will be found clustering around the mother bulb. These are detached and planted in a sandy compost to be grown on to flowering size, which takes two years.

Species. *Gethyllis afra*. It makes a bulb of about 2-in (5-cm) diameter with a long neck, and in its native Cape Province it blooms in December, in August in Britain and northern Europe. Its flowers are white with a red central stripe down the outside of each segment and they open star-like. They grow about 4 in (10 cm) above the soil. The leaves appear later, in spring in their native land, and are narrow and twisted.

Gethyllis ciliaris. A rare native of the flatlands of Raapenberg, it reached Europe towards the end of the nineteenth century. Though the bulbs are small, they have necks up to 5 in (12·5 cm) long from the basal part of which are formed fleshy roots. The flowers are white and are followed by spirally twisted leaves.

GLADIOLUS (Iridaceae)

A genus of about 300 species, distributed in one small area of the British Isles, in western and central Europe, the Canary Islands, western Asia, tropical and southern Africa. Known as the corn flag, it takes its name from the Latin *gladius*, a sword, an allusion to the shape of the leaves, which are plaited and terminate in a sharp point. The flowers are borne on spikes 2 to 3 ft (60 to 90 cm) tall, the flowers being arranged at regular intervals along the spike and all facing the same way. The three upper segments are larger than the three lower ones, while in *G. primulinus* the central uppermost petal is hooded. The spikes are 1- to 12- or more-flowered, the florets opening from the bottom upwards so that the spikes remain colourful for several weeks. The perianth tube is curved and funnel-shaped.

In his *Historie of Plants* (1597), Gerard mentioned *G. communis* and *G. segetum*, while Parkinson (1629) illustrates and describes *G. byzantinus*, the corn flag of Constantinople, introduced from Turkey late in the sixteenth century. The blooms are rich red and, as Parkinson mentions, they appear in August. This species was used in early hybridising. Sir Thomas Hanmer, writing shortly after Parkinson, mentions another red-flowered species, *G. aethiopica*, native of eastern Africa.

The Frenchman Lemoine was the first to improve the early species. He crossed *G. brenchleyensis*, raised in 1848, with *G. purpurea-auratus* and produced a race with beautiful butterfly markings on the petals. This he called *G. lemoinii*, and from it Max Leichtlin raised *G. leichtlinii*, later renamed *G. childsii* after the American who purchased his entire stock. It was an American, Arthur Kunderd, who in 1907 introduced the first gladiolus with ruffled petals. *G. gandavensis*, the Ghent gladiolus, was also used in the raising of some of the early hybrids. It was itself a hybrid of *G. cardinalis*, which was used to raise *G. colvillei*.

In 1904 Mr Frank Fox of Wimbledon discovered *G. primulinus* while working on the erection of a bridge across the Zambesi at the Victoria Falls. There, in the spray from the famous falls, protecting its organs of reproduction by a hooded petal, he found the small flowered pale-yellow gladiolus which (on account of its colour) was to be named *G. primulinus*.

Of easy culture and well adapted to the cooler climate of North America and Europe, the gladiolus stands supreme as a plant for late summer- and early autumn-flowering, its colour range being unique among garden flowers for it is obtainable in every conceivable shade, while the flowers are long-lasting in the garden and when cut.

Given an open, sunny situation where they are not troubled by strong winds, gladioli may be used anywhere in the garden, in the flower border or for bedding, while they may also be planted in large groups in the kitchen garden to provide cut bloom. The commercial grower will plant them by the acre, for with the dahlia they are the chief source of income during late summer and autumn, until the chrysanthemum comes into bloom.

Culture. The gladiolus has what may be called a double rooting system. When the corm is planted fibrous roots appear from around the circular marking at the base. It is those short, fibrous roots which sustain the corm in its early days until a new set of thick, fleshy roots appear, not from the base but from the top of the corm where the buds have appeared. It is these roots which feed the flower spikes and which build up the new corm which forms at the base of the flower stem on top of the original corm. As the season advances, the fibrous roots of the old corm will be replaced by the vigorous new roots which search down for moisture and food. Thus, where a flower spike of exhibition quality is required, it will be necessary to give the ground a thorough preparation, working the soil to a depth of two 'spits' (spades). Sufficient humus materials and plant food should be incorporated to provide for the building up of the new corm and at the same time, the formation of a flower spike of exhibition size.

To grow a large spike the gladiolus will require ample supplies of moisture and sufficient plant food to last until the corm is lifted in autumn. This means that quantities of humus must be provided, together with those materials which release their plant foods slowly and over a long period. Artificial fertilisers should not be used, apart from a little sulphate of potash to accentuate the colour of the florets. Nor must the corm be permitted to come into contact with rank manure, for this would cause it to decay.

Though gladioli are not particular as to soil, usually producing good spikes in a heavy soil as well as in one of a light, sandy nature, the better the condition it be brought into, the better the flower spikes. Drainage is of first importance, requiring greater attention than the provision of plant food.

A friable loam will require little by way of additional plant food and will usually be well-drained. A light soil will require larger quantities of humus. The gladiolus enjoys a neutral soil, so where there is a high lime content this may be neutralised by the addition of peat. The acid soil of a town garden, on the other hand, will benefit from a liberal dressing of lime.

Where growing spikes of exhibition quality, a top-size corm should be planted, one between 12 and 24 cm in size, which will be of almost 2-in diameter. For garden display, a 10- to 12-cm-size corm will be suitable, but guard against planting cheap corms which may be of doubtful quality. The corms should have a high crown and be plump rather than thin and shallow. Corms which are soft when pressed or are hollow at the top should not be planted. The most vigorous corms are those which have more recently been grown for the spawn or tiny cormlets which are to be found clustered around the base of mature corms. It

Fritillaria lutea maxima : Crown Imperial

Gladiolus: Hastings and new seedling

Gladiolus: Frank's Perfection

MINIATURE GLADIOLI

Gladiolus: Zylpha, Ellaline and new seedling

Gladiolus: Salmon Star

will, however, take at least three years before the corm is capable of producing a bloom of exhibition quality.

For an early crop, though the gladiolus will not withstand transplanting when once it has formed its root run, the corms may be started into growth in boxes of peat in the same way as begonias or potatoes. By sprouting early-flowering varieties, it is possible to have them in bloom in warmer parts by the first days of July, thus greatly extending the season.

A greenhouse, cold frame or the window of a warm room will prove suitable for sprouting, the corms being placed in shallow trays containing a layer of peat which is kept moist. The corms should not, however, be started until two or three weeks before they are due to be planted out. This will mean starting the corms around mid-March for planting out early in April, for the corms must have only just begun to sprout and must not have made more than the minimum of root growth when planted out.

The first days of April will be early enough for the first plantings. The corms must never be planted if the soil is wet and sticky following snow, frost or heavy rain. Where the soil is of a clay texture, planting should be delayed a few days until it has had time to become warmed by the sun's rays. There is nothing to be gained by planting too early in a soil that is still wet and cold.

Planting the early-, mid-season- and late-flowering varieties will ensure a continuation of bloom from early July until mid-October. A succession of bloom may also be obtained by planting early-flowering varieties over a period of five or six weeks, making one planting each week, beginning about 1st April.

For exhibition growing it is necessary to plant only those varieties which will open several florets at the same time, at least six open florets being necessary for a spike to gain an award. For garden display, it is preferable if the florets open at intervals, for this will prolong the display, while for commercial cut-flower purposes the spikes are cut with the lower florets only just showing colour, for they will open when in water. The best of the modern exhibition varieties are able to form as many as 20 to 25 buds to a spike, more than half of which will be fully open together, to present a most brilliant display on the show bench, and with certain varieties the florets will measure up to 6 in (15 cm) across.

As the earlier-flowering varieties will take approximately 90 days to reach perfection in southern gardens, the mid-season varieties 100 days and the late varieties about 120 days, it is possible to calculate the correct time for planting from the various show dates. To make certain of having a number of spikes in perfect condition at the correct time, it is advisable to spread out the planting over a period of about a week or 10 days, while the state of the soil must also be taken into consideration at planting time. Again, to be sure of having sufficient spikes of a variety on show day, at least six corms of each should be planted. Many of the white, cream and yellow varieties bloom early, so do the purple and smoky hues, while the dark reds and most of the pinks bloom late, though in each section there are exceptions. Northern growers should omit the

L

late-flowering varieties and concentrate on the early and mid-season varieties. Even the early-flowering varieties in the North will take a fortnight longer to come into bloom than where growing in the South. This means that it will be late in August before the mid-season varieties come into bloom from a mid-April planting and they will thus be at their best for the late shows.

Whether specially prepared beds have been made up or whether the whole area of ground has been brought into suitable cultivation, the best method of planting where bloom of exhibition quality is required is to take out a trench 6 in (15 cm) deep where the soil is light and sandy or 3 in (10 cm) deep where it is heavy and the ground low-lying. A thin layer of peat, sand or vermiculite should be placed at the bottom—using peat for light land—and into this the corms are gently pressed, spacing them 6 in (15 cm) apart. Too shallow planting in light land will mean that even the small-flowered types will require adequate staking at an early date. After planting, a covering of peat should be placed over and around the corms before the trench is filled in, taking care to round off the surface to enable rainwater to be drawn away readily if the soil is heavy or the ground low-lying. Into the soil should be mixed a quantity of wood ash or 1 oz per square yard of sulphate of potash. This should be given at planting time as potash is readily washed away by heavy rains and will be lost if applied in autumn.

Where planting groups of four or five in a border, approximately 1 square foot of soil should be removed to a depth of 6 in (15 cm) where the soil is light and sandy, or to a depth of 4 in (10 cm) where it is heavy. The sand or peat is spread

Planting gladiolus

over the soil to a depth of about 1 in (2·5 cm) into which the gladioli corms are pressed. The soil is then filled in and made level. This is a better method than planting by means of a trowel for it is possible to ensure that the base of the corm is in complete contact with the soil.

After about eight weeks when the plant has formed five or six leaves, it will be possible to feel the embryo flower spike by gently pressing the sheaf of leaves near the base. A hardness will denote that the spike is on its way and the plant must now be given copious amounts of moisture. Watering the ground to saturation point every day is necessary. Liquid feeding should also begin at this stage. This should consist of alternate applications of diluted manure water and soot water given once a week. Liquid manure in diluted form may be made by dissolving a bag of animal manure in a tub of water. Soot water is also made in this way.

Liquid feeding should be done during showery weather. If dry, it is best given just before the plants are watered. In this way the plant food is washed down to the roots before it can evaporate. For the same reason, the ground should be given a thorough soaking in the evening, for if the moisture does not penetrate to the roots they will turn towards the surface in search of it. Lack of moisture will mean a shorter flower spike and florets lacking substance, while the new corm will not fully develop. As this is of the utmost importance, feeding should also be continued almost until it is time to lift the corm. To prevent wastage, a circle is made in the soil around the plant about 3 in (7·5 cm) from the stem, and into this the manure water is poured.

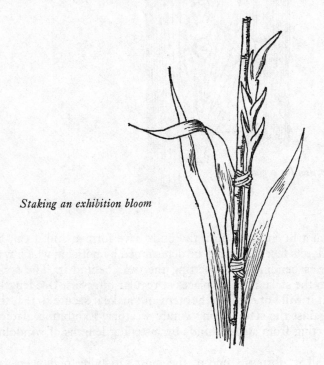

Staking an exhibition bloom

As the season advances lawn mowings or peat may be spread out over the bed to conserve moisture.

The large-flowering varieties will require staking, for, if growing exhibition-quality bloom, a slightly bent or twisted spike may spoil what may otherwise be one of outstanding form. Staking must be done efficiently. It must be remembered that the spikes will grow 5 or 6 ft (1·5 or 1·8 metres) tall and will carry up to two dozen flower buds, half of which will be open together. Those who have seen the flowers after heavy rain will realise how great a weight the stem has to support, and each stem should be given a stake. This may be a strong cane 5 or 6 ft (1·5 or 1·8 metres) in length or a stout stake which should be inserted well into the ground about 2 in (5 cm) away from the base of the stem so that it will not injure the corm.

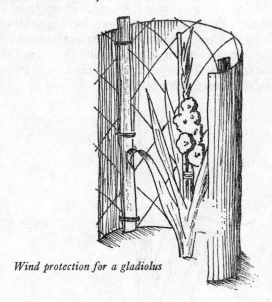

Wind protection for a gladiolus

The stake should not be inserted until the buds have formed and it can be seen which way the florets face. This may be determined by noticing which way the end of the spike is bending and inserting the cane behind it. The spike should be fastened to the stake in three places at regular intervals. Use lengths of broad raffia so that it will not cut into the stem and make it secure so that the petals cannot rub against the stem during windy weather. Exhibition gladioli may also need protecting from strong winds by fastening lengths of windolite around them.

The gladiolus in all its forms is one of the most satisfying of flowers for exhibiting, for it is doubtful if any other flower can reveal such beauty on a single stem. With modern varieties as many as a dozen florets, often almost 6 in (15 cm) in diameter, will be open at the same time to give the appearance of a sheaf of orchids.

There are usually classes for exhibiting gladioli at one's local shows, while the international shows arranged by the Royal Horticultural Society and by the British Gladiolus Society are open to entries from anywhere.

Growing for Cut Blooms. When growing for cut flower, the size of the corm calls for some consideration. In the most favourable districts and where the soil is light and friable, good spikes may be expected from an 8- to 10-cm corm. Where the soil is in good 'heart' a 10- to 12-cm corm will produce a spike of top quality, but planting the 12- to 14-cm size will not only be a safeguard against adverse soil conditions but will produce a spike capable of obtaining top prices on the wholesale market.

Where the corms are not to be protected do not plant too early. First allow the soil to become warmed by the sun's rays, and ensure that it is well-drained and is not in a sticky condition following frost and rain. Planting may be done with a blunt-nose trowel, making the hole about 4 in (10 cm) deep and sufficiently large as to allow the base of the corm to be in contact with the soil below it. Plant 2 in (5 cm) apart for the large-flowering varieties and 6 in (15 cm) apart for the miniatures. Stagger the rows to allow the plants space to develop.

If the trenches are made 6 in (15 cm) deep, no more than 4 in (10 cm) of soil should be placed over the corms. The remainder may be added when the plants have made about 6 in (15 cm) of growth. This will give them extra support against strong winds, for the spikes will not be given individual staking. Earthing up and the fact that they will tend to hold each other up by growing close to-gether will enable individual staking to be dispensed with.

After cutting the bloom—and this is best done with a sharp knife—the spikes should be removed to a cool room and placed in deep buckets with the lower 6 in (15 cm) of stem immersed in water. Here, they should remain for several hours, though this is not necessary where selling the bloom direct to local florists, who will place the spikes in water upon delivery. Where travelling a distance and where being consigned to the wholesale market, a long drink is essential, after which the stems should be wiped dry and the spikes made up into bunches of six. They should be arranged so that the buds face in the same direction. Place the spikes on a large sheet of sulphite paper on the bench and, when correctly arranged, tie them together with raffia immediately beneath the lower florets and again about 6 in (10 cm) from the end of the stems.

The bunches are placed in large-sized flower boxes made of cardboard, which are usually non-returnable, or in returnable wooden boxes which are 3 ft (90 cm) in length and 6 in (15 cm) deep. Each box will hold two dozen bunches of six spikes in each. The box is lined with white sulphite paper which extends beyond the ends of the box. The bunches are then placed in two rows of six at each end of the box so that the stems are to the centre. Immediately below the lower buds, lengths of cane are fixed to hold the bunches firm in the box, the canes being wedged against the sides. The extension paper is then turned over the spikes before the box is closed. The boxes should be clearly addressed with their contents shown. A box may be composed entirely of one variety, of a dozen bunches each of two varieties or even half a dozen bunches each of four varieties; but mixed bunches are not popular. Spikes that are bent, or where the florets are too advanced, are not required.

Lifting the Corms. Upon the successful lifting and storing of the corms depends the quality of next year's flowering spike. If the flower stem has been removed with too much foliage, the new corm will be deprived of nourishment and no matter how carefully the corms are lifted and stored, the next season's spike will be of greatly inferior quality, and will be quite unsuitable both for exhibition and the top-class florist trade. When growing for garden display, remove only the upper portion of the spike which has borne the flowers. At least five leaves should be allowed to remain on each plant after the spike has been removed. The corm will receive additional help if given regular applications of dilute manure water.

The growing plants should be fed for several weeks after the bloom has been removed and until the leaves begin to turn yellow in autumn. Liquid feeding should then end, for the corms must be as dry as possible when lifted. The Dutch growers plant their gladioli in siltland, which can be flooded to provide the plants with water during summer and drained when the corms are ready for lifting. This ensures the formation of a large corm, almost entirely free from soil particles upon lifting. Drying may then take place rapidly. Thus, decay does not have time to set in while the corms are damp. The plants are also allowed to retain all their foliage, only the bloom being removed. In this way a plump, clean and disease-free corm is produced.

Use a small garden fork for lifting, for a spade may cut the corms, causing serious damage. Dig deeply, and when lifting take care not to lose the cormlets. Then, taking each variety separately, tie the foliage together. Or where large numbers of a variety are grown, tie in bunches of not more than twenty—otherwise they will not dry quickly.

The bunches should be hung up in an open shed, in the same way as for drying onions and for about two weeks, so that surplus soil will dry out and may be readily removed. The less soil adhering to the corms the more rapidly will they dry and the less liable will they be to disease. As soon as the foliage has become dry, during which time the sap will have finished draining into the corms, cut away the leaves about 1 in (2·5 cm) above the crown or neck, taking care to ensure that thrips, which may be on the foliage, do not fall on to the corms. The foliage should be burnt.

The corms are then placed in an airy room for three weeks, preferably where a temperature of 60° F (16° C) can be maintained. If there is room available on the greenhouse bench this is ideal, provided ample ventilation is given. A free circulation of air will encourage the rapid drying of the corms which is essential if botrytis is not to gain a hold. If no greenhouse is available, place the corms on trays in a warm cupboard, which is left open to enable the moisture from the drying corms to escape. An airy loft, or attic, may also be used, but it must be remembered that at this time of year, the corms may take some time to dry, and the longer they take the more liable will they be to attack by disease. Corms lifted from light, sandy soil which may have been dry when they were harvested will, of course, dry out more rapidly than corms harvested from heavy land.

When quite dry, portions of the old corms and the old roots should be removed to leave a clean circular scar at the base of the new corms. From here the new fibrous roots will appear when the corms are planted again in spring. The corms should also have the brown husk or outer skin removed, for this will enable them to be inspected for disease. Also thrips will not be able to hide beneath the husk, making them more difficult to eradicate.

The cormlets should be removed with care to be placed with any others that might have been removed when lifted. When dry, small numbers may be placed in small paper bags upon which is written the name of the variety. For larger quantities use muslin bags. This is the most suitable method of storing both the cormlets and large corms, though with the latter it may not be practical to store large numbers in this way. Inside the muslin bag is placed a slip of paper containing the name of the variety. The bag is then tied at the top and hung up in a cool airy room. But first the corms should be inspected for disease. If only slightly affected, the parts may be cut away with a sharp knife, rubbing the cut portion with flowers of sulphur. Also both the corms and cormlets should be shaken up in bags containing powdered sulphur. This will prevent an outbreak of botrytis should the atmosphere of the storage room not be entirely free from moisture.

To guard against thrip, which will feed on the corms during storage and cover the areas with a brown cork-like tissue, all corms should be treated with naphthalene flakes before storage, used at a rate of 1 oz to every 100 corms.

Store the corms in a temperature of 50° F (10° C). A frost-free place is essential, but where the temperature does not exceed 45° F (7° C) there may be some risk of mildew in spite of all precautions.

Gladiolus Under Glass. The gladiolus does well under glass. When early bloom is required and there is no greenhouse available, the corms may be planted outdoors in prepared beds, where they are covered with cloches or with garden frames. A cold greenhouse will also bear its full quota of bloom in spring.

To bear bloom in a cold or in a gently warmed greenhouse, G. colvillei and G. nanus are planted. G. colvillei has for its parents G. cardinalis and G. tristis, the latter species having the greater influence on its offspring, for, like G. tristis, G. colvillei grows only about 18 in (45 cm) tall, the blooms being small and dainty, while they are spring-flowering. Plant the corms in October and only in the south-west is it advisable to do so without giving some form of protection. Even so, in a less mild than average winter, the plants may be disappointing outdoors. G. tristis may also be grown in the same way as G. colvillei and G. nanus, its creamy-white flowers having reddish-purple pencilling, while they possess a delicious fragrance. *G. colvillei* has crimson-purple flowers pencilled with white. There are several named varieties:

PEACH BLOSSOM. The graceful spikes are of delicate rose-pink, blotched with deeper rose and cream which makes the flowers popular with florists.

SPITFIRE. A magnificent variety, the blooms being of brilliant salmon-red.

THE BRIDE. It is one of the purest of all flowers, both the petals and the anthers being snow-white. It is, therefore, grown for bouquets during late spring when white flowers are usually scarce. For this reason, the bloom is grown in greenhouses and frames.

Gladiolus nanus follows *G. colvillei* in that it blooms during May and early June, thus almost closing the gap with those large-flowered varieties grown under cloches or in frames, and which will come into bloom early in July, a month before those which are grown unprotected. With the species *G. nanus*, the colour of the blooms varies from white through cream, blush pink, to carmine and scarlet but there are better forms:

AMANDA MAHY. This is perhaps the finest variety of the nanus group, the large, refined blooms being of brilliant orange-scarlet.

NYMPH. The blooms are white, blotched with carmine.

QUEEN WILHELMINA. The blooms, which are of a lovely shade of shell-pink, are produced with freedom.

ROMANCE. An introduction of great beauty, the flowers being of a lovely shade of soft salmon-pink with red blotches.

ROSEMARY. A new variety bearing bloom of rose-pink flaked with red.

Closely allied to the *G. nanus* group is *G. delicatissima*, also known as the blushing bride. It grows to a height of 2 ft (60 cm) and bears larger blooms than *G. nanus*. The blush-coloured flowers are flaked with white and carmine to produce a most colourful effect.

Also in bloom at the same time is *G. tubergenii*, which bears elegant loose spikes above strap-like foliage. The blooms, which are produced on 2-ft (60-cm) stems, are of purple-rose and have an attractive white throat. Like the others it is best grown under glass.

G. colvillei may be brought into bloom from the first days of April until early June, during which time those corms planted outdoors and covered with cloches will come into bloom. All the early-flowering species make good prices as cut flowers and, as they may be grown in pots outdoors in frames and do not need to be taken inside until early February, they are a useful crop to follow forced tulips and hyacinths. They will occupy the house for only about 12 weeks to make way for tomatoes. Or they may be grown entirely without heat in the cold greenhouse, though they will not come into bloom until early May when the house may be required for other crops.

The corms should be planted in 5-in (12·5-cm) pots at the end of September or early October, using two corms to each pot and planting them 3 in (7·5 cm) deep. They like a compost made up of:

    4 parts sterilised loam
    1 part well-decayed manure
    1 part silver sand
    1 part lime rubble.

With all the South African bulbs and corms such as the freesia, ixia and the sparaxis, the gladiolus species should not be placed in plunge beds, for it is important that the foliage grows sturdy from the beginning. After planting the corms, the pots are placed on a layer of ashes in a cold frame, the frame light being kept in place throughout autumn and winter for the plants require to be kept as dry as possible until growth begins. No water must, therefore, be given until the foliage has grown several inches tall, when the pots are ready to take indoors.

Make certain that the glass of the frame lights is kept clean, otherwise the foliage will grow weakly. The early-flowering gladioli, like freesias, require ample light and it is little use attempting to grow them under glass near to an industrial city owing to the atmosphere depriving the plants of the necessary light rays, for they will refuse to flower. For this reason, it is never advisable to take the pots indoors until mid-February, when there is a greater intensity of light than during the midwinter months.

The plants may be taken indoors in batches so that there will be a succession of bloom, though it will be necessary to have sufficient bloom to cut at one time to make up a box for the wholesale market, or to make it worth while to take the bloom to a local florist. The pots should be placed as near to the glass as possible. With the forcing-type house they are allowed to stand on the bench but with the Dutch light house, which has glass sides, the pots may be placed on the ground.

The plants require a free circulation of air and only gentle forcing. A temperature of between 50° and 55° F (10° to 13° C) is recommended, but though the appearance of the bloom may be delayed for 7 to 10 days, it is preferable to maintain a temperature of 48° F (9° C) for sturdier flower spikes are obtained when temperatures are moderate. If no heat is available, the plants should not be taken indoors until early March, for when once they begin to make growth it is easier to protect them when in the frame by covering with sacking during cold weather. The covering should be removed when conditions become milder.

When once the plants are indoors and ready to be brought into bloom, they should be watered so that the compost is made comfortably moist. It should be kept in this condition until they have finished flowering. Never give so much water that the compost remains cold and wet for any length of time. At all times the moisture should be slowly evaporating so that the roots do not receive more than they can actively utilise.

As the plants make growth, support them by placing two canes or sticks at the side of each pot to enable raffia to be taken around the foliage. This will prevent the flower spikes from leaning over and growing bent.

The early-flowering gladioli may also be grown in frames, planting the corms in pots any time between early October and early December. The pots should be inserted as deeply as possible into the soil of the frame so that there will be sufficient room for the plants to bloom. Varieties of *G. nanus* which grow no more than 15 in (37·5 cm) tall are most suitable for frame culture. The frame should be of sufficient depth to allow for flowering without the spike touching the glass, but as they come into bloom in May the light may be raised to allow fresh air to enter, and this will give additional room for the flowers to develop. The frame lights may be removed entirely on all warm, sunny days, but care should be taken to protect the blooms from being damaged by rain, replacing the lights whenever rain is imminent.

Propagation. Where facilities are available the best method of increasing one's stock is either by sowing seed, or by growing on the cormlets. Seed is sown under glass early in March, and if deep boxes are used there will be no need for transplanting—which will take up one's time and is resented by gladioli. For sowing the seed, use the John Innes compost.

The seed is small so must be handled with care, the best method being to tip out that which has been saved from each crossing into the palm of one hand and taking a pinch at a time, to scatter this over the surface in its own separate pot or box. When the box has been sown, lightly cover the seed with the dry compost and water carefully. A sheet of clean glass should then be placed over the box to hasten germination.

Where relying on the sun's rays to provide heat, the seed will begin to germinate at the end of April, or early in the month where given a temperature of 55° to 60° F (13° to 16° C). Maintain the compost in a moist condition, but if moisture is not continually evaporating, give no water or the seedlings may damp off. If the box is covered with glass this will help to maintain the compost in a moist condition, the glass should be removed when the plants are little more than 1 in (2·5 cm) tall.

Where there is a cold frame, the boxes should be moved to it early in May when the seedlings, like grass in appearance, are kept growing steadily throughout summer. They should be hardened off in the normal way for half-hardy plants, gradually admitting more air but protecting them from night frost until the month end when the boxes are allowed to stand out in the open. At all times the seedlings should be watered only when the compost begins to dry out. The young plants should be kept growing on until early October when they are lifted individually. The foliage will then be turning yellow, while they will have formed a tiny corm almost the size of a pea.

Cormlets raised from seed take two more years to reach flowering size, as will those saved from around the base of an established corm and removed when the corms are lifted. Where a stock is raised in this way, the corms will be fully acclimatised to the soil of one's garden and will possess a vigour rarely to be found in older corms. Bloom raised from cormlets grown to their third year will be of a quality unequalled from old imported corms.

To start them into growth, commencement should be made about 1st April. First soften their hard brown outer shell or covering. This is done by placing the cormlets in a jar and covering them with a solution of diluted Lysol (1 table-spoonful to a quart of water). After covering the corms with the solution leave them for 24 hours so that the shell becomes soft, while the Lysol acts as a safe-guard against thrip. Next, drain off the solution and empty the cormlets on to a tray, where the shell is removed by pressing between finger and thumb. Then in each jar place a layer of moist cotton wool, sand or peat into which the corm-lets are set. The jars should then be placed in a warm cupboard where all light is excluded and there they remain for 10 to 14 days, depending upon the degree of warmth and until they have begun to sprout. The cormlets must then be planted out without delay, mid-April being a suitable time, for by then the soil will be warm and the cormlets will grow away at once. Keeping the cormlets in a warm cupboard may be dispensed with, but sprouting them is halfway to success.

They are planted in drills 2 in (5 cm) deep over a layer of sand. Space the cormlets 3 or 4 in (7·5 to 10 cm) apart and allow 12 in (30 cm) between the drills to permit hoeing. After covering in the drills, all that is required is to keep the soil moist throughout summer, for the cormlets will not make growth if too dry. As soon as growth commences keep the hoe moving between the rows to prevent the appearance of weeds and 'panning' of the surface of the soil, which will deprive the cormlets of air. By the time the foliage has died back and the corms are ready for lifting in October, they will be about the size of crocus corms, almost 1 in (2·5 cm) in diameter. They should be dried and stored as previously described and the following year should be treated exactly as for fully grown corms, planting them in trenches 4 in (10 cm) deep and 6 in (15 cm) apart.

During the second season's growth it is advisable to feed the corms with liquid manure each week from the beginning of July so as to build up as large a corm as possible, to produce flower spikes the following season. By then the corms will be 10 to 12 cm in size and capable, where grown well, of producing a spike of exhibition quality.

For show purposes, the gladiolus is divided into three main sections:

(a) GRANDIFLORUS. This covers all Sections except the true Primulinus and Primulinus Grandiflorus groups.

    (i) Midget-flowered. The florets are not to exceed 1½ in in diameter.
    (ii) Miniature-flowered. Here the florets must be more than 1½ in but not exceeding 2½ in in diameter.

(iii) Small-flowered. In this group, the florets to be over $2\frac{1}{2}$ in but not exceeding 4 in in diameter.

(iv) Medium-flowered. The florets to be over 4 in but not exceeding 5 in in diameter.

(v) Large-flowered. Here the florets are to be over 5 in but not exceeding 6 in in diameter.

(vi) Giant-flowered. The florets to be over 6 in in diameter.

(*b*) PRIMULINUS. The florets to be hooded and not exceeding 3 in in diameter.

(*c*) PRIMULINUS GRANDIFLORUS. The florets to be hooded and over 3 in in diameter.

AMERICAN CLASSIFICATION

Miniatures	Florets under $2\frac{1}{2}$-in diameter
Small-flowered	$2\frac{1}{2}$- to $3\frac{1}{4}$-in diameter
Medium-flowered	$3\frac{1}{2}$- to $4\frac{3}{8}$-in diameter
Large-flowered	$4\frac{1}{2}$- to $5\frac{3}{8}$-in diameter
Largest-flowered	$5\frac{1}{2}$-in and larger

Species. *Gladiolus alatus*. Native of Cape Province where it is present on hilly slopes, especially after fires. It grows only 10 in (25 cm) tall and has four linear leaves, usually longer than the flower stem. The spike is four- or five-flowered, the blooms being of brick-red with the three lower lobes marked with pale yellow and they are sweetly scented. It is late-summer flowering in the British Isles and North America.

Gladiolus angustus. A rare species of the marshlands of Cape Province, it makes a corm only 1 cm in diameter and has four linear leaves, sheathing at the base. The narrow funnel-shaped flowers are white with a purple blotch on the lower petals and they appear as a two- to six-flowered spike 18 in (45 cm) long. Late summer-flowering.

Gladiolus atroviolaceus. Native of northern Turkey, where it blooms in damp meadowlands during midsummer, it has grass-like linear leaves and bears three to five flowers of violet-purple on a 2-ft (60-cm) stem.

Gladiolus aureus. Native of Cape Province, where it is found on lower slopes, it makes a corm 2 or 3 cm in diameter and has three leaves, the lower part of which are sheathing. It forms a three- to six-flowered spike about 2 ft (60 cm) tall, the florets being of rich golden-yellow with the upper part of the tube funnel-shaped.

Gladiolus blandus. Common on mountainous slopes in Cape Province, where it is known as the White Afrikaner, it makes a corm 3 cm in diameter and has four sword-like leaves. Its flowers are creamy-white with pink markings on the lower petals, and they are borne on a 3- to 10-flowered spike about 20 in (50 cm) tall. It blooms October to December in South Africa, in midsummer in the British Isles and North America.

Gladiolus brevifolius. Native of the Cape, where it is common on mountainous slopes, flowering there during April and May. It makes a 3-cm corm covered in a reddish fibrous tunic. The flowers are pale pink with a yellow blotch on the lower petals and they appear in a 6- to 10-flowered spike on 20-in (50-cm) stems.

Gladiolus byzantinus. Native of Turkey and Asia Minor, it forms a 2-cm corm and bears its bright magenta-red flowers in a 6- to 10-flowered spike during mid-summer. The flower stems are 30 in (75 cm) tall. There is a white form, *albus*, striking in its purity.

Gladiolus cardinalis. Native of Natal, where it grows in partial shade, its brilliant-red flowers appearing in a three- to six-flowered spike 2 ft (60 cm) high. Though not in bloom until late in July, it begins to grow early in winter and requires glass protection in the British Isles and North America, except in those gardens enjoying a favourable winter climate.

Gladiolus carinatus. Common about sandy flats in Cape Province, where it is known as the purple Afrikaner, it has a corm only 1 cm in diameter and has a sheathing leaf longer than the stem which attains a height of 18 in (45 cm). The blooms are borne in a two- to eight-flowered spike and are deep violet, with the scent of violets. It is usual for the lower petals to be marked with yellow.

Gladiolus carmineus. A rare native of Natal, it is known as the klip lily and bears its bright pink flowers on 12-in (30-cm) stems late in summer before the leaves. As it blooms early summer in the British Isles and, like *G. cardinalis*, begins to make growth before the end of winter, it should be grown in pots which are removed to the open as it comes into bloom. In the most sheltered gardens it may be grown in the rock garden.

Gladiolus caryophyllaceus. Native of Natal, it is the pink Afrikaner, but re-ceived its botanical name from the clove-like scent of its flowers. It is also *G. hirsutus*, its narrow red-margined leaves being covered in tiny hairs. The flowers are rose-pink, the lower petals striped with white, and they are borne in July in a three- to six-flowered spike.

Gladiolus childsii. A hybrid variety raised at Baden-Baden by Max Leichtlin but taking the name of the American John L. Childs, who purchased the stock. The plants grow 3 or 4 ft (90 cm to 1·2 metres) tall with branched stems which produce spikes 2 ft (60 cm) long with the individual blooms measuring 6 to 8 in (15 to 20 cm) across. The flowers appear in almost all the familiar gladiolus colourings, often speckled in the throat.

Gladiolus communis. Native of southern Europe, it was a familiar plant in Elizabethan gardens and was described by Gerard. It grows 2 ft (60 cm) tall, with narrow leaves, lance-shaped and ribbed, and it blooms in July, bearing bright rose-pink flowers in an elegant spike.

Gladiolus confusus. It is common in Cape Province on mountainous slopes, especially near Hout Bay, where it bears its inconspicuous yellowish-brown flowers in a one- to three-flowered spike during July and August. It blooms early in spring in the British Isles. The lower petals have a central stripe of maroon.

Gladiolus cruentus. A rare native of the slopes of the Drakensbergs, where it grows 3 ft (90 cm) tall and has long sword-like leaves. It blooms late autumn in the British Isles, its brilliant scarlet flowers spaced closely together on the spike. The side petals are blotched with white. It was used by the early hybridists to impart its red colouring.

Gladiolus cuspidatus. Native of Cape Province, where it is rare in damp places between Constantia and Steenberg, and flowering in December, in early autumn in the British Isles. It grows 12 in (30 cm) tall and bears a four- to seven-flowered spike. The flowers are creamy-white with small flakes on the lower petals, while the edges are elegantly waved. In warm parts it should be allowed to remain in the ground all the year, when it will increase rapidly.

Gladiolus debilis. It makes a small corm 1 to 2 cm in diameter, covered in coarse fibres. Native of mountainous slopes of Cape Province, where it is known as the painted lady, for its white flowers, borne in a one- to six-flowered spike, are splashed with crimson on the three lower lobes. At the base of each lobe is a purple mark.

Gladiolus dracocephalus. Native of Natal, it has pale-green leaves and in Britain blooms in spring and requires winter protection. The flowers are borne in a three- to six-flowered spike and are pale yellow, the lower petals being striped and spotted with purple.

Gladiolus gracilis. It is a common plant of sandy slopes of Cape Province, bearing scented flowers of pale pink or blue in a slender two- to six-flowered spike. The lower lobes are marked with cream. The deeply grooved leaves are almost round. It blooms early in summer in the British Isles and so requires winter protection with the corms growing in pots or boxes.

Gladiolus grandis. A rare native of mountainous slopes of Cape Province, where it is known as the large brown Afrikaner. It makes a small corm, the tunic being spiny at the base, while the leaves are narrow and rush-like with a prominent mid-rib or channel. It blooms early in summer, bearing five or six flowers in a loose spike. The flowers are coloured maroon, brown and dull yellow and have pointed petals. At night they emit a powerful carnation-like perfume. It requires winter protection in all but the warmest of gardens for it begins to make growth early in the year.

Gladiolus illyricus. A rare native of the British Isles, where it is to be found among bracken in the New Forest of Hampshire. It grows 12 in (30 cm) tall with short linear leaves, and it bears its magenta-purple flowers in July. The petals are attractively pointed.

Gladiolus macowanianus. Found in marshy places from Hout Bay to the south of Cape Peninsula, it makes a 2-cm corm and has four leaves, the two lower being 12 in (30 cm) long. The flowers are cream-coloured with red markings at the centre of the three lower lobes and are borne in a two- to six-flowered spike

2 ft (60 cm) tall. In their native land, they appear in October. In North America and northern Europe they bloom early in summer and require winter protection.

Gladiolus maculatus. Common on lower mountainous slopes of Cape Province, where it is known as the small brown Afrikaner, it makes a small corm with a netted tunic and has three or four leaves, the two lower being as long as the stem. The flowers are borne on a stem 2 ft (60 cm) tall and are pinkish-brown with pencil-like markings of darker brown and they are sweetly scented. It is spring-flowering in the British Isles and requires winter protection.

Gladiolus monticolus. Native of the Cape, where it is to be found near the top of Table Mountain, in bloom during January and February (in autumn in North America and northern Europe). It has two or three sword-like leaves, and it bears four to six cream-coloured flowers in a spike 2 ft (60 cm) tall. The three lower petals have red markings.

Gladiolus orchidiflorus. Native of Natal, where it blooms in spring. It blooms in midwinter in the British Isles, and so requires greenhouse protection. The flowers are small, of curious shape and are borne on a wiry stem 18 in (45 cm) tall. They are greyish-green, marked with brown at the centre and are sweetly scented.

Gladiolus ornatus. Native of Cape Province, where it is found in damp places, it is in bloom in September, in early summer in the British Isles and North America. It forms the smallest corm of all the species, less than 1 cm in diameter, and it has four leaves, the lower two sheathing at the base. The flowers are pale pink with a red and yellow butterfly mark on the lower lobes.

Gladiolus papilio. Native of Natal, it grows 20 in (50 cm) tall and bears its broad tubular drooping flowers in an elegant spike. The flowers are of greyish-purple, splashed with deeper purple and yellow. Flowering early in summer, it requires glass protection.

Gladiolus primulinus. Native of south-eastern Africa, of the rain-forest of the Victoria Falls, it makes a corm 2 to 3 cm in diameter and has strongly ribbed leaves 2 ft (60 cm) in length and 1 in (2·5 cm) wide. It bears clear primrose-yellow flowers on a two- to four-flowered stem 3 ft (90 cm) tall. The upper petal is hooded, bending over the reproductive organs to protect them from spray and so has been named maid of the mist. The primulinus hybrids have retained the form of the original species, having smooth-edged petals, the three outer petals being triangular. The large top inner petal falls over at the apex, the small lower petals (lobes) being slightly reflexed. The blooms are evenly spaced along the stem, there being more space between the blooms than with the large-flowered varieties, while the blooms are smaller, thus giving a more dainty effect to the spike. They come into bloom in July, before the large-flowered gladioli.

Gladiolus psittacinus. Common in Natal and Rhodesia, it was introduced early into Europe and was used by the first hybridists. It has sword-like leaves 12 in (30 cm) long and bears its flowers on a 3-ft (90-cm) stem. The flowers are almost bell-shaped and are borne 8 to 12 in a spike. They are of brilliant red, lined and spotted with yellow. It blooms in autumn. The variety *hookeri* bears up to 20 bright scarlet flowers to each spike.

Gladiolus purpureo-auratus. It was used by Lemoine to raise the first large-flowered hybrids. It is native of Natal with broad grey-green leaves 18 in (45 cm) long, and it increases by underground runners which form small corms at intervals. The flowers appear in August, 8 to 10 to a 3-ft (90-cm) spike, and they are pale yellow with a purple blotch on the lower petals.

Gladiolus quartineanus. Native of central Africa, it is a most striking species with long, narrow leaves, and bearing late in summer on a 3-ft (90-cm) stem large flowers of golden yellow heavily spotted with red.

Gladiolus recurvus. Native of Natal, it has rounded leaves, deeply veined, and early in summer bears six or seven flowers of pale yellow spotted with blue on a 2-ft (60-cm) spike. The flowers are violet-scented.

Gladiolus segetum. It is distributed in the Canary Isles, along the coast of southern Europe and as far east as Iran. It has small corms and is as hardy as *G. illyricus*, which it resembles, bearing bright carmine-purple flowers in loose spikes 12 in (30 cm) tall. It blooms in July.

Gladiolus tristis. A rare plant of marshy flats of the southern Cape Peninsula and of Natal, it is distinguished from *G. grandis* by the shorter perianth lobes, otherwise it is similar in botanical details. Its flowers are borne in a three- to six-flowered spike and are creamy-white, the three upper lobes having a mauve stripe, while the three lower have a yellow stripe. The flowers are sweetly scented at night and on dull days.

Varieties of the Gladiolus. VE—very early; E—early; M—mid-season; L—late.

Large-flowered.

ABU HASSAM (E). A magnificent violet-blue gladiolus, being a decided improvement on existing varieties of this colour, 10 flowers opening together, each being perfectly arranged on a sturdy stem.

ADORABLE (M). The sulphur-cream florets are slightly ruffled and have an amber-cream blotch in the throat. When in bud, the blooms have a slight greenish sheen. Eight florets open at one time out of a total of 20 on an extremely strong stem.

ADORATION (E). This is one of the finest of all pink gladioli and, flowering early, it is excellent for cutting. The salmon-pink florets are beautifully placed along the flower head.

ALBERT SCHWEITZER (L). The finest late red, the florets being large and broad and of fiery scarlet, the lower petal having a crimson throat flecked with white.

ARANJUEZ (VE). It bears flowers of soft orange colouring, shading to apricot down the throat. A strong-growing variety of delicate beauty, it is admired as a garden plant and as a cut flower.

ARISTOCRAT (E). A 'smoky' variety of great merit, the large florets having ideal placement and being of an unusual shade of strawberry-red flushed with grey.

ARTIST (E). It is one of the most beautifully coloured of all gladioli, the pale-lilac blooms being veined with white and flecked with purple.

ATHLONE (M). The florets are of an attractive shade of buff pink. On a 22-bud spike, 10 will be open at the same time, the straight-edged petals giving it a cool, chaste appearance.

ATLANTIC (M). It opens more florets at the same time than any other gladiolus and so has won many show awards. The colour is rich orange-scarlet.

BENARES (ML). A most unusual and valuable variety, in colour a beautiful almost even tone of clear dawn pink, showing a sharp crimson tongue against salmon-pink on two lower petals and with a cyclamen throat.

BERMUDA (ML). A truly wonderful gladioli, the large florets having a leathery texture and extremely ruffled petals. As many as eight open together, the blooms being of a lovely shade of pale salmon-pink with a white throat.

BIRD OF DAWNING (E). It forms a long tapering spike of ideal placement, the florets with their crinked petals being of soft mimosa yellow with lilac anthers in the arched throat.

BLACK CHERRY (M). Of classical form, the colour is glistening black-red. The florets open eight at a time on tall spikes to make it an outstanding exhibition variety.

BLOEMFONTEIN (L). Like so many of the pinks, it is late-flowering but is unsurpassed in its form and beauty. The florets open wide and are of a lovely shade of soft apricot pink.

BOW BELLS (VE). Outstanding for exhibition, as a cut flower and for garden display, it has won every possible award. Its heavily ruffled florets are of a lovely shade of pink with a buff undertone.

BURMA (ML). A large proportion of the best gladioli are late flowering and this is no exception. The rose-purple florets are extremely ruffled and have perfect placement, up to 10 blooms opening together.

CARNIVAL (M). A truly great variety, the large florets being of vivid scarlet accentuated by the clear icy white throat. The florets are ruffled, eight opening together.

CHINOOK (ML). It bears one of the largest spikes of all and opens up to 10 huge florets at one time. The blooms are of a glorious shade of bright salmon.

CIRCE (M). Clear-glowing tangerine, with crimson streaks behind a light throat, decisive light pencilling down the centre of each petal and numerous precise streaks of crimson against a sharp cream tongue on one lower petal. A superb variety with a perfection of form and finish hardly approached by any other.

CONNECTICUT YANKEE (M). For long a winner on the show bench, it opens eight florets together which have ideal double row placement. The blooms are of a lovely shade of deep pink with red throat blotches.

COVER GIRL (L). Has for long been a show winner in the United States. It is also a valuable cut-flower variety, the spikes being long and thin, the florets being plain edged and of clear soft salmon-pink.

ELIZABETH THE QUEEN (M). With Spic and Span, has won more awards at the American shows than any other variety. The blooms are of purest lavender and beautifully ruffled. Eight to ten florets will open together and have excellent placement. It has been widely used for breeding.

ERIDGE (M). An 'all-blue' gladiolus of exceptional merit, the colour being of an even tone of pale mauve-blue, slightly darker in the throat. Producing a medium-sized graceful spike, its nicely formed florets and perfect carriage add to its beauty.

EVANGELINE (L). Though late-flowering, this is one of the most popular of all gladioli. The enormous ruffled florets, which are of a lovely shade of light rose pink, open at least 10 together.

FIREBRAND (M). A variety of outstanding quality, opening 10 closely packed florets to a flower head. The colour is deep glowing red. A championship gladiolus.

FLORIST'S GLORY (M). One of the finest of the blue gladioli, the large, beautifully placed florets being of a lovely shade of clear lavender-blue, feathered with dark blue in the throat.

FLOWER SONG (E). It has a tall wiry stem along which are evenly spaced medium-sized florets of soft golden yellow, streaked with carmine in the throat.

FORGOTTEN DREAMS (M). A variety of charm, its creamy-white buds opening to broad florets of palest yellow edged with rose. As many as eight or nine florets open together and remain fresh for a considerable time.

GOLD PIECE (E). The outstanding exhibition yellow, the florets being of ideal placement and of pure gold, slightly ruffled at the edges and of velvet-like texture.

HAPPY END (E). Valuable as an early cut flower bearing an elegant spike which lasts well in water and when transported. The medium-sized florets are of a lovely shade of salmon-coral shaded cream in the throat.

HAWAII (M). Rich glowing blood-red with a sheen of richer crimson on the tongue of the lower petals. Extremely beautiful and impressive colour, it is a garden plant of distinction which blooms well in exposed districts. The petals are attractively edged with white.

HEIRLOOM (M). Ranks with Elizabeth the Queen as the best of its colour. It forms a long spike, while the florets, which are of deep, clear lavender and beautifully ruffled, open more together than any other variety. The florets are among the largest of all.

HENRIDE GREEVE (L). This glorious gladiolus may be regarded as the royal representative of this popular family. It bears very large flowers of a warm apricot-orange colour, seven or eight opening at a time, on a tall straight stem.

KING DAVID (M). Raised by Carlson in the United States it is one of the finest of all, the broad ruffled florets being of deepest purple with a silver picotee edge. Twenty-four buds make up the spike in a double row placement.

KING SIZE (ML). It is well named for the massive spikes reach a height of more than 6 ft (1·8 metres). The monster florets open together on a 26-bud flower spike. The blooms are of pale salmon-pink.

KONYNENBERG AND MARK'S BLUE (M). It forms a large exhibition spike of powerful colouring, the almost navy-blue buds opening to large broad flowers of deep petunia purple.

LANDMARK (M). A show bench favourite, for the florets, which are of a glorious shade of creamy-white, open up to 12 together, while the spike will carry as many as 24 buds.

LEIF ERIKSON (M). This magnificent cream variety with its pale green throat is a great exhibition favourite. On the 5- to 6-ft (1·5- to 1·8-metre) spike 10 florets will be open together, while eight more will be showing colour.

LIPSTICK (M). A most attractive gladiolus, 9 to 10 florets opening together on a 22-bud spike. The ruffled petals are of a charming shade of shell-pink, the blooms having great substance.

LITTLE PANSY (E). A most dainty and early-flowering variety for cutting, the light-blue florets having pansy-purple blotches. Sixteen buds make up the spike.

MARIA GORETTI (E). The finest white for early shows, making a spike of enormous size, the large florets being of icy-white, opening as many as 10 or more together.

MAX HAVELAAR (M). It forms a long spike of broad-petalled flowers of warm apricot, shaded gold at the centre and coppery orange at the petal edges. An ideal exhibitor's variety.

PACTOLUS (EM). Daffodil yellow with a broad vermilion and deep crimson tongue on two lower petals. A variety of outstanding colour, the beautifully formed florets being well arranged along the slender stem and producing a most graceful spike.

PATROL (M). One of the finest exhibition gladioli on account of its exquisite form, while it will open as many as a dozen florets together. The colour is rich buff-apricot shading to yellow in the throat. One of the easiest gladioli to bring to perfection.

PAUL PFITZER'S MEMORY (M). One of the outstanding 'blues', the broad petals, neatly folded back, being of rich pure lavender-blue with a silver sheen in the throat and lavender anthers.

PETER PEARS (M). The broad florets are set closely together along the stem to make a spike of great substance. The blooms are of rich tangerine shaded pink and overlaid with gold. The lower petals are shaded orange-red in the throat.

PICARDY (L). The charm of this variety arises from the glorious colour, salmon-pink with darker feathering on the lower petals. A magnificent gladiolus, which produces a strong stalk on which the florets are nicely arranged. A garden variety of exceptional merit, very showy as a cut flower and a perfect exhibition bloom. Though introduced 40 years ago, it is still grown for cutting, and has been more widely used for breeding than any other variety.

POPPY DAY (EM). A gladiolus of singular beauty, the colour being radiant scarlet of great intensity with a white line on the lower petal. It produces a large tall spike with seven or eight perfectly formed open florets, prettily ruffled and nicely arranged on a strong erect stem.

RAVEL (E). Undoubtedly one of the best blues yet produced, being pale blue with a mauve blotch on lower petals, six to eight flowers open at a time, which are of good substance and noble form and well placed on a tall erect stem.

REDCOAT (M). This may take over from Red Charm as the most popular red for exhibition. The clear light-red blooms are beautifully ruffled and open eight together, placement being ideal.

RHAPSODY IN BLUE (M). Probably the best blue raised by Konyenberg and Mark of Holland, for which colour they are justly famous. The handsome spikes are of exhibition quality, the blooms being of clear light blue.

ROSITA (M). A most attractive variety both for cutting and exhibition. The light-rose florets have a deeper rose blotch in the throat. The silver edge to the petals and the double row placement of the giant florets makes it outstanding.

SANS SOUCI (M). Fiery scarlet-red with a clear-yellow streak down the centre of the lower petal; a variety of wonderful charm. The flowers of excellent substance are perfectly set on the tall straight stem.

SCHÖNBRUNN (L). Though late-flowering it opens well in adverse weather, the blooms being of an attractive shade of creamy apricot, shading to coral at the petal edges, the lower petals being edged with gold.

SHOW GIRL (E). On account of its extreme earliness it is a valuable cut flower. The brick-red blooms, which are only about half the size of the exhibition varieties, have a creamy-yellow blotch in the throat.

SILHOUETTE (M). The large florets are of a most attractive shade of smoky-pink and grey which makes it ideal for cutting but forms rather too short a spike for exhibition.

SNOW PRINCESS (M). A white gladiolus, greenish in bud, which is outstanding for size and form. Colour, milky white with a tinge of green down the throat. Very strong spike, often 2 ft (60 cm) in length, bearing up to 20 florets.

SOUTHERN BELLE (E). A beautiful variety, excellent for cutting and exhibition. The blooms are of deep smoky-pink covered in a misty blue sheen. The florets are of leathery texture and have first-class placement.

SPIC AND SPAN (EM). Raised by Carlson in the United States, where it has been the most consistent show winner for a decade. The 3-ft (90-cm)-long flower heads will open 10 florets together. The colour is a bright deep pink with ruffled petals.

TEMPTRESS (M). A consistent winner in America and a most charming variety. The ruffled florets, which open as many as 10 together, are of a lovely shade of shell-pink.

TOULOUSE-LAUTREC (M). One of the most attractive of all, the medium-sized florets of salmon-pink being shaded with gold in the throat and marked with orange.

TUNIA'S ARISTOCRAT (L). One of Bott's best 'smokies', the florets having exhibition placement and being of a lovely shade of smoky-brown and slate, feathered red in the throat.

TUNIA'S CLASSIC (M). General effect is of light purple and salmon, freely flecked, with the tongue on one lower petal being deep cream, delicately pencilled with four strokes of crimson, and a light fawn throat. An extremely attractive and dainty variety, quite apart from any other.

WINSTON CHURCHILL (M). A gladiolus of glowing brilliancy, the large flowers are bright blood-red, slightly flecked, of unequalled beauty and perfect formation. A noble, handsome variety of distinct character which will produce a rich display in any position in the garden.

Butterfly Strain. The spikes grow 2 to 3 ft (60 to 90 cm) tall, the florets being only half the size of the large-flowered hybrids. While the petals are slightly ruffled, their beauty lies in their attractive throat markings, like exotic butterflies. Varieties:

ANECDOTE (M). Raised in the United States it has blooms of primrose yellow with deeper yellow fall petals.

ATTICA (E). The salmon-pink florets are flushed with yellow on the fall petals, which also have red markings. A fine exhibition variety as eight to nine florets open together.

BLUE GODDESS (M). A strong grower, the florets of silver-blue are shaded deeper blue at the edges, the lower petals having a cream-edged tongue of purple.

BUMBLE BOOGIE (M). It has extremely frilled petals of a warm shade of shrimp-pink with scarlet markings.

BUTTERFLY (M). A gladiolus of most unusual colouring, the blooms being of an exotic shade of rose-pink, the yellow throat being splashed with red.

CHINATOWN (E). One of the first to bloom, it bears smooth-petalled florets of rich tangerine with the lower petals shaded lime-green.

DAILY SKETCH (M). The petals are extremely ruffled and are coloured cream, with biscuit markings on the lower petals.

DESIRÉE (E). One of the most brilliantly coloured gladiolus, the blooms being of terra-cotta with a bright golden throat and crimson blotches on the fall petals.

FROLIC (E). It forms a long graceful spike, the florets having turned back petals. They are of bright red with purple and cream markings on the lower petals.

FROU-FROU (M). A pretty variety, the lavender-rose blooms have a yellow throat and faint white lines.

GIGI (M). The blooms with their ruffled petals form a pyramid, eight or nine opening together, and are of a lovely shade of wild-rose pink shaded with biscuit at the centre.

GREEN WOODPECKER (M). An outstanding exhibition variety, the cream-ground florets having a deep-green tint, offset by wine-red markings.

HERALD (ML). The heavily ruffled blooms are of deepest yellow flushed with orange and have a red blotch in the throat.

ICE FOLLIES (M). Particularly attractive, the beautifully ruffled blooms are ivory-white with amber markings in the throat.

LITTLE DIAMOND (EM). A superb introduction, the dainty deep amber blooms being overlaid reddish-orange and with a maroon throat.

MAGIC CARPET (M). The blooms are pale yellow flushed with apricot, the fall petals being of deeper yellow with a purple blotch.

MELODIE (E). A brilliantly coloured variety, the salmon-pink blooms being deeper at the petal edges, while they have a scarlet throat.

SOUTHPORT (E). A variety of charm, the ivory-white florets with their ruffled petals are flushed with gold at the centre.

SUMMER FAIRY (E). One of the finest, the clear salmon-pink blooms have cream fall petals and a maroon throat.

TOPOLINO (EM). A particular favourite having nicely frilled petals, the golden-yellow blooms having a scarlet blotch.

VIVALDI (M). Glows like a prairie fire, the deep-orange blooms having blood-red markings.

Miniatures. Raised in Canada by Mr Leonard Butt, the heavily ruffled petals being less than $2\frac{1}{2}$ in (6 cm) across. They have an orchid-like appearance.

BONNIE PRINCE (EM). The very ruffled well-placed florets are of a lovely shade of rose-pink and make this a charming variety for all occasions.

BO PEEP (E). Usually the first of the ruffled miniatures to bloom, the florets being of delicate buff-pink, stippled with red.

CORVETTE (E). One of Butt's best which opens as many as 10 florets together. The small, dainty florets are of vivid scarlet.

DAINTINESS (E). The petals are extremely ruffled with precise placement, the blooms being white with a cream throat.

GOLDETTE (M). It opens eight blooms together on a 20-bud spike, the petals being extremely ruffled and of clear rich yellow. An exhibition favourite.

HEART O'GOLD (E). Like Lavender and Gold, the florets are ruffled but of Primulinus placement, the creamy-white blooms having a striking golden throat.

LAVENDER AND GOLD (E). It always commands top prices at Covent Garden with its pale-lavender blooms with their moonlight yellow throat. Though ruffled, the blooms have Primulinus placement.

PICOTEE (E). Most striking in that the creamy-white petals have a crimson-red picotee edge, while the top petals are flushed with scarlet.

PINT SIZE (M). Ideal for the small garden, the tiny lavender blooms with their creamy-white throat opening eight together on an 18-bud spike.

STATUETTE (E). A beauty, opening eight blooms together and which are of pale yellow, stippled with rosy-red in the throat. Probably the best exhibition miniature.

TOYTOWN (E). It blooms very early, opening eight together on an 18-bud spike. The strikingly coloured blooms are scarlet with a yellow throat.

WEDGEWOOD (M). The blooms are of a lovely shade of lavender-pink with a cream throat and are larger than those of Butt's Miniatures.

ZIG-ZAG (L). The last of the miniatures to bloom, the small florets of red splashed with gold in the throat have zig-zag placement up the stem.

Primulinus. The flowers are spaced along the stem in ladder fashion. S—small primulinus; L—large primulinus.

ALICIDE (E). It forms a slender spike with florets of dazzling scarlet contrasting with the picotee edge of white.

ARIA (M, S). Outstanding, opening eight small florets together on a 17-bud spike. The attractive deep-pink blooms have a cream throat.

ATOM (M, S). Unique in its colour, the slightly frilled blooms being of orange-scarlet with a cream picotee edge. Healthy stocks are now difficult to obtain.

ATTRACTIE (M, L). One of Unwin's best, the ivory blooms being suffused with coral and with a crimson throat.

CANDY (E, L). Quite delightful, the apricot blooms being flecked with cream, the lower petals being marked with orange and with a crimson throat.

CAROLINE (M, L). Very lovely, the white blooms being flushed with pink, which deepens at the petal tips.

CHINESE LANTERN (M, S). The florets are more widely separated than usual and are of vivid flame-red with a bright-yellow throat.

CITRONELLA (M, S). One of the most dainty, the pale-yellow florets being held on long, slender stems.

COLUMBINE (M, L). A fine exhibition Primulinus of pink and white colourings, like icing sugar.

COMIC (M). A delightful colour combination of peach-pink flushed with orange, the lower petals being blotched with chestnut and with a narrow white line down the centre.

FASCINATION (M, L). Of beautiful colourings, the cerise-pink blooms having a cream throat feathered with scarlet.

FIERY KNIGHT (E, S). A beauty. The orange-red blooms with their deeper glowing throat present a velvet-like appearance.

FOREMOST (M, L). A most beautiful variety, the salmon-orange blooms deepening at the petal tips. The fall petals are of deeper orange, faintly lined with gold.

KATHLEEN FERRIER (M, L). A lovely variety, the deep salmon-pink blooms being flushed with orange and with rose markings in the throat.

LADY GUINEVERE (M). On its own for floral arrangement, the green buds opening to dainty florets of lime white flushed with ivory in the throat.

LEMONDROP (E, S). Quite lovely, the lemon-yellow blooms having deeper yellow shading in the throat.

MIKADO (M, L). Of unusual colouring, the salmony-biscuit blooms are flaked with slate and marked with red in the throat.

OSAGE (M, L). A show favourite, six florets opening together on a 16-bud spike and being nicely spaced. The blooms are of clear bright scarlet.

PAMELA MUMMERY (M, S). Introduced after having first been discarded to become a Gold Vase winner and one of the most popular of all Primulinus. The blooms are of a lovely shade of biscuit-salmon with a cream throat and waved petals.

PRIMROSE DAME (M, S). The spikes are dainty, the blooms of primrose-yellow with a deeper yellow throat.

RICHARD UNWIN (M, S). A beauty and Gold Vase winner. The blooms, which have excellent placement, are of chestnut-crimson with a cream stripe on the fall petals, while the petals have a velvety texture.

SCARLET MAID (E, S). Most striking in every way, the small, dainty blooms being of vivid scarlet-orange with a crimson throat.

URANUS (M, L). One of the few Primulinus 'smokies'. The smoky crimson blooms are offset by the small cream throat.

Face-up.

PICCOLO (E). One of the most dainty of the face-ups, the pure white blooms having a red blotch in the throat. The wiry stems make it valuable for indoor flower arrangement.

RED BUTTON (E). The best in this section, the long tapering stems having 20 or more buds. The bright scarlet blooms have attractive grey stamens.

T. E. WILSON (E). The blooms are of rich salmon-pink with a white throat, the florets being scarcely $1\frac{1}{2}$ in (4 cm) across, which makes this the smallest of all gladioli.

Multi-flowered. A strain evolved by Konynenberg and Mark and introduced in 1970, by crossing the early-flowering butterfly variety, Sympathique, with *G. nanus Floriade*. The raisers have named these new gladioli the Coronado strain, and from a single corm several flowering spikes are produced during July and August, or a month earlier, where March planting is possible. The flowers, which appear in all shades of pink, have the pretty ruffled daintiness of the parents.

Among the best varieties to date are Mavajo, which bears pink flowers, feathered with white; Belcanto, soft mauve pink with a purple blotch; and Nimrod, salmon-pink, feathered with purple.

GLORIOSA (Liliaceae)

A genus of five species of tuberous-rooted plants so named for the beauty of their flowers. They are plants for a warm greenhouse, climbing by means of their leaves, the tips acting like tendrils. They are native of tropical Africa and Asia and require a minimum night temperature of 60° F (16° C). The leaves are lance-shaped and dark glossy green, the flowers appearing singly in the axils of the upper leaves. The perianth consists of six narrow waved segments, which bend back to expose the six stamens and the ovary with its three-cleft stigma.

Culture. The plants may be grown up the rafters of a greenhouse or garden room warmed by central heating. The tubers are planted in February, using an 8-in (20-cm) pot to hold two or three tubers. The compost should consist of turf loam, leaf mould or peat and decayed cow manure in equal parts, to which a liberal sprinkling of sand is added to assist drainage. Plant the tubers 2 in (5 cm) deep and give no water until growth commences in spring, but maintain a night temperature of 60° F (16° C). The shoots are trained up the roof of a glasshouse along canes or wires and their foliage should be syringed daily. During summer, they will also require copious amounts of water and, as they come into bloom, a weekly application of dilute manure water. The flowers are long-lasting on the plant and also when cut for indoor decoration. They will bloom from mid-June until mid-September, depending upon the amount of sunshine they receive. The stems and foliage will then begin to die back, and water should be withheld until the plants are started into fresh growth in March, when the tubers are re-potted into fresh compost.

Propagation. Division of the tubers by cutting into pieces, each containing a bud or shoot is a reliable method. Dust the cut parts with sulphur before planting into 4-in (10-cm) pots for growing on. March is the most suitable time, when the old tubers have begun to sprout.

Plants may also be raised from seed sown in April in pans containing a compost made up of sterilised loam, peat and sand in equal parts. For reliable germination, a minimum temperature of 68° F (20° C) must be maintained and the compost kept moist. Under such conditions, the seed will germinate in four weeks, and as soon as large enough to handle, the seedlings are moved to 3-in (7·5-cm) pots containing a similar compost. Here they remain, kept comfortably moist and shielded from strong sunlight until the pots are filled with roots. The plants are then moved to larger pots in which they will bloom, but no flowers should be allowed to form the first summer. Then after a winter's rest, they are brought into bloom.

Gloriosa rothschildiana

Species. *Gloriosa carsonii*. It is found in Rhodesia and Tanzania and is more compact than other species, though the stems reach a height of 6 ft (1·8 metres) or more. The flowers have broad petals and are yellow, shading to red towards the base. It has small tubers.

Gloriosa rothschildiana. Discovered in Uganda, the flowers are large, the petals handsomely waved and of bright ruby-red, edged yellow and with yellow shading at the base. The petals incurve at the tips. The variety *citrina* has all-yellow flowers.

Gloriosa superba. Native of India and tropical eastern Africa, it is the latter, *G. superba africana*, that is grown in greenhouses. It was introduced into Europe in 1690 and has narrow flowers with wavy petals. The lower part is yellow, the upper part orange-red edged with yellow.

Gloriosa verschuurii. Native of tropical Africa, it sends up its stems to a height of 5 or 6 ft (1·5 to 1·8 metres) and bears broad petals which do not incurve as with *G. rothschildiana*. The segments are brilliant red edged with yellow.

Gloriosa virescens. Native of Mozambique, it grows 3 to 4 ft (about 1 metre) tall and has flowers of pale orange-yellow edged with deeper yellow.

GLOXINIA (Gesneriaceae)

A genus of six species, native of tropical South America and named after the botanist B. P. Gloxin. It is now separated from sinningia as its roots form a tuber and not a corm. The modern gloxinia hybrids have been evolved from *Sinningia speciosa*, introduced from Brazil in 1815. Only one or two species of *gloxinia* are in general cultivation. Flowering in the autumn, they are plants for a warm greenhouse or living-room.

Culture. Requiring a minimum night temperature of 60° F (16° C) the tubers are potted in March, using a compost made up of 2 parts fibrous loam and 1 part each leaf mould and decayed manure. The size of pot will depend upon age of the tuber, for they increase in size each year. Usually a 6-in (15-cm) pot is suitable. The top of the tuber should be inserted level with the surface of the compost, and to start it into growth, vigorous bottom heat and a humid atmosphere should be provided. During summer, water liberally and syringe the foliage daily, while shielding it from the midday sun. When the flower buds form, discontinue syringeing so as not to harm the blooms. The plants will remain colourful for about six weeks, at which point the leaves begin to die back. Gradually discontinue watering, and during winter lay the pots on their side and shield from frost.

Propagation. Gloxinias (and sinningias) are increased by division of the tubers (as for begonias), by leaf cuttings, or from seed. The tubers are divided when coming into growth early in summer. Use a sharp knife and make sure that each piece has an eye or shoot. Plant in a 3-in (7·5-cm) pot, moving later in summer to a larger pot in which the plants will bloom.

Plants may be raised from leaves removed in summer, inserting the stalks up to the base of the leaf in boxes of sandy compost (as for begonia). A propagating frame will encourage rapid rooting, a temperature of 70° F (21° C) and a humid atmosphere (to prevent transpiration) being necessary. The leaves should be shielded from the sun. Rooting will take place at the base of the leaf stalk in about four weeks, when they may be moved to small pots. By late autumn they will have formed a tuber. They are allowed to die back in winter and may be brought into bloom the following year.

The gloxinia may be raised from seed sown in June under glass. The seed is small and must be sown with care to prevent overcrowding. Use the John Innes compost, making the surface as fine and as level as possible, so that the seeds receive an equal amount of moisture. Sow with finger and thumb and do not cover the seed. After watering with a fine spray, place a sheet of glass over the pan and a piece of brown paper to shield the seed from the light and to hasten germination. Take care that the seeds do not become dry, watering as often as necessary, preferably from the base of the container and remove the paper as soon as the seeds have germinated. Transplant the seedlings when large enough to handle to the 3-in (7·5-cm) pot in which they will remain during their first summer, moving to larger pots the following spring. Do not plant the crown too deep. The lower leaves must be above soil level.

Species. *Gloxinia fimbriata* (syn. *G. glabra*). It grows only 9 in (22·5 cm) tall with dark-green leaves, and late in summer bears white trumpet-shaped flowers, shaded yellow in the throat and spotted with purple.

Gloxinia maculata insignis. It grows 18 in (45 cm) tall and is an elegant plant with large decorative leaves, bearing in August and September downy purple-blue funnel-shaped flowers which are scented.

Hybrid Varieties

Outstanding is Switzerland, a variety of great vigour, the large scarlet trumpets having a frilly edge of white. Grenadier is glowing scarlet and The Duchess, deep purple edged white. Three Dutch introductions, Gerda Lodder (scarlet), Lodder's Rose (pink), and Glory of Utrecht (violet) are also striking. Lovely too, is a Pink Princess, the white blooms being edged with pink; and Bacchus, bearing large trumpets of rich wine red. Blackmore and Langdon's Spotted Hybrids are remarkable in their diversity of colouring.

GRIFFINIA (Amaryllidaceae)

A genus of seven species native to Brazil, being the South American counterpart of the amaryllis of southern Africa. They are bulbous plants with broad stalked leaves, prominently veined and bear funnel-shaped flowers in a large umbel at the end of a stout scape. They are plants for a warm greenhouse, being more tender than amaryllis, requiring a minimum night temperature of 50° F (10° C) in winter. They bloom early in the year—unlike amaryllis, which blooms in autumn—and so they must be confined to a greenhouse or garden room.

Culture. As the bulbs increase in size annually, they require a larger pot every three years, one bulb being planted to each. Begin with a 4-in (10-cm) pot, for the bulbs should almost fill it, allowing only sufficient room for the bulb to grow larger. Use a compost made up of 2 parts fibrous loam and 1 part each leaf mould and dehydrated cow manure, to which is added a sprinkling of sand. Plant in September and start the bulbs into growth in a temperature of 60° F (16° C), giving only sufficient moisture to keep them growing. It is in summer that the plants should be rested, but as they are evergreen they must not be dried off. They continue to grow after flowering and until the end of June. Watering should then be reduced to a minimum until autumn, when the flower stems develop. Repotting is done soon after flowering.

Propagation. The offsets should be detached when the plants are repotted, pressing the bulblets into the surface of a sandy compost and using a 3-in (7·5-cm) pot. Here they remain for a year, when they are transplanted to larger pots, and will begin to bloom in about three years.

They may also be raised from seed and will bloom in five years. The seeds are sown in June using the John Innes compost and laying the seed on the surface. Water from the base and allow a day temperature of 65° F (18° C) when the seeds will germinate in about three months. The seedlings should not be disturbed until the following April, when they are moved to 3-in (7·5-cm) pots, planting one into each and using a compost made up of fibrous loam, leaf mould and sand in equal parts. After 12 months, the plants will be ready to move to a 4-in (10-cm) pot, in which they will remain until flowering.

Species. *Griffinia blumenavia.* It makes an ovoid bulb of 2-in (5-cm) diameter and has oblong leaves 6 in (15 cm) long and 3 in (7·5 cm) broad. It blooms in February and March, bearing six to nine lilac-pink flowers at the end of a 9-in (22·5-cm) scape. It is one of the easiest species to manage.

Griffinia hyacinthina. The bulbs measure 3 in (7·5 cm) across when fully mature, the oblong leaves being 9 in (22·5 cm) long and 3 in (7·5 cm) wide, with the stalk almost as long as the blade. It blooms in January, bearing 10 to 12 horizontal flowers of bright lilac-blue on a 15-in (37·5-cm) scape.

Griffinia liboniana. It forms a small round bulb. Its oblong leaves are 4 in (10 cm) long and 2 in (5 cm) wide. They are without stalks. It blooms later than others, in March and April, bearing six to eight lilac-mauve flowers on a 10-in (25-cm) stem.

Griffinia ornata. It was described in the *Gardener's Chronicle* in 1876 and is a most handsome species. It makes a large bulb 4 in (10 cm) in diameter and has large leaves 12 in (30 cm) long and 6 in (15 cm) broad, the base clasping the flower stem. The pale-lilac flowers are borne in a large umbel of 12 or more on a 12-in (30-cm) stem and are at their best in December.

GYNANDRIRIS (Iridaceae)

A genus of several species, present in both northern and southern Africa, and with *G. sisyrinchium* present along the coastline of southern Europe. The species resemble iris and morea and grow from a corm, not a bulb or rhizome like iris, with which the genus is often identified. The corm is globose, the tunic being made up of parallel fibres. The leaves, two in number, are linear and pointed, while the flowers are borne in terminal clusters, emerging from two colourless spathes (coloured in morea).

Culture. The plants require a warm sunny situation, like the base of a warm wall, for it is necessary for the corms to ripen thoroughly if they are to bloom well. In exposed gardens of northern Europe and North America they are best grown under glass, for they bloom early in summer, during May and June (in autumn in their native haunts). If growing in the open, plant the corms in the autumn, 4 in (10 cm) deep and 6 in (15 cm) apart and into a well-drained sandy soil. It is advisable to cover with glass to protect them from frost and heavy rain.

Where growing under glass, plant in March four or five corms to each pot and give no moisture until they come into growth. After flowering, gradually dry off, and during winter, keep in a frost-free room.

Propagation. They may be increased by detaching the cormlets and growing on in boxes of sandy soil until they reach flowering size in three or four years.

Species. *Gynandriris setifolia* (syn. *Morea xerospatha*). Native of South Africa, where it is a common plant of waysides, growing in poor sandy soil. It has twin basal leaves 15 in (37·5 cm) long and bears sweetly scented pale bluish-mauve flowers in terminal clusters.

Gynandriris sisyrinchium (syn. *Iris juncifolia*). Present in southern Europe from Spain to the Levant and east to Afghanistan. It grows 6 in (40 cm) tall with arched linear leaves, and early in summer bears fleeting flowers of pale blue in small terminal clusters.

H

HABRANTHUS (Amaryllidaceae)

A genus of 20 species, native of tropical and South America and closely related to hippeastrum. It is distinguished by its stamens of unequal length and also by the spathe which protects the pedicel. Mostly native of Chile and Peru, the plants require winter protection in the British Isles and North America in all but the most sheltered gardens of the south-west. The bulb is globose with a dark-brown tunic and from it arises its narrow linear leaves, often deeply channelled. The flowers are funnel-shaped and are borne singly on a 6-in (15-cm) stem.

Culture. Under glass, those flowering in early summer should be potted in September and those which bloom in autumn in March. Plant one bulb in a 6-in (15-cm) pot, in which it will remain for three to four years, during which time it will continue to increase in size. The plants require a compost made up of 2 parts fibrous loam and 1 part each leaf mould and decayed manure with a sprinkling of coarse sand. Being lime lovers, the plants will benefit from some lime rubble (mortar) in the compost. The bulbs vary in size, but the pot should not be too large—as a general rule it should be twice the diameter of the bulb. Plant firmly and so that the neck and shoulder of the bulb is above the level of the compost. Stand the pots in a frame or in deep boxes in the greenhouse with bulb fibre or leaf mould packed around and over them and kept moist. In a temperature of 60° F (16° C) the bulbs will soon begin to grow. The plants should be syringed regularly to maintain a humid atmosphere. Increase moisture supplies as the plants make growth, and as soon as the flower stems appear give a weekly application of dilute manure water until the flowers begin to fade. After flowering, withhold water gradually as the foliage dies back. Keep the plants almost dry and in a frost-free room during the dormant period.

In the open, plant in April, at the base of a sunny wall, first working into the soil some decayed manure and leaf mould and a liberal dressing of lime rubble. To encourage winter drainage, incorporate some grit or coarse sand while the soil is being prepared. Plant 4 in (10 cm) deep and 6 in (15 cm) apart and, to protect the plants from frost, cover with bracken during winter or give a thick mulch of decayed leaves.

Propagation. Bulbs which have occupied the pots for several years should be repotted into fresh compost and into a larger pot, when numerous offsets will be seen to have formed around the base of the original bulb. These are detached and planted into 3-in (7·5-cm) pots and after two years, they should be moved to 5-in (12·5-cm) pots in which they will bloom the following year.

Plants may be raised from seed sown in pans containing the John Innes compost. Freshly harvested seed will germinate quickly and if the seeds are sown ½ in (1·25 cm) apart or one to a 3-in (7·5-cm) pot in a temperature of 60° F (16° C) they will germinate in 10 to 12 days. The seedlings are kept growing until winter, when less moisture is given but water is not entirely withheld, while a night temperature of not less than 52° F (11° C) is maintained. Early in spring, the young plants are moved to larger pots and grown on for another year, when they are moved to 5-in (12·5-cm) pots in which they will come into bloom the following year.

Species. *Habranthus andersonii*. Native of Chile and Argentina, it has narrow pale-green leaves 6 in (15 cm) long, which appear before the flowers. The funnel-shaped flowers appear in June and are yellow, shaded with copper on the outside and are borne singly on a 6-in (15-cm) stem.

Habranthus brachyandrus. From a large ovoid bulb are produced the linear leaves 12 in (30 cm) long. They appear before the flowers which are of pale lilac-rose, shaded claret at the base and are borne singly on a 15-in (37·5-cm) stem, from July until September. It may be grown outside in a warm winter climate.

Habranthus robustus. Native of the hillsides around Buenos Aires, it has narrow grey-green deeply channelled leaves which with this species appear after the flowers. The flowers have funnels 3 in (7·5 cm) long and are borne on a slender scape 9 in (23 cm) tall. They are rosy-pink, shaded green in the throat and appear during August and September.

Habranthus versicolor. Native of Uruguay, it has linear leaves 12 in (30 cm) long, which appear after the flowers. It blooms from December until February, the flowers having 2-in (5-cm)-long tubes and opening to nearly 3 in (7·5 cm) across. They are white, shaded red at the tips of the petals and green at the base and are most striking.

HAEMANTHUS (Amaryllidaceae)

A genus of 50 species, native of tropical and southern Africa and of Socotra. It takes its name from *aima*, blood, and *anthos*, flower, the reference being to the vivid blood-red colouring of all its parts, hence its name blood flower. It is also known as the red Cape lily. The bulb is large and globular, and from it arise broad blunt-ended fleshy leaves. It bears globular flower heads, composed of numerous small flowers with prominent red stamens. They are surrounded by persisting membranous bracts and are borne on a 12-in (30-cm) stem. The plants are readily cultivated in a cool or warm greenhouse, while several species are suitable for planting outdoors, especially *H. katharinae*, which blooms late in summer. It is also the most reliable species for cool greenhouse culture.

Culture. For indoors, provide a compost made up of fibrous loam, peat or leaf mould and decayed cow manure in equal parts, to which is added some coarse sand or grit. The pot should be twice the circumference of the bulb and must be well crocked. Plant in March, one bulb to each pot and with the top of the bulb exposed. Start into growth in a temperature of 55° F (13° C) and give little moisture until active, increasing supplies with the rise in the natural temperature. Shade the plants from sunlight, and when the flower buds show colour remove to the window of a cool room where they will maintain their beauty for several weeks. After flowering, continue watering until the leaves begin to turn yellow. Moisture should then be withheld gradually until by the end of autumn the plants are dried off and given a rest, the pots being placed on their side in a frost-free room. They are started into growth again in spring and may occupy the pots for four or five years.

Several species make excellent plants for tubs, flowering in the open, the tubs being lifted indoors early in autumn and protected from frost. It is a suitable plant to accompany agapanthus.

Where growing in the open, plant at the base of a warm wall, in a soil made porous and enriched with some decayed manure such as old mushroom bed compost. Plant in April, 4 in (10 cm) deep and 12 in (30 cm) apart, and, where possible, cover the bulbs with cloches or with frame lights reared against the wall, to provide as high a temperature as possible when they are starting into growth. Keep the plants in a moist condition throughout summer and, after flowering, lift and store away from frost. Where winter frosts are not experienced, the bulbs may be left undisturbed for several years, protected by a winter covering of dead bracken or leaves.

Propagation. This is usually done by removing the offsets from around mature bulbs which may have occupied the pots for several years and are in need of repotting into fresh compost and a larger pot. The offsets should be planted into 3-in (7·5-cm) pots containing a similar compost for flowering-size bulbs. After a year, they are moved to larger pots and again each year until they reach flowering size, when they may remain undisturbed for several years. They should be dried off and rested each winter.

Species. *Haemanthus albiflos.* Native of Natal, it comes into bloom in June and is too tender for outdoor culture in the British Isles and northern Europe, though it may be brought into bloom in the sunny window of a warm room. It makes a bulb of 2-in (5-cm) diameter with short leathery tongue-shaped leaves 3 in (7·5 cm) broad, hairy at the margins. The flowers are greenish-white with a satin-like quality and are borne in dense umbels on a 9-in (22·5-cm) stem.

Gloxinia: Princess Mary

Gloxinia: Spotted

Hippeastrum: Minerva

The plant resembles *Allium ursinum*, the wild garlic, but is without its onion smell.

Haemanthus brevifolius. Native of the mountainous slopes of Kaffraria it forms a bulb 3 in (7·5 cm) thick, with twin leaves which follow the flowers. The leaves are 6 in (15 cm) long and almost as broad, while the soft-pink flowers are borne in an umbel 2 in (5 cm) across and on a 9-in (22·5-cm) stem. It blooms in midsummer.

Haemanthus cinnabarinus. Native of the Gold Coast, it forms a small bulb 1 in (2·5 cm) across, from which arise several oblong leaves 8 in (20 cm) long and deeply channelled. The bright-crimson flowers are borne in a dense umbel 3 in (7·5 cm) across and on a 12-in (30-cm) stem which arises between the leaves.

Haemanthus coccineus. Native of the Cape, where it is common about coastal scrublands, it blooms in March, in August and September in the British Isles and northern Europe. It bears twin tongue-shaped leaves, unspotted and up to 2 ft (60 cm) long, which develop when the flowers have formed. They die back at the end of autumn. The flowers with their linear segments are of brilliant red and are borne in dense umbels about 3 in (7·5 cm) across. They have red bracts and are held on stems 9 in (22·5 cm) tall, which are spotted with dark red. The plant requires long periods of sunshine in summer to ripen the bulb.

Haemanthus katharinae. Native of Natal, it has a large globular bulb and forms four or five stem leaves 9 in (22·5 cm) long, which narrow into a sheathing stalk. Each leaf has eight or nine veins on each side of the mid-rib. The flowers are salmon-orange and are borne on a 12-in (30-cm) stem to form a spherical umbel of about 8 in (20 cm) across. The prominent stamens add to its beauty. It is in bloom during July and August, sometimes later and makes an arresting display in a tub, against the whitewashed walls of a house.

Haemanthus magnificus. It is found among the rocks about Delagoa Bay and makes a large globular bulb up to 4 in (10 cm) in diameter and a leafy stem up to 2 ft (60 cm) tall and spotted with brown, which develops after the flower. The leaves are 12 in (30 cm) long and bright green with waved edges, while the bright-red flowers, like a shaving brush, are borne in a large umbel on a 12-in (30-cm) stem which arises from the side of the bulb. It blooms in June and July and needs greenhouse culture.

Haemanthus multiflorus. Native of Ethiopia and eastern Africa, it forms a bulb of 2-in (5-cm) diameter and makes a leafy stem, separate from the flower stem, with leaves 8 in (20 cm) long, narrowing into a sheathing stem. The flowers appear in July in a dense spherical umbel at a height of 12 in (30 cm). They have scarlet segments and green reflexed bracts.

Haemanthus natalensis. Native of Natal, it forms a bulb 3 in (7·5 cm) in diameter and a stem with eight or nine bright green leaves 12 in (30 cm) long, the lower leaves being marked on the underside with red. The flowers are greenish with orange stamens and are borne in a large round umbel 4 in (10 cm)

M

in diameter and held on a 12-in (30-cm) stem which arises from the side of the bulb. It blooms early in summer.

Haemanthus pubescens. Introduced from the Cape towards the end of the eighteenth century, it is now rare in the wild and in cultivation. It forms two strap-like leaves fringed with hairs; these are also hairy on both surfaces and blotched with red near the base. The flowers are crimson and are borne in a small umbel 2 in (5 cm) across and held on a 6-in (15-cm) stem. It is of dainty habit.

HEMEROCALLIS (Liliaceae)

A genus of 20 species of herbaceous plants, distributed across central Europe and in Asia and Japan. It takes its name from *homero*, a day, and *kallos*, beauty, the reference being to the flowers opening and remaining fresh but for a single day, hence its name, day lily. It has a short rhizomatous root from which grow thick fleshy roots and tufts of strap-like leaves 18 in (45 cm) long. The flowers are funnel-shaped and borne in clusters of 2 to 30 on 2- to 3-ft (60- to 90-cm) scapes. They bloom in June, July and August and have a long cylindrical tube with six spreading spoon-shaped segments. They are among the most colourful plants for the border, being of exceptional hardiness and easy culture. They grew in Gerard's London garden when they were known as asphodel lilies, for they have roots resembling that plant. Gerard in his *Herbal* wrote, 'these lilies do grow in my garden and also in the gardens of herbarists and lovers of fine and rare plants'. For the modern gardener there are many lovely hybrids descended from *H. flava* and *H. fulva* and varying in colour from blackish-red to orchid pink. The sweetly scented *H. flava* occupies a similar place in meadows of central Europe as does the cowslip in England and Ireland, while the flowers are of the same deep-yellow colouring.

Culture. The plants flourish in ordinary soil, in full sun or partial shade, but they require a soil containing some humus and decayed manure. The ground should be made ready early in spring, which is the most suitable planting time. Plant the roots 6 in (15 cm) deep to protect them from frost, and during their first season keep them well supplied with moisture. They will appreciate a mulch of decayed leaves and manure given in autumn each year.

Propagation. It will take the plants two years to become established, and before they will bloom well. They should be left untouched for at least six years before lifting and dividing. This may be done in autumn or spring, by placing two garden forks back to back and gently pressing them apart. The plants will divide readily, while the small pieces may be further split up by hand. Where possible, plant into newly prepared ground.

Species. *Hemerocallis aurantiaca.* Native of Japan, it grows 2 to 3 ft (60 to 90 cm) high, forming tufts of dark-green leaves and brilliant orange-red flowers.

This species was used to pass on its rich reddish colouring to many of the modern hybrids.

Hemerocallis flava. It is distributed across central Europe and Asia to Japan, where it inhabits low-lying meadows. It forms a tuft of deep-green leaves 2 ft (60 cm) in length and bears its flowers in large clusters on 3-ft (90-cm) stems. They are of richest yellow with a sweet scent, while the segments are without veins. It blooms during June and July, being the earliest species.

Hemerocallis fulva. Like *H. flava*, it is found across central Europe and Asia, as far as Japan, bearing large tufts of broad leaves 2 ft (60 cm) long and orange-yellow flowers on 3- to 4-ft (90-cm to 1·2-metre) stems. The flowers are 4 in (10 cm) across and have blunt segments with wavy margins. They appear in June. The form *flore plena* has double flowers of coppery-orange.

Hemerocallis graminea (syn. *H. minor*). It inhabits low-lying meadows from Siberia, across northern China to Japan, forming tufts of narrow grass-like leaves and bearing its scented yellow flowers tinted with green on 9-in (22·5-cm) stems. The three inner segments have waved margins.

Hybrid Varieties:

ENTICEMENT. An attractive variety, the creamy-white flowers being delicately tinted with pink and with pale green shading in the throat.

GREEN GODDESS. The flowers, which measure 4 in (10 in across), are of cool primrose yellow with overtones of chartreuse green and are enhanced by the blue-green foliage.

HALL CROFT. One of the most beautiful hybrids ever raised, the blooms having large broad petals of great substance and of rich coral-pink with yellow shading in the throat.

HAZEL POWELL. Its flowers with their reflexing petals open star-like and are of a lovely shade of soft glistening yellow. They are borne with freedom on branching stems.

JAKE RUSSELL. It grows 36 in (90 cm) tall with the broadest petals of any variety and of brilliant clear gold with a velvet-like sheen.

KATHLEEN ORMEROD. One of the best 'reds', the flowers of rich velvety crimson being borne on branching stems 2 to 3 ft (60 to 90 cm) tall.

NASHVILLE. A showy variety, bearing large heavily textured blooms which open flat with the segments widely spread out. They are of creamy-yellow with a red band in the throat.

ORANGE BEAUTY. It grows 3 ft (90 cm) tall and bears masses of brilliant-orange flowers which open continuously over a long period.

ORANGE BRIGHT. The large broad-petalled blooms are of vivid orange and are completely sun-proof.

PATRICIA FAY. It grows 30 inches (75 cm) tall and is one of the finest 'pinks', the blooms with their reflexing outer segments being of coral-pink with deeper veins and with yellow shading in the throat.

PINK PROGRESS. A first-class variety of branching habit, the large blooms being of soft buff-pink.

HERBERTIA (Iridaceae)

A genus of seven or eight species, native of South America and named in honour of Dean Herbert of Manchester, author of a monograph on Amaryllidaceae (1837). The corms are small and tunicated, the leaves narrow and linear, while the flowers are borne at the end of a short scape, the three inner segments being slightly clawed.

Culture. Growing about 9 in (22·5 cm) tall and remaining in bloom over a long period, they are delightful plants for a frame or cool greenhouse, several corms being planted in a 6-in (15-cm) pot or pan. Plant in March, 2 in (5 cm) deep and 3 in (7·5 cm) apart and in a compost made up of fibrous loam, peat and sand in equal parts. Give little moisture until growth commences, increasing supplies as the summer temperature rises. After flowering, dry off the plants and store during winter away from frost.

The corms of those species flowering late in summer, i.e. *H. pulchella*, may be planted in the open in a sunny border. Plant in April, 4 in (10 cm) deep and 6 in (15 cm) apart, and lift in autumn to dry off and winter away from frost. Only in those gardens enjoying a frost-free climate is it advisable to leave the corms in the ground, but where this is possible, they will increase like crocosmia (montbretia) and form large clumps.

Propagation. When the corms are lifted, cormlets will be seen clustering about the base of the original corm. These are detached, and after keeping them over winter safe from frost, plant in spring in boxes of sandy compost and grow on until flowering size, which will be in three or four years.

Species. *Herbertia amatorum.* Native of Uruguay, it has small brown-coated corms and tapering lance-shaped leaves 9 in (22·5 cm) long. It blooms in July, the deep violet-blue flowers measuring 2 in (5 cm) across with the outer blade-like segments opening flat.

Herbertia pulchella. The finest species, believed to grow only on one small island in the Bay of Maldonado, near the Straits of Magellan. The flowers are like small irises with three large 'fall' petals of brilliant purple-blue, marked with creamy-white, the inner segments being of shell pink and silvery-grey. It blooms during July and August on a 9-in (22·5-cm) stem, two stems usually appearing from one bulb.

HERMODACTYLUS (Iridaceae)

A genus of a single species, syn. *Iris tuberosa*, and native of southern Europe, extending from south-western France to Greece. It has a tuberous rootstock, like that of the dahlia, and four-sided leaves terminating in a point. The flowers are borne on hollow stems 12 in (30 cm) long and differ from iris in the unilocular ovary.

Culture. It is almost hardy but should be planted in a light sandy soil which is well-drained in winter and in a position where the summer sun can ripen the tubers to enable them to bloom well the following year. Plant the tubers 3 in (7·5 cm) deep and 6 in (15 cm) apart in July so that they become established before winter. Once planted, leave undisturbed for several years. Like almost all members of the iris family, the plants are happiest in a soil of high lime content and will appreciate a top-dressing of lime rubble (mortar) in autumn each year.

Propagation. It is increased by division of the tubers. This should be done towards the end of summer when the plant has begun to die back.

Species. *Hermodactylus tuberosus* (syn. *Iris tuberosa*). It forms thin tuberous roots and has linear four-sided leaves. The flowers appear towards the end of March in those gardens where hard frosts are absent, about a month later in more exposed gardens, and remain colourful for about two months. The flowers are borne on a 12-in (30-cm) stem and are of olive-green colouring. When closed they resemble the head of a snake, hence the name of snake's head iris. The falls are blackish-purple so the flower is interesting rather than colourful.

HESPERANTHA (Iridaceae)

A genus of about 50 species, native of tropical and southern Africa and taking its name from the Greek *hesperos*, evening, and *anthos*, a flower, for it opens its flowers at night and is sweetly scented. The small corms have a flat base and are covered in a hard fibrous tunic. The leaves are partly sheathing and strap-like. The flowers are white or pale yellow with a perianth of six equal-spreading segments.

Culture. In bloom during May and June, treat as for *Ixia* and *Homeria*. It may be grown outdoors only in those North American and European gardens enjoying a frost-free climate. Or plant in April when they will come into bloom early in July, two months later than usual. They require an open situation (though they are tolerant of shade) and a porous soil. Plant 4 in (10 cm) deep and 4 in (10 cm) apart.

For indoor flowering, plant in November, six corms to a 6-in (15-cm) pot, planting 1 in (2·5 cm) deep and 1 in (2·5 cm) apart. They require a compost made up of fibrous loam, peat and coarse sand in equal parts. Stand the pots in a closed frame or in a cool greenhouse during winter and give no water. Bring on the plants as they begin to grow early in spring, giving ample water but shielding from the sun when the flower buds begin to form. As with all plants of the ixia type, give plenty of fresh air on suitable occasions, for they are intolerant of excessive warmth and damp, humid conditions. After flowering, dry off gradually, and after a rest, bring on the plants again. They will scent a large greenhouse at night during early summer.

Propagation. It is readily increased from offsets which form at the base of the corms. These are detached in autumn and grown on in pans containing a sandy compost, to reach flowering size in three or four years.

Species. *Hesperantha buchrii.* Native of Natal, it is a dainty species, growing 9 in (22·5 cm) tall and bearing, in early summer, racemes of glistening white, shaded pale pink on the outside. The flowers open late afternoon and are scented at night.

Hesperantha pilosa. Present on damp slopes and in partial shade in Cape Province, where it makes a small globular corm and grows 12 in (30 cm) tall, the lower leaves with a long pilose and inflated sheath. The flowers are white and are borne in a five- to seven-flowered spike, in September in their native parts, in June in northern Europe.

Hesperantha radiata. Found on Signal Hill and Table Mountain, it makes a small corm and has five or six linear leaves. The flowers are pale yellow with the outer petals shaded red on the underside, and they are borne in a 5- to 10-flowered spike at a height of 12 in (30 cm).

Hesperantha spicata (syn. *H. cinnamomea*). It is present on the lower slopes of Signal Hill and it makes a corm 1 cm in diameter with four leaves, the lower two having waved margins. The flowers are white, shaded red on the underside and are borne in a 5- to 10-flowered spike on a stem 12 in (30 cm) long.

Hesperantha stanfordiae. Native of damp lower mountainous slopes at the Cape, it bears racemes of clear primrose-yellow flowers on 18-in (45-cm) stems during May and June in European gardens.

HESPEROCALLIS (Liliaceae)

A genus of a single species, native of the Californian desertlands and taking its name from *hesperos*, evening, and *kallos*, beauty, for the white flowers are sweetly scented when open at night. The plant is virtually unknown away from its native haunts but may prove sufficiently hardy in cooler climes to survive the winter if given a sunny situation and a well-drained soil.

Culture. Where growing indoors, plant the large round bulbs in sandy soil, three to a 6-in (15-cm) pot and 2 in (5 cm) deep. Plant in October, and after two months in a cool dark room or in the plunge bed, introduce to a warm greenhouse or garden room and bring slowly into bloom in spring.

Propagation. Usually by offsets, which form about the mother bulb and which are detached and grown on in a sandy compost in pots or pans in a frame or greenhouse.

Species. *Hesperocallis undulata.* It forms a large round bulb, which is edible and which buries itself in the desert sands to a depth of 18 in (45 cm). From the bulbs arise wavy leaves edged with white, and in April appear large white tubular flowers which are borne in umbels.

HEXAGLOTTIS (Iridaceae)

A genus of five species, native of southern Africa and taking its name from *hex*, six, and *glotta*, a tongue, in reference to the six lobes of the style. The corms are globose and covered with a tunic of woody fibres. The lower leaves are long; the upper short and sheathing. The flowers are yellow and unpleasantly scented and, though short-lived, open in succession at the end of the branched stems, where they appear in clusters during June and July.

Culture. Treat like *Homeria* and *Morea*, to which they are closely related. Plant the corms in April 3 in (7·5 cm) deep and 6 in (15 cm) apart in an open sunny situation. After flowering, the corms are lifted and hung up to dry, while the foliage is dying back, and they are then stored in boxes of dry sand or peat during winter, away from frost.

Indoors, the corms are planted in March in a cool greenhouse, four or five to a 6-in (15-cm) pot and in a compost made up of fibrous loam, peat and sand in equal parts. Plant the corms 1 in (2·5 cm) deep and 2 in (5 cm) apart and give little or no water until they begin to make growth. They will bloom towards the end of May and early in June. Afterwards, moisture is gradually withheld and the plants dried off. Store in winter away from frost, and repot the corms in March.

Propagation. Increase by detaching the small cormlets from the base of the old corm when lifting in autumn. They are kept in small boxes of dry sand during winter and planted in spring, into pots or pans containing a sandy compost. Space them 1 in (2·5 cm) apart and press the corms into the surface of the compost, watering when they begin to grow. Dry off in autumn and replant in spring into a similar compost. They will reach flowering size in four years.

Species. *Hexaglottis flexuosa.* Present on mountainous slopes in Cape Province, where it grows 15 in (37·5 cm) tall, the stem and branches being slightly curved. It has one to three lower leaves which grow nearly 2 ft (60 cm) in length, and its yellow, unpleasantly scented flowers grow in lax clusters.

Hexaglottis longifolia. It is found in damp places on Table Mountain and has five or six linear leaves, prominently veined. It bears its golden-yellow flowers in loose clusters, the outer perianth segments being longer than the inner. They have an unpleasant smell.

HIPPEASTRUM (Amaryllidaceae)

A genus of about 70 species, native of tropical America and known as the equestrian star-flower. It takes its name from *hippeus*, a knight on horseback, and *aston*, a star. From the large tunicated bulbs strap-like leaves arise, while the flowers are borne two to six on a hollow scape, usually about 12 in (30 cm) tall. Where a temperature of 60° F (16° C) can be provided, they will bloom in winter, and where 'prepared' bulbs are obtainable will come early into bloom.

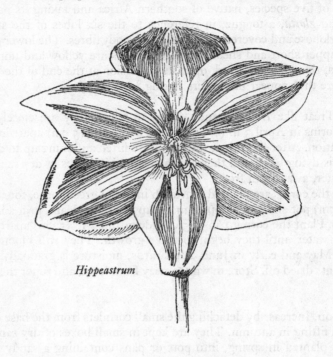

Hippeastrum

Where there is no heat but protection from frost can be given, they will bloom in spring. Several species and hybrid varieties may be grown outdoors in those gardens of the British Isles and North America which enjoy a mild winter climate. In America it is known as *Amaryllis hippeastrum*.

Culture. Where growing indoors, its culture commences in October with 'prepared' bulbs. A bulb of not less than 28 cm in circumference should be used, for it will bloom well its first year under glass. For outside, 26 cm is suitable. To encourage the bulb to make early growth, place the base of the bulb in a tray containing water and allow it to remain there for three or four days before potting. The pots should not be larger than twice the diameter of the bulb. The following January the bulbs should be repotted into a larger size, for by then they will also have grown larger. A 28- to 30-cm bulb may be expected to bear two flowering spikes.

Hippeastrums like a rich porous soil which will allow air to reach the roots.

The compost should be composed of fibrous loam, decayed manure (cow manure or old mushroom-bed compost) and grit in equal parts. Pack the compost firmly around the bulb, leaving the top exposed and with the compost just below the rim of the pot to allow for watering. To start into growth, give bottom heat either by placing them on a shelf above a radiator or on a mantelpiece above an open fire, where they will remain for several weeks, removing to a sunny window as soon as the flower spikes appear. Where a warm greenhouse is available, place the pots in deep boxes and pack moist peat around them. Stand the boxes above the hot pipes and, if possible, maintain a temperature of 65° F (18° C). This may be 10° F (5° C) lower without ill effect, though the bulbs will be later into bloom. As soon as the flower stems appear, which will be in about five weeks after potting, the temperature should not exceed 60° F (16° C).

While making growth, syringe the foliage frequently and water (at the top) as often as necessary, for hippeastrums are copious drinkers. To enhance the quality of bloom and to build up the bulb, give a twice weekly application of dilute manure water when once the flower stem is observed and until the plants are due to be rested. It is also advisable to wipe the leaves occasionally with clean water as most species are evergreen and in the home will collect dust. The leaves may grow up to 3 ft (90 cm) in length and will be 4 in (10 cm) wide. So that the flower stem grows straight where the plants are growing in a sunny window in the home, turn the pots several degrees each day. By regulating the temperature, it will be possible to have the bulbs in bloom from February until midsummer but always provide brisk bottom heat to start them into growth. Keep the bulbs supplied with water until the early autumn when the foliage begins to turn yellow and die back. Moisture is then withheld until early in the new year when the bulbs are repotted. With care in their cultivation, and this means removing the dead flowers before they can seed, the bulbs should remain healthy and free-flowering for many years, increasing in size until they attain a circumference of 36 cm or more.

Where growing outdoors, plant the bulbs in April, 4 in (10 cm) deep and in a sunny position such as at the base of a wall, where they may be protected from winter frost by covering them with bracken or with a frame light reared against the wall. *Hippeastrum pratense* is the best species for outdoor culture and will bloom during June and July.

Propagation. The plants are readily increased both from offsets and by seed. Upon lifting the bulbs for repotting in January, small offsets will be found clustered at the base. These are detached and grown on in boxes containing a sandy compost, when after 12 months they will be large enough to plant into small pots. Here they remain for another year, when they are moved to a larger pot. They will bloom in three to four years from the time of removal from the mother bulb.

Plants are readily raised from seed sown one to a 3-in (7·5-cm) pot. Sow when ripe in late summer and into a sandy loam, and if the greenhouse (or room) temperature does not fall below 60° F (16° C), the seed will germinate in about 10 days. Within a month the seedlings will have formed tiny bulbs, which with careful watering will begin to swell. During winter, they should be given only sufficient moisture to keep them alive and in spring will be ready to move to larger pots. They will bloom in three to four years from time of sowing.

Species and Varieties. *Hippeastrum advenum.* Native of Chile, it has narrow leaves of blue-green 15 in (37·5 cm) long and, as it flowers towards the end of summer, it is useful for outdoor culture in a warm border. The flowers with their long narrow petals are borne horizontally and are scarlet shaded with yellow.

Hippeastrum aulicum. Native of Brazil, it has large strap-shaped leaves and bears flowers with a tube up to 6 in (15 cm) long. It is bright crimson, shading to green at the base of the tube.

Hippeastrum bifidum. Present on the hillsides around Buenos Aires, it is almost hardy, but as it blooms in April is best given greenhouse protection in the British Isles and North America. Of easy culture, it bears large trumpets of clear orange-scarlet on a 15-in (37·5-cm) stem.

Hippeastrum candidum. Native of Argentina, it is one of the hardiest species and blooms during midsummer, bearing its elegant trumpets of purest white on a 2-ft (60-cm) stem. The flowers are scented.

Hippeastrum equestre. Like *H. reginae*, it is distributed throughout Mexico, South America and in several islands of the West Indies, where it is known as the Barbados lily. It is the oldest known species, first discovered in 1698, and where naturally established it grows with abandon from its stoloniferous bulbs, flowering throughout the year. It has strap-like leaves of brilliant green and bears bright-red flowers on a 12-in (30-cm) scape. In the British Isles, it blooms in summer. The variety *splendens* bears larger flowers of vivid scarlet.

Hippeastrum pratense. Native of Chile, it makes a smaller bulb than most species and has narrow leaves 12 in (30 cm) long. It bears two or three bright-scarlet blooms, shaded yellow at the base on a 12-in (30-cm) scape during spring and early summer.

Hippeastrum reginae. It is distributed throughout Mexico, South America and in several islands of the West Indies. In cultivation, it first flowered in 1728, on the birthday of Queen Caroline, in whose honour it was named. It has leaves 2 ft (60 cm) long, which appear after the flowers which are at their best during midsummer. They have a long tapering trumpet opening to 4 in (10 cm) across, and are brilliant scarlet with a white star in the throat.

Hippeastrum reticulatum. Native of Brazil, it is evergreen with broad strap-like leaves and it bears its mauve-pink flowers in autumn. The tubes measure 4 in (10 cm) in length. The variety *striatifolium* has a distinct white mid-rib.

Hippeastrum rutilum. Native of Venezuela, it has narrow leaves 15 in (40 cm) long and is the most free-flowering species, bearing in autumn several large blooms on each 12-in (30-cm) stem. They are bright crimson with pointed petals, the long elegant tube being shaded with green.

Hippeastrum vittatum. Introduced from the Chilean Andes in 1769, it is a vigorous species with large strap-like leaves and it bears its flowers on 2-ft (60-cm) stems. Each flower measures up to 6 in (15 cm) across and up to six appear on each scape. They are white, striped with magenta, while there is also a pure white form, *album*.

This species was used by a Prescot watchmaker, Arthur Johnson, who crossed it with *H. reginae* and raised the first hybrid in 1799. It was named *H. johnsonii*. It makes a large bulb from which arises a 2-ft (60-cm) scape bearing three or four tubular flowers of brilliant scarlet, streaked with white. From this plant de Graaf of Leiden raised a number of outstanding hybrid varieties known as the Dutch hybrids and bearing flowers of almost every known colour except blue. Of the named varieties, the following are worthy of a place in any collection:

ANNA PAVLOVA. Brilliant scarlet of outstanding form.

APPLEBLOSSOM. The large tubular flowers are of softest pink shading to white down the throat.

BELINDA. The broad-petalled flowers are of deep crimson shading to scarlet at the base of the petals.

BORDEAUX. Raised by W. S. Warmerhaven, the large solid blooms are of deep wine-red, exquisite under artificial light.

BOUQUET. A von Ludwig hybrid, the large refined blooms being of an attractive blend of salmon and begonia-pink.

DURANGO. The flowers with their long tubes are of clearest orange.

GLORIOUS VICTORY. A variety of merit, the long elegant trumpets are of salmon-orange, paler at the petal edges, darker in the throat.

HALLEY. The flowers open wide and are of vivid scarlet with a glistening frost-like appearance.

KING OF THE STRIPES. The large blooms with their long elegant tubes are white with broad stripes of velvet red.

LEGION STANDARD. The large blooms of rosy-red open wide to reveal a glistening white throat.

MARGARET ROSE. The blooms open wide but have a long slender tube and are of an unusual shade of deep shrimp-pink.

MINERVA. It bears a flower of beauty, being brick-red with veining of similar colouring from the end of the tube to the tips of the petals which have an edging of white.

MONT BLANC. The blooms are white, shaded green in the throat, which gives an appearance of icy-whiteness.

QUEEN OF THE WHITES. The large refined flowers are of purest white with a distinctive velvet-like sheen.

QUEEN SUPERIORA. Raised by van McEuwen, it is one of the finest hybrids, the large handsome blooms being of pure ox-blood red.

HOMERIA (Iridaceae)

A genus of about 35 species of corm-bearing plants, native of southern Africa and closely related to *Morea* and *Tigridia*. The corms are covered in woody fibres, while the one to three lower leaves are long and narrow. The flowers, which are fleeting, emerge from two green spathes and are borne at the end of a branched stem. The perianth segments are free and curve upwards to form a bell, then spread out. The inner segments are smaller than the outer, like *Tigridia*. It takes its name from *homereo*, to meet, in reference to the filaments which unite into a tube. Bulbils form in the axils of the lower leaves on several species, i.e. *H. bulbillifera*.

Culture. They may be treated like *Morea* and *Tigridia*, but, flowering early in summer, are grown in the open in the British Isles and northern Europe only in those gardens which are free from frost. Plant in September or in April, depending upon soil and situation, 6 in (15 cm) deep and 6 in (15 cm) apart and in a well-drained sandy soil from which excess moisture can drain. Choose a position at the base of a wall, sheltered by the eaves of a house and where the plants benefit from the early summer sunshine. Corms planted in spring will bloom later, spring planting being advisable where there is danger of late frosts. Water copiously while the plants are growing and dry off in autumn for storing in winter.

To bloom under glass, plant in pots containing a sandy compost, in November. Plant six corms to a 6-in (15-cm) pot, 1 in (2·5 cm) deep and 1 in (2.5 cm) apart and stand in a closed frame or in deep boxes in a greenhouse, plunged in peat and keeping almost dry until growth appears in spring. Then place on the greenhouse bench and water according to the weather and requirements of the plants. They will bloom early in May and when the foliage begins to die back, gradually withhold moisture and dry off, turning the pots on their side and placing beneath the bench until starting into growth again after the winter rest.

Propagation. The bulbils which form in the axils of the lower leaves of certain species may be detached towards the end of summer and grown on in pans containing a sandy compost, while, when lifting the plants, a new corm will have formed above the old one and this will bloom the following year.

Species. *Homeria bulbillifera*. Native of Cape Province where it is found on mountainsides, especially on Little Lion's Head, it makes a small corm covered in spiny fibres. It grows 16 in (40 cm) tall and forms bulbils in the axils of the leaves. The flowers are creamy pink and like those of the closely related *Ferraria* are unpleasantly scented.

Homeria collina. Native of Natal, it is the best and first known species, introduced in 1768. It grows 20 in (50 cm) tall, the stem having a long basal leaf, while the flowers of dark orange, blotched with purple and measuring about 2 in (5 cm) across, are borne three or four to each stem during June.

The variety *ochroleuca* bears flowers 3 in (7·5 cm) across and of a lovely soft pale yellow shading to orange. It is present on rocky ground from Table Mountain to Kalk Bay.

Homeria miniata. It is a common plant of mountainous slopes of Cape Province and is known as the red tulp. The corm is to be found surrounded by small cormlets, which are detached and grown on in a sandy compost, while bulbils form in the axils of the lower leaves. The flowers are of an unusual shade of salmon-pink, shaded yellow at the centre and are borne on 2-ft (60-cm) stems. They bloom in August and September in southern Africa, in May in the British Isles and northern Europe. They are scented.

HOMOGLOSSUM (Iridaceae)

A genus of 20 species, native of southern Africa, and taking their name from the Greek *omoios*, similar, and *glossa*, tongue, in reference to the shape and colour of the petals of certain species. The corms are small and are covered in a soft fibrous tunic; the slender stems having four or five sheathing leaves. The spikes are one- to five-flowered; the perianth tube being curved, the six lobes equal. The genus is closely related to *Antholyza*, which has six unequal segments, the upper being longer than the others.

Culture. Related also to *Gladiolus*, the plants require similar culture, being not quite hardy in the British Isles and northern Europe, while several species are winter-flowering, i.e. *Homoglossum priorii*, the Red Afrikaner, which blooms in May in its native land, in February in northern Europe. Plant the corms in September, four or five to a 6-in (15-cm) pot and in a sandy compost. Plant 1 in (2·5 cm) deep and 2 in (5 cm) apart. Until they begin to grow, water sparingly, while growing water only when necessary. Like freesias, they should be kept fairly dry. As they bloom at a height of 2 ft (60 cm), give some support as the flower stems begin to form. After flowering, dry off gradually and during summer give the plants a rest, placing the pots on their side.

Propagation. Usually from cormlets which form at the base of the older corms and which are grown on in pans in a sandy compost. They will attain flowering size in four years.

Species. *Homoglossum priorii*. Present among brushland in Cape Province, it has four or five leaves, the lower sheathing, and bears bright-red flowers during February and March in a one- to four-flowered spike. The variety *salteri* bears larger flowers of brilliant scarlet on a 2-ft (60-cm) stem.

Homoglossum watsonium. Similar to *H. priorii*, it grows 2 ft (60 cm) tall and has four leaves, each with a prominent mid-rib. It bears its bright-red flowers in

a two- to four-flowered spike, the perianth tube having a pouch in the middle.
Indoors in the British Isles it blooms in March.

HYACINTHUS (Liliaceae)

A genus of about 25 species, native of the Mediterranean countries and taking
their name from that of the youth Hyacinth, favourite of Apollo. The bulbs are
large, round and fleshy, covered in a brown tunic; the leaves are strap-like or
linear; the flowers borne in a loose raceme on a leafless scape, the perianth bell-
shaped, the segments joined part of the way to form a tube which distinguishes
it from scilla. *H. orientalis*, the florists' hyacinth, is that most often grown but it
was possibly *H. azureus* that Homer included among those flowers which formed
the couch of Juno. In Book 14 of the Iliad it is written:

> And clust'ring Lotus swell'd the rising bed,
> And sudden Hyacinths the turf bestrow,
> And flow'ry Crocus made the mountain glow

The large-flowered *H. orientalis* was introduced into England in 1560 from
Persia by Anthony Jenkinson and it quickly became popular. Parkinson in the
Paradisus describes several forms, including the White Roman, and a century
later Philip Miller tells that the Dutch growers had by then raised over 2,000
varieties. One, bearing a double bloom and called King of Great Britain, earned
for its raiser, Peter Voerheim, the equivalent of £100 for each bulb.

The florists' hyacinths were grown in pots for winter decoration, the scent of
the flowers also being appreciated to counteract the musty smell of badly ventilated apartments. Persy Bysshe Shelley in 'The Sensitive Plant' admirably
describes the perfume of the flowers:

> And the hyacinth purple and white and blue
> Which flung from its bells a sweet peal anew
> Of music so delicate, soft and intense,
> It was felt like an odour within the sense

Being hardy, all the species may be grown outdoors in all parts of the world
enjoying a temperate climate.

Culture. Most varieties make large bulbs up to 20 cm in circumference. Some,
while just as vigorous, produce a smaller bulb, 18 cm being the top size for the
yellow-flowering varieties. For forcing, an 18-cm bulb will be suitable; for
outside bedding, a bulb of 14 to 16 cm may be used. A properly ripened bulb
should possess a silvery sheen, and one perfectly sound will be firm when
pressed at the base. A bulb will be suspect if there is any degree of softness.

Bulbs of Roman hyacinths which will come into bloom before Christmas are
smaller, a forcing-size bulb being of 14 cm. It is not advisable to try to force
smaller bulbs, though, when grown under ordinary room conditions, a 16-cm

bulb will be satisfactory and a 12- to 13-cm size for the Roman hyacinths. It depends upon the temperatures to which they are to be subject.

It is possible to obtain bulbs specially prepared in Holland to flower a fortnight earlier than usual. This is done by earlier lifting and ripening of the bulbs and then placing them in cold storage. They are more expensive, but it is possible to have them in bloom by Christmas. The bulbs are not sent out until required for planting at the end of September.

Prepared hyacinths should be planted three to a bowl or one to a small pot. When growing commercially, the pots and bowls are obtained from a wholesaler, for buying per dozen or gross will prove more economical. Hyacinths enjoy a moist soil. They must not be allowed to suffer from too dry conditions or the flower spike will be stunted. Bulb fibre can be used with satisfactory results, but, as with all bulbs, where it is possible to make up a compost to the bulb's requirements, better results are obtained. A light loamy soil into which has been incorporated some coarse sand and moist peat will prove ideal. It is important when planting hyacinths to have the peat moist before mixing, if too dry the peat will take up moisture from the soil which is needed by the bulbs. The bulbs will also appreciate a sprinkling of bone meal worked into the compost. Potting should not be too firm or there will be a tendency for the bulbs to push themselves out of the compost as they form their roots. The bulbs should be so planted that their tops just show above the soil. As a rule, Roman hyacinths which reach England from France and are smaller-flowering should be planted early in September. As many as five or six Romans may be planted in a bowl of a size that would hold only three Dutch hyacinths.

When planting is completed the pots should, if possible, be placed under the protection of a wall and covered with either sand or weathered ashes for five or six weeks. Those living in a flat cannot use this method of rooting and must be content with placing the bowls in a dark cupboard or in a dry place which is cool. A cellar is ideal, for here the compost will not dry out and the bulbs, like those in the open, will require no watering after the soaking given at planting. It is essential with all bulbs, and none more so than hyacinths, that they should form a heavy rooting system before any attempt is made at forcing. If not, a thin or a stunted spike will result. Cool conditions while rooting takes place are necessary. Nor will the hyacinth stand up to hard forcing as soon as taken indoors. This must be done gradually. The Romans and the prepared bulbs will be taken indoors at the same time, about 1st November, and they should first be partially shaded with sacking or brown paper. After shaking the ash from the pots, first place them under the greenhouse bench for several days until they become accustomed to the light, while the temperature should be no more than $45°$ F ($7°$ C). Ventilate thoroughly at first, then gradually increase the temperature, giving the pots all the light possible and copious amounts of water. Growth will be rapid if the temperature be kept at a steady $60°$ F ($16°$ C) but never at any time allow the bulbs to lack moisture. They will require water most days and will appreciate some damping down of the floor at midday. Hyacinths grown in the home will not be subject to such a high degree of forcing, but the same rules apply. When the roots have formed, introduce them gradually to a warm room, while full exposure to strong light too soon may cause the leaf tips to turn brown and there may be stunting of the bloom. The pots should be placed in as light a position as possible as soon as acclimatised but not before, while the soil must always be kept moist.

As growth advances and the flower spike makes headway, it will be advisable to support it by means of a wire; but if the plants have been grown as described they will be sturdy and have a compact flower spike so that staking may not be necessary unless it appears that the bloom will be unduly heavy.

It is said that the hyacinth should be grown only indoors, where its fragrance, its earliness and the long life of the blooms make it the ideal indoor flower; that outdoors it is too stiff, too formal for an interesting display. Like the geranium, in its formality lies its charm for it is different in habit to most other spring-flowering bulbs. A bed of hyacinths massed together with a background of flowering cherries or against the silvery bark of the birch, or interplanted with aubretia or arabis, make a display of the utmost charm. Two-colour schemes are most attractive, using pink and blue, or purple and white hyacinths. Or the yellow-flowering variety, City of Haarlem, interplanted with purple aubretia, Dr Mules; or plant the white L'Innocence among a bed of pale-pink arabis; or carpeted with aubretia, Russell's Crimson.

The hyacinth's love of water is equally applicable to outside plantings and a sandy soil should be given humus such as decayed manure or peat. A dry, clay soil will rarely produce a large spike. Chopped seaweed is also an excellent form of humus. Heavy feeding is not necessary, but it is important to supply the moisture-holding humus, for dry weather often prevails when hyacinths are in bloom.

Mid-October is the most suitable time for planting. Plant the bulbs 6 in (15 cm) deep, and should the soil be on the heavy side, place around the bulbs some sand or peat. Planting distance will depend upon whether carpeting plants are being used. If not, plant the bulbs 9 in (23 cm) apart. If they are, plant 15 in apart. In the mixed border a few clumps of hyacinths will add colour and fragrance, and here they may be left in the ground year after year. If given a top-dressing of peat and decayed manure in midsummer they will continue to produce a spike of reasonable size for a number of years.

Plants that have flowered outdoors should have the dead blooms removed immediately they have completed their flowering. This will be when the blooms begin to turn brown. If they are allowed to form seed, they will exhaust the bulbs. Do not remove the stems, only the flower heads, for the stems contain sap that must drain back in the bulbs.

When the leaves have turned a yellow colour is the time to lift the bulbs. This will be late in May or early June, to make way for summer bedding plants.

Select a dry day for lifting and leave the bulbs on the bed exposed to the air for several hours. Then remove as much dry soil as possible and place in a dry, open shed for several weeks. The bulbs should be turned weekly as they are liable to sweat. If bulbs of 16-cm size have originally been used, they may be used again the following year and after that should be planted in a mixed border. It is more economical to purchase a large bulb which will produce a first-class bloom for two years. Bulbs which have been forced and possibly subject to high temperatures should be allowed to die down after flowering and should be shaken from the pots and dried off in the same way as those planted outside. They will be of little use for indoor planting again, nor will they give a bloom worthy of an outdoor display. They are best planted in the border in October, where they will produce spikes of indifferent size but will be useful for cutting or to give colour in the border.

Commercial growers on the Continent never replant again in the same beds for at least three years and it has been noticed that the bulbs do give a better display if planted in the same beds in alternate years, rather than for several years in succession.

Children will obtain enjoyment from growing indoor flowers in a narrow-necked glass bowl or jar and this method will clearly show the hyacinth's love for water. During October an 18-cm bulb is firmly placed into the neck of the glass container into which has been placed some rainwater. The bulb should be suspended just above the water-level; the base should not actually touch the water. It should be placed in a cellar or cupboard for a month and when taken out, will be found to have formed a mass of roots extending down into the water. Admittance to the light and to a warm room should be gradual, but it should be given a position of full light in ten days time. The bulbs will come into bloom early in the new year and are extremely ornamental, with the roots almost as attractive as the bloom.

Propagation. The hyacinth is a plant that is shy to increase, and even where bulblets are produced they take several years to reach flowering size. The requirements for building up the bulblets into flowering size is a rich, deeply cultivated sandy soil with a high water content. The two rarely go together, for a deep sandy soil is generally a dry soil. In Holland, however, the water-level is such that sufficient moisture is always in easy reach of the rooting system. Thus, they enjoy a warm, sandy soil and at the same time the necessary moisture for the rapid development of the bulbs.

If the mature bulbs are cut crosswise at the base to a depth of $\frac{1}{2}$ in before being planted, they will form a number of small bulblets at the place where the cut has been made. The mother bulbs are planted out during September but are not allowed to flower in the spring, the spike being removed when observed. Thus, the energy of the plant is devoted to the formation of bulblets. These bulblets are removed in early summer and grown on in beds, being continually fed with liquid manure water, and within three years will have reached flowering size. In England almost double the time will elapse before the bulbs reach the same size.

Species and Varieties. *Hyacinthus amethystinus.* The Spanish hyacinth, it is native of the Pyrenees and flowers in May and June. Farrer wrote that 'it stands bright among the loveliest bulbs we have and yet is one of the most rarely seen'. It has linear leaves and bears its bell-shaped flowers of clearest blue in a loose spike and on a 9-in (23-cm) stem. There is also a white form, *alba.*

Hyacinthus azureus (syn. *Muscari azureum*). Native of Asia Minor, it bears its flowers in a conical spike and they resemble those of *Muscari* to which it is closely related. They are bell-shaped and sky blue and appear during April on a 9-in (23-cm) stem. They are sweetly scented. There is a white form, *albus*, while *amphibolis* bears a large spike tightly packed with bell-shaped flowers of azure-blue.

Hyacinthus dalmaticus. Native of Yugoslavia, it is a delightful species for the rock garden, bearing, in April and May, dainty spikes of soft azure blue on 6-in (15-cm) stems.

Hyacinthus fastigiatus. Native of the mountains of Corsica, it makes a small oval bulb and on a 6-in (15-cm) stem bears five or six star-like flowers of purest white.

Hyacinthus orientalis. It is native of those countries of the Near East, especially Persia and Turkey, and is a charming plant, bearing a dozen or more nodding bells of palest mauve on stems 10 in (25 cm) long. The bells open like stars and diffuse about them a perfume equalled only by that of the stock. From this plant the enormous spikes of the Dutch or florists' hyacinths have been evolved, and from the variety *albus*, with its blooms of virginal whiteness, native of southern France, was raised the early flowering Roman hyacinth. Among the finest of the large-flowered hyacinths are:

ANN MARY. The large thick spikes are of clearest pink with perfect placement of the bells around the stem.

BEN NEVIS. The finest of the whites with a powerful balsam-like perfume, while the large ivory-white bells are fully double.

BISMARCK. Long in commerce, it has never been surpassed in its colour which is light porcelain-blue.

CITY OF HAARLEM. Later-flowering than most so that it will prolong the season. It forms a flower spike of great substance and of a lovely shade of soft creamy-yellow.

JAN BOS. It forms a magnificent spike of ox-blood red which does not fade in sunlight or as the spike ages.

KING OF THE BLUES. A magnificent late-flowering variety bearing an enormous spike of deep indigo, flushed with purple.

LADY DERBY. It forms a large broad spike of bright salmon-pink.

L'INNOCENCE. Probably more widely grown indoors than any variety, it forms the largest spike of all, with enormous bells of purest white.

MYOSOTIS. The finest of all the light-blue hyacinths, of forget-me-not colour with a silver centre.

ORANGE CHARM. It bears a large compact truss of an unusual shade of buff yellow shaded orange.

OSTARA. The finest in its colour, bearing a spike of exhibition form, its large bells being of clear dark blue.

PRINCESS IRENE. A variety of uncommon beauty, bearing a handsome spike of soft silvery pink.

SALMONETTA. From a small bulb, it forms a most attractive spike of soft salmon-orange.

SCARLET PERFECTION. The double form of Tubergen's scarlet, bearing a spike of perfect symmetry and of deepest scarlet.

YELLOW HAMMER. It forms a compact spike of a lovely shade of deep creamy-yellow.

Hyacinthus romanus. Not a true species but the French form of *H. orientalis* bearing creamy-white flowers in a loose spike at a height of 12 in (30 cm). It is usually grown under glass, when it will bloom between Christmas and Easter.

The multiflora hyacinths are derivatives of *H. romanus* and from each bulb produce numerous spikes of elegant, dainty form, making them ideal for a window box or for planting in bowls. They make a 16- to 17-cm bulb and come early into bloom. Five or six should be planted to a large bowl and when in bloom they will present an attractive feathery appearance. Borah bears azure-blue flowers; Rosalie, shell-pink; and Snow Princess, pure white. They are suitable for early forcing and may be brought into bloom for Christmas either in fibre or in water glasses.

Hyacinthus tabrizianus. Native of Persia, it is one of the rarest plants in cultivation, a single bulb being worth 50 new pence. It grows only 3 in (7·5 cm) tall and blooms in March, the tiny bell-shaped blooms being white, shaded with palest blue and they are deliciously scented.

HYMENOCALLIS (Amaryllidaceae)

A genus of about 50 species, native of Mexico and South America and closely related to *Pancratium*. It takes its name from the Greek *hymen*, a membrane, and *kallos*, beautiful; the reference being to the conspicuous corona at the centre of the flower which is formed by the stamen appendages uniting into a cup. It has ovoid tunicated bulbs with an extended neck and strap-like leaves of brightest green. The yellow or white flowers, borne in umbels of two to five, are mostly scented and appear at the end of a solid scape 12 to 18 in (30 to 45 cm) long. The perianth is funnel-shaped, the six stamens joined together by the membranous cup, having filaments which protrude beyond the corona. The outer segments are narrow and pointed, which give the flowers a spider-like appearance, hence its name, spider lily. It is a suitable plant for a cool or warm greenhouse or for a garden room, while several of the hardier species, e.g. *H. narcissiflora*, may be grown outdoors in a warm border and lifted in autumn; whilst it may be allowed to occupy the ground permanently where frost is no problem.

Culture. It requires similar cultural conditions to *Hippeastrum*—i.e. a compost made up of fibrous loam, leaf mould and decayed manure in equal parts, into which is mixed a liberal amount of grit. Plant early in March where a temperature of 55° to 60° F (13° to 16° C) can be provided, setting one bulb to a pot which should be twice the size of the bulb. Press the compost firmly around the bulb, just covering it. Give little moisture until growth begins, then increase supplies as the sun becomes warmer. Where no heat is available, planting should be delayed a month; as will the flowering time, for those planted in March will appear early in June (*Pancratium* in autumn). After flowering, maintain moisture supplies and give an occasional application of dilute liquid manure until the foliage begins to die back in autumn. Moisture is then withheld and the pots placed on their side in a frost-free room for the winter rest. The plants are started into growth again in spring and will require repotting every two or three years.

If growing outdoors, select the hardiest species and an open, sunny situation. Plant in April, 6 in (15 cm) deep and 9 in (22·5 cm) apart, and after the foliage dies back in autumn, either lift the bulbs and store in boxes of peat during winter, or protect them from frost by covering with a 6-in (15-cm) mulch of decayed leaves and strawy manure. The plants will require copious amounts of water in summer.

H. narcissiflora is a valuable plant for a garden tub which can be placed under cover and protected from frost during winter.

Propagation. Increase by removal of the offsets when the bulbs are repotted every two or three years. They are grown on as for *Hippeastrum* and will bloom in three or four years, depending upon their size. Plants may be raised from seed sown in April. The seeds are large and green-coated, and one should be sown in a 3-in (7·5-cm) pot containing a compost of sterilised loam and sand. They will readily germinate in a temperature of 60° F (16° C), and in 12 months the young plant will be ready to move to a larger pot, and into a flowering pot in another 12 months, when it will come into bloom after two more years. The young plants should be dried off in winter.

Species. *Hymenocallis amancaes*. Native only of the Hill of Amancaes near Lima in Peru. Though mature bulbs are less than 2 in (5 cm) through, they have a cylindrical neck 6 in (15 cm) long, from which arise bright-green leaves 18 in (45 cm) in length. The flowers which appear about mid-June are yellow, shaded green and with the staminal cup waved at the edges, while the outer segments are of pure golden yellow. The flowers, which are heavily scented, are borne two to four on a scape 18 in (45 cm) tall.

Hymenocallis andreana. It is found in the Andes of Ecuador at 10,000 ft, where the bulbs, of cricket or hockey ball size, grow among rocks. It has narrow pale-green leaves 12 in (30 cm) long, and on a 12-in (30-cm) scape it bears a solitary flower with a white staminal cup shaded green and with pure-white outer petals. It is almost hardy and blooms in July.

Hymenocallis festalis. Found in Venezuela, it closely resembles *H. undulata* and forms a large ovoid bulb with narrow oblong leaves, while the flowers are borne on a 2-ft (60-cm) scape. They have a wide staminal cup of glistening white and long slender outer segments which sweep back gracefully. The bloom is enhanced by the gold-tipped anthers.

Hymenocallis harrisiana. Native of Mexico, it makes a large ovoid bulb with an extended neck and increases by stolons. It has oblanceolate leaves 12 in (30 cm) in length and it comes into bloom before the end of May, thus requiring protection in the British Isles and northern Europe. The flowers have a short staminal cup and narrow outer segments 3 in (7·5 cm) long, which give the flower a spider-like appearance. The flowers are white and are borne during June and July in twos or threes on a 9-in (22·5-cm) stem.

Hymenocallis lacera (syn. *H. rotata*). Native of Florida and northern Mexico, it resembles *H. harrisiana* in that its bulb has an elongated neck, while it also increases by stolons which under natural conditions spread rapidly to form large plantations. The leaves grow 15 in (37·5 cm) long, while the flowers have a shallow staminal cup 2 in (5 cm) across and outer segments almost 4 in (10 cm) long. They are white and scented.

Hymenocallis narcissiflora (syn. *H. calathina*). Native of the Peruvian Andes, it forms a large globular bulb with a cylindrical neck. Its leaves are formed almost in a double row and grow up to 2 ft (60 cm) in length, while the flowers, borne in an umbel of two to five, have a wide staminal cup of purest white, waved at the edges. The lance-shaped outer segments are tinted with green and give the flowers a spider-like appearance. They appear in June and are heavily scented.

Hymenocallis speciosa. It has bulbs of 4-in (10-cm) diameter from which arise oblong bright-green leaves 18 in (45 cm) long. The flowers with their large white staminal cup and green-tinted tube 4 in (10 cm) long appear in May and June and are borne in umbels of two to five on a 15-in (37·5-cm) stem. They are powerfully scented. The hybrid Daphne bears large umbels of purest white flowers during June and July.

Hymenocallis tubiflora. Discovered in the valley of the Amazon, it has large ovoid bulbs with a long neck from which arise twin oblong leaves 8 in (20 cm) in length and 4 in (10 cm) wide. The flowers, borne three to six in an umbel, have a cylindrical tube 8 in (20 cm) long with a narrow staminal cup and outer segments 4 in (10 cm) in length. The flowers are pure white and possess extreme fragrance.

Hymenocallis undulata. Native of Venezuela, it has a large ovoid bulb and thin oblong leaves, which narrow into a stalk. The white flowers have a perianth tube 6 in (15 cm) long and a staminal cup 1 in (2·5 cm) deep, while the outer segments are 3 in (7·5 cm) long. The flowers appear in June and are borne in an umbel of 4 to 12 at the end of a 2-ft (60-cm) scape.

HYPOXIS (Amaryllidaceae)

A genus of about 100 species, native of North and South America, South-east Asia, tropical and southern Africa and Australia and taking their name from *hypo*, under, and *oxys*, sharp, referring to the spiny base of the seed pod. They are plants of the warmer parts and known as the star-grasses for they have narrow rush-like leaves covered with down and star-like flowers, borne singly or in clusters. Only two species—*H. stellata*, native of tropical and southern Africa, and *H. hirsuta* of North America—are grown as decorative plants. In the British Isles and northern Europe they should be confined to a cool greenhouse or sheltered garden.

Culture. Plant two or three bulbs to a 6-in (15-cm) pot in September and into a compost made up of loam, peat and sand in equal parts. Plant 1 in (2·5 cm) deep and 2 in (5 cm) apart and place in a cold frame until growth begins towards the year end. Then move into gentle warmth and water only when the compost becomes dry. The plants will bloom early in spring. They may be grown out-doors only in those gardens enjoying a mild winter climate, when they may be planted about the rock garden which they will enhance with their neat upright habit. Plant 4 in (10 cm) deep and 6 in (15 cm) apart in September and into a light, well-drained soil.

Propagation. The plants may be increased by division, which should be done immediately after flowering, or by removing the offsets in autumn when the plants are ready for repotting.

Species. *Hypoxis hirsuta.* It is to be found in fields and open woodlands from Maine to Texas, usually growing in a sandy soil and flowering in May and June with occasional blooms appearing in autumn. It forms a small ovoid bulb from which arise narrow linear leaves about 9 in (22·5 cm) long and one-eighth of an inch wide and covered in white hairs. The flowers are borne on a 6-in (15-cm) stem in an umbel of one to seven and they are bright yellow, shaded green on the outside, hence its name of the yellow star grass.

Hypoxis stellata. It forms a small round bulb and has grass-like leaves which appear along the stems. The flowers are white, often shaded blue, with six segments which open star-like to reveal a dark blue or black centre, enhanced by golden anthers. The flowers measure 1 in (2·5 cm) across and are borne in May and June (April under glass) on 6-in (15-cm) stems.

I

IPHEION (Amaryllidaceae)

A genus of 25 species, native of Mexico and South America, only one of which is in general cultivation. This is *I. uniflorum*, at some time in its history classed as *Milla, Triteleia, Brodiaea*. It is not to be confused with *Milla biflora*.

Culture. It is almost hardy and, as the bulbs are inexpensive, may be planted in generous drifts about the rock garden or shrubbery. It is happy in full sun or in partial shade. Plant in October 4 in (10 cm) deep and 4 in (10 cm) apart in a well-drained sandy soil. For indoor flowering, plant four to six bulbs to a 5-in (12·5-cm) pot in October, using a sandy loam. Give little or no water until the plants make growth and water sparingly throughout winter. Give only sufficient heat to keep out frost. After flowering, dry off gradually and allow the bulbs to remain in the pots for several years, but give them an annual top-dressing.

Propagation. Offsets may be removed from the parent bulb when repotting or if the bulbs are lifted from the open ground. They are grown on in boxes of sandy compost for two years when they may be planted out and will bloom in two more years.

Species and Varieties. *Ipheion uniflorum*. Native of Mexico and Argentina, it has narrow grass-like leaves and blooms outdoors in April, a month earlier under glass, bearing its white star-like flowers in a loose spike of five or six on a 6-in (15-cm) reddish-green stem. The flowers are scented. The variety *violacea* bears pale-blue flowers, while Wisley Blue, found in the gardens of the Royal Horticultural Society, bears flowers almost 2 in (5 cm) across and of deepest blue.

IRIS (Iridaceae)

A genus of about 300 species, native of the northern temperate regions of the world and taking their name from *iris*, the eye, in reference to the beauty of the flowers. The plants may be divided into two main groups: those with a woody rhizomatous rootstock, which are usually planted in the border; and those with pear-shaped bulbs, known as bulbous iris. Those with rhizomatous roots comprise the 'bearded' and 'beardless' iris and those of the 'oncocyclus' group, all bearing flowers of exceptional beauty for garden display. The bulbous iris, derived from *I. xiphium* and *I. xiphioides*, are widely grown commercially for their cut flowers, while those of dwarf habit, i.e. the *I. reticulata* group, are grown in pots and on the rock garden, where they bloom in winter and early in spring. They are plants with sword-like, linear or angular leaves; and flowers which emerge from sheathing scales on an erect scape. The three outer segments or 'fall' petals are reflexed and sometimes 'bearded' at the base, while the three inner segments known as 'standards' are erect. The three stamens are inserted at the base of the outer segments. The style arches over the stamens.

Culture (Rhizomatous section). The rhizomatous iris is among the most beautiful of all garden plants, at home in the mixed border or in a border to themselves. The plants require a deeply worked soil and some lime in their diet. This may be given in the form of lime rubble or mortar, while they like a soil that is well-drained in winter. They also require a position where the summer sunshine can ripen the rhizomes. This is essential if they are to bloom well each year.

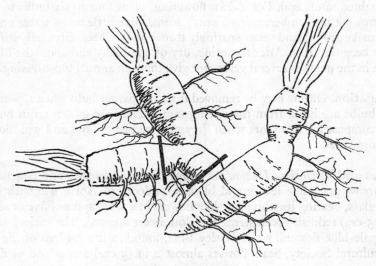

Dividing a rhizomatous iris

The flag iris is an excellent town garden plant being tolerant of deposits of soot and of a sulphur-laden atmosphere which will in no way harm the sword-like leaves. Usually, however, the plants are confined to a shady corner or to the shrubbery where sunlight may never reach them and where the soil is devoid of food, and so they are rarely seen in the same form as when planted in a well-prepared border.

The plants should be divided every four years as they quickly exhaust the soil. The most suitable time is late in July, after flowering, which commences mid–May. Or they may be lifted in October or in March—though no bloom can be expected that year.

The roots may be divided into sections by cutting them with a sharp knife, but each piece must have an 'eye' from which the leaves arise and from which the new plant can develop.

Set the pieces 2 ft (60 cm) apart, laying them just below the surface of the soil with the fibrous roots downwards and the top of the rhizome exposed to the sun.

The rhizomatous irises may be divided into three groups:

(i) The bearded iris, descended from *I. germanica*, with a creeping rootstock from which arise dark-green sword-like leaves 18 in (45 cm) long and an erect scape of several flowers. The flowers are like large orchids in shape and colour and have 'fall' petals which are bearded or crested.

(ii) The beardless iris. In this group is *I. stylosa*, the winter-flowering iris, and several other species whose large, handsome blooms are free of any beard.

(iii) The cushion or oncocyclus iris. Here the bud appears at the end of a short stolon, while the scape bears only a single flower of great size and beauty. The Regelia irises of this section bear more than one bearded flower to each scape. The plants like a well-drained gritty soil and shallow planting.

Rhizomatous Species and Varieties. *Iris acutiloba* (i). Native of the Caucasus, it has a slender creeping rootstock and narrow leaves. It is one of the cushion irises, growing 3 in (7·5 cm) high with broad falls of pale lilac with dark purple veins and black hairs at the base. The standards are erect and of pale lilac, waved at the margins.

Iris alberti (i). Native of Turkestan, it has sword-like leaves 2 ft (60 cm) long, and in May and June bears its flowers in loose panicles on stems of similar length. The standards are lilac; the falls white, veined with lilac and bronze. They are heavily bearded.

Iris albicans (i). At one time classed as a variety of *I. florentina* but now a separate species. Native of the Yemen, it is found about coastal areas, where it is planted to bind the sandy soil against erosion. It bears a pure-white flower.

Iris atropurpurea (iii). Native of Syria and Iran, it has sickle-shaped leaves 6 in (15 cm) long and flowers which have narrow falls, bearded with yellow and with black tips; the standards are large and coloured purple-black.

Iris aurea (ii). Native of the western Himalayas, it grows 4 ft (1·2 metres) tall and is readily raised from seed. The flowers are borne in two sessile clusters during June and are of brilliant golden-yellow throughout, the fall being waved at the edges.

Iris barnumae (iii). Present among the hills of Kurdistan, it grows only 4 in (10 cm) tall, bearing flowers of port-wine red, the falls being narrower than the standards and with a yellow beard. The yellow variety *sulphurea* emits the delicious scent of lily-of-the-valley.

Iris bartoni (i). Native of Afghanistan, it has sword-like leaves 18 in (45 cm) long and 2 in (5 cm) broad and it blooms in June, bearing its scented flowers in clusters of two or three. The creamy-white falls, and standards veined with green and purple with an orange beard, combine to make this a most interesting species.

Iris biflora (syn. *I. fragrans*) (i). Native of southern Europe, it has glaucous sword-like leaves and bears its flowers in April at a height of 15 in (37·5 cm). They are bright purple, the standards erect, the falls having a yellow beard and they are scented.

Iris biliotti (i). A rare native of Asia Minor, it has sword-like leaves, distinctly striped and 2 ft (60 cm) in length and it bears heavily scented flowers in June. The falls are 3 in (7·5 cm) long and are of reddish-purple, veined with black and with a pronounced white beard, the standards being of purple-blue with navy-blue veins.

Iris bismarckiana (iii). Native of the hills of northern Palestine, being especially prominent on Mount Lebanon, it bears a flower resembling *I. susiana*, the standards and falls being heavily spotted with purple on a cream ground. It is bearded at the base with black hairs and blooms in May on a 12-in (30-cm) stem.

Iris bracteata (i). Native of Oregon, it has leaves 2 ft (60 cm) long, glaucous on one side only, and bears its flowers on an angled stem, which is shorter than the leaves and with purple sheathing bracts. The flowers are palest yellow, the falls veined with blue.

Iris chamaeiris (i). A southern European species bearing its flowers on 6-in (15-cm) stems amidst a tuft of pale-green leaves. It blooms in April, the spoon-shaped falls being of brightest yellow, veined with brown and with a yellow beard. The narrow standards are pale yellow.

Iris cristata (ii). Native of the eastern United States, it grows 6 in (15 cm) tall, its flower stem appearing in April from a rosette of linear leaves. The flowers are amethyst-blue with a yellow crest on the falls and with crisped margins.

Iris douglassii (ii). Native of California, it forms a tuft of linear leaves from which arise, in June, flowers of primrose-yellow, the falls veined with lilac.

Iris duthiei (i). Native of north-western India, it has a knotty rhizomatous rootstock from which arises a tuft of yellowish leaves 2 ft (60 cm) in length, though the solitary flowers appear in May when the leaves are only making their appearance. The flowers with their horizontal falls are purple-lilac with darker veins and a white beard; the standards are also purple-lilac.

Iris flavescens (i). Native of south-eastern Europe and Afghanistan, it resembles *I. germanica* in its habit and sword-like leaves, while it bears its lemon-yellow flowers bearded with orange on a 3-ft (90-cm) stem.

Iris florentina (i). The Florentine iris, the roots of which, when dry, possess the fragrance of the violet and in medieval times were used as powder, to be placed among clothes and linen and to perfume the hair. The dry roots when burnt will perfume a musty-smelling room and if chewed, will sweeten the breath.

Iris foetidissima (iii). The Gladwin or roast beef iris, native of the British Isles and northern Europe, where it is to be found growing by the side of streams and damp meadows. It has a thick fleshy rootstock from which arise a tuft of sword-like leaves. It bears its flowers in June on stems 2 to 3 ft (60 to 90 cm) tall, which when crushed emit the smell of roasting beef. The flowers are purple-blue and are followed by seed pods which burst open when ripe to reveal large orange seeds for which the plant is worthy of a place in the woodland garden or for planting by the side of a pond.

Iris gatesii (iii). A rare native of the lower mountainous regions of Armenia and Asia Minor, it is known as the prince of irises, for it bears one of the most beautiful flowers of all plants. It has narrow dark-green foliage and bears its blooms in June on a 20-in (50-cm) stem. The standards are silvery-white, dotted with violet; the falls being cream, splashed with brownish-mauve. The flowers measure 5 in (12·5 cm) across and should be protected from wind for they bruise easily. Plant at the base of a wall in full sun and where it may remain dry in winter.

Iris germanica (i). The common flag or German iris is a native of central Europe and is the oldest iris in cultivation, believed to have been grown in the ninth century in the monastery garden of Reichenau by its Abbot, Walfred Strabo. It is one of the hardiest and toughest of plants, well-nigh indestructible but, though by its rugged constitution persisting through the years, it received little attention from breeders until the twentieth century. Though the modern flag irises are usually classed as being the offspring of *I. germanica*, this species has played little part in their raising in comparison with the scented *I. pallida*. Some varieties of outstanding beauty:

ALINE. It is an older variety, being a pure azure-blue self and carrying a more powerful perfume than any other.

BLUE RHYTHM. A mid-blue of outstanding beauty.

CLIFFS OF DOVER. Probably the finest white, the large ruffled blooms having a glittering frosted appearance.

CREAM CREST. One of the most exquisite of all irises with broad smooth petals of soft creamy-yellow.

CRINKLED GEM. The petals are crinkled and frilled, the colour being soft lavender, flushed rose and with a golden glow.

DEEP BLACK. One of the most striking of the dark irises, having violet-black standards and falls of velvet black and a violet beard.

EBONY QUEEN. Like a number of the darker-coloured irises, it is scented. The blue-black flowers have great substance and come into bloom before all others. 3 ft (90 cm).

ESTHER FAY. An outstanding iris, the large flowers of ruffled form being of flesh pink with a white blaze on the falls and an orange beard.

FASCINATION. A gorgeous iris to plant near those of dark colouring, for its flowers are of a lovely shade of dusky lilac-pink with a sweet perfume. 4 ft (1·2 metres).

FIRE MAGIC. It grows 40 in (1 metre) tall and is of branching habit, the flowers being of rich copper-red with a beard of bright yellow.

GIPSY LULLABY. Of compact habit, it has standards of bright butterscotch-yellow and falls of dusky purple-red, the whole flower being heavily ruffled.

GOLDEN GARLAND. A spectacular iris, the huge ruffled blooms having standards of canary yellow and falls of purest white with a broad margin of gold.

GRANADA GOLD. The large waved blooms are of velvety texture and of brilliant golden-yellow.

HAPPY BIRTHDAY. Of compact habit and well-branched, the large flowers are of bright flamingo-pink.

HARIETTE HALLOWAY. An iris of refined form, bearing ruffled flowers of great substance and of a lovely shade of medium blue with a sweet perfume.

HEARTBREAKER. One of the loveliest of the pinks, the huge blooms of superb texture, being deep pink with creamy overtones and with a bright-pink beard.

INSPIRATION. Though introduced in 1937, no iris bears a flower quite of the same rosy-cerise colouring and none has a sweeter fragrance. 3 to 4 ft (90 cm to 1·2 metres).

IVORY GLEAM. The large refined blooms are of solid ivory with touches of gold at the edges of the falls and diffusing a perfume like lily-of-the-valley.

JANE PHILLIPS. A pale blue of refinement and poise, the large flowers having ruffled fans.

LAGOS. Valuable in that, with Coastal Command, it is the latest iris to bloom, its large cream and gold flowers with their soft sweet perfume opening about mid-June to extend the season by several weeks.

LIMELIGHT. A most beautiful iris, the large ruffled blooms being of bright canary yellow with a flush of lime-green on the falls.

MAGGADAN. One of the most unusual and sweetly scented varieties. The standards are slate-blue, the ivory-white falls being flushed with grey. 3½ ft.

MANYUSA. With their exquisitely ruffled petals, the blooms are of soft orchid-pink with orange perfume. 3 ft (90 cm).

MARY RANDALL. A Dykes Medal winner, it is one of the most popular of the pinks, the flowers being of a deep rose-pink throughout and with a tangerine-red beard.

MATTIE GATES. A most attractive variety and one of the few yellows with pronounced perfume. The standards are of soft primrose-yellow, with the falls of brightest gold, blazoned with white. 3 ft (90 cm).

MOONBEAM. With Mattie Gates, it is the most richly scented of the yellow irises, the large blooms of clear sulphur-yellow having the scent of the lily-of-the-valley. Plant at the front of the border. 2 ft (60 cm).

MY HONEYCOMB. A variety of unusual beauty with standards of buff, amber and gold and flared falls of gold and tan with a central white blaze.

OLYMPIC TORCH. Of ideal branching habit, the flowers have a velvety texture and are of uniform golden-bronze.

PARTY DRESS. A flamingo-pink of ruffled charm and quality and with a brilliant orange beard.

RADIANT. This fine iris will be a valuable addition to the front of the border for its bright apricot-orange standards and terracotta falls ensure that it receives the attention it deserves. In addition, it is free-flowering and richly scented. 2½ ft (75 cm).

ROSE VIOLET. A front of the border bi-colour with rose-pink standards and violet falls, the bloom having great substance. Valuable for its lateness of flowering and its rich gardenia scent. 2 to 3 ft (60 to 90 cm).

SARAH ELIZABETH. The blooms are heavily ruffled and of great substance and of crystal-clear blue, free from any markings but with a metallic sheen.

STARSHINE. Tall-growing, its flowers have a delicate beauty unlike that of any other variety, being a subtle blending of soft blue, cream and buff, producing a pearl-like appearance.

STATEN ISLAND. Late flowering, it has old gold standards and wine red falls edged with gold.

Iris graminea (ii). It is to be found about lower alpine regions of central Europe and has linear leaves 18 in (45 cm) long and two-edge flower stems of only half that height. The flowers which measure 2 in (5 cm) across are borne in twos and emit the smell of ripe apricots. The falls are lavender, veined with violet and tipped with yellow, the standards being bright mauve. The long stamens are protected by the petal-like stigmas. This iris grows well in full sun or partial shade and is hardy anywhere.

Iris hexagona (ii). Native of the southern United States, it has sword-shaped leaves 3 ft (90 cm) in length and bears its flowers on forked stems 4 ft (1·2 metres) tall during April and May. They are of soft lilac with spoon-shaped standards and obovate falls.

Iris hoogiana (iii). It was discovered in central Asia by the brothers Hoog and was named in their honour by the late Mr W. R. Dykes, an authority on the genus. The flowers appear early in May, each bloom being 6 in (15 cm) across and borne on 18-in (45-cm) stems. They are of soft lavender-blue, almost devoid of markings. Bronze Beauty has a standard of violet and falls of deep purple, shading to bronzey-brown.

Iris hookeriana (i). A handsome native of Bengal with fleshy rhizomes and pale-green leaves which appear when the flowers die back. The flowers are borne two to a stem, the purple falls being heavily bearded with white hairs while the narrow standards are bluish-purple.

Iris iberica (iii). Native of the Caucasus, it was crossed with *I. korolkowii*, a bulbous iris, to raise several of the *Regelio-oncocyclus* hybrids. It has sickle-like leaves 4 in (10 cm) long and large broad flowers. The standards of pale lilac are marked with purple with the creamy-white falls spotted with black. It was widely used for hybridising by Sir Michael Foster early in the century.

Iris kaempferi (ii). It is beardless, the flowers having the appearance of clematis and varying considerably in size. They may be propagated by division immediately after flowering or by sowing the seed in moist soil where the plants are to bloom. If sown in September the plants will appear the following spring. The plants must be kept free of lime and they enjoy a soil of high acidity.

Iris korolkowii (iii). Native of Turkestan, it bears a flower which is strange and exciting being white, veined all over with purple-grey and with a blotch on the falls of velvety purple. It blooms in May on a 12-in (30-cm) stem and has glaucous linear foliage. The variety *violaceae* has flowers of pale-violet ground colour.

Iris lortetii (iii). Native of the Lebanon, it resembles *I. gatesii*. It has sword-like leaves and in June bears large flowers, the standards being of a beautiful shade of soft pink veined with mauve, while the falls are pale blue spotted with crimson, heavily so at the centre.

Iris lutescens (i). Native of southern Europe, it has glaucous sword-like leaves and stems on which it bears in May large yellow flowers, the falls being veined with purple-brown.

Iris missouriensis (ii). Native of the Rocky Mountains, it forms a tuft of linear leaves 12 in (30 cm) long which taper to a point, and it blooms in May, the large lilac-blue flowers being veined with purple, the falls delicately shaded with yellow.

Iris pallida (i). A flag iris similar to *I. germanica* and which has had a considerable influence on the raising of the modern hybrids. It is native of southern Europe and reached England during Elizabethan times. Gerard says it grew in his garden in Holborn with 'leaves much broader than any other [iris] and . . . with fair large flowers of a light blue or (as we term it) a watchet colour'. And he adds, 'the flowers do smell exceeding sweete, much like the orange flower'. To some, the perfume more nearly resembles vanilla; to others, it has been likened to civet.

Iris prismatica (ii). Closely resembling *I. versicolor*, it is found along the eastern United States and Canada, from Nova Scotia to Georgia, usually in damp meadows and marshy ground. It is a more slender species than *I. versicolor* and bears two or three narrow grass-like leaves and a flower stem 1 to 2 ft (30 to 60 cm) tall, at the end of which appear one or two flowers of deep blue, veined with yellow.

Iris pseudacorus (ii). The yellow or water iris, to be seen growing by the side of rivers and in marshlands throughout the British Isles and France, whose King Louis VII took the flower as his blazon during the Crusades and gave it his name, 'flower of (de) Louis'. It is the yellow 'vagabond flag' of Shakespeare's Antony and Cleopatra and it became the national symbol of medieval France— in heraldic language: 'Azure powdered with fleurs-de-lis or'. In 1339 when Edward III made claim to the throne of France and began hostilities against Philip VI (Philip of Valois), he took for his arms the three Plantagenet lions and the fleur-de-lis of France.

It is a delightful plant with a scented flower some 3 in (7·5 cm) across and of a soft shade of golden-yellow. The flowers are produced in succession from May until August amidst sword-like leaves. From the dried rhizomatous roots, a delicately scented oil, once used to adulterate oil of Acorus calamus, is obtained.

Iris sambucina (i). It is the 'elder-scented' iris of central Europe, forming tufts of glaucous leaves 18 in (45 cm) tall and bearing, in May and June, flowers on branching stems 2 ft (60 cm) high. The standards are dull yellow shaded with claret, the falls dull purple.

Iris sari (iii). It grows on the banks of the River Sari and blooms in May, its large handsome flowers resembling those of *I. gatesii*. It has sword-like leaves 6 in (15 cm) long and bears flowers of soft violet, spotted and veined with deeper violet, with the falls darker than the standards and with a dark-brown beard.

Iris sibirica (ii). It was grown in Elizabethan gardens and is native to all parts of Europe. It makes a pleasing waterside plant but will flourish in the border provided lime is not present. It has elegant grass-like foliage and bears two or three flowers together, of brightest lilac-blue.

Two outstanding varieties are Helen Aster, a rose-red, and Nottingham Lace, introduced in 1960, the wine-red flowers being laced with white.

Iris stolonifera (iii). Native of the Levant, it has grey sickle-shaped leaves and in June bears its handsome flowers. The standards are white, shaded violet and edged chocolate-brown; the falls also being edged with brown with lilac shading at the centre and a white beard.

Iris stylosa (syn. *I. unguicularis*) (ii). Native of Algeria, it has a thin rhizomatous rootstock from which arises a tuft of bright-green linear leaves 12 in (30 cm) high. As it blooms in January, it should be given as warm a position as possible such as the foot of a wall facing south and beneath the eaves of a house where the plant will be protected from excess winter moisture. It requires a poor, dry soil supplied with lime rubble. The scented flowers are of a most beautiful shade of sky blue, the variety *speciosa* being veined with white. The partially open buds, if taken indoors, will expand in water and remain fresh for a week or more.

Iris susiana (iii). The mourning iris, 'so fit for a mourning habit', wrote Parkinson. 'I think in the whole compasse of nature's store, there is none more pathetical . . . among all the flowers I know, coming neare into the colour of it.' It takes its name from the ruined city of Susa in Persia where it was discovered growing on old walls. The enormous flower is white, veined and marked with black. It must be given a dry, sunny situation. Gerard said 'it doth prosper well in my garden', and he likened its bloom to the ginny hen. He also called it the Turkey 'flower de luce', for it reached England from Constantinople early in the sixteenth century.

Iris tectorum (ii). Native of Japan, it has pale-green sword-shaped leaves 12 in (30 cm) long, and it blooms in May and June, on 12-in (30-cm) stems. The flowers are of brightest lilac, with the falls attractively crisped and veined with purple.

Iris variegata (i). Native of central Europe, it forms tufts of sword-like leaves

18 in (45 cm) long, shaded purple at the base, and it blooms in May, bearing its flowers on a glaucous stem 18 in (45 cm) high. The falls are of deep claret-red with a yellow beard, while the erect standards are of contrasting golden-yellow.

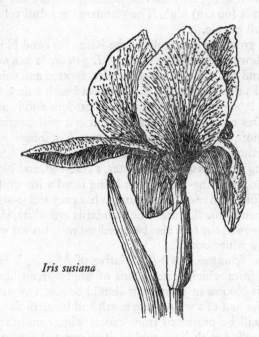

Iris susiana

Iris versicolor (ii). Native of the eastern United States and Newfoundland, where it is common by the side of streams and in damp meadows. It has glaucous sword-shaped leaves, and in May and June bears clusters of deep-purple flowers variegated with yellow and green.

Culture (bulbous section). The bulbous irises may also be divided into three main groups:

(i) Those of the reticulata group, which are distributed in Asia Minor and are characterised by the handsome netted tunics of the bulbs, by their dwarf habit and earliness to bloom. They have rush-like leaves and bear their flowers singly. They are mostly scented. They make admirable pot plants and are suitable for the rock garden.

(ii) Those of the Xiphium group, native of the Iberian Peninsular and north-western Africa. They have smooth tunics and bear their flowers on stems 2 ft (60 cm) tall. Of this group belong the English and Dutch irises, grown by the million each year for their cut bloom in spring and early summer.

Hyacinth: Lady Derby

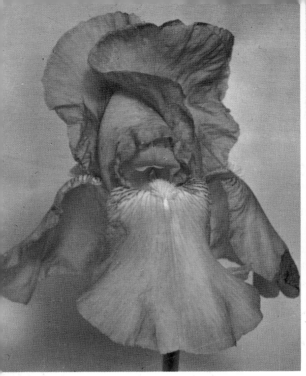

Iris: Jane Phillips

Iris: Blue Rhythm

Iris: Staten Island

Iris: Cliffs of Dover

(iii) The Juno irises of Bokhara, Turkey and Afghanistan. They are bulbous but also have thick fleshy roots and deeply channelled leaves which enclose the stem at the base. They are the most difficult of irises to maintain, requiring a rich diet and plenty of moisture while growing, but needing to be kept almost dry when resting.

Iris of the reticulata group will come into bloom outdoors early in February and are suitable for planting in short grass and on the rock garden, where they prove valuable on account of their earliness and neatness of foliage. They may be planted in small groups near grey stone, which shows off the rich purple, crimson and pale blue colours of the flowers to advantage. Alternatively, used as an edging to a border, they will come into bloom in February, at a height of only 6 in (15 cm). In the semi-shade of trees, particularly among silver birch, with their brightly coloured winter bark, the bulbs may be left untouched for several years, after which they are best lifted, divided and replanted in September. Plant the bulbs 2 in (5 cm) deep and 2 in (5 cm) apart outdoors, for their habit is neat and upright and they have only a few rush-like leaves. Though they like a soil containing peat or leaf mould and even a little decayed manure, lime rubble is the most important part of their diet, and plenty of mortar should be worked into the soil before the bulbs are planted in autumn. A dressing of lime rubble given in autumn will keep the bulbs healthy and free-flowering. When the blooms begin to die back they should be removed, to conserve the energies of the plant.

It is as a pot plant that the dwarf iris is at its best. Plant in September 7 in (2·5 cm) apart. As many as a dozen may be planted in an earthenware bowl. After two months in the plunge bed, or in a cool, dark place, they may be slowly introduced to the living-room. In early spring, their richly coloured blooms will scent a large room.

Irises of the Xiphium section may be planted in groups in the border and in prepared beds for cutting. Plant in October to ensure the early formation of roots and anchorage against frost.

One method is to prepare a bed 3 ft (90 cm) wide which will enable cutting of the blooms to be done easily. As irises like dry conditions in winter, a raised bed will suit them best. This should be made up in September, incorporating some sand and leaf mould. If the soil is light in texture, dig in some decayed manure, for although the iris enjoys dry conditions, some humus is essential to the formation of a tall, well-formed spike. If the ground lacks lime, rake in some lime rubble or a small quantity of hydrated lime; but the bed must be given two weeks to settle down, for bulbous irises are like onions and shallots in demanding a firm bed. To make certain that the bed is compact, it is as well to tread it all over a day or so before the bulbs are planted. Some growers plant in drills made 3 in (7·5 cm) deep, placing the bulbs 1 in (2·5 cm) apart. Another method is to plant as for shallots, pressing the bulbs into the soil so that their

N

noses may be seen above ground. Plant 2 in (5 cm) apart and in rows the same distance apart, so that they will hold up each other when coming into bloom and will require no staking other than placing a cane at the four corners of the bed and enclosing it with a length of twine. So as to ensure a firm bed, pull the garden roller over it after planting, provided the soil is not sticky. If it is, wait until it is friable.

The booms will be ready for cutting early in May, six months after planting, and they must be removed before the flower heads are fully opened. Several days may be saved, and every day means a more profitable crop, if the blooms are removed as soon as they show colour and allowed to stand in buckets of cold water for several hours before dispatching to market. The flower stems, being of a high water content, will continue to supply the blooms with moisture and they will continue to open. But a bloom which is too far open will bruise and rapidly deteriorate.

If a 7- to 8-cm-size bulb is planted as against the 6- to 7-cm size used for garden culture, and if the beds are watered with liquid manure once a fortnight, it will be possible to grow the same bulbs for a second season, though the blooms will be smaller. In order to help the bulbs as much as possible, it is advisable to leave a length of stem and a leaf rather than to cut the bloom at ground-level. Bulbous iris grown in the border for decoration should have the dead heads removed after flowering and the stem and foliage must be allowed to die down gradually.

In the border, plant in groups of six or more in separate colours and in alternate varieties. The Spanish and English types will prolong the season into July, and while these irises may not have commercial value, they are invaluable for early summer cutting for the home. They require similar treatment to Dutch iris, though the English iris enjoys a heavier and moister soil. They should be planted in a position sheltered from the prevailing winds on account of their growing tall. A wall or hurdle screen is ideal; the shelter of trees is not suitable, for the plants must have full sun.

The outdoor forcing of Dutch irises under frames and barn cloches is done by commercial growers to supply the early spring market. The same methods may also be used to provide early bloom for the home. The Dutch irises bloom well under glass outdoors and will bloom three weeks before uncovered bulbs. If the lights are placed on their sides and held in position by wooden stakes and over the top are also placed lights or lengths of polythene, the miniature greenhouse will provide the correct height for Dutch irises.

The bulbs are planted early in October and are covered in February, the plants coming into bloom in April. If a cool or heated greenhouse is to be used, the bulbs are planted either in large pots or deep boxes. They should be planted about 1st September in a mixture of loam, coarse sand and decayed manure. Old mushroom-bed manure is ideal, so are spent hops. Some lime rubble should also be added. As many as six bulbs may be planted into each large pot. If growing in boxes, plant the bulbs 2 in (5 cm) apart each way, using a 10- to 12-cm bulb. After planting and watering, the pots or boxes are stood outside in a plunge bed of ashes or sand until thoroughly rooted, which will take about two months. The first batch may then be taken indoors. Wedgwood will be the first and a temperature of just under 50° F (10° C) will be sufficient—indeed a temperature above 52° F (11° C) will be detrimental to the production of top-quality bloom. Only when the buds are showing colour should the temperature be increased to 55° F (13° C). At this period, the bulbs will need ample supplies of water and a well-ventilated atmosphere. Wedgwood taken indoors about 1st November should be ready for cutting by 1st March when grown in a temperature of 50° F (10° C). Later batches of Yellow Queen and Imperator will be taken indoors before the year end and will be in bloom from the end of March. Those growing outdoors under lights or cloches will bridge the gap until the unprotected Wedgwood is in bloom.

Bulbous Species and Varieties. *Iris alata* (iii). The Scorpion Iris, native of southern Europe and northern Africa, is winter-flowering, coming into bloom early in November and, though hardy in all but the most exposed gardens, its exquisite beauty is most appreciated in the shelter of the alpine house. Outdoors, it requires a well-drained soil and a sun-baked situation and, where sheltered from cold winds, it will continue to bloom until the new year. It has lance-shaped pale-green leaves 12 in (30 cm) long and bears its flowers on a 6-in (15-cm) stem. They are of bright lavender, the falls having a golden crest or keel, while the spoon-shaped standards spread out horizontally.

Iris bakeriana (i). Native of Persia and Iraq, it comes into bloom a week or so before all others in this section and is one of the most handsome of irises. Like *I. reticulata*, the flowers have the scent of violets. It has ovoid bulbs with an eight-ribbed tunic of pale brown and sharply pointed leaves 9 in (23 cm) in length. The flowers have standards of pale ultramarine-blue and broad spoon-shaped falls of white, blotched with deep blue and edged with violet. The flowers are borne on 6-in (15-cm) stems and are hardy and tolerant of adverse weather, though for the bulbs to be long-living they should be planted where excess winter moisture can readily drain away and where they may be baked by the summer sun.

Iris boissieri (ii). It is found about the Gerez Mountains of Portugal and Spain and is a handsome species though difficult to manage in the open and is best grown under glass where it can be dried off after flowering. It has linear leaves and bears its flowers in June on a 12-in (30-cm) stem. The standards are purple, shaded red at the base; the falls being of reddish-purple with a yellow beard.

Iris bucharica (iii). Native of Bokhara, it has long pale green leaves like those of the leek and from the axils arise white and yellow flowers on 12-in (30-cm) stems. The falls are tipped with yellow. It blooms in April.

Iris caucasica (iii). A delightful little iris, native of the Caucasus and the mountains of northern Persia, growing 6 in (15 cm) tall with bright-green leaves which taper to a point. It is one of the earliest of the Junos to bloom, flowering towards the end of February or early March, the pale lime-yellow flowers being 3 in (7·5 cm) across. The variety *major* bears larger flowers.

Iris danfordiae (i). Native of the Cilician Taurus, it requires a light, well-drained soil containing lime rubble, and a sunny position. Once established, do not disturb for it is from the newly formed bulblets that next season's flowers will arise. It bears golden-yellow flowers, speckled with brown, during February, being almost leafless at flowering time. It blooms on a 4-in (10-cm) stem and is untroubled by the severest weather, for the flowers will emerge through frozen snow. The bulb dies after flowering.

Iris filifolia (ii). Native of southern Spain and northern Africa, it resembles the Spanish iris in miniature when in bloom, also in its bulb and foliage. It has slender grass-like leaves and it bears its flower of bright uniform purple in June on a 12-in (30-cm) stem.

Iris fosteriana (iii). It is to be found about rocky hillsides in Afghanistan. It resembles the Xiphium group in its bulb, for it forms few fleshy roots, while its flowers and leaves resemble those of the Spanish iris. It blooms in March and has horizontal standards of bright mauve and pale-yellow falls, waved at the margin. The flowers are borne on a 12-in (30-cm) stem.

Iris graeberiana (iii). A rare native of Turkestan, bearing sheaths of leaves 12 in (30 cm) high and, from the axils, small flowers of silvery-mauve with cobalt-blue shading on the falls.

Iris histrio (i). Native of Syria and the Lebanon, it is usually the first of the reticulata group to bloom, after showing colour in January and bearing lilac-blue flowers with a white crest on the falls, on a 6-in (15-cm) stem.

Iris histrioides (i). One of the best of winter-flowering bulbs, coming into bloom as soon as the snow begins to melt and bearing its flowers before the leaves appear. It is tolerant of all weathers and, growing only 4 in (10 cm) tall, it is at its loveliest in pans in the alpine house or where planted in sunny pockets about the rock garden. It should be planted where the bulbs can be ripened (baked) by the summer sun, such as in a narrow border beneath the eaves of a house and facing south. The flowers are of bright ultramarine, spotted with black with a white crest on the falls. The form *major* bears larger flowers.

Iris juncea (ii). A delightful little Spanish iris from southern Spain and northern Africa, it blooms during June and is followed by rush-like leaves which grow 12 in (30 cm) long. The flower is of deepest golden-yellow, borne on a 12-in (30-cm) stem, and it has a powerful scent which is retained long after it is cut and placed in water.

Iris kolpakowskiana (i). Native of Turkestan, it is rare in the wild and in cultivation, for it is difficult to manage. It bears violet-scented flowers in March before the deeply channelled linear leaves have appeared. The flowers are borne on a 3-in (7·5-cm) stem, the standards being of soft lilac-purple, the falls of rich purple with a golden crest and purple veining.

Iris magnifica (syn. *I. vicaria*) (iii). Native of Turkestan, it is one of the finest of the Junos and one of the tallest, attaining a height of 2 ft (60 cm) with as many as 10 flowers appearing in April in rapid succession from the axils of the leaves. They are palest lavender with an orange crest on the falls.

Iris orchioides (iii). This beautiful orchid iris, found about the hillsides of Bokhara, has bulbs as large as a hen's egg. It has broad bright-green leaves from the axils of which are produced flowers with pale-yellow standards and deep yellow falls, with an orange crest at the centre. The variety *sulphurea* is pale uniform yellow; and *coerulea*, palest blue with a yellow ridge on the falls.

Iris persica (iii). It was depicted on the first plate of the *Botanical Magazine* in 1787, since when it has been growing in gardens but often with difficulty. It makes a bulb the size of a bantam's egg from which arises a stem 6 in (15 cm) high with two or three narrow leaves. The flowers appear in February and measure 3 in (7·5 cm) across. They are violet-scented and of an unusual shade of greenish-blue with a purple blotch at the tips of the falls and a yellow crest. For it to be long-living and free-flowering the bulbs must be grown where the summer sunshine can ripen them, but where the garden is exposed and the soil badly drained it is best grown in pans in the alpine house.

Iris reticulata (i). It is to be found on mountainous slopes from the Caucasus to northern Persia and as a pot plant and in the garden is one of the loveliest, being hardy and bearing its flowers of exquisite form and perfume from February until April, while the linear leaves will grow no taller than the flowers. The plants increase rapidly and bloom year after year. They are dark-purple flowers, like tiny Dutch irises held on 6-in (15-cm) stems. They are enhanced by an orange flash on the falls. There are several lovely varieties:

CANTAB. It bears flowers of brightest Cambridge blue with a brilliant orange crest on the falls.

CLAIRETTE. The result of a cross with *I. bakeriana*, it has standards of sky blue and falls of deeper blue with a white flake.

HARMONY. The flowers have both substance and durability and are of rich pansy purple with a central orange ridge on the falls.

JEANNINE. It bears sky-blue flowers of great clarity of colour.

J. S. DIJT. The earliest to bloom, the scented blooms are of reddish purple.

PAULINE. It bears a handsome bloom of brightest purple with a large white crest on the falls.

PURPLE GEM. Early to bloom, the standards are of ruby-purple, the falls purple-black spotted with white.

ROYAL BLUE. The blooms are large and of uniform Oxford blue.

VIOLET BEAUTY. The standards are of bright Parma violet, the falls having a conspicuous orange crest.

WENTWORTH. Sweetly scented and early, the blooms are of brightest royal purple, the falls crested with gold.

Iris sindjarensis (syn. *I. aucheri*) (iii). A beautiful species, native of the Djebel Sindjar Mountains of Mesopotamia, with long pear-shaped bulbs and leaves which narrow to a point. From the axils are borne, early in March, vanilla-scented flowers of a unique shade of slate-blue, the falls having a creamy-white crest veined with green.

Iris stenophylla (i). Native of the Cilician Taurus, it grows 4 in (10 cm) high and forms a tuft of grass-like leaves which are 2 in (5 cm) tall when the flowers appear in March. The blooms measure 4 in (10 cm) across and are of purple-mauve; the falls having a central line of yellow and a blotch of velvety black near the tips.

Iris tingitana (ii). This beautiful iris of Tangiers with its ovoid pointed bulbs, linear leaves and widely splayed standards and falls has been used in the breeding of the Dutch irises. The flowers appear in March and are borne on 2-ft (60-cm) stems. They are of deep blue, the falls having a bright-yellow keel. Slightly tender, it is advisable to grow it in pots under glass in all but those gardens enjoying a mild winter climate.

Iris vartani (i). It is found growing about the rocky hillsides around Nazareth and has ovoid heavily ridged bulbs from which arise horny-tipped leaves and flowers which measure 4 in (10 cm) across. Following a warm, dry summer, the first flowers will appear in October and continue through winter. They are of a lovely shade of lavender-blue, the falls having a white crest, while the claw is spotted with black. The flowers are borne on a 6-in (15-cm) stem and are almond scented. There is a white form, *alba*.

Iris willmottiana (iii). Native of the higher mountainous regions of Turkestan, it is rare in cultivation and in the wild. It has a large round bulb and blooms before the end of February at a height of 6 in (15 cm). The flowers are 2 in (5 cm) across and are palest blue, the falls being flecked with darker blue.

Iris winogradowii (i). It grows near the Black Sea and is similar to *I. histrioides* in habit and flowering time but its flowers are of a lovely shade of soft creamy-yellow, the falls having a central ridge of bright orange.

Iris xiphioides (ii). It is a parent of the English iris, though it is native of north-western Spain and the Pyrenees. It has also been used in the breeding of the Dutch hybrids. The bulbs have rough brown coats, while the leaves are broader than those of the Spanish iris. It blooms in July, being the latest in the section, its flowers of deepest blue having a golden keel. Varieties of English iris:

BLUE GIANT. The standards are deep purple-blue; the falls of similar colouring with a white blotch.

MANSFIELD. The blooms are of bright uniform wine purple.

MONT BLANC. Plant it with Mansfield for it has flowers of contrasting pure white.

Iris xiphium (ii). The Spanish iris, native of southern Spain, southern France and north-western Africa and parent (with *I. tingitana*) of the Dutch and

Spanish irises. It blooms in April and May, bearing its deep-purple flowers with a yellow crest on the falls, on slender 2-ft (60-cm) stems. Varieties of Spanish iris:

BLUE ANGEL. The flowers are rich mid-blue with a yellow blotch on the falls.

CAJANUS. A late-flowering variety of rich golden yellow, to bridge the gap between the Spanish and English irises.

CANARY BIRD. The finest of its colour, being bright canary yellow with an orange blotch on the falls and waved margins.

LA RECONNAISSANCE. It bears a flower of unusual colouring for bulbous irises, the blooms being of rich bronze with golden blotches.

PRINCE HENRY. A handsome variety with standards of purple-brown and falls of rich bronzey-brown with a striking golden blotch.

Iris xiphium

Varieties of Dutch iris:

BLUE CHAMPION. It has the largest flower of all irises in this group, being of clear cornflower blue with a yellow blotch on the falls.

BLUE TRIUMPHATOR. A superb variety and not one commonly grown. The blooms are of pure sky blue, delicately perfumed.

DOMINATOR. A Wedgwood 'sport' and equally good for forcing, bearing flowers of deepest blue.

GOLDEN HARVEST. This is the rich yellow iris, so plentiful in florists' shops during May.

IMPERATOR. The most widely grown of all Dutch irises, the colour being indigo blue.

JEANNE D'ARC. A variety of strong constitution, the bloom being of a rich Jersey cream.

LEMON QUEEN. The pale lemon-yellow blooms are of largest size.

PROFESSOR BLAAUW. The blooms are of rich gentian blue.

ROYAL YELLOW. The large refined blooms have standards of deep buttercup yellow with falls of sunflower yellow.

WEDGWOOD. Although always classed as a Dutch hybrid, it is a hybrid of *I. tingitana*. It bears pale-blue flowers and is the earliest blooming of all in this section.

WHITE PERFECTION. An outstanding white with the flowers held on stems 28 in (70 cm) in length.

IXIA (Iridaceae)

A genus of 45 species, native of southern Africa and taking its name from *ixia*, bird-lime, the reference being to the sticky juice present in the stems. The globose corms are either smooth or covered in a tunic of netted fibres. The erect sword-like leaves number five or six while the flowers are borne in a loose spike and are spirally arranged. They are salver-shaped with equal-spreading lobes. The style is usually longer than the perianth tube. Closely related to *Sparaxia* and *Tritonia*, in its native land it is known as the corn lily, being common in corn fields. It is hardy only in the mildest parts of the British Isles and North America; elsewhere it should be grown indoors and treated in the same way as freesias.

Culture. In warm, sheltered gardens, the corms may be planted out in October when they will bloom in June. Plant 4 in (10 cm) deep and 6 in (15 cm) apart, into a well-drained sandy soil into which some peat or leaf mould has been incorporated. To guard against frost damage, cover the ground with bracken (or decayed leaves) after planting. Remove this early in spring.

The corms may be planted into a sandy compost in a cold frame, the lights being closed until growth commences early in spring. They are then removed. Or plant in beds 3 ft (90 cm) wide, made at the base of a wall and in full sunlight. This is essential, for in shade the flowers will not open. Over the bed, frame lights may be reared against the wall and will keep away frost and excess winter moisture.

Ixias are lime lovers, and in soils of an acid nature lime rubble should be incorporated before planting. They are long-lasting flowers in the open and when cut and placed in water, but their cutting calls for judgement, for if cut too soon, before the blooms open, they may never do so, while those which may open too far have a habit of closing if remaining out of water for any length of time. For this reason, ixias are not grown commercially.

If growing indoors, plant in October in pots or deep boxes containing a sandy loam. Set the corms 2 in (5 cm) deep and 3 in (7·5 cm) apart, wintering them in a frame where they are plunged in ashes. Transfer to the greenhouse when growth begins towards the end of the year. In a temperature of 50° F (10° C) they will come into bloom during April or early in May, but, like freesias, they should be watered with care and given ample ventilation. As they produce their flowers on wiry stems 16 in (40 cm) tall, it is advisable to give them support by inserting thin canes around the pots or boxes and to which is fastened green twine. After the foliage begins to die down, withhold water and dry off so that the plants are given a rest period during late summer and autumn.

Propagation. Named varieties may be perpetuated by the removal of cormlets which are detached when the older corms are repotted in autumn. They are planted in pans or boxes of sandy compost, ½ in (1·25 cm) deep and 1 in (2·5 cm) apart and grown on undisturbed for two years, after which they may be planted in the compost in which they will bloom in 12 months time.

Ixias are readily raised from seed. Sow in spring, in boxes containing the John Innes compost. Water from the base, and after germination protect the seedlings from the sun. They should be left undisturbed, watering only when necessary for two years, when they are transplanted to deep boxes or pots in which they will bloom in two more years.

Species and Varieties. *Ixia maculata*. Known as the golden ixia, for its flowers are of deepest golden-yellow, it has erect sword-shaped leaves and bears its flowers in a 5- to 17-flowered spike. The variety *ochroleuca* has creamy yellow flowers with a brown ring around the centre. *I. maculata* is the hardiest species and increases rapidly in a sandy soil in a sunny position.

Ixia odorata. Native of Cape Province, where it is common around Hout Bay, flowering there in October—in June in Europe. Its leaves are arranged fan-wise, while it bears its pale-yellow flowers in a 7- to 17-flowered spike on a 16-in (40-cm) stem. The flowers are heavily scented.

Ixia polystachya. A vigorous species, growing 2 ft (60 cm) tall, with long sword-shaped leaves and bearing its sweetly scented flowers of creamy-white in a dense many-flowered spike. The flowers have a pale-blue eye, while there is also a yellow form, *flavescens*.

Ixia viridiflora. The green ixia, it has sword-like leaves arranged fan-wise and it bears on a 12-in (30-cm) stem a 5- to 15-flowered spike, the star-like flowers being brightest green, shaded Prussian blue and with a purple eye to provide an effect of great brilliance. It requires a well-drained soil and a warm situation for it to be long-living.

IXIOLIRION (Amaryllidaceae)

A genus of three species, native of central Asia, with grey-green linear leaves and bearing funnel-shaped flowers on slender 16-in (40-cm) stems. Closely resembling *Alstroemeria*, though not as showy, it requires similar culture, being not quite hardy in the cooler parts of the British Isles and northern Europe. It is known as the blue Altai or ixia lily.

Ixia viridiflora

Culture. It blooms from April until June and the bulbs should be planted outdoors in September, 6 in (15 cm) deep and 6 in (15 cm) apart in a well-drained sandy soil. Select a place at the base of a wall or a sunny border, or make a raised bed which will allow winter moisture to drain away quickly. A warm, sunny position should be chosen and into the soil dig some decayed manure to a depth of at least 12 in (30 cm) for, like *Alstroemeria*, the plants are heavy feeders. If it is possible to place a frame light over the bulbs in December, this will provide valuable protection against excess moisture. In all but the coldest parts, however, the plants will survive without protection, though they will appreciate a covering of bracken or decayed leaves.

Propagation. By removal of offsets in spring after the bulbs have flowered. These are planted one to a 3-in (7·5-cm) pot containing a mixture of loam, decayed manure and sand and grown on for two years, when they are planted out. They will come into bloom in two more years.

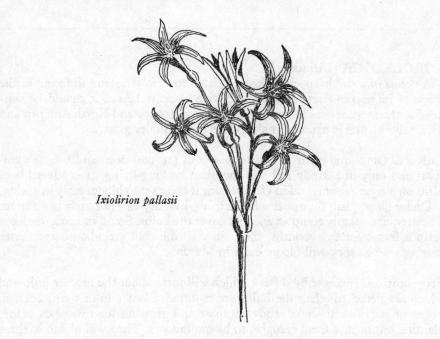

Ixiolirion pallasii

Species and Varieties. *Ixiolirion kolpakowskianum.* Native of central Asia where it grows up to an altitude of 6,000 ft, it has tufts of grey-green grass-like leaves and in April bears numerous bluish-white flowers on a slender 12-in (30-cm) stem.

Ixiolirion montanum. Found near the Caspian Sea, it forms a long-necked ovoid bulb and tufts of grass-like leaves. The flowers are pale lilac with the six reflexing segments having three to five ribs of darker lilac. The variety *ledebouri*, found only in Afghanistan, bears deep porcelain-blue flowers in a graceful umbel, while *pallasii*, which blooms in June at a height of 15 in (30 cm), has violet-blue flowers shaded with pink.

K

KOROLKOWIA (Liliaceae)

A genus of a single species, closely related to *Fritillaria* and differing in the shape of its nectar-secreting glands. Native of central Asia, it should be confined to the more sheltered gardens of northern Europe and North America and where the garden is exposed it should be grown under glass.

Culture. Outdoors, plant in short grass, 4 in (10 cm) deep and 6 in (15 cm) apart and only in a sandy soil will the plant be long-living. It is advisable to plant on a layer of sand and in October, for it comes into bloom early in spring.

Under glass, plant four or five bulbs to a 5-in (12·5-cm) pot early in autumn. They require a sandy compost and just cover the bulbs. Stand the pots outdoors or in a frame for two months, then move to the cold greenhouse and water sparingly when they will bloom early in March.

Propagation. Increase by offsets, which will form about the mother bulb and which are detached when the bulbs are repotted. Plant 1 in (2·5 cm) apart in boxes or pots containing a sandy compost and grow on for two years before planting out or into fresh compost to bloom indoors. They will bloom in three years.

Species. *Korolkowia sewerzowii.* Native of central Asia, it has round stems 12 in (30 cm) tall and has glaucous stem leaves. The drooping bell-shaped flowers are borne 4 to 10 to each stem and are coloured greenish-yellow on the inside, plum-purple on the outside with veining of olive green. The variety *bicolor* has a brown blotch at the base of each segment.

L

LACHENALIA (Liliaceae)

A genus of 65 species, native of southern Africa and taking their name from that of the eighteenth-century Swiss botanist, Werner de la Chenal. The plants are closely related to hyacinth and have tunicated ovoid bulbs and handsome fleshy leaves of bright green or grey-green, sometimes spotted with red or yellow. The tubular flowers are borne on an erect leafless scape as a many-flowered raceme and are drooping, the three inner segments being longer than the three outer and united at the base. It is named Cape cowslip or leopard lily from the markings on its foliage and requires similar culture to other Cape lilies. It is not quite hardy in the colder parts of Europe and North America, yet it is a plant of easy culture.

Culture. It may be grown in the open, that most suitable being *L. nelsonii*, the first hybrid, raised by Rev. John Nelson, which blooms early in summer. It requires a warm border and a sandy soil enriched with decayed manure. Plant the bulbs in September, 4 in (10 cm) deep and 8 in (20 cm) apart and protect them from frost by covering with decayed leaves. If undisturbed, the plants will eventually form large clumps.

Mostly late winter- and early spring-flowering, the plants may be grown in a warm greenhouse or garden room or are attractive growing in hanging baskets indoors. Plant early August in pots or pans of 5-in (12·5-cm) diameter to accommodate six bulbs and use a compost made up of 2 parts fibrous loam and 1 part each decayed manure and leaf mould, to which has been added a sprink-ling of coarse sand. Just cover the tops of the bulbs and water in, then stand in a frame or on a greenhouse bench, watering only when the compost begins to dry out. A minimum winter temperature of 46° F (8° C) is all that is necessary, and in the warmer parts of the British Isles, where frost is rarely experienced, artificial heat is not required.

Towards the year end, the plants will begin to make growth, and when the flower stems appear water once each week with dilute liquid manure until the foliage begins to die back towards the end of summer. Then withhold moisture gradually and dry off, placing the pots on their side under the greenhouse bench or in a shaded frame until time for repotting in August, or in September for the later-flowering species. The plants will resent forcing conditions and must be grown as cool as possible. With most types, it is necessary only to exclude frost, but gentle heat may be required to bring *L. pendula* into bloom for Christmas. With their dainty habit and freedom of flowering, lachenalias are among the most accommodating of all plants for the amateur's greenhouse or garden room.

Propagation. The plants will multiply rapidly, and each autumn, when re-potting, the old bulbs will have formed numerous offsets. These are detached and planted one to a 3-in (7·5-cm) pot containing a sandy compost, in which they are grown on for two years until reaching flowering size. They are then shaken from the pots and replanted in pans, six bulbs to each.

Lachenalias are readily raised from seed, which is black and glossy and should be sown in pans containing the John Innes compost. Sow in April, just covering the seed, and do not allow it to become dry. It will germinate in about four weeks. When the seedlings are large enough to handle, transplant to 3-in (7·5-cm) pots, one to each, and grow on, shielding from the midsummer sun-shine and keeping the compost moist. In 12 months transfer to larger pots containing a compost similar to that suggested for flowering-size bulbs and in which they will remain for two years. It is necessary to dry off and rest the bulbs each summer. They will reach flowering size in three or four years from sowing.

Species and Varieties. *Lachenalia glaucina*. Found at the Cape, where it blooms in August, in spring under glass in Europe. It has two strap-like leaves almost 12 in (30 cm) long and bears sweetly scented flowers of pale blue, pink, mauve and green in large racemes. The flowers are formed horizontally. The variety *parviflora* has smaller flowers in various shades of purple and blue.

Lachenalia mutabilis. Native of Natal, it blooms early in spring under glass, the pale blue of the unopened bells contrasting with the yellow of the older flowers. The flowers, which are borne on 9-in (22·5-cm) stems, have brilliant-blue tips.

Lachenalia orchioides. Present on mountainous slopes at the Cape, it has two spreading strap-shaped leaves and bears on a 9-in (22·5-cm) stem pale-yellow flowers, shaded blue at the base and sweetly scented. It blooms early in spring.

Lachenalia pearsonii. A hybrid, the two leaves being heavily spotted, likewise the flower stems, which attain a height of 18 in (45 cm) and are valuable for cutting. The unopened flowers are bronzey-brown, opening to yellow, and are edged with claret.

Lachenalia pendula. In its native South Africa it is found in sandy places, usually near the sea, and produces a large bulb. The two leaves grow erect and are bright green and unspotted, while the tubular flowers of vermilion and pale yellow tipped with green are pendulous and are borne in a many-flowered raceme. In bloom from Christmas until spring.

Lachenalia rubida. Found in sandy places by the sea at the Cape, it grows 8 in (20 cm) tall with two purple-spotted leaves which develop after flowering. The flowers are crimson, shaded yellow and tipped with purple.

Lachenalia tricolor (syn. *L. aloides*). Native of Natal and the Cape, it has broad fleshy leaves spotted with purple above, and it bears its tubular, pendulous blooms in a many-flowered raceme on a 12-in (30-cm) stem. The flowers are yellow, shaded green at the base, above which is a crimson band. The stem and the foliage is marked with purple. The variety *aurea*, often classed as a separate species, bears flowers of golden-orange, while *nelsonii* bears yellow flowers tinged with green and is the best form for planting outdoors.

LAPEYROUSIA (Iridaceae)

A genus of about 60 species, native of tropical and southern Africa and named after the French botanist Picot de la Peyrouse. The small conical corms are flat at the base and covered in a tunic of hard fibres. The one or two lower leaves are narrow and grass-like, the upper leaf being shorter and partly sheathing. The flowers are borne in a small spike at the end of a shortly branched stem. The perianth tube is cylindrical with the stamens inserted at the top. The star-shaped flowers are divided into six equal segments. Only two or three species have any garden value and in northern Europe and North America should be confined to those gardens which are free from winter frosts; otherwise grow them under glass.

Culture. Closely related to *Ixia*, it requires similar treatment. If growing out-doors, plant the corms 4 in (10 cm) deep and 6 in (15 cm) apart in a light sandy soil. Growing only 6 in (15 cm) tall, several species are suitable for the rock garden, where they enjoy the protection afforded by the stones just as where growing in granite crevices in the wild. Plant in April to bloom in August. When established, it soon makes a large clump.

Indoors, plant in March, six corms to a pan or pot filled with sandy compost. Place in a frame and give little moisture until growth begins, then water only when necessary. When the flower buds have formed, the pans may be trans-ferred to a sunny window and the flower spikes supported by small twigs. After flowering, dry off gradually and, for their winter rest, place in a frost-free room until spring when they are started into growth again.

Propagation. It is readily raised from seed sown in April in pans or boxes con-taining a sandy compost; or sow directly into a frame. Water sparingly and allow the foliage to die down naturally in autumn. In spring, transfer to pots or pans and bring into bloom.

Species. *Lapeyrousia corymbosa.* Common on mountainous slopes near the Cape, especially Signal Hill. It forms a small corm and has long spreading leaves, waved at the edges. The flowers are blue with a white star at the centre and are borne in dense corymbs on a 6-in (15-cm) much-branched stem.

Lapeyrousia cruenta. It makes a large corm from which arise narrow sword-like leaves and a flower stem 9 in (22·5 cm) tall. The flowers are of bright carmine-red with salmon shading and with a crimson blotch at the base of the three lower segments. They are borne 6 to 10 to a spike. The flowers all face the same way and appear at regular intervals along the stem, with about 1 in (2·5 cm) space between each, the flowers being held on short footstalks. They open from the bottom upwards and are long-lasting, in bloom from early August to the end of September.

Lapeyrousia fabricii. Common on sandy flats at the Cape, it forms a small corm covered in hard fibres and has spreading leaves with bulbils in the axils. The flowers, which appear in August, are cream, often shaded with pink, and they appear in a one- to four-flowered spike on a 12-in (30-cm) stem.

Lapeyrousia fistulosa. Present at the Cape, growing in cracks among the rocks on Lion's Head and forming a small corm covered in netted fibres. The two basal leaves are prostrate, while the creamy-white flowers, shaded mauve on the reverse, are scented and are borne singly on a 4-in (10-cm) stem.

LEUCOCORYNE (Alliaceae)

A genus of five species, native of the Chilean Andes and taking its name from *leukos*, white, and *koryne*, a club, referring to the anthers. They have small ovoid tunicated bulbs or corms, like those of the freesia, and they require similar culture. Like all members of the family, the plants have a garlic-like smell, with the exception of *L. ixioides odorata*, which emits a scent of ripe plums, this being one of the few sweetly scented blue flowers. The plants have narrow, almost prostrate leaves and bear their salver-shaped flowers in small umbels. They are known as glory of the sun. The flowers have three perfect stamens and three staminodes. As they bloom early in spring, they should be given protection in the British Isles and northern Europe.

Culture. Plant the bulbs early in September, four or five to a 6-in (15-cm) pot or pan, or plant in deep boxes to provide cut bloom for the home. They require a compost made up of fibrous loam, peat and sand in equal parts. Plant 1 in (2·5 cm) deep and 2 in (5 cm) apart and place the containers in a frame for several weeks until rooting has taken place, giving only the minimum amount of moisture. Towards the year end, transfer to a greenhouse or garden room, to a temperature of about 40° F (4° C), which will exclude frost and keep the plants growing slowly. Like freesias they will not tolerate any degree of forcing and, being native of the rarefied atmosphere of the Andes, they are intolerant of close, humid conditions. Give only sufficient moisture to keep the plants growing and shade from the sunlight. They will bloom from mid-March until May. After flowering, dry off gradually and give a period of rest before repotting in September.

Spanish Iris: Summertime, Copper Star, Delph Blue, Cajanus

Ixia

Lilium hansonii

Lilium candidum

Propagation. Usually by offsets which form around the base of the bulb and which are detached when the bulbs are repotted in autumn. The offsets are planted in boxes of sandy compost and grown on for two years until reaching flowering size.

Species. *Leucocoryne ixioides odorata.* Found on grassy mountainous slopes near the foot of the Chilean Andes, it forms two feeble-looking rush-like leaves from between which arises a wand-like stalk 16 in (40 cm) tall, bearing eight or nine salver-shaped flowers of rich cobalt blue with a glistening white star-shaped centre. They are scented, like freesias, but with spicy undertones.

LEUCOJUM (Amaryllidaceae)

A genus of 12 species, distributed in parts of the British Isles, across central and southern Europe to the Crimea, with several species present in Corsica and two in Morocco. It takes its name from *leukos*, white, and *ion*, a violet, from the violet-like perfume of *L. vernum*, the spring snowflake. Resembling the snowdrop in appearance and character, they have egg-shaped tunicated bulbs of about 1-in (2·5-cm) diameter and narrow strap-like leaves. The dangling bell-shaped flowers which have green markings at the tips of the segments differ from snowdrops in that the segments are equal or almost so. Not all are hardy in the most exposed gardens of northern Europe, several species requiring a frame or cool greenhouse.

Culture. Outdoors, they need a well-drained soil into which is incorporated peat or leaf mould, together with some grit. They may be planted in full sun or partial shade such as beneath mature trees in short grass, on a bank or about the rock garden, the hardy species resembling snowdrops in that they enjoy cool conditions.

Plant the bulbs of the spring and summer snowflakes in September, or lift and divide the clumps after flowering (as for snowdrops). The autumn snowflake is planted in March and, being native of Spain and Portugal, should be given a sheltered, sunny situation. Plant 3 in (7·5 cm) deep and 6 in (15 cm) apart and in groups of a dozen or more. Leave undisturbed to multiply each year.

Indoors, plant five or six bulbs to a pan or 6-in (15-cm) pot and for this purpose the winter- and early spring-flowering species *L. vernum* and *L. hyemale* (syn. *L. nicaeënse*) are most suitable. Plant 2 in (5 cm) deep into a sandy loam and in September, standing the pots in a darkened frame or in a plunge bed until rooting has taken place. Then transfer to the cold greenhouse or home, giving sufficient moisture to keep them growing. After flowering, do not dry off but move the pots to the open and take indoors again in October. Like many of the narcissus species, the leucojums bloom better when allowed to remain in the pots for several years until they exhaust the soil.

Propagation. The usual method is to lift and divide the clumps after flowering, splitting each into tufts of four or five bulbs and replanting without delay. Or lift the clumps when the foliage has turned brown. This is removed and the soil shaken from the bulbs which are then separated and graded, the larger bulbs being replanted, the smaller bulbs grown on in boxes of sandy compost for two years until they reach flowering size, when they are planted out. Where growing from seed, plants will take four to five years to bloom and the seed is slow to germinate. Sow in a sandy compost in September, only just covering the seed and placing the container in the open entirely unprotected. Germination will usually follow a period of hard frost. The seedlings should be undisturbed for 12 months, when they are transplanted to boxes of sandy compost and grown on for two years. They are then planted out and will bloom in two more years.

Species and Varieties. *Leucojum aestivum*. The summer snowflake, it is to be found in the British Isles, in France and across central Europe to the Black Sea and Asia Minor, being present in damp meadows and on river banks. The bulbs are egg-shaped, with a long neck from which arise blunt-ended strap-like leaves 12 in (30 cm) long and of vivid green. The flowers appear from the end of April until early June and are borne in an umbel of three or four on a leafless scape up to 18 in (45 cm) long. They measure about 1 in (2·5 cm) across and are bell-shaped and drooping, the pure white segments being tipped with jade green. The variety Gravetye, discovered by William Robinson in the grounds of his home Gravetye Manor in Sussex, has larger flowers.

Leucojum autumnale. It is present in Portugal and southern Spain and in Morocco. It has small round bulbs and slender grass-like leaves as against the strap-like leaves of *L. aestivum* and *L. vernum*. For this reason it was at one time classed as *Acis autumnalis*, and those species with linear leaves are now included in the Acis group. The flowers appear before the leaves, in September, and are usually borne singly on a 9-in (22·5-cm) stem. They are bell-shaped and white, delicately shaded with pink and tipped with green. Though native of warmer climes, they are hardy in the British Isles south of the Thames. The variety *pulchellum* forms its leaves with the flowers, the latter being held on long footstalks and borne in umbels of four or five.

Leucojum hyemale (syn. *L. nicaeënse*). It is found only on the French coast between Nice and Monaco and makes a small round bulb. It produces its long grass-like leaves with the flowers, in April and May. The flowers which are usually borne singly on a 6-in (15-cm) stem are white, lightly shaded with green.

Leucojum longifolium. Native of the mountainous parts of Corsica, it has a small brown tunicated bulb and forms grass-like leaves 12 in (30 cm) long which appear with the flowers in April. The flowers are small, held on long footstalks and are borne one to three in an umbel at the end of a 9-in (22·5-cm) stem. They are small and bell-shaped and pure white.

Leucojum roseum. One of the Acis group, it is autumn-flowering, resembling

L. autumnale except that it grows no more than 4 in (10 cm) tall, while its white flowers are tinted with rose-pink. The leaves are long and threadlike and appear after the flowers, which bloom during September and October. It is native of Corsica.

Leucojum tingitanum. Native of southern Spain and north-western Africa, it resembles *L. aestivum* in its broader leaves and flowering time. The pure-white flowers are borne on a 12-in (30-cm) stem and appear in April and May.

Leucojum trichophyllum. One of the Acis group. It is native of southern Spain and Morocco and blooms during winter and early spring. In the British Isles and northern Europe, it should be grown in the cool greenhouse. It has grass-like leaves, which appear with the flowers, which are white and are borne three or four on a 9-in (22·5-cm) stem.

Leucojum vernum. The spring snowflake, native of central Europe, extending from western France to southern Poland, it is a most accommodating plant, flourishing in all parts and under all conditions. It has a round green-skinned bulb of about 1-in (2·5-cm) diameter and forms strap-like leaves 9 in (22·5 cm) long and almost 1 in (2·5 cm) broad. Its flowers appear in March (February under glass) and remain colourful until May. They are drooping and bell-shaped with broad segments 1 in (2·5 cm) long and are white, tipped with green and have a sweet perfume. The variety *carpathicum* differs in that the bells are tipped with yellow and not green.

LIBERTIA (Iridaceae)

A genus of 10 species, native of Australasia and the South American Andes and named in honour of Marie Libert, a Belgian botanist. With *Patersonia*, it is the only representative of the family known in Australia and forms a creeping rhizomatous rootstock rather than a corm. Hardy in the British Isles only in the warmer parts, it forms a tufted plant with grass-like radical leaves and bears its flowers in paniculate clusters.

Culture. Outdoors, plant with ericas and rhododendrons for it prefers an acid soil, one which is light and well-drained and well supplied with peat. Plant in September, placing the small rhizomes 3 in (7·5 cm) below the surface and 6 in (15 cm) apart. Six rhizomes planted in a group will ensure an effective display. Protect from frost by covering with bracken or by heaping ashes over them. They will bloom early in summer.

Indoors, they will grow 2 ft (60 cm) high, and several rhizomes should be planted to a 6-in (15-cm) pot, using a compost made up of loam, peat and sand in equal parts. Plant in September and stand outdoors or in a frame, covering with ashes. Towards the year end, remove to a cool greenhouse and water with care, giving sufficient only to keep the plants growing. As they make height they will need supporting by fastening twine to canes inserted around the side of the pot. Indoors they will bloom early in spring.

Propagation. By division as the plants come into new growth in spring and before the flowering stems begin to form; or by lifting the roots in April and cutting into several pieces each with a leafy shoot. After dusting the cut portion with sulphur, replant without delay.

Species. *Libertia formosa*. Found on the island of Formosa and in Chile. From its rootstock arise dark-green sword-shaped leaves 12 in (30 cm) long and gracefully recurving. The white flowers appear in May and are borne in a long tapering spike over a period of six to eight weeks.

Libertia grandiflora. Native of New Zealand, it has long grass-like leaves and on a 2-ft (60-cm) stem bears spikes of white flowers resembling Sissyrinchium.

Libertia paniculata. Present in eastern Australia and New Zealand, it forms a tuft of flat grass-like leaves and bears its pure-white flowers in loose panicles. The bracts are small and membranous.

LILIUM (Liliaceae)

A genus of about 80 species, native of the Northern Hemisphere of both the Old and New Worlds. It takes its name from the Celtic *li*, white, probably from *L. candidum*, the Madonna lily, which bears flowers of glistening white and is one of the oldest of cultivated plants. Lilies have large bulbs with overlapping

Lilium candidum with prominent scales

scales and bear their flowers in a terminal umbel on a leafy scape. The leaves are lance-shaped, arranged in whorls or irregularly, the flowers drooping or horizontal; the perianth is funnel- or bell-shaped with six spreading or recurving segments, the three inner being broader than the three outer segments. Stamens six, with brown, red or orange anthers at the end of slender filaments.

The principal areas of distribution are North America, central Europe, the

Caucasus and Asia Minor; extending to the Himalayas and east to Nepal, western China, Burma, Japan and the Philippine Islands.

No plant is so versatile. The list of species and varieties covers a flowering period from May until September; some are tall-growing, some dwarf; some are suitable for lime-free soils, others thrive in a calcareous soil. Some species enjoy shade, others a position of full sun.

For planting in the shrubbery or herbaceous border, there is no more showy plant, and there are species for all positions. From the tall-growing *L. henryi*, which reaches a height of 6 ft, to the dwarf-growing *L. chalcedonicum*, which flowers at a height of 2 ft. The border is ideal for lilies, provided it is enriched with humus, for they love to have their roots in shade and their heads in the sunlight. In a lily border, they are more striking still and their perfume will be enjoyed about the whole garden, especially in the early evening. They may be planted in autumn or spring and, except for staking and an annual top-dressing, they will need no attention for many years, though they may require shelter from wind.

For the small courtyard or for the side of an entrance or porch, lilies look most attractive when planted in tubs containing a compost into which is incorporated plenty of peat to retain moisture. Here, those bulbs growing to a height of no more than 4 ft should be used. *Lilium speciosum* or *L. tenuifolium* are suitable, likewise *L. davidii*, Maxwell so that there should be at least one lily in bloom from mid-May until September. Plant half a dozen bulbs to a large tub.

Lilies, like most bulbs, enjoy a soil in which humus is plentiful. A mixture of old mushroom-bed manure and peat is suitable, or used hops. They enjoy a moisture holding compost, rather than a rich soil, and appreciate an annual top-dressing or mulch given in autumn. Not only will this retain moisture in the soil and keep down annual weeds, but many of the lilies are stem-rooting and a top-dressing is essential to maintain a vigorous plant. Should the soil be heavy peat, coarse sand and decayed leaves should be worked in. If growing in a shrubbery in the town garden, the soil will generally be of an acid nature and plenty of lime rubble should be given and the soil prepared to a depth of 9 in (22·5 cm).

Culture. Care must be taken in handling lily bulbs prior to their planting. They are usually received packed in dry peat, and it is unwise to remove them and expose them to drying winds until ready to plant. A lily bulb has a solid base known as the basal plate, to which the roots and the fleshy scales are attached. As it is the scales which store up nutrition, it is important that they do not become shrivelled. Also, handle them with care for, unlike tulips and most other bulbs, they are not protected by a tunic or covering and the scales are easily broken.

Where the soil is heavy, the bulbs should be planted on to a layer of sand to assist drainage, while they should also be given a covering of sand before the soil is filled in. As a rule, the early summer-flowering bulbs should be planted early in autumn; those flowering in July, August and September may be planted in spring. If the soil tends to be heavy, plant all lilies in spring.

Planting depths vary. *L. davidii* should be planted 8 in (20 cm) deep, while *L. candidum* requires shallow planting. It should be set so that the top of the bulb is 1 in (2·5 cm) below the surface of the soil. Not all lily bulbs are of the

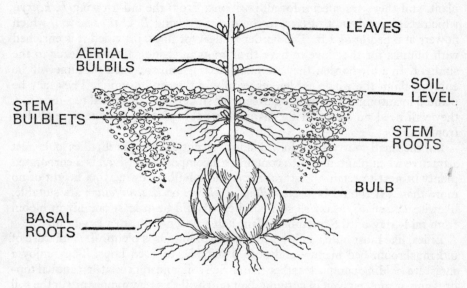

Lily bulb showing basal roots and underground stem roots

same size, but in general they should be planted two or three times deeper than their diameter, which will be about 4 in (10 cm). Plant 12 to 18 in (30 to 45 cm) apart depending upon habit. At first, the bulbs will begin to form basal roots, which provide the plant with nutrition as it begins to grow. Then, as the flowering stem lengthens, it forms underground stem-roots which provide additional nourishment, and the stems will produce further roots above soil level. It is therefore advisable to give a top-dressing up to the stem as it makes growth. This should consist of decayed manure and leaf mould.

Before planting, study the requirements of each species, for some do better in shade, others in full sun. Some are lime tolerant, while others require a lime-free soil.

If growing in an exposed situation, support by inserting canes close to each stem when 2 ft (60 cm) tall and carefully make secure with raffia.

After flowering, the blooms should be removed as soon as they die back. This

TABLE XXIV. *Culture characteristics (figures in brackets after the names denote their division of classification)*

Species	Height	In bloom
Shade-loving:		
L. amabile (9)	2 to 3 ft (60 to 90 cm)	July–August
L. auratum (9)	6 to 9 ft (1·8 to 2·7 metres)	August–September
Aurelian hybrids (6a)	4 to 5 ft (1·2 to 1·5 metres)	July–August
Bellingham hybrids (4)	5 to 6 ft (1·5 to 1·8 metres)	July–August
L. canadense (9)	3 to 4 ft (90 cm to 1·2 metres)	July–August
L. davidii (9)	4 to 5 ft (1·2 to 1·5 metres)	July–August
L. duchartrei (9)	2 to 3 ft (60 to 90 cm)	July–August
L. hansonii (9)	3 to 4 ft (90 cm to 1·2 metres)	June
L. henryi (9)	5 to 6 ft (1·5 to 1·8 metres)	August–September
L. lankongense (9)	2 to 3 ft (60 to 90 cm)	July–August
L. martagon (9)	3 to 4 ft (90 cm to 1·2 metres)	June–July
Olympic hybrids (6a)	4 to 5 ft (1·2 to 1·5 metres)	July–August
L. pardalinum (9)	4 to 5 ft (1·2 to 1·5 metres)	July–August
L. parryi (9)	4 to 5 ft (1·2 to 1·5 metres)	May–June
L. regale (9)	3 to 4 ft (90 cm to 1·2 metres)	July–August
L. rubellum (9)	12 to 16 in (30 to 40 cm)	June–July
L. speciosum (9)	3 to 6 ft (90 cm to 1·8 metres)	August
L. superbum (9)	5 to 6 ft (1·5 to 1·8 metres)	July–August
L. tigrinum (9)	4 to 5 ft (1·2 to 1·5 metres)	August–September
L. wardii (9)	3 ft (90 cm)	July–August
Sun-loving:		
L. brownii (9)	3 to 4 ft (90 cm to 1·2 metres)	July–August
L. carniolicum (9)	2 to 3 ft (60 to 90 cm)	May–June
L. chalcedonicum (9)	3 ft (90 cm)	July
L. dauricum (9)	2 ft (60 cm)	July–August
L. pomponium (9)	3 ft (90 cm)	June
L. pumilum (9)	1 to 2 ft (30 to 60 cm)	May–June
Lime tolerant:		
L. amabile (9)	2 to 3 ft (60 to 90 cm)	July–August
L. canadense (9)	3 ft (90 cm)	July–August
L. candidum (9)	3 to 4 ft (90 cm to 1·2 metres)	June–July
L. cernuum (9)	1 to 2 ft (30 to 60 cm)	June–July
L. chalcedonicum (9)	3 ft (90 cm)	July–August
L. concolor (9)	1 to 2 ft (30 to 60 cm)	May–June
L. croceum (9)	3 to 4 ft (90 cm to 1·2 metres)	June–July

Table XXIV—*Continued*

Species	Height	In bloom
Lime tolerant—(contd.)		
L. davidii (9)	5 to 6 ft (1·5 to 1·8 metres)	July–August
L. hansonii (9)	3 to 4 ft (90 cm to 1·2 metres)	June
Harlequin hybrids (1c)	4 to 5 ft (1·2 to 1·5 metres)	June–July
L. henryi (9)	5 to 6 ft (1·5 to 1·8 metres)	August–September
L. humboldtii (9)	4 to 5 ft (1·2 to 1·5 metres)	July
L. lankongense (9)	2 to 3 ft (60 to 90 cm)	July–August
L. martagon (9)	3 to 4 ft (90 cm to 1·2 metres)	June–July
Mid-Century hybrids (1a)	2 to 3 ft (60 to 90 cm)	June–July
L. monadelphum (9)	3 to 4 ft (90 cm to 1·2 metres)	June
Olympic hybrids (6)	4 to 5 ft (1·2 to 1·5 metres)	July
L. pumilum (a)	1 to 2 ft (30 to 60 cm)	May–June
L. pyrenaicum (9)	2 to 3 ft (60 to 90 cm)	May–June
L. regale (9)	3 to 4 ft (90 cm to 1·2 metres)	July–August
L. sargentiae (9)	3 to 4 ft (90 cm to 1·2 metres)	August
L. testaceum (9)	4 to 5 ft (1·2 to 1·5 metres)	July
L. tigrinum (9)	4 to 5 ft (1·2 to 1·5 metres)	August–September
Prefer lime-free soil:		
L. amabile (9)	2 to 3 ft (60 to 90 cm)	July–August
L. auratum (9)	6 to 9 ft (1·8 to 2·7 metres)	August–September
L. pardalinum (9)	4 to 5 ft (1·2 to 1·5 metres)	July–August
L. superbum (9)	5 to 6 ft (1·5 to 1·8 metres)	July–August
Suitable for the wild garden:		
Aurelian hybrids (6a)	4 to 5 ft (1·2 to 1·5 metres)	July–August
Bellingham hybrids (4)	5 to 6 ft (1·5 to 1·8 metres)	July–August
L. canadense (9)	3 to 4 ft (90 cm to 1·2 metres)	July–August
L. hansonii (9)	3 to 4 ft (90 cm to 1·2 metres)	June
L. henryi (9)	5 to 6 ft (1·5 to 1·8 metres)	August–September
L. pardalinum (9)	4 to 5 ft (1·2 to 1·5 metres)	July–August
L. pyrenaicum (9)	2 to 3 ft (60 to 90 cm)	May–June
L. rubellum (9)	12 to 15 in (30 to 37·5 cm)	June
L. speciosum (9)	3 to 6 ft (90 cm to 1·8 metres)	August
L. testaceum (9)	4 to 5 ft (1·2 to 1·5 metres)	July

will prevent them from seeding, which may shorten the life of the bulb. Remove only the bloom, so that the stem and leaves may continue to play their part in nourishing the bulb. When the stems have died back in autumn, remove them with care and top-dress with a mixture of finely riddled loam, leaf mould and decayed manure. If severe frost threatens, cover the ground with bracken or leaves, which must be removed when frost has departed.

Growing in Pots. Indoors, many species and varieties make admirable pot plants for greenhouse or garden room but they require plenty of light. Many of the hardy garden lilies may be grown under cool conditions, when they will bloom early in summer and here they may be seen to perfection, free from rain

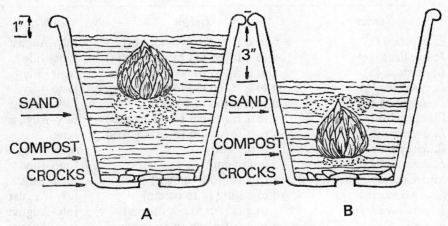

Pot culture of lilies: (A) basal rooting (B) Stem rooting

marks, while many will scent the greenhouse with their perfume. *L. longiflorum* and *L. candidum* are both grown in large quantities for the Easter trade in cut bloom and require to be grown in a temperature of 60° F (16° C). Their culture is usually in the hands of specialist growers.

Large pots are necessary for all lilies and, as they form stem roots, ample space must be allowed for top-dressing as growth progresses. Rather than plant one bulb to each small pot, it is better to use a large pot and to plant three or four bulbs in each. Deep planting and constant top-dressing is the secret of success with *L. longiflorum*, while correct drainage and a moisture-holding compost is essential for success with all indoor lilies. The pots should be well 'crocked' and 4 in (10 cm) of compost should be placed over the crocks. This should be composed of turf loam passed through a sieve, to which is added 1 part each of peat and sand. Do not use manure. If the bulbs are just covered with compost, there will be a 4-in (10-cm) space to be filled up as they make growth. For Easter- and early summer-flowering, the bulbs are potted in October and stood in a cold frame until the end of the year. The lights should be covered with sacking to keep out frost. In introducing lilies to a warm greenhouse or room, this must be done gradually.

After flowering the bulbs should be slowly dried off, bearing in mind that more bulbs are spoilt through giving insufficient care at this time than through any other cause. Water should be gradually withheld until the foliage has turned completely yellow. The bulbs should then be removed and placed in boxes of peat in a cool, dry room until spring, when they may be planted in the border. A 20-cm bulb should be used for indoor cultivation.

TABLE XXV. *Lilies suitable for pot culture*

Species	Height	In bloom
L. auratum (9)	6 to 9 ft (1·8 to 2·7 metres)	July–August
L. candidum (9)	3 to 4 ft (90 cm to 1·2 metres)	June–July
L. cernuum (9)	1 to 2 ft (30 to 60 cm)	June–July
L. croceuum (9)	3 to 4 ft (90 cm to 1·2 metres)	June–July
L. dauricum (9)	2 to 3 ft (60 to 90 cm)	July–August
Fiesta hybrids (1c)	3 to 4 ft (90 cm to 1·2 metres)	July–August
L. hansonii (9)	3 to 4 ft (90 cm to 1·2 metres)	June
L. longiflorum (9)	3 ft (90 cm)	April–May
L. maculatum (9)	12 in (30 cm)	June–July
Mid-Century hybrids (1a)	2 to 3 ft (60 to 90 cm)	June–July
L. nepalense (9)	18 to 24 in (45 to 60 cm)	July–August
L. pardalinum (9)	4 to 5 ft (1·2 to 1·5 metres)	July–August
L. regale (9)	3 to 4 ft (90 cm to 1·2 metres)	July–August
L. rubellum (9)	12 to 15 in (30 to 45 cm)	June
L. speciosum (9)	3 to 6 ft (90 cm to 1·8 metres)	August
L. testaceum (9)	4 to 5 ft (1·2 to 1·5 metres)	July

Propagation. Lilies are among the easiest of bulbous plants to propagate, some species coming into bloom within two years, e.g. *L. amabile*. They may be propagated:

(i) By division of established clumps, separating the bulbs as for narcissus. This may be done in autumn, or in spring if the soil is heavy, though autumnal lifting is preferable and is necessary for *L. candidum*. The soil should be carefully scraped from about the base of the stems as they die back. Then carefully lift with a garden fork and divide them by hand so as not to damage the scales. If it is possible to replant at once, do so for in this way the scales will not shrivel. Handle the bulbs with care for if the scales are damaged, the bulb will lose vitality. Those bulbs with loose scales, e.g. *L. amabile*, are particularly liable to damage.

(ii) By bulbils which appear at the axils of the leaves. These are detached early in autumn when ripe and planted in shallow drills in the open ground, in a frame or in boxes 3 in (7·5 cm) deep. An 'open' compost should be used and the drills lined with peat. Plant 1 in (2·5 cm) deep and 2 in (5 cm) apart and leave for two years before disturbing, removing any flowers which may form. They may then be planted into their flowering quarters. While growing in summer, do not allow the bulbils to lack moisture.

(iii) By scales. These are removed from the bulbs in autumn and placed flat on a layer of sphagnum moss, peat and sterilised loam (made moist) in a seed pan. Cover with compost and keep moist. The pans may be placed in the window of a warm room or in a frame. Plump broad scales should be used and these will produce from one to four bulbils at the base of each scale. As soon as they have formed roots, remove and replant into 3-in (7·5-cm) pots containing sterilised loam and coarse sand in equal parts. This will be in about 12 weeks after the scales are planted but they may be induced to form bulbils more quickly if grown in a propagator and in a temperature of 65° F (18° C).

(iv) From seed. By this method a virus-free stock may be inexpensively formed, but the plants will take longer to come into bloom. *L. longiflorum*, however, will bloom within 18 months of sowing.

For saving seed, the pods are removed when brown, just before they open. Place those of each species into a small box to complete the drying process, then after shaking the seeds from the pods, sow in boxes or pans containing the John Innes compost or in raised beds in the open. Sow thinly, just sprinkling the seed with compost. When the surface is dry, water from the base so that excessive moisture does not come into contact with the germinating seed. Some lilies— e.g. *L. longiflorum*, *L. concolor*, *L. davidii*—germinate rapidly, while others, e.g. *L. auratum*, may take a year or more. If there is no sign of a cotyledon for some time, it should not be thought that germination has failed.

Where sowing in boxes or pans, the seedlings will be ready to transplant when they have grown 1 in (2·5 cm) above the surface of the compost, and this is done with a smooth-ended dibber, taking care not to damage the roots. They should be moved to 3-in (7·5-cm) pots containing a compost made up of sterilised loam, peat and coarse sand in equal parts. The young plants may be grown on in a frame, shielded from the summer sunlight and kept moist.

If the seed is sown outdoors, it is preferable to allow the seedlings to remain for 18 months before removing to trenches of prepared compost, where they will remain for another 12 months.

Species and Varieties. The classification of lilies as adopted by the Royal Horticultural Society and the North American Lily Society is followed. Approximate flowering times are given at the end of the description of each variety or selected clone.

DIVISION 1. ASIATIC HYBRIDS. *Subdivision 1a.* Lilies with upright flowers, borne singly or in umbels. Most are stem rooting and should be planted 4 to 5 in (10 to 12·5 cm) deep and about 15 in (37·5 cm) apart, either in sun or dappled shade. Lilies of this section are of compact habit. They are the Mid-century hybrids raised by Mr Jan de Graaf at the Oregon Bulb Farm, U.S.A.

CINNABAR. It may be forced or grown in a cool greenhouse and does well outdoors, bearing its cinnabar-red flowers on a 2-ft (60-cm) stem. June.

CROESUS. The large goblet-shaped blooms are of brilliant golden-yellow and possess great substance. A hybrid of vigour and freedom of flowering growing 3 ft (90 cm) tall. June to July.

DESTINY. A free-flowering lily bearing blooms of soft lemon-yellow with dark brown contrasting spots. It grows 3 ft (90 cm) tall. June.

ENCHANTMENT. A vigorous and easy grower, good under glass and in the garden, the large cup-shaped flowers, borne on 30-in (75-cm) stems, being of bright nasturtium-red with the petals attractively reflexed. June.

HARMONY. One of the finest of this section, growing 30 in (75 cm) tall and bearing its orange flowers in large umbels.

JOAN EVANS. The latest to bloom of the Mid-Century hybrids, it bears six to nine flowers on each stem. They are of brightest yellow spotted with maroon. July.

RUBY. Of compact habit, growing only 20 in (50 cm) tall, it bears bright scarlet flowers amidst an abundance of rich deep-green foliage. June.

Subdivision 1b. Here, the flowers face outwards, otherwise they are similar in habit and need the same culture as group 1a.

BRANDYWINE. It grows 3 ft (90 cm) tall, the flowers having broad petals of great substance and of rich orange-red with tiny spots of blood red. June.

CORSAGE. It grows 3 ft (90 cm) tall and is one of the most attractive of lilies, bearing 12 or more flowers on each stem and of a lovely shade of creamy-yellow shading out to pink at the petal edges. June to July.

FIRE KING. Of vigorous habit, it bears its flowers in generous umbels of 20 or more. They are of bright orange-red spotted with purple. July.

ORANGE TRIUMPH. It bears large bell-shaped flowers of orange-yellow (spotted with purple at the centre) in umbels of 10 to 12 on 2-ft (60-cm) stems. June.

PAPRIKA. Excellent under glass, the flowers of rich paprika-red being of great substance and borne on 3-ft (90-cm) stems. June.

PROSPERITY. Its flowers of clear lemon yellow contrast effectively with the dark-green foliage and with red-flowering lilies growing nearby. June.

Subdivision 1c. They bear their flowers in pendant fashion on long pedicels. Otherwise as 1a and 1b, though they usually bloom early July rather than June.

AMBER GOLD. One of the finest of the hybrid lilies, growing 3 ft (90 cm) tall and bearing on each stem 10 to 12 Turk's cap blooms of buttercup-yellow spotted maroon and with broad thick-textured petals. July.

BURNISHED ROSE. A Patterson hybrid of sturdy constitution and bearing scented flowers in shades of copper, orange and rose with spots of dark crimson. June to July.

DISCOVERY. It forms a large Turk's cap with the lilac-pink petals rolled gracefully back, the centre of the flowers being pink, overlaid cream. July.

EDNA KEAN. A vigorous and free-flowering lily, bearing umbels of glowing orange-red flowers with gracefully reflexed petals. This variety possesses extreme hardiness. June.

FUGA. One of the most striking of all garden lilies, growing 3 ft (90 cm) tall and bearing as many as 20 flowers to each stem. They are of an unusual shade of burnt orange with tiny dots of black sprinkled about the broad petals. June to July.

GARNET. The large handsome flowers are of a striking shade of garnet-red, speckled with maroon, each stem carrying up to 20 blooms 4 in (10 cm) across. It has grey-green foliage. July.

LEMON QUEEN. A lily of great hardiness and easy culture, the nodding lemon-yellow flowers being spotted with brown, while each bloom measures 4 in (10 cm) across. July.

PANAMINT. The flowers measure 5 in (12·5 cm) across and are of an unusual shade of greenish-yellow, speckled with red, the gracefully reflexing petals having great substance.

PINK CHARM. One of the most compact in the section and a lily of delightful charm, bearing medium-sized blooms of clear shell-pink with a creamy-white centre and spotted with red. July.

SONATA. It grows 3 ft (90 cm) tall and bears a large Turk's cap of enormous substance, the cream base being overlaid with shades of salmon and pink and with deeper colouring at the centre, while it is lightly spotted maroon. July.

WHITE GOLD. Of compact habit, the creamy-white flowers, which open soft apricot and which are spotted with black, have a cool appearance in the heat of summer. July.

DIVISION 2. Hybrids mostly raised in Holland by van Tubergen, derived from *L. martagon* and *L. hansonii* both of which bear nodding Turk's cap flowers, held on long pedicels. They are woodland plants, requiring a neutral or slightly acid soil and dappled shade. They are stem rooting and should be planted 4 in (10 cm) deep in a soil containing humus. The flowers open in June and are borne at intervals along the stem rather than in clusters or umbels. The segments reflex gracefully.

ACHIEVEMENT. Raised from *L. martagon album*, it bears similar flowers of ivory-white, but is a plant of greater vigour, forming a large clump and growing well almost anywhere. It grows 3 ft (90 cm) tall. June.

JACQUES DIJT. It grows 5 to 6 ft (1·5 to 1·8 metres) tall, each stem carrying up to 20 blooms of elegantly recurving flowers of waxy-white, lightly spotted with purple.

JUPITER. It grows 5 to 6 ft (1·5 to 1·8 metres) tall, bearing up to 20 flowers to each stem. The blooms are of lilac-purple, spotted with brown to make this a lily of distinction. June to July.

MARHAN. A hybrid of *L. martagon album* bearing flowers of great beauty, being of rich yellowish-orange, heavily spotted with red.

MRS R. O. BACKHOUSE. Bearing up to 30 blooms on a robust stem of pyramidal habit, the flowers are of rich orange-yellow lightly spotted with purple.

QUEEN OF THE NIGHT. It grows only 2 to 3 ft (60 to 90 cm) tall and is the most compact in this section, the flowers being of crimson-maroon flecked with yellow, the reverse of the reflexed petals being of lighter colouring. June to July.

DIVISION 3. Hybrids of *L. candidum*. Like the species, they should be planted in August or September, not more than 1 in (2·5 cm) below the surface of the soil. *L.* × *testaceum* is possibly a natural hybrid of *L. candidum* and *L. chalcedonicum* which are to be found growing in the same part of the world. It is the oldest known hybrid, offspring of the two oldest known lilies and is one of the most handsome in cultivation, lime-loving like its parents. It bears 6 to 12 flowers of apricot-yellow with prominent orange anthers to each stem. They have the same wax-like appearance as *L. candidum* and the same sweet perfume. June to July.

DIVISION 4. American hybrids, derived from *L. parryi* and *L. pardalinum* and from other species of North American lilies. They may be planted in full sun or in partial shade and are semi-rhizomatous, forming only a few stem roots, these mostly at the base of the stem. They require a well-drained compost and are planted 4 in (10 cm) deep. They are tall-growing and bloom in July.

AFTERGLOW. Growing up to 6 ft (1·8 metres) tall, it bears several large flowers on each stem. They are of deepest crimson with contrasting gold shading at the centre and are heavily spotted maroon. It increases rapidly and soon makes a large clump. June to July.

BELLINGHAM HYBRIDS. A strain of immense beauty, the flowers with their gracefully reflexing petals being of various shades of garnet, maroon, orange and yellow with maroon spots and bearing up to 20 flowers on a 6-ft (1·8-metre) stem.

BUTTERCUP. It grows 3 to 4 ft (90 cm to 1·2 metres) tall and bears scented flowers of bright buttercup-yellow with large maroon markings that make this one of the finest of all yellow lilies, the blooms retaining their form for a long time.

DEL NORTE HYBRIDS. This lovely strain bears flowers in all shades of pink from shell-pink to pale burgundy and have a sweet perfume. The flowers are held on long stiff pedicels and are borne five to nine on a 5-ft (1·5-metre) stem. July.

OLIVER WYATT. A *L. parryi* hybrid, it is one of the most beautiful of all lilies, the long cylindrical buds opening to large handsome blooms of richest gold flushed with orange, the recurving petals being broad and of heavy texture. The flowers are lightly spotted with brown, while the anthers are large and of deepest orange.

SHUKSAN. One of the Bellingham hybrids and one of the best. It grows 3 ft (90 cm) tall and bears up to 20 large reflexed blooms to each stem. They are of soft orange, lightly flushed with scarlet and with maroon spots. July.

DIVISION 5. The Longiflorum hybrids. They have the qualities of *L. longiflorum* and are best suited to warm greenhouse culture. None are as yet available in the British Isles.

DIVISION 6. Trumpet hybrids. Derived from Asiatic species, excluding *L. auratum* and *L. speciosum*. They are subdivided into four groups.

Subdivision 6a. Represented by funnel-shaped flowers derived from *L. brownii* and *L. regale*. They are mostly July- to August-flowering and are borne in umbels of 12 to 20 at the end of 5- to 6-ft (1·5- to 1·8-metre) stems. They should be planted 4 in (10 cm) deep, in a soil containing plenty of humus, and they are stem-rooting. Plant in partial shade or with some shade at the base.

AURELIAN HYBRIDS. Raised by de Graaf, from *L. henryi* and the Aurelianense crosses of Mons Debras, they bear their large elegant trumpets in shades of golden-yellow, apricot and white, shaded yellow at the centre. July to August.

BLACK DRAGON. The enormous trumpets are borne 12 or more to a stem and are pure white inside, shaded purple-brown on the outside and with delicious perfume, while they are borne on long pedicels in candelabra fashion. July.

CARRERA STRAIN. A group of lilies bearing white trumpets, shaded yellow in the throat and which are pale green in the bud stage. July.

GOLDEN CLARION STRAIN. The long cylindrical buds open to large trumpets in all shades of yellow, from primrose to deep buttercup, while several are striped on the reverse with wine-red. Of vigorous habit, they grow well almost anywhere. July to August.

GREEN DRAGON. One of the most beautiful lilies, the large white trumpets are shaded in the throat and on the reverse with chartreuse green to give a cool and distinctive appearance. July to August.

LIMELIGHT. One of the Aurelian hybrids, its long elegant trumpets of soft yellow are shaded on the reverse with lime-green. When fully open, the flower measures 6 in (15 cm) across. July to August.

OLYMPIC HYBRIDS. Raised at the Oregon Bulb Farms, from *L. brownii*, *L. sargentiae* and other trumpet species, the colours range from greenish-white to soft pink, shaded on the exterior with chocolate or wine, while the flowers are sweetly scented. July.

PINK FRILLS. It is well named, for its flowers are of a refreshing shade of wild-rose pink, its petals attractively frilled and curled. August.

ROYAL GOLD. The glistening golden trumpets enhanced by the orange anthers present a picture of great beauty at the back of the border. The blooms, on long pedicels, are borne in large handsome trusses. July.

VERONA. The elegantly formed trumpets of deep fuchsia-pink have green shading in the throat and are offset to perfection by the grey-green foliage. July.

Subdivision 6b. The flowers open flat rather than trumpet-shaped and face outwards rather than downwards. They grow 5 to 6 ft (1·5 to 1·8 metres) tall and are stem-rooting. They may be planted in full sun or partial shade.

FIRST LOVE. It bears six to eight blooms in a well-balanced head, each flower being more than 6 in (15 cm) across when fully open. The outer edges of the segments are shell pink, fusing into gold, which in turn shades into green in the throat.

MME EDW. DEBRAS. The large broad-petalled blooms open flat and are of a lovely shade of soft lime green. July.

REGINA. Up to eight or nine flowers form the well-proportioned head, the blooms opening to 6 in (15 cm) across and of a lovely shade of soft sulphur yellow. August.

Subdivision 6c. Hybrids with pendant flowers, otherwise the same as 6a and 6b as to habit and culture.

GOLDEN SHOWERS STRAIN. The flowers have pointed petals and open almost star-like. They are of deepest yellow with a brown reverse, as many as 20 blooms appearing on each stem. July to August.

GOLDEN SPLENDOUR. The deepest yellow of all the Asiatic hybrids, the flowers having a maroon stripe down each petal on the reverse. August.

Subdivision 6d. Hybrids opening flat and star-like, otherwise as 6a, 6b, 6c.

BRIGHT STAR. It grows only 3 ft (90 cm) tall and bears up to 16 widely opened blooms to each stem. They are of silvery-white with a contrasting orange star at the centre of each, while the segments are attractively frilled at the margins.

SILVER SUNBURST. It bears as many as 30 flowers to each stem yet is not overcrowded. The blooms have waxy-white petals and are shaded green in the throat so that they contrast admirably with lilies of richer colouring. August.

STARDUST. It bears up to 20 flowers on a 3- to 4-ft (90-cm to 1·2-metre) stem and they are glistening white with a brilliant orange star-shaped centre and with green shading in the throat. The blooms open to more than 6 in (15 cm) across. August.

WHIRLYBIRD. It grows 3 to 4 ft (90 cm to 1·2 metres) tall, bearing large flowers which measure 8 in (20 cm) across when open. They are ivory-white, shaded and veined at the centre with orange that also runs out towards the edges of the petals. July.

DIVISION 7. Oriental hybrids. Lilies derived mostly from *L. auratum* and *L. speciosum*, the two most important species of Japan. The section is sub-divided into four main groups.

Lily: Destiny

Lily: Limelight

Lily: African Queen

Muscari azureum

Subdivision 7a. Oriental hybrids bearing trumpet-shaped flowers. Rare.

Subdivision 7b. Hybrids bearing bowl-shaped flowers derived from *L. auratum* and *L. speciosum*. August-flowering, they grow to a height of 3 to 4 ft (90 cm to 1·2 metres) and are stem-rooting. They require a soil containing plenty of leaf mould and an open, sunny situation. They are the 'queens' of all lilies, bearing flowers of exquisite beauty:

AMERICAN EAGLE. One of the most beautiful of all lilies bearing an enormous flower of pure white heavily spotted with red and shaded with green on the reverse. The ends of the petals curl over in a most attractive fashion. It is deliciously scented. August.

APOLLO. The large blooms measure 8 in (20 cm) across and are of creamy white with a deep red band down each petal, which is heavily dotted with crimson. August.

ARABIAN NIGHTS. One of the darkest and most striking of all lilies, the segments being heavily banded with blackish-mauve and of velvet-like texture. July to August.

CRIMSON BEAUTY. A lily of extreme beauty, the open flowers measuring 9 in (22·5 cm) across, the pure-white blooms having a central band of crimson to each segment, while they are lightly dotted with maroon. August.

EMPRESS OF CHINA. A lily of great dignity, the large flowers of ivory-white are spotted with crimson and shaded lime green in the throat. The flowers measure 9 in (22·5 cm) across when fully open and are sweetly scented. August.

EMPRESS OF INDIA. A most striking lily, bearing flowers of intense crimson-red, shaded on the reverse with deep pink and, when fully open, measuring 10 in (25 cm) across. August.

EMPRESS OF JAPAN. A magnificent lily, the enormous flowers of pure white being spotted with maroon and with a golden band at the centre of each petal which gives the flower a warm tone. August.

RED RUBY. Easy in pots and tubs and in the garden, it is one of the finest in the section, the large flowers of crimson-red having contrasting white margins to the petals which gracefully recurve at the tips. August.

Subdivision 7c. Hybrids with blooms which are recurving rather than bowl-shaped, otherwise similar in habit and cultural requirements to 7b.

IMPERIAL CRIMSON. A lily of beauty in which the crimson colouring varies in intensity. The petals have a silvery-white margin which encloses the crimson colouring, while the petals recurve gracefully. August.

JULIAN WALLACE. Raised in Australia by Mr Roy Wallace from a variety of *L. speciosum*, the blooms when open measure 8 in (20 cm) across and are of an enchanting shade of rosy-red with white margins. They are heavily spotted with crimson. Ten to twelve fragrant blooms appear on each stem. August.

LAVENDER PRINCESS. One of the finest in this section, the large ivory-white flowers are spotted with lavender-grey and are shaded with lavender towards the tips of each petal. Scented, it does well anywhere. August.

o

SWAN LAKE. A beautiful hybrid, the large pure-white blooms with their gracefully recurving segments are shaded green in the throat and have a wax-like appearance. August.

Subdivision 7d. Hybrids with flat flowers, otherwise similar in habit and cultural requirements to 7b and 7c.

BLACK BEAUTY. The flowers which measure 5 in (12·5 cm) across are borne with great freedom, as many as 40 or more appearing on a single stem. They are of crimson-red with a green star-shaped centre.

JAMBOREE STRAIN. It bears its handsome blooms in profusion and they are rosy-pink and white, stippled with crimson and have exotic perfume. The petals fold back flat and star-like to give it an orchid-like appearance. August.

JOURNEY'S END. It was raised in New Zealand, the large rose-coloured blooms having a thin white margin to the petals which sweep back to reveal a flat star-like bloom. August.

WINSTON CHURCHILL. A New Zealand hybrid, flowering on a 3- to 4-ft (90-cm to 1·2-metre) stem, the large blooms being of deep purple-red of velvet-like texture and open to more than 6 in (15 cm) across. July.

DIVISION 8. All hybrids not provided for in divisions 1 to 7.

DIVISION 9. The true species and their varieties, which vary as to their cultural requirements, also in their habit and flowering times.

Lilium amabile. Native of Korea, it is of the Martagon type, requiring a gritty well-drained soil and partial shade, though it is lime tolerant. Plant 6 in (15 cm) deep. It bears two to six reflexed scarlet-red flowers to each 3- to 4-ft (90-cm to 1·2-metre) downy stem. The flowers are heavily spotted with black and possess an oriental perfume. They are stem-rooting and make small ovoid bulbs with loose scales. They should be planted to the front of a border or in the dappled shade of woodland clearings.

The variety *luteum* has flowers of deep golden yellow, borne on a 2-ft (60-cm) stem. Planted together, the two provide pleasing contrasts. July.

Lilium auratum. The golden-rayed lily of Japan, introduced into Britain in 1862. It requires shelter from strong winds and, as it is not as hardy as some species, the large round bulbs being frost tender, it needs planting 6 in (15 cm) deep. Plant in March, in a well-drained peaty soil, for the bulbs will not tolerate excess moisture while dormant. Also, the hair-like basal stem roots require a well-nourished but 'open' soil in which to develop. It will be long-living only under these conditions.

The glistening white blooms have broad golden bands at the centre of each petal and are spotted with purple, while at the base are to be found short purple hairs. The flowers are borne 10 to 30 on a 6-ft (1·8-metre) purple stem, scenting the autumnal air, while they remain longer in bloom than any lily. They open to 10 in (25 cm) across. August and September.

The variety *platyphyllum* bears flowers which open to 12 in (30 cm) across and are more heavily spotted, while *virginale* is almost pure white, the band spotting being of palest yellow. *Rubro-vittatum* has a crimson band down the petals and is heavily spotted with crimson; and *pictum* has white flowers with crimson-tipped petals. The variety Little Gem grows only 16 in (40 cm) tall and has a broad red flush down the centre of each petal.

Lilium bakerianum. Native of Burma and south-western China, it has greenish-white bell-shaped flowers and petals which fold back to reveal heavy sprinklings of purple inside the throat. It grows 3 to 4 ft (90 cm to 1·2 metres) high and bears one to six blooms to each stem. It requires plenty of moisture when making growth in early summer but, if growing outdoors, it should be covered with a cloche in winter to protect it from excess moisture. Plant in March, 5 in (12·5 cm) deep in a warm border and mulch frequently. The blooms are heavily scented. July and August.

The variety *delavayi* has flowers with a greenish-yellow ground colour and which are more heavily marked than the type.

Lilium bolanderi. Its home is northern California and Oregon, and it is difficult to manage elsewhere. It grows 3 to 4 ft (90 cm to 1·2 metres) tall and bears its bluish-green leaves in four whorls of 12 or more and three to seven bell-shaped blooms on each stem. They are of a unique shade of velvety-purple, slightly spotted and shaded burgundy-red on the outside. Plant the bulbs 4 in (10 cm) deep in semi-shade and in a soil containing plenty of peat or leaf mould. June.

Lilium brownii. Native of western and central China, it was the first of the Chinese lilies to reach Britain, while it is possibly the finest of the trumpet lilies. It has a large bulb, which is flat both at the top and bottom and which turns orange when out of the ground for any length of time. The scales are brittle and readily break away and so should be handled with care. Plant 6 in (15 cm) deep, preferably on its side if the soil is heavy. It grows 3 to 4 ft (90 cm to 1·2 metres) tall with purple-spotted stems and it bears its trumpet-shaped flowers horizontally. They are satiny white, sometimes with a purple stripe down the inside of the petals and are heavily shaded rosy-purple on the reverse. The trumpets measure 8 in (20 cm) in length and open wide to reveal prominent brown anthers. They are borne five or six to a stem and are delicately scented. They grow best in a lime-free soil and in partial shade. July.

The variety *viridulum* from central China is more heavily scented, while the flowers are more funnel-shaped than the type with reddish-brown anthers. It has also a grey-green stem. The form *australe*, to be found growing in the hills around Hong Kong is difficult to establish in European and American gardens and is best grown under glass. The flowers are only lightly shaded on the reverse and open 6 in (15 cm) wide.

Lilium bulbiferum (syn. *L. aurantiacum*). It is also known by the name of its variety, *croceum*. Native of the mountains of central Europe, it is one of the easiest lilies to manage, not being fastidious as to soil or situation, though it should be planted 8 in (20 cm) deep. It is to be seen at its best in the wild garden or shrubbery, where it sends up its leafy stems to a height of 5 or 6 ft (1·5 to 1·8 metres), at the end of which it bears clusters of reddish-orange, cup-shaped flowers. It is propagated from the bulbils which form at the axils of the leaves.

The variety *croceum* (syn. *L. croceum*) was grown in gardens of Elizabethan days. Gerard described it as 'deep orange in colour, spotted with black (at the base)'. It is a familiar cottage garden plant of northern Ireland for it is the orange lily, symbol of the Order of the Ulster Orangemen, who still celebrate the victory of William of Orange in 1691. Once planted, the bulbs should not be disturbed but allowed to form large clumps from which will arise a profusion of flowers in July.

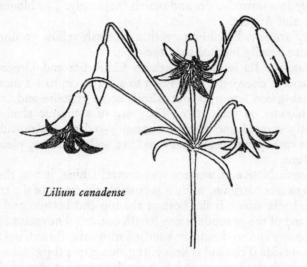

Lilium canadense

Lilium canadense. It is a lily of deciduous woodlands and damp meadows of eastern North America, to be found from Nova Scotia to Georgia and Alabama, growing 4 to 5 ft (1·2 to 1·5 metres) tall from a large white globose bulb. It bears its leaves in whorls of 4 to 10, and they are about 6 in (15 cm) long and 1 in (2·5 cm) wide, with rough veins on the underside. The flowers are borne on long pedicels, four or five to each stem and nod in the summer breezes. They are orange-yellow, spotted with black with the petals swept back. Increasing by stoloniferous bulbs, it enjoys a lime-free soil and dappled shade. Plant the bulbs in September, 6 in (15 cm) deep in a soil well provided with peat or leaf mould. It blooms in July. The variety *coccineum* bears reddish flowers.

Lilium candidum. It is the white lily of the East, the madonna lily, so named for its purity and sweet perfume. It was depicted more than any other flower in the paintings of the masters, while to the poets, the white lily served to typify all that was good and beautiful. It reached England early in her history and is shown on a tenth-century miniature of Queen Etheldreda of Ely; also in the Arms of the Borough of Marylebone and of Corpus Christi College, Cambridge. Gerard mentioned that 'our English White Lily groweth in most gardens'. It was so common at the time that he believed it to be a native plant. It remains the only pure-white lily and is seen at its loveliest growing with blue delphiniums or against a background of evergreens.

It is native of the Balkans, Asia Minor and Palestine and may be the 'lily of the field' mentioned in the Bible. It is found naturally on grassy slopes and requires a soil containing lime rubble. The large white bulbs are planted in September, the only time of year when it is dormant, for soon after planting it produces its basal leaves which persist through winter. It also requires shallow planting, with the top of the bulb just below the surface of the soil. It must also be protected from strong sunlight at the base of the stem yet will in no way tolerate woodland shade. Hence, it is found at its best in cottage gardens, in the company of other plants which provide the necessary shelter at the base. In such gardens it has remained healthy for centuries. Plant the bulb on its side and on a layer of sand to enable excess moisture to drain away.

The flowers with their spreading segments, open wide to reveal the golden anthers. They are borne 10 to 20 to a 4- to 5-ft (1·5-metre) stem and are at their best during late June and July, scenting the garden with their soft, sweet perfume.

The variety *salonikae* differs in that the segments are more spreading, while it blooms about a fortnight earlier.

Lilium catesbaei. A rare native of the swamplands of Florida, it is the most tender of all and requires a frost-free garden—otherwise it must be grown under glass in gentle warmth. It makes a small bulb which dies after flowering but leaves behind a small offset, rather like *Iris danfordiae*, so that an established plantation will always produce some bloom. Plant the bulbs in September, 4 in (10 cm) deep in a soil containing leaf mould, and in September the following year it will bear two to five orange-scarlet blooms spotted with brown, on purple stems 18 in (45 cm) tall. Soon after planting it will form basal leaves like *L. candidum*, which persist through winter and until the flower stem dies back.

Lilium cernuum. It is native of northern Korea and Manchuria and is a charming lily, bearing two to six lilac-pink Turk's caps on slender stems 18 in (45 cm) tall. It has lilac anthers and a soft, sweet perfume. It enjoys similar conditions to *L. candidum*, i.e. the company of other plants, to give shelter to its roots. But it likes a porous, leafy soil and no lime. Plant 4 in (10 cm) deep. To be long-living, the flowers should be removed as soon as they fade. June and July.

Lilium chalcedonicum. It is the famous scarlet Turk's-cap lily, present throughout the Near East, which Gerard said 'groweth wild in the fields many days journey beyond Constantinople (Chalcedon)'. It then grew in every garden with the Madonna lily, yet is now one of the rarest of lilies. It sends up to a height of 3 to 4 ft (90 cm to 1·2 metres) a stem clothed in silver-margined leaves, and it bears 6 to 10 Turk's-cap blooms of glossy sealing-wax red, which are sweetly scented, while the petals roll back to expose brilliant-red stamens. Its flowers are the most vividly red of all lilies and they bloom at the same time as *L. candidum*, providing an exciting contrast. It also requires a similar soil and situation, though it should be planted 4 in (10 cm) deep as it forms basal stem roots. The variety *maculatum* is spotted with black at the base of the petals. June and July.

Lilium columbianum (syn. *L. nitidum*). It is found about mountainous slopes of British Columbia and Oregon and is a dainty species, bearing its golden-orange flowers dotted with purple on 2-ft (60-cm) stems. The flowers have reflexed petals of martagon type and as many as 40 or more blooms may appear on each stem, though 20 to 30 is the usual number. It grows well anywhere but prefers the semi-shade of an open woodland and a soil containing peat or leaf mould. Plant 4 in (10 cm) deep. July and August.

Lilium concolor. Native of Manchuria and northern China, it is a charming lily for the rock garden and for small pots, bearing its unspotted flowers of brilliant red on 18-in (45-cm) stems. The star-like blooms are borne in umbels of five to seven. Plant 4 in (10 cm) deep in a sunny position and in a well-drained gritty soil to provide efficient winter drainage for it to be long-living. The variety Coridion bears lemon-yellow flowers spotted with brown, which are a pleasing contrast to the type. May and June.

Lilium carniolicum. A rare native of south-eastern Europe, of Yugoslavia and Albania, and much resembling the scarlet Turk's-cap in the colour of its flowers, though they are of martagon type, appearing two to six on a 2-ft (60-cm) stem. Plant the small white bulbs 4 in deep. May and June.

Lilium dauricum. It is native of Siberia, Mongolia and north-eastern China and is now rare in cultivation. It is stoloniferous, like *L. bulbiferum*, sending up its flower stems some distance from the original planting. It does well in all soils and in any situation. It bears its urn-shaped flowers in a terminal umbel at the end of a 2-ft (60-cm) stem, the blooms being of brilliant red, spotted with black and with yellow shading in the throat. June and July.

Lilium davidii. Native of western China and Tibet, it perpetuates the name of Father Pierre David, a Franciscan monk and intrepid plant collector in western China. It grows 5 to 6 ft (1·5 to 1·8 metres) tall, its stem running underground before turning upwards. The flowers are deep orange-scarlet with reflexing martagon-type petals spotted with black, and are borne 10 to 20 on long pedicels. The variety *willmottiae* (syn. *L. willmottiae*) is better known, for it is more free-flowering than the type and bears its flowers on a graceful arching stem. Maxwell, raised in Canada in 1928 is a variety of similar but stiffer habit.

Though stem-rooting, these lilies do better if not planted more than 3 in (7·5 cm) deep. They require a well-drained acid soil and an open, sunny situation, and for them to be long-living they should not be allowed to set seed. July and August.

Lilium duchartrei. It was discovered by Father David in high mountainous woodlands in western China and is a beautiful lily, known as the marbled martagon. It increases by stolons and may travel far without inducement to bear flowers so when planting the small round bulbs 3 in (7·5 cm) deep, enclose them on each side with slates, with one below the bulb to contain it. It prefers a soil containing leaf mould. It bears nodding white flowers marbled with purple and with purple spots at the margin of the attractively reflexing petals. July.

Lilium formosanum. Native of Formosa, it bears funnel-shaped flowers about 6 in (15 cm) long, the segments curling back at the tips. The flowers are white with a central line of green and with purple shading on the reverse. They are borne five or six to a 5- to 6-ft (1·5- to 1·8-metre) stem. The scented flowers are enhanced by the dark-green stems and glossy leaves, which are borne in abundance at the base. It is valuable for under-glass culture and will withstand forcing. Outside, the bulbs should be planted 4 in (10 cm) deep and, like *L. candidum*, they should accompany other plants, to provide shade at the base. It is moisture-loving and requires a soil containing some peat or leaf mould.

Price's variety grows only 15 in (37·5 cm) tall and bears two or three flowers on each stem. The segments are shaded deep purple-brown on the reverse and are scented. June and July.

Lilium grayii. Present on hilly slopes of North Carolina and Tennessee, bearing two to six nodding blooms on a slender 3-ft (90-cm) stem. The flowers are bell-shaped and dull red with flared petals, shaded yellow in the throat and spotted with brown. It is stoloniferous and should be planted 3 in (7·5 cm) deep in a lime-free and well-drained soil, though moisture is essential during growing time. It does well by the side of a pond or stream. July.

Lilium hansonii. It is to be found on one small island off Korea and is one of the best of garden lilies, being long-living and happy in most soils. The large round bulb is yellowish white and should be planted 8 in (20 cm) deep, preferably in semi-shade. It bears orange martagon-type flowers on 4- to 5-ft (1·2- to 1·5-metre) stems which are clothed in whorls of dark-green leaves. The flowers are borne 10 to 12 to a stem and are held on long pedicels which causes them to nod in the breezes. As it makes early growth, it should be planted in autumn with low shrubs or herbaceous plants such as paeonies which will provide protection in spring with their foliage.

Crossed with *L. martagon*, a number of beautiful hybrids (Division 2) have been raised by van Tubergen and by Miss Isabella Preston of the Horticultural Station, Ottawa. *L. hansonii* and its hybrids is lime-tolerant if in limited amounts but does better in a slightly acid soil. June.

Lilium henryi. It was found by Professor Henry in a limestone gorge in Hupeh Province of China and is one of the loveliest and most accommodating of all lilies. The reddish-brown bulbs should be planted 8 in (20 cm) deep, for it forms numerous bulbils at the base of the stem below ground. It likes partial shade, and in a neutral soil (it does not like peat) it will bear up to 50 large Turk's cap blooms on a 5- to 6-ft (1·5- to 1·8-metre) stem. The flowers are of rich golden orange with the broad petals folded back and are enhanced by a bunch of long bright-green stamens. It is tolerant of a small amount of lime in the soil and will come into bloom within two years of sowing seed which germinates readily. It blooms late, in August.

Lilium humboldtii. A lily of the pinewoods of the Sierra Nevadas, it usually grows best in a moist neutral soil and in partial shade, but, like all American species of the Pacific coast, it is difficult to establish in gardens. The brilliant reddish-orange flowers, prettily flecked with maroon, are borne 10 to 12 to a 5- to 6-ft (1·5- to 1·8-metre) stem, the upper part of which is clothed in whorls of leaves.

It forms one of the largest bulbs of all lilies, weighing half a pound or more. It usually takes two years to bloom after planting 4 in (10 cm) deep and until it has formed its new basal roots for it is not stem rooting. July.

The variety *magnificum* is easier to manage. It has orange flowers so heavily spotted with maroon as to give it a mahogany appearance.

Lilium japonicum. Present in woodlands, growing in volcanic ash in several regions of Japan—and this is how to grow it in gardens. Plant the small bulbs 6 in (15 cm) deep in a gravelly soil but in one containing peat or leaf mould for it requires to be well-drained in winter yet must have ample supplies of moisture in summer. It is suitable for a cool greenhouse. The flowers are funnel-shaped and of a lovely shade of soft shell pink with red anthers. They are borne two to five on a slender stem 2 ft (60 cm) tall. July.

Lilium kelloggii. It is of Pacific North America and is a most elegant lily, bearing its flowers on long pedicels and in pyramid form on slender 3- to 4-ft (90-cm to 1·2-metre) stems. The flowers with their reflexed petals open waxy white but with age turn mauve-pink. They are heavily spotted with maroon and have the fragrance of honey.

The bulbs are oval with long thin scales and as they form no stem roots should be planted only 2 in (5 cm) deep. They require a peaty soil (disliking lime) and a position of semi-shade. May and June.

Lilium lankongense. It grows wild in the mountainous regions of Yunnan and is long living in the garden, bearing as many as 20 to 30 Turk's cap flowers of rosy mauve, spotted with crimson on a 2-ft (60-cm) stem. The flowers are heavily scented and have pointed segments which are strongly recurving.

Plant the pinkish-white bulb 4 in (10 cm) deep in a soil containing plenty of humus and in a position of partial shade. The stems run underground for some distance before turning upwards. August.

Lilium leichtlinii. A rare Japanese lily bearing Turk's cap flowers of bright lemon yellow spotted with wine red and on slender stems 3 ft (90 cm) tall. It is tender and must be confined to sheltered gardens, while it is not suitable for pots on account of its wandering habit. The small bulb should be planted 6 in (15 cm) deep, in a well-drained soil and in an open situation. August.

The variety *maximowiczii* which grows 2 ft (60 cm) tall and blooms mid-July is easier to establish. It bears 8 to 10 brilliant orange Turk's cap flowers on a graceful slender stem and, like the type, will not grow in a soil containing lime.

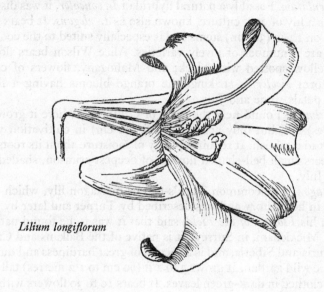

Lilium longiflorum

Lilium leucanthum. Native of the high rainfall regions of western China, it is difficult to establish away from the western parts of Britain, for it requires not only copious amounts of moisture but also a frost-free climate. It bears three to five sweetly scented trumpet-shaped flowers of ivory-white, shaded yellow inside, green on the outside on leafy stems 3 to 4 ft (90 cm to 1·2 metres) tall. The large ball-shaped bulbs should be planted 4 in (10 cm) deep. August.

Lilium longiflorum. The Easter lily, native of Japan and one of the best lilies to grow in a cool greenhouse or in gentle heat. It will bloom within 18 months of sowing the seed. It bears horizontal or slightly drooping white trumpets, shaded green in the throat and with delicious scent. They appear in umbels of three to six and on stems 2 to 3 ft (60 to 90 cm) tall. In the more exposed parts it should be planted 6 in (15 cm) deep in an open, porous soil and it is one of the few oriental lilies to be lime-tolerant. July to August in the open; April under glass.

Mount Everest and Holland's Glory bear larger trumpets than those of the type and of glistening white, the latter being the best for outside planting. The variety Croft, which grows only 20 in (50 cm) tall is suitable for growing in pots in a small greenhouse.

Lilium mackliniae. It was discovered on the borders of India and north-western Burma by Kingdon Ward, and is a rare and beautiful lily, bearing nodding bowl-shaped flowers of creamy-white with wine-red markings at the base. Growing only 12 in (30 cm) tall, it is a delightful lily for the alpine house or rock garden. Early June.

Lilium × maculatum. Possibly a natural hybrid of *L. concolor*, it was discovered in Japan and is a lily of easy culture, known also as *L. elegans*. It bears red and yellow flowers on 12-in (30-cm) stems and is especially suited to the cool greenhouse. There are a number of lovely varieties. Alice Wilson bears flowers of clear lemon-yellow spotted with black; and Mahogany, flowers of crimson-brown. The form *bicolor* is striking, the orange blooms having a fiery-red margin to the petals. June and July.

Lilium maritimum. Found near the coast of California, where it grows up to 6 ft (1·8 metres) tall, but only achieving 2 ft (60 cm) in cultivation where it proves difficult to establish. It requires plenty of moisture about its roots during summer. It bears small bell-shaped flowers of deepest crimson, shaded orange in the throat. July.

Lilium martagon. The common Turk's-cap or martagon lily, which reached England early in her history and was described by Turner and later by Gerard. Rev. Johns, in his *Flowers of the Field*, said that it was to be found naturalised in woods near Mickleham, in Surrey. It is native of the Balkans and Caucasus, also of Manchuria and Siberia, and is a species of great hardiness and durability, at its best in the wild garden. It grows 3 to 4 ft (90 cm to 1·2 metres) tall and has a downy stem clothed in dark-green leaves. It bears 10 to 30 flowers with acutely recurving petals of pinkish purple or claret red, with darker shading on the reverse, while the flowers are heavily dotted in the throat with purple.

The small, pointed bulbs should be planted in October, after flowering and setting them 6 in deep. Ordinary leafy soil is suitable and, if in partial shade in the company of foxgloves and primroses, they will seed themselves freely. It has been freely used in hybridising, and crossing with *L. hansonii* produced numerous lovely hybrids of Division 2. July.

The scarce variety *dalmaticum*, bears larger flowers of deep purple on 4- to 5-ft (1·2- to 1·5-metre) stems, while *album* bears 30 to 40 flowers of waxy-white in a pyramidal head and is an admirable companion. Another variety, *pilosiusculum* of northern Russia and Siberia, has flowers of dull purple, covered on the reverse with small hairs.

Lilium medeoloides. A Japanese lily with leaves of wheel-like precision appearing halfway up the 16-in (40-cm) stem. The dainty reflexed flowers are of deep apricot or brick red, spotted with crimson while they usually appear one, two or three to each stem. It requires partial shade and a soil containing peat or leaf mould. August.

Lilium michauxi. The fragrant Carolina lily, native of south-eastern United States and bearing on a 2-ft (60-cm) stem two to seven reflexed flowers of brilliant orange (or yellow) heavily dotted with purple. It requires a moist soil and one free of lime, when it will be hardy and long-lasting. August.

Lilium michiganense. A rare Turk's cap lily to be found in damp meadows of eastern North America and known as the Michigan and Iowa Lily. It bears four to eight orange-red flowers on a 3- to 4-ft (90-cm to 1·2-metre) stem, the blooms being dotted with purple. It requires an open, sunny situation and a soil retentive of summer moisture. The stoloniferous bulbs should be planted 4 in (10 cm) deep in a lime-free soil. July.

Lilium monadelphum. Native of the Caucasus, it requires plenty of moisture about its roots and may take several years to establish itself, when it will prove to be hardy and long-living. It bears 20 to 30 nodding Turk's cap flowers to each 4-ft (1·2-metre) stem and they are of bright golden yellow, lightly dotted with orange. The pointed petals fold back in star-like fashion.

The variety *szovitzianum*, discovered in the Balkans, has orange instead of yellow pollen, while the stamens are not united as in the type. For this reason it is often classed as a separate species. Both plants require a soil containing lime but one retentive of summer moisture. July.

Lilium neilgherrense. The most southerly of all lilies, native of southern India. In the British Isles and North America it should be grown under glass except in sheltered gardens. It has another distinction in that it is the largest lily, its fragrant white trumpets measuring 10 in (25 cm) or more in length. They are shaded pale yellow on the reverse with petals reflexed at the tips. Borne on a 2-ft (60-cm) stem, the flowers resemble *L. longiflorum*. Where growing in pots, firm planting is necessary. August and September.

Lilium nepalense. Native of Nepal, it is too tender for British and North American gardens except where most favourably situated. The large trumpet-shaped flowers are of pale lime green marked with crimson in the throat and are heavily scented, unpleasantly so as the flowers fade. The plant spreads by underground stolons from which arise the stems, often 2 ft (60 cm) away from the mother bulb. They grow 3 ft (90 cm) tall, at the end of which the flowers appear in umbels of one to three. The plant increases by underground bulbils. In pots, plant 5 or 6 in (12·5 to 15 cm) deep in a mixture of leaf mould, sterilised loam and coarse sand.

The variety *concolor* is without the crimson markings and grows only 20 in (50 cm) tall. It may be grown in the alpine house or in a sunny nook of the rock garden. August.

Lilium nevadense (syn. *L. parviflorum*). It resembles the most common of Californian lilies, *L. pardalinum*, and like it, it is to be found on the lower slopes of the Sierra Nevadas, growing in a moist loamy soil. It bears 10 to 18 sweetly-scented blooms of orange, tipped with red on a 2-ft (60-cm) stem. It differs from *L. padalinum* in its broader segments, which are blunt ended rather than pointed. The bulbs are small and should be planted 3 in (7·5 cm) deep. July.

Lilium nobilissimum. Native of Japan, it is rare in the wild and in cultivation, requiring a light soil and semi-shade. It is also suitable for growing under glass. It bears large trumpets of frosty whiteness surrounded by dark-green leaves which provide a striking contrast. It bears one to three horizontal or drooping scented flowers on a 2-ft (60-cm) stem. Plant the round white bulbs 4 in (10 cm) deep. It is stem-rooting and lime-tolerant. May and June.

Lilium occidentale. A Turk's cap lily from northern California, resembling *L. pardalinum*. It has small orange-red flowers, shaded green in the throat and crimson at the tips of the segments. The throat is spotted with crimson. It bears up to 20 flowers on a 3- to 4-ft (90-cm to 1·2-metre) stem, while the leaves are borne in whorls. It requires a lime-free soil and a position of partial shade. July.

Lilium papilliferum. Native of limestone hills of western China and Tibet, it grows 12 in (30 cm) tall and bears elegant little Turk's cap flowers of purple-maroon with brown anthers. The flowers are scented. It requires an open situation and a well-drained soil containing lime. Plant 4 in (10 cm) deep. August.

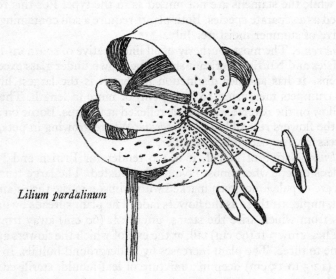

Lilium pardalinum

Lilium pardalinum. The panther lily, native of Pacific North America, where its brilliantly coloured flowers are found in deciduous woodlands. It requires partial shade and a well-drained leafy soil, where its rhizomatous bulb will increase rapidly. Plant 4 in (10 cm) deep and it will usually be necessary to lift and divide the bulbs every six years. It bears orange-red flowers, heavily spotted at the centre, in a raceme of 20 to 30, and the recurving segments are touched with crimson at the tips. The blooms are held on 5- to 6-ft (1·5- to 1·8-metre) stems, which are clothed in whorls of bright-green leaves.

The variety *giganteum* bears crimson-red flowers, strongly recurving, the centre being shaded with gold and with crimson-red anthers. June and July.

Lilium parryi. A lily of beauty from the mountains of Pacific North America, bearing sweetly scented funnel-shaped flowers of brilliant yellow on a stem 5 to 6 ft (1·5 to 1·8 metres) tall. Twenty or more flowers make up the head. The leaves are pale-green and borne in whorls. It requires a soil containing plenty of peat or leaf mould. Plant the rhizomatous bulbs in autumn 4 in (10 cm) deep for it blooms early and over a long season. June to August.

Lilium parvum. It is from the Sierra Nevadas, bearing flowers of deep yellow or orange on a slender stem 2 to 3 ft (60 to 90 cm) tall. The segments reflex slightly at the tips, while the flowers are held upright. It forms a small rhizomatous bulb, which should be planted 3 in (7·5 cm) deep in autumn, into a well-drained soil containing some peat or leaf mould. June and July.

Lilium philadelphicum. Native of the eastern United States, where it is known as the red lily or American flame lily, it has a reputation for being one of the most difficult lilies to grow. It should be lifted and divided when in full bloom. It is found in dry thickets from Ontario to North Carolina and makes a bulb of 1-in (2·5-cm) diameter increasing by stolons. It bears its leaves in whorls of three to eight on a 2-ft (60-cm) stem and its flowers in umbels of one to five. The spreading segments are of reddish-orange, spotted with purple at the base. June and July.

Lilium philippinense. At one time it was considered a variety of *L. formosanum*. It is usually grown under glass in the British Isles and North America, though may be grown outside in sheltered gardens. Native of the Philippine Islands, it bears one of the largest trumpets of all, sometimes 10 in (25 cm) in length. The sweetly scented snow-white flowers are streaked with red on the reverse and are shaded green at the base. They measure 6 in across the mouth and are borne one to three on a slender 2-ft (60-cm) scape.

For pots use a 14- to 16-cm bulb; 12- to 14-cm for outside, where it should be planted 6 in (15 cm) deep.

The variety White Superior, often grown by commercial growers as a substitute for *L. longiflorum*, bears pure-white flowers, while those of Pink Perfection are shaded pink on the outside. August and September.

Lilium polyphillum. A rare native of the lower slopes of the western Himalayas, it is equally rare in gardens. It bears, on a 3- to 4-ft (90-cm to 1·2-metre) stem, 2 to 10 creamy-yellow flowers which curl back at the mouth to reveal a greenish-yellow throat. The flowers are scented and are borne among numerous dark-green leaves. It forms a narrow pointed bulb which should be planted 6 in (15 cm) deep into a soil which has been prepared to a depth of at least 18 in (45 cm).

Lilium pomponium. Native of the Maritime Alps of southern Europe, where it grows in a sparse and unshaded soil, it resembles *L. chalcedonicum* in that its Turk's cap flowers are of brightest scarlet, while its leaves are margined with silver. The flowers are borne 2 to 10 on a 2-ft (60-cm) stem. They are pendulous with heavily reflexing petals and emit an unpleasant fox-like smell.

The small oval bulbs, of the size of a bantam's egg, are planted 4 in (10 cm) deep in poor soil containing plenty of lime rubble (mortar) and in an open position. They may take three years to bloom, and once established should not be disturbed. June.

Lilium primulinum (syn. *L. ochraceum*). Native of northern Burma, it should be grown under glass in Britain and North America except in the most favourable parts. The type bears large drooping yellow flowers with funnels 6 in (15 cm) long, but it is the variety *ochraceum* that is usually grown. This bears smaller flowers with its segments, reflexed at the tips, shaded with green and with a purple patch in the throat. The flowers are borne two to eight on a 2-ft (60-cm) stem which runs underground for 12 in (30 cm) or more before turning upwards. Where growing in pots, this can be prevented by firm planting and by surrounding the bulb with slates.

The variety *burmanicum* grows 6 ft (1·8 metres) tall and bears bright-yellow flowers with wine-red markings in the throat. It makes a better pot plant than *ochraceum* as its stems grow straight up, but it needs room to attain full stature. It is stem-rooting and should be planted 4 in (10 cm) deep in the pots. The flowers have scent of an 'eastern' quality. July.

Lilium pumilum (syn. *L. tenuifolium*). Native of Mongolia and Siberia, it is a martagon-type lily of great charm, bearing one to six or more coral-red flowers on a wiry stem 18 in (45 cm) tall. It likes to have its head in the sun and its roots in shade, for it is stem-rooting and enjoys the company of paeonies and dwarf shrubs. Plant the bulbs (of 8- to 10-cm size and with few broad scales) 4 in (10 cm) deep in a soil containing leaf mould. Golden Gleam, which bears flowers of rich golden yellow, is more free-flowering and a suitable companion. It often bears 20 or more flowers on a single stem and grows true from seed. May and June.

Lilium pyrenaicum. Present on lower grassy slopes of the Pyrenees, it is one of the more easily managed of lilies and one of the most valuable in the garden for it is early to bloom. It bears 3 to 12 drooping Turk's cap flowers of greenish yellow, heavily spotted with black on a 2-ft (60-cm) stem, the blooms being enhanced by the scarlet anthers. Plant it anywhere and in any soil and it will flourish, increasing as the years go by, as it has done in cottage gardens since its introduction. Its only fault is its unpleasant perfume. Plant 4 in (10 cm) deep. May and June.

Lilium regale. Since its discovery in 1910 by E. H. Wilson on the borders of China and Tibet, it has remained the most popular lily for it does well under glass and in the garden where it soon becomes established and increases rapidly. Its strong flexible stems, which reach a height of 5 to 6 ft (1·5 to 1·8 metres), are crowned with 20 or more funnel-shaped flowers of glistening white, shaded yellow in the throat and with a heavy but pleasing perfume. The flowers are arranged in wheel fashion and are borne horizontally so that their beauty may be seen from all sides. The petals reflex at the tips to reveal a golden throat while the flowers are shaded wine red on the reverse. It has golden anthers. As it makes growth early, it should not be planted where the foliage may be caught by cold winds. Protect from cold winds by planting it with low shrubs or evergreens. Plant the orange-coloured bulbs, which will withstand many degrees of frost, 6 in (15 cm) deep and mulch them each year. For indoor flowering, bulbs of 22 to 24 cm are used; a 20- to 22-cm bulb being suitable for outdoor planting. This lily is lime-tolerant.

The variety *album* bears pure-white blooms and should be grown where supplying the cut-flower trade. June and July.

Lilium rubellum. It was discovered by E. H. Wilson in Japan at a height of 8,000 feet, where it is covered in a blanket of snow for six months of the year. It bears one to four fragrant funnel-shaped flowers on a 20-in (50-cm) stem which is clothed in dark-green leaves which set off the pink satin-like flowers to advantage. The three inner petals are of soft pink, the three outer being of rose pink with wine-pink shading on the reverse. It is like *L. regale* in that it comes early into leaf and so should be protected from frost and cold winds by using other plants for low cover. Plant the small white bulbs 6 in (15 cm) deep and into a lime-free soil containing peat or leaf mould. May and June.

Lilium rubescens. A rare and difficult lily from Pacific North America, where it grows in pine forests and requires a well-drained acid soil. It bears tubular flowers of waxy-white, which turn pink as they age and which are upwards-facing. They are held on a 2- to 3-ft (60- to 90-cm) stem. The segments open wide and reflex to display golden anthers, while they are scented. The narrow lance-shaped leaves are borne in whorls, while as many as 20 to 30 flowers appear on a stem. The oval-shaped bulb has loose pointed scales which easily break off and it must be treated with care. Plant 2 in (5 cm) deep in September in a peaty soil. July.

Lilium sargentiae. Discovered by E. H. Wilson on the borders of Tibet and China, growing near *L. regale*—which it greatly resembles, though the flower is longer and more tubular than that of *L. regale*. It is of brilliant white, shaded yellow in the throat and borne 2 to 12 on a 3- to 4-ft (90-cm to 1·2-metre) grey-green stem. The scented flowers are shaded purple on the reverse and are distinguished from *L. regale* by the purple tip of the stigma. The rather broad leaves are formed at the top of the stem.

Though the bulb has broad overlapping scales to protect it from winter moisture, it will perish if the ground is wet while it is dormant. It should be planted beneath the overhanging eaves of a house and in a gritty soil. Failing this, grow it in a cool greenhouse.

Outdoors, plant the bulbs 5 in (12·5 cm) deep for it is stem rooting. August.

Lilium speciosum. Native of Japan, it is classed with *L. longiflorum* and *L. formosanum* as a 'florists'' lily, at one time being grown in large numbers for the cut-flower trade. The long trumpet-shaped flowers are white, heavily spotted with crimson, while the tips of the segments curl back slightly. The flowers are borne 4 to 12, or 30 or more in their native land, to a stem 3 ft (90 cm) tall and usually clothed in glossy dark-green leaves.

The bulbs, which vary in colour from yellowish-brown to mahogany have overlapping scales and should be planted 6 in (15 cm) deep in a deeply cultivated soil, free from lime. For indoor culture, use a 20- to 22-cm bulb; 18- to 20-cm for outdoor planting. Those produced in Holland will be free from virus and less dry than those imported from the east. They will withstand gentle forcing. August and September.

There are numerous varieties, *album* being the most widely grown for cutting. Its broad petals are waved at the margins while it has a pale-green band radiating from the centre. Ellabee is similar but slightly larger, while as many as 15 blooms appear on a stem. As with all the florists' lilies, the blooms will last at least 10 days in water.

Also lovely is Cinderella, the whole bloom being flushed peach-pink but shading out to blush-pink at the petal tips, while Lucie Wilson bears flowers of soft rose-pink, edged white and spotted red in the throat. Grand Commander bears blooms of glowing crimson, edged white, and Uchida Kanoka is of similar colouring. These are varieties of *L. speciosum rubrum*, which bears large trumpets measuring 8 in (20 cm) across, of ruby-red with a broad white margin. The 'red' varieties grow 4 ft (1·2 metres) tall and are easier to grow than the type.

Lilium sulphureum (syn. *L. myriophyllum*). Native of northern Burma, it is rare in cultivation because it blooms so late outdoors when the plants may be cut down by adverse weather. It is best grown under glass, but here again its height of 6 to 7 ft (1·8 to 2·1 metres) makes it difficult to accommodate in the small greenhouse. For all that, it is a lily of superb beauty, the large elegant trumpets being of a lovely shade of rich cream, tinted with pink on the outside and with a soft sweet perfume. It is stem-rooting and does well in pots. The bulbs should be planted 6 in (15 cm) deep outside, in a position where the late summer sunshine can reach it and in a well-drained soil. September and October.

Lilium superbum. Native of the coastal areas of Pacific North America, where it is known as the swamp lily, it resembles *L. pardalinum* in that its Turk's cap flowers are of brilliant orange, shading to red at the tips. At the centre, it is flushed with yellow and spotted crimson-brown. The flowers are larger than those of *L. pardalinum* and are borne 15 to 30 in pyramidal form on a 6-ft (1·8-metre) stem. The large red anthers contribute to the brilliance of the flowers, which open from a triangular-shaped bud.

Plant the large round bulbs, which increase by stolons, 2 in (5 cm) deep and in an acid soil containing some peat. They require plenty of moisture while growing. July and August.

Lilium taliense. Discovered in Yunnan, it is a lily of martagon type, bearing its flowers on slender hairy stems 3 to 4 ft (90 cm to 1·2 metres) tall. The blooms, with their strongly recurving segments, are white, spotted with purple and borne 6 to 12 to a stem, to which they are attached by horizontal pedicels. They are scented. They are found growing in limestone soils but are tolerant of all soils. Plant the small yellow bulbs 4 in (10 cm) deep and mulch frequently. Mrs Alice Maxwell in her book *Lilies in their Homes* states that this lily must not be propagated by scales, for if descaled it will perish. July and August.

Lilium × *testaceum* (syn. *L. excelsum*). The Nankeen Lily, believed to be a natural hybrid of *L. candidum* and *L. chalcedonicum*. It bears pendulous Turk's cap flowers of pale apricot-orange with long projecting scarlet anthers. As many as 10 to 12 flowers are borne on a 3- to 4-ft (90-cm to 1·2-metre) stem. The blooms have the same sweet scent of *L. candidum*.

Plant the yellow bulbs in September, 2 in (5 cm) deep in an open position and in a well-drained soil containing lime rubble, for it resembles its parents in its liking for lime. June and July.

Lilium tigrinum. The tiger lily, native of Japan, was introduced early in this century. It requires a lime-free soil. In parts of eastern United States, it has become naturalised, while its large white bulbs were at one time consumed by the peoples of Japan and eastern China as a staple food. The flowers are orange-red with black markings, while the petals of the bell-shaped flowers curl back sharply. They are borne 12 to 20 to a 3- to 4-ft (90-cm to 1·2-metre) stem and, like *L. martagon*, is suitable for planting in grass or in clearings in deciduous woodlands. Plant 6 in (15 cm) deep in a porous soil and mulch frequently, for it forms numerous stem roots. A flowering bulb will be of 16- to 18-cm size.

The variety *splendens* has larger flowers of salmon orange spotted with black, while *flaviflorum* has flowers of deep clear yellow with black dots and, with its slender pointed petals, is one of the most handsome of lilies. The rare double form, *flore plena*, has six circles of petals instead of the usual three and they are of brilliant orange-red. August and September.

Lilium tsingtauense. Native of Korea and south-eastern China, its flower is a symphony in orange, for all its parts are of the same colour. It bears four to eight flowers with reflexed petals on a 2-ft (60-cm) stem clothed in whorls of glossy green leaves.

It requires a lime-free soil containing plenty of peat or leaf mould, and a position of partial shade. Plant the white oval bulbs 2 in (5 cm) deep, either in pots or in the open ground. June and July.

Lilium vollmeri. It has brilliant orange-red flowers heavily spotted with purple-black, while the segments curl back. It is native of Pacific North America and bears two or three flowers on a 2-ft (60-cm) stem. Plant the bulbs 3 in (7·5 cm) deep in a soil containing plenty of peat. This lily is difficult to establish. July.

Lilium wallichianum. Native of Nepal, it should be grown under glass except in those gardens favourably situated. It bears its horizontal funnel-shaped flowers, which measure 6 in (15 cm) or more across, on a 2-ft (60-cm) stem. The flowers are creamy-white, shaded green on the outside and with delicious scent.

Outside, the bulbs should be planted 6 in (15 cm) deep in a gravel soil fortified with liberal amounts of peat or leaf mould, for though, requiring a well-drained soil in winter, it needs plenty of summer moisture. August and September.

Lilium wardii. It was discovered by Captain Kingdon Ward in Tibet in 1924, growing at an altitude of 10,000 ft and bearing 30 or more purple-pink martagon-type flowers on a 3-ft (90-cm) stem. The scented blooms are spotted with purple while the purple anthers have orange pollen.

Plant the pink bulbs 4 in (10 cm) deep in a peaty soil free from lime and mulch each year. July and August.

Lilium washingtonianum. Its home is Pacific North America and it is one of the more difficult lilies to establish. It has large egg-shaped bulbs from each of which arises a 4-ft (1·2-metre) stem, clothed in whorls of dark-green leaves and bearing carnation-scented flowers in a large raceme. They are white, turning pink, rosy-red and maroon with age, so that in each raceme there will be flowers showing each degree of pink colouring. Plant the bulbs 10 in (25 cm) deep in partial shade, in a lime-free but gravelly soil. June and July.

Lilium wigginsii (syn. *L. roezlii*). Native of Pacific North America, it has a rhizomatous rootstock and bears Turk's cap flowers of bright yellow, spotted with black on a 2-ft (60-cm) stem. The lance-shaped leaves are borne in whorls all the way up the stem. Plant 3 in (7·5 cm) deep in a lime-free soil. June and July.

LIRIOPSIS (PLAGIOLIRION) (Amaryllidaceae)

A genus of three species, native of South America and taking their name from the Greek *leirion*, a lily, which the flowers resemble. It is a plant requiring warm greenhouse culture in the British Isles. It has a brown tunicated globular bulb and oblong leaves. The flowers are white and are borne in summer.

Culture. Plant two or three bulbs to a 5-in (12·5-cm) pot containing a compost made up of fibrous loam, leaf mould and dehydrated cow manure in equal parts. Plant the bulbs 1 in (2·5 cm) deep, early in the year. Provide a temperature of 55° F (13° C), watering sparingly until growth commences, then increase supplies as the leaves appear. The plants come into bloom late in June and continue until the end of August, when they are dried off gradually and the pots placed on their sides in a frost-free place until it is time to start them into growth again.

Propagation. By removal of the offsets when the bulbs are repotted in alternate years. They are planted in 3-in (7·5-cm) pots in a sandy compost and grown on for two years, after which they will have attained flowering size.

Species. *Liriopsis horsmannii.* It was discovered in the Peruvian Andes in 1883 by Mr F. Horsman of Colchester and is the best-known species. It makes a globular bulb 2 in (5 cm) through from which arise oblong leaves 9 in (23 cm) long and 4 in (10 cm) broad, blunt at the end. The flowers are like small white lilies and are borne in umbels of four to six on a 12-in (30-cm) stem.

LITTONIA (Liliaceae)

A genus of eight species, native of tropical and southern Africa and named in honour of Dr Litton, Professor of Botany at Trinity College, Dublin. It is tuberous-rooting, climbing by means of leaf tendrils, like Gloriosa. It requires a greenhouse or garden room for its culture in the British Isles and northern Europe where it may be trained along canes supported by wires fixed across the roof. The flowers, shaped like small tulips, are produced at the axils of the leaves during summer and are less conspicuous than those of Gloriosa.

Culture. The tubers are potted early in spring, one to a 4-in (10-cm) pot, using a compost made up of fibrous loam, peat and decayed manure in equal parts, to which has been added a sprinkling of grit or sand. Cover the tubers with 2 in (5 cm) of compost and give the minimum of moisture until growth begins, increasing supplies as the sun becomes warmer. As the slender stems lengthen, they will require support and this is provided by 6-ft (1·8-metre) canes fixed at an angle into the pot and fastened to wires across the greenhouse roof. The plants require plenty of fresh air during summer and liberal amounts of moisture. During the heat of summer, the plants will benefit from a daily syringe. After flowering, the stems die back and watering must be gradually discontinued. The tubers are then removed from the pots and stored in boxes of peat in a frost-free place.

Propagation. This is done in spring when the plants are starting to make growth, by lifting and dividing the tubers with a sharp knife.

Species. *Littonia modesta.* Native of Natal, it is the only species in general cultivation. It forms a stem 5 to 6 ft (1·5 to 1·8 metres) in length and climbs by means of the tendrils at the end of the bright-green stalkless leaves. The yellowish-orange flowers are borne in July and August from the axils of the leaves and resemble small tulips, opening star-like with their pointed segments.

LLOYDIA (Liliaceae)

A genus of 20 species, closely related to Calochortus and named after William Lloyd, a botanist who discovered the first species growing on a rocky ledge in the Snowdon Range in his native Wales. Completely hardy, it may be planted about the alpine garden and in any partially shaded nook.

Culture. The small scaly bulbs should be planted 2 in (5 cm) deep in September, and in a well-drained shingly soil. Plant 6 to 8 in (15 to 20 cm) apart.

Propagation. It is increased by offsets which form about the mother bulb. These are detached when the plants are lifted in autumn and may be replanted where they are to bloom.

Species. *Lloydia serotina.* Known as the Snowdon lily, it is low-growing with round grass-like basal leaves 9 in (23 cm) long, and in May and June bears small solitary flowers of creamy-white, veined outside with purple on a 4-in (10-cm) stem. The flowers with their pointed segments open star-like.

LYCORIS (Amaryllidaceae)

A genus of 10 species, to be found from western China to Japan and named after a lady in Roman history. Closely allied to *Nerine*, it has a large tunicated bulb with a short neck and strap-like leaves. At the end of a stout scape are borne funnel-shaped flowers with attractively waved petals. In the British Isles and North America it should be grown in the open only in those gardens enjoying a frost-free climate, though *L. radiata* and *L. squanigera* have been known to survive several degrees of frost.

Culture. In the open, select a border where the bulbs will be baked by the summer sunshine and where they may be kept as dry as possible when forming their flower buds and during winter. A bed at the base of a wall, in full sun and beneath the eaves of a house, is suitable. The soil should be well-drained and contain some decayed manure, together with peat or leaf mould. Plant the bulbs (as for *Nerine*) early in August before the flower stems appear, placing them on a layer of sand to assist with drainage. The neck of the bulb should be just above soil level. Plant 12 in (30 cm) apart and do not disturb for several years when each year the bulbs will increase in size and form numerous offsets which will attain flowering size in about four years. The leaves die down before the flower buds appear in August when moisture should be withheld. After flowering, the bulbs should be covered with leaves and where possible with a frame light reared against the wall, though the *Lycoris* is more tolerant of winter moisture than *Amaryllis* and *Hippeastrum*. New leaves will form early in the year.

Indoors, plant one bulb to a 5-in (12·5-cm) pot, using a compost made up of fibrous loam, peat and decayed manure in equal parts and to which has been added a liberal sprinkling of sand or grit. Plant in July or early in August with the neck of the bulb just above the level of the compost. Water sparingly until the flowers appear then give an occasional application of dilute manure water. After flowering, the leaves will begin to form, and during winter and spring give only sufficient moisture to keep the plants growing. Frost should be excluded by placing the pots in a living-room of the home (if the greenhouse is unheated) where the night temperature does not fall below 40° F (4° C). High temperatures are to be avoided. As with *Nerine*, allow the plants a two-month rest period from the time the leaves fade in June until the flower stems appear in

August. At this time and until after the flowers have formed, moisture should be withheld.

The plants should remain in the pots for several years, top-dressing with fresh loam and cow manure each year after the leaves have died back.

Propagation. By offsets which are detached when the bulbs are ready for re-potting after four or five years. This is done early in August. The offsets are planted one to a 3-in (7·5-cm) pot containing a mixture of fibrous loam and sand. They are grown on for two years, giving them the necessary rest, when they will be ready to plant into 5-in (12·5-cm) pots in which they will bloom in two more years.

The plants (like *Nerine*) are readily raised from seed sown in April. This should be scattered over the surface of the John Innes compost. Keep in a moist condition and transplant to 3-in (7·5-cm) pots (one to each) in about 18 months. Here they will remain for 12 months, when they are moved to 5-in (12·5-cm) pots in which they will bloom in two more years.

Species and Varieties. *Lycoris aurea* (syn. *Nerine aurea*). Native of western China, it is known as the golden spider lily, the bright golden-yellow flowers appearing in an umbel on an 18-in (45-cm) scape. The funnel-shaped flowers have narrow wavy segments and measure about 3 in (7·5 cm) across.

Lycoris incarnata. Native of central China and northern Japan, it bears its funnel-shaped flowers of soft salmon-pink veined with blue in a large umbel of 6 to 12 and on a 16-in (40-cm) scape. The segments are only slightly waved but have a soft sweet perfume.

Lycoris radiata. Outstanding in its beauty, it was introduced from Japan in 1750 and is the hardiest species. The flowers are bright orange-red and scent-less, attractively reflexed and borne on a 15-in (37·5-cm) stem. The variety *alba* (syn. *L. albiflora*) bears creamy-white flowers, while *carnea* has white flowers tinted with pink.

Lycoris sanguinea. It is native of Japan and blooms three or four weeks earlier than other species. It has bright crimson-red flowers which measure about 2 in (5 cm) across and which are borne in a small umbel on an 18-in (45-cm) stem.

Lycoris squamigera. One of the best, being almost hardy and bearing large umbels of sweetly scented flowers of rosy-lilac pencilled with blue on a 2-ft (60-cm) scape and which appear after the narrow strap-like leaves.

Lycoris sprengeri. Native of southern Japan, it has long-stalked flowers of rich mauve-pink, without a distinct tube above the ovary. They are borne on 12-in (30-cm) stems.

Lycoris straminea. Native of western China, it is closely related to *L. aurea* and bears, on a 2-ft (60-cm) scape, straw-coloured flowers shaded with pink.

M

MASSONIA (Liliaceae)

A genus of 45 species of small bulbous plants, native of South Africa and named in honour of Frank Masson, a botanist who travelled widely there at the end of the eighteenth century. The flowers are borne late in spring, in umbels or clusters between twin opposite leaves, the flower stem being absent or almost so. They are best grown under glass in the British Isles and northern Europe.

Culture. Plant three or four bulbs to a 6-in (15-cm) pot or pan containing a compost made up of fibrous loam, leaf mould and grit. Plant in September, 1 in (2·5 cm) deep and stand in a frame, covering with ashes until late November. Then transfer to a cool greenhouse or shake away the ash and allow them to remain in the frame to bloom late in spring or early in summer.

Propagation. By the removal of offsets from around the older bulbs when re-potting in autumn. They are planted in boxes containing a gritty compost until reaching flowering size in about three years.

Species. *Massonia amygdalina*. It has short oval leaves and in April and May bears clusters of pure-white flowers which emit an almond-like scent, resembling heliotrope.

Massonia jasminiflora. The two oval leaves spread over the ground and between them there appears in spring, an almost stemless umbel of white star-like flowers, tipped with green.

Massonia muricata. Native of Natal, it has roundish heart-shaped leaves and bears pure-white flowers in small clusters.

Massonia pustulata. It forms three oval fleshy leaves (instead of the usual two), which are covered on the surface with white pustules, and in April it bears clusters of white flowers on a 1-in (2·5-cm) stem.

MEDEOLA (Liliaceae)

A genus of a single species, native of North America and taking its name from Medea, the sorceress, for its supposed medicinal qualities. It was introduced into Britain from Virginia in 1759. It grows in moist woodlands from Nova Scotia to Florida. It is known as cucumber root for the short rhizomatous root-stock has a pleasant refreshing smell of cucumber when lifted and when cut.

Culture. Plant in partial shade and in a moist soil. It may be grown with *Trillium*, to which it is closely related, or with Solomon's seal, which also enjoys a damp soil with plenty of leaf mould. Plant the rhizomes 12 in (3 cm) apart in autumn, just below the surface of the soil.

Propagation. By division of the rootstock (like Solomon's seal) which is done in autumn after the foliage has died down, or in spring. Dust the cut portion of the rhizome with sulphur before replanting.

Species. *Medeola virginiana.* From a rootstock 3 in (7·5 cm) long, it forms a slender, erect, unbranched stem 18 in (40 cm) tall, covered in down and with a whorl of leaves at the middle. The leaves are 3 in (7·5 cm) long and 1 in (2·5 cm) wide, narrowing at the base where they are often coloured red. The flowers are yellow, the perianth segments being ½ in (1·25 cm) long, and are borne in an umbel of three to nine during June. They are followed by a dark-blue fruit, a berry of about ½-in (1·25-cm) diameter.

MERENDERA (Liliaceae)

A genus of 10 species, native of the eastern Mediterranean, Ethiopia and India, their name being the Spanish for *Colchicum*, to which they are closely related. *M. montana* is known as the Pyrenees meadow saffron. They have swollen tunicated bulb-like corms, like those of *Colchicum* but smaller, and narrow leaves. They usually appear after the flowers, which are funnel-shaped and differ from *Colchicum* in the absence of a perianth tube. They are less hardy than the *Colchicum* and less robust and should be grown in the alpine garden or to the front of a shrubbery in the warmer gardens of northern Europe and North America, or in the alpine house or frame.

Culture. Outdoors, they require a soil retentive of summer moisture but which is well-drained in winter. Add sand or grit to assist drainage and leaf mould to make the soil retentive of moisture during dry weather. Plant the corms 2 in (5 cm) deep early in July, for they bloom from early August until the end of May—depending upon species—thus giving a long succession of bloom if several species are planted.

Indoors, plant five or six corms to each pan or 6-in (15-cm) pot, using a gritty compost which incorporates some leaf mould and a small quantity of de-hydrated cow manure. Plant the corms in July, 1 in (2·5 cm) deep and place in an open frame or on a veranda until they have formed their roots, then remove to a cool greenhouse or cover with frame lights which should be opened whenever weather permits. The plants require cool conditions but are best protected from winter rains, mist and hard frost. They are most attractive and worthy of some care in their culture. After flowering, stand outdoors early in summer and where they remain until autumn.

Propagation. Disturb the plants as little as possible, lifting and dividing every four or five years, the most suitable time being in July after the leaves have died back and before the flowers of *M. montana* begin to appear. Plant the corms into pans or boxes containing a sandy compost, where they will remain for two years, after which they are planted into their flowering quarters.

Merenderas grow steadily from seed but will take four or five years to reach flowering size. Sow in spring in a frame or in boxes of sandy compost, just covering the seed and keeping it moist. When the young leaves die back the following summer, place some manure over them, repeating this the following year. In three years, the corms will be large enough to plant out. Alternatively, plant in pots in which they will bloom within two years.

Species. *Merendera filifolia.* Native of the Balearic Islands and of Algeria, it requires glass protection in the British Isles and northern Europe, where it will bloom in September. It makes a small corm with an extended neck and has filiform leaves which appear with the flowers. The blooms are rose-pink and are borne about 2 in (5 cm) above the ground.

Merendera montana. Native of the Pyrenees, it resembles *Bulbocodium vernum* but blooms in August and September. It makes a small corm and has narrow curved leaves which appear in October after the flowers and remain green throughout winter. The flowers are rosy mauve and open about 3 in (7·5 cm) above soil level.

Merendera persica (syn. *M. robusta*). Present in Persia and Afghanistan and north-eastern India, it blooms in spring, the leaves appearing with purple-pink flowers which are enhanced by their anthers of brilliant green.

Merendera sobolifera. It is found from Bulgaria east to Afghanistan and has an irregular rhizomatous corm mottled with purple. The linear leaves appear early in spring with the flowers which are pale rosy-lilac, the narrow claw-like petals giving them a spidery appearance.

Merendera trigyna (syn. *M. caucasica*). Native of the Caucasus and the Middle East, it has narrow leaves which appear with the flowers in April and May. The flowers are white or pale lilac, tinted with rose pink and with narrow petals 4 in (10 cm) long. It is scented.

MELASPHAERULA (Iridaceae)

A genus of a single species, native of Cape Province and taking its name from *melas*, black, and *sphaerula*, a ball, a reference to the colour of the small black corms, which are almost spherical with numerous cormlets clustering round the base. They are covered in leathery fibres. The leaves are lanceolate and grasslike; the flowers small and creamy-white with the perianth lobes free to the base. It is hardy only in the mildest parts of the British Isles and northern Europe and, as it blooms in spring, is best grown in a cool greenhouse.

Culture. Plant six corms to a 6-in (15-cm) pot containing a compost made up of fibrous loam, leaf mould and sand in equal part. Plant in September 1 in (2·5 cm) deep and stand the pots in a frame and plunge into ashes. Give little or no water until growth begins. Transfer the pots to the greenhouse in November and water sparingly until the plants make growth in spring. The flowers may require staking as they grow 18 in (45 cm) tall. After flowering, allow the foliage to die down, then place outdoors in a sunny position and rest during late summer and autumn.

Propagation. After two years in the pots, shake out the corms when the foliage has died down and remove the small corms to be found clustering about the base. Plant into pans or boxes containing sandy compost and grow on for two years before planting into flowering-size pots.

Species. *Melasphaerula graminea* (syn. *M. ramosa*). Common on lower mountainous slopes near the Cape, it has bright-green grass-like leaves 12 in (30 cm) long and bears creamy-white star-like flowers with purple veins in a branching panicle.

MORAEA (Iridaceae)

A genus of about 100 species, native of tropical and southern Africa and Madagascar and named in honour of the British botanist Robert Moore. It has a globose corm covered in a woody tunic. The lower leaves are long and narrow, the upper short and sheathing. The flowers are borne in terminal clusters and, though fleeting, open successively from two green spathes. The perianth segments are free (in ixia, united into a tube) with the blades spreading, the three inner being shorter than the three outer. It is known as the butterfly iris and requires a sunny situation where it will bloom in May. *M. spathulatum*, which blooms in July, is more tolerant of rain and cold than ixia and freesia and may be grown in the open south of a line drawn from Chester to King's Lynn in Britain.

Culture. Outdoors, provide a sheltered, sunny position and a well-drained soil containing some sand or grit and either peat or leaf mould. Plant in September 3 in (7·5 cm) deep and 6 in (15 cm) apart, preferably in raised beds beneath a sunny wall which will permit the corms to be covered during winter with a frame light reared against the wall. After flowering, the foliage will die down gradually when moisture should be withheld.

For indoor culture, plant five or six corms to a 6-in (15-cm) pot containing a compost made up of fibrous loam, peat or leaf mould and sand in equal parts. Plant in September 1 in (2·5 cm) deep and allow the corms two months outdoors or in a frame to make root growth. Then remove to a cool greenhouse where the temperature does not exceed 42° F (5° C) or fall below 38° F (3° C). Water sparingly during winter. Indoors, the plants will bloom early in spring; a month later (in May) outdoors, while several species are summer-flowering. After flowering, dry off and allow the corms several months rest before starting them into growth again in autumn.

Propagation. Usually by offsets, which are detached when the corms are re-potted in autumn. They are grown on in pans or boxes containing a sandy compost for two years then planted into pots in which they will flower the following year.

Plants raised from seed will take four or five years to bear bloom. Sow in June in pans or boxes containing a compost made up of sterilised loam, peat and sand in equal parts and only just cover the seed. Water sparingly when once the seed has germinated, and allow the plants to remain in the containers for two years before moving the corms to boxes containing a similar compost in which they are planted 1 in (2·5 cm) apart. They are grown on for another two years to reach flowering size.

Species. *Moraea bicolor.* Native of Natal, it bears its flowers on a 3-ft (90-cm) stem. They are pale yellow with purple spots at the base of each segment.

Moraea ciliata. Common on mountainous slopes at the Cape, it has a short stem, enclosed by the leaves and has pubescent spathes. The flowers are lilac with a pubescent triangular patch on the outer segments. They bloom in July and August—in spring in the British Isles—and are scented.

Moraea decussata. Frequent on sandy flats near the Cape, it has a corm covered in bristly fibres and three or four leaves, crisped at the margins. The flowers are yellow, sweetly scented with an orange blotch on the outer segments. They bloom in spring in the British Isles.

Moraea iridioides. Native of Natal. From its rhizomatous rootstock arises a tuft of narrow sword-like leaves and white flowers borne on 3- to 4-ft (90-cm to 1·2-metre) stems. They have a yellow blotch at the base and a downy central 'claw'.

Moraea odorata. Native of the Cape, where it is found only rarely near Grassy Park, opening its flowers each day at 3 p.m. They remain open until late evening to be pollinated by moths. The two lower leaves are 2 ft (60 cm) in length, while the white flowers are held on 18-in (45-cm) stems. The flowers are powerfully scented and at the Cape appear in December.

Moraea papilionaceae. Present on grassy slopes at the Cape, it has three pubescent leaves and bears flowers of yellowish-brown with a yellow mark on the outer segments. They appear in April and May and are scented.

Moraea pavonia (syn. *M. glaucopis, M. tricuspidata, Iris pavonia*). Native of Cape Province, where it is found in damp fields, usually growing beneath trees, and is known as the peacock iris, for at the base of each petal of the snow-white blooms is a circle of peacock blue surrounded with purple, like the 'eyes' on a peacock's tail. The variety *lutea* has yellow flowers, and, with the type, is the parent of numerous hybrids.

Moraea ramosissima (syn. *M. ramosa*). With *M. spathacea*, it is the hardiest species and, flowering midsummer, may be grown outdoors in the British Isles. Native of the Cape, where it is to be found at Newlands and on Table Mountain, it has small corms covered by spiny fibres, while its basal leaves bear cormlets in the axils. The flowers are dull yellow, borne on 2-ft (60-cm) stems, and they have a strong lily-like scent. They are shaded blue at the base and appear in long succession.

Moraea spathacea. Though native of the Transvaal it is almost hardy in the British Isles and has been known to withstand several degrees of frost. It has leaves 3 to 4 ft (90 cm to 1·2 metres) long, and its flowers, which are borne during May and June, appear on 3-ft (90-cm) stems. They are brilliant yellow with a 'claw' at the base and are scented. They are followed by handsome seed pods which may be used for floral decoration.

Moraea villosa. It is one of the peacock moraeas, resembling *M. pavonia*, and from it have been raised many hybrids. The lilac flowers have the peacock 'eye' or half circle of greenish-blue surrounded with black at the base and are borne on wiry stems 2 ft (60 cm) tall. The hybrids bear flowers of white, scarlet, orange and bronze, all with the peacock 'eye'.

MUSCARI (Liliaceae)

A genus of about 60 species, native of southern and central eastern Europe and western Asia and taking their name from *moschos*, musk, referring to the musk-like scent of *M. moschatum*. From the tunicated bulbs arise channelled linear leaves and dense racemes of urn-shaped flowers, usually of purple or blue and held on a leafless scape 4 to 9 in (10 to 22·5 cm) tall. Depending upon species, they bloom from February until June, are hardy and multiply rapidly. Flowering with daffodils, they should be planted with them in short grass or in the shrubbery to form a carpet of blue. They are also delightful planted in groups about the rock garden. *M. azureum* and *M. armeniacum* are charming with *Primula vulgaris*, the common yellow primrose and provide a pleasing contrast to those bearing white flowers—such as Buckland White with its bronze-tinted foliage or the compact Snow Cushion, which forms a mat of brilliant green studded with white star-like flowers. Alternatively, plant blue primroses —Blue Riband is the finest—with white-flowered muscari, and among them the miniature daffodils such as *Narcissus cyclamineus* Peeping Tom.

Since the tiny conical flowers of *M. botryoides* resemble black grapes in their colour and have a grape-like 'bloom', the muscari came to be known as the grape hyacinth. Of this plant Gerard said that it smelled 'strong . . . yet not unpleasant'. Ruskin wrote of it in more romantic terms. It was 'as if a cluster of grapes and a hive of honey had been distilled and pressed together in one small boss of celled and beaded blue'. The white variety *alba*, was known to Parkinson as pearls of Spain for it is a plant of southern Spain and was grown in Elizabethan gardens.

There are numerous interesting forms of the muscari, none more so than *M. comosum monstrosum*, described by the American writer Louise Wilder 'as a quaint monstrosity'. Gerard called it the 'fair-headed hyacinth' because of its twisted filaments of purple and gold. The feather hyacinth, as it is known, is a cottage garden favourite and will bear its violet-blue and gold 'feathers' in May. It has a plume-like appearance. *M. moschatum*, with its dingy flowers, is a species to grow in pots indoors. What it lacks in beauty it makes up in its rich incense-like perfume, which will scent a room for weeks.

Culture. Outdoors, plant 7- to 8-cm bulbs in September, 3 in (7·5 cm) deep and 4 in (10 cm) apart, preferably in groups of 6 to 12 and on a bed of sand to assist drainage. They like a gritty soil enriched with a little decayed manure and some peat or leaf mould and are happy in full sun or in partial shade, where they may accompany primulas.

Where growing indoors, plant five or six bulbs of 8-cm size to a 6-in (15-cm) pot containing a compost made up of fibrous loam, decayed manure and leaf mould, to which is added some sand or grit. Plant 1 in (2·5 cm) deep and 2 in (5 cm) apart in September, placing the pots in a dark, cool place or in the plunge bed outdoors, where they remain for eight weeks. Then remove to a cool greenhouse or warm room where the temperature does not exceed 50° F (10° C). Water only occasionally, and after flowering dry off gradually as the foliage dies back and place the pots beneath the greenhouse bench or outdoors beneath the eaves of a house, where they remain until time for repotting in autumn.

Propagation. They increase freely from offsets which form about the old bulbs and are detached upon lifting after four or five years, by which time they will have attained considerable size. From bulbs grown in pots, the offsets will be smaller and should be grown on in boxes of sandy compost for two years until reaching flowering size.

Plants may be raised from seed sown in April in a frame or in pans containing a sandy compost. They will germinate in about six weeks. The plants are grown on for 18 months before moving the bulblets to pots or boxes containing a compost made up of fibrous loam, leaf mould and sand in equal parts. Here they are grown on for two more years until ready to plant out and will bloom within four or five years of sowing.

Species and Varieties. *Muscari ambrosiacum.* Native of Asia Minor, it is closely related to *M. moschatum*. Like that species it was named for the sweet perfume of its flowers, the upper 'grapes' being of soft lilac, the lower cream-coloured with a brown rim to the little bells.

Muscari argaei album. It is late-flowering, from early May until mid-June, while the flowers remain fresh for several weeks. They are white, like tiny spikes of chalk and are borne on 4-in (10-cm) stems.

Muscari armeniacum. Native of south-western Europe and Asia Minor, it will make a bulb up to 10 cm in circumference and will also increase by self-sown seed. A brilliant blue form is known as Early Giant, for the 9- to 10-cm bulbs will permit gentle forcing in a temperature of 58° F (14° C) when plants in bloom in pots find a ready sale. The flowers of cobalt blue with a white rim are borne in large spikes on a 9-in (22·5-cm) stem during April and May. They are scented. There are also several varieties of merit. Cantab bears flowers of soft sky-blue on a 6-in (15-cm) stem while Blue Spike bears double flowers of medium blue in ball-shaped heads resembling *Primula denticulata*.

Muscari botryoides. Native of southern France and Italy, it is known as the Italian grape hyacinth and bears globular flowers of navy-blue with a white rim. It grows 6 in (15 cm) tall and blooms during April and May. The white form *album*, which is native of southern Spain, bears a small cylindrical spike of pure-white bells. It has an unusual perfume, described by Parkinson as 'like into starch when it is made new and hot'. The flower is shown in the painting of spring flowers by J. Marellus (1614–81) now in the Fitzwilliam Museum, Cambridge.

Muscari comosum. Native of south-eastern Europe, it is known as the tassel hyacinth and has narrow strap-like leaves. It bears its flowers in a cluster at the end of a 16-in (40-cm) stem during May and June, being one of the latest to bloom. At the top of the cluster are sterile purple flowers, which grow upwards, with green fertile flowers below and which hang downwards, to give it a tassel-like appearance. It is scented.

In the variety *monstrosum* (syn. *plumosum*), the flowers are all sterile and purple-blue in colour and have been converted into a mass of slender twisted filaments giving the flower heads a feathery appearance, hence its name of the feather hyacinth. It lasts long in bloom and also when cut and used for indoor decoration.

Muscari conicum. Native of Persia and western Asia, it bears a conical spike on a 9-in (22·5-cm) scape during April, the bright-blue flowers being fertile, the pale-blue flowers sterile; and it remains fresh for several weeks. Heavenly Blue, which may be a variety, bears a tightly packed spike of gentian blue.

Muscari latifolium. Native of south-eastern Europe, it is a strong grower, its flowers appearing in April and May on a 15-in (37·5-cm) stem, which arises from a solitary broad, arum-like leaf, like a pale green spathe shielding a dark-blue tongue. The bud pushes up to open pale blue and sterile at the top, dark blue beneath. The bells hang down to give it a lightness and informality unknown among others.

Muscari massayanum. Native of Persia, it is the rarest and most striking of all. It grows only 6 in (15 cm) tall and has delicate filaments of vivid carmine at the tip, passing to crimson and to crimson-brown, a combination of colours unique in the world of floriculture. It blooms during May and June and is a treasure in the alpine garden.

Muscari moschatum (syn. *M. suaveolens*). It is the musk hyacinth of Asia

Minor which has given its name to the genus. It forms a large bulb and has broad leaves, while it bears its flowers on an 8-in (20-cm) scape. They are of dull olive-green, later changing to an uninteresting shade of yellowish-brown but with a delicious scent. Several in a pan will scent a large room for weeks during spring.

The variety *flavum* (syn. *M. macrocarpum*), native of the islands of the Aegean, has large flowers of yellowish-green, tipped with purple, later turning to clear yellow and borne in a loose spike. *Major* is slightly larger still in all respects and *minor* is more compact. It bears its greyish flowers in small spikes on a 6-in (15-cm) stem and diffuses a pungent incense-like scent. It may be planted in a trough garden beneath a window which may be opened whenever the weather permits, so that the scent of the blooms may drift indoors. The musk hyacinths require a sunny position.

Muscari neglectum. Native of southern Europe, it forms a large bulb and bears, early in summer, dense clusters of blackish-blue grape-like flowers on an 8-in (20-cm) stem. The flowers, borne with freedom, are enhanced by the white rim and they are sweetly scented, while the foliage is brilliant green. It blooms in May and June.

Muscari paradoxum. Native of the Caucasus, it makes a large bulb and has strap-like leaves nearly 18 in (45 cm) long. It blooms in May and June, its deep-purple flowers, tinted peacock green on the inside, appearing in a thick broad spike on an 8-in (20-cm) stem.

Muscari pinardii. A rare tassel-flowered species from Cilicia, which requires scree conditions or the shelter of an alpine house or frame. It bears its flowers on an 8-in (20-cm) stem. They are composed of grey filaments with the tips brilliant blue. It blooms late in May and in June.

Muscari polyanthum. Native of northern Greece, it is one of the first to bloom, the navy-blue flowers borne in a dense spike on a 6-in (15-cm) stem. The form *album* is one of the best of the white-flowered *muscari*, having the same neat habit as the type so that it is a valuable plant for the alpine garden. Its short spikes of creamy white retain their beauty for several weeks from mid-March to early May.

Muscari racemosum. The starch hyacinth, which is distributed throughout Europe including the British Isles. It has rather weak, slender channelled leaves 8 in (20 cm) long, and in March bears short cylindrical spikes of purple-blue flowers which smell strongly of ripe plums.

Muscari tubergenianum. Discovered in north-western Persia and introduced by van Tubergen of Haarlem. It is known as the Oxford and Cambridge grape hyacinth. The buds are deep turquoise-blue, of a colour unknown in any other flower, while they open to reveal a spike of sky blue at the top, navy blue below. It blooms during April and May on an 8-in (20-cm) scape, several arising from one bulb. The broad leaves lie flat on the ground. It is a valuable alpine garden species.

N

NARCISSUS (Amaryllidaceae)

A genus of 60 species, native of Europe, the Mediterranean and western Asia and named by Linnaeus in honour of the youth in Greek mythology who was changed into the flower. Species known as 'daffodils' have a large trumpet in contrast to the small-cupped forms known as 'narcissus'. They have tunicated bulbs and narrow strap-like leaves (rush-like in *N. juncifolium*), while the flowers of white, yellow or pink have six spreading segments with a central corona varying in size and shape from being shallow and scarcely noticeable to one 2 in (5 cm) long and 1 in (2·5 cm) wide, of trumpet shape.

As early as 1548 Turner mentioned the wild daffodil, *N. pseudo-narcissus*, and Gerard had this to say about it: 'It is most common in our country gardens. . . . The flower groweth at the top, of a yellowish white colour with a yellow crown or circle in the middle tinues; we have them all and every one of them in our London gardens in great abundance.'

During Elizabethan times, wild daffodils grew so profusely around London that the women of Cheapside sold the flowers made up into large bunches, to those in the city who were unable to grow their own. This daffodil has a long trumpet of deepest yellow and has the same woodland or moss-like fragrance as the primrose. It is early-flowering, hence its name, Lent lily.

The poet Shelley described the narcissus as 'the fairest flower among them all'—and for their numerous delightful forms and their long-flowering season, daffodils must be the most popular of all spring flowers, sharing pride of place with the primrose. Perhaps the popularity of the daffodil derives from it being a flower native to Britain; like the primrose with which it keeps company, flowering throughout spring and early summer. Nowhere are the two plants happier than when growing in short grass, given the protection of trees or shrubs which provide the dappled shade both so much enjoy. In a coppice, wild garden or orchard, they may be rewarded in abundance using the more inexpensive and old-established varieties such as Sir Watkin and Golden Spur, listed by William Robinson in *The English Flower Garden* (1883). He tells that these varieties will treble themselves the second year after planting. This freedom of flowering and the fact that they will grow in shade, increasing each year in any average soil containing some humus, contributes greatly to their high esteem. But perhaps it is the fact that they require almost no attention when once planted makes the daffodil and narcissus so valuable to the modern gardener, who must now cultivate his own garden with the minimum of attention and with little or no outside help. Apart from an occasional top-dressing of peat when the bulbs are growing in soil devoid of humus and the removal of the dead flower heads, the bulbs may be left in their original position for years. The wide variety of forms gives it an added attraction. All are valuable for pot culture and the dainty dwarf species are ideal for rockery or for planting round the roots of large trees. Planted towards the front of a shrubbery, a daffodil border is most beautiful, the bulbs being set out in groups of six or a dozen, using as many different types and varieties as possible.

Where planting for garden display and for commercial cut flower, thought must be given to those varieties which increase most rapidly and which bear the most flowers from a bulb.

Experiments to assist growers were carried out over a number of years at the Rosewarne Experimental Station of the Ministry of Agriculture. Their findings were published in 1970 and most interesting reading do they make. The rate of increase in bulbs was measured by weight increase, after the bulbs have been growing for two years; while the numbers of flowers per bulb was recorded in the second season after planting single nosed bulbs (rounds).

Variety	Section	Weight increase	Blooms per bulb
		(per cent)	
Beryl	6	270	4·2
Binkie	1d	281	4·5
Carlton	2a	223	2·2
Edward Buxton	3a	243	4·3
Fortune	2a	145	2·1
Golden Ducat	4	127	1·3
Golden Harvest	1a	200	2·4
Ice Follies	2c	350	2·5
Joseph McLeod	1a	309	1·8
King Alfred	1a	154	2·0
Mount Hood	1c	217	2·0
Peeping Tom	6	220	4·0
Snipe	6	276	4·1
Sweetness	7	415	4·5

In yellow trumpets, Joseph McLeod increased in weight by 309 per cent and Golden Harvest by 200 per cent as against 154 per cent by King Alfred. In the white trumpet section, Mount Hood increased by 217 per cent; and in white cups, Ice Follies had the greatest increase of all, with a 350 per cent increase in weight and 2·5 blooms per bulb. But among the most free-flowering are the N. cyclamineus hybrids—Snipe, Beryl and Peeping Tom—which averaged four

Narcissus canaliculatus

Narcissus triandus albus

Narcissus February Gold with Snowdrop and *Anemone blanda*

blooms or more from each bulb and should be more widely planted if only for their exceptional freedom of flowering.

Culture. A well-drained soil, deeply worked and containing some humus is ideal for the narcissus. The plant will in no way tolerate a waterlogged soil. The bulbs grow and flower best in a soil containing leaf mould in the natural state, such as is to be found in woodlands, though the best bloom is obtained from those bulbs planted away from the hungry roots of tall trees. Dappled shade will enable the bloom to remain in a fresh condition for as long a period as possible and will prevent fading should the weather be unduly sunny. An ideal position is between rows of orchard trees, in soil of fibrous loam which has received an occasional top-dressing of peat or decayed manure. Animal manure must not come in direct contact with the bulbs though wool shoddy, decayed leaves, peat or hop manure worked into the soil will help to retain the necessary moisture about the bulbs. Wet, clay soil may be lightened and made suitable for daffodils by incorporating a quantity of grit before opening up the texture with humus materials. Woodland soil will be suitable for planting without any special preparation for the daffodil prefers a soil which is slightly acid.

When planting in the border or in beds, the ground should be prepared early in August, so that it is allowed time to settle before the bulbs are set out early in September. Just before, the ground should be given a light dressing with wood ash and a 2-oz per square yard dressing of steamed bone flour, which should be raked into the soil. Established beds, or bulbs planted in short grass will also benefit from a yearly dressing with bone flour and a peat mulch given in February, just before the foliage appears above ground. When planting with members of the primrose family, such as blue primroses or blue polyanthus, which are so effective used with Golden Harvest or King Alfred daffodils, the plants should be placed in position immediately after the bulbs are planted 5 in (12·5 cm) deep and 8 in (20 cm) apart. If the ground is used for summer bedding plants, these may be left in position and planting of the beds delayed until early October, though early planting for daffodils is preferable. The great advantage of growing in an orchard or a shrub border is that the bulbs may be planted at the correct time and left undisturbed. Also, the blooms will be afforded some protection from cold and often strong winds during spring.

Where bulbs are planted in an orchard, it will not be possible to cut the grass until the foliage has died down in July. The grass may then be cut short to facilitate gathering of the fruit in autumn.

It is not advisable to plant daffodils on a lawn which is to be frequently cut. Preferably, plant the bulbs along the edge of the lawn if there is no other place available and this strip can be left uncut until the foliage has died back in July.

When growing for profit, the bulbs should be planted either in prepared beds or in an orchard; but in either case the beds should be made 3 to 4 ft (90 cm to 1·2 metres) wide to enable picking to be done easily. So that staking will not be

P

necessary, plant the bulbs 4 in (10 cm) apart each way. If Dutch lights are to be used for covering the beds, use a 4-ft (1·2-metre) light and make the beds just under 4 ft (1·2 metres) wide.

What size bulb to plant is often a question of speculation. Daffodils and narcissi are advertised as 'double-nose 1', 'double-nose 2', 'double-nose 3' and 'rounds'. There is approximately 50p per 100 difference in the price. First size double-nose bulbs are of enormous proportions and will produce several flowers. The 'double-nose 2' size are cheaper and generally used for cool-house or home culture in pots. 'Rounds' are suitable for garden culture, while large 'rounds' are generally used for forcing. As with all bulbs, the firm, virile, round bulb of good average size is the most suitable for planting for cool conditions indoors and for open-air culture under glass. Often the monster top-size bulbs have lost their vitality and have become too acclimatised to their original surroundings to be entirely satisfactory. Mr Guy Wilson has suggested that a good-sized offset will produce a top-quality bloom if given cool treatment. The skin should be clean, light brown and smooth, and the bulbs be quite firm when gently pressed with the thumb. Small rounds will be suitable for outdoor planting if they measure up to this standard.

Bulbs planted in borders or in beds which may remain undisturbed, should be lifted and divided every three years. This is not vital if one is pressed for time during September, but it should be the rule where possible and where bloom of exhibition quality is required. The offsets should be removed and planted in a nursery bed and the bulbs, which will have now formed clusters of good-sized bulbs, should be carefully pulled apart and replanted into ground which has previously been prepared. This work of lifting, dividing and replanting may be done any time after the leaves have turned yellow and died down. Some growers utilising cloches or frames for early bloom, plant the bulbs early in August to allow them as long a time as possible in the ground, before covering them with glass early in the new year.

Most of the well-known exhibitors will lift and divide the bulbs in July before new root action commences, for they contend that once this begins, the check will seriously impair the ability of the bulbs to produce a bloom of top quality the following spring. But the daffodil is one of the most accommodating of all plants, and may even be planted as late as December, though the blooms will be later in appearing in spring and will lack quality. If the bulbs are to remain out of the ground for any length of time, they should be placed on shallow trays in a dry but cool room. If sending bulbs through the post, pack them in dry peat to prevent bruising

Daffodils and narcissi are ideal for growing under barn cloches or frames, for they do not grow too tall. The bulbs should be planted in August. If cloches are used, two rows may be placed side by side with a path between each double row. One method is to cover the beds with straw and soil or ashes during early autumn, in order that moisture may be retained and a strong rooting system formed. The covering is removed towards the year's end when the rows are covered with glass.

As soon as the plants have finished flowering the glass is removed; and when the foliage has died down, this is removed and burnt and the bed given a top-dressing with peat and old mushroom bed compost.

When growing daffodils in the home garden, alongside a path or in beds near the house, any untidiness of the leaves may be overcome while dying back if they are tied loosely together into knots. Or again, where time for gardening is limited, the leaves may be pegged down at ground-level with wire sprigs and the summer bedding plants set out between the leaves early in June.

Indoors there is no happier flower than the daffodil when given cool treat-ment. True, more forced daffodils are sold in the early new year than any other flower—forced that is in temperatures around 56° F (13° C)—but it is only under cool conditions, where a temperature of between 40° and 48° F (4° and 9° C) is maintained to keep out frost and prevent mildew, that the daffodil reaches perfection. Under such conditions, the plants may receive that in-dividual attention which each variety demands and it is only thus that the delicate whites and pinks and creams of the modern varieties can be seen at their best, shielded from soot deposits, soil splashings and strong winds which out-doors will cause bruising of the flowers. The daffodil is at its best under con-ditions somewhere between those required for the snowdrop and the tulip; a cold, damp atmosphere it does not enjoy, neither is it happy in considerable heat. In a cool living-room or warm greenhouse, the plants will bloom to per-fection from February until late April, if varieties for successional flowering are selected. For home culture top-size or double-nose bulbs are planted in 5-in (12·5-cm) pots, four bulbs to each; or earthenware bowls are equally effective. A compost of good fibrous loam to which is added a small quantity of peat and some coarse sand is ideal. As the bulbs have a tendency to decay at the base, ample drainage must be provided. To keep the compost sweet, place a few pieces of charcoal at the bottom of the pot.

Now comes the crucial point. More often than not, daffodil bulbs are then placed in a darkened cupboard in a room which is too warm for them. For from 12 to 14 weeks, absolutely cool conditions are essential from the time the bulbs are planted about 1st September. It must be remembered that daffodils require a very long period for the formation of their rooting system and while this is taking place, almost ice-cold conditions are necessary. Where possible, the home grower should place the pots outdoors away from the sunlight; alternatively, a cellar will be suitable and there the bulbs must remain until they have become well rooted and made about 2 in (5 cm) of top growth. This will mean taking them indoors about mid-December onwards, depending upon the variety. All too often impatience will cause them to be placed in too warm a room, or they are brought from the darkness before the bulbs are sufficiently well rooted, with the result that the foliage turns yellow and no bloom appears. When placing the pots outdoors, cover them with 6 in (15 cm) of ashes or soil to keep them dark. Plant the bulbs firmly, with the tops showing just above soil-level. When growing for cut bloom, it is usual to plant in strong wooden boxes with the bulbs almost touching each other. The boxes are placed outdoors and covered in ashes as described.

Bowl culture of narcissus

Early in January, or (for certain varieties) just before Christmas, if a warm greenhouse is available, the soil or ashes are carefully shaken away and the pots or boxes are first placed in a position of partial shade—under a greenhouse bench or in a semi-darkened position in a living-room—where they remain for ten days to become accustomed to the light. The compost should be kept moist and more water given as the bulbs are brought on either by the heat of the sun or from the artificial warmth of living-room or greenhouse. As they reach flowering stage, copious amounts of water will be required.

The blooms should be supported by inserting thin sticks or canes around the pots or boxes as soon as the buds show the first sign of colour. Staking is essential for all but the dwarf-growing species, which must be an additional reason for using pots instead of bowls, which are often too shallow to allow for efficient staking.

Where the blooms are to be cut they should be removed before they are fully open, and where they have to travel a distance for exhibition or sale, they should be allowed to stand in rainwater for a full 24 hours before packing. Flowers growing in the open and which are required in bloom as soon as possible should be cut the moment the buds show colour and placed in water in a slightly warmed room or greenhouse. There they will open in 48 hours with a saving of at least two to three days on the time taken if left to open outdoors. This may enable the bloom to be marketed on a Thursday or Friday, which is the best selling time of the week, rather than on the Monday or Tuesday, which would otherwise be so if the blooms were not cut and taken indoors.

Consideration must be given to the performance of each variety when grown indoors commercially. Double-nose bulbs of Golden Harvest will cost more per 1,000 than Carlton. Both are excellent selling varieties; but under forcing conditions Carlton will take a full month to yield its full quota of blooms but Golden Harvest will require only three weeks; which will mean that the greenhouse space may be more quickly utilised for another crop. Again, the size of bulbs is another consideration; Golden Harvest makes a mature bulb of almost half the size of that of King Alfred, which means that almost double the number of bulbs can be accommodated in the same area of the greenhouse and will yield double the amount of bloom.

Earliness in forcing is another factor. Golden Spur may be forced from early December and will be clear of the greenhouse by mid-February to allow another variety to be forced while prices are still profitable; and with the high price of fuel, prices obtained from a quick-maturing variety will be enhanced by the use of less fuel. Only by growing and experimenting with several new varieties each season can the commercial grower determine which will prove most profitable.

The use of low-storage temperatures will induce earliness of flowering, but time of lifting the bulbs is important, for there is danger of damaging them through cooling in temperatures of less than 48° F (9° C). The Dutch growers lift at the end of July and keep the bulbs in a temperature of 48° F (9° C) until late September. The bulbs should be boxed as soon as possible after arrival and kept as cool as possible until taken into a temperature of just under 60° F (16° C) at the end of November. They will then come into bloom early in the new year.

Daffodils sold in pots must be grown as cool as possible so that fluctuations of temperatures will not cause trouble. They, too, should be marketed with the buds just showing colour so that the purchaser may have the added enjoyment of seeing the blooms open. White tissue paper should be wrapped round the pots and the foliage and buds should also be enclosed by the paper.

After indoor-grown bulbs have finished flowering, those grown in heat should be planted in trenches in some out-of-the-way corner or in the woodland garden, where they will produce smaller blooms. They may take a year to recover. Bulbs grown under cool conditions are allowed to die back by gradually withholding water. The bulbs should then be removed from the pots, cleaned and replanted in the open in August when they will be none the worse for flowering indoors.

For the rock garden and for planting around the roots of young trees; as an edging to a path or border; in the alpine garden for window-box, and especially in pans for the alpine house or cold frame, the dainty species which bloom on stems no taller than 6 in (15 cm) will make a delightful display during April. They are inexpensive and so easily grown in any fibrous loam to which has been added some peat and coarse sand or shingle. Small pockets should be prepared on the rock garden to take four or five bulbs, which are planted in September after the rockery has been thoroughly cleaned and the established plants stripped of any straggling growth. When using a window-box or tub it is not always convenient to plant before mid-October, which will not be too late as the miniatures do not seem to require so long a season to make root growth.

Propagation. Most species and varieties increase rapidly by means of offsets. The large-flowering varieties should be lifted and divided every five or six years, this being done immediately after the foliage has completely died back. The offsets are removed and will be of all sizes for they continue to grow and increase in size each year. Every offset can be replanted 6 to 8 in (15 to 20 cm) apart and even the smallest will come into bloom in three or four years.

The species are best lifted and divided whenever the clumps become large and overcrowded, and this should be done in May, when they have flowered and before the foliage begins to die down, as for snowdrops. The clumps are lifted and divided into small groups of three or four bulbs, to be replanted immediately with the foliage above ground level. By this method there should be no loss of bloom the following season as there will usually be if dividing is left until autumn.

Species and Varieties. The order follows the Royal Horticultural Society classification.

I. TRUMPET NARCISSI. Distinguishing characters: One flower to a stem: trumpet or corona as long as, or longer than the perianth segments.

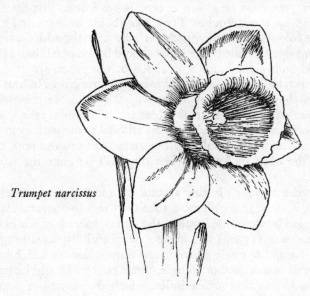

Trumpet narcissus

I(*a*). *Yellow Trumpets*. Perianth coloured; corona coloured, not paler than perianth.

ARCTIC GOLD. Award of Merit 1963. Of outstanding quality with broad overlapping perianth petals and a large trumpet deeply serrated at the mouth. The colour is deep golden-yellow throughout.

CROMARTY. Of faultless form, the broad, smooth, flat perianth standing at right-angles to the neatly flanged and serrated trumpet; colour, deep self-gold; free-flowering and of splendid habit. It does well in a town garden.

DUTCH MASTER. After King Alfred, possibly the finest all-round yellow trumpet yet introduced, fine in pots and for forcing, and outstanding in the garden. It has deep overlapping petals and a large serrated trumpet. It has no faults and does well anywhere.

GARRON. A magnificent flower that combines refinement of quality and colour with immense size, having a broad, slightly waved perianth of smoothest velvety texture and thick substance, and a beautifully serrated trumpet. Colour is deep, clear primrose yellow.

GOLDCOURT. A first-class exhibition flower of perfect form and quality. The whole flower is pure glistening gold throughout.

GOLDEN HARVEST. A first-class yellow trumpet of good colour, large size and refined form. The trumpet is deep golden-yellow set off by an overlapping perianth of clear yellow. Excellent for garden decoration and for forcing.

HUNTER'S MOON. It bears a refined trumpet arrayed in graded tints of clear shining, cool, luminous lemon. Vigorous, free-blooming and durable, it is a sheer delight for cutting, a most beautiful garden plant and exquisite in pots.

JOSEPH MCLEOD. It multiplies more rapidly and bears more bloom for the area of ground it occupies than any yellow trumpet. It bears a bloom of immense size with overlapping perianth and deeply frilled trumpet.

KING ALFRED. A superb all-round trumpet daffodil; 24 in (60 cm) in height and bearing a flower of great substance. The colour is deep golden yellow. It is first-rate for forcing.

KINGSCOURT. Bred from Royalist, it forms a large flower of faultless form, and of uniform rich deep golden yellow. The flat smooth perianth is of immense breadth and has a perfectly balanced bell-mouthed trumpet. For years rated in the Royal Horticultural Society Daffodil Year Book ballot as the best exhibition yellow trumpet.

LEINSTER. One of the best yellow trumpets, making a large flower of ideal show form with a broad, flat perianth standing at right-angles to the beautifully balanced trumpet, well-flanged and frilled at the mouth. The colour is a pleasing clear deep self-lemon. A tall and vigorous grower it is good in pots.

MAGNIFICENCE. A favourite for pots and garden decoration, being the earliest of the large trumpets to bloom. It has overlapping perianth petals, attractively waved and a large, deeply serrated trumpet.

MOONSTRUCK. One of the famous lemon-yellow trio which includes Leinster and Hunter's Moon. With Broughshane it is the largest daffodil, its blooms measuring 6 in (15 cm) across, the broad perianth petals of lemon-yellow placed at right-angles to the huge trumpet of similar colouring.

ULSTER PRINCE. A yellow of the highest quality and of great substance with broad pointed perianth petals and a well-proportioned trumpet, beautifully serrated.

UNSURPASSABLE. One of the largest-flowered trumpet daffodils, of deep golden-yellow throughout. A striking flower and first-class garden plant.

VIRTUE. One of the best of all exhibition daffodils, bearing a bloom of faultless symmetry and quality with a broad, smooth, flat perianth standing at right-angles to the straight-sided nicely flanged and serrated trumpet. The flower is of firmest texture and of clear, brilliant golden yellow. Slow to increase and, like its pollen parent Crocus, needs good conditions.

I(b). Bi-colour Trumpets. Perianth white; corona coloured.

FORESIGHT. A flower of first-class form and good quality with a broad, flat, erect milk-white perianth and a perfectly proportioned neatly flanged golden trumpet. The first to open outdoors.

INISHKEEN. Possibly the finest of the bi-coloured trumpets, with broad overlapping perianth petals and a sharply contrasting trumpet of old gold, attractively serrated at the edge.

KARAMUDLI. It forms a bloom of exhibition quality with broad erect perianth petals of purest white and a well-proportioned trumpet of soft yellow.

NEWCASTLE. Named in honour of the town in County Down, it is a bi-colour of superb proportions with smooth flat overlapping perianth segments each at right-angles to the golden trumpet with its expanded roll.

PRESIDENT LEBRUN. Pure white perianth with large creamy trumpet. A very fine bi-colour variety of good substance. A valuable variety for pots and bowls.

QUEEN OF THE BICOLORS. One of the most free-flowering of all garden daffodils with broad overlapping perianth petals and bearing a long elegant trumpet of palest yellow.

TROUSSEAU. One of the very finest daffodils in existence, of superb quality and perfect form. It has a broad, flat, pure-white perianth and well-proportioned straight trumpet which opens soft yellow.

I(c). White Trumpets. Perianth white; corona white, not paler than the perianth.

BEERSHEBA. One of the finest and largest white trumpets yet raised. The flowers are of perfect form and texture. The flower stems long. The flower is of the purest white; very free and vigorous.

BROUGHSHANE. A giant white of perfect form and balance, the trumpet being widely flanged and frilled. The flower is of immense substance and exceptionally durable. It is carried on a strong stem 2 ft (60 cm) high, while the foliage measures 2 in (60 cm) in width.

CANTATRICE. Headed the list as an exhibition white trumpet in the Royal Horticultural Society ballot from 1946 to 1954. A flower of smooth texture with a clean-cut even perianth, standing out from the well-balanced perfectly smooth, slender trumpet; clear white throughout.

EMPRESS OF IRELAND. Voted the finest white trumpet by the Royal Horticultural Society panel of experts in the 1960's, it is well named for it is in every way a beauty with broad well-proportioned perianth petals of purest white, while the balanced trumpet is attractively frilled.

GLENESK. It bears a bloom of noble proportions, more than 5 in (12·5 cm) across, the perianth petals smooth and wax-like and with a beautifully serrated trumpet of glistening white.

KANCHENJUGA. The bloom has the biggest and broadest perianth segments, forming an almost perfect circle, and a magnificent widely flanged and serrated trumpet. The perianth is pure white, the trumpet palest lemon passing to white.

MOUNT HOOD. A white trumpet variety with well-proportioned blooms of great substance. The growth is tall and vigorous. It does well in pots. A notable newcomer to the white trumpet section which does well anywhere.

RASHEE. The flower is ice-white throughout, with broad pointed perianth petals and a trumpet with a deeply rolled flange at the mouth.

SILVER WEDDING. It bears a medium-sized bloom of purest white of charm and refinement with a smooth, sharp-pointed perianth, and a slender trumpet.

I(d). *Other Colours*. Any colour combination not falling into (a), (b) or (c) above.

BINKIE. A reverse bi-colour of excellent form and balance with broad flat perianth petals and a well-proportioned trumpet. On first opening, the flower is clear pale yellow with the crown gradually passing to white.

RUSHLIGHT. A flower and stem of exceptional sturdiness, with a broad, flat perianth of brightest yellow, shading to white at the base and an elegant trumpet of creamy white with a lemon frill.

SPELLBINDER. It bears a large handsome flower of luminous greeny-lemon with the perianth petals shading out to white at the base and with a white broad trumpet attractively shaded lemon at the edge.

II. LARGE-CUPPED NARCISSI

II(a). Perianth coloured; corona coloured, not paler than the perianth.

ADAMANT. It has a well-formed smooth perianth of deep saffron-yellow and a medium-sized rich saffron-orange crown frilled at the margin. A flower of unique and striking colouring.

AIR MARSHALL. A large bloom with broad perianth petals of intense yellow with a straight cup of orange-scarlet, beautifully frilled at the mouth.

ARANJUEZ. A flower of the very highest quality with a smooth, clear-yellow, round perianth of exceptional texture and a shallow deep-yellow crown, widely margined deep orange-red.

ARMADA. Outstanding in the garden and for early work in pots with smooth flat perianth petals of deepest yellow and with a deep cup of tangerine-orange.

CARBINEER. A magnificent flower of great substance with broad, flat, bright, rich-yellow perianth and deep bright orange-red cup.

CARLTON. It has a broad, overlapping, flat perianth 5 in (12·5 cm) in diameter and a large expanded cup, frilled at the mouth; the whole flower being clear, soft yellow. Excellent for forcing and garden decoration.

CEYLON. Sunproof and of beautiful form, the smooth flat perianth petals are of intense gold with almost a metallic sheen and with a contrasting crown of orange-red.

CORNISH FIRE. A flower of quality with a yellow perianth and well-proportioned crown of intense orange-scarlet. It is a strong grower.

DAMSON. It has a broad, overlapping, creamy-white perianth of excellent form; the base of the segments being suffused with yellow, while the cup is long and solid and deep red throughout.

FORTUNE. A giant Incomparabilis of perfect form and gorgeous colour, borne on a tall, strong stem. It has a flat, overlapping perianth of great substance and of a clear brilliant yellow colour, with a large and bold crown of glowing coppery orange. Very early.

GALWAY. A tall strong-stemmed variety, bearing an intense golden flower bordering on trumpet proportions with a broad, smooth perianth and well-flanged trumpet crown. A magnificent garden plant and grand for exhibition.

HAVELOCK. Deepest yellow throughout, it is a flower of perfect form, the perianth broad and overlapping, 4 in (10 cm) in diameter. One of the finest for exhibition or garden, it is tall and early-flowering.

HELIOS. The perianth is deep primrose yellow, the cup deep yellow, darkening to orange as it expands. A flower of fine form it is one of the earliest. Splendid for bowls and forces well.

INDIAN SUMMER. It has a broad, smooth perianth of great substance and of deepest golden yellow, and a well-proportioned, rather shallow cup of intensely vivid deep orange-scarlet.

KILLIGREW. A flower of wonderful quality with a bright-yellow perianth and a large orange-red cup.

LEPRECHAUN. A small flower of jewel-like brilliance with a deep clear lemon-gold perianth, and small goblet-shaped ruby-red cup.

MISSOURI. One of the best in its class with broad perianth petals of shining gold and with a straight cup of orange-scarlet which is fadeless in the strongest sunlight.

ROUGE. A completely new colour break, the pale-yellow perianth overlaid pinkish-buff, while the expanded cup is of bright brick-red. It attracts immediate attention wherever shown.

RUSTOM PASHA. One of the aristocrats of this section with large flowers of intense colouring. The large flat perianth is deep golden yellow, while the crown is of the most brilliant orange-red, which is absolutely sunproof.

SCARLET ELEGANCE. A red and yellow Incomparabilis of merit for garden and forcing. The perianth is clear yellow and the cup of rich red. Tall and vigorous.

II(b). Perianth white; corona coloured (including pink).

ALICANTE. The large refined flower has a broad creamy-white perianth and a large solid cup of apricot-orange.

BELISANA. One of the best in its section with broad perianth petals of purest white and a large flat orange cup, attractively frilled.

BRUNSWICK. It has a broad, flat white perianth and finely formed well-balanced crown of palest lemon, shading to a paler colour at the centre and of lasting quality.

COVERACK PERFECTION. A flower of charm, with a broad white perianth and wide shallow saucer crown. The ground colour is white, while it is edged and flushed pale gold and salmon and has a faint tinge of green behind the anthers.

DEBUTANTE. Remarkable in every way, with broad perianth petals of velvet-like texture and glistening white and with a large crown of soft pink shaded biscuit-buff.

DUKE OF WINDSOR. Outstanding with its thick waxy perianth petals of purest white and broad cup of apricot-orange, beautifully ruffled at the rim.

EASTER BONNET. It bears a large flower of richest colouring with broad white petals and a creamy-white trumpet heavily frilled with salmon pink.

EDDY CANZONY. In every way one of the best in its group with a broad, flat perianth of great substance and a ruffled crown of soft yellow shaded with orange.

FANCY FREE. A variety with a difference with broad overlapping perianth petals of icy-white and a corona of palest citron, edged with salmon orange.

FERMOY. A magnificent and striking flower of great size and fine quality; it has a large pure-white perianth of great substance and well-proportioned beautifully frilled bowl-shaped crown, bright orange-red at the mouth, shading to gold in the base.

FINTONA. One of the late Mr Guy Wilson's finest pinks, with a broad white perianth and a crown of palest yellow which changes to deep rose pink with age.

FLAMENCO. A large flower with round, flat, overlapping, creamy-white perianth, and large wide-expanded orange crown. One of the best sunproof red and white narcissi.

GREEN ISLAND. Headed the list in the Royal Horticultural Society Daffodil Year Book ballot 1946–50 as the best in its section, bearing a flower of large size, great substance and smoothest texture. It has smooth rounded white segments of such width that they form an almost complete circle; well-proportioned shallow bowl-shaped frilled cup, greenish white at the base inside, passing to white, which in turn passes to a band of clear, cool, greenish lemon at the margin.

IRISH ROSE. One of the best of the pinks, with a broad perianth of glistening white and a short frilly crown of apple-blossom pink.

JOHN EVELYN. It has a large solid white perianth of great substance; 3 in (7·5 cm) broad and overlapping, with flat soft-yellow cup. An outstanding cut flower.

KILWORTH. An outstandingly fine large dark-red and white flower, with broad white perianth and perfectly proportioned bowl-shaped crown of intense orange-red with a touch of green in the eye.

LEMON CUP. A variety of charm with a broad, flat perianth of glistening white and a broad heavily frilled crown of soft greenish lemon.

LINGERING LIGHT. It bears a good-sized flower of great refinement, with a spreading pure-white perianth of delicate texture, and well-proportioned shallow bowl-shaped crown, flushed pale apricot-pink.

LOUISE DE COLIGNY. It should be in every collection for its delightful perfume and charm. The pure-white perianth is slightly reflexing, while the dainty trumpet-shaped crown is of a lovely shade of soft apricot pink.

MAIDEN'S BLUSH. It has pure-white overlapping petals of outstanding texture and a trumpet-shaped crown of soft blush pink shaded rose at the edge.

MOYIENA. It bears a pink-cupped flower with a pure-white perianth and a pink cup, deeper and rather more coppery in tone than any variety.

MRS R. O. BACKHOUSE. A lovely variety with perianth of ivory-white and well-proportioned slim, long trumpet of apricot pink, changing to shell pink at the deeply fringed edge. Early.

PASSIONALE. Outstanding in every way, the ice-white perianth petals being pointed and overlapping, while it bears a large expanding cup of soft rose pink which does not fade.

PERSONALITY. It bears a large flower of noble proportions and of exhibition quality, the pure-white perianth being flat and smooth, while the pale-lemon corona is clean-cut at the rim.

PINKEEN. Perfectly symmetrical, very smooth, flat, overlapping, clean-cut white perianth of exceptional substance. Crown sometimes faintly flushed peachy pink when fully developed.

PINK RIM. It is one of the most attractive of pink daffodils, bearing a solid, well-formed flower with a white perianth and a cup of soft ivory with a distinct cream rim.

RED HACKLE. A magnificent and brilliant red and white of fine habit and beautiful form. It has a broad, rather pointed, very slightly reflexing, pure-white perianth; frilled bowl-shaped crown of solid, intense, deep orange-red.

ROSARIO. From Australia and one of the finest of Mr Radcliffe's famous pink-crowned daffodils. It has a broad, smooth, pure-white perianth. The trumpet-shaped crown which is gracefully flanged and frilled is of very pale soft primrose, flushed and overlaid throughout with shell pink. In some seasons it comes entirely pink.

ROSE OF TRALEE. One of the best of a remarkable series of pink-crowned seedlings raised from the self-fertilised White Sentinel. The flower of beautiful form has a pure-white perianth, pointed at the tips and a long, nicely flanged crown of rosy apricot pink.

ROSEWORTHY. It is one of the brightest of the pinks, with a solid white perianth and a well-proportioned cup of rich deep pink.

SALMON TROUT. A pink of unequalled charm, the medium-sized blooms being of perfect form and solid texture, able to stand up to all weathers, while the trumpet-shaped corona is of brilliant salmon pink.

STRAY PINK. A most attractive variety of neat and dainty habit with broad pointed perianth petals and a trumpet-shaped corona of brightest rose pink.

TUDOR MINSTREL. It bears a bloom 5 in (12·5 cm) across and has won every award on the show bench. Its broad white perianth petals being of smoothest texture, while the large frilled cup is of a unique shade of soft yellowish orange.

WILD ROSE. One of the brightest pinks to date, as the cup is rosy pink to the base, the colour being retained till the flower dies. Not a large flower, but of attractive form.

WOODLEA. Its trumpet is so long that it could be classed in section I(a). It

445

bears a flower of classic proportions with broad white perianth petals and a trumpet of rich rosy apricot, frilled at the mouth.

II(c). Perianth white; corona white, not paler than the perianth.

CARNLOUGH. A constant winner at overseas shows. It is a distinct flower of strong sturdy habit, fine size and superb quality, with a broad, flat pure-white perianth. On first opening the crown is faintest citron with a frill of soft coral pink.

COURAGE. It has an immense water-lily-like flower of splendid substance and quality and purest clear white throughout; a great broad-pointed perianth and large, long crown, slightly flanged at the mouth.

GENTILITY. It bears a medium-sized flower of perfect form, with broad pointed perianth petals of milky white and a corona with a slight flange.

GREENLAND. A most lovely flower of perfect proportion and of splendid substance. It is of pure ice white throughout, with an entrancing tint of cold sea green in the base.

ICE FOLLIES. It has a large circular perianth of ivory-white and a flat corona of palest cream which turns pure white to form a flower of great beauty, while it is most free-flowering and increases rapidly.

KILLALOE. A striking and immense pure-white flower, with broad flat perianth segments of fine substance. The large cup is beautifully flanged and frilled at the mouth.

MURMANSK. It bears a large flower of solid texture with a broad reflexing perianth and trumpet of great substance, the whole bloom being of icy white.

OSLO. It bears a most beautiful flower of perfect form with a broad, flat perianth and well-balanced frilled crown. It is a flower of splendid substance and purest white throughout.

SHINING WATERS. It is the first of the all-whites to bloom and is valuable for garden and pot culture. It has broad pointed perianth petals and a large corona of frosty whiteness.

SLEVEEN. A variety of great beauty and of exhibition quality bearing broad pointed perianth petals which are at right-angles to the corona, the whole flower being of icy-whiteness enhanced by the blue-green foliage.

III. SMALL-CUPPED NARCISSI.

Distinguishing characters: one flower to a stem: cup or corona not more than one-third the length of the perianth segments.

III(a). Perianth coloured; corona coloured, not paler than the perianth.

APRICOT DISTINCTION. A novelty of exquisite colouring, the perianth being of a most unusual shade of rich apricot, with a cup of brilliant orange.

BALLYSILLAN. It bears an early and brilliant cupped flower of fine quality with clear yellow perianth of smooth, firm texture and a shallow vivid deep-red cup.

CHUNGKING. The finest red and yellow small-cupped narcissus bearing a magnificent large, tall-stemmed flower of fine quality with a broad, clear, rich golden perianth and perfectly proportioned intense deep vivid-red shallow crown.

EDWARD BUXTON. The perianth with its broad rounded petals is of a lovely shade of soft lemon yellow, the cup deep yellow with a broad margin of orange. Extremely free-flowering, it increases rapidly.

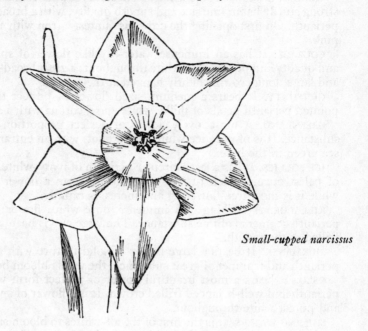

Small-cupped narcissus

JEZEBEL. One of the most brilliantly coloured of all narcissi, the perianth being of reddish gold with a shallow crown of brick red.

THERM. A variety of striking beauty with broad pointed perianth petals of richest yellow and a shallow corona of deep ruby-red.

III(b). Perianth white : corona coloured.

BLARNEY. One of the most distinct and charming of its type, bearing a large flower with a firm, satin smooth, snow-white perianth and flat salmon-orange crown with narrow primrose rim.

CROWN DERBY. The flowers have a large, broad pure-white perianth and well-proportioned golden yellow crown, handsomely edged with a striking ribbon of deep orange-red. It holds its colour better than any and is a vigorous grower.

DREAMLIGHT. One of the best in its group, with a large circular perianth of glistening white and cup also of white, edged cerise.

MATAPAN. The earliest in this section, the medium-sized flowers having smooth flat perianth and flat crown of intense crimson.

MISTY MOON. An exquisite flower, having a large pure-white perianth and a large eye, with a greyish-white centre and the outer half a halo of soft pale salmon orange.

REPRIEVE. One of the latest (with Frigid and Portrush) of all narcissi and should be grown with Matapan to prolong the display at either end. The circular perianth is white with a slight shading of green, while the small cup is of palest lemon, shaded green at the centre.

III(c). Perianth white: corona white, not paler than the perianth.

BRYHER. A most handsome variety with broad overlapping petals making a perianth of perfect symmetry and of purest white, while the cup is also white with a slight tinting of green.

CHINESE WHITE. It bears a large flower of faultless form and quality; pure white throughout, except for a faint touch of green in the eye. It has a broad circular satin-smooth perianth of great substance, 4 in (10 cm) in diameter, and with a perfectly proportioned shallow-fluted saucer crown. A superb flower, quite unique which created a sensation when winning the Engleheart Cup.

FOGGY DEW. It is half-sister to Chinese White with a broad, rounded, much overlapping, pure-white perianth of fine substance and quality, and a smallish frilled white crown with a deep sage-green centre.

PORTRUSH. A lovely late-flowering variety, with broad, flat pure-white perianth of great substance and almost flat white crown with deep-green eye. Tall, vigorous plant with good stem, and very free of bloom. It is a valuable market flower, coming at the end of the season.

IV. DOUBLE NARCISSI. Distinguishing character: double flowers.

EARLYCHEER. It grows only 6 in (15 cm) tall and is at its loveliest on a sunny bank or on the rock garden, bearing clusters of small globular flowers of ivory white, intermingled with petals of palest yellow and is sweetly scented.

albus plenus odoratus. The old Double White *poeticus* which bears sweetly scented gardenia-like flowers of snowy whiteness during May and June but may take a year to become established before it does so.

FAIRNESS. A tall, vigorous grower bearing symmetrical flowers of palest yellow intermingled with petals of orange and red to produce a flower of great beauty.

FEU DE JOIE. A very distinct and beautiful flower. The long perianth petals are pure white; the short petals being of a brilliant orange-scarlet. The flower is fully double, which makes it lovely for decoration. Tall, strong, free and early.

GOLDEN DUCAT. A double 'sport' of King Alfred, the entire bloom being of the same brilliant golden yellow as its famous 'parent'.

INGLESCOMBE. Full double flowers of a buttery primrose yellow, with broad rounded petals. The finest double-yellow daffodil.

MARY COPELAND. It has a pure-white perianth with segments of glowing orange-scarlet. One of the most beautiful of all doubles.

ROSE OF MAY. A beautiful form of the old *poeticus*, flowering early and bearing symmetrical blooms of rich creamy white.

SANTA CLAUS. It makes a flower of great substance and perfect symmetry with flat overlapping outer petals 3 in (7·5 cm) across and of purest whiteness, the centre petals also being white, while the flower has a powerful sweet perfume. Late-flowering.

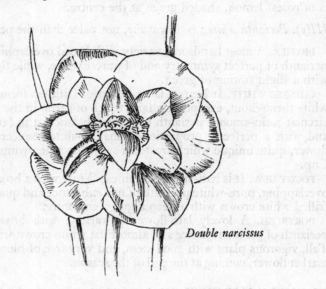

Double narcissus

SNOWBALL. Very double, its beautifully shaped flowers are like pure-white gardenias, with a tight centre which opens slowly so that it retains its beauty for sometime.

SWANSDOWN. A double with a great future as a commercial cut flower with broad overlapping outer petals of purest white with feathery white centre petals.

TEXAS. Large fully double flowers, circular in form, petals rich yellow, interspersed with fiery orange segments. Ideal for forcing.

WHITE LION. A variety of beauty and distinction, the large overlapping segments being of waxy-white with the centre petals intermingled with pale yellow.

V. TRIANDRUS NARCISSI. Distinguishing characters: characteristics clearly evident.

N. triandrus. Native of the Iberian Peninsula, it was known to cottage gardeners as Ganymedes Cup. The bulbs are of less than 1-in (2·5-cm) diameter from which arise slender round leaves and drooping white flowers borne in clusters of three to nine on 6-in (15-cm) stems. The perianth petals bend back

Nerine bowdenii

Ranunculus

Scilla campanulata

Schizostylis coccinea

Sprekelia formosissima

to reveal a globular corona, like tear-drops from a distance, hence its other name of the angel's tears daffodil.

The form *albus*, bearing clear-white flowers was discovered on the borders of Spain and Portugal by the late Mr Peter Barr. Another form, *concolor*, bears flowers of soft yellow, while *loideleurii*, which is found on the Isles of Glenan off the south-western coast of France, bears larger flowers than those of *albus* but of the same pure whiteness.

VI. CYCLAMINEUS NARCISSI. Distinguishing characters: clearly evident.

Narcissus cyclamineus. Like *N. triandrus* it is native of Spain and Portugal and it has broader upright leaves and a bloom with reflexing perianth segments and a long cylindrical corona, serrated at the edge, like an inverted trumpet. It requires a damper soil than *N. triandrus* and should be planted in the partial

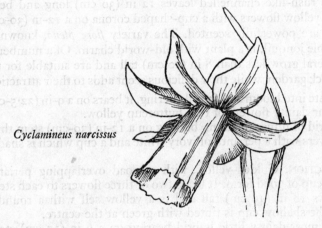

Cyclamineus narcissus

shade of an orchard or by the side of water. The species has imparted its delightful charm to a number of hybrid varieties which bloom at least a month before those of *N. triandrus*. All are delightful in pots in the alpine house or cold frame.

BERYL. It bears a drooping flower of a primrose-yellow colour and with a globular orange cup and is of very dwarf habit.

CHARITY MAY. Increases rapidly and is a most attractive form with broad overlapping but much reflexed perianth petals of soft clear yellow, and a corona which is beautifully frilled.

FEBRUARY GOLD. Outstanding in every way, having a lemon-yellow reflexed perianth and a bright-yellow trumpet frilled at the edge.

JENNY. One of the finest hybrids, with its gracefully reflexing perianth and long elegant cup of purest white.

LE BEAU. It has drooping flowers of softest yellow with a long graceful trumpet, and is ideal for pots.

LITTLE WITCH. Growing 6 in (15 cm) tall and in bloom in March, it is a most dainty variety of deep yellow throughout, with a long trumpet and extremely reflexed perianth.

MARCH SUNSHINE. Follows February Gold into bloom and has a perianth of canary yellow, which is only slightly reflexing, and a long elegant trumpet shaded with orange. Free-flowering and quite outstanding.

PEEPING TOM. Naturalises well and blooms in March, the perianth petals being slightly reflexed with a long narrow trumpet of rich golden yellow.

VII. JONQUILLA NARCISSI. Distinguishing characters: characteristics of any of this group clearly evident.

Narcissus jonquilla. The sweet-scented jonquil, native of southern Spain and Algeria, which has rush-like channelled leaves 12 in (30 cm) long and bears three to six golden-yellow flowers with a cup-shaped corona on a 12-in (30-cm) stem. The flowers are powerfully scented. The variety *flore pleno*, known as Queen Anne's double jonquil, is a plant with old-world charm. Of a number of lovely hybrids, several grow less than 8 in (20 cm) tall and are suitable for the alpine house and rock garden, while their delicious scent adds to their attraction.

BABY MOON. Late into bloom and free-flowering, it bears on a 9-in (22·5-cm) stem three or four dainty flowers of rich buttercup yellow.

CHERIE. A hybrid of unusual charm, bearing on a 12-in (30-cm) stem three or four small flowers with a perianth of ivory white and a cup which is shaded with pink.

GOLDEN PERFECTION. Golden-yellow with a broad overlapping perianth and large golden cup of good form. It bears two or three flowers to each stem.

HESLA. It grows 18 in (45 cm) tall and is a yellow self with a rounded perianth, while the shallow cup is tinted with green at the centre.

LINTIE. It is a most dainty little hybrid bearing on a 6-in (15-cm) stem, three or four flowers with a yellow perianth and orange cup.

ORANGE QUEEN. A beautiful hybrid, bearing on a 9-in (22·5-cm) stem three or four sweetly scented flowers of deep golden orange throughout.

SWEETNESS. It has broad pointed perianth petals of golden yellow and a goblet-shaped corona of similar colouring. It increases more rapidly than any other narcissus.

SWEET PEPPER. A hybrid of great beauty and intense colouring, bearing three or four blooms to each stem, the perianth petals being richest golden yellow with a corona of brilliant orange-red.

TITTLE-TATTLE. It is one of the latest jonquils to bloom, bearing two or three flowers to each stem with a perianth of clear yellow and a shallow corona of golden orange.

TREVITHIAN. A beautiful jonquil, carrying a large cluster of pale self-lemon-yellow flowers. It is early-flowering and forces well.

VIII. TAZETTA NARCISSI. Distinguishing characters clearly evident.

Narcissus tazetta. The polyanthus or bunch-flowered narcissus referred to by the poets of ancient Greece and widely distributed across southern Europe, Syria and Persia, and across central China to Japan. It has a bulb of 2-in (5-cm) diameter and four to six narrow leaves 12 in (30 cm) long. The flowers measure

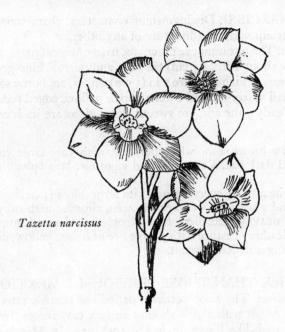

Tazetta narcissus

1 to 2 in (2·5 to 5 cm) across and are almost flat with a shallow corona, and circular. They are white with a pale-yellow corona and are sweetly scented. They are borne four to eight to a 12-in (30-cm) stem. Of a number of lovely bunch-flowered hybrids, all are sweetly scented. They may be grown in bowls of pebbles and water, like the Paper White, to be placed in a sunny window immediately after planting.

BRIDAL CROWN. A double form of great beauty, the flowers being of purest white and borne three to five to a stem.

CRAGFORD. A notable new Poetaz variety. Creamy-white perianth. With rich-orange eye and bearing three to four flowers on a stem. A splendid variety to grow in bowls for it can be brought into bloom by Christmas.

EARLY SPLENDOUR. Free-flowering and a vigorous grower, it has a pure-white overlapping perianth and a deep-orange corona, while it bears up to eight blooms on a 15-in (38-cm) stem.

GERANIUM. A splendid variety, with pure-white perianth and geranium-red cup. An excellent variety for growing in bowls for late display.

MARTHA WASHINGTON. Pure-white, well-overlapping perianth with clear-orange crown, two or three flowers on a stem. The flowers are much larger than those of any other Poetaz.

SCARLET GEM. A showy and attractive Poetaz for growing in pots. The perianth is primrose yellow enhanced by a deep-orange cup.

IX. POETICUS NARCISSI. Distinguishing characters: characteristics of the *Narcissus poeticus* group without admixture of any other.

Narcissus poeticus. The pheasant eye narcissus, native of most parts of southern Europe, with bulbs about 1 in (2·5 cm) through and narrow blue-green leaves 12 in long. The flowers, which measure 2 in (5 cm) across, are borne solitary and are white with a small saucer-shaped corona of pale yellow, edged red. They are borne in May and early June and are sweetly scented, as are its several lovely hybrids.

ACATEA. It has a broad snow-white perianth with very large yellow cup, broadly margined dark red. Very early and vigorous. It is splendid for pots and bowls.

CANTABILE. A beauty in every respect, its large blooms having a frosty-white perianth and a large eye of emerald green, rimmed with ruby red.

WINIFRED VAN GRAVEN. Excellent for indoor or garden culture, the large blooms being of leathery texture with a large eye of lemon yellow, edged with scarlet and carrying a delicious scent.

X. SPECIES OTHER THAN THOSE PREVIOUSLY MENTIONED.

Narcissus bulbocodium. The hoop petticoat daffodil of south-western Europe and north-western Africa with bulbs about 1 in (2·5 cm) across, from which arise three or four rush-like leaves 12 in (30 cm) long. In March they bear solitary flowers of brightest yellow on 8-in (20-cm) stems. The flowers have narrow lance-shaped perianth segments and a broad corolla like the speaker of an old-fashioned gramophone. It enjoys a sunny situation and a light sandy soil and may take a year to become established before it blooms but will soon form a large clump and once established will bloom profusely.

The form *citrinus* bears pale citron-coloured flowers, while *conspicuus* bears flowers of deep golden yellow. *Romieuxii* bears sulphur-yellow flowers and is earlier to bloom, often showing colour before the end of February outdoors. Likewise *monophyllus*, native of northern Africa and bearing flowers of purest white. It is perfectly hardy and forms only a single leaf. The variety *tenuifolius* grows only 4 in (10 cm) tall and bears tiny hooped flowers of richest gold. All are delightful subjects for the alpine house or frame.

Narcissus calcicola. One of the jonquils, its natural habitat being the hilly country around Lisbon. It is a rare species of charm, bearing three or four sweetly scented blooms on a 6-in (15-cm) stem. They are of deepest yellow, larger than those of *N. juncifolius* to which it is closely related.

Narcissus canaliculatus. Native of southern Europe, Sicily and the Near East, it is possibly a sub-species of *N. tazetta*, with which it is closely connected. It blooms in April and usually is shy with its flowers until established. It bears four to six blooms to each 9-in (22·5-cm) stem and they measure 1 in (2·5 cm) across with perianth segments of purest white and with a tiny cup of richest yellow. It is scented.

Narcissus gracilis. Native of southern France, it is one of the jonquils with rush-like leaves and bears three to five flowers to each stem. The flowers have an intoxicating scent and are of pale sulphur yellow. They appear late in May or early June, extending the season with the early-flowering species to give six months of colour.

Narcissus juncifolius. The rush-leaf jonquil of the Pyrenees with bulbs less than 1 in (2·5 cm) across which should be given the shelter of rockery stones or the protection of a cool greenhouse or frame. It does not respond to open-ground planting. It has slender rounded leaves 6 in (15 cm) long and bears its bright golden flowers in umbels of three to five on a 5-in (12·5-cm) stem. The flowers with their tiny cup-shaped coronas are sweetly scented and appear in April.

Narcissus minimus (syn. *N. asturiensis*). Native of the Pyrenees, it is one of the smallest of all bulbous plants, growing less than 3 in (7·5 cm) tall. It blooms in February—January under glass, where it should be grown to protect it from rain. The flower is of purest golden yellow with the perianth petals attractively twisted, while the miniature trumpet is beautifully frilled.

Narcissus minor. Native of Portugal, it is a bi-colour trumpet daffodil in miniature with leaves 4 in (10 cm) long. It blooms on 6-in (15-cm) stems. The perianth petals are twisted and are of pale sulphur yellow with an extended trumpet-shaped corona of deeper yellow. The double form *plenus* (Rip van Winkle), discovered in Ireland, has a trumpet of pale yellow tinted with green.

Narcissus odorus. Believed to be a natural hybrid of the jonquil, it has been growing in British gardens since Tudor times and is a delightful plant, known as the campernelle. It has the rush-like leaves of the jonquil and the same delicious scent. Its golden-yellow star-like blooms are borne in clusters of three to five on 8-in (20-cm) stems. There is also a double form, known as Queen Anne's Irish campernelle with the same sweet perfume which can be picked up at a distance.

Narcissus pseudo-narcissus. The Lent lily of English woodlands about which Shakespeare wrote in *A Winter's Tale*. It has bulbs 1 to 2 in (2·5 to 5 cm) through and narrow blue-green leaves 12 in (30 cm) long. The first flowers appear in March and are borne on 12-in (30-cm) stems, the perianth petals being sulphur yellow, while the plaited trumpet-like corona is of lemon yellow.

The sub-species *lobularis*, the Tenby daffodil, native of southern Europe, blooms a month earlier, its flowers being of golden yellow, while *palladiflorus*, of the Pyrenees, bears flowers of uniform lemon yellow. Two others of beauty are *nobilis*, a bi-colour of vigour with an orange-yellow trumpet; and *moschatus*

(*N. cernuus* of earlier garden books), which blooms in April, its drooping flowers of silvery white having twisted petals and a plaited corona 1 in (2·5 cm) across. Both bloom on a 6-in (15-cm) scape.

A natural hybrid, *N. johnstonii*, the result of a cross between *N. triandrus* and the Lent lily and discovered in Spain, is a rare and charming plant, known as the Queen of Spain's daffodil. It bears a lemon-yellow flower with the interesting reflexed petals of *N. triandrus* and the flowers are borne on 12-in (30-cm) stems.

A hybrid, possibly with *N. minor*, called W. P. Milner is one of the finest of all miniature trumpet daffodils for growing in pans under glass, when it will bloom in February. It has twisted perianth segments and a long trumpet of palest sulphur yellow, the flowers being borne on 10-in (25-cm) stems.

Narcissus rupicola. A rush-leaved jonquil of the Pyrenees, requiring similar conditions to *N. juncifolius* and *N. jonquilla*. It has glaucous three-sided leaves 6 in (15 cm) long and bears solitary flowers on a 4-in (10-cm) stem. They are bright golden yellow with a shallow six-lobed corona and are sweetly scented.

Narcissus serotinus. Native of southern Europe and northern Africa, it has rush-like leaves and blooms early in autumn, bearing one or two flowers to a 6-in (15-cm) scape. The perianth segments are white, with a saucer-like corona of pale yellow. Like all the rush-leaf species, it requires a sun-baked situation for it to bloom well.

Narcissus scaberulus. A rare native of Portugal and closely related to other rush-leaf jonquils. The leaves lie almost flat on the ground, while the flowers are the smallest of all the narcissi, measuring less than 1 in (2·5 cm) across. They are of deepest orange with a large corona for so small a bloom. They open in March and are borne one or two to a 6-in (15-cm) stem.

Narcissus viridiflorus. Native of Gibraltar and Morocco, it is one of the rush-leaf jonquils known to Tudor gardeners and unusual in that it blooms in October and November. Again, it is unique in its colouring, bearing a bloom of soft greenish yellow on an 8-in (20-cm) stem before the appearance of the foliage. It should be grown in pans under glass wherever the early winter climate may be expected to be against it flowering to the perfection it will attain under glass.

Narcissus watieri. Native of the Atlas Mountains, it is a rush-leaf species bearing single flowers of purest white on a 4-in (10-cm) scape but unlike the other jonquils, the flower has no scent. It is at its best in small pans under glass or in the alpine garden.

NEMASTYLIS (Iridaceae)

A genus of 45 species, native of Mexico and North America and taking its name from *nema*, a thread, and *stylos*, a column, the reference being to its slender style. They are plants with narrow sword-like sheathing leaves and bear flowers resembling *Tigridia*. They are suitable only to those gardens with a mild winter climate, for they bloom early in summer and need to occupy the ground during winter.

Culture. Outdoors, the corms are planted in October, 4 in (10 cm) deep and 6 in (15 cm) apart, in a well-drained soil containing some grit and enriched with decayed manure. Plant in raised beds which should be covered with a thick mulch of decayed leaves during winter to protect the corms from frost.

Where growing indoors, plant three to four corms to each 6-in (15-cm) pot containing a gritty compost enriched with some dehydrated cow manure. Plant in October 1 in (2·5 cm) deep and stand the pots in a closed frame during winter. Early in February, move to a cool greenhouse in which the temperature does not exceed 45° F (7° C) and water sparingly as the plants make growth. They will bloom towards the end of April and early May, and as they make height they should be supported. After flowering, place the pots in a dry sunny position outdoors for the corms to ripen and repot in October.

Propagation. Cormlets will be seen clustering about the base of the old corms when repotting. These are detached and grown on in boxes of sandy compost. They will reach flowering size in three or four years.

Species. *Nemastylis coelestina.* The finest species, with narrow sword-like leaves 15 in (38 cm) long and bearing small bright-blue flowers on 2-ft (60-cm) stems.

Nemastylis geminiflora. It has narrow upright leaves and bears on a 2-ft (60-cm) stem, purple-blue flowers from twin spathes.

NERINE (Amaryllidaceae)

A genus of 30 species of bulbous plants, native of tropical and southern Africa and named after Nerine, a water nymph of Greek mythology. Closely related to *Amaryllis*, they have strap-like leaves arranged in two ranks. The leaves appear after the flowers, which are borne in a 2- to 20-flowered umbel on an erect slender scape, usually about 2 ft (60 cm) tall. They are funnel-shaped with spreading segments, attractively waved and with erect stamens. Long-lasting when cut or as a pot plant, the flowers are at their loveliest under artificial light.

Culture. These species which bloom early in autumn are suitable to grow outdoors in a sunny border such as beneath the over-hanging eaves of a house where they may be protected from frost by rearing a frame light over them. However, as the plants make foliage during winter, they should be grown outdoors only where a mild winter climate can be expected. If the leaves are damaged at this time, the bulbs will not bloom and will quickly perish. Plant in July, 9 in (22·5 cm) apart and so that the neck of the bulb is about 3 in (7·5 cm) beneath the surface of the soil. They require a light well-drained soil into which has been dug some decayed manure, old mushroom bed compost being ideal. Give no water and cover with a frame light after planting. This is left in position until danger of frost damage to the leaves has passed in May. The leaves will die back during summer and from then onwards, water copiously and once each week with dilute liquid manure until the flowers begin to die back in October. *N. bowdenii* and its varieties is the most suitable species for growing in the open in Britain and North America.

Where growing indoors, use a pot which is double the diameter of the bulb. Crock well and provide a compost made up of fibrous loam, leaf mould, decayed manure and sand in equal parts. Plant in July or early August when the bulbs are dormant, i.e. just before the appearance of the flower spike. The neck of the bulb should be just above the level of the compost. Plant firmly and place the pots as near to the glass as possible. Those species flowering early will require no heat to bring them into bloom, but after flowering they will require a minimum night temperature of 45° F (7° C) during winter while they make new foliage. This they will begin to do after flowering at the year end. From the time the flower spike appears until the leaves have begun to die back early in summer (May), the plants need water but this should be withheld when the leaves begin to wither and for three months the plants are given a complete rest. The pots should be placed in a sunny position outdoors, protected from rain, a cold frame being ideal, or they should be stood in a sunny window or on a shelf in the greenhouse or garden room for the bulbs to ripen. Watering may recommence early in August when the flower spike will soon appear. After flowering, the process is repeated, the bulbs being repotted every fourth year.

Propagation. When the bulbs are repotted (a larger-sized pot must be used as the bulbs continue to increase in size), numerous offsets will have formed around the mother bulb. These are detached and planted in small pots containing a sandy compost and grown on for three years until they reach flowering size. Plants may also be increased from seed sown in spring in a temperature of 55° F (13° C). They will germinate readily if sown on the surface of a gritty compost and in autumn may be moved to 3-in (7·5-cm) pots in which they remain for 12 months, before being moved to larger pots. They will reach flowering size in three or four years.

Species and Varieties. *Nerine angustifolia*. Almost hardy, it may be grown in a cold greenhouse or frame. It has narrow leaves 9 in (22·5 cm) long and bears its rich pink flowers in an umbel of six to ten on a 2-ft (60-cm) scape which is covered in grey hairs.

Nerine bowdenii. Native of Cape Province, it has thick glossy leaves 12 in (30 cm) long and bears in September, a large umbel of pale-pink flowers with recurving segments 3 in (7·5 cm) long and which have a dark-pink line down the centre. The hardiest species, the leaves begin to appear before the flowers fade. There are several outstanding varieties: Blush Beauty, bearing flowers of soft shell-pink, and Pink Triumph which is much later into bloom (October), bearing flowers of silvery-pink in umbels of 6 to 10.

Nerine filifolia. Discovered in south-western Cape Province in 1879. It has filiform leaves which persist almost throughout the year so that the plant requires little or no rest period. The flowers appear in late October and are borne on a 20-in (50-cm) scape in an umbel of eight to ten. They are bright rosy-red with incurving petals.

Nerine flexuosa. It has bright-green leaves 12 in (30 cm) long, which appear with the flowers in September. The flowers are pale-pink with waved petals and are borne in a large umbel of 12 to 20 on a 3-ft (90-cm) scape. The variety *alba*, discovered in Cape Province in 1795, bears pure-white flowers, while *sandersoni* has flowers with less-waved petals.

From *N. flexuosa alba*, van Tubergen's raised a number of hybrids of merit by crossing with *N. sarniensis*, var. *corusca major*. Ancilla bears a large umbel of deep carmine-red flowers on a stem 2 to 3 ft (60 to 90 cm) tall; while Bettina bears neyron-rose flowers during October and November in a large globular head measuring 6 in (15 cm) across.

Nerine humilis. Closely resembling *N. flexuosa*, it has narrower leaves which are deeply channelled and bears rosy-red flowers in an umbel of 10 to 12 on a 12-in (30-cm) scape. The narrow perianth segments recurve at the ends.

Nerine masonorum. It is a species of compact and dainty habit, bearing its soft-pink flowers on a 6-in (15-cm) scape during August and September and is a delightful plant for a warm pocket of the rock garden. It is ideal for the alpine house, bearing its flowers in a dainty umbel of four to six. It is almost evergreen and requires no rest period.

Nerine moorei. It has bright-green leaves 12 in (30 cm) long and $\frac{1}{2}$ in (1·25 cm) broad and bears bright-scarlet flowers in an umbel of 6 to 10 on a flattened scape 10 to 12 in (25 to 30 cm) tall. The flowers are enhanced by their wavy segments.

Nerine pudica. It has narrow glaucous leaves 9 in (22·5 cm) long and bears umbels of ivory-white flowers on a 12-in (30-cm) scape. Each segment has a red line down the centre.

Nerine sarniensis. The Guernsey Lily, so called because the first bulbs to reach Europe were washed up on the coast of Guernsey where they took root in the sand and have since been cultivated commercially there. Native of the Cape, where it grows on rocky ledges above 500 ft and blooms during April and May—in September and October in the British Isles. It has narrow bright-green leaves and bears bright-crimson flowers with crescent-shaped segments crisped at the margins, and in umbels of 10 to 12 on a slender 16-in (40-cm) scape. The flowers are as if sprinkled with gold dust. The variety *corusca major* bears flowers of fiery orange and has broader leaves, while *profusa* bears large flowers of deepest crimson.

Nerine undulata (syn. *N. crispa*). Closely related to *N. sarniensis*, it is almost hardy in the British Isles and is in bloom during October. The pale-pink flowers have elegantly waved segments and are borne in umbels of 8 to 10 on a 12-in (30-cm) scape.

NOMOCHARIS (Liliaceae)

A genus of 16 species, closely related to *Lilium*, with bulbs without tunics and with thin narrow leaves arranged along the stem in whorls. The segments of the flowers, which are held on long pedicels, are divided to the base and open flat and face downwards. Native of the Himalayas and western China, it was discovered growing at a height of 10,000 ft by Mr Reginald Farrer. It is rare in cultivation.

Culture. It requires similar conditions as in its native land—i.e. a cold winter followed by long periods of warm sunshine to ripen the bulbs. An open situation is therefore essential. It also requires a well-drained soil, containing humus and grit. Plant the bulbs in September, 9 in (22·5 cm) apart and 4 in (10 cm) deep, but the best method of obtaining a stock is to raise plants from seed and grow on in pots for at all stages of growth they resent transplanting.

Propagation. Seed of most species now in cultivation is obtainable from Messrs Thompson and Morgan of Ipswich and it will germinate quickly. In April, sow the contents of a packet in a pan filled with the John Innes compost. Sow thinly, just covering with compost, and keep comfortably moist but giving little or no moisture in winter. During this time, the pans are best kept in a frame to which plenty of fresh air is admitted. In two years time, carefully knock from the pan the seedlings and the compost adhering to the mass of fibrous roots, and, without disturbing, plant where they are intended to bloom. Keep moist during their first summer outdoors until established, when they may be expected to bloom the following year. Where conditions are suitable, the plants will readily seed themselves to replace those which die off each year.

Species. *Nomocharis aperta.* Native of Tibet and western China, it grows 2 ft (60 cm) tall and in June bears four to six pale-pink pendulous flowers held on long pedicels. Both the inner and outer segments have a crimson blotch at the base.

Nomocharis farreri. Native of northern Burma, it grows 3 ft (90 cm) tall, the stems being clothed in whorls of narrow leaves, while the white flowers, blotched with purple at the base of each segment open to 4 in (10 cm) across.

Nomocharis mairei. Native of western China, it grows 2 ft (60 cm) tall, its large white flowers being heavily spotted with purple, while the inner segments are heavily fringed. The variety *candida*, rare in cultivation has pure-white flowers devoid of markings.

Nomocharis meleagrina. Native of eastern Tibet and Yunnan, its large white flowers, borne on a 3-ft (90-cm) stem are heavily marked with crimson-purple spots resembling the snake's-head fritillary, hence its botanical name.

Nomocharis pardanthina. Native of western China, it resembles *N. mairei* except in the absence of fringing to the inner segments. The pale-pink flowers are blotched with crimson at the base of each inner segment and are borne eight to ten on a 3-ft (90-cm) stem.

Nomocharis saluenensis. Native of the western Himalayas, it grows 3 ft (90 cm) tall and bears five or six large flowers of deep rose-pink, which open saucer-shaped, the three inner segments being blotched at the base.

NOTHOLIRION (Liliaceae)

A genus of six species, closely related to *Lilium* and *Fritillaria*, the bulbs being distinguished from those of *Lilium* by the smaller number of scales, while it also has a long basal leaf which protects the dormant flower spike. The flowers resemble those of *Nomocharis*, being funnel-shaped and nodding and borne on long pedicels, though they do not open flat as with *Nomocharis*. *Notholirion* is native of the Himalaya regions, extending from Afghanistan to western China. The plants require similar cultural conditions but are of more tender habit and as they produce their basal leaf in midwinter they should be confined to those gardens where frost and rain are not excessive.

Culture. Outdoors, the bulbs should be planted 4 in (10 cm) deep and 12 in (30 cm) apart in September, in an open sunny situation and in a well-drained sandy soil with plenty of humus. Plant near to low shrubs which will provide the basal leaf in winter with protection from frost and cold winds, for if the foliage is harmed, the plants may fail to bloom as the dormant flower spike is enclosed within the broad basal leaf.

Where the garden is exposed, the plants are grown in pots under glass, one bulb to a 5-in (12·5-cm) pot containing a sandy compost. *N. macrophyllum* is the most suitable species to grow under glass, for it grows only 16 in (40 cm) tall and blooms during April and May. The bulbs should be planted in September 2 in (5 cm) deep, giving only sufficient moisture to maintain plant growth during winter but increasing supplies as the flower spike forms early in spring. After flowering, the bulb dies away but leaves behind numerous bulbils which form inside the scales, and in the wild serve to propagate the species.

Propagation. Upon lifting the old bulb late in summer when most species have finished flowering, the bulbils are detached and planted in boxes containing a sandy compost in which they are grown for two years. They are then moved to individual pots where they remain for two more years to attain flowering size.

Species. *Notholirion bulbuliferum.* Native of Tibet and Nepal, it was so named for the multitudes of bulbils it produces. Its funnel-shaped flowers are of a lovely shade of pinkish-mauve tipped with green and as many as 20 to 30 appear on a 5 to 6-ft (1·5 to 1·8-metre) stem. It blooms during July and August.

Notholirion campanulatum. Native of northern Burma, it forms a basal leaf almost 2 ft (60 cm) in length and bears its crimson bell-shaped flowers in an umbel of 20 or more at the end of a 3- to 4-ft (90-cm to 1·2-metre) stem. Each segment is tipped with green, while each flower is more than 2 in (5 cm) long. It is midsummer flowering.

Notholirion macrophyllum. Native of Nepal, it is too tender to grow outdoors in Britain and should be confined to the alpine house, where it will bloom in April and May. The funnel-shaped flowers of lilac-mauve are borne six to eight on a wiry stem 15 in (37·5 cm) tall, the basal leaf being of similar length.

Notholirion thomsonianum (syn. *Fritillaria thomsonianum*). Native of the alpine meadows of the Himalayas, it is one of the most handsome plants in cultivation, bearing its scented mauve flowers in a large umbel of 30 or more at the end of a 3- to 4-ft (90-cm to 1·2-metre) stem. As it blooms in April and May, it is best grown under glass except in those gardens enjoying a warm winter climate. It produces a large irregular bulb.

NOTHOSCORDUM (Alliaceae)

A genus of 35 species of bulbous plants, native of North America and taking their name from *nothes*, spurious, and *scordon*, garlic, in allusion to its close affinity to that plant. Most species are hardy with flat narrow leaves and bear their flowers in umbels at the end of a leafless scape. They are distinguished from *Allium* by the united perianth segments.

Culture. Outdoors, they may be planted in the shrubbery or border where they will bloom from May until July depending upon species. Plant in groups of six for maximum effect, setting the garlic-like bulbs 3 in (7·5 cm) deep and 6 in (15 cm) apart. They require a light sandy soil of an open nature, though containing some humus for the retention of summer moisture. Plant in September and do not expose the bulbs until ready to plant.

Propagation. Increase by offsets which form at the point where the fleshy roots are attached to the bulb. They are planted in pots or boxes of sandy compost and grown on for three years to flowering size.

Species. *Nothoscordum fragrans.* The best species for garden culture, it has linear lance-shaped leaves and bears its umbels of scented bell-shaped flowers on an 18-in (45-cm) stem. The flowers are white, keeled outside with mauve and are long-lasting. In bloom during May and June.

Nothoscordum inordorum. It bears its white bell-shaped flowers, keeled with purple, during June and July on an 18-in (45-cm) scape and is scentless.

O

ORNITHOGALUM (Liliaceae)

A genus of about 150 species, native of the temperate regions of the Old World, more especially of Europe, northern and southern Africa and Asia Minor. The bulbs are tunicated with radical leaves, while the flowers are borne in clusters or racemes at the end of short leafless scapes. The segments are either free or joined at the base and are star-shaped; the stamens are free from the perianth. The flowers are yellow or white, often grey-green on the outside. Several species possess extreme hardiness, though native of warmer parts. They first reached England during the Middle Ages, brought back by returning Crusaders, and by the end of the sixteenth century a dozen species were under cultivation, including *O. arabicum*, known to Parkinson as the great star-flower of Arabia with a smell which is 'pretty sweet but weak'. Another is *O. umbellatum*, the Star of Bethlehem of cottage gardens, so called because its white starry flowers have covered the hillsides around Bethlehem since earliest times. They may be the 'Dove's dung' mentioned in the Book of Kings for the flowers do resemble small pieces of bird's dung when seen dotted about the rocks. It is said that the bulbs were eaten in times of famine after roasting, for if eaten raw they are poisonous. Parkinson says that when roasted they have the taste of sweet chestnuts.

Culture. The hardy species will grow anywhere: in short grass which does not require cutting until late summer, in the shrubbery, about the rock garden and in open woodlands, where they should be planted in large groups, for many species are most inexpensive. They are valuable in that several species will make a bold display early in summer when the scillas and late flowering muscari are at an end. The more tender *O. arabicum* and *O. subcucullatum*, which bloom in May, should be given a sheltered but sunny situation or be grown under glass.

All require a well-drained soil containing some humus to retain summer moisture and they do well on limestone land. They increase by bulblets and self-sown seed. Plant the bulbs in October 3 in (7·5 cm) deep and 4 in (10 cm) apart in groups of a dozen or more, setting them on a layer of coarse sand to assist drainage. The most suitable species for planting in short grass are *O. narbonense*, *O. fimbriatum* and *O. nutans*, which bloom early in spring, thus extending the season. They will have died back by mid-July, allowing the grass to be cut. Each of these species is tolerant of partial shade. They may also be grown in pots or pans in a cold frame or greenhouse or in a sunny window in the home. Plant 1 in (2·5 cm) deep early in October, six bulbs to each pan and in a gritty compost, then place in a darkened room or in an outside plunge bed for two months to become well rooted before gradually introducing to the light. They bloom during March and April without the aid of any heat.

The South African species, *O. thyrsoides* (chincherinchee) and *O. graminifolium*, which bear their flowers at the end of 2-ft (60-cm) stems and are grown commercially there for indoor decoration, should be planted in deep boxes (or pots) filled with a gritty compost and brought into bloom in a temperature of 40° to 45° F (4° to 7° C) for early spring-flowering. The plants will bloom later where there is no artificial warmth. Plant the bulbs 2 in (5 cm) deep and 3 in (7·5 cm) apart and place the boxes beneath the bench or in a darkened frame for the bulbs to root, during which time they should be given little or no moisture. Another batch may be planted in the new year to bloom under glass later in summer, but if the greenhouse is needed for other purposes, the boxes may be removed to the open, when fear of frost damage has passed, and where, in a sunny position, the plants will bloom in July. They will require ample supplies of moisture as they make growth. If the stems are cut when the flowers are just fully open, they will remain fresh for several months if the ends of the stems are waxed.

Propagation. They are increased by offsets which form around the parent bulb. These are removed in autumn when the clumps are divided and grown on in boxes of sandy compost for two years, when they are planted out and will come into bloom the following year. They are also raised from seed and many of the hardier species will seed themselves if left undisturbed. Seed is sown in a sandy compost in pans or boxes in spring, just covering with compost and keeping moist. Sow thinly and add a thin layer of compost the following summer (15 months after sowing) when the foliage has died down. Place the boxes outdoors for another 15 months before planting out the bulbs to bloom the following year.

Species. *Ornithogalum arabicum.* The Arabian star-flower, native of Asia Minor, eastern Africa and Arabia. It has a large ovoid bulb and thick broad basal leaves. It blooms early in summer, and in the British Isles and northern Europe should be confined to a cool greenhouse or to a garden enjoying a warm winter climate. The glistening white flowers with the ovary of contrasting jet-black and yellow anthers are borne on a 2-ft (60-cm) stem in racemes of 12 or more, each flower measuring more than 1 in (2·5 cm) across. It rivals the chincherinchee as a cut flower, for if the ends of the stems are waxed, the flowers will retain their freshness for several months.

Ornithogalum balansae. Valuable for the trough or rock garden, also for pots for flowering in March and April, it bears umbels of pure-white flowers striped on the outside with grey-green on 6-in (15-cm) stems. Like all the species, the flowers remain fresh for several weeks.

Ornithogalum fimbriatum. Native of south-eastern Europe and Asia Minor, it is the first to bloom in March or in February in a sheltered garden. It bears white star-shaped flowers in a small umbel on a 6-in (15-cm) stem, each segment being edged with green.

Ornithogalum graminifolium. Found on flats in Cape Province, where it blooms in January; in early autumn in the British Isles. It forms a large globose corm, with an extended neck covered in the fibrous sheaths of the bases of the old leaves which are narrow and grass-like with a deep groove. The creamy-white flowers have a thin green dorsal line and are borne in an erect 2- to 12-flowered inflorescence.

Ornithogalum hispidum. Native of Cape Province, where it is common on rocky slopes, flowering in January—early in autumn in the British Isles. Plant the globose bulbs, which form bulbils at the base, in April. It resembles *O. lacteum* in that the leaves are hairy at the margins and die before the flowers appear. The flowers are white with a grey-green dorsal stripe and they appear in a 6- to 12-flowered inflorescence on a 12-in (30-cm) stem.

Ornithogalum lacteum. Native of the Cape, where it is found on rocky slopes above Camps Bay and on Lion's Head, it has leathery lance-shaped leaves which in their natural haunts have died back by flowering time. The margins of the leaves are heavily fringed. At the Cape, it bears large white flowers in a many-flowered raceme on a 15-in (37·5-cm) stem during November—in July in the British Isles where in the more exposed gardens it is grown under glass.

Ornithogalum latifolium. Native of Asia Minor, it has broad leaves, almost 2 in (5 cm) wide and pale green. It bears small white star-shaped flowers in a long raceme on a stem 2 ft (60 cm) tall during midsummer. It is a valuable plant for the border.

Ornithogalum montanum. Present on mountainous slopes of south-eastern Europe and in Turkey and Syria. Completely handy, it has broad leaves and bears its flowers during May and June in a dense cluster of 20 to 30 or more on an 18-in (45-cm) stem. The flowers are white, the outer surface being almost entirely shaded with jade-green.

Ornithogalum narbonense. Though native of the eastern Mediterranean, it is hardy in the British Isles, where it blooms in April and May, bearing small milky-white flowers, striped with green on the outside on 18-in (45-cm) stems. The leaves are broad and shorter than the scape.

Ornithogalum nutans. Native of the woodlands of southern Europe, but long naturalised in parts of the British Isles, it enjoys partial shade and is in bloom from mid-April until early June, happy in the company of bluebells. It bears its silvery-grey flowers shaded jade-green on the outside, on 15-in (37·5-cm) stems and in umbels of six to nine, which carry a soft sweet mossy perfume. It is valuable for orchard planting or in long grass anywhere.

Ornithogalum pilosum. Common on rocky slopes at the Cape, where it blooms in October, it has ovoid bulbs covered in a black outer tunic, and broad leaves which have usually withered at flowering time. The flowers are white with broad perianth segments, shaded with jade-green on the outside. They are borne in a lax 5- to 15-flowered inflorescence on a 12-in (30-cm) stem.

Ornithogalum nutans

Ornithogalum pyramidale. Native of south-western Europe, it blooms during May and June, bearing a spike thickly set with star-like white flowers, striped with green on the outside and held on a 2-ft (60-cm) stem. It has bright green lance-shaped leaves.

Ornithogalum pyrenaicum. Native of the Pyrenees and southern France and long naturalised in the British Isles. During Tudor times it was grown as a commercial crop around Bath, the young shoots being cut and made into bundles, to be eaten as a substitute for asparagus, hence its name, Bath asparagus. The flowers vary in colour, being pale yellow or grey-green, rather than white. They are borne in a long pointed spike during May and June.

Ornithogalum saundersii. Native of the Transvaal, where it is known as the giant summer chincherinchee, it requires greenhouse protection or a warm garden in the British Isles. It comes into bloom in June and continues until August, the large creamy-white flowers with a greenish-black centre, opening in

(*Above*) *Leucocoryme irioides*. (*Below*) *Lilium candidum*, the Madonna Lily.

Lilium regale

Lilium auratum

Muscari botryoides album

Muscari tubergenianum

(*Above*) *Narcissus bulbocodium conspicuus*, Hoop-petticoat Daffodil.
(*Below*) *Narcissus telamonius plenus*, Double Daffodil Van Sion

(*Above left*) Daffodil, Music Hall. (*Above right*) *Narcissus triandrus albus*, Angel's Tears Daffodil. (*Below left*) Narcissus La Riante – pure white perianth, the cup being large, flat, and a brilliant orange scarlet. (*Below right*) Narcissus, Semper Avanti.

(*Above left*) *Narcissus poetaz*, Cheerfulness. (*Above right*)
Narcissus tazetta, Geranium – each stem carries 4–6 white
blooms with bright orange-red cups. (*Below left*) Trumpet
narcissus, Dutch Master – rich gold flower having perfectly
shaped trumpet, the flange deeply and evenly notched.
(*Below right*) Narcissus, Mrs R. O. Backhouse – the original
pink daffodil.

(*Above*) Bulbs of Ornithogalum species compared in size with a matchbox
Ornithogalum pyramidale   *Ornithogalum arabicum*
Ornithogalum umbellatum   *Ornithogalum nutans*
(*Below*) *Ornithogalum umbellatum*, Star of Bethlehem – pure white star-like blooms in great profusion.

Ornithogalum nutans – star-like blooms of soft green with white margins.

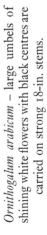

Ornithogalum arabicum – large umbels of shining white flowers with black centres are carried on strong 18-in. stems.

Oxalis adenophylla – dainty pink flowers sitting upon neat
mats of grey-green foliage.

Polianthes tuberosa

Puschkinia scilloides, Lebanon Squill

(*Above*) *Scilla tubergeniana* – delicate silver-blue flowers make an attractive subject in the rock garden. (*Below*) *Scilla sibirica*, Spring Beauty – the finest of all Scillas, producing a succession of vivid blue flowers on several strong stems.

Planting tulips and narcissi
in fibre

Late Double Tulip, Nizza –
clear yellow petals flamed
with scarlet

Lily-flowered Tulip, China Pink

Tulipa tarda – each bulb produces several star-shaped flowers of creamy white with a golden centre.

Tulipa turkestanica – from four to eight on a stem, the open flowers are star-like, creamy white with rich brown stamens.

Tulipa kaufmanniana,
Water-lily Tulip

Tulipa biflora – creamy
white star-like blooms

(*Above*) Springtime colour: tulips and wallflowers. (*Below*) Beds of tulips underplanted with winter-flowering pansies.

long succession. The scape arises to a height of 3 to 4 ft (90 cm to 1·2 metres) or more from a rosette of grey-green leaves.

Ornithogalum subcucullatum. Native of south-western Europe, the leaves die back before it blooms in June, the snow-white star-like flowers being borne in dense racemes on an 18-in (45-cm) stem. In the British Isles it should be grown in a cool greenhouse or in those gardens with a mild winter climate.

Ornithogalum thyrsoides. The chincherinchee, an anomatopoeic word used to describe the sound of the south winds as they blow through the flowers in the hedgerows of Cape Province. In the British Isles and northern Europe it may be grown under glass to bloom in spring and early summer or outdoors late in summer from a spring planting in those gardens which do not experience late frosts. It has broad leaves and bears its large pure-white flowers with brown centres and yellow stamens up to half as long as the perianth segments, in a dense raceme on 2-ft (60-cm) stems. Plant in autumn to bloom under glass.

Ornithogalum tricophyllum. A rare native of the eastern Mediterranean, it has a small globose bulb and prostrate narrow leaves, deeply channelled. The flowers are white and are borne in a 5- to 10-flowered corymb on a 6-in (15-cm) scape. It is rare in cultivation.

Ornithogalum umbellatum. The star of Bethlehem, to be found about the rocky hillsides of the ancient city and throughout the Middle East. It is now naturalised in a few meadows in southern England, its flowers opening at noon and closing at about 5 p.m. It has narrow leaves 6 to 8 in (15 to 20 cm) long, and from late in April until June it bears clusters of white star-like flowers, striped with green on the outside. Eight to ten blooms appear on a 6-in (15-cm) stem.

OXALIS (Geraniaceae)

A genus of about 800 species, many of them tuberous and cosmopolitan in their distribution. They chiefly inhabit South America and southern Africa, where the roots of several are used as food. The leaves are usually three-lobed and clover-like (*O. enneaphylla* has up to 20 leaflets); the flowers tubular or bell-shaped. Both the leaves and flowers close up in dull weather and at night. Stamens 10; five short and five long. The flower is remarkable in that the styles and stamens are of three different lengths. (See Nicholas Jacquin's *Monograph of the Oxalis*, 1794.) The tuberous roots or bulbs are covered in dark-brown tunics and shaggy hairs. The sorrels, as they are called, may be used about the rock garden, planted in sunny corners or in a trough, while those of more tender habit are grown in the alpine house.

Culture. They like a slightly acid soil, one containing peat or leaf mould and some grit to encourage drainage, for their natural habitat is lower mountainous slopes in full sun.

The bulb-like rootstock should be planted 3 in (7·5 cm) deep, the spring-flowering species in October, while those that bloom in autumn are planted in

Q

spring. Plants grown in small pots by alpine plant specialists may be planted out at any time between March and October, for there will be no root disturbance. During summer, the plants should not be allowed to lack moisture. Indoors, plant as described according to season of flowering and in a compost made up of fibrous loam, leaf mould or peat and sand in equal parts, setting the tubers 1 in (2·5 cm) deep and 2 in (5 cm) apart. Artificial heat is not necessary but water sparingly during winter. In spring, admit plenty of fresh air and shade the plants from the direct rays of the sun to prevent leaf scorch. Early in summer, the containers may be placed outside until late autumn.

Propagation. They are readily increased by division of the tubers in spring and from seed which is sown in pans of sandy compost. Germination is rapid, and often self-sown seedlings will appear around the parent plants. These may be transplanted when large enough to handle, to boxes containing a compost made up of loam, leaf mould and sand in equal parts. Here they remain for 12 months until ready to move to individual pots, to bloom the following year.

Species. *Oxalis adenophylla.* Native of the Chilean Andes, it has a bulbous rootstock covered in matted fibres and has crinkled grey-green foliage formed like a fan from the centre of which arise in May and June, goblet-shaped flowers of creamy-pink with a maroon eye. They open flat.

Oxalis bowiei. Native of Cape Province where it is common on sandy ground, it has a small scaly bulb and downy leaves divided into three blunt heart-shaped leaflets. In July and August appear large cup-shaped flowers of rich rosy-purple with a swollen yellow tube. The plant was once raised in large numbers in small pots under glass for summer bedding.

Oxalis brasiliensis. Though native of Brazil, it is almost hardy in the British Isles if given a sunny nook in the rock garden or it is lovely under glass. It grows only 3 in (7·5 cm) tall with trifoliate leaves and bears large crimson-red flowers in May and June.

Oxalis cernua. A common native of the Cape, it has a bulb which is vertically ridged and has leaves with long hairs below and with purple zoning above. It blooms in spring, bearing 8 to 10 golden-yellow flowers in an umbel.

Oxalis enneaphylla. Native of the Falkland Islands, it has fan-shaped leaves of silvery-grey about which nestle blush-white goblets nearly 2 in (5 cm) across and scented. It is in bloom from May until August and grows 2 to 3 in (5 to 7·5 cm) tall.

Oxalis falcata. Native of Cape Province, where it blooms in May—in winter under glass in Britain. It forms an ovoid bulb covered in a smooth black tunic and has leaves with linear leaflets. The flowers are pale rose with a yellow tube and a pubescent corolla.

Oxalis hirta. Native of Cape Province, the bulb is large and covered in a thin brown tunic. The leaves are sessile, crowded on the upper part of the trailing stems and covered in short hairs. The flowers are of glowing purple, often with a buff margin on the underside. In the British Isles and northern Europe, it blooms in November and December and must be grown under glass.

Oxalis incarnata. Native of the Cape, it forms an ovoid bulb covered in a smooth brown tunic and leaves which are whorled. The flowers are of medium size, pale mauve in colour with a green tube and they bloom throughout summer on short erect stems. The plant enjoys a cool soil and semi-shade.

Oxalis lobata. Native of the Chilean Andes, it is almost hardy and blooms in autumn, when it comes into life after dying back early in summer. It has grey-green trifoliate leaves and bears large flowers of golden yellow spotted with red.

Oxalis luteola. Native of Cape Province, it is stemless with a long ovoid tuber and trifoliate leaves. The flowers are large, of brilliant yellow, sometimes with brown margins on the underside and appear intermittently almost throughout the year.

Oxalis magellanica. It is found on the coast near the Straits of Magellan and forms a mat of bronzey-green leaves, studded with short-stemmed flowers of gleaming white.

Oxalis variabilis (syn. *O. purpurea*). It forms a large black ovoid bulb and rounded leaflets which are purple on the underside. The large purple flowers (sometimes lilac, pink or white) have a swollen yellow tube and appear in November. It is a beautiful plant for the alpine house.

Oxalis violacea (syn. *Ionaxalis violacea*). Native of North America, where it is present in woodlands and thickets from Massachusetts to Florida, it has a brown scaly bulb and several slender-stemmed trifoliate leaves. The flowers are rosy purple and appear in May and June in umbels of 3 to 10 on a 6-in (15-cm) stem.

P

PAMIANTHE (Amaryllidaceae)

A genus of a single species, native of Peru and named in honour of Major Pam, its introducer. It is distinguished from Pancratium by its sheathing leaf bases. An evergreen, it must be grown in a warm greenhouse in the British Isles and northern Europe, where it can be given a minimum winter temperature of 50° F (10° C).

Culture. Plant the bulbs in September, one to a 5-in (12·5 cm) pot containing a compost made up of fibrous loam, peat and decayed manure in equal parts with a sprinkling of sand. Plant firmly with the extended neck just above the level of the compost. Give little or no water until the roots have formed and place the pots in a cool room. Then introduce to a temperature of 50° to 55° F (10° to 13° C) and increase moisture as the leaves appear, followed by the flower spike early in March. After flowering, stand the pots outside when there is no fear of late frosts and give only sufficient moisture to keep the leaves from 'flagging'. Top-dress in autumn and place the pots in a temperature of 50° F (10° C) to bring them into bloom again early next year.

Propagation. Usually by offsets, which, upon lifting the bulbs every third year, will have formed around the mother bulb. They are detached and planted in small pots containing a sandy compost, in which they are grown for two years. They are then moved to larger pots and will bloom in two more years.

Species. *Pamianthe peruviana.* Native of the Peruvian Andes, it forms a large oval bulb covered in a brown tunic which has an extended neck, really a false stem, made up of the sheathing bases of the leaves. The flowers are white with a long green tube and a central corona about 2 in (5 cm) across. They are scented and appear early in March on a 2-ft (60-cm) scape.

PANCRATIUM (Amaryllidaceae)

A genus of 15 species of bulbous plants, native of southern Europe, central Asia, tropical Africa and India, and closely related to *Hymenocallis*. It takes its name from *pan*, all, and *kratys*, powerful, the reference being to its medicinal qualities. From the extended neck of the bulb arises a rosette of strap-like leaves and umbels of scented white flowers, remarkable for their central staminal cup resembling the corona of narcissus, while the six narrow outer petals converge into an elongated tube. Most species require warm greenhouse culture but those which are native of the Mediterranean region are sufficiently hardy to be grown outdoors in those gardens of the British Isles with a mild winter climate.

Culture. The best for outdoor culture is *P. illyricum* which blooms early in summer. It requires an open, sunny situation where the bulbs will ripen without which they will not bloom. Plant in October, 6 in (15 cm) deep and 12 in (30 cm) apart in a well-drained soil enriched with decayed manure and to which some peat or leaf mould has been added. The bulbs should be given a covering of decayed leaves to protect them against frost, but as they bloom before the end of May, plant only where late frosts are not experienced. To assist with winter drainage it is advisable to plant the bulbs on a layer of sand. The plants will require ample supplies of moisture as they make growth in spring and should not be disturbed for at least four years.

Indoors, plant one bulb to a 5-in (12·5-cm) pot using a compost made up of fibrous loam, leaf mould, dehydrated cow manure and silver sand in equal parts, leaving the neck of the bulb exposed. Pot firmly, *P. illyricum* in October, *P. maritimum* in March, and provide a minimum night temperature of 55° F (13° C). Water sparingly during winter but increase supplies in spring and early summer. After flowering, gradually withhold water while the foliage dies back and place the pots on their side for the bulbs to ripen. They are given a top-dressing in autumn before starting into growth again. Indoors, *P. illyricum* will bloom towards the end of April and *P. maritumum* during July and August.

Propagation. By offsets, which will have formed around the mother bulb and which are detached when the bulbs are lifted in October. They should be planted into 3-in (7·5-cm) pots containing a sandy compost, in which they are grown for two years before being planted out or moved to larger pots in which they will bloom after another two years.

Species. *Pancratium canariense.* Native of the Canary Islands, it has broad strap-like glaucous leaves and in autumn bears pure-white flowers in a large umbel of 8 to 12 on a 2-ft (60-cm) scape. The staminal cup is short, the petals narrow and reflexed. In the British Isles it should be grown under glass except in the warmest gardens.

Pancratium illyricum. It is found among the sand dunes of Mediterranean bays of southern Europe, being prominent near St Tropez. It has a large pear-shaped bulb with a neck almost 12 in (30 cm) long, encased in brown scales. The lance-shaped leaves are covered in glaucous farina, while the powerfully scented snow-white blooms appear in June in an umbel of 8 to 12 on an 18-in (45-cm) scape.

Pancratium maritimum. It is found along the Mediterranean coast, where it is known as the sea lily or sea daffodil on account of the staminal cup. It has brown-coated, pear-shaped bulbs and lance-shaped glaucous leaves which are evergreen. The large powerfully scented translucent white flowers are borne in umbels of four to eight on a 15-in (38-cm) stem. The flowers have a long perianth tube, while the staminal cup is longer than in others.

Pancratium sickenbergerii. It is found in furrows of the desert lands of Egypt and Arabia and has a bulb 1 in (2·5 cm) through with a long neck. It blooms in September in an umbel of four to eight, the white flowers being small with the perianth segments short. They are borne on a 12-in (30-cm) scape, to be followed by spirally curled leaves. It is not in general cultivation.

Pancratium tortuosum. It is found about the coral rocks along the coast of Egypt and northern Africa and around the Isle of Elba, where it forms a small globose bulb with a cylindrical neck. The leaves are twisted and appear in a tuft of 8 to 12 at the same time as the flowers in January. The white flowers are larger than of other species and are borne two to five in an umbel on a 12-in (30-cm) scape.

Pancratium verecundum. Native of northern India, it has a bulb 2 in (5 cm) through with a cylindrical neck and strap-like leaves 18 in (45 cm) long. It blooms in autumn, two to six pure-white flowers appearing on a 15-in (37·5-cm) scape.

PARADISIA (Liliaceae)

A genus of a single species, native of the alpine regions of central Europe and closely related to *Anthericum*. It was named St Bruno's lily in honour of the founder of the Carthusian Order and is a plant of extreme hardiness, with a short rhizomatous rootstock and fleshy roots. It blooms early in summer and is a valuable plant for a sunny border or for the rock garden.

Culture. It requires a well-drained sandy loam enriched with some decayed cow manure and, as it blooms early in summer, it is necessary to plant the roots 2 in (5 cm) deep and 9 in (22·5 cm) apart in October.

Propagation. By division of the tuberous roots in autumn, replanting at once so that the roots do not become dry.

Species. *Paradisia liliastrum.* It forms a tuft of fleshy leaves channelled on the upper surface, while its white funnel-shaped flowers, which emit a soft sweet perfume, are borne in May and June in a one-sided raceme at a height of 2 ft (60 cm). The spoon-shaped segments are tipped with green.

PHAEDRANASSA (Amaryllidaceae)

A genus of six species, native of the Andes of Peru and Ecuador and named from two Greek words *phaidros*, gay, and *anassa*, a queen, a reference to the brilliant colouring of the flowers. It has large ovoid bulbs 2 in (5 cm) through, covered in a brown tunic and stalked oblong leaves, produced after (or at the same time as) the flowers, early in summer. The flowers with their long tubes and extended stamens are borne in a loose umbel on a 2-ft (60-cm) scape. In the British Isles and the cooler parts of North America the plants are given the protection of a greenhouse or garden room.

Culture. Plant the bulbs singly in a 5-in (12·5-cm) pot in late October, using a compost made up of fibrous loam, leaf mould and sand in equal parts. Plant firmly with the top of the bulbs at soil level and after allowing the bulbs four or five weeks in a cool place to form roots, introduce them to a temperature of 45° F (7° C), increasing supplies of water when the flower stems appear. The plants require only sufficient warmth to exclude frost and to keep them growing for they are almost hardy. The leaves form at the same time as the flowers or shortly after, and watering should be maintained until they die down late in autumn. The plants should then be given a rest until repotted and started into growth again early in spring, but during winter they should be kept in a frost-free place.

Propagation. When repotting, detach the small offsets from around the mother bulb and plant into boxes of sandy compost in which they remain for two years. They are then moved to 3-in (7·5-cm) pots and grown on for another two years until they reach flowering size, when they are moved to a 5-in (12·5 cm) pot.

Species. *Phaedranassa carmioli.* Native of the Peruvian Andes, it is more tender than other species and should be given a temperature of 52° F (11° C). It forms a large brown-coated bulb almost 3 in (7·5 cm) through and has large oblong leaves 12 in (30 cm) long and 4 in (10 cm) broad with 6-in (15-cm) stalks. The flowers are borne on a 2-ft (60-cm) scape during May and June and in a loose umbel of 12 or more. They are tubular and of bright red, shaded with green at the base and with a green rim around the mouth.

   Phaedranassa chloracea. It is found at a height of 12,000 ft in the Andes of Ecuador, forming a large bulb 3 in (7·5 cm) through and with lance-shaped leaves 12 in (30 cm) long. The drooping tubular flowers are borne in summer in a loose umbel of 6 to 12 on a 3-ft (90-cm) scape and are brilliant red, edged with green.

   Phaedranassa lehmannii. Native of the Andes of Colombia and Ecuador, where it grows at an altitude of 7,000 to 10,000 ft, it has an ovoid bulb 2 in (5 cm) through and bright-green leaves 9 in (22·5 cm) long. The bell-shaped flowers are borne on a 2-ft (60-cm) scape and are scarlet with green shading at the base of the tube but without the green edge.

PLACEA (Amaryllidaceae)

A genus of five species, native of South America, the plants having tunicated bulbs and narrow grey-green leaves. The flowers resemble *Pancratium* in that they have a funnel-shaped corona which is formed at the base of the oblong segments. Flowering early in summer, the plants should be grown under glass in the British Isles and northern Europe.

Culture. It is a plant which is rare in cultivation, for it does not take to the confined space of a pot. Instead it should be grown in deep boxes or in a border under glass, though in those parts enjoying a warm winter climate it may be grown in a cold frame. The bulbs should be planted in October 2 in (5 cm) deep and 4 in (10 cm) apart, in a compost made up of fibrous loam, decayed manure and coarse sand in equal parts. Give little or no moisture until growth commences early in the new year, when supplies are increased according to temperature. In winter, the temperature of the greenhouse should be around 55° F (13° C) by day and 50° F (10° C) by night. Indoors, at these temperatures, the plants will begin to bloom early in May, a month later in a frame. They remain long in bloom, after which they should be dried off gradually and given a rest until late in autumn, when they are started into growth again.

Propagation. After two or three years it will be found that offsets will have formed about the mother bulbs. These are detached when the plants are dormant in autumn and planted in boxes of sandy compost in which they remain for two years, before being moved to a border or frame in which they will bloom.

Species. *Placea grandiflora.* Native of the Andes of Chile, it forms a bulb 1 in (2·5 cm) through, from which arise three pointed linear leaves 18 in (45 cm) long. The flowers are white with the outer segments striped with red. They are borne in May on a 12-in (30-cm) scape.

Placea ornata. Native of the Chilean Andes, it has an ovoid bulb 1 in (2·5 cm) through, from which arise two narrow leaves 12 in (30 cm) long and a 9-in (22·5-cm) scape on which are borne four to six white flowers, striped with purple and with claw-shaped outer segments.

POLIANTHES (Amaryllidaceae)

A genus of a single species, native of Mexico and taking its name from *poly*, many, and *anthos*, flower, on account of its abundance of flowers. It is the poet Shelley's 'sweet tuberose, the sweetest flower for scent that blows'. During Victorian times the tuberous-rooted bulbs, covered with the old leaf bases, were imported from southern Italy, to be grown by specialists in heated glasshouses almost the whole year round, while few conservatories were without its pleasantly scented flowers. The linear leaves are channelled and spotted with brown on the underside. The flowers are white and funnel-shaped and appear in a terminal raceme on a 2-ft (60-cm) stem during July and August where growing outdoors or in an unheated greenhouse.

Culture. The tubers may be brought into bloom in a temperature of 60° F (16° C) during the winter months; or where there is no heat, they will bloom in summer from an early spring planting. Plant one tuber to a 5-in (12·5-cm) pot, using a compost made up of fibrous loam, sand, leaf mould or peat and dehydrated cow manure in equal parts. Plant firmly, just covering the nose of the bulb and keep the compost moist. Where a temperature of 65° F (18° C) and a moist atmosphere is provided, retarded bulbs may be brought into bloom within eight weeks. They require copious amounts of moisture and after flowering will take a year before they bloom again. The tubers may be grown in a cool greenhouse or garden room and will bloom late in summer, when the flowers will remain fresh for several weeks, scenting the room with their lily-like perfume.

Plants may also be brought into bloom outdoors. They should be started into growth in 4-in (10-cm) pots under glass from a March planting to be set out in their flowering quarters early in June when there is no fear of frost. Plant 9 in (22·3 cm) apart in a warm border, leaving the top of the tubers exposed and where they may be ripened by the sun. They require a soil containing some decayed manure and peat or leaf mould. During summer, give plenty of moisture. They will bloom during August and September. After flowering, the tubers are lifted and stored over winter in boxes of peat or sand until started into growth again in March. In a sunless summer, the tubers will not ripen sufficiently to be worth keeping for another year.

Species and Varieties. *Polianthes tuberosa.* Native of Mexico, it makes a large bulbous-like tuber and has channelled leaves. The funnel-shaped flowers open star-like and are borne in an elegant raceme of 20 or more at the end of a 2-ft (60-cm) scape. The variety *gracilis* has narrower leaves and bears flowers with longer tubes, while The Pearl, which bears double flowers of pearly white, is that most often cultivated for the florist trade. The flowers are larger than those of the type.

POLYGONATUM (Liliaceae)

A genus of 50 species of perennial plants, native of the Northern Hemisphere and taking its name from *poly*, many, and *gonu*, a knee, the reference being to the many joints of the stems. Its country name, Solomon's seal, is derived from the curious seal-like markings which the shoots leave on the rhizomatous root as they die back in autumn. From the roots arise graceful wand-like stems clothed in alternate or opposite lance-shaped leaves arranged in ladder-like fashion, hence another name, ladder-to-heaven. From the axils of the leaves are borne, on short stalks, nodding flowers of greenish white. The perianth is tubular or bell-shaped enclosing six stamens. It is a plant of deciduous woodlands, flowering in May and June. In Tudor times, a toilet water was distilled from the flowers of *P. odoratum*, which has the rich smell of the tuberose.

Culture. Plant the rhizomes in November, just below the soil surface and 12 in (30 cm) apart. They require a leafy soil, retentive of summer moisture.

The plants may be gently forced into bloom indoors by lifting the roots in November and planting them 1 in (2·5 cm) deep in pots containing a sandy soil. Place in the dark or in a plunge bed until Christmas, then introduce to a temperature of 45° F (7° C). Water sparingly at first, increasing supplies as the sun's warmth increases and admit plenty of air, except when the weather is cold. They will come into bloom early in spring.

Propagation. Lift and divide the rootstock in November. Each severed portion should have a terminal bud. After rubbing the cut part with flowers of sulphur, replant.

Species. *Polygonatum biflorum*. Native of eastern Canada and the United States, it grows 2 ft (60 cm) tall and has dark-green lance-shaped leaves from the axils of which are produced pairs of drooping greenish-white bell-shaped flowers.

Polygonatum multiflorum. The common Solomon's seal, native of the British Isles, which produces, in May and June, graceful arching stems 2 ft (60 cm) tall. These are furnished with oblong stem-clasping leaves of dark green and white tubular flowers, waisted at the middle and edged with green. The form *flore pleno* bears double flowers, and *roseum* has flowers tinted with pink.

Polygonatum odorum. Known as the angular Solomon's seal, it is to be found on limestone land in western England, where it forms a short angular stem 10 to 12 in (25 to 30 cm) tall, clothed in alternate lance-shaped leaves. The flowers, which are not waisted, are borne in June, singly or in pairs and are greenish white with a powerful lily-like scent.

Polygonatum officinale. A dainty species, native of the limestone woodlands of southern England. It grows 12 in (30 cm) tall with stem-clasping leaves, and in May and June bears greenish-white flowers followed by blue-black berries.

Polygonatum oppositifolium. Native of the Himalayas, it grows 3 ft (90 cm) tall with opposite leaves which taper to a point. The drooping flowers are borne in corymbs during April and May and are greenish white, striped with red. They are followed by red berries.

Polygonatum roseum. Native of Siberia, it has a furrowed stem 3 ft (90 cm) tall, clothed in opposite lance-shaped leaves 4 in (10 cm) long from the axils of which appear, in pairs, rose-pink flowers. In bloom May and June.

PUSCHKINIA (Liliaceae)

A genus of two species, native of the hilly terrain extending from the Lebanon to Afghanistan and named in honour of the Russian botanist, Puschkin. The plants have tunicated bulbs and strap-like leaves and bear their flowers in a loose raceme on a leafless scape. Possessing extreme hardiness, *P. scilloides*, the striped squill, is one of the best of small bulbous plants and may be naturalised beneath mature trees or planted in generous drifts towards the front of a shrubbery. Also, as it grows 6 in (15 cm) tall, it is an ideal plant for the rock garden. In the open, it blooms during April and May. Indoors, in small pots or pans, it blooms in March over several weeks.

Culture. It requires a well-drained gritty soil, similar to that in which it grows in its natural haunts, where the plants are to be found in damp ravines. The soil should contain ample supplies of peat or leaf mould to retain summer moisture. It is also a lime-lover and grows best where lime rubble (mortar) is incorporated in the soil. Plant in October 3 in (7·5 cm) deep and 3 in (7·5 cm) apart and in groups of 20 to 30 for maximum effect. It will increase rapidly from offsets.

Indoors, plant six to eight bulbs to a 5-in (12·5-cm) pot or pan containing a compost made up of fibrous loam, leaf mould and sand in equal parts. Plant in October, 1 in (2·5 cm) deep and 3 in (7·5 cm) apart and place the container in the dark or in a plunge bed outdoors for two months, until the bulbs have formed their roots. Then move indoors, to a greenhouse or inside the home, where the plants should be grown, watering only when necessary to maintain the compost in a moist condition. After flowering, place the plants outdoors, where the foliage will gradually die back. The bulbs may be repotted in October or planted in the open ground to bloom in spring.

Propagation. When the bulbs are lifted, the numerous offsets are detached and planted in boxes of sandy compost to grow on for two years. They may then be planted out and will come into bloom within 18 months.

Species. *Puschkinia scilloides* (syn. *P. libanotica*): Native of the Lebanon, Persia and Afghanistan, it has a round bulb 1 in (2·5 cm) through, covered in a brown tunic and dark-green strap-like leaves. It blooms in April and May, bearing its bell-shaped flowers in racemes of 6 to 12 on a stem 6 in (15 cm) tall. The flowers are pale blue and open flat, to reveal a blueish-green stripe down the centre of each petal. It has six stamens, with the filaments united into a cup or corona. There is a rare white form, *alba*.

R

RANUNCULUS (Ranunculaceae)

A genus of about 400 species of annual or perennial plants, some aquatic, and taking their name from *rana*, a frog, which denotes their liking for marshy land. *R. asiaticus*, the ranunculus, has claw-like tuberous roots which may be dried and stored like those of bulbous plants and so it is included here. It was discovered near Constantinople by the Vizier Cara Mustapha and brought to the attention of the Sultan, who sent his emissaries to search the Near East for others. It reached France during the reign of Louis IX and grew in the garden of his mother, Blanche of Castille, but there is no mention of the plant being in England until Elizabethan times. Gerard tells us that 'my lord and master, the Rt Hon. the Lord Treasurer had plants sent to him', while others arrived from Syria '. . . for our gardens, where they flourish as in their own country'. During the eighteenth century it had become a florists' flower, there being two main forms, the turban and the Persian, the latter being descended from a dark-red form called by Philip Miller, *R. sanguineus*. Miller said that the blooms of the ranunculus are so large and of such rich colours 'as to vie with the carnation itself'. By 1792, Maddock listed over 800 varieties and said that seed never produced two flowers alike; yet by 1850 Glenny said that it had become 'a neglected flower', for it demanded care with its cultivation, which an industrial age did not permit. Being only half-hardy, the ranunculus requires protection, for it blooms early in summer and should be planted in October, or early in March, depending upon soil and situation. It is thus suitable only for those gardens enjoying a mild winter and spring climate and should be planted in autumn only where winter frost is absent. In those gardens less favourably situated, the tubers may be planted in April, when they will bloom in June.

Culture. The plants require an open sunny situation and a well-drained soil containing leaf mould and decayed cow manure. It is usual to grow in beds for display or for cutting, planting the tubers in drills as for anemones. The drills are made with the back of a rake, 4 in (10 cm) apart and 3 in (7·5 cm) deep, the tubers being spaced 3 in (7·5 cm) apart. Line the drills with sand before planting claws downwards with the 'bud' at the top. Scatter more sand over them before filling in the drills and raking level. When growth can be seen, hoe between the rows to suppress weeds and to aerate the ground, while the soil must be kept moist. As soon as the flower stalks appear, water once each week with dilute liquid manure which will encourage the flower stems to grow sturdy and help to build up the tubers. They will bloom over a period of five to six weeks, after which the foliage will begin to yellow and die back. The tubers should then be lifted. Allow them to dry before carefully shaking off the soil and storing in boxes of sand away from frost.

Propagation. Offsets will form around the older tubers and these are removed upon lifting. Plant in boxes of sandy soil in spring and grow on for 12 months until reaching flowering size, when they are planted out. They are also raised from seed sown in April in boxes of sandy soil or in a frame. Sow thinly and keep the compost moist. In 12 months time, transplant the seedlings to another part of the frame, spacing them 1 in (2·5 cm) apart, and grow on for two years, keeping the seedlings moist and give an occasional watering with dilute liquid manure. During cold weather it is advisable to cover the frame lights with sacking to exclude frost, and at this time give no water. The tubers will be ready to plant in their flowering quarters when three years old.

Species and Strains. *Ranunculus asiaticus*. It has claw-like tuberous roots and ternate or bi-ternate leaves divided into deeply toothed segments. The flowers, in shape like small pompone dahlias, are borne on 12-in (30-cm) stems. In form like the pompone dahlia, they have the same brilliance. The so-called turban form, which bears flowers of brilliant scarlet spotted with gold, is known to French growers as *turban doré*. The Turkish ranunculuses are now known as paeony-flowered on account of their size, being semi-double and obtainable in scarlet, gold, orange and white. The Scottish form is a derivation of the old Persian ranunculus, the blooms being spotted and edged with gold. The Florentine strain, one of the best to raise from seed, bears flowers in attractive art shades as well as those of more brilliant colouring.

REINECKEA (Liliaceae)

A genus of two species, native of eastern Asia and named in honour of the German horticulturist, Johanne Reineck. It has a creeping rhizomatous rootstock, from which arises a tuft of narrow leaves 10 in (25 cm) long and terminating in a point. Its tubular flowers are borne in dense spikes on a 12-in (30-cm) stem during April and May.

Culture. It requires an open, sunny situation and a well-drained soil containing some peat or leaf mould. A sunny border is a suitable place to plant it. Plant the creeping rhizomatous roots in October, 3 in (7·5 cm) deep and 12 in (30 cm) apart.

Propagation. Increase by division of the rootstock in autumn.

Species. *Reineckea carnea*. Native of eastern China and Japan, it is perennial. From the rootstock arises a tuft of narrow lance-shaped leaves and spikes of flesh-coloured flowers which appear in April and May. The flowers are tubular with six oblong segments and are scented.

RIGIDELLA (Iridaceae)

A genus of four species, native of Mexico and Gautemala and so named because of their stiff upright flower stem. Closely related to *Tigridia* and flowering early in summer, they are best grown under glass in the British Isles and northern Europe, though *R. flammea*, the best-known species, attains a height of 3 ft (90 cm) and is not suitable for the small greenhouse.

Culture. Plant the corms in November, 2 in (5 cm) deep into pots or boxes of sandy compost and in a temperature of 45° F (7° C). Water sparingly until growth commences, and as the flower stem forms provide support. After flowering, dry off, then remove the corms from the compost and store in a frost-free room until ready to use again.

Propagation. Usually from offsets which form at the base of the corm and which are removed when they are lifted. They are grown on in boxes of sandy compost until reaching flowering size in two years.

Species. *Rigidella flammea*. Native of Mexico, it has plaited leaves 20 in (50 cm) long, sheathing at the base, and early in summer bears large umbels of drooping scarlet flowers with the outer segments striped with purple.

ROMULEA (Iridaceae)

A genus of about 90 species, native of southern Europe and northern and southern Africa and named in honour of Romulus, founder of Rome. The corms are small, flat at the base and covered in a hard fibrous tunic. The leaves are leathery and grass-like, while the crocus-like flowers are borne in clusters of two to several from the leaf axils which are usually below ground. Those species of the Mediterranean regions are almost hardy in the British Isles and northern Europe, those of South African origin requiring a mild winter climate. Plant in a sunny position, for the flowers will open only in sunlight. They are at their best grown in pans and given the protection of a cool greenhouse, where they bloom early in spring.

Culture. Outdoors, plant the corms in groups of six to eight in sunny pockets in the rock garden or to the front of the shrub border. They are also attractive in short grass but must not be planted in shade. Plant in October in a well-drained soil, 3 in (7·5 cm) deep and 3 in (7·5 cm) apart.

Indoors, plant six corms to a pot or pan, using a compost made up of fibrous loam and coarse sand, but no manure. Plant 2 in (5 cm) deep and 2 in (5 cm) apart in October and give no water until the corms begin to make growth in spring. It is one of the best of bulbous plants for indoor culture in full light, for the blooms, though short lived, open over several weeks and their colouring is unique. After flowering, place the pots outdoors, where the foliage will die back gradually, and take indoors again late autumn before the frosts.

Propagation. This is usually by seed sown under glass in April in pans containing a sandy compost. By keeping the compost moist, germination will be in about two months, but allow the plants to remain in the pans for two years, until reaching flowering size, when they are replanted into containers in which they will bloom. When the young foliage dies down, give little or no water until it makes new growth in spring.

Species. *Romulea bulbocodiodes.* Native of the Cape, where it appears on the sun-baked ground of mountainous slopes, its pale-yellow flowers are stemless with a long perianth tube. At the Cape it blooms during August and September, April and May in the British Isles.

Romulea bulbocodium. A common plant of southern France (and Italy), where it grows near the coast, usually in sand dunes. Indoors it bears small chalice-shaped flowers of brightest purple on 6-in (15-cm) stems during March and April, a month later in the open.

Romulea clusiana. Native of southern Spain, it resembles *R. bulbocodium* in its purple flowers, shaded yellow at the base, but they are larger and are almost stemless.

Romulea elegans. Native of the Cape, present on Kenilworth flats, the leaves and peduncles emerging directly from the corm. The flowers are white, shaded reddish green at the base of the outer segments.

Romulea hirsuta. Present at the Cape, it is common on Signal Hill and Lion's Head. It forms a pea-size corm and bears filiform leaves covered in minute hairs. The flowers are magenta-red, shaded yellow at the base.

Romulea requienii. Native of Corsica and Sardinia, it is almost hardy and in April bears large chalice-shaped flowers of deep violet on 3-in (7·5-cm) stems.

Romulea rosea. Native of Cape Province, where it is present on grassy flats, it has a stem enclosed in the leaf bases below ground, the small mauve or white flowers opening star-like, the outer segments shaded with green at the base and faintly striped with purple.

Romulea sabulosa. Native of Natal, it is one of the best of the genus, with bristle-like leaves and globular flowers of cherry-red, veined with crimson and with a satin-like sheen.

Romulea triflora. Common at the Cape, it has basal leaves and two to five cauline leaves from the axils of which the peduncles arise. The globular flowers are of deep golden yellow with a long perianth tube. It blooms August and September at the Cape, May in the British Isles.

S

SANDERSONIA (Liliaceae)

A genus of a single species, native of Natal and named in honour of Mr J. Sanderson, first secretary of the Natal Horticultural Society. Of trailing habit and closely related to *Gloriosa*, it should be grown in a warm greenhouse or garden room where, climbing by leaf tendrils, it may be trained up a pillar or trellis—or the stems may be supported by stakes inserted around the side of a pot. It has a small tuberous root, and in its native land bears bell-shaped blooms at Christmas, hence its name, Christmas bells. In the British Isles it blooms from July until September.

Culture. It requires protection from winter frosts and rain, and where grown indoors may be left in its pot undisturbed, to come into new growth each spring. Alternatively, the roots may be lifted when the plant dies back in autumn, to be stored in boxes of sand during winter and started into growth again in spring. Plant in April, one tuber to a 4-in (10-cm) pot, into a compost made up of fibrous loam, leaf mould, decayed manure and coarse sand in equal parts. Plant 2 in (5 cm) deep and water copiously as the sun increases in strength. In autumn, the stems will die back, when the plants should be dried off. Where no winter warmth is available, the tubers are best lifted and stored in boxes of sand in a frost-free room.

In the warmest parts, the roots may be planted at the base of a warm wall in early April and the stems grown against a trellis, up which they will climb to a height of 6 ft (1·8 metres). The roots are lifted and stored when the plants die back in autumn.

Propagation. By division of the small tubers in spring, treating the cut part with flowers of sulphur and replanting immediately.

Species. *Sandersonia aurantiaca*. Native of Natal, it forms a short tuberous rootstock from which arise climbing stems up to 6 ft (1·8 metres) long with lance-shaped leaves. The flowers, inflated like small balloons and in shape like a cardinal's cap, are borne at the leaf axils on wire-like stems and droop down. They are of deep golden-orange and are borne several to a stem.

SCHIZOSTYLIS (Iridaceae)

A genus of two species, native of most parts of southern Africa and taking its name from *schizo*, to cut, and *stylos*, a column, in reference to the thread-like styles. It is almost hardy in the British Isles, but as it blooms from late September until Christmas, it should either be grown indoors or planted only in those gardens enjoying a warm autumnal climate.

Culture. Indoors, plant the corms (really a swollen rhizome) in April, 2 in (5 cm) deep and 2 in (5 cm) apart in pots or deep boxes which may be allowed to stand outdoors at the foot of a warm wall until they begin to bloom in September. Then lift indoors to a sunny greenhouse or garden room, where, in a temperature of 42° F (5° C) they will bloom until Christmas. The spikes remain fresh in water for several weeks. The compost is of fibrous loam, peat and decayed manure, to which is added a sprinkling of sand. After flowering, protect the plants from frost and keep the compost just moist. In April, they may be placed in the open to repeat the process.

Where growing outdoors in a warm border, where the plants are to bloom late in autumn, plant in April 4 in (10 cm) deep and 3 in (7·5 cm) apart in a sandy soil containing peat or leaf mould. If possible, place a frame light over the blooms in autumn to protect them from adverse weather.

Propagation. Plants that have been undisturbed for two or more years will have formed a tuft of leaves and stems, at the base of which is a swollen rhizome. This is divided in spring and replanted.

Species and Varieties. *Schizostylis coccinea.* The only species in general cultivation, it has sheathing sword-like leaves and bears elegant spikes of crimson-red flowers on a 2-ft (60-cm) stem. The flowers open flat and measure 2 in (5 cm) across. The variety Mrs Hegarty bears flowers of rose red and Viscountess Byng, shell pink.

SCILLA (Liliaceae)

A genus of about 80 species, native of temperate Europe, Asia and northern and southern Africa and taking their name from *squilla*, a squill. They have tunicated bulbs and strap-like leaves and bear their usually bell-shaped flowers on leafless scapes from early spring until autumn. Possessing extreme hardiness, they are among the best of all bulbous plants for the garden and may be planted in short grass or about the rock garden, while those flowering early are attractive in the alpine house or cold frame. The taller-flowering woodland species, including the bluebell, are now classified under *Endymion*.

Culture. With few exceptions, they are hardy in the British Isles and northern Europe and flourish in any well-drained soil, in full sunlight or partial shade.

Plant the early spring- and summer-flowering species in October—associating them with chionodoxas, winter aconite and muscari—and the late summer- and autumn-flowering species in March. Plant in drifts, 3 in (7·5 cm) deep and 4 in (10 cm) apart. The scillas require a well-drained soil, and it is advisable to plant the bulbs on a layer of sand. A 7- to 8-cm bulb will bear flowers in its first year and is the most suitable size for outdoor planting. A 6- to 7-cm bulb may take 18 months to come into bloom. Where planting in a trough or in the rock garden, plant in groups of six or more.

Indoors, plant 7- to 9-cm bulbs for best results, six to a pot or pan containing a compost made up of fibrous loam, leaf mould and coarse sand in equal parts. Plant the winter- and spring-flowering species in September 1 in (2·5 cm) deep and 2 in (5 cm) apart and place the pot in a plunge bed or cupboard in a cool room until rooting has taken place. Early November remove the containers to a cold greenhouse or frame or into a room heated to 50° F (10° C) and water only when necessary, giving just enough to keep the compost moist and the bulbs growing. In gentle heat they begin to bloom early in the year. Where no artificial heat is available, water sparingly and the bulbs will bloom a month or so later. At all times, provide a buoyant atmosphere.

Propagation. The clumps may be lifted and divided every four or five years. This is done when the foliage has died back late in summer; with the autumn-flowering species, in spring. Lift as for snowdrops, dividing each clump into several portions or into single bulbs, those which are small being planted out in

TABLE XXVI. *Flowering times of the hardy scillas*

Species	Time	Height
Scilla amoena	April–May	6 in (15 cm)
S. autumnalis	August–September	9 in (22·5 cm)
S. bifolia	March–April	9 in (22·5 cm)
S. bithynica	March–April	12 in (30 cm)
S. hyacinthoides	July–August	15 in (37·5 cm)
S. italica	April–May	15 in (37·5 cm)
S. lilio-hyacinthus	May–June	12 in (30 cm)
S. monophylla	May–June	6 in (15 cm)
S. messanaica	April–May	6 in (15 cm)
S. odorata	May–June	9 in (22·5 cm)
S. peruviana	May–June	9 in (22·5 cm)
S. pratensis	May–June	12 in (30 cm)
S. sibirica	March–April	6 to 8 in (15 to 20 cm)
S. tubergeniana	February–April	4 to 6 in (10 to 15 cm)
S. verna	April–May	6 to 8 in (15 to 20 cm)

drills 2 in (5 cm) deep and lined with sand. The bulblets are spaced 1 in (2·5 cm) apart and are grown on for two years until large enough to plant in their flowering quarters.

They are also readily raised from seed sown in boxes or pans of sandy compost in spring. Sow thinly, just covering with compost, and place in a frame until germination has taken place, then remove to a partly shaded position outdoors, keeping the compost moist while the plants are growing. They may remain in the boxes or pans for two years, after which they will have reached 1 cm in diameter. They are then dried off and in autumn sown like peas in shallow drills where they remain for two more years before being planted in their permanent quarters. They will then have reached 5 to 6 cm and will bloom the following year, five years after sowing the seed.

Species. *Scilla amoena.* The Byzantine or star squill of south-eastern Europe, it makes a round bulb with a purple tunic and has deeply channelled leaves 9 in (22·5 cm) long. It bears bright indigo star-like flowers in a dainty raceme on a 6-in (15-cm) stem during April and May.

Scilla autumnalis. Native of the British Isles and northern Europe, it bears its flowers before the leaves, during August and September. The star-like flowers are of pale lilac-rose and are borne on 9-in (22·5-cm) stems.

Scilla bifolia. Native of the lower mountainous slopes of central Europe, where it grows in pockets of shingle, it has two or more narrow bronzey-green leaves and blooms in March and April, a month earlier under glass. It bears large star-like flowers of deep gentian-blue in a raceme of six to eight on a 9-in (22·5-cm) stem, the flowers having long pedicels so that they dangle and dance in the spring breezes.

There are a number of varieties: *praecox* is early-flowering, while *taurica* bears flowers of deepest violet. For contrast, plant the white, *alba. Rosea* bears blooms of soft shell pink. Where undisturbed, the plants seed freely and increase from offsets to form large clumps.

Scilla bithynica. Native of south-eastern Europe and Asia Minor, it has lance-shaped leaves and bears its violet-blue flowers in a dense raceme on a 12- to 15-in (30- to 37·5-cm) stem during March and April.

Scilla cooperi. The South African squill, it is native of Natal and forms long narrow leaves, striped and spotted at the base with purple. It blooms in April, bearing bright-purple bell-shaped flowers in a raceme of 40 to 50 on a 9-in (22·5-cm) stem.

Scilla hyacinthoides. It is native of coniferous woodlands of southern Europe and makes a large bulb 2 in (5 cm) through. The leaves grow 18 in (45 cm) long and are broad and glossy; while the scented flowers are lilac-blue and borne in a dense raceme on a 15-in (37·5 cm) scape. In bloom July and August.

Scilla italica (syn. *Endymion italica*). It is to be found across southern France and into northern Italy. It has strap-like leaves 6 to 8 in (15 to 20 cm) long and bears its pale-blue flowers in dense racemes on a 15-in (37·5-cm) stem. It blooms in April and May, the colour of the flowers being intensified by the purple stamens, while it is scented.

Scilla lilio-hyacinthus. Native of the Pyrenees, it has large scaly bulbs like those of the lily and broad strap-like leaves of brilliant green. The bright-blue star-like flowers appear in May and June and are borne on a 12-in (30-cm) scape.

Scilla monophylla. Native of Portugal, it extends the display into midsummer, bearing its spike of cobalt-blue in a loose raceme on a 6-in (15-cm) stem. It forms a solitary leaf 9 in (22·5 cm) long at the same time as the flowers.

Scilla messanaica. Native of Greece and south-eastern Europe, it has leaves 6 to 8 in (15 to 20 cm) long and 1 in (2·5 cm) broad and it is April-flowering, bearing small star-shaped flowers of richest blue in a compact raceme on a 6-in (15-cm) stem.

Scilla natalensis. Native of Natal, where it is known as the blue squill, it requires glasshouse culture in the British Isles and northern Europe. It blooms early in autumn, bearing deep blue bell-shaped flowers on stems up to 3 ft (90 cm) tall.

Scilla odorata. Native of northern Spain and Portugal, it blooms with *S. monophylla* and bears its flowers of a lovely shade of sky blue on a 9-in (22·5-cm) stem. It is scented and blooms early summer.

Scilla peruviana. Known as the Cuban lily but in no way connected with either Cuba or Peru, being native of southern Europe and northern Africa and probably taken west by the Spaniards. It forms a rosette of glaucous strap-shaped leaves 9 in (22·5 cm) long and margined with hairs, while its flowers are borne in a gobular umbel 6 in (15 cm) across, composed of a large number of bright-blue, star-like blooms. At first, the flower heads seem to rest on the leaves, the scape lengthening as the flowers open. The bulbs, which measure 2 in (5 cm) across, should be planted 4 in (10 cm) deep, as it is the least hardy of the Mediterranean species. The pure-white form, *alba*, is equally fine. It is in bloom in May and June.

Scilla pratensis. Native of south-eastern Europe, especially of those countries bordering the Adriatic, it has narrow leaves 12 in (30 cm) long and early in summer bears its lilac-blue bell-shaped flowers in a dense raceme on a 12-in (30-cm) scape. The flowers are scented.

Scilla sibirica. The Siberian squill and the best-known member of the family. It is one of the earliest to bloom, flowering in a sunny nook during the first days of March, a month earlier under glass. From its large oval bulb it forms three or four strap-like leaves 6 in (15 cm) long and several 6- to 8-in (15- to 20-cm) stems of drooping bell-shaped flowers which open star-like and are of porcelain blue, striped with deeper blue. It is one of the best for planting in short grass and also for forcing in gentle heat.

An outstanding form is Spring Beauty (*atrocoerulea*), which bears flowers twice the size of the type and of a lovely shade of delphinium blue. Being sterile, the flowers retain their beauty for several weeks. A 9- to 10-cm bulb should be used for growing indoors in heat. The white form should be planted with it for contrast.

Scilla tubergeniana. Native of northern Persia and Afghanistan, from whence it was introduced by van Tubergens, it is a species of great merit and, like *S. sibirica*, bears several spikes to each bulb—thus four or five bulbs to a pot will provide a display of beauty, each spike bearing three or four blooms. The flowers resemble *Puschkinia* (with which it grows) in that they are of a unique shade of soft Cambridge blue, with darker stripes down each petal. They are borne from mid-February to early April on stems 4 in (10 cm) long. The flower spikes appear just before the strap-like leaves of richest green. With the variety Zwanenburg, the dark stripes are more pronounced and the flowers slightly larger.

Scilla verna. Native of the British Isles and northern Europe, it usually grows on grassy slopes in sight of the sea and is known as the spring squill. It has narrow upright leaves and bears, in April and May, short spikes of mauve-coloured star-like flowers on a 6-in (15-cm) stem.

Scilla villosa. Native of Morocco, it has upright leaves 6 to 8 in (15 to 20 cm) tall, hairy at the margins and on the underside, while the blue star-like flowers appear in spring in dense racemes on a 6-in (15-cm) stem. It is best grown in the alpine house or frame.

SMITHIANA (NAEGELIA) (Gesneraceae)

A genus of eight species, native of Mexico and originally named *Naegelia* after Karl Naegel, the German botanist. It is closely related to *Achemenes* and has underground catkin-like rhizomes covered with leaf scales. Its soft hairy leaves are of velvet-like appearance while it bears tubular flowers in tall trusses, late in summer and in autumn. A number of handsome hybrids have been evolved.

Culture. It requires a compost made up of fibrous loam, peat, decayed manure and silver sand in equal parts, and, to maintain a succession of bloom, make two plantings, one in March, another in May. Plant 1 in (2·5 cm) deep and space out the tubers 3 in (7·5 cm) apart if more than one is to be planted in a pot. They should be given a night temperature of not less than 55° F (13° C) and must be watered sparingly until growth begins, then increase supplies according to natural temperatures. Syringe the foliage daily to keep it free from red spider and to provide the humid conditions it enjoys. Those from a March planting will bloom towards the end of July. Shade from the sun. After flowering, the stems and foliage will die down; moisture should be withheld and the plants stored in a temperature of 45° F (7° C) in winter. The pots should be placed on their side or the tubers shaken out and stored in boxes of sand.

Propagation. It is readily increased by splitting the rhizomes, which should be done in spring, replanting afterwards, or by rooting the leaves, inserting the stalks up to the blade at the side of a pot. Use a sandy compost, which should be kept moist, and protect from the sun. The leaf cuttings are taken in July and rooted in a temperature of 60° to 65° F (16° to 18° C), syringeing them twice daily to prevent too rapid evaporation of moisture and to prevent them wilting.

Hybrid Varieties

ABBEY. The foliage is rich velvety green, the tubular flowers creamy white, shaded on the outside with salmon pink and borne on stems 15 in (37·5 cm) long.

KAREN FRANKLIN. A hybrid of great beauty with bronzey green foliage and bearing flowers of golden yellow.

ORANGE KING. It has dark-green foliage and flowers of a uniform clear-orange colour.

PINK DOMINO. It bears long tubular flowers of dusky pink, white inside and speckled with pink. They are enhanced by the dark-green foliage.

SANTA CLARA. An outstanding variety with dark-bronze foliage and bearing flowers of rich apricot, creamy white inside.

SCARLET EMPEROR. It has dark-green foliage and bears flowers of crimson-red, the inside being yellow, speckled with red.

SPARAXIS (Iridaceae)

A genus of four species, native of southern Africa and taking their name from *sparasso*, to tear, in allusion to the torn spathe. Closely related to *Ixia* and requiring similar culture, they bloom in early summer in the British Isles, but in all but the warmest parts should be grown under glass. The corm is small with a tunic composed of straw-coloured netted fibres, while the narrow leaves are arranged in two ranks. The flowers are borne in a few-flowered spike. The bracts are colourless. The perianth tube is funnel-shaped, with the stamens directed to one side.

Culture. Indoors, plant five or six corms to a 5-in (12·5-cm) pot or pan, using a compost made up of fibrous loam, leaf mould and coarse sand in equal parts. Plant the corms 1 in (2·5 cm) deep early in September, placing the pots in a frame for about six weeks until the roots have developed, during which time they should receive little or no moisture. Then move to a greenhouse heated to 45° F (7° C) and water only when the compost begins to dry out. After flowering, dry off gradually as the foliage dies back and place the pots on their side, repotting in autumn.

Outdoors, select a warm, sheltered border and plant the corms early in September 4 in (10 cm) deep and 4 in (10 cm) apart, in a well-drained soil.

Cover with bracken or leaves until early March, when growth will appear above ground. The protective covering should then be removed. The 16-in (40-cm)-tall stems should be supported by inserting twigs about them. After flowering the foliage will begin to die back and is removed when quite brown. During summer, keep the corms as dry as possible.

Propagation. Usually by offsets, removed from around the base of the corm when lifted dormant in September. The cormlets are planted in boxes of sandy soil, where they remain for two years while reaching flowering size.

Species. *Sparaxis grandiflora*. Native of Cape Province, it has six to eight basal lance-shaped leaves and bears deep-violet or cream-coloured flowers, shaded violet on the outside on a wiry stem 18 in (45 cm) tall. The flowers have wedge-shaped segments and measure about 2 in (5 cm) across. The variety *liliago* has white flowers.

Sparaxis tricolor. Native of Natal, where it blooms in September, in May in the British Isles. It has lance-shaped leaves and bears its flowers in a dainty spike on a 15-in (37·5-cm) stem. They are bright orange-red, shaded yellow at the centre and are long lasting when cut and in water.

Of several handsome varieties, *alba maxima* bears large flowers of purest white; Fire King, brilliant scarlet; Sulphur Queen, soft yellow; and Honneur de Haarlem, cerise-pink with a black centre.

SPREKELIA (Amaryllidaceae)

A genus of a single species, native of Mexico and named in honour of Dr Sprekel, the German botanist. It is also known as the Jacobean lily or Aztec lily. It has tunicated bulbs 2 in (5 cm) thick and narrow strap-like leaves 18 in (45 cm) long, while its bright-red flowers appear in July and August on 12-in (30-cm) stems. It is hardy outdoors in the British Isles and North America only in those gardens not troubled by winter frosts, otherwise it should be grown indoors to bloom early in summer.

Culture. Outdoors, plant the bulbs early September in a warm border, 4 in (10 cm) deep and 6 in (15 cm) apart, or in April in more exposed parts. Water copiously while the bulbs are growing, and after flowering allow the plants to dry off, if possible by covering the bulbs with glass, or with decayed leaves or bracken to a depth of 6 in (15 cm). Alternatively, lift the bulbs in autumn, store in sand in a frost-free room and plant out in April.

Indoors, plant the bulbs in September, one to a 5-in (12·5-cm) pot containing a compost made up of fibrous loam, leaf mould and decayed manure in equal parts, to which is added some sand. As with *Hippeastrum*, from which it differs in its irregular flower, the bulbs must not be given too large a pot. Plant so that the upper portion and neck is exposed above the level of the compost and place in a plunge bed for six weeks to form roots. Then grow on in a temperature of 55° F (13° C), increasing moisture supplies as the plant continues to grow. Indoors it will bloom in April and May, but a later planting may also be made in an unheated house early in spring, when the bulbs will bloom late in summer. After flowering, allow the foliage to die back gradually by withholding moisture and give the plants a rest period in full sun to ripen the bulbs.

Propagation. Repot every three or four years, and when so doing, remove the offsets which will have formed about the mother bulb. Plant those of small size in boxes of sandy compost; the larger in a 3-in (7·5-cm) pot to grow on to flowering size in three or four years.

Species. *Sprekelia formosissima.* It has ovoid bulbs with an extended neck and narrow strap-like leaves 18 in (45 cm) long. The bright-red flowers are borne singly (occasionally in twos) on a leafless scape 12 in (30 cm) tall. Each flower measures about 6 in (15 cm) across and has irregular segments, the three upper being narrow and clawed, the lower drooping and broader. The filaments are also red.

STENOMESSON (Amaryllidaceae)

A genus of 20 species, native of tropical South America and taking their name from two Greek words, *stenos*, narrow, and *merson*, middle, in allusion to the flowers being contracted in the middle. Mostly native of the Andes of Peru and Ecuador, where they grow at altitudes of 10,000 ft, they have round bulbs 2 in (5 cm) through and narrow lance-shaped leaves. The flowers are borne in an umbel on the top of a leafless scape 12 to 18 in (30 to 45 cm) tall and appear early in summer.

Culture. They require indoor culture in Britain, the bulbs being planted early in the new year, one to a 5-in (12·5-cm) pot. Like *Hippeastrum*, they enjoy restricted conditions and may be allowed to occupy the pots for three to four years before repotting. Provide a compost made up of fibrous loam, leaf mould and decayed manure in equal parts, to which is added some sand or grit. The plants should be started into growth by vigorous bottom heat, after which the temperature should be reduced to 52° F (11° C). The leaves appear with or shortly after the flowers. During growth, the plants require plenty of moisture but shade from the sun when they come into bloom. After flowering, the leaves die back, when the pots should be taken outside and placed on their side in a sunny position for the bulbs to rest and ripen. They are taken indoors and started into growth again early in November.

Propagation. When repotting, offsets should be removed from around the old bulbs and planted into 3-in (7·5-cm) pots containing a sandy compost. Here, they grow on for two years until reaching flowering size, when they are moved to larger pots to bloom.

Species. *Stenomesson aurantiacum.* Native of Ecuador, it forms a round bulb 1 to 2 in (2·5 to 5 cm) through, from which arise strap-like leaves and orange funnel-shaped flowers 2 in (5 cm) long, borne two to four on a 15-in (37·5-cm) scape.

Stenomesson croceum. It has bright-green leaves and bears its drooping pale-yellow flowers in an umbel of four to six, their long tubes being dilated in the middle.

Stenomesson humile. Native of Peru, it bears a solitary flower of orange-red, which stands erect and has a tube 3 in (7·5 cm) long, striped with yellow. The flowers are borne on a 9-in (22·5-cm) scape in April and May.

Stenomesson incarnatum. It makes a large long-necked bulb and is the finest species, with strap-like leaves 15 in (37·5 cm) long, which are formed with the red flowers, borne three or four to a 15-in (37·5-cm) scape. The flowers are slightly drooping and have a tube 4 in (10 cm) long.

The variety *trichromum* bears scarlet flowers with a central green stripe down each segment, while *fulvum* bears flowers of brownish-yellow.

Stenomesson luteo-viride. It makes a large bulb 3 in (7·5 cm) through and forms its leaves early in summer, with the flowers, which are pale yellow tipped with green, with a tube 2 in (5 cm) long.

Stenomesson viridiflorum. It has a large ovoid bulb 2 in (5 cm) through with a long cylindrical neck and forms its lance-shaped leaves with the flowers which are borne on a scape 2 ft (60 cm) tall. The flowers have a curved tube 3 in (7·5 cm) long and are entirely green, borne in an umbel of two to four.

STERNBERGIA (Amaryllidaceae)

A genus of eight species, native of the Caucasus and Asia Minor and named in honour of Count Sternberg, the German botanist. They have black tunicated bulbs with long necks and strap-like leaves which usually appear after the flowers. The yellow crocus-like flowers appear in autumn (with one exception). They differ from crocus in that they have six stamens; three in crocus.

Culture. The plants are shy to flower in cultivation, except where conditions suit them. They require an open, sun-baked soil which is well-drained and are best confined to those gardens enjoying a mild winter climate. The bulbs should be planted in a dry sunny corner for they will survive with the minimum amount of moisture. They grow well in a limestone soil, in which they are found growing under natural conditions. Add leaf mould and decayed manure. Plant the bulbs in June (*S. fischeriana* in October), 4 in (10 cm) deep and 6 in (15 cm) apart. They may be planted to the front of a shrubbery, in a sunny pocket in the rock garden, or to the front of a narrow border beneath the eaves of a house. The bulbs should be left undisturbed for six to eight years to form

large clumps, and it is only after two or three years that they begin to bloom
well.

Indoors, plant the autumn-flowering species in April or May, four or five
bulbs to a pot or pan, in a compost made up of fibrous loam, leaf mould and
lime rubble in equal parts. Plant the bulbs 2 in (5 cm) deep and place in a plunge
bed or cool, dark room for six weeks for the roots to form, then remove to a
sunny position outdoors and give only sufficient moisture to keep them growing.
They may be taken indoors to bloom when they will be much appreciated at
this time. After flowering, keep the plants growing until late spring, then
gradually withhold moisture as the leaves begin to die back. With most species,
the leaves do not appear until after the flowers and will persist until spring. Do
not repot the bulbs for several years, for, like many of the family Amaryllidaceae,
they bloom better when pot-bound.

Propagation. After five or six years, lift the clumps when the leaves have died
back and divide them, at the same time removing the offsets which form around
the larger bulbs. These are planted one to a 3-in (7·5-cm) pot containing a
sandy compost and are grown on for two years before being planted out, when
they will bloom in two years time.

Species. *Sternbergia clusiana* (syn. *S. macrantha*). Native of Turkey and Syria,
where it grows on mountainous slopes, it makes a large bulb with an extended
neck and grey-green strap-like leaves 12 in (30 cm) long, which appear early in
spring and persist until midsummer, dying back before the flowers appear late
in August. The flowers are like golden-yellow goblets, enclosed in a sheath
which is the extended tunic of the bulb. They open star-like and persist until
late autumn.

Sternbergia colchiciflora. Native of south-eastern Europe and Asia Minor, it
has narrow leaves which appear early in spring and persist until the end of
summer when the flowers appear. They are stemless and palest yellow, with
narrow segments, and when open, almost sit on the soil. They are scented.

Sternbergia fischeriana. Native of south-eastern Europe, Turkey, Persia and
Kashmir. It is unusual in the genus in that it is spring-flowering, while several
large canary-yellow flowers appear from one bulb. The flowers have a short
tube and a stem 6 in (15 cm) long. The segments are more rounded at the tips
than with others.

Sternbergia lutea. The best-known species and that most easily grown. Native
of south-eastern Europe, Palestine and Persia, it is believed to be the 'lily of the
fields' of Biblical days and blooms on grassy slopes. It has a large pear-shaped
bulb and strap-like leaves which appear with or immediately after the flowers
in early autumn. The flowers are deep golden yellow and chalice-shaped,
opening star-like. The variety *angustifolia* has narrower leaves and smaller
flowers. It is native of Greece and south-eastern Europe and is very free-flower-

ing. It is very much more expensive than the type. The variety *sicula* has pale-green leaves and flowers with pointed segments.

STREPTANTHERA (Iridaceae)

A genus of two species, closely related to *Ixia* and *Sparaxis*, but differing in its twisted anthers. Native of southern Africa. The corms are small and covered in coarse fibres, while the leaves are arranged fanwise, as in *Freesia*. The flowers are borne several on a 10-in (25-cm) stem during May and June.

Culture. It may be grown outside in Britain only in those gardens which have a favourable winter climate, for it blooms early in summer and must occupy the ground through winter. Plant the corms in October, 4 in (10 cm) deep and 4 in (10 cm) apart in a sunny border and in a well-drained soil.

Indoors, plant five or six corms to a pot or pan containing a compost made up of fibrous loam, leaf mould and coarse sand in equal parts. Plant in October and place in a frame or cool room for several weeks for the corms to form roots during which time they need little or no moisture. Then move to the greenhouse or garden room in a temperature of 42° to 45° F (5° to 7° C) and water sparingly, increasing supplies as the plants make growth in spring. After flowering, dry off the plants before placing the pots outdoors on their side to rest.

Propagation. By the cormlets which form at the base of the older corms and which are detached when repotting in October. Grow on the cormlets in boxes of sandy compost for two years until they reach flowering size.

Species. *Streptanthera cuprea.* Native of Natal, it has lance-shaped leaves arranged in two ranks and bears on a 12-in (30-cm) stem copper-coloured flowers with a black centre. The perianth lobes spread out and overlap. The variety *coccinea* bears glowing orange flowers, while Zwanenburg has maroon-red flowers shaded yellow at the centre.

Streptanthera elegans. It has a small corm and lance-shaped leaves arranged in two ranks, while the flowers, borne two or more to a 9-in (22·5-cm) stem, are white with a large purple centre surrounded by a black ring covered in yellow spots.

SYNNOTIA (Iridaceae)

A genus of five species, native of southern Africa and closely related to *Sparaxis*. The corms are small with a tunic of straw-coloured fibres and lanceolate leaves formed in two ranks. The flowers are borne in a two- to three-flowered spike. The upper lobes are arched; the lower spreading. Named in honour of W. Synot, a collector of plants in Cape Province.

Culture. It blooms in August and September in its natural haunts; in early summer in Britain, where it is grown under glass. Plant in October, three or four corms to a 5-in (12·5-cm) pot containing a sandy compost, and place in a frame for six weeks for the corms to form roots. Then remove to a temperature of 45° F (7° C), increasing supplies of moisture as the plants make growth. After flowering, dry off. During the latter weeks of summer, give the corms a rest by placing the pots on their side and withhold moisture.

Propagation. When the corms are repotted in October, detach the cormlets which cluster around the base of the older corms and grow on in boxes of sandy compost for two years until they reach flowering size.

Species. *Synnotia bicolor* (syn. *S. villosa*). Native of Cape Peninsula, where it is found on Lion's Head. It makes a small corm with six or seven basal leaves and two cauline leaves which are partly sheathing. The flowers are cream-coloured with the uppermost lobe purple and they carry a soft sweet perfume. The three lower lobes incurve at the margins.

Synnotia meterlerkamfiae. Native of Natal, it has six or seven basal leaves and bears its flowers in a loose spike on a 12-in (30-cm) stem. They are deep violet flaked with orange on the lower petals.

SYRINGODEA (Iridaceae)

A genus of eight species, native of Natal and taking their name from *syringodes*, fistula, in allusion to the slender perianth tube. Only one species, *S. pulchella*, is in general cultivation and in Britain and northern Europe and may be grown under glass or in a warm pocket in the rock garden.

Culture. Plant five or six bulbs to a pot or pan containing a compost made up of loam, leaf mould and sand in equal parts. Plant early in spring, 1 in (2·5 cm) deep and 2 in (5 cm) apart. After a month in a cool place for the corms to form roots, remove to a frame or greenhouse and increase moisture as the plants make growth. After flowering, dry off and place the pots on their side beneath the greenhouse bench or in a frost-free room in winter. Repot and start into growth again in spring.

Outdoors, plant the corms 2 in (5 cm) deep and 3 in (7·5 cm) apart in April, in a well-drained soil and in an open, sunny position. Lift the corms late in autumn after flowering and store in boxes of sand during winter, away from frost.

Propagation. By cormlets which, when lifting the old corms, will be found clustering at the base. Detach and plant in boxes of sandy compost where they will grow on for two years until reaching flowering size.

Species. *Syringodea pulchella*. It makes a small round corm from which arise stiff grass-like leaves 4 in (10 cm) long. It blooms early in autumn, bearing on a 6-in (15-cm) stem mauve-coloured flowers with wedge-shaped segments and a cylindrical tube.

T

TECOPHILAEA (Amaryllidaceae)

A genus of two species, native of the Andes of Chile and Peru, and requiring greenhouse protection in all but the warmest gardens. They take their name from that of Tecophilo, daughter of the Italian botanist, Professor Colla, friend of the botanist Botero, who discovered and named the plant in her honour.

Culture. In its natural habitat it blooms in November, in March in the British Isles and northern Europe. Where grown outdoors it must occupy the ground over winter. It needs a well-drained soil, containing plenty of shingle or grit and enriched with some decayed manure. It grows on ground manured by sheep in its native land. Plant the corms in October, 6 in (15 cm) deep and 4 in (10 cm) apart, preferably on a layer of sand and at the foot of a sunny wall or in a pocket in the rock garden. Plant in small groups for maximum effect and cover with a cloche to protect the corms from excess winter moisture. Of such exquisite beauty are the flowers that it may be desirable to retain the cloche covering until after the blooms have faded.

Indoors, they will bloom in February and March and should be planted five or six corms to a large pot or pan, in a compost made up of fibrous loam, peat or leaf mould and dehydrated cow manure, to which has been added a liberal sprinkling of sand. Plant the corms 2 in (5 cm) deep and 2 in (5 cm) apart in October and place under the bench for four or five weeks for the corms to root. No heat is necessary to bring them into bloom; in a temperature of 45° F (7° C) they will bloom early in February. Give only sufficient moisture to prevent the compost from drying out. After flowering, dry off and place the pans outside in a sunny position, preferably beneath the eaves of a house, where the bulbs will ripen until taken indoors again late in autumn.

Propagation. By offsets which are removed from the base of the corms upon lifting every three or four years. The cormlets are grown on in boxes of sandy compost for two years until they reach flowering size. They may also be raised from seed sown in May in pans containing a sandy compost. Here the cormlets remain for two years before being moved to small pots in which they grow on for two more years to reach flowering size.

Species. *Tecophilaea cyanocrocus.* Native of the Chilean Andes, it makes a small corm with a reticulate tunic and has glossy linear channelled leaves 4 in

(10 cm) long which curl over at the end. The flowers are borne on 6-in (15-cm) stems and with their six pointed segments open star-like and about 2 in (5 cm) across. They are of rich gentian blue and have a soft sweet perfume. The variety *leichtlinii* has flowers of deeper blue with a large white centre.

TIGRIDIA (Iridaceae)

A genus of 12 species, native of Mexico and Peru and named after the tiger because of the spots in the throat of the flowers (though they are leopard-like rather than tiger-like). The corms are large, bulbous and covered in brown scales, while the narrow leaves are plaited like those of *Gladiolus*. The large outer petals of the flowers form a deep cup 2 in (5 cm) across and then open flat or horizontal to about 4 in (10 cm) across, the three inner petals being small. The filaments are united to form a long cylindrical tube, the stamens and stigma protruding 1 in (2·5 cm) or more beyond the cup. The flowers last only for a day, but others take their place in long succession over six to eight weeks. Those occupying the ground in winter in those gardens enjoying a mild climate, will bloom in July; those from a spring planting flower in August and September. Alternatively, they may be grown under glass to bloom in June.

Culture. In warm gardens the corms are planted in October. They require a well-drained soil and a sunny situation. Plant the corms 4 in (10 cm) deep and 6 in (15 cm) apart, preferably in groups of a dozen or more so that though the blooms are fleeting, there will be a colourful display for almost two months. To assist drainage, plant on a layer of sand, and to protect the corms from frost, cover the ground with leaves or bracken until growth commences in spring.

In colder gardens, plant early in April. They will bloom two months later and when the foliage dies back in autumn, lift the corms as for *Gladiolus*. After drying, store through the winter in boxes of sand or peat in a frost-free room and where mice cannot prove troublesome.

Indoors, plant five or six corms to a 5-in (12·5-cm) pot containing a compost made up of fibrous loam, leaf mould and decayed manure in equal parts. Make a planting in October to bloom early in summer and another early in the year, to continue the display when those planted outdoors in spring will bloom late in summer. Give little or no moisture while the corms are rooting, but increase supplies as they make growth and begin to bloom. Heat is not necessary, but in a temperature of 45° to 48° F (7° to 9° C) the corms will bear bloom within five months. Since the stems grow 18 in (45 cm) tall, support should be given.

After flowering, dry off and place the pots on their sides outdoors for the corms to ripen and rest during late summer. In autumn, the corms are repotted and started into growth again. Whether growing indoors or outside, *tigridias* will benefit from a weekly application of dilute manure water from the time the flower stem appears.

Propagation. When the corms are lifted in autumn, small cormlets will be seen clustering at the base. These are detached and grown on as for *Gladiolus* and will reach flowering size in three or four years. Plants which are growing in the open and have occupied the ground for several years may be increased by division either after the foliage has died back in autumn or when starting new growth in April, after the manner of *Montbretia* (*Crocosmia*).

Plants may also be raised from seed sown in boxes or pans of sandy compost in May, or into a frame. Treat like *Ixia* and grow on for two years, topping up with fresh compost when they die back in autumn. They should be moved to 3-in (7·5-cm) pots when about three years old and will bloom within five years of sowing.

Species. *Tigridia curvata*. It has short plaited leaves and bears flowers on a stem less than 12 in (30 cm) tall. They are yellow, spotted with purple at the centre, while the inner segments are brown and are also heavily spotted.

Tigridia pavonia. Native of southern Mexico and Peru, it is the peacock tiger flower with leaves 18 in (45 cm) long, while it bears its flowers on a branched stem up to 2 in (5 cm) tall. The flowers measure up to 6 in (15 cm) across with a deep cup, while the outer segments are violet at the base, shading to scarlet at the tips and with yellow zones. The variety *alba grandiflora* bears large white flowers spotted with crimson at the centre, while *alba immaculata* is free of spots. *Canariensis* has yellow flowers spotted with crimson and *lutea immaculata* bears unspotted yellow flowers. Strikingly conspicuous is *speciosa*, its scarlet flowers having a yellow centre, while *carminea* bears flowers of carmine red.

Tigridia pringlei. It resembles *T. pavonia*, differing in its broader blade-like segments. Native of northern Mexico, its flowers are of brilliant-scarlet, blotched with crimson, and they form a more shallow cup than *T. pavonia*.

Tigridia violacea. It has narrow plaited leaves 12 in (30 cm) tall and bears its flowers on a branching stem of similar height. The outer segments are violet, marked with red at the base; the inner segments being spotted with purple.

TRILLIUM (Liliaceae)

A genus of 30 species, native of the western Himalayas, China and Japan but mostly of eastern United States, Canada and Newfoundland. They take their name from *trilix*, triple, for all parts of the flower are in threes. Herbaceous perennials with rhizomatous roots, they are to be found in deciduous woodlands, enjoying the cool, leafy soil and shade, hence their name of wood lilies. The finest and most showy is *T. grandiflorum*, the wake robin or snow trillium, which is also the most free-flowering. The three outer segments of each species are green, the three inner being white, yellow or purple. They occasionally stand erect, though they are usually horizontal, some being stemless while others have long peduncles.

Culture. Of extreme hardiness, the *Trilliums* require a soil which is retentive of moisture, one containing ample supplies of peat or leaf mould and where the plants are shaded from the direct rays of the sun. An open woodland or spinney suits them well, where, like Solomon's seal, the plants may be left undisturbed for many years. Plant in October, 4 in (10 cm) deep and 6 to 8 in (15 to 20 cm) apart, firming the soil about the rhizomes.

Propagation. Most species are slow to increase, but after five years they will be ready to divide. This is done in autumn when the plants with their cluster of rhizomes are lifted and divided, the pieces being replanted immediately to ensure that they do not dry out.

Plants may also be raised from seed, but even fresh seed takes 18 to 20 months to germinate and the young plants will not bloom until five or six years old. Sow thinly in boxes or pans containing the John Innes compost, which should be kept moist. When large enough to handle, transplant the seedlings to small pots, one to each, containing a compost made up of loam, leaf mould and sand in equal parts and here they are grown on for two years, after which they are planted out where they are to bloom. This they will do in two more years.

Species. *Trillium cernuum.* The nodding wood lily or bashful Ben, native of eastern North Africa, and to be found from Ontario southwards to Missouri. It grows 9 in (22·5 cm) tall with rhombus-shaped sessile leaves 6 in (15 cm) long. In April and May it bears scented drooping snow-white flowers, usually in threes on a 6-in (15-cm) stem. The flowers, which are borne at the end of a short peduncle, when open measure 1 in (2·5 cm) across, the oblong-lanceolate petals being rolled back and waved at the margins. The white ovary ripens to a dark-red berry.

Trillium chloropetalum (syn. *T. giganteum*). It is represented in the states of Washington, Oregon and California and resembles *T. sessile*, though is of more robust habit, growing 12 in (30 cm) tall with broad ovate leaves 6 in (15 cm) long, mottled with purple and brown. The flowers are variable, ranging in colour from purple to pink, from green to pale yellow and are about twice the size of those of *T. sessile*.

Trillium erectum (syn. *T. foetidum*). It is present in open woodlands and thickets from Nova Scotia to Tennessee and has a thick, short rootstock and broad dark-green leaves. It is known as birthroot, for its roots were used to assist in childbirth. The flowers open 2 in (5 cm) across and are claret purple, as if polished. They have a most unpleasant smell to attract flies for their pollination, yet they have a strange beauty in the half light of the woodlands. Known in America as wet dog because of their smell, the flowers are borne on 18-in (45-cm) stems and are held on a peduncle 4 in (10 cm) long.

The variety *blandum* has creamy-white flowers which do not have the unpleasant smell of the type. *Viridiflorum* bears greenish-white flowers and *luteum*, flowers of soft clear yellow.

Trillium govanianum. Native of the Himalayas, it forms a long slender stem and has ovate bright-green leaves 3 in (7·5 cm) long. The flowers with their purple petals stand erect for a considerable time and have long stigmas.

Trillium grandiflorum. The wake Robin, it is distributed on wooded slopes from Quebec to North Carolina. It has a scarred rootstock from which arises an unbranched stem 16 in (40 cm) tall, bearing at the top three pale-green broadly ovate leaves and strongly veined white flowers, which open to 3 in (7·5 cm)

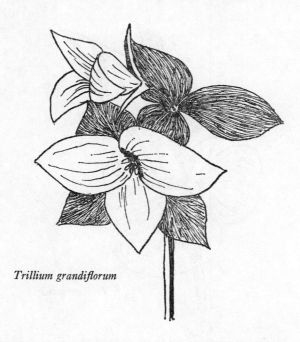

Trillium grandiflorum

across. The segments have wavy margins. It blooms in May and June and is also known as the snow trillium. It is more tolerant of drier conditions than other species.

Trillium luteum. Found only in the reserve of the Cherokee Indians in North Carolina, it has stout stems and ovate purple-mottled leaves. The stalkless flowers are large and of bright greenish yellow with a delicious lemon-like perfume, the long pointed petals retaining an erect position.

Trillium nivale. A dainty species, native of mountainous woodlands of Ohio and not exceeding 6 in (15 cm) in height. The ovate leaves are 1 in (2·5 cm) long, while the white flowers, striped with pink at the base, are no more than 1 in (2·5 cm) across with short oblong petals. It is a delightful plant for the rock garden.

Trillium pusillum. Native of eastern America, it resembles *T. nivale* in its

R

dainty habit, growing 6 in (15 cm) tall with oblong, sessile leaves and petals which are about 1 in (2·5 cm) long and terminate in a point. They are white, turning pink with age.

Trillium recurvatum. Native of Mississippi and Arkansas, where it is known as the prairie lily, it has ovate-acute leaves with long petioles and bears white flowers, shaded maroon and turning purple with age. It grows 9 in (22·5 cm) tall and blooms early in summer.

Trillium sessile

Trillium sessile. Native of open woodlands of North America, it has thick stems and stalkless oval leaves mottled with pale and dark green. The flowers with their narrow petals of deep purple are also stemless and remain erect for some time. It bears its scented flowers early in spring. The variety *viridiflorum* bears flowers of greenish yellow.

Trillium smallii. Native of the moist woodlands of southern Japan, it grows 9 in (22·5 cm) tall with stalkless rhomboid leaves, while the purple-brown flowers have a short arching peduncle.

Trillium stylosum (syn. *T. nervosum*). Native of rocky slopes of the south-eastern United States, where it grows 18 in (45 cm) tall, it has oval leaves, and bears nodding pink-tinted flowers which appear in April and May. The three styles are united from the base to the middle.

Trillium tschonoskii. It is found in mountainous woodlands of Japan and Korea and has five-nerved rhombic leaves borne at the end of an 18-in (45-cm) stem. The flowers are white with a slender peduncle and open to about 2 in (5 cm) across. The variety *violaceum* has rosy-mauve petals.

Trillium undulatum. The painted wake Robin, it is distributed in open woodland throughout Ontario and Newfoundland and south to Georgia. It has a slender stem 18 in (45 cm) tall at the end of which it bears three bluish-green wax-like leaves which turn to copper-brown and white flowers, painted with purple veins at the base of the segments which open to 2 in (5 cm) across. The flowers appear in May and are followed by a three-angled bright-red berry.

TRITONIA (Iridaceae)

A genus of about 50 species, native of tropical and southern Africa and taking their name from *triton*, a weathercock, in allusion to the variable direction of the stamens. Closely allied to *Ixia* and *Freesia* and requiring similar culture, it has a fibrous-coated globose corm and narrow sword-shaped leaves borne in two ranks above the sheathing bases. The flowers, which are excellent for cutting, appear in arching spikes like *Montbretia* (*Crocosmia*). Only one species, *T. crocata* and its varieties, is widely cultivated and, as it blooms early in summer, it should be grown under glass in Britain and North America, in all but those gardens enjoying a mild winter climate.

Culture. Indoors, plant five or six corms to a 5-in (12·5-cm) pot, or plant in boxes containing a 6-in (15-cm) depth of compost, to provide cut bloom for the home. The compost should consist of fibrous loam, peat and sand in equal parts. Plant the corms 2 in (5 cm) deep and 2 in (5 cm) apart in October and stand in a frame or beneath the greenhouse bench for about four weeks until rooting has taken place, during which time give little moisture. Then place on the greenhouse bench, giving sufficient moisture to keep the plants growing and provide a temperature of 42° to 45° F (5° to 7° C) during winter and early spring. Twigs should be used to support the stems. Under glass they will bloom during April and May. After flowering, allow the foliage to die back, then place the pots outdoors in full sun and give little moisture. In autumn shake the corms from the old compost and repot.

Outdoors, plant the corms in October where the garden enjoys a mild winter climate. Select an open, sunny situation. The soil must be well-drained and contain some grit or coarse sand. Plant 4 in (10 cm) deep and 4 in (10 cm) apart, placing the corms on a layer of sand to assist drainage.

In exposed gardens either delay planting until April (when the plants will bloom during late summer) or cover with cloches or frame lights if planted in autumn. If planting in spring, lift the corms in autumn when the foliage has died back and after drying, store in boxes of sand in a frost-free place.

Propagation. When lifting, a large corm will be seen to have formed beneath the old corm as for *Gladiolus*, and these are detached and grown on. The plant also increases by underground rhizomes, corms being produced at the nodes so that when established, they will form a large clump and a mass of corms of all sizes. Smaller corms take two years to bloom.

Corms may also be raised from seed sown under glass in April in boxes containing a sandy compost. Germination will take several weeks. When the young plants die back cover with 1 in (2·5 cm) of compost and do not disturb for another 12 months. Then shake the young corms from the compost and replant into boxes or pots containing the growing compost. They will bloom three or four years after sowing the seed.

Species. *Tritonia crispa.* Rare on the lower slopes of Table Mountain, it has leaves which are crisped at the margins, while it bears pale pink flowers in a four- to six-flowered spike. The three lower lobes are shaded and striped with red, the perianth tube being curved.

Tritonia crocata. Native of Cape Province, where it is a rare plant of the lower slopes of Lion's Head, flowering there in December—in early summer in Britain. It makes a corm 1·5 cm in diameter and bears its flowers on a slender branched stem 18 in (45 cm) tall. The flowers are of tangerine-yellow and borne in a two-ranked spike, the three lower lobes marked with red at the base. They are broadly funnel-shaped with a long cylindrical tube, the stamens being directed to one side.

Of a number of varieties of merit, Isabella bears amber-coloured flowers, shaded pink, and Prince of Orange has flowers of purest orange. Roseline bears flowers of deep pink on 2- to 3-ft (60- to 90-cm) stems. Salmon Queen is salmon-orange and Tearose has spikes of rich cream shaded yellow at the centre.

Tritonia hyalina. Native of Natal and Cape Province, it is more tender than others in cultivation and should be grown under glass in Britain. It bears flowers of soft salmon pink in an elegant spike. The flowers are transparent at the base.

Tritonia scillaris. It is present at the Cape on rocky slopes around Hout Bay, where it is prominent after fires. It makes a small corm 1 cm in diameter and has six erect leaves. The flowers are borne in short spikes, spirally arranged and are pale pink with a long perianth tube. In bloom during September and October in their native land; in early summer in the British Isles.

TROPAEOLUM (Geraniaceae)

A genus of about 90 species of annual or perennial plants, native of Mexico and tropical South America, some of which have a tuberous rootstock and a climbing or rambling habit. They have attractively lobed leaves and helmet-shaped flowers composed of five petals, fringed or bearded at the base and with eight anther-bearing stamens. The flowers of the climbing nasturtiums are mostly orange or yellow, occasionally blue; sometimes spotted, and with a long spur. Several species grow well outdoors in Britain and northern Europe but only under conditions in which they grow in their natural habitat—i.e. in a cool leafy soil with some shade at the roots, but where they are able to pull themselves up into the sunlight to bloom. For this reason several species enjoy the cool climatic conditions of Scotland and the north-eastern coast of England but few other places of Britain.

Culture. They may be planted against a trellis or like clematis, they may be allowed to pull themselves up through other climbing plants or young conifers whose dark-green foliage accentuates the brilliant colouring of the *Tropaeolum* flowers, while they provide shade for the roots. They may also be planted against a northerly wall, together with climbing or rambler roses or with other wall plants among which they will climb and bear their small dainty flowers throughout summer.

Plant in spring, placing the tubers 4 in (10 cm) deep and 12 in (30 cm) apart and they will almost immediately send up their thread-like stems covered in shamrock-like leaves. They require a soil containing plenty of peat or leaf mould and one that is well-drained in winter, for the tuberous rootstock will decay if excess moisture cannot drain away. Plant the tubers on a layer of sand, and in bleak gardens cover after planting with decayed leaves to protect the tubers from hard frost. However, it is hot, dry conditions that may kill them rather than cold. The plants enjoy a summer mulch of peat or leaf mould.

Plants may be grown indoors, to be trained against a trellis or over the greenhouse roof, and they are suitable for a garden room in summer. They may be grown up canes inserted in the pots in which the tubers are planted early in spring. Provide a soil containing plenty of leaf mould and sand to keep the compost 'open'. At all times the plants should be kept moist at the roots. Plant the tubers 2 in (5 cm) deep, two or three to a 5-in (12·5-cm) pot and fix the canes fanwise for maximum effect. The plants should be shaded from the direct rays of the sun and ventilated freely.

Propagation. By division of the tubers when lifting in autumn or spring, replanting immediately to prevent the tubers shrivelling from exposure; or by seed which is difficult to germinate. The seed is sown singly in 3-in (7·5-cm) pots in June under glass and germination may take 12 months. When established, the young plants are moved (with the soil ball intact) to larger pots, from which they are planted out into their flowering quarters with the soil ball unbroken as they resent root disturbance.

Species. *Tropaeolum azureum.* A rare and beautiful species, native of the Chilean Andes with small round tubers from which arise slender stems up to 6 ft (1·8 metres) tall, clothed in pale-blue 'helmets' borne on long pedicels.

Tropaeolum moritzianum. Native of the Colombian Andes, it has a large tuberous root and peltate leaves which measure up to 6 in (15 cm) across. The flowers appear in July and are brilliant yellow, veined with red.

Tropaeolum pentaphyllum. It is present on the hillsides around Buenos Aires and has a round brown-skinned tuber from which arise, to a height of 5 to 6 ft (1·5 to 1·8 metres), purple stems clothed in palmately cut leaves. It bears scarlet flowers in June and July.

Tropaeolum polyphyllum. Native of Chile, it is more tender than others and of weaker habit. Plant on top of a wall down which it will trail with its long graceful stems and handsomely cut grey-green leaves. It blooms midsummer, its brilliant yellow flowers being spotted with red.

Tropaeolum speciosum. Known as the Chilean flame flower. Against a white-washed wall in the company of other plants, it presents a display of great brilliance during July and August. It has long tubers of irregular shape from which arise wire-like stems to a height of 6 or 7 ft (about 2 metres), clothed in six-lobed peltate leaves of brightest green and multitudes of small long-spurred, flame-coloured flowers.

Tropaeolum tricolor. Native of Chile, it has a small round ruber covered in a brown skin and will send up its stems to a height of 8 to 9 ft (2·4 to 2·7 metres). The leaves are divided into six oblong lobes, while the flowers are of brilliant orange with a scarlet calyx and tipped with black.

Tropaeolum tuberosum. Native of Peru, it blooms from July until late September and grows up to 8 to 9 ft (2·4 to 2·7 metres) tall with yellow tubers and leaves divided into five lobes. The whole plant is covered in flowers of golden yellow, veined with red and with entire or toothed petals.

TULIPA (Liliaceae)

A genus of about 100 species, mostly native of south-eastern Europe and the Near East and taking their name from *tulbend*, the Turkish word for turban, which the flowers resemble both in their shape and colouring. The first species, probably a natural hybrid, was brought from Constantinople to Augsburg in 1559, by Conrad Gesner and it was named *T. gesneriana* after himself. It reached England at a later date. Richard Hakluyt writing in 1582 said: 'Within these four years there have been brought into England from Austria, divers kinds of flowers called tulipas.' Gerard also confirmed its date of introduction as 1578.

The tulip has a brown tunicated bulb and broad or linear leaves. The flowers are borne single or rarely in twos or threes on an erect scape and are bell-shaped, the perianth consisting of six distinct segments, free or arranged in two circles of three. Stamens six, shorter than the segments; stigma three-lobed; capsule three-celled and many-seeded.

For spring and early summer bedding, the tulip, with its rich oriental colourings, stands supreme. The most dwarf of the *Kaufmanniana* hybrids and single and double early-flowering varieties may be used in window-boxes and in small beds, with the Cottage and Darwin tulips for the border or large beds where they are usually under-planted with polyanthuses, forget-me-nots or wallflowers of contrasting colours. Tulips may be planted to bloom from March until the end of June and indoors from Christmas until Easter, while the species will be seen at their loveliest in the alpine house or on the rock garden.

Tulip bulbs are measured in centimetres of circumference around the fattest part of the bulb, graded according to size and it is advisable to plant to size rather than as 'garden-size' or 'forcing-size' bulbs.

For outdoor planting use a 10- to 11-cm bulb for a top-size bloom, though a 9- to 10-cm bulb will give a bloom of reasonable quality. For indoors, use a 10- to 11-cm bulb for cool-house culture and an 11- to 12-cm bulb for forcing. Not only have tulips the widest colour range of all flowers and a longer flowering time but they also are of such diverse habit, ranging in height from the 3 in (7·5 cm) of *T. aucheriana* to the 30 in (75 cm) of Darwin tulip, Farncombe Sanders.

Culture. The tulip enjoys a heavier soil than most other bulbs, one which may be described as a heavy loam but which is well-drained in winter. When growing for commercial cut flower, earliness to bloom—which is all-important—may be assisted by lightening the soil with humus such as peat or leaf mould or old mushroom-bed compost. As tulips do not grow well in soil that has continually been used for tulips, the ground should be deeply worked, bringing up to the surface the lower soil and it is to this that is added the various humus-forming materials. Tulips being grown in large unheated houses and frames require similar treatment when planted in beds but must be given ample water before planting in November. Where it can be obtained, a quantity of wood ash will be beneficial, or give 1 oz per square yard of sulphate of potash.

Tulips are unlike narcissus in that they must be given individual attention as to time of planting and correct depths. Many varieties grow better from an early November planting, yet the well-known Inglescombe Yellow and Golden Harvest prefer to be planted early October. Planting depths vary too. William Copeland and William Pitt, both Darwins, are happy in a soil depth of no more than 3 in (7·5 cm); the cherry-red King George V likes 4 in (10 cm) of soil over it, and Farncombe Sanders, which makes a large bulb, likes a 5-in (37·5-cm) covering and some growers plant it 8 in (20 cm) deep. As a general rule 5 in (12·5 cm) seems to suit most—1 in (2·5 cm) deeper in light soil, an inch shallower in clay soil. In the warmer parts of Britain where tulip fire disease may be troublesome, the bulbs are planted early December, and it is said that deeper planting will help to keep the trouble at a minimum. Plant with a wide trowel so that no air pocket is left beneath the bulb. They may be spaced 9 in (22·5 cm) apart. When growing for cutting, the beds should be planted 5 to 6 ft (1·5 to 1·8 metres) wide with a path down either side to allow for ease in cutting.

Tulips bruise easily and care should be taken in handling the bulbs. They should be firm and clean, with the skin rich brown in colour. Do not expose them to the elements at planting time more than is necessary. After planting, the topsoil should be raked over to leave a bed with a fine tilth. Planting late in autumn will mean that very little attention will be given the beds, nothing more than hoeing between the bulbs in spring when growth commences.

Cloche and cold-frame culture calls for care in planting distances. Here, the bulb may be set 4 in (10 cm) apart and in rows of the same distance, a barn-type cloche taking three rows. November planting is preferable for cloche work, for the plant should not become too tall too soon. If it is necessary to remove the cloches while the weather is cold, the cloches will have lost much of their value, for uncovered plants will have almost caught up with those that began under cloches.

One method of growing under cloches is to take out a trench 8 in (20 cm) deep and into the bottom 4 in (10 cm) is worked some sand, peat and a little decayed manure. Into this the bulbs are planted, a depth of 4 in (10 cm) being allowed above the compost level in the trench to give extra room before the cloches are removed. The bulbs are covered in early February. They will make rapid growth in the early spring sunshine, protected from frost and cold winds. The glass is removed early in April, possibly to cover early strawberries.

If tulips are allowed to remain in the ground after they have finished flowering, they will deteriorate to a point where only a tiny, short-stemmed bloom will be seen, but many of the bulbs will be suitable for a second season's flowering if carefully lifted in early June and if not allowed to set seed after flowering. Those who grow tulips for bulb sale in Lincolnshire and in Holland remove the flower head immediately it shows colour in the bud so that the energies of the plant can be directed entirely to the bulb.

Remove the flower heads when they begin to fade. A garden fork is used to lift the bulbs. A trench 6 in (15 cm) deep should be made in a spare piece of ground, which has been enriched with some decayed manure. At the bottom of the trench should be placed some sand and peat and on to this the bulbs are placed with their foliage exposed and the bulbs covered with soil. As it is desired to dry off the bulbs as soon as possible, all excess moisture should be withheld. The bulbs are then cleaned and the foliage removed. They should be sorted for any decayed bulbs and healthy offsets are removed for later planting and growing on. The bulbs should be stored in a cool, dry room or shed. 'Prepared' bulbs may be forced early. These bulbs will have been kept in cold storage in England and must be planted within 48 hours of being received. The method of 'preparing' is to subject the bulbs to a temperature of 75° F (24° C) for two weeks immediately after lifting. They are then kept for eight weeks at a temperature of only 47° F (8° C). This cooling not only hastens the appearance of the bloom but also causes more rapid root formation of the bulb when planted. As it is important to use the bulbs within a few hours of coming out of storage, they should be 'prepared' in England rather than in Holland.

The amateur will plant either in pots or bowls containing prepared bulb fibre or in a compost of soil, sand and peat which is sterile and contains neither disease spores nor weeds. Make the peat thoroughly moist, otherwise it will be almost impossible to bring to the desired condition after the bulbs are planted. Four or five bulbs to a bowl is usual and they should be of 12-cm size. When in the bowls, the tops should be just covered with the compost. If a layer of peat is placed at the bottom of the bowl, it will assist drainage. To keep the compost sweet, add several pieces of charcoal. Handle the bulbs carefully as tulips bruise easily. After planting, water lightly so that none remains at the bottom of the bowl to stagnate; then place in a darkened cupboard or cellar for six weeks. Those with ground near the house may stand out the bulbs, covering them with fibre or soil.

Tulips should be introduced to warmth and light gradually. A large proportion of failures are the result of the bowls being taken from complete darkness and a cool place and plunged straight into the strong light and warmth of a greenhouse, conservatory or large, sunny window. At first a temperature of 48° F (9° C) is sufficient and this can be increased to 60° F (16° C) by raising it about a degree each day. Likewise where a cool house is being used for growing on the bulbs for cutting in boxes. These will usually follow chrysanthemums, which will have finished flowering by the year end. The Darwins will be used and they may be taken indoors early in January to bloom in March. When first introduced to the greenhouse they should be shaded, either by hessian canvas nailed to the sash bars of the house or by sheets of brown paper placed over the boxes. The shading may be removed after 10 days, though in a greenhouse the hessian stretched over the inside of the roof will help to keep out frost and should remain in position until early March, when the spring sunshine will bring the bulbs into bloom.

In the heated greenhouse the temperature may safely be raised to 65° F (18° C) for all forcing varieties as soon as the flower buds are observed, but at this temperature opening of the buds will be rapid and care must be taken that they do not become too open before marketing.

As a general rule, the short-stemmed varieties should be given some shade almost throughout their period in the greenhouse, while the Darwins and all long-stemmed varieties are grown on without shade when under forcing conditions.

Care must be taken when growing on a large scale to determine the exact forcing requirements of the various varieties. It will not do to select a variety for forcing merely because its colour is attractive. For instance, the striking golden yellow and red Prince Carnival will not stand forcing at all, and if early bloom is required for cutting, then select the orange-red Prince of Austria, which may be forced at a temperature of 80° F (27° C) when acclimatised to the warm house, in preference to Rising Sun, which may be forced into bloom after Prince of Austria.

Again, the Darwin varieties William Pitt and William Copeland may be forced in a constant temperature of 72° F (22° C), whereas for most Darwins, the maximum temperature should be about 58° F (14° C).

A word should be said about fluctuations in temperatures, which will be fatal
to all bulbs. A constant temperature of 55° F (12° C) is better than one which
might fluctuate between 50° and 68° F (10° and 20° C), while draughts in the
home will frequently cause the formation of a badly drooping bloom or of a
yellowing of the foliage. If the temperature in a warm room or greenhouse falls
suddenly, the rate at which the plant loses water by evaporation is slowed up.
The roots, however, continue to work in the warm soil, taking in water which
cannot be transpired. The cells of the plant become waterlogged and cannot
support the bloom, with the result that it falls over, making it a total loss.
Careful watering, correct ventilation and a constant temperature make for
success in tulip forcing.

The commercial grower will use mass-production methods. The bulbs will
be set out in boxes 6 in (15 cm) deep and of a size which can be comfortably
handled to hold about three dozen bulbs. A 1-in (2·5-cm) space must be left
between the bulbs for air circulation, for bulbs being forced must contend with
conditions of considerable heat and high humidity, both of which will encourage
disease unless there is a free circulation of air. Commercial bulb boxes should be
drilled with holes, one to every 6 square inches, to make for correct drainage.

A clean virgin loam mixed with some coarse sand and moist peat should be
used. The soil should preferably have been taken from a depth of 10 in (25 cm)
to ensure freedom from disease and weed seeds. The bulbs are planted with the
tops just below the soil level. The boxes are then placed outdoors over a bed of
clinker or crushed brick to ensure satisfactory drainage. Over the boxes is
placed a 4-in (10-cm) covering of ashes, sand or soil to exclude the light and to
prevent the bulbs from drying out. They will rarely need any watering, rain and
heavy dews providing all that is necessary. They remain in the open until the
correct times for taking into heat or the cool-house. The covering of soil or
ash is then knocked away, taking care not to injure the growing points of the
bulbs which will be about 2 in (5 cm) tall. The gradual introduction to heat and
light is essential.

Propagation. By offsets, when bulbs growing in the open are lifted after
flowering. The offsets are detached and planted either in boxes of sandy compost or outdoors in a prepared bed in a position of full sunlight. Plenty of sand
and peat should be worked to a fine tilth. Plant the bulblets early in September
2 in (5 cm) deep and 3 in (7·6 cm) apart. Here they will remain for two years,
during which time they must always be kept moist. To encourage them to make
size, they should be watered with dilute liquid manure once a week during the
spring and summer months. The flowers must be removed as soon as they form
so that the total energies of the plant are directed to the bulb. It will also be
necessary to keep the ground free of weeds, which is done by hand. After two
years, the bulbs may be lifted, dried and stored during winter, to be planted out
in autumn in beds where they are to bloom.

Species and Varieties. *Tulipa acuminata* (syn. *T. cornuta*). The horned tulip of the Pyrenees, to be found across southern Europe to the Levant. It grows 18 in (45 cm) tall and bears flowers of yellow and red with narrow twisted petals up to 3 in (7·5 cm) in length. It blooms in May.

Tulipa aucheriana. Native of the mountainous regions of northern Persia, it has a small ovoid bulb and broad pale-green leaves which lie prostrate on the soil. The flowers, which are borne on a 3-in (7·5-cm) stem, are of a lovely shade of shell pink shaded yellow at the base. They open star-like and are scented. In bloom in March and April, it is charming in the alpine house.

Tulipa batalinii. Native of Turkestan and the Levant, it grows 6 in (15 cm) tall and has narrow grey-green leaves which extend beyond the flowers. It blooms during March and April, bearing dainty flowers of soft primrose-yellow with pointed segments. Free from any shading and having golden anthers, it is the most completely yellow of all tulips and is suitable for alpine house or rock garden, where it will form a large clump.

The variety Bronze Charm bears large flowers of apricot and bronze, while Bright Gem bears yellow flowers flushed with salmon-pink.

Tulipa biflora. Native of the Caucasus, it has narrow pale-green leaves and bears two to five tiny urn-shaped flowers on a 3-in (7·5-cm) stem. The flowers are white with a yellow centre and are shaded green and pink on the outside. They open star-like, and under glass come into bloom before the end of February, this being one of the earliest tulips.

Tulipa borszczowi. Native of central Asia extending from Bokhara to Persia, it is a most handsome species, in bloom early in April and bearing its flowers on a 12-in (30-cm) stem. They have the three inner petals deep yellow, while the outer petals are red on the outside and edged with yellow.

Tulipa clusiana. The lady tulip, grown by Clusius in 1607 and named after him. Native of Persia and Afghanistan. Like *T. sylvestris*, it spreads by underground runners. It has narrow dark-green leaves, three or four of which are stem leaves, and bears its flowers on slender 15-in (37·5-cm) stems. The segments are white striped with pink on the inside, red on the outside and have a dark blue centre. With its narrow pointed segments it opens star-like and is attractive used for floral arrangement. It blooms well only following a hot, dry summer.

Tulipa didieri. Its origin is unknown, but it is a tulip of great beauty with grey-green leaves and bearing its flowers on 15-in (37·5-cm) stems. The flowers are scarlet, margined with gold and shaded black at the base, the petals reflexing as they unfold. Sir Daniel Hall believed it to be a form of *T. praecox*. In bloom April and May.

Tulipa eichleri. Native of southern Russia and Turkestan, it is one of the most beautiful of tulips, with broad greyish-blue leaves waved at the margins and with two or three narrow stem leaves. It bears its bell-shaped flowers on a 15-in (37·5-cm) stem. They open to 4 in (10 cm) across, are scarlet shaded grey on the exterior and black and yellow at the centre. The anthers are also black. The perianth segments are broad but taper to a reflexed needle-like point. In bloom in April and May.

Tulipa fosteriana. Native of Bokhara and northern Persia, it is one of the most striking of all species and the chief parent of the Darwin tulips. It has broad grey-green leaves and bears its velvety scarlet flowers on a 12-in (30-cm) stem, being at its best in April. The bloom, which is the largest of all tulips, is enhanced by the black blotch at the base of the petals and the shining black anthers. It is long-lasting only where lifted in June and baked in the sun.

There are a number of beautiful hybrid varieties to use for bedding, for window boxes, and for the rock garden, while they also give a striking display in pots. Approximate height in inches and centimetres appear after each name:

CANTABA (10 in, 25 cm). It has glossy bright-green leaves which contrast with the flowers of brilliant scarlet. Long-lasting, it is one of the best for pot culture.

CANOPUS (20 in, 50 cm). The tallest-flowering in this section, it bears a large bloom of brilliant scarlet which is untroubled by adverse weather.

CHARTRES (18 in, 45 cm). First offered in 1968, it has beautifully mottled leaves and bears large blood-red flowers, edged yellow and shaded crimson at the base.

COPENHAGEN (18 in, 45 cm). It has broad grey-green leaves, handsomely mottled with purple and bears orange-scarlet flowers edged with yellow.

EASTER PARADE (15 in, 37·5 cm). The large golden-yellow blooms are shaded red on the exterior and have a black base.

FEU SUPERBE (18 in, 45 cm). A hybrid of *T. fosteriana* and a Mendel tulip, it has flowers of brightest orange, shaded yellow at the base and with greyish-black markings.

GOLDEN EAGLE (12 in, 30 cm). It has large oval-shaped flowers of buttercup-yellow with a scarlet 'flash' at the centre of the outside of the petals and black shading at the base.

JUAN (18 in, 45 cm). A 1967 introduction, its leaves being handsomely mottled, while it bears flowers of purest orange, shaded yellow at the base.

PASSION (12 in, 30 cm). An outstanding bedding tulip, bearing on sturdy stems, creamy-white flowers shaded carmine on the outside.

PINKEEN (18 in, 45 cm). A variety of rich colouring, the long elegant flowers being of an unusual shade of orange-cerise-pink, turning rose pink as the flower ages.

PRINCEPS (18 in, 20 cm). One of the most compact varieties, bearing brilliant scarlet flowers of velvet-like texture.

RED EMPEROR (syn. MME LEFEBRE) (15 in, 37·5 cm). No tulip is of more brilliant colouring, its large almost globular flowers being of clearest vermilion-scarlet, shaded black and yellow at the base.

RED RIBAND (15 in, 37·5 cm). An outstanding bedding variety, long-lasting in bloom, its poppy-red flowers shaded black at the base. A *T. fosteriana* × Mendel tulip hybrid.

ROCKERY BEAUTY (8 in, 20 cm). Ideal for the rock garden with its urn-shaped flowers of dazzling orange-scarlet and attractively pointed petals.

SIR DANIEL (12 in, 30 cm). Named in honour of Sir Daniel Hall, famed for his monograph on the tulip. It was raised, like all with mottled foliage, from a crossing with *T. greigii*. The flower is large, of exquisite shape and of pale primrose yellow, shaded black at the base.

TOULON (18 in, 45 cm). First offered in 1968 and raised by van Tubergen, its leaves are handsomely mottled with brown, while its flowers of deep orange are edged with yellow and shaded brown at the base.

WHITE EMPEROR (syn. PURISSIMA) (18 in, 45 cm). An ideal companion to Canopus or Juan for its enormous flowers are of purest white.

Tulipa gesneriana. The earliest known tulip, discovered in Persia during the reign of Elizabeth I. It has broad lance-shaped glaucous leaves and bears large crimson-scarlet flowers which are sweetly scented. It has a black base, while the variety *fulgens* has yellow shading at the centre. It blooms in May on a 9-in (22·5-cm) stem.

Tulipa greigii. Discovered in the same part as *T. fosteriana*, with which it has been frequently crossed, it makes a large bulb and has broad glaucous green leaves, heavily mottled and striped with purple, brown or yellow, its variety Red Riding Hood being outstanding in this respect and worthy of planting for its foliage alone. The flowers, which open early in April, are of vivid orange marked with red on the outside and with a black base, the segments reflexing at the tips.

Crossed with *T. fosteriana*, it has produced some outstanding hybrids described under *T. fosteriana*; also a series of hybrids of merit when crossed with *T. kaufmanniana*, while the form *aurea*, bearing golden-yellow flowers, makes a striking companion to the type. Hybrid varieties include:

CAPE COD (8 in, 20 cm). A variety of brilliance with mottled leaves and yellow flowers, shaded bronze on the interior and apricot outside. At the centre of each petal is a scarlet stripe.

DONNA BELLA (12 in, 30 cm). The creamy-yellow flowers are blotched with scarlet at the base and shaded carmine on the exterior.

DREAMBOAT (9 in, 22·5 cm). The leaves are purple mottled, the flowers being of soft salmon flushed on the outside with amber.

FRESCO (12 in, 30 cm). The leaves are but faintly mottled, while the flowers are of rosy-red shading out to cream at the petal edges.

ORATORIO (8 in, 20 cm). It has broad, heavily mottled leaves and flowers of an interesting shade of rose pink.

ORIENTAL SPLENDOUR (15 in, 37·5 cm). A magnificent variety, the large leaves being striped with brown, while the flowers of carmine red are edged with lemon yellow.

PANDOUR (8 in, 20 cm). The foliage is daintily mottled, while the creamy-yellow flowers are flushed and striped on the outside with carmine red.

PERLINA (12 in, 30 cm). A hybrid of beauty, the leaves being heavily mottled, while the flowers of porcelain-rose are shaded lemon yellow at the base.

PLAISIR (6 in, 15 cm). Owing to its compact habit, it is ideal for window-boxes and small beds. Its foliage is flecked with mahogany red while the flowers of vermilion red shade out to yellow at the petal edges.

PRIMA DONNA (14 in, 35 cm). A most striking hybrid, the flowers of richest scarlet being shaded on the outside with geranium red and chocolate brown at the base.

RED RIDING HOOD (8 in, 20 cm). A striking variety for small beds, the broad leaves being heavily striped purple-brown, against which the large urn-shaped flowers of oriental red make a striking contrast.

ROYAL SPLENDOUR (syn. MARGARET HERBST) (18 in, 45 cm). A big tulip for a large bed or border, to which it will add a splash of brilliant colour with its flowers of scarlet-orange.

SALMON-JOY (10 in, 25 cm). It bears a bloom of unique colouring, the interior being azalea pink with the segments edged white; the exterior being pale yellow with a broad mark of salmon pink on the outside.

YELLOW DAWN (12 in, 30 cm). A hybrid of brilliance, the flowers of oriental yellow being flushed with rose red on the outside and with scarlet blotches at the base.

Tulipa hageri. It is present on Mount Parnassus in Greece and is a dainty species, bearing tiny flowers of cherry red painted yellow on the outside on 8-in (20-cm) stems. It has brown anthers and olive-green pollen. Occasionally more than a single flower is to be seen to a stem, and they are at their best in April and May. The form *splendens* bears three to five coppery-bronze flowers on each stem, while *nitens* bears flowers of orange-red shaded on the outside with bronze and green.

Tulipa hoogiana. Native of central Asia, it was discovered by the brothers Hoog on behalf of Messrs van Tubergen who named it in their honour. It has a large bulb and narrow glaucous leaves and in May bears large bell-shaped flowers of crimson-scarlet blotched with green at the base of the petals.

Tulipa humilis (syn. *T. pulchella*). Like *T. aucheriana*, to which it is closely related, it is native of the mountains of northern Persia and bears pale-green leaves which lie flat on the ground. The flowers are of magenta pink, borne on a 3-in (7·5-cm) stem and open star-like to reveal a yellow centre. It grows best protected from excess winter moisture in the alpine house, where it will bloom in February. The variety *violacea* bears flowers of brightest purple.

Tulipa ingens. Native of Turkestan, it has never taken to garden cultivation and is now virtually unobtainable. Nor has it much to recommend it, growing 18 in (45 cm) tall and bearing in May a loose flower of brilliant glossy red with black anthers.

Tulipa kaufmanniana. Native of Turkestan, it is known as the water-lily tulip for, when fully open, its blooms resemble a *Nymphaea* and are among the most handsome of all tulips, with narrow reflexing segments of creamy-white, shaded on the outside carmine-pink and with a yellow base, while the variety *coccinea* is brilliant red. The blooms are borne on 4- to 8-in (10- to 20-cm) stems above handsome broad glaucous-green leaves. It is one of the earliest to bloom, in a sheltered nook of the rock garden, showing colour before the end of February and remaining in bloom until mid-April. With its short stiff stems and elegant urn-shaped blooms, it is untroubled by adverse weather and should be used for bedding in exposed gardens. The bulbs may be left undisturbed for many years where the soil is friable and well-drained and will increase by offsets. Those hybrid varieties developed from crossing with *T. greigii* show the attractively mottled foliage of the species:

ALFRED CORTOT (8 in, 20 cm). Above its beautifully mottled leaves are borne long graceful blooms of glowing scarlet with a black base.

ANCILLA (6 in, 15 cm). The flowers are pure white inside, shaded rose-pink on the exterior and seem to sit on the pale-green foliage when opening wide, like water-lilies.

BERLIOZ (6 in, 15 cm). A variety of outstanding beauty, the large blooms being of uniform clear yellow of velvet-like texture.

CESAR FRANCK (8 in, 20 cm). The deep golden-yellow blooms are shaded with scarlet on the exterior to make it one of the most striking of all.

CIMAROSA (6 in, 15 cm). The flowers are of a lovely shade of salmon orange, shaded buff on the outside and with a jet-black centre.

CORAL SATIN (6 in, 15 cm). Planted with blue primroses, it provides a charming display when in bloom, for it is of an exquisite shade of coral pink with a satin-like sheen.

FRITZ KREISLER (8 in, 20 cm). A distinct variety, the creamy-pink flowers being heavily shaded on the outside with apricot-rose and with a deep-yellow base.

GAIETY (4 in, 10 cm). It opens like a huge water-lily backed by dark-green leaves, the flowers being creamy-white shaded pink on the outside and with a large orange base.

GOLDEN EARRINGS (9 in, 22·5 cm). The dark-green leaves are marked with purple, while the long urn-shaped flowers are of golden yellow, flushed with scarlet on the exterior.

JOHANN STRAUSS (6 in, 15 cm). The foliage is stippled with purple-brown, while the creamy-white flowers are flushed with carmine on the exterior.

JOSEF KAFKA (5 in, 12·7 cm). A beautiful hybrid, its foliage striped with purple, while the deep golden-yellow flowers are heavily shaded scarlet on the outside.

LADY ROSE (8 in, 20 cm). A rare and beautiful hybrid, the long elegant blooms being of a lovely shade of soft satiny pink.

MENDELSSOHN (4 in, 10 cm). The flowers are the largest in this section and are creamy-white shaded on the outside with rose.

ORANGE BOY (5 in, 12·5 cm). Very early and of short, sturdy habit, the large handsome blooms are of clear bright orange.

ORIENTAL BEAUTY (10 in, 25 cm). It has marbled foliage and bears flowers of pure vermilion red of velvet-like texture.

ROBERT STOLZ (5 in, 12·5 cm). A variety of merit, its broad leaves being stippled with purple, while the flowers are of clearest orange-scarlet with a black base.

SHAKESPEARE (6 in, 15 cm). Of unusual colouring, being of a pleasing blend or salmon, apricot and orange, shaded red on the exterior.

SOLANUS (10 in, 25 cm). Early to bloom, the flowers are deep yellow, blotched and shaded scarlet on the exterior.

SHERANZA (10 in, 25 cm). An introduction of great beauty, the flowers being large and of bright red with a striking golden base.

STRESA (6 in, 15 cm). It has mottled leaves, while its flowers of rich Indian yellow are shaded red on the outside.

TARTINI (6 in, 15 cm). The leaves are mottled with bronze, while the white flowers are shaded crimson on the exterior.

THE FIRST (6 in, 15 cm). The earliest tulip to bloom, the ivory-white flower being heavily shaded with a broad band of scarlet on the outside.

Tulipa kolpakowskiana. Native of Turkestan, it grows 8 in (20 cm) tall and is worthy of a place in the rock garden for its long elegant flowers, 3 in (7·5 cm) across and borne in April, are of a striking shade of golden yellow, shaded on the outside with cherry red and with black stamens. The lance-shaped glaucous leaves grow 12 in (30 cm) long. The variety *coccinea* bears red flowers.

Tulipa lanata. Native of northern Persia and Asia Minor, it is tall-growing, reaching to a height of 18 in (45 cm) and requires a sun-baked situation for it to be successful. It increases by stolons and where it is happy will form a large colony which, when in bloom in April, is an arresting sight. The blooms are large and of brilliant scarlet-orange with a jet-black centre. Hairs are present on the bulb and flower stem and at the tips of the segments.

Tulipa linifolia. Native of Bokhara and northern Persia, it is recognised by its narrow grey-green leaves, waved at the margins and shaded with red. The 9-in (22·5-cm)-long stems are also red, while the flowers, borne during May and early June, are of brilliant clear scarlet with pointed segments and black anthers.

Tulipa marjolettii. A tulip of doubtful ancestry, native of northern Italy where it blooms in May and June, being one of the latest. It grows 20 in (50 cm) tall with broad leaves, while its soft primrose-yellow flowers are shaded red on the outside. It makes an attractive and long-lasting cut flower.

Tulipa mauriana. One of the *neo-tulipae*, like *T. marjolettii*. Native of Savoy and bearing on 16-in (40-cm) stems its elegant flowers of glowing red, shaded yellow at the base.

Tulipa maximowiczii. Native of Bokhara and northern Persia where it grows on grassy slopes, it differs from *T. linifolia* in that it blooms 10 days earlier and has green flower stems, while its narrow grey-green leaves stand more upright. It bears its scarlet flowers, shaded yellow on the outside, from late April until

Tulipa kaufmanniana : Heart's Delight

Tulipa kaufmanniana : Shakespeare

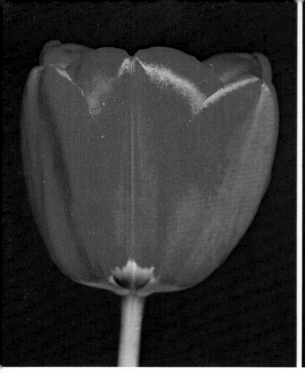
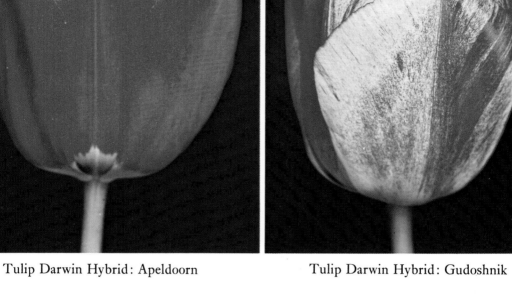

Tulip Darwin Hybrid: Apeldoorn   Tulip Darwin Hybrid: Gudoshnik

Tulipa greigii : Trinket

Triumph Tulip: Garden Party

Tulipa greigii : Plaisir

the end of May on 8-in (20-cm) stems. The inner segments remain erect, while the outer reflex.

Tulipa montana (syn. *T. wilsoniana*, *T. cuspidata*). It is a beautiful species. from Palestine, northern Persia and Afghanistan with glaucous leaves, waved and shaded red at the margins like those of *T. linifolia*, while both species have a tuft of hairs growing from the top of the bulb. It enjoys scree conditions, where the ground is well-drained in winter and is one of the latest tulips to bloom, being at its best in May. It bears scarlet flowers shaded with purple at the base and has golden stamens.

Tulipa orphanidea. Native of south-eastern Greece and Turkey, it will add a touch of distinction to the rock garden in April with its orange-bronze flowers, shaded green at the centre and borne on graceful stems 12 in (30 cm) high. The flowers have green anthers, while the leaves are narrow and shaded crimson at the margins. They form a rosette from which arises the flower stem. The recently discovered variety, *flava*, bears flowers of a brilliant clear-yellow colour and, as it increases rapidly, is one of the most inexpensive of tulips.

Tulipa ostrowskiana. A rare tulip from Turkestan with dull-green lance-shaped leaves and bearing in May, on a slender 8-in (20-cm) stem, a flower of pillar-box red, shaded yellow and green at the base and with attractively pointed reflexing petals.

Tulipa persica. In spite of its name, its natural habitat is unknown. It has narrow dark-green leaves margined with red, which form a flat rosette, and it bears sweetly scented urn-shaped flowers of brightest yellow, usually two or three to a 9-in (22·5-cm) stem during May and June. The outer segments are shaded green on the outside.

Tulipa polychroma. Native of the Near East, extending from Egypt to northern Persia, it is one of the most rare of cultivated tulips, a single bulb being worth £1. It is a tiny gem for the alpine house, where it blooms towards the end of February, bearing on a 6-in (15-cm) stem three to five dainty white star-like flowers, tinted blue-grey on the outside and having a large yellow centre. It forms two broad basal leaves.

Tulipa praecox. A neo-tulip (possibly a hybrid and not a species) of the vine-yards of Savoy, bearing in March on an 18-in (45-cm) stem crimson blooms which open to 12 in (30 cm) across to reveal a centre of greenish yellow with a black base.

Tulipa praestans. Native of Bokhara, it blooms early in April and is one of the most outstanding species, its large round bulbs covered in a parchment-like skin. The stem and the leaves, with their raised mid-rib, are covered in minute hairs to give them a greyish appearance. The scarlet flowers are of an unusual dull hue and are borne singly or in clusters of six to ten at the end of a 12-in (30-cm) scape. The variety Fusilier has flowers of intense orange-scarlet, while Zwanenburg is vermilion red with long pointed buds like those of a poinsettia.

Tulipa primulina. Native of the mountains of eastern Algeria, it closely resembles *T. sylvestris* with its long narrow leaves and drooping bell-shaped flowers of primrose yellow flushed pink on the outside. Though suitable for naturalising, the flowers open only in sunlight. They are scented and borne on 12-in (30-cm) stems during May.

Tulipa pulchella. A dwarf species of Asia Minor growing 4 in (10 cm) tall and in bloom at the end of March. It has glabrous strap-like leaves and urn-shaped flowers which open flat. They are of a unique purple colour, shaded green on the outside with a basal blotch of blue surrounded with a margin of white. The blue anthers add to its beauty.

Tulipa saxatilis. A distinctive species, native of the mountains of Crete, with leaves of glossy green, unlike those of any other species. It requires a dry, sunny situation such as a stony pocket at the top of a rock garden in full sun, where it should be planted 8 in (20 cm) deep and left undisturbed to increase by stolons. The leaves appear in winter and it blooms in May, bearing from one to three lilac-pink cup-shaped flowers shaded yellow at the centre, on a 12-in (30-cm) stem. For it to bloom well, its root run should be restricted by planting the bulbs in a pocket enclosed by slates inserted just below soil level to form a square with one slate forming the base.

Tulipa schrenki. Native of the Levant, it is a rare and beautiful species with a crimson-red flower tipped with gold, reminiscent of a Duc van Thol tulip. It grows only 6 in (15 cm) tall and blooms in April. It is best confined to the scree or alpine house. It dies back quickly after flowering.

Tulipa sprengeri. Native of the mountainous woodlands of Turkey and northern Persia, it is the latest tulip to bloom, opening in June when others have finished flowering. It is happiest in partial shade. Growing 12 in (30 cm) tall, it may be naturalised in long grass, which should not be cut until the end of summer. It has glossy bright-green leaves which remain upright and bears large ball-shaped flowers of clear glowing scarlet with golden anthers. Where happy, it will seed itself.

Tulipa stellata. A rare species, native of Afghanistan and the western Himalayas, and closely resembling *T. clusiana* with its long elegant flower, borne on a slender 9-in (22·5-cm) stem. It is white, striped red on the outside and with yellow shading at the base instead of blue. The flowers, which appear towards the end of April, open star-like.

The variety *chrysantha*, usually classed as a separate species, bears flowers which are more heavily flushed with pink on the outside and are shaded with yellow at the base.

Tulipa suaveolens. Native of Bokhara, it is believed to be the parent of the early single tulip. It has broad pale-green leaves and bears scented flowers of bright scarlet, edged yellow on 6-in (15-cm) stems. In bloom in March.

Tulipa sylvestris. Native of damp meadowlands of the British Isles and southern Europe and spreading freely by underground stolons, it is suitable for naturalising in orchards and beneath young trees. Here, it will increase rapidly and bloom during April and May, bearing one or two flowers on thin wiry stems 16 in (40 cm) tall. It has narrow grey-green leaves 9 in (22·5 cm) long and bears golden-yellow flowers shaded green and pink on the outside and which nod gracefully. They are scented but more so in the Italian form, *florentina odorata*, while the variety Tabriz, native of Persia, bears fragrant flowers of a delicate shade of lemon yellow and are larger than those of the Eureopan forms. It is also more free-flowering.

Tulipa tarda (syn. *T. dasystemon*). Native of Turkestan, it is one of the finest species for the alpine house or rock garden, being hardy and of easy culture. It has bright-green shining leaves which lie flat on the ground to form a rosette, and it bears its flowers three to five to a stem in March and April. The flowers are yellow inside, white on the outside and are heavily shaded with yellow and green. The anthers are golden-yellow. With their elegantly pointed petals, the flowers open star-like, resembling water-lilies and remain colourful over a long period.

Tulipa triphylla. Native of Bokhara, it makes a small bulb and has three or four sickle-shaped leaves, above which it bears on 9-in (22·5-cm) stems citron-yellow urn-shaped flowers, shaded green on the outside. In bloom in May.

Tulipa tubergeniana. It was discovered south of the Caucasus by the Hoog Brothers for van Tubergens and is closely related to *T. fosteriana*—with the same broad glaucous leaves. It bears large bright-scarlet blooms blotched with black at the centre, the segments being broad at the base, sharply pointed at the tips. It blooms late in April and in May on 12-in (30-cm) stems.

Tulipa turkestanica. Native of Turkestan, it is closely related to *T. biflora* and has glaucous lance-shaped leaves. It bears large white flowers, tinted green on the outside and with a yellow base on a slender stem 9 in (22·5 cm) tall. The flowers are borne three to nine to a stem and open star-like. They appear from the end of February until early April and are enhanced by the orange filaments and black anthers.

Tulipa undulatifolia. Native of Asia Minor, it is a handsome species with grey-green lance-shaped leaves, waved at the margins. It bears, in April, crimson-red bell-shaped flowers, shaded green on the outside and on 6-in (15-cm) stems.

Tulipa urumiensis. A rare native of northern Persia, closely related to *T. tarda*. It forms a rosette of broad leaves which lie prostrate on the ground, and it bears in April three to five blooms to each stem. They are of deep buttercup yellow, lightly shaded bronze on the outside and open like small water-lilies. They are borne on 3-in (7·5-cm) stems.

Tulipa viridiflora. Discovered in Turkestan early in the seventeenth century and believed to be a variety of *T. gesneriana*, or a natural hybrid, rather than a separate species. It has large green flowers striped and margined with yellow.

The form *praecox* blooms early in May, a fortnight earlier than the type, the flowers having attractively frilled petals. A selection of *viridiflora* hybrids:

ANGEL (14 in, 35 cm). A tulip of exquisite beauty, ideal for floral arrangement, the flowers being slim and elegant and of soft apple green, edged with white.

ARTIST (9 in, 22·5 cm). The most compact variety, suitable for window-box and tub, the flowers with their twisted petals being of all shades of the artist's palette, a combination of terra-cotta, salmon, green and cream, passing to green with age.

CHERIE (10 in, 25 cm). A compact grower, its cream-coloured flowers have serrated petals and a wide blaze of orchid green on the exterior.

COURT LADY (14 in, 35 cm). Delightful for flower arrangement, the blooms with their pointed petals are ivory white with a blaze of leaf green on the exterior.

GREENLAND (12 in, 30 cm). A vigorous grower, it rivals Artist in the diversity of its colouring, the rose-red flowers shading off to pale yellow at the petal edges and with a broad-green central stripe down the outer petals.

HOLLYWOOD (9 in, 22·5 cm). An Artist 'sport' of similar habit, the bright-crimson flower being attractively feathered with green.

HUMMING BIRD (12 in, 30 cm). An outstanding bedding tulip, the broad petals which terminate into a point are reflexed when open and are of brilliant yellow with a wide blaze of leaf green on the exterior.

PIMPERNEL (18 in, 45 cm). A tulip of fascinating charm with pointed reflexed petals and of a glowing carmine pink, shading to crimson at the tips with green at the base and with a wide green blaze on the exterior.

Tulipa whittallii. It is the tetraploid form of *T. hageri* and is native of Greece where it blooms in March. The dark-green leaves are edged with crimson, while the globular flowers are of brilliant orange, shaded yellow and green at the base and on the outside, with green tips to the petals. The flowers are borne on 12-in (30-cm) stems and are among the most showy of all tulips. It increases rapidly.

SINGLE EARLY TULIPS. One of the earlier forms of the tulip, derived from *T. gesneriana* and *T. suaveolens*, both scented species which have passed on this admirable quality to most of this group. Growing 12 to 14 in (30 to 35 cm) high and flowering in April and early May, these tulips are valuable for bedding, especially in those gardens which are less favourably situated and where spring-flowering plants are late into bloom and thus may be at their best when it is time to set out the summer bedding plants. The early tulips are also valuable for windswept gardens on account of their low habit and are most attractive planted in small beds. They are also much in demand for early forcing and for growing in pots and bowls. The single earlies may also be planted with the later-flowering Darwins so as to extend the display from early April until mid-June.

Varieties of single early tulips:

APRICOT BEAUTY (15 in, 37·5 cm). A variety of unusual charm, equally handsome in the garden and under artificial light, the blooms being of a lovely shade of rosy apricot which in bright light takes on a golden glow.

ARABIAN MYSTERY (14 in, 35 cm). Striking in pots or in the garden, its broad-petalled blooms of royal mauve tipped with white are long-lasting and have a mysterious eastern quality about them. Early.

BELLONA (15 in, 37·5 cm). One of the finest of all bedding tulips and a suitable companion for Prince of Austria and Dr Plesman. It bears large bell-shaped flowers of golden yellow with a delicious perfume. Medium-early.

BRILLIANT STAR (12 in, 30 cm). Outstanding for indoor culture and for bedding, the flowers being of refined form and of dazzling orange-scarlet. Very early.

CASSINI (15 in, 37·5 cm). A fine bedding tulip, the flowers being large, of deepest velvet crimson and poised on a sturdy stem. Medium-early.

CHRISTMAS MARVEL (14 in, 35 cm). An outstanding variety bearing bloom of bright cherry pink. It is one of the best of all tulips for forcing.

COLEUR CARDINAL (12 in, 30 cm). The flowers are of deep cardinal red with long-lasting qualities and of great substance.

DIANA (12 in, 30 cm). Excellent for forcing and for bedding, it is one of the earliest to bloom, its pure-white flowers having a velvet-like texture. Early.

DOCTOR PLESMAN (15 in, 37·5 cm). A variety of beauty, bearing heavily scented flowers of glowing scarlet and held on long sturdy stems. Medium-early.

GALWAY (15 in, 37·5 cm). A little-known variety but one of charm, the bright-orange flowers being shaded green at the base and with black stamens. Medium-early.

GENERAL DE WET (12 in, 30 cm). Unsurpassed for forcing and valuable for bedding, the large flowers being of fiery orange stippled with scarlet. A Prince of Austria 'sport'. Medium-early.

IBIS (14 in, 35 cm). A variety with a difference, the large well-formed flowers being of deep rose-pink shading to silver white at the margin. Medium-early.

KEIZERSKROON (15 in, 37·5 cm). One of the earliest named tulips still in cultivation and unsurpassed for bedding, the scarlet blooms having a deep edge of golden yellow to give a striking bi-colour effect. Medium-early.

MONTPARNASSE (15 in, 37·5 cm). A Bellona 'sport' and possessing the same bedding qualities. The blooms are of deep mustard yellow, stippled with red on the exterior.

MON TRÉSOR (12 in, 30 cm). When forced, one of the first to bloom, the sweetly scented flowers being of deep golden yellow. Early.

PETER PAN (12 in, 30 cm). It bears a bloom of exquisite shape and colouring, being deepest pink shading to cream at the margins and with a cream blaze at the centre of the petals.

PRINCE CARNIVAL (15 in, 37·5 cm). A Prince of Austria 'sport' with the same sweet scent. The blooms are yellow inside, scarlet outside and of great substance. Medium-early.

PRINCE OF AUSTRIA (15 in, 37·5 cm). An outstanding tulip bearing large orange-scarlet blooms of perfect form and sweet scent. Medium-early.

PRINCESS IRENE (12 in, 30 cm). A variety of unusual colouring, the large handsome blooms being of salmon orange with buff markings on the exterior. Medium-early.

SUNBURST (14 in, 35 cm). The blooms are large and of deep golden yellow with broad carmine stripes on the outer petals to make it a most striking variety for bedding. Medium early.

TRANCE (15 in, 37·5 cm). A vigorous grower, bearing its large broad-petalled blooms of fiery red on sturdy stems.

VAN DER NEER (12 in, 30 cm). A tulip of unusual colouring and great beauty, the large refined blooms being of soft violet purple. Medium-early.

VERMILION BRILLIANT (12 in, 30 cm). An outstanding forcing tulip of neat habit, bearing sweetly scented flowers of dazzling scarlet. Early.

COTTAGE OR SINGLE TULIPS. Introduced about 1885, having been discovered growing in old cottage gardens by William Hartland of Cork and Peter Barr of London. The attention of the gardening public was first drawn to these tulips in 1896 when William Hartland exhibited his collection in Cork. Later that year he published his *Little Book of Irish Grown Tulips*, in which he listed and described many interesting varieties. Later, a number which came to be included in this group were discovered in cottage gardens in France and Holland. Growing from 20 to 30 in (50 to 75 cm) tall, they have egg-shaped blooms which are at their loveliest during May when they reveal an elegance of form displayed by few other tulips. They may be used for bedding or planted in groups in the border.

ADVANCE (24 in, 60 cm). The first of the cottage tulips to bloom—if it can be called a cottage tulip, for it is a hybrid of *T. greigii*. The flowers of brilliant scarlet-cerise, shaded blue at the base, are borne on strong erect stems and show colour before the end of April.

BEVERLEY (22 in, 55 cm). One of the most beautiful of all tulips, the colour being a distinct shade of clear orange-flame.

BLUSHING BRIDE (22 in, 55 cm). Its large oval blooms are of an unusual shade of soft lemon-cream flushed with rose towards the petal edges.

BOND STREET (24 in, 60 cm). A handsome tulip bearing large blooms of deep buttercup yellow with a deep-orange flush to the petal edges.

CARRARA (20 in, 50 cm). The finest of the pure whites, bearing large flowers of exquisite texture. It may be brought into bloom under glass from February.

CHAPPAQUA (28 in, 70 cm). Late into bloom, being at its best early in June, the large cherry-rose blooms possess enormous substance. Award of Merit.

DIDO (28 in, 70 cm). Outstanding in any collection, its cherry-red blooms being flushed and margined with orange, while they are sweetly scented.

EASTER QUEEN (26 in, 65 cm). One of the best of bedding tulips, bearing blooms of enormous size and of glowing orange with a yellow flush at the base and centre of the outer petals.

ELSIE ELOFF (30 in, 75 cm). Tall-growing, it bears large oval blooms of a delicate shade of clear golden yellow, deepening towards the edge.

FORTUNE'S GIFT (28 in, 70 cm). At its best flowering above a bed of blue violettas, its rose-pink blooms being shaded with salmon and with a flush of gold at the centre.

GOOD GRACIOUS (24 in, 60 cm). A variety of beauty, bearing large egg-shaped blooms of salmon pink shading to yellow towards the petal edges.

GRENADIER (16 in, 40 cm). A tulip of brilliance, the large blooms being of intense scarlet shaded gold at the base and with a sweet perfume.

G. W. LEAK (24 in, 60 cm). Outstanding in every way, the large blooms being of clear geranium scarlet with a contrasting golden base.

HENRY FORD (26 in, 65 cm). It bears a large handsome bloom of unusual colouring, being mushroom-coloured on the outside, flecked with rose and crimson scarlet on the inside.

IVORY GLORY (22 in, 55 cm). Plant it with Marshall Haig for striking contrast, its enormous globular blooms of ivory white being of velvet-like texture.

JOAN CRUICKSHANK (24 in, 60 cm). Long-lasting in the garden and when cut the upper half of the bloom is deep rose, contrasting with the lower part, which is ivory white.

KINGSCOURT (24 in, 60 cm). An ideal bedding tulip, it bears a large flower of glowing crimson red which does not fade.

LOUIS XIV (30 in, 75 cm). The large handsome blooms are of rich royal purple edged with golden bronze.

MARSHALL HAIG (26 in, 65 cm). One of the best of bedding tulips, the blooms being large, of brilliant scarlet and of heavy texture.

MAUREEN (30 in, 75 cm). The long oval blooms are white, flushed with cream at the centre of each petal and with golden anthers.

MOTHER'S DAY (24 in, 60 cm). A delightful companion for Marshall Haig, it is a symphony in yellow, being of primrose colouring with golden anthers.

MRS J. SCHEEPERS (24 in, 60 cm). A yellow of outstanding texture, the long oval-shaped blooms being of soft clear yellow of velvet-like texture.

PALESTRINA (20 in, 50 cm). With its compact habit and long-lasting qualities, it is one of the best of bedding tulips, the large blooms being of soft salmon pink flushed with old rose.

PRINCESS MARGARET ROSE (20 in, 50 cm). A valuable bedding tulip, its golden-yellow flowers having a clear edge of brightest rose. It is late-flowering.

ROYAL PORCELAIN (24 in, 60 cm). The enormous ivory-white flowers are strikingly edged with deep rosy red.

SORBET (24 in, 60 cm). The large handsome blooms are ivory-white, shaded with rose and orange and with a creamy-white base.

SOUTHERN CROSS (28 in, 70 cm). The enormous lemon-coloured blooms are shaded with bronze on the outside.

YUMA (28 in, 70 cm). Late and long-lasting, the large globular blooms are of brilliant geranium red, edged orange.

EARLY DOUBLE TULIPS. Double tulips first appeared in 1664 and, with their large globular flowers which open wide, they greatly resemble paeonies. Retaining their form for several weeks, showing tolerance of adverse weather and growing only 10 to 12 in (25 to 30 cm) tall, they are valuable for bedding, for window-box display and for early forcing. Outdoors, they come into bloom early in April. One of the first to appear was Murillo, bearing sweetly scented flowers, a quality it has passed on to its numerous 'sports'.

Double tulip

AGA KHAN (10 in, 25 cm). A variety of attractive colouring, bearing flowers of soft golden yellow, shaded orange at the petal edges and opening to a rich apricot amber. Medium-early.

ALL GOLD (12 in, 30 cm). Excellent as a pot plant and for bedding, the large blooms are of uniform golden yellow. Medium-early.

COURONNE D'OR (12 in, 30 cm). One of the earliest doubles, known in 1770 and bearing large handsome flowers of golden yellow flushed with orange. Medium-early.

DANTE (10 in, 25 cm). One of the most striking tulips, its flowers of ox-blood red opening wide like paeonies. Plant it with Schoonoord. Medium-early.

DAVID TENIERS (10 in, 30 cm). A magnificent variety, bearing large blooms of violet-purple, at their loveliest planted with the yellow van der Hoeff. Medium-early.

ELECTRA (12 in, 30 cm). Excellent for forcing or bedding, the flowers are of a unique shade of bright carmine purple. A Murillo 'sport', it is scented. Medium-early.

EL TOREADOR (12 in, 30 cm). A variety of unusual colouring, bearing large handsome blooms of deepest salmon, shaded orange. Early.

FIRE DOME (12 in, 30 cm). One of the best of the scarlet bedding tulips, the large blooms being of intense vermilion. Early.

GOLDEN DUCAT (11 in, 28 cm). A 'sport' of Scarlet Cardinal, bearing large blooms of rich golden yellow. Early.

GOYA (12 in, 30 cm). A Murillo 'sport' bearing flowers of flame red shaded on the outside with warm salmon rose and yellow at the base. Medium-early.

JAN VERMEER (12 in, 30 cm). An Orange Nassau 'sport', itself a 'sport' of Murillo and a most striking bedding tulip, bearing large blooms of deep cardinal red edged with yellow. Medium-early.

JEAN PIERRE LAURENS (12 in, 30 cm). A Murillo 'sport' bearing bloom of deep mauve-pink, shading to lilac rose at the petal edges. Medium-early.

MADAME TESTOUT (12 in, 30 cm). The finest of all double pink tulips, the large handsome blooms being of rich warm rose pink. Medium early.

MARECHAL NIEL (12 in, 30 cm). An old favourite of great beauty, the soft lemon-yellow blooms being delicately tinted with orange on the outside. Early.

MARQUETTE (12 in, 30 cm). A Murillo 'sport' of striking beauty, the scarlet blooms being edged with gold. Early.

MURILLO (12 in, 30 cm). An old favourite, bearing white flowers tinted with pink. The form *maxima* may be brought into bloom 10 days early in heat, while it is taller-growing and a valuable cut flower. Medium-early.

ORANGE NASSAU (12 in, 30 cm). A Murillo 'sport' and for long a most effective bedding tulip, bearing large blooms of orange scarlet with mahogany shading on the outside. Medium-early.

PEACH BLOSSOM (12 in, 30 cm). An early Murillo 'sport', the large full blooms being of bright rose pink shaded cream on the outside. Early.

SCARLET CARDINAL (12 in, 30 cm). The earliest double for forcing and bedding, the large blooms being of brilliant orange scarlet shaded with crimson. Early.

SCHOONOORD (12 in, 30 cm). A Murillo 'sport' and the best double white tulip both for forcing and bedding, the large blooms being of glistening white.

TEAROSE (11 in, 27·5 cm). A Murillo 'sport' for bedding, bearing blooms of primrose yellow flushed outside with apricot and orange. Early.

VAN DER HOEFF (12 in, 30 cm). A Murillo 'sport' and the finest pure-yellow double for forcing and bedding. Medium-early.

WILHELM KORDES (12 in, 30 cm). A Murillo 'sport' named in honour of the famous German rose grower and bearing flowers of cadmium yellow, shaded orange and red. Early.

WILLEMSOORD (12 in, 30 cm). An Electra 'sport' of unusual charm, the large blooms being of similar carmine red colouring, edged white. Medium-early.

WILLIAM OF ORANGE (12 in, 30 cm). A bedding variety of distinction, the soft orange-coloured blooms being flushed on the outside with coppery red. Medium-early.

LATE DOUBLE TULIPS (PAEONY-FLOWERED). They follow the double early tulips into bloom, being at their best during May. They bear larger flowers than the early doubles and on stems 16 to 24 in (40 to 60 cm) tall, twice the height. Suitable for planting in groups in the border, especially among clumps of *Anchusa myosotidiflora*, a perennial plant which bears sprays of bright blue forget-me-not flowers early in summer. Also for tub culture, planted with early-flowering double or single tulips to prolong the display when they will give at least two months of bloom.

BRILLIANT FIRE (18 in, 45 cm). One of the most brilliant tulips, the large globular blooms being of bright cherry red, shaded coppery orange towards the petal tips.

EROS (24 in, 60 cm). It bears its heavily scented paeony-like flowers of deep old rose on long sturdy stems and remains colourful for several weeks.

EVE (syn. GERBRAND KIEFT) (18 in, 45 cm). It is one of the loveliest of all tulips, being of deep glowing purple crimson, edged with silvery white and is long-lasting.

GOLD MEDAL (18 in, 45 cm). A companion for Brilliant Fire, its blooms are the largest of all the doubles and of pure deep golden yellow throughout.

GRAND NATIONAL (18 in, 45 cm). The multi-petalled bloom of clear creamy yellow, shaded red on the outside, opens like a large bowl.

HERMIONE (20 in, 50 cm). A beautiful variety, excellent in all weathers and bearing a large refined bloom of soft lilac pink, lovely under artificial light.

LILAC PERFECTION (18 in, 45 cm). It bears a most lovely flower for floral arrangement, the large handsome blooms being of deep creamy pink, the outer petals shaded lilac.

MOUNT TACOMA (20 in, 50 cm). The peerless white flowers resemble Chinese tree paeonies when open, and when cut and placed in water remain fresh for more than a week.

NICE CARNIVAL (18 in, 45 cm). A Nizza 'sport' bearing a neat refined flower of snowy white, prettily striped with red. In addition, the leaves are beautifully striped with white.

NIZZA (18 in, 45 cm). A variety of charm, the large creamy-yellow flowers being striped and feathered with crimson.

ORANGE TRIUMPH (20 in, 50 cm). The flowers, opening to 9 in (22·5 cm) across, are of richest orange with a contrasting wire edge of gold.

LILY-FLOWERED TULIPS

LILY-FLOWERED TULIPS. Introduced in 1915 from a cross between the hybrid *T. retroflexa* and a Cottage tulip. *T. retroflexa* was raised in 1863 by William van der Winne by crossing *T. gesneriana* with *T. acuminata* which has long pointed petals, a feature of this group which gives the flowers so elegant an air where used for floral decoration. Tall-growing and May-flowering, they are best grown in groups in the border where, with their distinctive lines, they make their handsome contribution to the early summer display:

ALADDIN (20 in, 50 cm). It forms a long slim flower with gracefully reflexed petals of clearest crimson red with a narrow golden rim at the edges.

ARCADIA (24 in, 60 cm). The flower is especially long and reflexing and of rich golden yellow.

ASTOR (25 in, 62·5 cm). The flowers are of a most unusual shade of amber, tinted with salmon pink and bronze.

BALLAD (20 in, 50 cm). Unique in its colouring, being soft violet mauve with a contrasting silver-white margin.

CHINA PINK (22 in, 55 cm). An outstanding bedding tulip with broad reflexing petals of deep satin pink shaded deeper pink on the outside.

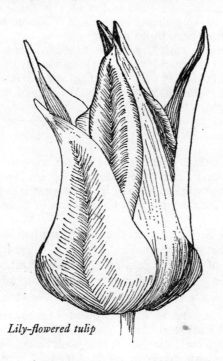

Lily-flowered tulip

CLARICE (24 in, 60 cm). Plant it with Red Shine or Queen of Sheba for it bears gracefully reflexing flowers of soft lemon yellow.

ELLEN WILLMOTT (20 in, 50 cm). Its long tapering flowers of soft primrose yellow have a delicious perfume and are untroubled by wet weather.

GISELA (22 in, 55 cm). An outstanding bedding tulip bearing a large but refined bloom of warm rose pink, flushed with salmon pink towards the petal edges.

HEDWIG VATTER (18 in, 45 cm). A compact variety of a new colour combination, the large handsome blooms being of deepest orange, shaded cochineal.

INIMITABLE (24 in, 60 cm). One of the longest-lasting of all tulips when cut and in water, it is equally long-lasting in the garden. The slim elegant blooms are deep buttercup yellow.

JACQUELINE (26 in, 65 cm). The tallest in the group (with Mrs Moon), the flowers being of deep pink, shading to softer pink and silvery pink at the petal edges. The long tapering blooms are borne on wiry stems.

KIRUNA (24 in, 60 cm). The elegant flowers, of brilliant geranium red, are a perfect companion to Inimitable and are fadeless in the hottest weather.

LEICA (24 in, 60 cm). Most beautiful in form and colour, the handsome flowers being of soft creamy white with elegantly reflexing petals.

MARIETTE (22 in, 55 cm). The blooms are thin-waisted in bud form, slowly expanding to resemble water-lilies and of a lovely shade of soft salmon pink.

MAYTIME (20 in, 50 cm). Plant it with Ellen Willmott, for its flowers of lilac mauve associate most beautifully with it.

MRS MOON (26 in, 65 cm). One of the tallest in this section, bearing large urn-shaped flowers of canary yellow smelling sweetly of almonds.

QUEEN OF SHEBA (18 in, 45 cm). One of the most arresting tulips, the large blooms with their gracefully reflexed petals being of scarlet-bronze with a distinct edge of golden yellow.

RED SHINE (20 in, 50 cm). The best pure-red lily-flowered tulip, the long shapely blooms being of deepest ruby red with a glossy shine on the outside of the petals.

SIDONIE (20 in, 50 cm). Should be grown in the company of yellow-flowering varieties, with which its rich wine-red flowers provide a pleasing contrast.

WHITE TRIUMPHATOR (28 in, 70 cm). Tall-growing, it bears a large handsome bloom, urn-shaped and reflexing at the tips and of glistening pure white.

PARROT TULIPS. So called from the fringed feather-like petals and unique colourings of red, orange, steel blue and green. The first Parrot tulip appeared in 1665 but the first of the modern named varieties, Fantasy, was found in the nursery of van Tubergens in Holland, being a 'sport' of the Darwin tulip, Clara Butt. Almost all are Darwin 'sports' and bloom at the same time.

BLUE PARROT (24 in, 60 cm). The blooms are of enormous size and of bright violet blue flushed with steel blue.

FANTASY (22 in, 56 cm). The bright rose-pink blooms with their deeply cut petals are feathered with pale green on the outside. There is also a rare double form of similar colouring.

FARADAY (22 in, 56 cm). A Fantasy 'sport', bearing creamy-white blooms instead of pink and with the same green featherings.

GAY PRESTO (24 in, 60 cm). A Cordell Hull 'sport', the white flowers being heavily marked with red, while the petals are deeply lascinated to produce a striking effect.

KAREL DOERMAN (20 in, 50 cm). The blooms are of remarkable size and of deep cherry red, the unevenly waved petals being edged with yellow.

MERRIMENT (20 in, 50 cm). An Ossi Oswalda 'sport' and one of the finest Parrots, bearing soft creamy-yellow flowers flushed carmine, with the petals deeply frilled.

ORANGE FAVOURITE (22 in, 55 cm). One of the sweetest scented of all tulips and one of the most colourful, the blooms being orange scarlet, tinted with rose and with apple-green outer featherings.

RED PARROT (28 in, 70 cm). Tall-growing, the brilliant scarlet-red blooms

are of enormous size, while both the inner and outer petals are deeply lascinated.

TEXAS FLAME (18 in, 45 cm). A Texas Gold 'sport', the blooms being of
brilliant golden yellow, flamed with carmine and with green shading at the
base.

TEXAS GOLD (18 in, 45 cm). The clear golden-yellow blooms have red markings about the waved petal edges, while the outside of the petals is feathered
with apple green.

WHITE PARROT (20 in, 50 cm). A most beautiful tulip, the blooms being of
pure snow-white throughout and of enormous size.

FRINGED TULIPS. May-flowering tulips, which have now been grouped
separately from the Parrots, for the edges of their petals are fringed rather than
deeply cut, while they are without the green markings of the Parrots. They are
also of more compact habit, growing 12 to 18 in (30 to 45 cm) tall.

BURGUNDY LACE (18 in, 45 cm). The flower is long and urn-shaped rather
than globular and of rich maroon red with a neat fringe.

FRINGED BEAUTY (12 in, 30 cm). Outstanding for bowl culture and for
bedding, the flowers are of ox-blood red with a golden fringe to the petals.

FRINGED FLAMINGO (12 in, 30 cm). The medium-sized flowers are of soft
flamingo pink, heavily fringed milky white.

FRINGED LILAC (18 in, 45 cm). The large flowers are of rich violet throughout
but with deeper violet shading at the base.

GEMMA (12 in, 30 cm). Fringed Flamingo in reverse, the large blooms being
creamy white with a fringe of flamingo pink.

NEW LOOK (18 in, 45 cm). The large blooms of ivory white are flushed rose
pink near the daintily fringed petal edges and inside the bloom.

SOTHIS (18 in, 45 cm). It should be planted with Gemma for contrast. The
heavily fringed blooms are of deep uniform scarlet red.

MULTIFLOWERED TULIPS. A group of hybrid tulips originally raised
from *T. tubergeniana* and a multi-flowered species. They grow 24 to 28 in
(60 to 70 cm) tall and bear three to six flowers which branch from the main
stem, so that for bedding display, the bulbs may be planted 10 in (25 cm) apart
and will be most economical:

CLAUDETTE (20 in, 50 cm). It bears four or five large flowers of ivory white
edged with cerise on a sturdy branching stem.

EMIR (24 in, 60 cm). An outstanding introduction, bearing three or four
large blooms of brilliant oriental red to each stem.

GEORGETTE (24 in, 60 cm). It has plenty of broad pale-green leaves and
bears four or five large flowers on a much-branched stem. The blooms are
of clearest yellow with a wire edge of red.

MONS MOTTET (20 in, 50 cm). It forms three or four elegant blooms of ivory-
white held well above healthy dark-green foliage.

ORANGE BOUQUET (24 in, 60 cm). Planted with Georgette, the effect is most striking, for it bears four or five large flowers of brilliant orange scarlet shaded yellow at the base.

ROSY MIST (24 in, 60 cm). The handsome blooms open blush white changing to shell pink as the flowers age. Four or five large blooms appear on each stem.

WALLFLOWER (26 in, 66 cm). A cottage garden variety of charm, bearing flowers of the same colour as the wallflower, deep mahogany brown, shaded yellow at the base and as many as five or six medium-sized flowers to each stem.

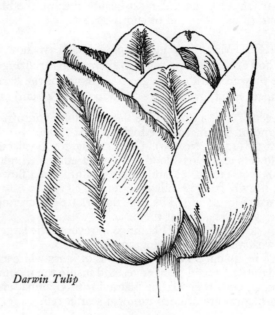

Darwin Tulip

DARWIN TULIPS. Considered to be the 'king' of tulips, the first of this important group were discovered in 1886 by Monsieur J. Langlart, an amateur gardener of Lille in France, and they were introduced to commerce by Messrs Krelage of Haarlem about the year 1900. The blooms have short rounded petals which open to large cups, almost square or rectangular in outline, while they embrace every known tulip colour. Growing up to 3 ft (90 cm) tall, they bloom in May and early June, later than other tulips and hold their blooms on robust stems. They will respond to gentle forcing in pots though the old varieties Rose Copeland and William Copeland may be forced hard from early in the year. Varieties of merit include:

ABERDEEN (28 in, 70 cm). The blooms are large and refined and of an attractive shade of silvery pink merging into silvery grey at the edges.

AFTERGLOW (28 in, 70 cm). The large handsome flowers are of apricot orange, shaded rose at the centre of the petals and pale orange at the edges.

ANJOU (24 in, 60 cm). It bears large refined blooms of soft lemon yellow shading to cream at the petal edges.

ARISTOCRAT (30 in, 75 cm). Well named for the blooms are enormous and are of rosy purple, shading out at the edges.

BLUE HILL (28 in, 70 cm). With its large flowers of rich amethyst blue, it is especially attractive when in bloom above a bed of yellow violas.

CHARLES NEEDHAM (24 in, 60 cm). The finest red Darwin and probably the best of all red tulips, the large handsome blooms being of ox-blood red which do not fade whatever the weather.

CLARA BUTT (24 in, 60 cm). Still unsurpassed in its colour, the blooms being of a lovely shade of salmon rose, shaded at the base with blue-grey.

DORRIE OVERALL (30 in, 75 cm). A tall grower and bearing a bloom of immense size, of rich lilac blue shading to paler blue at the edges.

ECLIPSE (22 in, 55 cm). A variety of rich colouring, being of bright crimson maroon, shaded black at the base and of velvet-like texture.

EVELYN HOWARD (28 in, 70 cm). A most refined tulip, the bloom being of soft lilac pink, shading to creamy lilac at the edges and with a cream base.

FARNCOMBE SANDERS (30 in, 75 cm). Of vigorous habit, it bears an immense bloom of geranium red with a contrasting white base.

FLORENCE NIGHTINGALE (22 in, 55 cm). Of compact habit and perfect poise, it makes an arresting sight when in small beds for the blooms are of bright vermilion, free from shading.

FLYING DUTCHMAN (28 in, 70 cm). The handsome blooms with their broad petals are of richest cherry red, flushed with scarlet at the centre of the petals.

GOLDEN AGE (24 in, 60 cm). For long one of the finest of 'yellow' tulips, the large handsome blooms being of deep buttery yellow shaded orange at the edges.

GOLDEN HIND (24 in, 60 cm). A handsome variety, remarkable for the intense golden yellow of its blooms, as if painted with gold-leaf.

HEATHER HILL (28 in, 70 cm). Well-named, for at a distance the large blooms of heather pink are like hilltops crowned with heather.

UNSURPASSABLE (28 in, 70 cm). Its large elegant blooms are of a lovely shade of purest lilac.

LA TULIPE NOIRE (24 in, 60 cm). The black tulip of ancient origin, its large cup-shaped blooms being of darkest maroon-black and of velvet-like texture.

MAGIER (25 in, 62·5 cm). One of the 'great' tulips, bearing a bloom of unrivalled beauty, long lasting in the garden and as a cut flower. The flowers are of milky white, shaded with purple at the edges.

MAMASA (24 in, 60 cm). A tulip of substance, its large blooms of buttercup yellow held on sturdy stems.

MR VAN ZYL (26 in, 65 cm). It bears flowers of delicate soft pink, shading to paler pink at the edges.

ORANGE COCADE (24 in, 60 cm). One of the most handsome of tulips bearing large blooms of brightest orange shaded with cream.

OSSI OSWALDA (24 in, 60 cm). Known as the chameleon tulip, for its colour changes with its age. The large blooms open creamy white with a rose flush at the petal edges. Later, it turns to a clear and uniform shade of rose pink.

PARADISE (22 in, 55 cm). A gay and effective variety, the blooms or glistening ivory white having a broad edge of claret red and shaded claret on the inside.

PERRY COMO (24 in, 60 cm). It holds its enormous blooms on sturdy, erect stems above broad apple-green leaves, while the flowers of bright strawberry rose are shaded gold at the base.

PINK SUPREME (26 in, 65 cm). It bears a flower of deep glowing pink shading to silvery pink at the edges.

QUEEN OF THE BARTAGONS (28 in, 70 cm). The best of the old Bartagon tulips now superseded by others of greater vigour, it remains one of the most beautiful of all, bearing globular blooms of pure salmon pink.

SCARLET LEADER (28 in, 70 cm). An outstanding tulip bearing an immense bloom of pure geranium red.

SCARLETT O'HARA (30 in, 75 cm). Plant it with Snowpeak for contrast for it bears a huge bloom of pure unfading scarlet.

SILVER WEDDING (30 in, 75 cm). An elegant and long-lasting tulip, bearing large handsome blooms of soft chrome yellow shading to creamy yellow at the edges.

SNOWPEAK (28 in, 70 cm). Plant it with a red Darwin or above a bed of red polyanthus, for it is the best white, the huge square blooms being held on tall sturdy stems above dark-green foliage.

SWEET HARMONY (26 in, 65 cm). The large handsome blooms are of lemon yellow, shading out to ivory and with golden anthers.

THE BISHOP (30 in, 75 cm). The finest of all purple tulips, the large globular blooms being of uniform purple as if varnished or polished and held on long sturdy stems.

DARWIN HYBRIDS. The crossing of the Darwin tulip with *T. fosteriana* has resulted in a group of outstanding beauty and garden value, growing less than 2 ft (60 cm) tall and coming into bloom before the end of April, thus being intermediate between the early-flowering tulips and the later-flowering Darwins. The flowers are larger than those of any other tulip and have a brilliance of colour more pronounced than any other tulip.

APELDOORN (24 in, 60 cm). It bears large oval blooms of orient red with a contrasting golden base.

BEAUTY OF APELDOORN (24 in, 60 cm). Its flowers are large and refined and of creamy yellow flushed with soft orange.

BIG CHIEF (24 in, 60 cm). Strikingly lovely, the huge blooms being of brilliant scarlet flushed lilac rose on the outside and glowing orange scarlet on the inside.

DOVER (24 in, 60 cm). The blooms are of enormous size and are vivid scarlet with a black base surrounded by a ring of gold.

GUDOSHNIK (24 in, 60 cm). The handsome oval bloom is of a colour which almost defies description, being of creamy apricot lightly streaked rose red and with black anthers.

GOLDEN SPRINGTIME (24 in, 60 cm). A beautiful variety to accompany the reds, the large globular blooms being of deepest uniform yellow.

HOLLAND'S GLORY (20 in, 50 cm). The finest scarlet bedding tulip ever introduced, the huge globular blooms being of soft orange scarlet and held above bottle-green foliage.

JEWEL OF SPRING (24 in, 60 cm). 'Sport' of Godoshnik, the large blooms of sulphur yellow are neatly edged with red.

LEFEBRE'S FAVOURITE (22 in, 55 cm). The rich scarlet bloom with its golden base carries a brilliant oriental lustre and attracts the eye from a distance.

PRESIDENT KENNEDY (25 in, 62·5 cm). The tallest in the section, it is one of the finest tulips in cultivation, the large blooms of golden yellow being over-laid with soft rose pink.

MENDEL TULIPS. The result of a cross between the Duc van Tol and Darwin tulip and introduced in 1909 by Krelage, they grow less than 18 in (45 cm) tall and are intermediate flowering. They are valuable for a windswept garden and those colder gardens where the later-flowering tulips interfere with summer bedding schemes.

APRICOT BEAUTY (15 in, 37·5 cm). Outstanding as a cut flower or for garden display, the almost globular blooms are of a lovely shade of apricot salmon.

BEAUTY OF VOLENDAM (16 in, 40 cm). The flowers are of attractive form and are white, feathered with crimson purple.

DEBUTANTE (12 in, 30 cm). Of compact habit, it is a 'sport' of Orange Wonder and bears a large bloom of glowing salmon orange, edged with yellow.

GOLDEN OLGA (16 in, 40 cm). The large blooms are of deep carmine red, edged with gold.

HER GRACE (18 in, 45 cm). A most attractive tulip bearing a large ivory-white bloom, edged with deep pink.

JOHN GAY (16 in, 40 cm). The long tapering blooms are of brilliant scarlet shaded with orange.

KRELAGE'S TRIUMPH (17 in, 42·5 cm). For early forcing and for bedding, the large blooms being of geranium red shaded black at the base.

MIMOSA (18 in, 45 cm). The only pure yellow in this group, the large globular blooms being of the colour of the sun.

OLGA (16 in, 40 cm). Excellent for early forcing, the blooms are of glowing scarlet, edged white.

ORANGE WONDER (18 in, 45 cm). A wonderful tulip of long-lasting qualities, forcing well and of brilliant colouring, being clearest orange.

PINK TROPHY (18 in, 45 cm). The finest pink in this group, the large handsome blooms being of deep pink flushed with rose.

VAN DER EERDEN (18 in, 45 cm). The blooms, of elegant form, are of deep glowing scarlet throughout.

TRIUMPH TULIPS. Raised from single early and Darwin tulips, they are mid-season flowering with the habit of the Darwins, bearing their bloom on

S

2-ft (60-cm) stems and with the Mendels. Their cone-shaped blooms and harmonious colourings make them among the most handsome of tulips, ideal for bedding.

AUREOLA (26 in, 65 cm). Outstanding in the border, the large scarlet blooms of velvet-like texture being broadly margined with gold.

ADORNO (24 in, 60 cm). The long pointed urn-shaped blooms are of rich salmon orange, edged with shades of bronze and yellow.

BRUNO WALTER (18 in, 45 cm). A variety of charm, its honey-amber blooms shaded with gold at the petal edges being sweetly scented.

DREAMLAND (20 in, 50 cm). The cone-shaped blooms are almost rectangular and are of rose pink with a broad cream 'flame' up the centre of each petal.

DUTCH PRINCESS (20 in, 50 cm). A distinct and charming bedder, the blooms being of glowing orange lightly touched with gold on the outside.

ELMUS (28 in, 70 cm). A strong grower bearing flowers of warm cherry red deeply edged with white.

FIRST LADY (26 in, 65 cm). It bears a large bloom of velvet-like texture, of reddish-violet, flushed purple.

GARDEN PARTY (16 in, 40 cm). One of the finest of bedding tulips, bearing elegant cone-shaped blooms of ivory white with a broad edge of carmine pink.

HIGH SOCIETY (20 in, 50 cm). The large blooms are of glowing salmon orange shading out to golden orange.

JOHANNA (20 in, 50 cm). A variety of exquisite colouring, bearing large flowers of deep salmon pink.

K. AND M.'S TRIUMPH (24 in, 60 cm). One of the finest of red tulips, the large globular blooms being of intense ox-blood red and of velvet-like texture.

MARY HOUSLEY (20 in, 50 cm). A lovely tulip with broad petals and of rich buttercup yellow, shaded apricot on the outside.

MERRY WIDOW (24 in, 60 cm). The flowers have enormous substance and are of deep glowing red with a fine but distinct white edge.

ORANGE SUN (22 in, 55 cm). The finest pure-orange tulip ever raised, the large blooms having great substance.

ORANGE WONDER (20 in, 50 cm). It bears a bloom of exceptional quality, being of coral orange with a silvery sheen on the outside, and is scented.

ORIENT EXPRESS (22 in, 55 cm). A handsome tulip bearing large blooms of glowing scarlet which are long-lasting and resistant to adverse weather.

PARIS (20 in, 50 cm). One of the most colourful, the orange-scarlet shading out to brilliant gold at the petal edges.

PINK GLOW (20 in, 50 cm). A tulip of substance, the large blooms being of rich glowing pink.

PRINCESS BEATRIX (20 in, 50 cm). An outstanding bedding tulip, the orange-scarlet flowers being edged with yellow.

PROMINENCE (16 in, 40 cm). It bears large egg-shaped blooms of crimson red of velvety texture.

REFORMA (20 in, 50 cm). It will brighten the darkest corner with its large cone-shaped blooms of buttercup yellow and is especially right for planting near evergreens.

ROSE KORNEFORUS (24 in, 60 cm). Its large globular flowers are of heather pink, deeper at the centre of the petals and shading out to silvery purple at the edges.

SULPHUR GLORY (24 in, 60 cm). Tall growing and in every way right to accompany Orange Sun, the blooms being of uniform chrome yellow.

FEATHERED AND FLAMED TULIPS. Their history goes back to 1560. By the beginning of the seventeenth century, fantastic prices were being paid for those flowers which were 'broken' in colour instead of being self-coloured (breeders). In 'broken' flowers the colour becomes concentrated into various parts of the flower, leaving the rest of the flower white or yellow. Once this happens, the bulb and its offsets retain this characteristic when the bloom is said to be either feathered or flamed. When the colour is confined to the petal edges it is known as feathering, for it resembles the feathers of a bird. Where the colour runs up the centre of each petal and then branches out towards the edges, it is said to be flamed, though feathering of the edges is also present and the same variety may be both feathered and flamed, e.g. Sir Joseph Paxton. Those cultivated by the florists of old were distinguished by their purity of base and ground colour and correct markings. Broken tulips increase less freely than the unbroken forms (breeders), while they usually have less vigour—hence most have died out over the years. Those remaining are prized by collectors, especially those having a pure-white base and known as 'roses'. They were mostly Cottage tulips that took on this breaking, the condition being rare among Darwins. Those tulips streaked with red, pink or purple on a white ground are known as Bybloemens; those with a yellow ground are known as Bizarres. The Rembrandt tulips are Darwins which have taken on this unusual characteristic. 'Breaking' is believed to be due to a virus, hence their lack of vigour.

ABSOLON (Bizarre) (26 in, 65 cm). The ground colour is deep yellow, feathered and flamed mahogany, the blooms being of beautiful globular shape.

BELIE QUEEN (Bizarre) (22 in, 55 cm). The feathering is of mahogany and bronze over a clear-yellow ground.

BOUQUET ROYAL (Bizarre) (20 in, 50 cm). One of the best, the large globular blooms being feathered and flamed rich purple bronze.

CORDELL HULL (Rembrandt) (22 in, 55 cm). It bears a large globular bloom of blood red, feathered and flamed pure white.

DAINTY MAID (Bybloemen) (18 in, 45 cm). One of the most attractive in this section with purple feathering on a white ground.

GOLDEN HAWK (Bizarre) (20 in, 50 cm). The ground is clear yellow, feathered with bronze and mahogany.

LORD FREDERICK CAVENDISH (Bizarre) (20 in, 50 cm). An old florists' tulip still in existence and bearing a handsome bloom, feathered and flamed red on a white ground.

MADAME DE POMPADOUR (Rembrandt) (18 in, 45 cm). A variety of charm, the pure-white flower being flamed with purple.

MAY BLOSSOM (Bybloemen) (18 in, 45 cm). The large cup-shaped blooms are lightly feathered with purple on a cream ground.

PALJAS (Bybloemen) (20 in, 50 cm). One of the best in the section, the large pure-white blooms being feathered with red.

SIR JOSEPH PAXTON (Bybloemen) (18 in, 45 cm). An outstanding tulip, its large globular blooms being feathered and flamed red on a white ground.

UNION JACK (Rembrandt) (24 in, 60 cm). A striking bedding tulip, the globular flower of ivory white being flamed with raspberry red, the base being shaded with blue.

U

URCEOLINA (Amaryllidaceae)

A genus of five species, native of the Peruvian Andes and taking its name from *urceolus*, a pitcher or urn. They have tunicated bulbs about 2 in (5 cm) through and lance-shaped leaves, while the drooping urn-shaped flowers are borne in umbels of six to ten on a leafless scape. In the British Isles, the plants are best given greenhouse culture for they bloom early in summer.

Culture. Provide a compost made up of fibrous loam, leaf mould and dehydrated manure in equal parts. Add to it a sprinkling of sand. Plant in October, three or four bulbs to a 5-in (12·5-cm) pot and place beneath the greenhouse bench or in a cool room for five to six weeks for the bulbs to root. Then introduce to a temperature of 45° F (7° C) and water sparingly until growth commences in spring, when supplies may be increased. After flowering, the plants are rested during late summer and autumn, placing the pots on their side and withholding moisture. They should be given a sunny situation for the bulbs to ripen. They are then shaken from the pots, cleaned and repotted and allowed to form new roots before starting into growth again; or they may be allowed to remain in the pots for another year, topping up with fresh compost. They require the minimum amount of heat and may be grown cool throughout.

Propagation. By offsets, which after two years will have formed about the mother bulb and may be removed when repotting. They are planted one to a 3-in (7·5-cm) pot in a sandy compost and grown on for two or three years until reaching flowering size.

Species. *Urceolina pendula.* The only species in general cultivation, it is native of the Andes of Peru and Bolivia and has pointed leaves 12 in (30 cm) long and 6 in (15 cm) broad. The drooping urn-shaped flowers are bright yellow, the slightly reflexed petal tips being shaded green on the outside. They are borne in umbels of 8 to 12 at the end of a 12-in (30-cm) scape.

URGINEA (Liliaceae)

A genus of about 100 species, native of the Mediterranean, northern and southern Africa and India and named after Beni Urgin, a place (or tribe) in Algeria. They have large tunicated bulbs and narrow strap-like leaves, often of rosette formation, while the star-like flowers are borne in an erect truss on stems 6 in to 3 ft (15 to 90 cm) tall. *U. maritima*, the sea onion, supplies the squill of commerce (used in cough mixtures), the vapour of the cut bulb bringing tears to the eyes, as with the onion.

Culture. Only one species, *U. maritima*, is afforded general garden cultivation. It should be confined to those gardens enjoying a mild winter climate, where the bulbs may be planted in the border and left undisturbed. The bulbs must be handled with care, preferably using gloves, for the juice may cause blistering of the hands. Plant in October 6 in (15 cm) deep and 8 in (20 cm) apart in a soil containing some peat and sand or grit to assist drainage. It is on sandy, stony ground near the sea that the bulbs are found in northern Africa. A heavy mulch of decayed leaves given in November will protect the bulbs from frost damage.

Propagation. If the bulbs are lifted in autumn when three or four years old, a number of offsets will be found around the older bulbs. These are detached and replanted where they are to bloom—which they will do in 18 months.

Species. *Urginea altissima*. It is rare at the Cape on Lion's Head and makes a large ovoid bulb from which arise six to eight lance-shaped leaves 12 in (30 cm) long. The flowers are white, keeled with purple, and are borne in a dense truss on a stem 2 ft (60 cm) tall.

Urginea filifolia. Native of southern Africa, where it is found growing in sand or shingle close to the sea, it has a bulb about 1 in (2·5 cm) through with a paper-like outer coat and six to nine dark-green wiry leaves which appear with the flowers. It blooms in August and September in its native land, in early summer in Britain. Its white flowers shaded purple on the outside are borne in a raceme of 8 to 16.

Urginea flexuosa. Native of the Cape, where it is found growing in damp peaty soil. It has a flattened bulb and two leaves which appear with the white flowers. They are shaded reddish purple on the outside and borne in a short raceme.

Urginea maritima (syn. *U. scilla*, *Scilla maritima*). Native of the coast of northern Africa, from Algeria to Egypt, where it grows in sandy pockets among rocks by the seashore. It has a large ovoid bulb up to 6 in (15 cm) across covered in a white tunic, from which arises a rosette of fleshy grey-green leaves, usually appearing in autumn after the flowers have faded. The bulbs grow in clumps of 50 or more, covering more than 1 square foot of ground. From the centre of the rosette appears a leafless scape 3 to 4 ft (about 1 metre) tall, covered to half its length in small white flowers, striped with green, while the scape is often purple.

V

VALLOTA (Amaryllidaceae)

A genus of a single species, native of southern Africa and named in honour of Monsieur Vallot, a French botanist. It has a large ovoid bulb, bright evergreen strap-shaped leaves 2 ft (60 cm) in length and bears eight or nine funnel-shaped flowers on a leafless scape 2 ft (60 cm) tall. It differs from *amaryllis* in its more regular perianth and, like that plant, it is suitable for cultivating in the window of a living-room where it will bloom during August and September. It is happy in semi-shade.

Known as the Scarborough lily, it was discovered at Martequar Kloof in 1773 by Francis Masson. In the *Scarborough Evening News*, it has been suggested that the plant received its name because the bulbs were brought to the Yorkshire seaport by a Mr John Woodall, whose boat made frequent runs to Cape Town early in the nineteenth century. It is believed that the bulbs first grew in his garden in Manor Road, Scarborough. Shortly after, the plant was to be found in the window of many a seaman's cottage home in the town.

Culture. Like *Hippeastrum* and *Amaryllis*, the bulbs continue to increase in size and attain large proportions, often cracking the pots in which they grow, though they bloom better when pot-bound. Use a 14- to 16-cm bulb and plant one to a 5-in (12·5-cm) pot. Within three or four years, it will have grown large enough to fill the pot, when it will begin to push itself out of the soil. It must then be moved to a larger pot. Crock the pots before placing at the bottom a 1-in (2·5-cm) layer of compost on which the bulb will rest. The compost should consist of fibrous loam, leaf mould, decayed manure and grit in equal parts. The compost is packed around the bulb, the top and neck of which are left exposed. The compost level should be 1 in (2·5 cm) below the rim of the pot to allow for watering. Plant early in summer, giving little moisture until rooting has taken place, during which time they should be grown as cool as possible. They will soon begin to form their leaves, but will not usually bloom until the following year. The plants should never be completely dried off, but in May and June each year reduce moisture to a minimum and place the pots outside, beneath the overhanging eaves of a house or on a bench in the garden room in full sun to allow the bulbs to ripen. At the end of June, increase supplies of moisture when the flower stem will begin to form. The plants may then be placed in a window in the home, keeping the compost moist during autumn and winter.

Propagation. After the plants have occupied the pots for several years, numerous leek-like offsets will have formed around the parent bulb. These may be sending up a flowering stem while still attached. The plant should be shaken from the pot with the soil ball intact and the offsets carefully removed, taking care not to damage the thick fleshy roots which will have filled the pot and will be seen at the top, having pushed themselves up from the base into a tangled mess. When replanting the old bulb, do so with care so that the roots are undamaged. Mid-summer, before the plants come into bloom, is the most suitable time to remove the offsets. They are planted in small pots, moving the bulbs to larger pots in which they will bloom as they make growth. With care in their culture, the plants will remain vigorous for many years and are attractive even when not in bloom, the foliage being enhanced by the large globular seed receptacles of glossy green which measure 1 in (2·5 cm) across, though these are best removed to conserve the energies of the plant.

Species. *Vallota speciosa* (syn. *V. purpurea*). Native of Cape Province, it is one of the easiest of plants to manage indoors, for once established it is almost indestructible. It forms at the neck, a dozen or more strap-like leaves of brilliant glossy green, 20 in (50 cm) long and sheathing at the base. They are kept healthy and clean by occasionally wiping with a damp cloth. From the neck arises late in July a hollow glossy green leafless scape up to 1 in (2·5 cm) through and 18 in (45 cm) long, at the end of which is an umbel of eight to ten funnel-shaped flowers of vermilion red, 3 in (7·5 cm) across. Several open together in succession and are followed by glossy green seed pods. A specially selected form, developed in Holland, has large flowers, six to eight opening together and these are followed by others so that the plants remain colourful for six weeks or more.

VELTHEIMIA (Liliaceae)

A genus of six species, native of southern Africa and named in honour of Count Veltheim, a patron of botany in the eighteenth century. It has a large bulb covered in scales and fleshy leaves, attractively waved and borne in rosette fashion. The flowers appear in a drooping conical truss on a leafless scape. It requires greenhouse culture in Britain and northern Europe but only the minimum amount of heat. *V. glauca* blooms midwinter and *V. viridifolia* early in spring. Both species are suitable for the sunny window of a living-room.

Culture. Plant the bulbs in September, one to a 5-in (12·5-cm) pot containing a compost made up of fibrous loam, peat and decayed manure in equal parts, to which a sprinkling of sand is added. Place in a cool room for four weeks for the roots to form and before introducing to a temperature of 45° F (7° C) in which the plants grow during winter. Water sparingly, giving only sufficient moisture to keep the plants growing and taking care not to splash the foliage. After flowering, dry off the bulbs and place the pots on their side in a sunny position for the bulbs to ripen. They should be started into growth again early in autumn.

Propagation. When the bulbs are shaken from the pots after two years, offsets will be found around the mother bulb. These are removed, planted in small pots and grown on for two years in a sandy compost. They are then moved to a larger pot containing a compost made up of fibrous loam, peat and decayed manure, in which they remain for another two years, when they begin to bloom.

They may also be propagated by inserting the base of the leaves around the side of a pot or pan so that the leaves are in an upright position. The compost should be composed of equal parts peat and sand and must be kept moist. Syringe the leaves daily, to prevent rapid evaporation of moisture, while in sunny weather they should be shielded from the direct rays of the sun. In six to eight weeks bulbils will form at the base of the leaf where inserted in the compost. These are detached when the leaves die back and are grown on as offsets until they reach flowering size.

Species. *Veltheimia glauca*. Native of Natal and western Cape Province, it forms a large ovate bulb and a rosette of broad strap-shaped leaves of glaucous green, sheathing at the base and with deeply waved edges. The flowers are pendulous and are borne in a tubular truss. They are white, spotted with crimson and borne in December and March at the end of a 16-in (40-cm) scape.

Veltheimia viridiflora (syn. *V. capensis*). Native of Cape Province, it was introduced in 1759 by Linnaeus. It has a large ovoid bulb and a rosette of strap-like leaves 12 in (30 cm) long and waved at the edges. The flowers droop down, 50 to 60 comprising the inflorescence which is borne at the end of a 12-in (30-cm) scape. They are pinkish red, spotted with pale yellow and shaded green at the edge.

There was no variation in colour until, in 1956, van Tubergens raised Rosalba, which has white flowers shaded with shell pink. It won an Award of Merit at Chelsea Show in 1962.

W

WATSONIA (Iridaceae)

A genus of 60 or more species, native of southern Africa and Madagascar, known as the southern bugle lily, and named in honour of Dr Watson, a London apothecary. They have large globular fibrous-coated corms and sword-like leaves arranged fanwise, while they bear their flowers—which resemble those of *Antholyza* and *Crocosmia* (*Montbretia*)—in tall spikes of 6 to 12. The perianth tube is curved—the lower part cylindrical, the upper part funnel-shaped; the stamens inserted halfway down the tube; the style branches six. Not entirely hardy in the British Isles and northern Europe, the plants require similar culture to *Gladiolus* and *Crocosmia*.

Culture. Mostly flowering in their native lands during October and November, they bloom early in summer in Britain. However, *W. beatricis*, which is ever-green, is late summer-flowering. This species, with those that bloom late in summer and which die back after flowering, may be grown outdoors, being treated like *Crocosmia*. The corms are lifted in autumn and stored in a frost-free place. Those evergreen species should be grown where their foliage will be untroubled by winter frosts, in those gardens situated on the western part of Britain. They require plenty of moisture about their roots in summer and must be given an open, sunny situation and a well-drained soil containing some humus and grit. The evergreen species will appreciate some decayed manure in the soil at planting time in April. Plant the corms 4 in (10 cm) deep and 4 in (10 cm) apart, but allowing 8 in (20 cm) for the evergreen species which will eventually form large clumps. *W. densiflora* is a valuable species to plant for commercial cut bloom, the tall flower spikes of rich pink blossoms meeting with a ready sale in August.

The plants will require abundant moisture while growing, indeed the rare *W. stanfordiae* enjoys almost bog-like conditions in its natural haunts and may be planted by the waterside. The flower stems will be stunted if the plants lack moisture. They may require staking, for, with the exception of *W. humilis*, they grow between 3 and 4 ft (90 cm and 1·2 metres) tall. If planted in circular groups of six or more, twine fastened to canes inserted around each group in triangular form will prove efficient. After flowering, discontinue watering; and after the leaves have turned brown and died back, lift and dry the corms and store during winter. Water should not be entirely withheld from the evergreen species,

The early summer-flowering species should be grown in pots under glass, either in a cold greenhouse or in a frame. Plant four or five corms to a 5-in (12·5-cm) pot in November, 2 in (5 cm) deep and the same apart and in a compost made up of fibrous loam, decayed manure and grit in equal parts. Stand the pots in a frame and around them pack peat or ashes. Give no water while rooting takes place. Early in the year transfer to greenhouse or garden room and commence watering according to temperature. Heat is not necessary, but if it is required to bring the plants into bloom earlier, a temperature of 45° F (7° C) may be provided. At all times give plenty of fresh air. After flowering, allow the foliage to die back and place the pots outside on their side for the corms to ripen. Repot towards the end of autumn and start into growth again.

Propagation. Usually by means of cormlets, which are detached when the corms are repotted. Plant in boxes of sandy compost and grow on for two years until reaching flowering size.

The evergreen species should be lifted and divided in spring every fourth year.

Watsonias are also readily raised from seed sown in a sandy compost in spring. They should be allowed to remain undisturbed for two years. Cover them with a 1-in (2·5-cm) layer of compost (as for *Ixia*) after the young plants die back. The young corms may then be planted into the pots in which they will bloom, some three or four years after sowing the seed.

Species. *Watsonia aletroides*. Native of south-eastern Cape Province, it has narrow sword-shaped leaves and bears its spikes of brick-red flowers in May and June on a 2-ft (60-cm) stem. The flowers are tubular and more drooping than with other species and in the British Isles should be grown under glass.

Watsonia alpina. Native of the Transvaal, it is late summer-flowering and may be grown outdoors and lifted in autumn. It is a dainty species with deep pink bell-shaped flowers borne on a slender 2-ft (60-cm) stem. It has a large globose corm.

Watsonia angusta. It requires ample supplies of moisture about its roots and in the wild is usually to be found by the side of water. It has narrow lance-shaped leaves arranged in two rows, the lower leaves glaucous and it bears scarlet flowers in a 10- to 20-flowered lax spike. The perianth tube is long and cylindrical, the lobes narrow, opening star-like.

Watsonia ardernei. In bloom June and July, it is one of the more easily managed species, bearing large spikes of glistening white funnel-shaped flowers on a 3-ft (90-cm) stem.

Watsonia beatricis. Native of the Cape and Natal, it is an evergreen of great beauty with narrow sword-like leaves, while it bears its flowers in a long graceful raceme on 3- to 4-ft (90-cm to 1·2-metre) stems. The flowers, which open to

2 in (5 cm) across, vary in colour from orange pink to flame and terra-cotta. It blooms in September.

Watsonia comptonii. A common species of the marshlands around Simonstown. It is evergreen, requiring plenty of moisture in summer. It has two or three basal leaves 12 in (30 cm) long and bears its flowers in a lax raceme. They are orange, the perianth tube streaked white on the inside and with arching stamens.

Watsonia densiflora. Common in Orange Free State, it is late summer-flowering and, like *W. meriana*, bears its flowers on two sides of the 2-ft (60-cm) stem. The flowers, which are borne horizontally, have a long tube and are deep pink. When open the flowers almost touch each other.

Watsonia galpinii. A rare Cape species, it is late summer-flowering and is evergreen, requiring plenty of moisture about its roots in summer. It bears its tubular flowers of scarlet-orange in a slender spike and on a stem 2 ft (60 cm) tall.

Watsonia humilis. Native of the Cape, where it is common on sandy flats, it has two rows of narrow lance-shaped leaves 12 in (30 cm) long, and in mid-summer bears on an 18-in (45-cm) stem an 8- to 10-flowered spike of pale magenta flowers which are faintly scented.

Watsonia marginata. It grows on grassy slopes around Camps Bay and has lance-shaped leaves 2 ft (60 cm) long with prominent yellow margins. It bears, on a 3- to 4-ft (90-cm to 1·2-metre) stem, drooping flowers of lilac-pink or pale magenta in a densely packed spike. It is sweetly scented.

Watsonia meriana. Native of Natal, it is one of the hardier species with lance-shaped leaves strongly nerved, and early in summer bears flowers of deep orange pink arranged on two sides of the stem. The flowers are funnel-shaped with a curved cylindrical tube and are borne on a 2-ft (60-cm) stem.

Watsonia pyramidata (syn. *W. rosea*). It is the common pink Watsonia, present on grassy slopes of Cape Province where it is prominent after fires. It has six to eight glossy green leaves and bears its flowers on a 3-ft (90-cm) branching stem during midsummer. The flowers are funnel-shaped with spreading lobes and are of bright rose pink. The stamens and style are directed to one side. In those gardens enjoying a favourable winter climate, it may be left to form a large clump.

Watsonia spectabilis. Native of Cape Province, it is the earliest to bloom and should be grown under glass. It has dark-green lance-shaped leaves and bears, on a 20-in (50-cm) stem, drooping flowers of orange-red.

Watsonia stanfordiae. Native of Cape Province, it is evergreen and requires plenty of moisture about its roots. Like *W. beatricis*, it blooms late in summer, bearing its rosy-crimson flowers on 3- to 4-ft (90-cm to 1·2-metre) branched stems.

Watsonia tubularis. Present at the Cape, where it is found in damp places, it has sword-like leaves with a prominent mid-rib and bears its flowers of coral-pink in a loose many-flowered spike. The perianth tube is long and cylindrical, with the stamens and style arched under the upper lobe.

Z

ZEPHYRANTHES (Amaryllidaceae)

A genus of about 40 species, native of North and South America, Cuba and the West Indies and taking its name from *zephyros*, west wind, the reference being to the New World (in the west), their natural habitat. They have tunicated bulbs and narrow strap-like leaves, while they bear their erect urn-shaped flowers on hollow stems. Closely related to *Hippeastrum*, they require similar culture and—with the possible exception of *Z. candida*, which blooms in autumn—should be given a sunny position preferably in the rock garden and a soil enriched with humus and decayed manure. The soil should also be well drained. Plant the bulbs in April, 4 in (10 cm) deep and 6 in (15 cm) apart and do not disturb. Each year the blooms will increase in number as the plants form large clumps. After flowering, mulch with decayed manure and leaf mould, and during summer give the growing plants plenty of moisture.

Indoors, plant four or five bulbs to a 5-in (12·5-cm) pot or pan, using a compost composed of fibrous loam, leaf mould and decayed manure in equal parts. Add a liberal sprinkling of sand or grit. Plant *Z. atamasco* in October, for it blooms in spring; and the others in March, for they are late summer-flowering. Plant so that the top of the bulbs are level with the top of the compost and allow 2 in (5 cm) between each. Place in a cool room for several weeks for the bulbs to root, then gradually introduce to the greenhouse or garden room, admitting plenty of air and watering copiously as soon as the flower stems appear late in summer. Several species bloom with or just before the leaves. After flowering, allow the foliage to die back by drying off gradually, and during spring and early summer place the pots on their side in a sunny position to enable the bulbs to get a thorough baking and a long rest. Then bring into fresh growth by resuming watering about midsummer. The plants will benefit from a mulch of loam and decayed manure each year after resting but do not remove the bulbs from the pots. Like *Hippeastrum*, they flower best if pot-bound and should occupy the pots for five or six years.

Propagation. By offsets, which form about the mother bulb in large numbers and are detached when the older bulbs are ready for lifting or repotting which should be done only occasionally. Large offsets may be planted in their flowering pots; those of smaller size being grown on for two years in boxes of sandy compost until reaching flowering size. This plant resents being dried off and is best increased by division after flowering, being replanted without delay.

Species. *Zephyranthes atamasco.* Native of damp meadowlands of Virginia, it has bright-green leaves and bears pure-white flowers on 12-in (30-cm) stems during April and May. The flowers have broad segments terminating into a point and open flat and star-like. In the bud state they are tinted or striped with pink.

Zephyranthes aurea. Native of Peru, it is rare in cultivation and has narrow leaves about 12 in (30 cm) long and blooms late in summer, bearing orange-yellow funnel-shaped flowers on 12-in (30-cm) stems. When open, the blooms measure 3 in (7·5 cm) across.

Zephyranthes candida. The swamp lily of La Plata, it is the most satisfactory species for British gardens, where it proves almost hardy but will not be free-flowering until established, when it should never be disturbed. It has a large ovoid bulb covered in a dark-brown tunic and long round leaves, almost rush-like. It blooms in August and October, bearing its pure-white flowers with long narrow pointed segments on 9-in (22·5-cm) stems. The variety *major* has flowers which measure 4 in (10 cm) long and 2 in (5 cm) across, almost twice the size of the type. The flowers have orange anthers.

Zephyranthes citrina. Native of the swamplands of Guyana, it is tender and, though flowering early in autumn, requires greenhouse culture in Britain. It has stolon-bearing bulbs and narrow pale-green leaves, while it bears small bright lemon-yellow flowers on a two-edged scape. Crossed with *Z. candida*, it has produced a lovely hybrid, Ajax, which bears pale-yellow flowers.

Zephyranthes grandiflora (syn. *Z. carinata*). Native of the West Indies and Mexico, it requires cool greenhouse or room culture in Britain and blooms from early August until late September, bearing its rose-pink flowers on a 9-in (22·5-cm) stem amidst graceful rush-like leaves. The flowers, which are 2 in (5 cm) long, are enhanced by the golden anthers.

Zephyranthes robusta. It is present on rocky slopes around Buenos Aires and produces its rush-like grey-green leaves after the flowers, which appear in July and August. The blooms are deep rose red, about 3 in (7·5 cm) long and are borne in a 9-in (22·5-cm) scape. They retain their beauty for several weeks.

Zephyranthes rosea. Native of the mountains of Cuba, it closely resembles *Z. atamasco* but is autumn-flowering. It has bright-green linear leaves and bears small rosy-red flowers 1 in (2·5 cm) long, which are held on a 6-in (15-cm) stem. They open crocus-like.

Zephyranthes tubispatha. Native of the Blue Mountains of Jamaica and of Cuba, it has narrow linear leaves 12 in (30 cm) long. In July and August it bears white flowers shaded green at the base, with the segments opening flat as with *Z. atamasco*, the pedicel being longer than the spathe.

ZYGADENUS (Liliaceae)

A genus of 15 species, native of north-western America and Siberia and taking its name from *zygos*, a yoke, and *aden*, a gland, the reference being to the glands on the perianth. The plants have a bulbous-like rootstock and bear tufts of narrow grass-like leaves amidst which arises a 2-ft (60-cm) scape bearing a loose raceme of yellow or greenish-white flowers.

Culture. Closely related to *Camassia*, the plants require similar open woodland conditions and are at their best in an orchard or spinney where they bloom in the filtered sunlight of early summer. Plant in October, 3 in (7·5 cm) deep and 9 in (23 cm) apart in groups of five or six and leave undisturbed for a number of years. They require a soil with plenty of peat or leaf mould to retain summer moisture. If growing in grassland, do not cut the grass about the plants until they have died back in autumn.

Propagation. By offsets which are freely formed about the old bulbs. These are removed when the clumps are lifted after several years and are replanted. Those of larger size will bloom in two years.

Species. *Zygadenus angustifolius.* Native of north-western America, it has short grass-like leaves and bears a raceme of small white flowers which later turn purple, on 18-in (45-cm) stems.

Zygadenus fremontii. Native of north-western America, it has attractive basal leaves and bears its pale-yellow flowers in a large raceme at the end of a stout stem 2 ft (60 cm) tall. The flowers open star-like and measure 1 in (2·5 cm) across, making this the most attractive species.

APPENDIX A

Planting Depths (Outdoors)

---

1 in (2·5 cm) *(with the top of the bulb 1 in below the surface)*

Anemone blanda
Anemone coronaria
Anemone stellata
Cardiocrinum giganteum
Chlidanthus fragrans
Crinum americanum (neck at soil
    level)
Crinum asiaticum
Crinum bracteatum
Crinum latifolium
Crinum longifolium
Crinum macowani
Crinum moorei
Crinum pedunculatum
Cyclamen africanum
Cyclamen cilicium
Cyclamen creticum
Cyclamen cyprium
Cyclamen graecum
Cyclamen libanoticum
Cyclamen orbiculatum
Cyclamen pseudo ibericum
Cyclamen neapolitanum
Cyclamen repandum
Cyclamen rohlfsianum
Iris acutiloba
Iris alberti
Iris albicans
Iris atropurpurea
Iris barnumae
Iris biflora
Iris biliotti
Iris bismarkiana

Iris bracteata
Iris chamaeiris
Iris cristata
Iris douglassii
Iris duthiei
Iris flavescens
Iris florentina
Iris foetidissima
Iris gatesii
Iris germanica
Iris graminea
Iris hexagona
Iris hoogiana
Iris hookeriana
Iris iberica
Iris kaempferi
Iris korolkowii
Iris lortetii
Iris lutescens
Iris missouriensis
Iris pallida
Iris prismatica
Iris sambucina
Iris sari
Iris siberica
Iris stolonifera
Iris stylosa
Iris susiana
Iris tectorum
Iris variegata
Iris xiphioides
Iris xiphium
Lilium candidum

Lycoris aurea
Lycoris radiata
Lycoris sanguinea
Medeola virginiana
Polygonatum biflorum

Polygonatum multiflorum
Polygonatum odorum
Polygonatum officinale
Polygonatum oppositifolium
Polygonatum roseum

2 in (5 cm)

Eranthis cilicica
Eranthis hyemalis
Eranthis pinnatifida
Eranthis tubergenii
Exohebia fraterna
Exohebia parviflora
Iris danfordiae
Lilium rubescens
Lilium × testaceum
Lilium tsingtauense
Lloydia serotina
Merendera filifolia
Merendera montana
Merendera sobolifera
Merendera trigyna
Narcissus bulbocodium
Narcissus calcicola
Narcissus canaliculatus

Narcissus cyclamineus
Narcissus gracilis
Narcissus jonquilla
Narcissus juncifolius
Narcissus watieri
Narcissus minimus
Narcissus minor
Narcissus poeticus
Narcissus pseudo-narcissus
Narcissus rupicola
Narcissus scaberulus
Narcissus serotinus
Narcissus tazetta
Narcissus triandrus
Narcissus viridiflorus
Paradisia liliastrum
Ranunculus asiaticus

3 in (7·6 cm)

Allium accuminatum
Allied affatunense
Allium albopilosum
Allium album
Allium amabile
Allium beesianum
Allium coeruleum
Allium flavum
Allium giganteum
Allium kansuense
Allium korataviense
Allium moly
Allium narcissiflorum
Allium oreophilum
Allium pulchellum

Allium rosenbachianum
Allium tibeticum
Allium triquetrum
Allium ursinum
Anemone nemorosa
Anthericum liliago
Anthropodium cirrhatum
Anthropodium candidum
Bulbocodium vernum
Camassia cusickii
Camassia esculenta
Camassia fraseri
Camassia leichtlinii
Camassia quamash
Chionodoxa lucilae

Chionodoxa sardensis
Convallaria majalis
Crocus aërius
Crocus aleppicus
Crocus ancyrensis
Crocus asturicus
Crocus aureus
Crocus balansae
Crocus baryi
Crocus biflorus
Crocus byzantinus
Crocus cambessedesii
Crocus cancellatus
Crocus candidus
Crocus carpetanus
Crocus caspius
Crocus chrysanthus
Crocus clusii
Crocus corsicus
Crocus dalmaticus
Crocus danfordiae
Crocus etruscus
Crocus evijicii
Crocus fleischeri
Crocus goulimyi
Crocus graveolens
Crocus hartmannianus
Crocus hyemalis
Crocus imperati
Crocus karduchorum
Crocus korolkowi
Crocus laevigatus
Crocus leichtlinii
Crocus longiflorus
Crocus minimus
Crocus niveus
Crocus nudiflorus
Crocus ochroleucus
Crocus olivieri
Crocus pulchellus
Crocus salzmannii
Crocus sativus
Crocus scharojani

Crocus sieberi
Crocus speciosus
Crocus suaveolens
Crocus susianus
Crocus suterianus
Crocus tamasinianus
Crocus tournefortii
Crocus veluchensis
Crocus vernus
Crocus versicolor
Crocus vitellinus
Crocus zonatus
Dierama pulcherrima
Disporum hookeri
Disporum lanuginosum
Disporum menziesii
Endymion hispanica
Endymion non-scriptus
Erythronium albidum
Erythronium americanum
Erythronium californicum
Erythronium citrinum
Erythronium dens-canis
Erythronium grandiflorum
Erythronium hartwegii
Erythronium hendersonii
Erythronium montanum
Erythronium oregonum
Erythronium purpurescens
Erythronium revolutum
Erythronium tuolumnense
Ferraria undulata
Fritillaria acmopetala
Fritillaria armena
Fritillaria askabadensis
Fritillaria aurea
Fritillaria camschatcensis
Fritillaria caucasica
Fritillaria cirrhosa
Fritillaria citrina
Fritillaria crassifolia
Fritillaria delphinensis
Fritillaria discolor

Fritillaria divieri
Fritillaria gracilis
Fritillaria graeca
Fritillaria involucrata
Fritillaria liliacea
Fritillaria meleagris
Fritillaria oranensis
Fritillaria pallidiflora
Fritillaria persica
Fritillaria pontica
Fritillaria pudica
Fritillaria pyrenaica
Fritillaria recurva
Fritillaria sibthorpiana
Fritillaria thunbergii
Fritillaria verticillata
Gagea lutea
Hexaglottis flexuosa
Hexaglottis longifolia
Hyacinthus amethystinus
Hyacinthus azureus
Hyacinthus dalmaticus
Hyacinthus tabrizianus
Iris alata
Iris bakeriana
Iris bucharica
Iris caucasica
Iris fosteriana
Iris graeberiana
Iris histrio
Iris histrioides
Iris kolpakowskiana
Iris magnifica
Iris orchioides
Iris persica
Iris reticulata
Iris sindjarensis
Iris vartani
Iris winogradowii
Leucojum aestivum
Leucojum autumnale
Leucojum hyemale
Leucojum longifolium

Leucojum roseum
Leucojum tingitanum
Leucojum trichophyllum
Leucojum vernum
Libertia formosa
Libertia grandiflora
Libertia paniculata
Lilium davidii
Lilium duchartrei
Lilium grayi
Lilium kelloggii
Lilium nevadense
Lilium parvum
Lilium vollmeri
Lilium wigginsii
Moraea decussata
Moraea iridioides
Moraea pavonia
Moraea spathacea
Moraea villosa
Muscari ambrosiacum
Muscari argaei
Muscari armeniacum
Muscari botryoides
Muscari comosum
Muscari conicum
Muscari latifolium
Muscari massayanum
Muscari moschatum
Muscari paradoxum
Muscari pinardii
Muscari polyanthum
Muscari racemosum
Muscari tubergenianum
Ornithogalum montanum
Ornithogalum narbonense
Ornithogalum nutans
Ornithogalum pilosum
Ornithogalum pyramidale
Ornithogalum pyrenaicum
Ornithogalum umbellatum
Oxalis adenophylla
Oxalis brasiliensis

Oxalis enneaphylla
Oxalis lobata
Oxalis magellanica
Oxalis violacea
Puschkinia scilloides (formerly
    P. *libanotica*)
Reineckia carnea
Romulea bulbocodium
Romulea clusiana
Scilla amoena
Scilla autumnalis
Scilla bifolia
Scilla bithynica

Scilla hyacinthoides
Scilla italica
Scilla menophylla
Scilla messanaica
Scilla odorata
Scilla pratensis
Scilla sibirica
Scilla tubergeniana
Scilla verna
Zygadenus angustifolius
Zygadenus fremantii
Zygadenus glaucus

4 in (10 cm)

Acidanthera bicolor
Allium neapolitanum
Allium roseum
Allium schubertii
Bessera elegans
Bloomeria aurea
Bobartia filiformis
Bobartia gladiata
Bobartia indica
Bulbinella rossii
Calochortus albus
Calochortus amabilis
Calochortus benthamii
Calochortus clavatus
Calochortus coeruleus
Calochortus elegans
Calochortus leichtlinii
Calochortus lilacinus
Calochortus luteus
Calochortus macrocarpus
Calochortus maweanus
Calochortus purdyi
Calochortus venustus
Chasmanthe aethiopica
Colchicum agrippinum
Colchicum alpinum
Colchicum atropurpureum
Colchicum autumnale

Colchicum bowlesianum
Colchicum byzantinum
Colchicum catacurzenium
Colchicum cilicicum
Colchicum decaisnei
Colchicum doerfleri
Colchicum giganteum
Colchicum luteum
Colchicum macrophyllum
Colchicum sibthorpii
Colchicum speciosum
Colchicum stevenii
Colchicum tenorii
Colchicum triphyllum
Colchicum troodi
Colchicum variegatum
Cooperia drummondii
Cooperia pedunculata
Cypella gracilis
Cypella herbertii
Cypella peruviana
Cypella plumbea
Drimia pusilla
Fritillaria pinardii
Galanthus byzantinus
Galanthus caucasicus
Galanthus corcyrensis
Galanthus elwesii

Galanthus fosteri

Galanthus graecus

Galanthus ikariae

Galanthus nivalis

Galanthus plicatus

Galaxia gramminea

Galaxia ovata

Geissorhiza humilis

Geissorhiza inflexa

Geissorhiza juncea

Geissorhiza ovata

Geissorhiza secunda

Geissorhiza setacea

Gethyllis afra

Gethyllis ciliaris

Gladiolus alatus

Gladiolus angustus

Gladiolus atroviolaceus

Gladiolus aureus

Gladiolus blandus

Gladiolus byzantinus

Gladiolus carinatus

Gladiolus carmineus

Gladiolus caryophyllaceus

Gladiolus communis

Gladiolus cruentus

Gladiolus cuspidatus

Gladiolus illyricus

Gladiolus monticolus

Gladiolus ornatus

Gladiolus primulinus

Gladiolus psittacinus

Gladiolus purpureo-auratus

Gladiolus segetum

Habranthus brachyandrus

Habranthus robustus

Haemanthus katharinae

Herbertia amatorum

Herbertia pulchella

Hermodactylus tuberosus

Hippeastrum advenum

Hippeastrum candidum

Hypoxis hirsuta

Ipheion uniflorum

Iris juncea

Iris tingitana

Iris willmottiana

Ixia maculata

Ixia odorata

Ixia polystachya

Ixia viridiflora

Korolkowia seurgowii

Lapeyrousia corymbosa

Lapeyrousia cruenta

Lapeyrousia fabricii

Lapeyrousia fistulosa

Lilium bolanderi

Lilium carniolicum

Lilium cernuum

Lilium chalcedonicum

Lilium columbianum

Lilium concolor

Lilium dauricum

Lilium formosanum

Lilium humboldtii

Lilium lankangense

Lilium leucanthum

Lilium mackliniae

Lilium maritimum

Lilium medeoloides

Lilium michauxi

Lilium michiganense

Lilium monadelphum

Lilium nobilissimum

Lilium occidentale

Lilium papilliferum

Lilium pardalinum

Lilium parryi

Lilium pomponium

Lilium primulinum

Lilium pumilum

Lilium pyrenaicum

Lilium taliense

Lilium wardii

Nemastylis coelestina

Nemastylis graminiflora

Nerine bowdenii
Nomocharis aperta
Nomocharis farreri
Nomocharis mairei
Nomocharis meleagrina
Nomocharis pardanthina
Nonocharis saluenensis
Notholirion bulbuliferum
Notholirion campanulatum
Nothoscordum fragrans
Nothoscordum inodorum
Schizostylis coccinea
Trillium cernuum
Trillium chloropetalum
Trillium erectum
Trillium govanianum
Trillium grandiflorum
Trillium luteum
Trillium nivale
Trillium pusillum
Trillium recurvatum
Trillium sessile

Trillium smallii
Trillium stylosum
Trillium tschonoskii
Trillium undulatum
Tritonia crocata
Tropaeolum azureum
Tropaeolum moritzianum
Tropaeolum pentaphyllum
Tropaeolum polyphyllum
Tropaeolum speciosum
Tropaeolum tricolor
Tropaeolum tuberosum
Watsonia alpina
Watsonia beatricis
Watsonia densiflora
Watsonia galpinii
Watsonia humilis
Watsonia marginata
Watsonia meriana
Watsonia pyramidata
Watsonia stanfordiae

5 in (12·7 cm)

Albuca nelsonii
Belamcanda chinensis
Crocosmia aurea
Crocosmia masonorum
Crocosmia pottsii
Cyclamen europeum
Lilium bakerianum
Narcissus, Garden hybrids
Scilla peruviana

Sternbergia clusiana
Sternbergia colchiciflora
Sternbergia fischeriana
Sternbergia lutea
Tigridia curvata
Tigridia pavonia
Tigridia violacea
Zephyranthes candida

6 in (15 cm)

Agapanthus umbellatus
Alstroemeria aurantiaca
Alstroemeria chilensis
Alstroemeria haemantha
Alstroemeria ligtu
Alstroemeria pelegrina
Alstroemeria pulchella

Amaryllis belladonna
Antholyza ringens
Asphodelus luteus
Asphodelus ramosus
Babiana bainsii
Babiana hyemalis
Babiana plicata

Babiana stricta
Babiana tubiflora
Brodiaea bridgesi
Brodiaea californica
Brodiaea coccinea
Brodiaea congesta
Brodiaea crocea
Brodiaea grandiflora
Brodiaea hyacinthina
Brodiaea ixioides
Brodiaea laxa
Brodiaea minor
Brodiaea peduncularis
Brodiaea pulchella
Brodiaea rosea
Bulbine alooides
Bulbine asphodelioides
Bulbine favosa
Bulbine mackeni
Calostemma luteum
Fritillaria imperialis
Galtonia candicans
Galtonia clavata
Galtonia princeps
Gladiolus cardinalis
Homeria bulbifera
Homeria collina
Homeria miniata
Hymenocallis andreana
Hymenocallis narcissiflora
Ixiolirion kolpakowskianum
Ixiolirion montanum
Lilium amabile
Lilium auratum
Lilium brownii
Lilium canadense
Lilium japonicum
Lilium leichtlinii
Lilium longiflorum
Lilium martagon
Lilium neilgherrense
Lilium philadelphicum
Lilium philippinense

Lilium regale
Lilium rubellum
Lilium speciosum
Lilium sulphureum
Lilium tigrinum
Lilium wallichianum
Pancratium illyricum
Pancratium maritimum
Tecophilaea cyanocrocus
Tulipa acuminata
Tulipa aucheriana
Tulipa batalinii
Tulipa biflora
Tulipa borszczowi
Tulipa clusiana
Tulipa eichleri
Tulipa fosteriana
Tulipa, Garden hybrids
Tulipa gesneriana
Tulipa greigii
Tulipa hageri
Tulipa hoogiana
Tulipa humilis
Tulipa ingens
Tulipa kaufmanniana
Tulipa kolpakowskiana
Tulipa lanata
Tulipa linifolia
Tulipa maximowiczii
Tulipa montana
Tulipa orphanidea
Tulipa ostrowskiana
Tulipa persica
Tulipa polychroma
Tulipa praestans
Tulipa primulina
Tulipa pulchella
Tulipa saxatilis
Tulipa schrenki
Tulipa sprengeri
Tulipa stellata
Tulipa suaveolens
Tulipa sylvestris

Tulipa tarda
Tulipa triphylla
Tulipa tubergeniana
Tulipa turkestanica
Tulipa undulatifolia
Tulipa urumiensis

Urginea altissima
Urginea filifolia
Urginea flexuosa
Urginea maritima
Urginea salteri

8 to 10 in (20 to 25 cm)

Lilium hansonii
Lilium henryi

Lilium napalense
Lilium washingtonianum

7 to 8 in (18 to 20 cm)

Hyacinthus orientalis

Bulbs and their Habitat

Species	Habitat	Colour	Height
Achimenes antirrhina	Mexico	Orange	3 ft (90 cm)
Achimenes bella	Brazil	Mid blue	2 ft (60 cm)
Achimenes coccinea	Jamaica	Red	15 in (37·5 cm)
Achimenes ghiesbreghti	Mexico	Crimson	16 in (40 cm)
Achimenes grandiflora	Mexico	Purple	15 in (37·5 cm)
Achimenes harveyi	Jamaica	Orange	12 in (30 cm)
Achimenes hirsuta	Guatemala	Rose	15 in (37·5 cm)
Achimenes jaureguia maxima	Brazil	White	12 in (30 cm)
Achimenes longiflora major	Guatemala	White	12 in (30 cm)
Achimenes patens major	Mexico	Purple	15 in (37·5 cm)
Achimenes pedunculata	Mexico	Yellow	3 ft (90 cm)
Achimenes tubiflora	Buenos Aires	White	18 in (45 cm)
Acidanthera aequinoctialis	Sierra Leone	White	3 to 4 ft (90 cm to 1·2 metres)
Acidanthera bicolor	Abyssinia	Cream	18 in (45 cm)
Acidanthera candida	Eastern Africa	White	18 in (45 cm)
Agapanthus pendulinus	South Africa	Dark blue	5 to 6 ft (1·5 to 1·8 metres)
Agapanthus umbellatus	South Africa	Hyacinth blue	2 ft (60 cm)
Albuca elwesii	Eastern Africa	Green	12 in (30 cm)
Albuca nelsonii	Natal	White	4 to 5 ft (1·2 to 1·5 metres)
Allium accuminatum	North-west America	Lilac-pink	12 in (30 cm)
Allium affatunensis	Northern Persia	Lilac	3 ft (90 cm)
Allium albopilosum	Persia	Lilac-pink	2 ft (60 cm)
Allium album	Siberia	White	18 in (45 cm)
Allium amabile	Yunnan	Rosy red	6 in (15 cm)
Allium beesianum	North-western China	Pale blue	9 in (22·5 cm)
Allium coeruleum	Siberia	Mid blue	2 ft (60 cm)
Allium elatum	Central Asia	Rosy lilac	3 ft (90 cm)
Allium flavum	Southern Europe	Buff	12 in (30 cm)
Allium giganteum	Siberia	Deep lilac	3 to 4 ft (90 cm to 1·2 metres)
Allium kansuense	Kansu	Blue	6 in (15 cm)
Allium karataviense	Turkestan	Lilac-grey	12 in (30 cm)
Allium moly	Southern Europe	Yellow	12 in (30 cm)
Allium narcissiflorum	S. Italy	Ruby-red	6 in (15 cm)
Allium neapolitanum	S. Italy	White	12 in (30 cm)
Allium oreophilum	Turkestan	Carmine	6 in (15 cm)
Allium pulchellum	Southern Europe	Violet-rose	2 ft (60 cm)
Allium rosenbachianum	Central Asia	Purple	3 to 4 ft (90 cm to 1·2 metres)
Allium roseum	Mediterranean	Rose pink	9 in (22·5 cm)
Allium schubertii	Israel	Rosy red	2 ft (60 cm)
Allium tibeticum	Tibet	Blue	6 in (15 cm)

Species	Habitat	Colour	Height
Allium triquetrum	Southern Europe	Greeny-white	12 in (30 cm)
Allium ursinum	British Isles	White	16 in (40 cm)
Alstroemeria aurantiaca	Chile, Peru	Orange	3 ft (90 cm)
Alstroemeria brasiliensis	Brazil	Red-bronze	3 ft (90 cm)
Alstroemeria chilensis	Chile	Red pink	2 ft (60 cm)
Alstroemeria caryophyllea	Brazil	Scarlet	9 in (22·5 cm)
Alstroemeria haemantha	Chile	Scarlet	3 ft (90 cm)
Alstroemeria ligtu	Chile	Various	2 ft (60 cm)
Alstroemeria pelegrina	Peru	Lilac	12 in (30 cm)
Alstroemeria pulchella	Brazil	Wine red	3 ft (90 cm)
Amaryllis belladonna	South Africa	Rose pink	20 in (50 cm)
Ammocharis falcata	Southern Africa	Rose pink	18 in (45 cm)
Anemone apennina	Southern Europe	Sky blue	6 in (15 cm)
Anemone biflora	Kashmir	Lilac	6 in (15 cm)
Anemone blanda	Greece	Blue	6 in (15 cm)
Anemone coronaria	Southern Europe	Various	12 in (30 cm)
Anemone fulgens	Pyrenees	Scarlet	10 in (25 cm)
Anemone nemorosa	British Isles	White	6 in (15 cm)
Anemone palmata	Southern France	Yellow	6 in (15 cm)
Anemone ranunculoides	South-eastern Europe	Yellow	6 in (15 cm)
Anemone stellata	Southern Europe	Various	12 in (30 cm)
Anthericum liliago	Southern Europe	White	2 ft (60 cm)
Anthericum ramosum	Southern Europe	White	20 in (50 cm)
Antholiza ringens	Southern Africa	Scarlet	18 in (45 cm)
Arthropodium candidum	Australasia	White	6 in (15 cm)
Arthropodium cirrhatum	Australasia	White	3 ft (90 cm)
Asphodelus luteus	South-eastern Europe	Yellow	3 ft (90 cm)
Asphodelus ramosus	Southern Europe	White	4 to 5 ft (1·26 to 1·5 metres)
Aspidistra lurida	China, Japan	White	18 in (45 cm)
Babiana bainsii	Cape Province	Blue	6 in (15 cm)
Babiana disticha	Southern Africa	Pale blue	12 in (30 cm)
Babiana hyemalis	Cape Province	Pale blue	6 in (15 cm)
Babiana plicata	Southern Africa	Violet	4 in (10 cm)
Babiana stricta	Cape Province	Blue	10 in (25 cm)
Babiana tubiflora	Cape Province	Cream	9 in (22·5 cm)
Belamcanda chinensis	China	Red	3 ft (90 cm)
Bessera elegans	Mexico	Orange	2 ft (60 cm)
Bloomeria aurea	California	Yellow	12 in (30 cm)
Bobartia filiformis	Southern Africa	Yellow	18 in (45 cm)
Bobartia gladiata	Southern Africa	Yellow	2 ft (60 cm)
Bobartia indica	Southern Africa	Lemon	20 in (50 cm)
Bomarea caldasiana	Ecuador	Yellow, brown	cl.
Bomarea carderi	Colombia	Pink	cl.
Bomarea edulis	Cuba	Pink	cl.
Bomarea frondea	Colombia	Crimson	cl.
Bomarea patacocensis	Ecuador	Scarlet	cl.
Bravoa bulliana	Mexico	White	2 ft (60 cm)
Bravoa geminiflora	Mexico	Coral red	18 in (45 cm)
Broadiaea bridgesi	Oregon	Lilac-pink	18 in (45 cm)
Brodiaea californica	California	Rosy lilac	18 in (45 cm)
Brodiaea coccinea	California	Crimson	2 ft (60 cm)
Brodiaea congesta	California	Blue	3 to 4 ft (90 cm to 1·2 metres)
Brodiaea crocea	California	Yellow	8 in (20 cm)
Brodiaea grandiflora	British Columbia	Violet-blue	6 in (15 cm)

Species	Habitat	Colour	Height
Brodiaea hyacinthina	Missouri	Violet	18 in (45 cm)
Brodiaea ixioides	California	Yellow	18 in (45 cm)
Brodiaea laxa	California	Mauve	2 ft (60 cm)
Brodiaea minor	British Columbia	Violet-blue	3 in (7·5 cm)
Brodiaea peduncularis	California	Blush white	20 in (50 cm)
Brodiaea pulchella	North-west America	Violet-blue	15 in (40 cm)
Brodiaea rosea	North-west America	Rosy red	4 in (10 cm)
Brunsvigia gigantea	Cape Province	Red	20 in (50 cm)
Brunsvigia josephinae	Cape Province	Scarlet	18 in (45 cm)
Bulbine alooides	Cape Province	Yellow	10 in (25 cm)
Bulbine asphodelioides	Cape Province	Yellow	10 in (25 cm)
Bulbine favosa	Cape Province	Yellow	12 in (30 cm)
Bulbine mackeni	Cape Province	Yellow	12 in (30 cm)
Bulbinella floribunda	Southern Africa	Cream	3 ft (90 cm)
Bulbinella hookeri	New Zealand	Yellow	20 in (50 cm)
Bulbinella rossii	New Zealand	Yellow	3 to 4 ft (90 cm to 1·2 metres)
Bulbocodium vernum	Central European Alps	Rosy mauve	4 in (10 cm)
Caliphruria hartwegiana	Bogota	White	12 in (50 cm)
Callipsyche aurantiaca	Peru	Yellow	2 ft (60 cm)
Callipsyche bicolor	Peru	Orange	12 in (30 cm)
Callipsyche eucrosioides	Peru	Yellow	2 ft (60 cm)
Callipsyche mirabilis	Peru	Yellow	3 ft (90 cm)
Calochortus albus	California	Pinkish white	18 in (45 cm)
Calochortus amabilis	California	Yellow	12 in (30 cm)
Calochortus benthamii	California	Lemon	6 in (15 cm)
Calochortus clavatus	California	Yellow	3 ft (60 cm)
Calochortus coeruleus	California	Blue	5 in (12·5 cm)
Calochortus elegans	California	Greenish white	6 in (15 cm)
Calochortus leichtlinii	California	Green, red	18 in 45 cm)
Calochortus lilacinus	California	Lilac	6 in (15 cm)
Calochortus luteus	California	Yellow	18 in (45 cm)
Calochortus macrocarpus	British Columbia	Violet	15 in (37·5 cm)
Calochortus maweanus	California	Cream	6 in (15 cm)
Calochortus nitidus	California	White	18 in (45 cm)
Calochortus purdyi	California	White	12 in (30 cm)
Calochortus venustus	Southern California	Yellow	18 in (45 cm)
Calochortus weedii	Southern California	Yellow	18 in (45 cm)
Calostemma album	Eastern Australia	White	18 in (45 cm)
Calostemma luteum	Eastern Australia	Yellow	16 in (40 cm)
Calostemma purpureum	Eastern Australia	Rosy purple	20 in (50 cm)
Camassia cusickii	Oregon	Mid blue	3 ft (90 cm)
Camassia esculenta	Oregon	Dark blue	2 ft (60 cm)
Camassia fraseri	Oregon	Pale blue	18 in (45 cm)
Camassia leichtlinii	Oregon	Cream	3 to 4 ft (90 cm to 1·2 metres)
Camassia quamash	North-west America	Dark blue	2 ft (60 cm)
Cardiocrinum cathayanum	Western China	Cream	3 to 4 ft (90 cm to 1·2 metres)
Cardiocrinum cordatum	Japan	Ivory white	6 ft (1·8 metres)
Cardiocrinum giganteum	Assam	White	10 ft (3 metres)
Chasmanthe aethiopica	Ethiopia	Scarlet	3 ft (90 cm)
Chasmanthe floribunda	Cape Province	Orange	2 ft (60 cm)
Chionodoxa cretica	Crete	Pale blue	9 in (23 cm)
Chionodoxa gigantea	Turkey	Blue	6 in (15 cm)
Chionodoxa luciliae	Turkey	Blue	6 in (15 cm)

Species	Habitat	Colour	Height
Chionodoxa nana	Crete	Pale blue	3 in (7·5 cm)
Chionodoxa sardensis	Sardinia	Blue	4 in (10 cm)
Chionodoxa tmoli	Asia Minor	Dark blue	3 in (7·5 cm)
Chlidanthus fragrans	Argentine	Yellow	12 in (30 cm)
Clivia gardeni	Natal	Orange	18 in (45 cm)
Clivia miniata	Natal	Scarlet	18 in (45 cm)
Clivia nobilis	Natal	Scarlet	12 in (30 cm)
Colchicum agrippinum	Levant	Lilac	4 in (10 cm)
Colchicum alpinum	European Alps	Rosy lilac	1 in (2·5 cm)
Colchicum autumnale	British Isles	Mauve-pink	2 in (5 cm)
Colchicum bowlesianum	Salonica	Lilac-pink	12 in (30 cm)
Colchicum byzantinum	Asia Minor	Lilac-pink	6 in (15 cm)
Colchicum catacuzenium	Greece	Lilac-pink	1 in (2·5 cm)
Colchicum cilicicum	Asia Minor	Purple	6 in (15 cm)
Colchicum decaisnei	Syria	Pale pink	1 in (2·5 cm)
Colchicum doerfleri	Macedonia	Lilac-rose	2 in (5 cm)
Colchicum giganteum	Greece	Rosy mauve	10 in (25 cm)
Colchicum luteum	Northern India	Yellow	1 in (2·5 cm)
Colchicum macrophyllum	Crete	Lilac	6 in (15 cm)
Colchicum sibthorpii	Greece	Lilac	6 in (15 cm)
Colchicum speciosum	Greece	Crimson-purple	12 in (30 cm)
Colchicum stevenii	Palestine	Rosy mauve	3 in (7·5 cm)
Colchicum tenorii	Italy	Rosy mauve	3 in (7·5 cm)
Colchicum triphyllum	Morocco	Rosy lilac	2 in (5 cm)
Colchicum troodi	Cyprus	Lilac	2 in (5 cm)
Colchicum variegatum	Greece	Rosy lilac	3 in (7·5 cm)
Convallaria majalis	Northern Europe	White	6 in (15 cm)
Cooperia drummondii	Texas	White	9 in (22·5 cm)
Cooperia pedunculata	Texas	White	12 in (30 cm)
Crinum amabile	Sumatra	Red	2 ft (60 cm)
Crinum americanum	Southern United States	White	2 ft (60 cm)
Crinum asiaticum	South-eastern Asia	Greenish white	3 ft (90 cm)
Crinum bracteatum	Seychelles	White	12 in (30 cm)
Crinum latifolium	Tropical Asia	Greenish white	18 in (45 cm)
Crinum longifolium	Natal	Pinkish white	12 in (30 cm)
Crinum macowani	Natal	Lilac-pink	2 ft (60 cm)
Crinum moorei	Natal	Rose pink	2 ft (60 cm)
Crinum pedunculatum	Queensland	Greenish white	3 ft (90 cm)
Crocosmia aurea	Natal	Golden orange	2 ft (60 cm)
Crocosmia masonorum	Natal	Orange-red	2 ft (60 cm)
Crocosmia pottsii	Natal	Orange-yellow	3 ft (90 cm)
Crocus aerius	Asia Minor	Lilac-blue	4 in (10 cm)
Crocus aleppicus	Palestine	White	3 in (7·5 cm)
Crocus ancyrensis	Turkey	Orange	3 in (7·5 cm)
Crocus asturicus	Northern Spain	Violet	5 in (12·5 cm)
Crocus aureus	Balkans	Orange	3 in (7·5 cm)
Crocus balansae	Smyrna	Orange	4 in (10 cm)
Crocus biflorus	South-eastern Europe	Silvery lilac	4 in (10 cm)
Crocus boryi	South-western Greece	White	3 in (7·5 cm)
Crocus byzantinus	Hungary	Purple	4 in (12·5 cm)
Crocus cambressedesii	Majorca	Lilac	3 in (7·5 cm)
Crocus cancellatus	Greece	White, grey	3 in (7·5 cm)
Crocus candidus	Levant	Creamy yellow	4 in (10 cm)
Crocus carpetanus	Portugal	Lilac-grey	1 in (2·5 cm)
Crocus caspius	Caspian Sea	White	3 in (7·5 cm)
Crocus chrysanthus	South-eastern Europe	Orange-yellow	4 in (10 cm)

Species	Habitat	Colour	Height
Crocus clusii	Portugal	Purple	3 in (7·5 cm)
Crocus corsicus	Corsica	Cream, purple	6 in (15 cm)
Crocus cvijicii	Albania	Lemon-yellow	3 in (7·5 cm)
Crocus dalmaticus	Jugoslavia	Greyish lilac	4 in (10 cm)
Crocus danfordiae	Asia Minor	Pale yellow	2 in (5 cm)
Crocus etruscus	Tuscany	Greyish mauve	4 in (10 cm)
Crocus fleischeri	Asia Minor	White	3 in (7·5 cm)
Crocus goulimyi	Southern Greece	Pale lilac	4 in (10 cm)
Crocus graveolens	Syria	Golden yellow	3 in (7·5 cm)
Crocus hartmannianus	Cyprus	Lilac-purple	4 in (10 cm)
Crocus hyemalis	Palestine	White	3 in (7·5 cm)
Crocus imperati	Naples	Lilac-mauve	4 in (10 cm)
Crocus karduchorum	Kirdistan	Lilac-pink	5 in (12·5 cm)
Crocus korolkowi	Turkestan	Greenish yellow	3 in (7·5 cm)
Crocus laevigatus	Greece	White	3 in (7·5 cm)
Crocus leichtlinii	Asia Minor	Greenish yellow	3 in (7·5 cm)
Crocus longiflorus	Southern Italy	Violet	5 in (12·5 cm)
Crocus minimus	Corsica	Purple	2 in (5 cm)
Crocus niveus	South-western Greece	White	5 in (12·5 cm)
Crocus nudiflorus	Pyrenees	Purple	4 in (10 cm)
Crocus ochroleucus	Syria	Cream	4 in (10 cm)
Crocus olivieri	Bulgaria	Orange	3 in (7·5 cm)
Crocus pulchellus	Turkey	Lavender	3 in (7·5 cm)
Crocus salzmannii	Gibraltar	Pale lilac	3 in (7·5 cm)
Crocus sativus	Asia Minor	Purple-red	4 in (10 cm)
Crocus scharojani	Southern Russia	Orange	3 in (7·5 cm)
Crocus sieberi	Crete	Lilac-maroon	5 in (12·5 cm)
Crocus speciosus	Central Europe	Lavender-blue	5 in (12·5 cm)
Crocus suaveolens	Southern Italy	Lilac-mauve	4 in (10 cm)
Crocus susianus	Crimea	Orange	4 in (10 cm)
Crocus suterianus	Central Asia Minor	Orange	3 in (7·5 cm)
Crocus tomasinianus	South-eastern Europe	Lavender-blue	4 in (12·5 cm)
Crocus tournefortii	Greek islands	Rosy lilac	4 in (10 cm)
Crocus veluchensis	Greece	Pale lilac	4 in (10 cm)
Crocus vernus	Southern Europe	Purple	4 in (10 cm)
Crocus versicolor	Southern Europe	Pale mauve	4 in (10 cm)
Crocus vitellinus	Syria	Golden yellow	4 in (10 cm)
Crocus zonatus	Southern Europe	Rosy mauve	4 in (10 cm)
Cyclamen africanum	Northern Africa	Rose red	6 in (15 cm)
Cyclamen cilicium	Lebanon	Pale pink	6 in (15 cm)
Cyclamen creticum	Crete	White	4 in (10 cm)
Cyclamen cyprium	Cyprus	Pink	4 in (10 cm)
Cyclamen europeum	Europe	Carmine	6 in (15 cm)
Cyclamen graecum	Crete, Rhodes	Lilac-pink	6 in (15 cm)
Cyclamen libanoticum	Mount Lebanon	Salmon pink	6 in (15 cm)
Cyclamen neapolitanum	Southern Italy	Mauve-pink	6 in (15 cm)
Cyclamen orbiculatum	Caucasus	Reddish purple	6 in (15 cm)
Cyclamen persicum	Syria	Blush white	6 in (15 cm)
Cyclamen pseudo-ibericum	Turkey	Violet	6 in (15 cm)
Cyclamen repandum	Southern Italy	Rosy lilac	4 in (10 cm)
Cyclamen rohlfsianum	North Africa	Dark red	4 in (10 cm)
Cypella gracilis	Argentine	Yellow	2 ft (60 cm)
Cypella herbertii	Brazil	Orange-yellow	18 in (45 cm)
Cypella peruviana	Peru	Yellow	18 in (45 cm)
Cypella plumbea	Mexico	Grey-blue	3 ft (90 cm)
Cyrtanthus angustifolius	Cape Province	Orange	12 in (30 cm)

Species	Habitat	Colour	Height
Cyrtanthus huttoni	Cape Province	Red	12 in (30 cm)
Cyrtanthus lutescens	Cape Province	Yellow	15 in (37·5 cm)
Cyrtanthus mackenii	Natal	Apricot, pink	10 in (25 cm)
Cyrtanthus obliquus	Cape Province	Red	2 ft (60 cm)
Cyrtanthus o'brienii	Natal	Scarlet	16 in (40 cm)
Cyrtanthus sanguineus	Natal	Cherry red	9 in (22·5 cm)
Cyrtanthus spiralis	Eastern Africa	Red	12 in (30 cm)
Cyrtanthus tuckii	Eastern South Africa	Orange	12 in (30 cm)
Dierama pulcherrima	Southern Africa	Red	5 to 6 ft (1·5 to 1·8 metres)
Dipcadi hyacinthiflora	Cape Province	Greenish brown	2 ft (60 cm)
Dipcadi longifolium	Mozambique	Greenish blue	3 ft (90 cm)
Dipcadi serotinum	Southern Spain	Greenish brown	9 in (22·5 cm)
Disporum hookeri	North America	Greenish yellow	12 in (30 cm)
Disporum lanuginosum	North America	Greenish yellow	12 in (30 cm)
Disporum menziesii	North America	Greenish white	2 ft (60 cm)
Drimia elata	Southern Africa	Silvery green	18 in (45 cm)
Drimia pusilla	Southern Africa	Greenish brown	12 in (30 cm)
Endymion hispanica	Spain	White, blue, pink	18 in (45 cm)
Endymion non-scriptus	British Isles	Blue	18 in (45 cm)
Eranthis cilicica	Greece	Yellow	2 in (5 cm)
Eranthis hyemalis	Western Europe	Pale yellow	2 in (5 cm)
Eranthis pinnatifida	Northern Japan	White	1 in (2·5 cm)
Erythronium albidum	Eastern United States	White	9 in (22·5 cm)
Erythronium americanum	Eastern United States	Pale yellow	9 in (22·5 cm)
Erythronium californicum	California	Cream	9 in (22·5 cm)
Erythronium citrinum	Oregon	Creamy yellow	6 in (15 cm)
Erythronium dens-canis	Eastern Europe, Siberia	Purple	6 in (15 cm)
Erythronium grandiflorum	Central United States	Golden yellow	9 in (22·5 cm)
Erythronium hartwegii	California	Pale yellow	6 in (15 cm)
Erythronium hendersonii	Oregon	Lavender	6 in (15 cm)
Erythronium montanum	Oregon	Cream	6 in (15 cm)
Erythronium oregonum	Oregon	Creamy white	6 in (15 cm)
Erythronium purpurascens	Montana	Pale yellow	6 in (15 cm)
Erythronium revolutum	California	Pink, brown	6 in (15 cm)
Erythronium tuolumnense	Oregon	Golden yellow	10 in (25 cm)
Eucharis amazonica	Colombia	White	2 ft (60 cm)
Eucharis candida	Columbia	White	18 in (45 cm)
Eucharis mastersi	Colombia	White	12 in (30 cm)
Eucharis sanderi	Colombia	White	18 in (45 cm)
Eucomis bicolor	Natal	Greenish white	15 in (37·5 cm)
Eucomis pole-evansii	Transvaal	Greenish yellow	5 to 6 ft (1·5 to 1·8 metres)
Eucomis nana	Natal	Brownish green	9 in (22·5 cm)
Eucomis punctata	Natal	Cream	20 in (50 cm)
Eucomis undulata	Natal	Cream	18 in (45 cm)
Eucrosia bicolor	Ecuador	Yellow	12 in (30 cm)
Eurycles cunninghami	Queensland	White	12 in (30 cm)
Eurycles sylvestris	Northern Australia	White	15 in (37·5 cm)
Eustephia coccinea	Peru	Crimson	15 in (37·5 cm)
Exohebea fraterna	Southern Africa	Cream	18 in (45 cm)
Exohebea parviflora	Southern Africa	Yellow-maroon	18 in (45 cm)
Ferraria undulenta	Southern Africa	Purple-brown	15 in (37·5 cm)
Freesia refracta	Southern Africa	Cream	18 in (45 cm)
Fritillaria acmopetala	Levant	Bronzey green	6 in (15 cm)
Fritillaria armena	Turkey	Yellow and maroon	9 in (22·5 cm)

Species	Habitat	Colour	Height
Fritillaria askabadensis	Caucasus	Greenish yellow	3 ft (90 cm)
Fritillaria aurea	Caucasus	Yellow and brown	4 in (10 cm)
Fritillaria camschatcensis	Northern China, Japan	Purple	12 in (30 cm)
Fritillaria caucasica	Caucasus	Mahogany	12 in (30 cm)
Fritillaria cirrhosa	Himalayas	Purple	2 ft (60 cm)
Fritillaria citrina	Asia Minor	Pale yellow	6 in (15 cm)
Fritillaria crassifolia	Syria	Purple	15 in (37·5 cm)
Fritillaria delphinensis	Southern France	Purple	6 in (15 cm)
Fritillaria discolor	Turkey	Yellow	12 in (30 cm)
Fritillaria gracilis	Eastern Adriatic	Greenish yellow	12 in (30 cm)
Fritillaria graeca	Greece	Olive green	6 in (15 cm)
Fritillaria imperialis	Turkey	Yellow, orange	3 ft (90 cm)
Fritillaria involucrata	Southern France	Wine red	12 in (30 cm)
Fritillaria liliacea	Northern California	Creamy green	9 in (22·5 cm)
Fritillaria meleagris	France	Purple	12 in (30 cm)
Fritillaria olivieri	Persia	Green	12 in (30 cm)
Fritillaria oranensis	North-western Africa	Purple	12 in (30 cm)
Fritillaria pallidiflora	Siberia	Creamy yellow	9 in (23 cm)
Fritillaria persica	Persia	Violet	3 ft (90 cm)
Fritillaria pinardii	Turkey	Purple	9 in (22·5 cm)
Fritillaria pontica	Balkans	Yellow, purple	18 in (45 cm)
Fritillaria pudica	Rocky Mountains	Yellow	6 in (15 cm)
Fritillaria pyrenaica	Pyrenees	Purple-brown	20 in (50 cm)
Fritillaria recurva	Oregon	Orange	2 ft (60 cm)
Fritillaria ruthenica	Black Sea shores	Wine purple	2 ft (60 cm)
Fritillaria sibthorpiana	Bulgaria	Yellow	6 in (15 cm)
Fritillaria thunbergii	Northern China Japan	Creamy yellow	12 in (30 cm)
Fritillaria verticillata	Northern China, Japan	Cream	2 ft (60 cm)
Gagea lutea	Northern Europe	Greenish yellow	6 in (15 cm)
Galanthus byzantinus	Western Turkey	White and green	6 in (15 cm)
Galanthus caucasicus	Caucasus	White	9 in (23·5 cm)
Galanthus corcyrensis	Sicily	White and green	6 in (15 cm)
Galanthus elwesii	Western Turkey	White, green	6 in (15 cm)
Galanthus fosteri	Lebanon	White and green	12 in (30 cm)
Galanthus graecus	Northern Greece	White and green	6 in (15 cm)
Galanthus ikariae	Nikaria	White, green	6 in (15 cm)
Galanthus nivalis	British Isles	White and green	4 in (10 cm)
Galanthus plicatus	Southern U.S.S.R.	White and green	6 in (15 cm)
Galaxia gramminea	Cape Province	Yellow	1 in (2·5 cm)
Galaxia ovata	Cape Province	Yellow	1 in (2·5 cm)
Galtonia candicans	Natal	Greenish white	5 to 6 ft (1·5 to 1·8 metres)
Galtonia elavata	Natal	Creamy white	3 ft (90 cm)
Galtonia princeps	Natal	Greenish white	3 ft (90 cm)
Geissorhiza humilis	Cape Province	Yellow	10 in (25 cm)
Geissorhiza inflexa	Cape Province	Yellow	18 in (45 cm)
Geissorhiza juncea	Cape Province	Cream	18 in (45 cm)
Geissorhiza ovata	Cape Province	Cream	8 in (20 cm)
Geissorhiza secunda	Cape Province	Purple-blue	9 in (22·5 cm)
Geissorhiza setacea	Cape Province	Ivory	9 in (22·5 cm)
Geissorhiza umbrosa	Cape Province	White	15 in (37·5 cm)
Gesneria blassii	Brazil	Cinnabar red	6 in (15 cm)
Gesneria donkelaari	Peru	Red	8 in (20 cm)
Gesneria douglasii	Peru	Red	8 in (20 cm)
Gesneria lindleyi	Brazil	Pink	8 in (20 cm)
Gesneria macrantha	Brazil	Red	6 in (15 cm)

Species	Habitat	Colour	Height
Gesneria naegelioides	Brazil	Pink	8 in (20 cm)
Gesneria pendulina	Mexico	Scarlet	8 in (20 cm)
Gethyllis afra	Cape Province	White and red	4 in (10 cm)
Gethyllis ciliaris	Cape Province	White	4 in (10 cm)
Gladiolus alatus	Cape Province	Brick red	10 in (25 cm)
Gladiolus angustus	Cape Province	White	18 in (45 cm)
Gladiolus atroviolaceus	Northern Turkey	Violet-purple	2 ft (60 cm)
Gladiolus aureus	Cape Province	Yellow	2 ft (60 cm)
Gladiolus blandus	Cape Province	Creamy white	20 in (50 cm)
Gladiolus brevifolius	Cape Province	Pink	20 in (50 cm)
Gladiolus byzantinus	Asia Minor	Magenta	2 to 3 ft (60 to 90 cm)
Gladiolus cardinalis	Natal	Scarlet	2 ft (60 cm)
Gladiolus carnatus	Cape Province	Violet	18 in (45 cm)
Gladiolus carmineus	Natal	Pink	12 in (30 cm)
Gladiolus communis	Southern Europe	Bright rose	2 ft (60 cm)
Gladiolus confusus	Cape Province	Yellow-brown	18 in (45 cm)
Gladiolus caryophyllaceus	Natal	Rose pink	2 ft (60 cm)
Gladiolus cruentus	Cape Province	Scarlet	3 ft (90 cm)
Gladiolus cuspidatus	Cape Province	Cream	12 in (30 cm)
Gladiolus debilis	Cape Province	Crimson	18 in (45 cm)
Gladiolus dracocephalus	Natal	Yellow	2 ft (60 cm)
Gladiolus gracilis	Cape Province	Pink-cream	2 ft (60 cm)
Gladiolus grandis	Cape Province	Maroon-brown	18 in (45 cm)
Gladiolus illyricus	British Isles	Magenta	12 in (30 cm)
Gladiolus macowanianus	Cape Province	Cream	2 ft (60 cm)
Gladiolus maculatus	Cape Province	Pink-brown	2 ft (60 cm)
Gladiolus monticolus	Cape Province	Cream	2 ft (60 cm)
Gladiolus orchidiflorus	Natal	Green-brown	18 in (45 cm)
Gladiolus ornatus	Cape Province	Pink	18 in (45 cm)
Gladiolus papilio	Natal	Purple-yellow	2 ft (60 cm)
Gladiolus primulinus	South-eastern Africa	Yellow	2 ft (60 cm)
Gladiolus prismatosiphon	Cape Province	Pink	18 in (45 cm)
Gladiolus psittacinus	Natal	Red	2 ft (60 cm)
Gladiolus purpureo-auratus	Natal	Yellow	3 ft (90 cm)
Gladiolus quartineanus	Central Africa	Yellow	3 ft (90 cm)
Gladiolus recurvus	Natal	Yellow	2 ft (60 cm)
Gladiolus segetum	Southern Europe	Carmine-purple	12 in (30 cm)
Gladiolus tristis	Cape Province	Cream	2 ft (60 cm)
Gladiolus villosus	Cape Province	Pink	2 ft (60 cm)
Gloriosa carsonii	Tanzania	Yellow	6 ft (1·8 metres)
Gloriosa rothschildiana	Uganda	Red and yellow	6 ft (1·8 metres)
Gloriosa superba	Central Africa	Orange and yellow	6 ft (1·8 metres)
Gloriosa verschuurii	Central Africa	Red and yellow	6 ft (1·8 metres)
Gloriosa virescens	Mozambique	Orange and yellow	6 ft (1·8 metres)
Gloxinia fimbriata	Brazil	White and purple	9 in (45 cm)
Gloxinia maculata	Brazil	Purple-blue	18 in (45 cm)
Gynandriris sisyrinchium	Southern Europe	Pale blue	6 in (15 cm)
Habranthus andersonii	Chile	Yellow, copper	6 in (15 cm)
Habranthus brachyandrus	Chile	Lilac, claret	15 in (37·5 cm)
Habranthus robustus	Buenos Aires	Rose pink	9 in (22·5 cm)
Habranthus versicolor	Uruguay	White, green	12 in (30 cm)
Haemanthus albiflos	Natal	Greenish white	9 in (22·5 cm)
Haemanthus brevifolius	Eastern Africa	Pink	9 in (22·5 cm)
Haemanthus cinnabarinus	Gold Coast	Crimson	12 in (30 cm)
Haemanthus coccineus	Cape Province	Red	9 in (22·5 cm)

T

Species	Habitat	Colour	Height
Haemanthus katharinae	Natal	Salmon orange	12 in (30 cm)
Haemanthus magnificus	Cape Province	Scarlet	2 ft (60 cm)
Haemanthus multiflorus	Abyssinia	Scarlet	12 in (30 cm)
Haemanthus natalensis	Natal	Green, orange	12 in (30 cm)
Haemanthus pubescens	Cape Province	Crimson	6 in (15 cm)
Haemanthus puniceus	Transvaal	Scarlet	9 in (22·5 cm)
Herbertia amatorum	Uruguay	Violet-blue	9 in (22·5 cm)
Herbertia pulchella	Bay of Maldonado	Violet-blue	9 in (22·5 cm)
Hermodactylus tuberosus	Southern Europe	Olive green	12 in (60 cm)
Hesperocallis undulata	California	White	6 in (15 cm)
Hesperantha buchrii	Natal	White, pink	9 in (22·5 cm)
Hesperantha pilosa	Cape Province	White	12 in (30 cm)
Hesperantha radiata	Cape Province	Pale yellow	12 in (30 cm)
Hesperantha spicata	Cape Province	White, red	12 in (30 cm)
Hesperantha stanfordiae	Cape Province	Pale yellow	18 in (45 cm)
Hexaglottis flexuosa	Cape Province	Yellow	15 in (37·5 cm)
Hexaglottis longifolia	Cape Province	Yellow	15 in (37·5 cm)
Hippeastrum advenum	Chile	Scarlet, yellow	12 in (30 cm)
Hippeastrum aulicum	Brazil	Crimson red	12 in (30 cm)
Hippeastrum bifidum	Argentina	Orange-scarlet	15 in (37·5 cm)
Hippeastrum candidum	Argentina	White	2 ft (60 cm)
Hippeastrum equestre	Mexico	Scarlet	12 in (30 cm)
Hippeastrum pratense	Chile	Scarlet, yellow	12 in (30 cm)
Hippeastrum reginae	Mexico	Scarlet	12 in (30 cm)
Hippeastrum reticulatum	Brazil	Mauve-pink	12 in (30 cm)
Hippeastrum rutilum	Venezuela	Crimson-red	12 in (30 cm)
Hippeastrum vittatum	Chile	White, magenta	2 ft (60 cm)
Homeria bulbillifera	Cape Province	Creamy-pink	16 in (40 cm)
Homeria collina	Natal	Orange	20 in (50 cm)
Homeria miniata	Cape Province	Salmon	2 ft (60 cm)
Homoglossum priorii	Cape Province	Red	2 ft (60 cm)
Homoglossum watsonium	Cape Province	Red	2 ft (60 cm)
Hyacinthus amethystinus	Spain	Blue	9 in (22·5 cm)
Hyacinthus orientalis	Persia	Blue	9 in (22·5 cm)
Hyacinthus azureus	Asia Minor	Blue	9 in (22·5 cm)
Hyacinthus dalmaticus	Yugoslavia	Blue	6 in (15 cm)
Hyacinthus romanus	Southern Europe	Creamy white	12 in (30 cm)
Hyacinthus tabrizianus	Persia	White, blue	3 in (7·5 cm)
Hymenocallis amancaes	Peru	Yellow	18 in (45 cm)
Hymenocallis andreana	Ecuador	White	12 in (30 cm)
Hymenocallis festalis	Venezuela	White	2 ft (60 cm)
Hymenocallis harrisiana	Mexico	White	9 in (22·5 cm)
Hymenocallis lacera	Mexico	White	9 in (22·5 cm)
Hymenocallis narcissiflora	Peru	White	2 ft (60 cm)
Hymenocallis speciosa	Peru	White, green	15 in (37·5 cm)
Hymenocallis tubiflora	Brazil	White	12 in (30 cm)
Hymenocallis undulata	Venezuela	White	2 ft (60 cm)
Hypoxis hirsuta	Eastern United States	Yellow	6 in (15 cm)
Hypoxis stellata	Southern Africa	White, blue	6 in (15 cm)
Ipheion uniflorum	Mexico, Argentina	White	6 in (15 cm)
Iris acutiloba	Turkestan	Lilac	3 in (7·5 cm)
Iris alata	Northern Africa	Lavender	6 in (15 cm)
Iris alberti	Turkestan	Lilac, white	2 ft (60 cm)
Iris albicans	Southern Europe	White	2 ft (60 cm)
Iris atropurpurea	Syria	Purple	6 in (15 cm)

Species	Habitat	Colour	Height
Iris aurea	Western Himalayas	Yellow	3 to 4 ft (90 cm to 1·2 metres)
Iris bakeriana	Persia	Blue, white	6 in (15 cm)
Iris barnumae	Kurdistan	Wine purple	4 in (10 cm)
Iris bartoni	Afghanistan	Cream	3 ft (90 cm)
Iris biflora	Southern Europe	Purple	15 in (37·5 cm)
Iris biliotti	Asia Minor	Reddish purple	2 ft (60 cm)
Iris bismarkiana	Mount Lebanon	Cream, purple	12 in (30 cm)
Iris boissieri	Portugal	Reddish purple	12 in (30 cm)
Iris bracteata	Oregon	Yellow	20 in (50 cm)
Iris bucharica	Bokhara	White, yellow	12 in (30 cm)
Iris caucasica	Caucasus	Yellow	6 in (15 cm)
Iris chamaeiris	Southern Europe	Yellow	6 in (15 cm)
Iris cristata	Eastern United States	Blue	6 in (15 cm)
Iris danfordiae	Caucasus	Yellow	3 in (7·5 cm)
Iris douglassii	California	Yellow	18 in (45 cm)
Iris duthiei	North-western India	Purple-mauve	2 ft (60 cm)
Iris filifolia	Southern Spain	Purple	12 in (30 cm)
Iris flavescens	South-eastern Europe	Yellow	3 ft (90 cm)
Iris florentina	Southern Europe	White	2 ft (60 cm)
Iris foetidissima	British Isles	Purple-blue	3 ft (90 cm)
Iris fosteriana	Southern U.S.S.R.	Mauve, yellow	12 in (30 cm)
Iris gatesii	Asia Minor	Cream, violet	20 in (50 cm)
Iris germanica	Central Europe	Purple	3 ft (90 cm)
Iris graeberiana	Turkestan	Silvery mauve	12 in (30 cm)
Iris graminea	Central Europe	Mauve	9 in (23 cm)
Iris hexagona	Eastern United States	Lilac	3 to 4 ft (90 cm 1·2 metres)
Iris histrio	Syria	Lilac-blue	6 in (15 cm)
Iris histrioides	Asia Minor	Ultramarine	4 in (10 cm)
Iris hoogiana	Central Asia	Lavender	18 in (45 cm)
Iris hookeriana	Bengal	Purple-blue	9 in (22·5 cm)
Iris iberica	Caucasus	Creamy lilac	6 in (15 cm)
Iris juncea	Southern Spain	Yellow	12 in (30 cm)
Iris kaempferi	Japan	Purple-blue	2 ft (60 cm)
Iris kolpakowskiana	Turkestan	Purple	3 in (7·5 cm)
Iris korolkowi	Turkestan	White, purple	12 in (30 cm)
Iris lortetii	Lebanon	Pinkish blue	18 in (45 cm)
Iris lutescens	Southern Europe	Yellow	2 ft (60 cm)
Iris magnifica	Turkestan	Lavender	2 ft (60 cm)
Iris missouriensis	Central United States	Lilac-blue	18 in (45 cm)
Iris orchioides	Bokhara	Yellow	2 ft (60 cm)
Iris pallida	Southern Europe	Lilac	3 ft (90 cm)
Iris persica	Persia	Greenish blue	6 in (15 cm)
Iris prismatica	Eastern United States	Blue	18 in (45 cm)
Iris reticulata	Northern Persia	Purple	6 in (15 cm)
Iris sambucina	Central Europe	Yellow, purple	2 ft (60 cm)
Iris sari	Cilicia	Violet	6 in (15 cm)
Iris siberica	Siberia	Lilac-blue	2 ft (60 cm)
Iris sindjarensis	Mesopotamia	Slate blue	9 in (22·5 cm)
Iris stenophylla	Cilicia	Purple	4 in (10 cm)
Iris stolonifera	Levant	White, lilac	6 in (15 cm)
Iris stylosa	Algeria	Sky blue	12 in (30 cm)
Iris susiana	Levant	Grey	12 in (30 cm)
Iris tectorum	Japan	Lilac	12 in (30 cm)
Iris tingitana	Tangiers	Dark blue	2 ft (60 cm)

Species	Habitat	Colour	Height
Iris variegata	Central Europe	Yellow, red	18 in (45 cm)
Iris vartani	Palestine	Lavender blue	6 in (15 cm)
Iris versicolor	Eastern United States	Purple	2 ft (60 cm)
Iris willmottiana	Turkestan	Pale blue	6 in (15 cm)
Iris winogradowi	Southern U.S.S.R.	Creamy yellow	4 in (10 cm)
Iris xiphioides	North-western Spain	Dark blue	2 ft (60 cm)
Iris xiphium	Southern Spain	Purple	2 ft (60 cm)
Ixia maculata	Cape Province	Yellow	15 in (37.5 cm)
Ixia odorata	Cape Province	Pale yellow	15 in (37.5 cm)
Ixia polystachya	Cape Province	Creamy white	12 in (30 cm)
Ixia viridiflora	Cape Province	Green, blue	12 in (30 cm)
Ixiolirion kolpakowskianum	Central Asia	Bluish white	12 in (30 cm)
Ixiolirion montanum	Southern Russia	Lilac	15 in (37.5 cm)
Korolkowia sewerzowii	Central Asia	Yellow, plum	12 in (30 cm)
Lachenalia glaucina	Cape Province	Blue, lilac	12 in (30 cm)
Lachenalia mutabilis	Natal	Blue, yellow	9 in (22.5 cm)
Lachenalia orchioides	Cape Province	Yellow, blue	9 in (22.5 cm)
Lachenalia pearsonii	Southern Africa	Bronze, yellow	18 in (45 cm)
Lachenalia pendula	Southern Africa	Orange, yellow	9 in (22.5 cm)
Lachenalia rubida	Cape Province	Crimson	8 in (20 cm)
Lachenalia tricolor	Natal	Yellow, green	12 in (30 cm)
Lapeyrousia corymbosa	Cape Province	Blue	6 in (15 cm)
Lapeyrousia cruenta	Cape Province	Carmine red	9 in (22.5 cm)
Lapeyrousia fabricii	Cape Province	Cream	12 in (30 cm)
Lapeyrousia fistulosa	Cape Province	Creamy white	4 in (10 cm)
Leucocoryne ixioides	Chile	Blue	15 in (37.5 cm)
Leucojum aestivum	Northern Europe	White, green	18 in (45 cm)
Leucojum autumnale	Southern Spain, Morocco	White, green	9 in (22.5 cm)
Leucojum hyemale	Southern France	White, green	6 in (15 cm)
Leucojum longifolium	Corsica	White	9 in (22.5 cm)
Leucojum roseum	Corsica	White, pink	4 in (10 cm)
Leucojum tingitanum	Southern Spain	White	12 in (30 cm)
Leucojum trichophyllum	Morocco	White	9 in (22.5 cm)
Leucojum vernum	Central Europe	White, green	9 in (22.5 cm)
Libertia formosa	Formosa, Chile	White	2 ft (60 cm)
Libertia grandiflora	New Zealand	White	2 ft (60 cm)
Libertia paniculata	New Zealand	White	2 ft (60 cm)
Lilium amabile	Korea	Scarlet	3 ft (90 cm)
Lilium auratum	Japan	White, yellow	6 ft (1.8 metres)
Lilium bakerianum	Burma, West China	Greenish white	3 to 4 ft (90 cm to 1.2 metres)
Lilium bolanderi	Western United States	Purple	3 to 4 ft (90 cm to 1.2 metres)
Lilium brownii	Western Central China	White, purple	3 to 4 ft (90 cm to 1.2 metres)
Lilium bulbiferum	Central Europe	Reddish orange	5 to 6 ft (1.5 to 1.8 metres)
Lilium candidum	Asia Minor	White	4 to 5 ft (1.2 to 1.5 metres)
Lilium canadense	Eastern United States	Orange-yellow	3 to 4 ft (90 cm to 1.2 metres)
Lilium carniolicum	Yugoslavia	Scarlet	2 ft (60 cm)
Lilium catesbaei	South-eastern United States	Orange-scarlet	18 in (45 cm)
Lilium cernuum	Korea	Lilac-pink	18 in (45 cm)

Species	Habitat	Colour	Height
Lilium chalcedonicum	Asia Minor	Scarlet	3 to 4 ft (90 cm to 1·2 metres)
Lilium columbianum	Western United States	Golden orange	2 ft (60 cm)
Lilium concolor	Manchuria	Scarlet	18 in (45 cm)
Lilium dauricum	Mongolia	Scarlet	2 ft (60 cm)
Lilium davidii	Western China	Orange-scarlet	5 to 6 ft (1·5 to 1·8 metres)
Lilium duchartrei	Western China	White, purple	3 to 4 ft (90 cm to 1·2 metres)
Lilium formosanum	Formosa	White, purple	5 to 6 ft (1·5 to 1·8 metres)
Lilium grayi	Eastern United States	Red	3 ft (90 cm)
Lilium hansonii	Korea	Orange	4 to 5 ft (1·2 to 1·5 metres)
Lilium henryi	Central China	Golden orange	5 to 6 ft (1·5 to 1·8 metres)
Lilium humboldtii	Western United States	Reddish orange	5 to 6 ft (1·5 to 1·8 metres)
Lilium japonicum	Japan	Shell pink	3 ft (90 cm)
Lilium kelloggii	Western United States	Mauve-pink	3 to 4 ft (90 cm to 1·2 metres)
Lilium lankongense	Western China	Rosy mauve	2 ft (60 cm)
Lilium leichtlinii	Japan	Lemon yellow	3 to 4 ft (90 cm to 1·2 metres)
Lilium leucanthum	Central China	Ivory white	3 to 4 ft (90 cm to 1·2 metres)
Lilium longiflorum	Japan	White	3 ft (90 cm)
Lilium mackliniae	North-western Burma	Ivory white	12 in (30 cm)
Lilium maritimum	Western United States	Crimson	2 ft (60 cm)
Lilium martagon	Caucasus	Pinkish purple	3 to 4 ft (90 cm to 1·2 metres)
Lilium medeoloides	Japan	Apricot, red	16 in (40 cm)
Lilium michauxi	South-eastern United States	Orange	2 ft (60 cm)
Lilium michiganense	Eastern United States	Orange-red	3 to 4 ft (90 cm to 1·2 metres)
Lilium monadelphum	Caucasus	Bright yellow	3 to 4 ft (90 cm to 1·2 metres)
Lilium neilgherrense	Southern India	White	3 ft (90 cm)
Lilium nepalense	Nepal	Lime green	3 ft (90 cm)
Lilium nevadense	Western United States	Orange	3 ft (90 cm)
Lilium nobilissimum	Japan	White	2 ft (60 cm)
Lilium occidentale	Western United States	Orange-red	3 to 4 ft (90 cm to 1·2 metres)
Lilium papilliferum	Western China	Purple-maroon	12 in (30 cm)
Lilium pardalinum	Western United States	Orange-red	5 to 6 ft (1·5 to 1·8 metres)
Lilium parryi	Western United States	Yellow	5 to 6 ft (1·5 to 1·8 metres)
Lilium parvum	Western United States	Yellow	3 ft (90 cm)
Lilium philadelphicum	Eastern United States	Orange-red	2 ft (60 cm)
Lilium philippinense	Philippine Islands	White	2 ft (60 cm)
Lilium polyphillum	Himalayas	Cream	3 to 4 ft (90 cm to 1·2 metres)
Lilium pomponium	Southern Europe	Scarlet	3 ft (90 cm)
Lilium primulinum	Northern Burma	Yellow	3 ft (90 cm)

Species	Habitat	Colour	Height
Lilium pumilum	Mongolia	Coral red	18 in (45 cm)
Lilium pyrenaicum	Pyrenees	Greenish yellow	2 ft (60 cm)
Lilium regale	Tibet	White	5 to 6 ft (1·5 to 1·8 metres)
Lilium rubellum	Japan	Pink	20 in (50 cm)
Lilium rubescens	Western United States	White	3 ft (90 cm)
Lilium sargentiae	Tibet	White	3 to 4 ft (90 cm to 1·2 metres)
Lilium speciosum	Japan	White	3 ft (90 cm)
Lilium sulphureum	Northern Burma	Cream	6 to 7 ft (1·8 to 2·1 metres)
Lilium superbum	Western United States	Orange-red	6 ft (1·8 metres)
Lilium taliense	Western China	White	3 to 4 ft (90 cm to 1·2 metres)
Lilium × testaceum	Unknown	Apricot	3 to 4 ft (90 cm to 1·2 metres)
Lilium tigrinum	Japan	Orange	3 to 4 ft (90 cm to 1·2 metres)
Lilium tsingtauense	Korea	Orange	2 ft (60 cm)
Lilium vollmeri	Western United States	Orange	2 ft (60 cm)
Lilium wallichianum	Himalayas	White	3 ft (90 cm)
Lilium wardii	Tibet	Purple-pink	3 ft (90 cm)
Lilium washingtonianum	Western United States	Pinkish white	3 to 4 ft (90 cm to 1·2 metres)
Lilium wigginsii	Western United States	Yellow	3 ft (90 cm)
Liriopsis horsmannii	Peru	White	12 in (30 cm)
Littonia modesta	Southern Africa	Yellowish orange	6 ft (1·8 metres)
Lloydia serotina	British Isles	Creamy white	4 in (10 cm)
Lycoris aurea	Western China	Yellow	18 in (45 cm)
Lycoris incarnata	Western China	Salmon pink	15 in (37·5 cm)
Lycoris radiata	Japan	Orange-red	15 in (37·5 cm)
Lycoris sanguinea	Japan	Crimson	18 in (45 cm)
Lycoris sprengeri	Japan	Mauve-pink	12 in (30 cm)
Lycoris squamigera	Japan	Rosy lilac	2 ft (60 cm)
Lycoris staminea	Western China	Buff-pink	2 ft (60 cm)
Massonia amygdalina	Southern Africa	White	3 in (7·5 cm)
Massonia jasminiflora	Southern Africa	White, green	1 in (2·5 cm)
Massonia muricata	Southern Africa	White	2 in (5 cm)
Massonia pustulata	Southern Africa	White	1 in (2·5 cm)
Massonia sanguinea	Southern Africa	White	2 in (5 cm)
Medeola virginiana	Eastern United States	Yellow	15 in (37·5 cm)
Melasphaerula graminea	Cape Province	Creamy white	18 in (45 cm)
Merendera filifolia	Balearic Isles	Rose-pink	2 in (5 cm)
Merendera montana	Pyrenees	Rosy mauve	3 in (7·5 cm)
Merendera persica	Persia	Purple-pink	3 in (7·5 cm)
Merendera sobolifera	Bulgaria	Rosy lilac	3 in (7·5 cm)
Merendera trigyna	Caucasus	Lilac-pink	3 in (7·5 cm)
Moraea bicolor	Natal	Pale yellow	3 ft (90 cm)
Moraea ciliata	Cape Province	Lilac	2 ft (60 cm)
Moraea decussata	Cape Province	Yellow	2 ft (60 cm)
Moraea iridioides	Natal	White	3 to 4 ft (90 cm to 1·2 metres)
Moraea odorata	Cape Province	White	18 in (45 cm)
Moraea papilianacea	Cape Province	Yellow-brown	2 ft (60 cm)
Moraea pavonia	Cape Province	White	3 ft (90 cm)
Moraea ramosissima	Cape Province	Yellow	2 ft (60 cm)

Species	Habitat	Colour	Height
Moraea spathacea	Transvaal	Yellow	3 ft (90 cm)
Moraea villosa	Cape Province	Lilac	2 ft (60 cm)
Muscari ambrosiacum	Asia Minor	Lilac, cream	6 in (15 cm)
Muscari argaei	Asia Minor	White	4 in (10 cm)
Muscari armeniacum	South-eastern Europe	Cobalt blue	9 in (22·5 cm)
Muscari botryoides	Southern Europe	Navy blue	6 in (15 cm)
Muscari comosum	South-eastern Europe	Purple	15 in (37·5 cm)
Muscari conicum	Persia	Blue	9 in (22·5 cm)
Muscari latifolium	South-eastern Europe	Dark and light blue	15 in (37·5 cm)
Muscari massayanum	Persia	Carmine crimson	6 in (15 cm)
Muscari moschatum	Asia Minor	Olive green	8 in (20 cm)
Muscari neglectum	Southern Europe	Blue-black	8 in (20 cm)
Muscari paradoxum	Caucasus	Purple	8 in (20 cm)
Muscari pinardi	Cilicia	Grey-blue	8 in (20 cm)
Muscari polyanthum	Greece	Creamy white	6 in (15 cm)
Muscari racemosum	Northern Europe	Purple-blue	4 in (10 cm)
Muscari tubergenianum	Persia	Dark and light blue	8 in (20 cm)
Narcissus bulbocodium	South-western Europe	Yellow	8 in (20 cm)
Narcissus calcicola	Portugal	Yellow	6 in (15 cm)
Narcissus canaliculatus	Sicily	White, yellow	9 in (22·5 cm)
Narcissus cyclamineus	Portugal	White	9 in (23 cm)
Narcissus gracilis	Southern France	Yellow	6 in (15 cm)
Narcissus juncifolius	Northern Spain	Yellow	5 in (12·5 cm)
Narcissus jonquilla	Southern Spain	Yellow	12 in (30 cm)
Narcissus minimus	Northern Spain	Yellow	3 in (7·5 cm)
Narcissus minor	Portugal	Yellow	6 in (15 cm)
Narcissus poeticus	Southern Europe	White	12 in (30 cm)
Narcissus pseudo-narcissus	British Isles	Yellow	12 in (30 cm)
Narcissus rupicola	Northern Spain	Yellow	4 in (10 cm)
Narcissus scaberulus	Portugal	Orange	6 in (15 cm)
Narcissus serotinus	Northern Africa	White, yellow	6 in (15 cm)
Narcissus tazetta	Southern Europe	White	12 in (30 cm)
Narcissus triandrus	Spain	White	8 in (20 cm)
Narcissus viridiflorus	Morocco	Green	8 in (20 cm)
Narcissus watieri	Morocco	White	4 in (10 cm)
Nemastylis coelestina	Mexico	Bright blue	15 in (38 cm)
Nemastylis graminiflora	Mexico	Purple-blue	2 ft (60 cm)
Nerine angustifolia	Natal	Deep pink	2 ft (60 cm)
Nerine appendiculata	Natal	Pale pink	2 ft (60 cm)
Nerine bowdenii	Cape Province	Pale pink	2 ft (60 cm)
Nerine filifolia	South-western Cape Province	Rose red	20 in (50 cm)
Nerine flexuosa	Cape Province	Pale pink	3 ft (90 cm)
Nerine humilis	Natal	Rose red	12 in (30 cm)
Nerine masonorum	Natal	Pale pink	6 in (15 cm)
Nerine moorei	Cape Province	Scarlet	12 in (30 cm)
Nerine pudica	Natal	Ivory white	12 in (30 cm)
Nerine sarniensis	Cape Province	Crimson	15 in (37·5 cm)
Nerine undulata	Cape Province	Pale pink	12 in (30 cm)
Nomocharis aperta	Tibet	Pale pink	2 ft (60 cm)
Nomocharis farreri	North Burma	White, purple	3 ft (90 cm)
Nomocharis mairei	Western China	White, purple	2 ft (60 cm)
Nomocharis meleagrina	Tibet	White, crimson	3 ft (90 cm)
Nomocharis pardanthina	Western China	Pale pink	3 ft (90 cm)
Nomocharis saluenensis	Tibet	Rose pink	3 ft (90 cm)
Nothoscordum fragrans	Southern United States	White, mauve	18 in (45 cm)

Species	Habitat	Colour	Height
Nothoscordum inordorum	Southern United States	White	18 in (45 cm)
Notholirion bulbuliferum	Tibet	Pink-mauve	5 to 6 ft (1·5 to 1·8 metres)
Notholirion campanulatum	Northern Burma	Crimson	4 ft (1·2 metres)
Notholirion macrophyllum	Nepal	Lilac-mauve	15 in (37·5 cm)
Notholirion thomsonianum	Tibet	Lilac-mauve	4 ft (1·2 metres)
Ornithogalum arabicum	Arabia	White	2 ft (60 cm)
Ornithogalum balansae	Middle East	White, grey	6 in (15 cm)
Ornithogalum fimbriatum	South-eastern Europe	White	6 in (15 cm)
Ornithogalum graminifolium	Cape Province	Creamy white	18 in (45 cm)
Ornithogalum hispidum	Cape Province	White, green	12 in (30 cm)
Ornithogalum lacteum	Cape Province	White	15 in (37·5 cm)
Ornithogalum montanum	South-eastern Europe	White, green	18 in (45 cm)
Ornithogalum narbonense	Eastern Mediterranean	White	18 in (45 cm)
Ornithogalum nutans	Southern Europe	Silver grey	15 in (37·5 cm)
Ornithogalum pilosum	Cape Province	White, green	12 in (30 cm)
Ornithogalum pyramidale	South-eastern Europe	White, green	2 ft (60 cm)
Ornithogalum pyrenaicum	Pyrenees	Pale yellow	2 ft (60 cm)
Ornithogalum saundersii	Transvaal	Creamy white	3 to 4 ft (90 cm to 1·2 metres)
Ornithogalum subcucullatum	South-western Europe	White	18 in (45 cm)
Ornithogalum thyrsoides	Cape Province	White	2 ft (60 cm)
Ornithogalum tricophyllum	Eastern Mediterranean	White	6 in (15 cm)
Ornithogalum umbellatum	Middle East	White	6 in (15 cm)
Oxalis adenophylla	Chile	Creamy pink	4 in (10 cm)
Oxalis bowiei	Cape Province	Rose-purple	6 in (15 cm)
Oxalis brasiliensis	Brazil	Crimson	3 in (7·5 cm)
Oxalis cernua	Cape Province	Yellow	4 in (10 cm)
Oxalis enneaphylla	Falkland Isles	Blush white	3 in (7·5 cm)
Oxalis falcata	Cape Province	Rose pink	4 in (10 cm)
Oxalis hirta	Cape Province	Purple	3 in (7·5 cm)
Oxalis incarnata	Cape Province	Mauve	4 in (10 cm)
Oxalis lobata	Chile	Yellow	3 in (7·5 cm)
Oxalis luteola	Cape Province	Yellow	4 in (10 cm)
Oxalis magellanica	Straits of Megellan	White	4 in (10 cm)
Oxalis variabilis	Cape Province	Purple	3 in (7·5 cm)
Oxalis violacea	North America	Rosy purple	6 in (15 cm)
Pamianthe peruviana	Peru	White	2 ft (60 cm)
Pancratium canariense	Canary Isles	White	2 ft (60 cm)
Pancratium illyricum	Southern European coast	White	18 in (45 cm)
Pancratium maritimum	Southern European coast	White	15 in (37·5 cm)
Pancratium sickenbergerii	Egypt	White	12 in (30 cm)
Pancratium tortuosum	Northern Africa	White	12 in (30 cm)
Pancratium verecundum	Northern India	White	15 in (37·5 cm)
Paradisis liliastrum	Central Europe	White	2 ft (60 cm)
Phaedranassa carmioli	Peru	Red, green	2 ft (60 cm)
Phaedranassa chloracea	Ecuador	Red, green	2 ft (60 cm)
Phaedranassa lehmannii	Ecuador	Red, green	2 ft (60 cm)
Polianthes tuberosa	Mexico	White	2 ft (60 cm)
Polygonatum biflorum	Canada	Greenish white	2 ft (60 cm)
Polygonatum multiflorum	Northern Europe	Greenish white	2 ft (60 cm)
Polygonatum odorum	British Isles	Greenish white	12 in (30 cm)
Polygonatum officinale	Northern Europe	Greenish white	12 in (30 cm)
Polygonatum oppositifolium	Himalayas	Greenish white	3 ft (90 cm)

Species	Habitat	Colour	Height
Polygonatum roseum	Siberia	Rose pink	3 ft (90 cm)
Puschkinia scilloides	Near East	Blue striped	6 in (15 cm)
Ranunculus asiaticus	Persia	Various	9 in (22·5 cm)
Reineckia carnea	China, Japan	Flesh	12 in (30 cm)
Rigidella flammea	Mexico	Scarlet	3 ft (90 cm)
Romulea bulbocodioides	Cape Province	Pale yellow	3 in (7·5 cm)
Romulea bulbocodium	Southern Europe	Purple	6 in (15 cm)
Romulea clusiana	Southern Spain	Purple	2 in (5 cm)
Romulea elegans	Cape Province	White	3 in (7·5 cm)
Romulea hirsuta	Cape Province	Magenta	3 in (7·5 cm)
Romulea requienii	Corsica	Violet	3 in (7·5 cm)
Romulea rosea	Cape Province	Mauve	3 in (7·5 cm)
Romulea sabulosa	Natal	Cherry red	3 in (7·5 cm)
Romulea triflora	Cape Province	Golden yellow	3 in (7·5 cm)
Sandersonia aurantiaca	Natal	Orange-yellow	5 to 6 ft (1·5 to 1·8 metres)
Schizostylis coccinea	Southern Africa	Crimson	2 ft (60 cm)
Scilla amoena	South Eastern Europe	Indigo	6 in (15 cm)
Scilla autumnalis	British Isles	Lilac-rose	9 in (22·5 cm)
Scilla bifolia	Central Europe	Gentian blue	9 in (22·5 cm)
Scilla bithynica	Asia Minor	Violet-blue	12 in (30 cm)
Scilla cooperi	Natal	Purple	9 in (22·5 cm)
Scilla hyacinthoides	Southern Europe	Lilac-blue	15 in (37·5 cm)
Scilla italica	Northern Italy	Pale blue	15 in (37·5 cm)
Scilla lilio-hyacinthus	Pyrenees	Blue	12 in (30 cm)
Scilla menophylla	Portugal	Cobalt blue	6 in (15 cm)
Scilla messanaica	Greece	Blue	6 in (15 cm)
Scilla natalensis	Natal	Deep blue	3 ft (90 cm)
Scilla odorata	Spain	Pale blue	9 in (22·5 cm)
Scilla peruviana	Southern Europe	Blue	8 in (20 cm)
Scilla pratensis	Dalmatia	Lilac-blue	12 in (30 cm)
Scilla sibirica	Siberia	Pale blue	8 in (20 cm)
Scilla tubergeniana	Persia	Blue striped	4 in (10 cm)
Scilla verna	British Isles	Mauve	6 in (15 cm)
Scilla villosa	Morocco	Blue	6 in (15 cm)
Sparaxis grandiflora	Cape Province	Violet/Cream	18 in (45 cm)
Sparaxis tricolor	Natal	Orange-red	15 in (37·5 cm)
Sprekelia formosissima	Mexico	Red	12 in (30 cm)
Stenomesson aurantiacum	Ecuador	Orange	15 in (37·5 cm)
Stenomesson coccineum	Peru	Red	15 in (37·5 cm)
Stenomesson croceum	Peru	Yellow	15 in (37·5 cm)
Stenomesson humile	Peru	Orange	9 in (22·5 cm)
Stenomesson incarnatum	Peru	Red	12 in (30 cm)
Stenomesson luteo-viride	Peru	Yellow, green	16 in (40 cm)
Stenomesson viridiflorum	Ecuador	Green	2 ft (60 cm)
Sternbergia clusiana	Turkey, Syria	Yellow	4 in (10 cm)
Sternbergia colchiciflora	South-eastern Europe	Pale yellow	3 in (7·5 cm)
Sternbergia fischeriana	Turkey, Persia	Pale yellow	6 in (15 cm)
Sternbergia lutea	Middle East	Yellow	4 in (10 cm)
Streptanthera cuprea	Natal	Copper	10 in (25 cm)
Streptanthera elegans	Natal	White	10 in (25 cm)
Synnotia bicolor	Cape Province	Cream, purple	12 in (30 cm)
Synnotia meterlerkampiae	Cape Province	Violet	12 in (30 cm)
Syringodea pulchella	Natal	Mauve	6 in (15 cm)
Tecophilaea cyanocrocus	Chile	Blue	6 in (15 cm)
Tigridia curvata	Mexico	Yellow	12 in (30 cm)

Species	Habitat	Colour	Height
Tigridia pavonia	Mexico, Peru	Violet, red	18 in (45 cm)
Tigridia pringlei	Northern Mexico	Scarlet	18 in (45 cm)
Tigridia violacea	Mexico	Violet, red	12 in (30 cm)
Trillium cernuum	Eastern North America	White	6 in (15 cm)
Trillium chloropetalum	North-western United States	Purple	12 in (30 cm)
Trillium erectum	Eastern North America	Purple	18 in (45 cm)
Trillium govanianum	Himalayas	Purple	15 in (37·5 cm)
Trillium grandiflorum	Eastern North America	White	15 in (37·5 cm)
Trillium luteum	North Carolina	Yellow	15 in (37·5 cm)
Trillium nivale	Ohio	White, pink	6 in (15 cm)
Trillium pusillum	Eastern North America	White	8 in (20 cm)
Trillium recurvatum	Southern North America	White	9 in (22·5 cm)
Trillium sessile	Eastern North America	Purple	16 in (40 cm)
Trillium smallii	Japan	Purple	9 in (22·5 cm)
Trillium stylosum	South-eastern United States	Pink	16 in (40 cm)
Trillium tschonoskii	Japan, Korea	White	18 in (45 cm)
Trillium undulatum	Eastern North America	White, purple	18 in (45 cm)
Tritonia crispa	Cape Province	Pink	18 in (45 cm)
Tritonia crocata	Cape Province	Orange-yellow	18 in (45 cm)
Tritonia hyalina	Natal	Salmon pink	15 in (37·5 cm)
Tritonia scillaris	Cape Province	Pink	18 in (45 cm)
Tropaeolum azureum	Chile	Pale blue	6 ft (1·8 metres)
Tropaeolum moritzianum	Colombia	Yellow	6 ft (1·8 metres)
Tropaeolum pentaphyllum	Buenos Aires	Scarlet	5 to 6 ft (1·5 to 1·8 metres)
Tropaeolum polyphyllum	Chile	Yellow	3 ft (90 cm)
Tropaeolum speciosum	Chile	Scarlet	6 ft (1·8 metres)
Tropaeolum tricolor	Chile	Orange	9 ft (2·7 metres)
Tropaeolum tuberosum	Peru	Yellow	9 ft (2·7 metres)
Tulipa acuminata	Pyrenees	Yellow, red	18 in (45 cm)
Tulipa aucheriana	Persia	Pink	3 in (7·5 cm)
Tulipa batalinii	Levant	Pale yellow	6 in (15 cm)
Tulipa biflora	Caucasus	White	3 in (7·5 cm)
Tulipa borszczowi	Central Asia	Yellow, red	12 in (30 cm)
Tulipa clusiana	Persia	White, pink	15 in (37·5 cm)
Tulipa eichleri	Southern U.S.S.R.	Scarlet	15 in (37·5 cm)
Tulipa fosteriana	Central Asia	Scarlet	12 in (30 cm)
Tulipa gesneriana	Persia, Turkey	Crimson	9 in (22·5 cm)
Tulipa greigii	Central Asia	Orange	9 in (22·5 cm)
Tulipa hageri	Greece	Cherry red	8 in (20 cm)
Tulipa hoogiana	Central Asia	Crimson	9 in (22·5 cm)
Tulipa humilis	Northern Persia	Magenta pink	3 in (7·5 cm)
Tulipa ingens	Turkestan	Scarlet	18 in (45 cm)
Tulipa kaufmanniana	Turkestan	White, pink	6 in (15 cm)
Tulipa kolpakowskiana	Turkestan	Yellow, red	8 in (20 cm)
Tulipa lanata	Northern Persia	Orange-scarlet	18 in (45 cm)
Tulipa linifolia	Northern Persia	Scarlet	9 in (22·5 cm)
Tulipa maximowiczii	Northern Persia	Scarlet	8 in (20 cm)
Tulipa montana	Northern Persia	Scarlet	9 in (22·5 cm)
Tulipa orphanidea	Greece, Turkey	Orange-bronze	12 in (30 cm)
Tulipa ostrowskiana	Turkestan	Scarlet	8 in (20 cm)
Tulipa persica	Northern Persia	Yellow	9 in (22·5 cm)

Species	Habitat	Colour	Height
Tulipa polychroma	Northern Persia	White	6 in (15 cm)
Tulipa praestans	Bokhara	Scarlet	12 in (30 cm)
Tulipa primulina	Eastern Algeria	Pale yellow	12 in (30 cm)
Tulipa pulchella	Asia Minor	Purple	4 in (10 cm)
Tulipa saxatilis	Crete	Lilac-pink	12 in (30 cm)
Tulipa schrenki	Levant	Crimson	6 in (15 cm)
Tulipa sprengeri	Turkey	Scarlet	12 in (30 cm)
Tulipa stellata	Afghanistan	White, red	9 in (22·5 cm)
Tulipa sylvestris	British Isles	Yellow	15 in (37·5 cm)
Tulipa tarda	Turkestan	Yellow, white	3 in (7·5 cm)
Tulipa suaveolens	Bokhara	Scarlet	6 in (15 cm)
Tulipa triphylla	Bokhara	Yellow	9 in (22·5 cm)
Tulipa tubergeniana	Bokhara	Scarlet	12 in (30 cm)
Tulipa turkestanica	Turkestan	White	9 in (22·5 cm)
Tulipa undulatifolia	Asia Minor	Crimson	6 in (15 cm)
Tulipa urumiensis	Northern Persia	Yellow	4 in (10 cm)
Urceolina pendula	Peru	Yellow	12 in (30 cm)
Urginea altissima	Cape Province	White, purple	12 in (30 cm)
Urginea filifolia	Cape Province	White, purple	12 in (30 cm)
Urginea flexuosa	Cape Province	White, purple	12 in (30 cm)
Urginea maritima	Northern Africa	White, green	12 in (30 cm)
Urginea salteri	Cape Province	White, purple	12 in (30 cm)
Vallota speciosa	Cape Province	Vermilion	15 in (37·5 cm)
Veltheimia glauca	Cape Province	White	15 in (37·5 cm)
Veltheimia viridiflora	Cape Province	Pink	12 in (30 cm)
Watsonia aletroides	Cape Province	Brick red	2 ft (60 cm)
Watsonia alpina	Transvaal	Pink	2 ft (60 cm)
Watsonia angusta	Cape Province	Scarlet	2 ft (60 cm)
Watsonia ardernei	Natal	White	3 ft (90 cm)
Watsonia beatricis	Natal	Flame	4 ft (1·2 metres)
Watsonia comptonii	Cape Province	Orange	2 ft (60 cm)
Watsonia densiflora	Orange Free State	Pink	2 ft (60 cm)
Watsonia galpinii	Cape Province	Orange	2 ft (60 cm)
Watsonia humilis	Cape Province	Magenta	18 in (45 cm)
Watsonia marginata	Cape Province	Lilac-pink	4 ft (1·2 metres)
Watsonia meriana	Natal	Orange-pink	2 ft (60 cm)
Watsonia pyramidata	Cape Province	Rose pink	4 ft (1·2 metres)
Watsonia spectabilis	Cape Province	Orange-red	20 in (50 cm)
Watsonia stanfordiae	Cape Province	Crimson	3 to 4 ft (90 cm to 1·2 metres)
Watsonia tubularis	Cape Province	Coral pink	2 ft (60 cm)
Zephyranthes atamasco	Virginia	White	12 in (30 cm)
Zephyranthes aurea	Peru	Orange-yellow	12 in (30 cm)
Zephyranthes citrina	Guyana	Lemon yellow	12 in (30 cm)
Zephyranthes grandiflora	West Indies	Rose pink	9 in (22·5 cm)
Zephyranthes robusta	Buenos Aires	Rose red	9 in (22·5 cm)
Zephyranthes rosea	Cuba	Rose red	6 in (15 cm)
Zephyranthes tubispatha	Jamaica	White	9 in (22·5 cm)
Zephyranthes verecunda	Mexico	White	6 in (15 cm)
Zygadenus angustifolius	North America	White	18 in (45 cm)
Zygadenus fremontii	North America	Pale yellow	2 ft (60 cm)
Zygadenus glaucus	North America	White	2 ft (60 cm)

APPENDIX C

Planting and Flowering Times for Outdoor Cultivation

Species	Planting depth	When to plant	Flowering time
Acidanthera bicolor	4 in (10 cm)	End April	September–October
Acidanthera tubergenii	4 in (10 cm)	End April	September
Agapanthus umbellatus	6 in (15 cm)	April	August–October
Albuca nelsonii	5 in (12·5 cm)	September	May–June
Allium accuminatum	3 in (7·5 cm)	September	July–August
Allium affatunense	3 in (7·5 cm)	September	May–June
Allium albopilosum	3 in (7·5 cm)	September	June–July
Allium album	3 in (7·5 cm)	September	June–July
Allium amabile	3 in (7·5 cm)	September	July–August
Allium beesianum	3 in (7·5 cm)	September	July–August
Allium coeruleum	3 in (7·5 cm)	September	June–July
Allium flavum	3 in (7·5 cm)	September	July–August
Allium giganteum	3 in (7·5 cm)	September	June–July
Allium kansuense	3 in (7·5 cm)	September	August
Allium karataviense	3 in (7·5 cm)	September	May–June
Allium moly	3 in (7·5 cm)	September	May–June
Allium narcissiflorum	3 in (7·5 cm)	September	June–July
Allium neapolitanum	4 in (10 cm)	September	May–June
Allium oreophilum	3 in (7·5 cm)	September	June–July
Allium pulchellum	3 in (7·5 cm)	September	May–June
Allium rosenbachianum	3 in (7·5 cm)	September	May–June
Allium roseum	4 in (10 cm)	September	June–July
Allium schubertii	4 in (10 cm)	September	June–July
Allium tibeticum	3 in (7·5 cm)	September	June–July
Allium triquetrum	3 in (7·5 cm)	September	May–June
Allium ursinum	3 in (7·5 cm)	September	May–June
Alstroemeria aurantiaca	6 in (15 cm)	April	July–August
Alstroemeria chilensis	6 in (15 cm)	April	August–September
Alstroemeria haemantha	6 in (15 cm)	April	August–September
Alstroemeria ligtu	6 in (15 cm)	April	July–August
Alstroemeria pelegrina	6 in (15 cm)	April	July–August
Alstroemeria pulchella	6 in (15 cm)	April	July–August
Amaryllis belladonna	6 in (15 cm)	May	September–October
Anemone apennina	2 in (5 cm)	September	March–April
Anemone biflora	2 in (5 cm)	September	April–May
Anemone blanda	1 in (2·5 cm)	September	February–April
Anemone coronaria	1 in (2·5 cm)	All year	All year
Anemone fulgens	2 in (5 cm)	All year	All year
Anemone nemorosa	3 in (7·5 cm)	October	April–June
Anemone palmata	2 in (5 cm)	October	April–June
Anemone ranunculoides	2 in (5 cm)	October	March–May
Anemone stellata	1 in (2·5 cm)	All year	All year

Species	Planting depth	When to plant	Flowering time
Anthericum liliago	3 in (7·5 cm)	September	May–August
Antholiza ringens	6 in (15 cm)	September	May–June
Arthropodium candidum	3 in (7·5 cm)	March	July–August
Arthropodium cirrhatum	3 in (7·5 cm)	March	June–July
Asphodelus luteus	6 in (15 cm)	March	June–August
Asphodelus ramosus	6 in (15 cm)	March	June–August
Babiana bainsii	6 in (15 cm)	April	June–July
Babiana disticha	6 in (15 cm)	April	June–July
Babiana hyemalis	6 in (15 cm)	April	June–July
Babiana plicata	6 in (15 cm)	April	June–July
Babiana stricta	6 in (15 cm)	April	June–July
Babiana tubiflora	6 in (15 cm)	April	June–July
Belamcanda chinensis	5 in (12·5 cm)	April	July–August
Bessera elegans	4 in (10 cm)	April	July–September
Bloomeria aurea	4 in (10 cm)	April	June–July
Bobartia filiformis	4 in (10 cm)	April	June–July
Bobartia gladiata	4 in (10 cm)	April	June–July
Bobartia indica	4 in (10 cm)	April	June–July
Brodiaea bridgesi	6 in (15 cm)	October or March	June–July
Brodiaea californica	6 in (15 cm)	October or March	June–July
Brodiaea coccinea	6 in (15 cm)	October or March	June–July
Brodiaea congesta	6 in (15 cm)	October or March	June–July
Brodiaea crocea	6 in (15 cm)	October or March	June–July
Brodiaea grandiflora	6 in (15 cm)	October or March	June–July
Brodiaea hyacinthina	6 in (15 cm)	October or March	June–July
Brodiaea ixioides	6 in (15 cm)	October or March	June–July
Brodiaea laxa	6 in (15 cm)	October or March	June–July
Brodiaea minor	6 in (15 cm)	October or March	June–July
Brodiaea peduncularis	6 in (15 cm)	October or March	June–July
Brodiaea pulchella	6 in (15 cm)	October or March	June–July
Brodiaea rosea	6 in (15 cm)	October or March	June–July
Bulbine alooides	6 in (15 cm)	April	July–August
Bulbine asphodelioides	6 in (15 cm)	April	July–August
Bulbine favosa	6 in (15 cm)	April	July–August
Bulbine mackeni	6 in (15 cm)	April	July–August
Bulbinella floribunda	4 in (10 cm)	April	August–September
Bulbocodium vernum	3 in (7·5 cm)	October	February–March
Calochortus albus	4 in (10 cm)	October	May–June
Calochortus amabilis	4 in (10 cm)	October	May–June
Calochortus benthamii	4 in (10 cm)	October	July–August
Calochortus caeruleus	4 in (10 cm)	October	July
Calochortus clavatus	4 in (10 cm)	October	June–July
Calochortus elegans	4 in (10 cm)	October	June–July
Calochortus leichtlinii	4 in (10 cm)	October	June–July
Calochortus lilacinus	4 in (10 cm)	October	June–August
Calochortus luteus	4 in (10 cm)	October	July
Calochortus macrocarpus	4 in (10 cm)	October	July–August
Calochortus maweanus	4 in (10 cm)	October	July
Calochortus purdyi	4 in (10 cm)	October	June–July
Calochortus venustus	4 in (10 cm)	October	June–July
Calostemma luteum	6 in (15 cm)	April	June–July
Camassia cusickii	3 in (7·5 cm)	September–October	May–June
Camassia esculenta	3 in (7·5 cm)	September–October	June–July
Camassia fraseri	3 in (7·5 cm)	September–October	June–July
Camassia leichtlinii	3 in (7·5 cm)	September–October	June–July
Camassia quamash	3 in (7·5 cm)	September–October	June–July

Species	Planting depth	When to plant	Flowering time
Cardiocrinum giganteum	1 in (2·5 cm)	April	July–August
Chasmanthe aethiopica	4 in (10 cm)	May	July–August
Chionodoxa sardensis	3 in (7·5 cm)	September–October	March–April
Chlidanthus fragrans	1 in (2·5 cm)	April	July–August
Colchicum agrippinum	4 in (10 cm)	July	August–October
Colchicum alpinum	4 in (10 cm)	July	August–October
Colchicum atropurpureum	4 in (10 cm)	July	September–December
Colchicum autumnale	4 in (10 cm)	July	September–December
Colchicum bowlesianum	4 in (10 cm)	July	October–November
Colchicum byzantinum	4 in (10 cm)	July	August–November
Colchicum catacurzenium	4 in (10 cm)	July	March–April
Colchicum cilicicum	4 in (10 cm)	July	October–November
Colchicum decaisnei	4 in (10 cm)	July	November–December
Colchicum doerfleri	4 in (10 cm)	July	February–March
Colchicum giganteum	4 in (10 cm)	July	October–November
Colchicum luteum	4 in (10 cm)	July	February–March
Colchicum macrophyllum	4 in (10 cm)	July	November–December
Colchicum sibthorpii	4 in (10 cm)	July	September–November
Colchicum speciosum	4 in (10 cm)	July	September–October
Colchicum stevenii	4 in (10 cm)	July	November–December
Colchicum tenorii	4 in (10 cm)	July	October–November
Colchicum triphyllum	4 in (10 cm)	July	February–March
Colchicum troodi	4 in (10 cm)	July	October–November
Colchicum variegatum	4 in (10 cm)	July	December–February
Convallaria majalis	3 in (7·5 cm)	October	May–June
Cooperia drummondii	4 in (10 cm)	April	June–July
Cooperia pedunculata	4 in (10 cm)	April	June–July
Crinum americanum	Neck at soil level	May	July–August
Crinum asiaticum	Neck at soil level	May	July–August
Crinum bracteatum	Neck at soil level	May	July–August
Crinum latifolium	Neck at soil level	May	May–June
Crinum longifolium	Neck at soil level	May	June–July
Crinum macowani	Neck at soil level	May	May–June
Crinum moorei	Neck at soil level	May	July–August
Crinum pedunculatum	Neck at soil level	May	June–July
Crocosmia aurea	5 in (12·5 cm)	May	July–October
Crocosmia masonorum	5 in (12·5 cm)	May	July–October
Crocosmia pottsii	5 in (12·5 cm)	May	July–October
Crocus aërius	3 in (7·5 cm)	October	March–April
Crocus aleppicus	3 in (7·5 cm)	September	January–February
Crocus ancyrensis	3 in (7·5 cm)	September	January–March
Crocus asturicus	3 in (7·5 cm)	July	October–November
Crocus aureus	3 in (7·5 cm)	September	February–March
Crocus balansae	3 in (7·5 cm)	September	February–March
Crocus biflorus	3 in (7·5 cm)	September	February–March
Crocus boryi	3 in (7·5 cm)	July	November–December
Crocus byzantinus	3 in (7·5 cm)	June	September–October
Crocus cambessedesii	3 in (7·5 cm)	July	September–March
Crocus cancellatus	3 in (7·5 cm)	July	September–October
Crocus candidus	3 in (7·5 cm)	October	March–April
Crocus carpetanus	3 in (7·5 cm)	September	February–March
Crocus caspius	3 in (7·5 cm)	July	October–February
Crocus chrysanthus	3 in (7·5 cm)	September	January–March
Crocus clusii	3 in (7·5 cm)	July	October–November
Crocus corsicus	3 in (7·5 cm)	October	March–April
Crocus cvijicii	3 in (7·5 cm)	October	March–April

Species	Planting depth	When to plant	Flowering time
Crocus dalmaticus	3 in (7·5 cm)	October	February–March
Crocus danfordiae	3 in (7·5 cm)	October	February–March
Crocus etruscus	3 in (7·5 cm)	October	March–April
Crocus fleischeri	3 in (7·5 cm)	September	January–February
Crocus goulimyi	3 in (7·5 cm)	July	September–October
Crocus graveolens	3 in (7·5 cm)	September	February–March
Crocus hartmannianus	3 in (7·5 cm)	October	February–March
Crocus hyemalis	3 in (7·5 cm)	July	December–January
Crocus imperati	3 in (7·5 cm)	September	January–February
Crocus karduchorum	3 in (7·5 cm)	July	October–November
Crocus korolkowi	3 in (7·5 cm)	October	March–April
Crocus laevigatus	3 in (7·5 cm)	September	December–February
Crocus leichtlinii	3 in (7·5 cm)	October	February–March
Crocus longiflorus	3 in (7·5 cm)	July	October–November
Crocus minimus	3 in (7·5 cm)	October	March–April
Crocus niveus	3 in (7·5 cm)	July	November–December
Crocus nudiflorus	3 in (7·5 cm)	July	October–November
Crocus ochroleucus	3 in (7·5 cm)	July	September–October
Crocus olivieri	3 in (7·5 cm)	October	March–April
Crocus pulchellus	3 in (7·5 cm)	July	November–December
Crocus salzmannii	3 in (7·5 cm)	July	October–November
Crocus sativus	3 in (7·5 cm)	July	October–November
Crocus scharojani	3 in (7·5 cm)	June	August–October
Crocus sieberi	3 in (7·5 cm)	September	January–March
Crocus speciosus	3 in (7·5 cm)	July	October–November
Crocus suaveolens	3 in (7·5 cm)	October	March–April
Crocus susianus	3 in (7·5 cm)	September	February–March
Crocus suterianus	3 in (7·5 cm)	October	March–April
Crocus tomasinianus	3 in (7·5 cm)	September	February–March
Crocus tournefortii	3 in (7·5 cm)	July	November–December
Crocus veluchensis	3 in (7·5 cm)	September	February–March
Crocus vernus	3 in (7·5 cm)	October	March–April
Crocus versicolor	3 in (7·5 cm)	September	February–March
Crocus vitellinus	3 in (7·5 cm)	September	December–February
Crocus zonatus	3 in (7·5 cm)	July	September–November
Cyclamen africanum	1 in (2·5 cm)	July	September–November
Cyclamen cilicium	1 in (2·5 cm)	July	September–November
Cyclamen creticum	1 in (2·5 cm)	September–October	April–May
Cyclamen cyprium	1 in (2·5 cm)	July	August–October
Cyclamen europeum	5 in (12·5 cm)	June	July–October
Cyclamen graecum	1 in (2·5 cm)	July	September–October
Cyclamen libanoticum	1 in (2·5 cm)	September–October	March–April
Cyclamen neapolitanum	1 in (2·5 cm)	June	August–October
Cyclamen orbiculatum	1 in (2·5 cm)	July	December–March
var: *atkinsii*	1 in (2·5 cm)	July	December–March
var: *coum*	1 in (2·5 cm)	July	December–March
Cyclamen pseudo-ibericum	1 in (2·5 cm)	September	January–March
Cyclamen repandum	1 in (2·5 cm)	September–October	March–May
Cyclamen rholfsianum	1 in (2·5 cm)	July	September–October
Cypella gracilis	4 in (10 cm)	May	July–August
Cypella herbertii	4 in (10 cm)	April–May	July–August
Cypella peruviana	4 in (10 cm)	April–May	August
Cypella plumbea	4 in (10 cm)	May	August–September
Dierama pulcherrima	3 in (7·5 cm)	April	August–October
Disporum hookeri	3 in (7·5 cm)	October	May–June
Disporum lanuginosum	3 in (7·5 cm)	October	June

Species	Planting depth	When to plant	Flowering time
Disporum menziesii	3 in (7·5 cm)	October	June–July
Drimia pusilla	4 in (10 cm)	April	July–August
Endymion hispanica	3 in (7·5 cm)	October	May–June
Endymion non-scriptus	3 in (7·5 cm)	October	May–June
Eranthis cilicica	2 in (5 cm)	October	February–April
Eranthis hyemalis	2 in (5 cm)	October	January–March
Eranthis pinnatifida	2 in (5 cm)	October	February–March
Eranthis tubergenii	2 in (5 cm)	October	February–March
Erythronium albidum	3 in (7·5 cm)	October	April–May
Erythronium americanum	3 in (7·5 cm)	October	April–May
Erythronium californicum	3 in (7·5 cm)	October	March–April
Erythronium citrinum	3 in (7·5 cm)	October	March–April
Erythronium dens-canis	3 in (7·5 cm)	October	March–April
Erythronium grandiflorum	3 in (7·5 cm)	October	April–May
Erythronium hartwegii	3 in (7·5 cm)	October	March–April
Erythronium hendersonii	3 in (7·5 cm)	October	March–April
Erythronium montanum	3 in (7·5 cm)	October	March–April
Erythronium oregonum	3 in (7·5 cm)	October	March–April
Erythronium purpurascens	3 in (7·5 cm)	October	March–April
Erythronium revolutum	3 in (7·5 cm)	October	April–May
Erythronium tuolumnense	3 in (7·5 cm)	October	April–May
Exohebia fraterna	2 in (5 cm)	April	July–September
Exohebia parviflora	2 in (5 cm)	April	July–September
Ferraria undulenta	3 in (7·5 cm)	April	June–August
Fritillaria acmopetala	3 in (7·5 cm)	October	March–May
Fritillaria armena	3 in (7·5 cm)	October	April–May
Fritillaria askabadensis	3 in (7·5 cm)	October	April–May
Fritillaria aurea	3 in (7·5 cm)	October	April–May
Fritillaria camschatensis	3 in (7·5 cm)	October	May–June
Fritillaria caucasica	3 in (7·5 cm)	October	April–May
Fritillaria cirrhosa	3 in (7·5 cm)	October	May–June
Fritillaria citrina	3 in (7·5 cm)	October	May–June
Fritillaria crassifolia	3 in (7·5 cm)	October	May–June
Fritillaria delphinensis	3 in (7·5 cm)	October	April–May
Fritillaria discolor	3 in (7·5 cm)	October	April–May
Fritillaria gracilis	3 in (7·5 cm)	October	May–June
Fritillaria graeca	3 in (7·5 cm)	October	April–May
Fritillaria imperialis	6 in (15 cm)	March	May–June
Fritillaria involucrata	3 in (7·5 cm)	October	May–June
Fritillaria liliacea	3 in (7·5 cm)	October	May–June
Fritillaria meleagris	3 in (7·5 cm)	October	April–May
Fritillaria olivieri	3 in (7·5 cm)	October	May–June
Fritillaria oranensis	3 in (7·5 cm)	October	May–June
Fritillaria pallidiflora	3 in (7·5 cm)	October	May–June
Fritillaria persica	3 in (7·5 cm)	October	May–June
Fritillaria pinardii	4 in (10 cm)	October	May–June
Fritillaria pontica	3 in (7·5 cm)	October	April–May
Fritillaria pudica	3 in (7·5 cm)	October	April–May
Fritillaria pyrenaica	3 in (7·5 cm)	October	April–May
Fritillaria recurva	3 in (7·5 cm)	October	June–May
Fritillaria sibthorpiana	3 in (7·5 cm)	October	April–May
Fritillaria thunbergii	3 in (7·5 cm)	October	May–June
Fritillaria verticillata	3 in (7·5 cm)	October	May–June
Gagea lutea	3 in (7·5 cm)	October	March–May
Galanthus byzantinus	4 in (10 cm)	September	January–February
Galanthus caucasicus	4 in (10 cm)	September	January–February

Species	Planting depth	When to plant	Flowering time
Galanthus corcyrensis	4 in (10 cm)	September	December–January
Galanthus elwesii	4 in (10 cm)	September	March–April
Galanthus fosteri	4 in (10 cm)	September	March–April
Galanthus graecus	4 in (10 cm)	September	April–May
Galanthus ikariae	4 in (10 cm)	September	March–April
Galanthus nivalis	4 in (10 cm)	September	January–March
Galanthus plicatus	4 in (10 cm)	September	February–March
Galaxia gramminea	4 in (10 cm)	October	June–July
Galaxia ovata	4 in (10 cm)	October	June–July
Galtonia candicans	6 in (15 cm)	April	August–September
Galtonia clavata	6 in (15 cm)	April	August–September
Galtonia princeps	6 in (15 cm)	April	August–September
Geissorhiza humilis	4 in (10 cm)	April	July–August
Geissorhiza inflexa	4 in (10 cm)	April	July–August
Geissorhiza juncea	4 in (10 cm)	April	July–August
Geissorhiza ovata	4 in (10 cm)	April	July–August
Geissorhiza secunda	4 in (10 cm)	April	June–July
Geissorhiza setacea	4 in (10 cm)	July–August	July–August
Geissorhiza umbrosa	4 in (10 cm)	April	July–August
Gethyllis afra	4 in (10 cm)	April	July–August
Gethyllis ciliaris	4 in (10 cm)	April	July–August
Gladiolus alatus	4 in (10 cm)	April	August–September
Gladiolus angustus	4 in (10 cm)	April	August–September
Gladiolus atroviolaceous	4 in (10 cm)	April	August–September
Gladiolus aureus	4 in (10 cm)	April	August–September
Gladiolus blandus	4 in (10 cm)	April	July–August
Gladiolus byzintinus	4 in (10 cm)	April	July–August
Gladiolus cardinalis	6 in (15 cm)	October	July–August
Gladiolus carinatus	4 in (10 cm)	April	July–August
Gladiolus carmineus	4 in (10 cm)	October	July–August
Gladiolus caryophyllaceus	4 in (10 cm)	April	July–August
Gladiolus communis	4 in (10 cm)	April	July–August
Gladiolus cruentus	4 in (10 cm)	April	September–October
Gladiolus cuspidatus	4 in (10 cm)	April	August–September
Gladiolus grandis	4 in (10 cm)	October	June–July
Gladiolus illyricus	4 in (10 cm)	October	July–August
Gladiolus monticolus	4 in (10 cm)	April	August–September
Gladiolus ornatus	4 in (10 cm)	April	July–August
Gladiolus primulinus	4 in (10 cm)	April	July–August
Gladiolus psittacinus	4 in (10 cm)	April	September–October
Gladiolus purpureo-auratus	4 in (10 cm)	April	July–August
Gladiolus segetum	4 in (10 cm)	April	July–August
Habranthus brachyandrus	4 in (10 cm)	April	July–September
Habranthus robustus	4 in (10 cm)	April	August–September
Haemanthus katharinae	4 in (10 cm)	April	July–September
Herbertia amatorum	4 in (10 cm)	April	July–August
Herbertia pulchella	4 in (10 cm)	April	July–August
Hermodactylus tuberosus	4 in (10 cm)	July	March–April
Hesperantha buchrii	6 in (15 cm)	April	July
Hesperantha pilosa	6 in (15 cm)	April	July
Hesperantha radiata	6 in (15 cm)	April	July
Hesperantha spicata	6 in (15 cm)	April	July
Hesperantha stanfordiae	6 in (15 cm)	April	July
Hexaglottis flexuosa	3 in (7.5 cm)	April	June–July
Hexaglottis longifolia	3 in (7.5 cm)	April	June–July
Hippeastrum advenum	4 in (10 cm)	April	August–September

Species	Planting depth	When to plant	Flowering time
Hippeastrum candidum	4 in (10 cm)	April	July–August
Homeria bulbilifera	6 in (15 cm)	September, March	June–July
Homeria collina	6 in (15 cm)	September, March	June–July
Homeria miniata	6 in (15 cm)	September, March	May–June
Hyacinthus amethystinus	3 in (7·5 cm)	September	May–June
Hyacinthus azureus	3 in (7·5 cm)	September	April–May
Hyacinthus dalmaticus	3 in (7·5 cm)	September	April–May
Hyacinthus orientalis	6 in (15 cm)	September	May–June
Hyacinthus tabrizianus	3 in (7·5 cm)	September	March–April
Hymenocallis andreana	6 in (15 cm)	April	July–August
Hymenocallis narcissiflora	6 in (15 cm)	April	June–July
Hypoxis hirsuta	4 in (10 cm)	September	May–June
Ipheion uniflorum	4 in (10 cm)	October	April–May
Iris acutiloba	1 in (2·5 cm)	July	May–June
Iris alata	3 in (7·5 cm)	April	November–March
Iris albicans	1 in (2·5 cm)	July	May–June
Iris alberti	1 in (2·5 cm)	July	May–June
Iris atropurpurea	1 in (2·5 cm)	June	May–June
Iris bakeriana	3 in (7·5 cm)	September	February–March
Iris barnumae	1 in (2·5 cm)	June	April–May
Iris biflora	1 in (2·5 cm)	July	April–May
Iris biliotti	1 in (2·5 cm)	July	May–June
Iris bismarkiana	1 in (2·5 cm)	June	May
Iris boissieri	4 in (10 cm)	September	June
Iris bracteata	1 in (2·5 cm)	July	May–June
Iris bucharica	3 in (7·5 cm)	September	April–May
Iris caucasica	3 in (7·5 cm)	September	February–March
Iris chameiris	1 in (2·5 cm)	June	April
Iris cristata	1 in (2·5 cm)	July	April–May
Iris danfordiae	2 in (5 cm)	September	February–April
Iris douglassii	1 in (2·5 cm)	July	May–June
Iris duthiei	1 in (2·5 cm)	July	May
Iris flavescens	1 in (2·5 cm)	July	May–June
Iris filifolia	4 in (10 cm)	September	June
Iris florentina	1 in (2·5 cm)	July	May–June
Iris foetidissima	1 in (2·5 cm)	July	May–June
Iris fosteriana	3 in (7·5 cm)	September	March–April
Iris gatesii	1 in (2·5 cm)	July	June
Iris germanica	1 in (2·5 cm)	July	May–June
Iris graminea	1 in (2·5 cm)	July	May–June
Iris graeberiana	3 in (7·5 cm)	September	March–April
Iris hexagona	1 in (2·5 cm)	July	April–May
Iris histrio	3 in (7·5 cm)	September	January–March
Iris histrioides	3 in (7·5 cm)	September	February–March
Iris hoogiana	1 in (2·5 cm)	June	May
Iris hookeriana	1 in (2·5 cm)	July	May–June
Iris iberica	1 in (2·5 cm)	June	May
Iris juncea	4 in (10 cm)	September	June–July
Iris kaempferi	1 in (2·5 cm)	September	July–August
Iris kolpakowskiana	3 in (7·5 cm)	September	March–April
Iris korolkowi	1 in (2·5 cm)	June	May
Iris lortetii	1 in (2·5 cm)	July	June
Iris lutescens	1 in (2·5 cm)	July	May–June
Iris magnifica	3 in (7·5 cm)	September	April–May
Iris missouriensis	1 in (2·5 cm)	July	May–June
Iris orchioides	3 in (7·5 cm)	September	March–April

Species	Planting depth	When to plant	Flowering time
Iris pallida	1 in (2·5 cm)	July	June
Iris persica	3 in (7·5 cm)	September	February–April
Iris prismatica	1 in (2·5 cm)	July	May–June
Iris reticulata	3 in (7·5 cm)	September	February–April
Iris sambucina	1 in (2·5 cm)	July	May–June
Iris sari	1 in (2·5 cm)	June	May
Iris siberica	1 in (2·5 cm)	July	May–June
Iris sindjarensis	3 in (7·5 cm)	September	March–April
Iris stenophylla	2 in (5 cm)	September	March–April
Iris stolonifera	1 in (2·5 cm)	July	June
Iris stylosa	1 in (2·5 cm)	July	January–March
Iris susiana	1 in (2·5 cm)	July	April–May
Iris tectorum	1 in (2·5 cm)	July	May
Iris tingitana	4 in (10 cm)	September	March–April
Iris variegata	1 in (2·5 cm)	July	May–June
Iris vartani	3 in (7·5 cm)	April	October–February
Iris versicolor	1 in (2·5 cm)	July	May–June
Iris willmottiana	4 in (10 cm)	September	February–April
Iris winogradowii	3 in (7·5 cm)	September	February–March
Iris xiphioides	1 in (2·5 cm)	October	July
Iris xiphium	1 in (2·5 cm)	September	April–May
Ixia maculata	4 in (10 cm)	October	June
Ixia odorata	4 in (10 cm)	October	June
Ixia polystachya	4 in (10 cm)	October	June
Ixia viridiflora	4 in (10 cm)	October	June
Ixiolirion kolpakowskianum	6 in (15 cm)	September	April–June
Ixiolirion montanum	6 in (15 cm)	September	May–June
Korolkowia sewergowii	4 in (10 cm)	October	April–May
Lapeyrousia corymbosa	4 in (10 cm)	April	August–September
Lapeyrousia cruenta	4 in (10 cm)	April	August–September
Lapeyrousia fabricii	4 in (10 cm)	April	August–September
Lapeyrousia fistulosa	4 in (10 cm)	April	August–September
Leucojum aestivum	3 in (7·5 cm)	September	May–June
Leucojum autumnale	3 in (7·5 cm)	March	September–October
Leucojum hyemale	3 in (7·5 cm)	September	March–May
Leucojum longifolium	3 in (7·5 cm)	September	April–May
Leucojum roseum	3 in (7·5 cm)	March	September–October
Leucojum tingitanum	3 in (7·5 cm)	September	April–May
Leucojum trichophyllum	3 in (7·5 cm)	September	March–April
Leucojum vernum	3 in (7·5 cm)	September	March–May
Libertia formosa	3 in (7·5 cm)	September	May–June
Libertia grandiflora	3 in (7·5 cm)	September	May–June
Libertia paniculata	3 in (7·5 cm)	September	May–June
Lilium amabile	6 in (15 cm)	Spring/Autumn	July
Lilium auratum	6 in (15 cm)	March	August–September
Lilium bakerianum	5 in (12·5 cm)	March	July–August
Lilium bolanderi	4 in (10 cm)	Spring/Autumn	June
Lilium brownii	6 in (15 cm)	March	July
Lilium bulbiferum	8 in (20 cm)	September–October	June–July
Lilium canadense	6 in (15 cm)	September–October	July
Lilium candidum	1 in (2·5 cm)	September	June–July
Lilium carniolicum	4 in (10 cm)	September–October	May–June
Lilium catesbaei	4 in (10 cm)	September–October	September
Lilium cernuum	4 in (10 cm)	Spring/Autumn	June–July
Lilium chalcedonicum	4 in (10 cm)	Spring/Autumn	June–July
Lilium concolor	4 in (10 cm)	September–October	May–June

Species	Planting depth	When to plant	Flowering time
Lilium columbianum	4 in (10 cm)	Spring/Autumn	July–August
Lilium dauricum	4 in (10 cm)	September–October	June–July
Lilium davidii	3 in (7·5 cm)	Spring/Autumn	July–August
Lilium duchartrei	3 in (7·5 cm)	Spring/Autumn	July
Lilium formosanum	4 in (10 cm)	September–October	June–July
Lilium grayi	3 in (7·5 cm)	September–October	July
Lilium hansonii	8 in (20 cm)	September–October	June–July
Lilium henryi	8 in (20 cm)	Spring/Autumn	August
Lilium humboldtii	4 in (10 cm)	Spring/Autumn	July
Lilium japonicum	6 in (15 cm)	Spring/Autumn	July
Lilium kelloggii	3 in (7·5 cm)	September–October	May–June
Lilium lankongense	4 in (10 cm)	Spring/Autumn	August
Lilium leichtlinii	6 in (15 cm)	March	August
Lilium leucanthum	4 in (10 cm)	March	August
Lilium longiflorum	6 in (15 cm)	March	July–August
Lilium mackliniae	4 in (10 cm)	September–October	June
Lilium maritimum	4 in (10 cm)	Spring/Autumn	July
Lilium martagon	6 in (15 cm)	October	July
Lilium medeoloides	4 in (10 cm)	Spring/Autumn	August
Lilium michauxi	4 in (10 cm)	Spring/Autumn	August
Lilium michiganense	4 in (10 cm)	Spring/Autumn	July
Lilium monadelphum	4 in (10 cm)	Spring/Autumn	July
Lilium neilgherrense	6 in (15 cm)	March	August–September
Lilium nepalense	8 in (20 cm)	March	July–August
Lilium nevadense	3 in (7·5 cm)	Spring/Autumn	July
Lilium nobilissimum	4 in (10 cm)	September–October	May–June
Lilium occidentale	4 in (10 cm)	September–October	July
Lilium papilliferum	4 in (10 cm)	Spring/Autumn	August
Lilium pardalinum	4 in (10 cm)	Spring/Autumn	June–July
Lilium parryi	4 in (10 cm)	September–October	June–August
Lilium parvum	3 in (7·5 cm)	September/October	June–July
Lilium philadelphicum	6 in (15 cm)	June–July	June–July
Lilium philippinense	6 in (15 cm)	March	August–September
Lilium pomponium	4 in (10 cm)	September–October	June
Lilium primulinum	4 in (10 cm)	September–October	July
Lilium pumilum	4 in (10 cm)	September–October	May–June
Lilium pyrenaicum	4 in (10 cm)	September–October	May–June
Lilium regale	6 in (15 cm)	Spring/Autumn	June–July
Lilium rubellum	6 in (15 cm)	September–October	May–June
Lilium rubescens	2 in (5 cm)	September–October	July
Lilium sargentiae	5 in (12·5 cm)	Spring/Autumn	August
Lilium speciosum	6 in (15 cm)	Spring/Autumn	August–September
Lilium sulphureum	6 in (15 cm)	Spring/Autumn	September–October
Lilium superbum	2 in (5 cm)	Spring/Autumn	July–August
Lilium taliense	4 in (10 cm)	September–October	July–August
Lilium × testaceum	2 in (5 cm)	September–October	June–July
Lilium tigrinum	6 in (15 cm)	Spring/Autumn	August–September
Lilium tsingtauense	2 in (5 cm)	September–October	June–July
Lilium vollmeri	3 in (7·5 cm)	Spring/Autumn	July
Lilium wallichianum	6 in (15 cm)	Spring/Autumn	August–September
Lilium wardii	4 in (10 cm)	Spring/Autumn	July–August
Lilium washingtonianum	10 in (25 cm)	Spring/Autumn	June–July
Lilium wigginsii	3 in (7·5 cm)	Spring/Autumn	June–July
Lloydia serotina	2 in (5 cm)	September	May–June
Lycoris aurea	1 in (2·5 cm)	August	August–September
Lycoris radiata	1 in (2·5 cm)	August	August–September

Species	Planting depth	When to plant	Flowering time
Lycoris sanguinea	1 in (2·5 cm)	August	July–August
Medeola virginiana	1 in (2·5 cm)	September	May–June
Merendera filifolia	2 in (5 cm)	July	September–October
Merendera montana	2 in (5 cm)	July	August–September
Merendera sobolifera	2 in (5 cm)	July	April–May
Moraea decussata	3 in (7·5 cm)	September	May–June
Moraea iridioides	3 in (7·5 cm)	September	May–June
Moraea pavonia	3 in (7·5 cm)	September	May–June
Moraea spathacea	3 in (7·5 cm)	September	May–June
Moraea villosa	3 in (7·5 cm)	September	May–June
Muscari ambrosiacum	3 in (7·5 cm)	September	May–June
Muscari argaei	3 in (7·5 cm)	September	May–June
Muscari armenaicum	3 in (7·5 cm)	September	April–May
Muscari botryoides	3 in (7·5 cm)	September	April–May
Muscari comosum	3 in (7·5 cm)	September	May–June
Muscari conicum	3 in (7·5 cm)	September	April–May
Muscari latifolium	3 in (7·5 cm)	September	April–May
Muscari massayanum	3 in (7·5 cm)	September	May–June
Muscari moschatum	3 in (7·5 cm)	September	March–April
Muscari paradoxum	3 in (7·5 cm)	September	May–June
Muscari pinardi	3 in (7·5 cm)	September	May–June
Muscari polyanthum	3 in (7·5 cm)	September	March–May
Muscari racemosum	3 in (7·5 cm)	September	March–April
Muscari tubergenianum	3 in (7·5 cm)	September	April–May
Narcissus bulbocodium	2 in (5 cm)	June–July	March–April
Narcissus calcicola	2 in (5 cm)	June–July	April
Narcissus canaliculatus	2 in (5 cm)	June–July	April
Narcissus cyclamineus	2 in (5 cm)	June–July	April
Narcissus gracilis	2 in (5 cm)	June–July	May–June
Narcissus jonquilla	2 in (5 cm)	June–July	April
Narcissus juncifolius	2 in (5 cm)	June–July	April
Narcissus minimus	2 in (5 cm)	June–July	February–March
Narcissus minor	2 in (5 cm)	June–July	February–March
Narcissus poeticus	2 in (5 cm)	September	May–June
Narcissus pseudo-narcissus	2 in (5 cm)	June–July	March–April
Narcissus rupicola	2 in (5 cm)	June–July	March–April
Narcissus scaberulus	2 in (5 cm)	June–July	March–April
Narcissus serotinus	2 in (5 cm)	June–July	September–October
Narcissus tazetta	2 in (5 cm)	September	March–April
Narcissus triandrus	2 in (5 cm)	June–July	April
Narcissus viridiflorus	2 in (5 cm)	June–July	October–November
Narcissus watieri	2 in (5 cm)	June–July	February–March
Nemastylis coelestina	4 in (10 cm)	October	May–June
Nemastylis graminiflora	4 in (10 cm)	October	May–June
Nerine bowdenii	4 in (10 cm)	July	September–October
Nomocharis aperta	4 in (10 cm)	September	June–July
Nomocharis farreri	4 in (10 cm)	September	June–July
Nomocharis mairei	4 in (10 cm)	September	June–July
Nomocharis meleagrina	4 in (10 cm)	September	June–July
Nomocharis pardanthina	4 in (10 cm)	September	June–July
Nomocharis saluenensis	4 in (10 cm)	September	May–June
Notholirion bulbuliferum	4 in (10 cm)	September	July–August
Notholirion campanulatum	4 in (10 cm)	September	July–August
Nothoscordum fragrans	4 in (10 cm)	September	May–June
Ornithogalum montanum	3 in (7·5 cm)	October	May–June
Ornithogalum narbonense	3 in (7·5 cm)	October	April–June

Species	Planting depth	When to plant	Flowering time
Ornithogalum nutans	3 in (7·5 cm)	October	April–June
Ornithogalum pilosum	3 in (7·5 cm)	October	April–June
Ornithogalum pyramidale	3 in (7·5 cm)	October	May–June
Ornithogalum pyrenaicum	3 in (7·5 cm)	October	May–June
Ornithogalum umbellatum	3 in (7·5 cm)	October	May–June
Oxalis adenophylla	3 in (7·5 cm)	October	May–June
Oxalis brasiliensis	3 in (7·5 cm)	October	May–June
Oxalis enneaphylla	3 in (7·5 cm)	October	May–August
Oxalis lobata	3 in (7·5 cm)	April	August–October
Oxalis magellanica	3 in (7·5 cm)	October	June–August
Oxalis violacea	3 in (7·5 cm)	October	May–June
Pancratium illyricum	6 in (15 cm)	October	June–July
Pancratium maritimum	6 in (15 cm)	April	August–September
Paradisia liliastrum	2 in (5 cm)	October	May–July
Polygonatum biflorum	1 in (2·5 cm)	November	May–June
Polygonatum multiflorum	1 in (2·5 cm)	November	May–June
Polygonatum odorum	1 in (2·5 cm)	November	May–June
Polygonatum officinale	1 in (2·5 cm)	November	May–June
Polygonatum oppositifolium	1 in (2·5 cm)	November	May–June
Polygonatum roseum	1 in (2·5 cm)	November	May–June
Puschkinia libanotica	3 in (7·5 cm)	October	April–May
Ranunculus asiaticus	2 in (5 cm)	October/March	April–May
Reineckia carnea	3 in (7·5 cm)	October	April–May
Romulea bulbocodium	3 in (7·5 cm)	October	April–May
Romulea clusiana	3 in (7·5 cm)	October	April–May
Schizostylis coccinea	4 in (10 cm)	April	September–November
Scilla amoena	3 in (7·5 cm)	October	April–May
Scilla autumnalis	3 in (7·5 cm)	March	August–September
Scilla bifolia	3 in (7·5 cm)	October	March–April
Scilla bithynica	3 in (7·5 cm)	October	March–April
Scilla hyacinthoides	3 in (7·5 cm)	October	July–August
Scilla italica	3 in (7·5 cm)	October	April–May
Scilla menophylla	3 in (7·5 cm)	October	May–June
Scilla messanaica	3 in (7·5 cm)	October	April–May
Scilla odorata	3 in (7·5 cm)	October	May–June
Scilla peruviana	5 in (12·5 cm)	October	May–June
Scilla pratensis	3 in (7·5 cm)	October	May–June
Scilla sibirica	3 in (7·5 cm)	October	March–April
Scilla tubergeniana	3 in (7·5 cm)	October	February–April
Scilla verna	3 in (7·5 cm)	April–May	October–December
Sternbergia clusiana	5 in (12·5 cm)	June	September–November
Sternbergia colchiciflora	5 in (12·5 cm)	June	September–October
Sternbergia fischeriana	5 in (12·5 cm)	October	April–May
Sternbergia lutea	5 in (12·5 cm)	June	August–October
Tecophilaea cyanocrocus	6 in (15 cm)	October	March–April
Tigridia curvata	5 in (12·5 cm)	October/April	May–July
Tigridia pavonia	5 in (12·5 cm)	October/April	May–July
Tigridia violacea	5 in (12·5 cm)	October/April	May–July
Trillium cernuum	4 in (10 cm)	October	April–May
Trillium chloropetalum	4 in (10 cm)	October	April–May
Trillium erectum	4 in (10 cm)	October	May–June
Trillium govanianum	4 in (10 cm)	October	April–May
Trillium grandiflorum	4 in (10 cm)	October	May–June
Trillium luteum	4 in (10 cm)	October	May–June
Trillium nivale	4 in (10 cm)	October	March–April
Trillium pusillum	4 in (10 cm)	October	March–April

Species	Planting depth	When to plant	Flowering time
Trillium recurvatum	4 in (10 cm)	October	April–May
Trillium sessile	4 in (10 cm)	October	April–May
Trillium smallii	4 in (10 cm)	October	April–May
Trillium stylosum	4 in (10 cm)	October	April–May
Trillium tschonoskii	4 in (10 cm)	October	April–May
Trillium undulatum	4 in (10 cm)	October	May–June
Tritonia crocata	4 in (10 cm)	October	May–June
Tropaeolum azureum	4 in (10 cm)	April	June–July
Tropaeolum maritzianum	4 in (10 cm)	April	July–August
Tropaeolum pentaphyllum	4 in (10 cm)	April	June–July
Tropaeolum polyphyllum	4 in (10 cm)	April	June–July
Tropaeolum speciosum	4 in (10 cm)	April	July–August
Tropaeolum tricolor	4 in (10 cm)	April	July–August
Tropaeolum tuberosum	4 in (10 cm)	April	July–September
Tulipa acuminata	6 in (15 cm)	October	May–June
Tulipa aucheriana	6 in (15 cm)	October	March–April
Tulipa batalinii	6 in (15 cm)	October	March–April
Tulipa biflora	6 in (15 cm)	October	February–March
Tulipa borszczowi	6 in (15 cm)	October	April
Tulipa clusiana	6 in (15 cm)	October	April
Tulipa eichleri	6 in (15 cm)	October	April–May
Tulipa fosteriana	6 in (15 cm)	October	April
Tulipa gesneriana	6 in (15 cm)	October	May
Tulipa greigii	6 in (15 cm)	October	April
Tulipa hageri	6 in (15 cm)	October	April–May
Tulipa hoogiana	6 in (15 cm)	October	May
Tulipa humilis	6 in (15 cm)	October	February–March
Tulipa ingens	6 in (15 cm)	October	May
Tulipa kauffmanniana	6 in (15 cm)	October	February–April
Tulipa kolpakowskiana	6 in (15 cm)	October	April–May
Tulipa lanata	6 in (15 cm)	October	April–May
Tulipa linifolia	6 in (15 cm)	October	May–June
Tulipa maximowiczii	6 in (15 cm)	October	April–May
Tulipa montana	6 in (15 cm)	October	May
Tulipa orphanidea	6 in (15 cm)	October	April–May
Tulipa ostrowskiana	6 in (15 cm)	October	April–May
Tulipa persica	6 in (15 cm)	October	May–June
Tulipa polychroma	6 in (15 cm)	October	February–March
Tulipa praestans	6 in (15 cm)	October	April
Tulipa primulina	6 in (15 cm)	October	May
Tulipa pulchella	6 in (15 cm)	October	March–April
Tulipa saxatilis	6 in (15 cm)	October	May
Tulipa schrenki	6 in (15 cm)	October	April
Tulipa sprengeri	6 in (15 cm)	October	June
Tulipa stellata	6 in (15 cm)	October	April–May
Tulipa suaveolens	6 in (15 cm)	October	March–April
Tulipa sylvestris	6 in (15 cm)	October	April–May
Tulipa tarda	6 in (15 cm)	October	March–April
Tulipa triphylla	6 in (15 cm)	October	May
Tulipa tubergeniana	6 in (15 cm)	October	April–May
Tulipa turkestanica	6 in (15 cm)	October	March–April
Tulipa undulatifolia	6 in (15 cm)	October	April
Tulipa urumiensis	6 in (15 cm)	October	April
Urginea altissima	6 in (15 cm)	October	May–June
Urginea filifolia	6 in (15 cm)	October	May–June
Urginea flexuosa	6 in (15 cm)	October	May–June

Species	Planting depth	When to plant	Flowering time
Urginea maritima	6 in (15 cm)	October	May–June
Urginea salteri	6 in (15 cm)	October	May–June
Watsonia alpina	4 in (10 cm)	April	August–September
Watsonia beatricis	4 in (10 cm)	April	August–September
Watsonia densiflora	4 in (10 cm)	April	August–September
Watsonia galpinii	4 in (10 cm)	April	August–September
Watsonia humilis	4 in (10 cm)	April	July–August
Watsonia marginata	4 in (10 cm)	April	July–August
Watsonia meriana	4 in (10 cm)	April	June–July
Watsonia pyramidata	4 in (10 cm)	April	June–July
Watsonia stanfordiae	4 in (10 cm)	April	August–September
Zephyranthes candida	5 in (12·5 cm)	April	September–October
Zygadenus angustifolius	3 in (7·5 cm)	October	May–June
Zygadenus fremantii	3 in (7·5 cm)	October	May–June
Zygadenus glaucus	3 in (7·5 cm)	October	May–June

APPENDIX D

Flowering Times for Indoor Bulbs

Species	When to Plant	Flowering Time
Achimenes	February–May	May–October
Acidanthera candida	March–April	August–September
Albuca nelsonii	September–October	May–June
Alstroemeria brasiliensis	September–October	February–March
Alstroemeria caryophyllea	September–October	February–March
Amaryllis belladonna	March–April	August–September
Ammocharis falcata	May–June	November–December
Antholyza ringens	January–February	May–June
Asparagus plumosus	April	May–June
Asparagus sprengeri	April	May–June
Babiana stricta	March	May–June
Belamcanda chinensis	March	May–June
Bessera elegans	March	June–August
Bomarea corderi	March	June–August
Bravoa geminiflora	October	May–June
Brunsvigia gigantea	April	July–September
Caliphruria hartwegiana	October	May–June
Callipsyche aurantiaca	March, September	August
Callipsyche bicolor	September	April–May
Callipsyche eucrosioides	September	May, September
Callipsyche mirabilis	September	June, December
Chasmanthe floribunda	September	May–June
Chlidanthus fragrans	March	June–July
Clivia gardeni	May	January–March
Clivia miniata	October	May–June
Clivia nobilis	October	May–June
Cooperia drummondii	February	May–June
Crinum amabile	May	November–December
Crinum asiaticum	March	July–August
Crinum latifolium	March	July–August
Crinum longifolium	November	May–June
Crinum moorei	March	July–August
Crinum pedunculatum	March	July–August
Crinum × powellii	March	June–September

Species	When to Plant	Flowering Time
Cyclamen africanum	June	September–October
Cyclamen persicum	June	October–January
Cyrtanthus angustifolius	March	July–August
Cyrtanthus huttoni	February	May–June
Cyrtanthus lutescens	February	May–June
Cyrtanthus mackenii	October	March–April
Cyrtanthus obliquus	February	May–June
Cyrtanthus o'brienii	March	June–July
Cyrtanthus odorus	March	July–August
Cyrtanthus sanguineus	March	July–August
Cyrtanthus spiralis	April	October–November
Cyrtanthus tuckii	March	July–August
Drimia elata	October	February–March
Eucharis amazonica	March	November–April
Eucharis candida	March	November–March
Eucharis mastersi	March	November–March
Eucharis sanderi	March	November–March
Eucomis bicolor	March	August–September
Eucomis nana	March	July–August
Eucomis pole-evansii	March	August–September
Eucomis punctata	March	July–August
Eucomis undulata	March	August–September
Eucrosia bicolor	October	March–May
Eurycles cunninghami	October	June–August
Eurycles sylvestris	October	June–August
Eustephia coccinea	October	April–May
Ferraria undulenta	January	April–June
Freesia refracta	May	December–March
Gesneria blassii	All year	All year
Gesneria douglasii	All year	All year
Gesneria lindleyi	All year	All year
Gesneria macrantha	All year	All year
Gesneria pendulina	All year	All year
Gesneria tuberosa	All year	All year
Gloriosa carsonii	February	June–September
Gloriosa rothschildiana	February	June–September
Gloriosa superba	February	June–September
Gloriosa verschuurii	February	June–September
Gloriosa virescens	February	June–September
Gloxinia fimbriata	March	July–August
Gloxinia maculata	March	August–September
Griffinia blumenavia	September	February–March

Species	When to Plant	Flowering Time
Griffinia hyacinthina	September	January–February
Griffinia liboniana	September	March–April
Griffinia ornata	September	December–January
Griffinia parviflora	September	February–March
Gynandriris sisyrinchium	March	May–June
Habranthus andersonii	September	May–June
Habranthus brachyandrus	March	July–September
Habranthus robustus	March	August–September
Habranthus versicolor	August	December–January
Haemanthus albiflos	March	June–July
Haemanthus brevifolius	March	June–July
Haemanthus cinnabarinus	March	June–July
Haemanthus coccineus	March	August–September
Haemanthus katharinae	March	July–August
Haemanthus magnificus	March	June–July
Haemanthus multiflorus	March	July–August
Haemanthus natalensis	March	June–July
Haemanthus pubescens	March	June–July
Haemanthus puniceus	March	July–August
Herbertia amatorum	March	July
Herbertia pulchella	March	July
Hesperantha buchrii	November	May–June
Hesperantha pilosa	November	May–June
Hesperantha radiata	November	May–June
Hesperantha spicata	November	May–June
Hesperantha stanfordiae	November	May–June
Hesperocallis undulata	October	April–May
Hexaglottis flexuosa	April	June–July
Hexaglottis longifolia	April	June–July
Hippeastrum bifidum	September–October	April–May
Hippeastrum candidum	October–January	July–August
Hippeastrum equestre	September–October	June–September
Hippeastrum pratense	September–October	April–May
Hippeastrum reginae	September–October	June–July
Hippeastrum reticulatum	October–January	July–August
Hippeastrum rutilum	October–January	July–August
Hippeastrum vittatum	September–October	June–September
Homeria bulbillifera	November	May
Homeria collina	November	May
Homeria miniata	November	May
Homoglossum priorii	September	February–March
Homoglossum watsonium	September	February–March

Species	When to Plant	Flowering Time
Hyacinthus orientalis	September	December–April
Hyacinthus romanus	September	December–April
Hymenocallis amancaes	April	June–July
Hymenocallis andreana	April	July–August
Hymenocallis festalis	April	June–July
Hymenocallis harrisiana	April	June–July
Hymenocallis lacera	April	June–July
Hymenocallis narcissiflora	April	June–July
Hymenocallis speciosa	April	June–July
Hymenocallis tubiflora	April	June–July
Hymenocallis undulata	April	June–July
Hypoxis hirsuta	September	April–May
Hypoxis stellata	September	April–May
Ipheion uniflorum	October	March–April
Ixia maculata	October	April–May
Ixia odorata	October	April–May
Ixia polystachya	October	April–May
Ixia viridiflora	October	April–May
Korolkowia sewerzowii	September	March–April
Lachenalia glaucina	August	March–May
Lachenalia mutabilis	August	March–May
Lachenalia orchioides	August	March–May
Lachenalia pearsonii	August	March–May
Lachenalia pendula	August	December–March
Lachenalia rubida	August	March–May
Lachenalia tricolor	August	March–May
Lapeyrousia corymbosa	March	July–September
Lapeyrousia cruenta	March	July–September
Lapeyrousia fabricii	March	July–September
Lapeyrousia fistulosa	March	July–September
Leucocoryne ixioides	September	March–May
Leucojum hyemale	September	March–May
Leucojum trichophyllum	September	March–May
Libertia formosa	September	April–May
Libertia grandiflora	September	April–May
Libertia paniculata	September	April–May
Liriopsis horsmannii	March	July–August
Littonia modesta	March	July–August
Lycoris aurea	August	July–August
Lycoris incarnata	August	July–August
Lycoris radiata	August	July–August
Lycoris sanguinea	August	July–August

Species	When to Plant	Flowering Time
Lycoris sprengeri	August	July–August
Lycoris squamigera	August	July–August
Lycoris straminea	August	July–August
Massonia amygdalina	September	April–May
Massonia jasminiflora	September	April–May
Massonia muricata	September	April–May
Massonia pustulata	September	April–May
Massonia sanguinea	September	April–May
Melasphaerula graminea	September	April–May
Merendera persica	July–August	April–May
Merendera trigyna	July–August	April–May
Moraea bicolor	September	March–April
Moraea decussata	September	March–April
Moraea odorata	September	March–April
Moraea papilionacea	September	March–April
Moraea pavonia	September	March–April
Moraea ramosissima	September	March–April
Moraea spathacea	September	March–April
Moraea villosa	September	March–April
Muscari moschatum	September	March–May
Muscari massayanum	September	March–May
Muscari pinardii	September	March–May
Nemastylis coelestina	February	May
Nemastylis graminiflora	February	May
Nerine angustifolia	July–August	September–November
Nerine appendiculata	July–August	September–November
Nerine bowdenii	July–August	September–October
Nerine filifolia	July–August	October–November
Nerine flexuosa	July–August	September–October
Nerine humilis	July–August	September–October
Nerine masonorum	July	August–September
Nerine moorei	July–August	October
Nerine sarniensis	July–August	September–October
Nerine undulata	July–August	October
Notholirion macrophyllum	September	April–May
Notholirion thomsonianum	September	April–May
Ornithogalum arabicum	September	May–July
Ornithogalum balansae	September	March–April
Ornithogalum graminifolium	September	August–September
Ornithogalum lacteum	September	June–July
Ornithogalum saundersii	September	June–August
Ornithogalum subcucculatum	September	June–August

Species	When to Plant	Flowering Time
Ornithogalum thyrsoides	September	May–June
Oxalis bowiei	September	July–September
Oxalis cernua	September	April
Oxalis falcata	August	November–January
Oxalis hirta	April	November–December
Oxalis variabilis	August	November–January
Pamianthe peruviana	September	March–April
Pancratium canariense	March	September–October
Pancratium illyricum	October	June–July
Pancratium maritimum	March	August–September
Pancratium sickenbergerii	March	September–October
Pancratium verecundum	March	September–October
Phaedranassa carmioli	October	May–June
Phaedranassa chloracea	October	May–June
Phaedranassa lepmannii	October	May–June
Polianthes tuberosa	All year	All year
Rigidella flammea	November	May–June
Romulea bulbocodium	October	March–April
Romulea bulbocoidoides	October	April–May
Romulea clusiana	October	March–April
Romulea elegans	October	April–May
Romulea hirsuta	October	April–May
Romulea requienii	October	April
Romulea rosea	October	April–May
Romulea subulosa	October	April–May
Romulea triflora	October	May
Sandersonia aurantiaca	April	July–September
Schizostylis coccinea	April	September–November
Scilla cooperi	October	April–May
Scilla natalensis	March	August–September
Scilla villosa	October	April–May
Sparaxis grandiflora	October	April–June
Sprekelia formosissima	October	July–August
Stenomesson aurantiacum	January	May–June
Stenomesson coccineum	March	July–August
Stenomesson croceum	January	May–June
Stenomesson humile	January	April–May
Stenomesson incarnatum	January	May–June
Stenomesson luteo-viride	January	May–June
Stenomesson viridiflorum	January	May–June
Streptanthera cuprea	October	May–June
Streptanthera elegans	October	May–June

Species	When to Plant	Flowering Time
Synnotia bicolor	October	April–June
Synnotia meterlerkampiae	October	April–June
Syringodea pulchella	March	August–September
Tecophilaea cyanocrocus	October	February–March
Tigridia curvata	October–February	May–July
Tigridia pavonia	October–February	May–July
Tigridia pringlei	October–February	May–July
Tigridia violacea	October–February	May–July
Tritonia crocata	October	April–May
Tritonia crispa	October	April–May
Tritonia hyalina	October	April–May
Tritonia scillaris	October	April–May
Urceolina pendula	October	May–June
Vallota speciosa	May	August–September
Veltheimia glauca	September	December–March
Veltheimia viridiflora	September	December–March
Watsonia aletroides	November	May–June
Watsonia ardernei	November	June–July
Watsonia spectabilis	November	April–May
Zephyranthes atamasco	November	April–May
Zephyranthes aurea	March	August–September
Zephyranthes citrina	March	August–September
Zephyranthes grandiflora	March	August–September
Zephyranthes robusta	March	July–August
Zephyranthes rosea	March	August–September
Zephyranthes tubispatha	March	July–August

APPENDIX E

Bulbs with Scented Flowers

Species	Colour	Scent	In bloom
Achimene tubiflora	White	Sweet	June–September
Acidanthera aequinoctialis	White	Sweet	September–October
Acidanthera bicolor	Cream	Violet	September–October
Acidanthera candida	White	Violet	September–October
Albuca nelsonii	White	Lily	June–July
Allium neapolitanum	White	Violet	May–June
Alstroemeria caryophyllea	Scarlet	Clove	February–March
Alstroemeria ligtu	Various	Sweet	July–August
Amaryllis belladonna	Rose pink	Lily	September–October
Anthericum liliago	Yellow	Lily	May–June
Babiana bainsii	Blue	Mossy	May–June
Babiana disticha	Pale blue	Soft	May–June
Babiana hyemalis	Blue	Mossy	January–February
Babiana plicata	Violet	Soft	May–June
Babiana stricta	Blue	Mossy	May–June
Babiana tubiflora	Cream	Soft	May–June
Bulbine favosa	Yellow	Jasmine	July–August
Cardiocrinum cordatum	White	Lily	July–August
Cardiocrinum giganteum	White	Lily	July–August
Chlidanthus fragrans	Yellow	Lily	July–August
Convallaria majalis	White	Lily	May–June
Cooperia drummondii	White	Lily	May–June
Crinum amabile	Red	Sweet	November–December
Crinum americanum	White	Sweet	July–August
Crinum asiaticum	Greenish	Lily-like	July–August
Crinum bracteatum	White	Lily-like	July–August
Crinum latifolium	Greenish	Sweet	May–June
Crinum longifolium	Pinkish white	Sweet	June–July
Crinum macowani	Lilac pink	Sweet	May–June
Crinum moorei	Rose pink	Sweet	July–August
Crinum pedunculatum	Greenish	Sweet	June–July
Crocus chrysanthus	Lilac mauve	Primrose	January–March
Crocus graveolens	Yellow, brown	Unpleasant (beetles)	February–March
Crocus imperati	Lilac mauve	Primrose	January–March
Crocus laevigatus	White	Sweet	October–March
Crocus leichtlinii	Yellowish green	Sweet	February–March
Crocus longiflorus	Violet	Honeysuckle	October–November
Crocus suaveolens	Lilac	Violet	March–April
Crocus versicolor	Pale mauve	Sweet	February–March
Crocus vitellinus	Yellow	Sweet	December–February
Cyclamen africanum	Rose red	Sweet	September–November
Cyclamen cilicium	Pale pink	Vanilla	September–November
Cyclamen creticum	White	Clove	April–May
Cyclamen cyprium	Pale pink	Vanilla	August–October

Species	Colour	Scent	In bloom
Cyclamen europeum	Carmine	Musk	July–October
Cyclamen libanoticum	Salmon pink	Vanilla	March–April
Cyclamen pseudo-ibericum	Violet	Sweet	March–April
Cyclamen repandum	Blush white	Sweet	March–May
Cyrtanthus lutescens	Yellow	Lily	May–June
Endymion hispanica	White	Balsamic	May–July
Endymion non-scriptus	Blue	Balsamic	May–June
Eranthis, Guinea Gold	Yellow	Sweet	February–March
Eucharis amazonica	White	Lily	November–April
Eucharis candida	White	Lily	November–March
Eucharis sanderi	White	Lily	November–March
Eucomis punctata	Cream	Lily	July–August
Exohebia parviflora	Yellow-maroon	Sweet	July–September
Ferraria undulenta	Purple-brown	Unpleasant	May–July
Fritillaria citrina	Yellow	Mossy	April–May
Fritillaria imperialis	Orange, yellow	Foxy	April–May
Fritillaria liliacea	Cream	Indol	April–May
Freesia refracta	Cream	Violet	All year
Galanthus ikariae	White and green	Mossy	March–April
Galanthus nivalis	White and green	Sweet	February–March
(Arnotts Seedling)			
Galtonia candicans	White	Soft	August–September
Gethyllis afra	White and red	Sweet	July–August
Gethyllis ciliaris	White	Sweet	July–August
Gladiolus alatus	Brick red	Sweet	August–September
Gladiolus carinatus	Violet	Violet	August–September
Gladiolus caryophyllaceus	Rose pink	Clove	July–August
Gladiolus grandis	Maroon-yellow	Clove	May–June
Gladiolus maculatus	Pink-brown	Sweet	April–May
Gladiolus orchidiflorus	Green-brown	Sweet	December–January
Gladiolus recurvus	Yellow	Violet	June–July
Gladiolus tristis	Creamy white	Clove	May–June
Gloxinia maculata	Purple-blue	Sweet	August–September
Gynandriris sisyrinchium	Pale blue	Sweet	May–June
Hemerocallis lutea	Yellow	Sweet	June–July
Hesperantha buchrii	White	Sweet	June–July
Hesperantha pilosa	White	Sweet	June–July
Hesperantha radiata	Pale yellow	Sweet	June–July
Hesperantha spicata	White, red	Sweet	June–July
Hesperantha stanfordiae	Pale yellow	Sweet	June–July
Hesperocallis undulenta	White	Sweet	April–May
Hexaglottis flexuosa	Yellow	Unpleasant	June–July
Hexaglottis longifolia	Yellow	Unpleasant	June–July
Hippeastrum candidum	White	Sweet	July–August
Homeria bulbilifera	Creamy pink	Unpleasant	July–August
Homeria miniata	Salmon	Sweet	May–June
Hyacinthus azureus	Blue	Balsamic	April–May
Hyacinthus orientalis	Blue	Balsamic	December–May
Hyacinthus tubrizianus	White	Sweet	March–April
Hymenocallis andreana	White	Sweet	July–August
Hymenocallis amancaes	Yellow	Sweet	June–July
Hymenocallis festalis	White	Sweet	June–July
Hymenocallis harrisiana	White	Sweet	June–July
Hymenocallis lacera	White	Sweet	June–July
Hymenocallis narcissiflora	White	Sweet	June–July
Hymenocallis speciosa	White, green	Sweet	June–July

U

Species	Colour	Scent	In bloom
Hymenocallis tubiflora	White	Sweet	June–July
Hymenocallis undulata	White	Sweet	February–March
Ipheion uniflorum	White	Sweet	March–April
Iris bakeriana	Blue, white	Violet	February–March
Iris barnumae	Wine purple	Lily of the Valley	May
Iris bartoni	Cream	Vanilla	June
Iris biflora	Purple	Sweet	April–May
Iris biliotti	Purple	Sweet	May–June
Iris florentina	White	Violet	May–June
Iris germanica	Purple	Sweet	May–June
Iris graminea	Mauve	Apricot	May–June
Iris hoogiana	Purple	Tea rose	February–April
Iris juncea	Yellow	Sweet	June–July
Iris kolpakowskiana	Purple	Sweet	March–April
Iris pallida	Lilac	Orange	June
Iris persica	Purple	Almond	February–April
Iris reticulata	Purple	Violet	February–April
Iris sambucina	Claret purple	Elder	May
Iris sindjarensis	Slate blue	Vanilla	March–April
Iris stylosa	Sky blue	Primrose	January–March
Iris vartoni	Lavender	Almond	October–February
Ixia odorata	Pale yellow	Sweet	April–May
Lachenalia glaucina	Pale blue	Sweet	April–May
Lachenalia orchioides	Pale yellow	Sweet	March–May
Leucocoryne ixioides	Blue	Plums	March–May
Leucojum vernum	White, green	Violet	March–May
Lilium amabile	White, yellow	Indol	August–September
Lilium auratum	White, yellow	Sweet	August–September
Lilium bakerianum	Greenish-white	Heavy	July–August
Lilium brownii	White, purple	Soft	July
Lilium candidum	White	Sweet	June–July
Lilium cernuum	Lilac-pink	Soft	June–July
Lilium duchartrei	White, purple	Soft	June–July
Lilium formosanum	White, purple	Sweet	June–July
Lilium leucanthum	White	Sweet	August
Lilium longiflorum	White	Sweet	July–August
Lilium nepalense	Lime green	Heavy	July–August
Lilium papilliferum	Purple-maroon	Sweet	August
Lilium parryi	Yellow	Sweet	June–August
Lilium philippinense	White	Sweet	August–September
Lilium regale	White	Sweet	June–July
Lilium rubellum	Rose	Sweet	May–June
Lilium rubescens	White	Sweet	July
Lilium sargentiae	White	Sweet	August
Lilium speciosum	White	Sweet	August–September
Lilium sulphureum	Cream	Sweet	September–October
Lilium taliense	White	Sweet	July–August
Lilium × testaceum	Apricot	Sweet	June–July
Lilium wallichianum	Cream	Sweet	August–September
Lilium wardii	Purple-pink	Sweet	July–August
Lycoris sprengeri	Mauve, pink	Sweet	August–September
Lycoris squamigera	Rosy lilac	Sweet	August–September
Lycoris straminea	Buff, pink	Sweet	August–September
Merendera trigyna	White, rose	Sweet	April–May
Moraea ducussata	Yellow	Sweet	May–June
Moraea odorata	White	Sweet	May–June

Species	Colour	Scent	In bloom
Moraea papilianacea	Brick red	Sweet	May–June
Moraea ramosissima	Dull yellow	Lily	May–June
Moraea spathacea	Yellow	Sweet	May–June
Muscari ambrosiacum	Lilac, cream	Musk	April–May
Muscari botryoides	Navy blue	Starch	April–May
Muscari comosum	Purple	Sweet	May–June
Muscari conicum	Brilliant blue	Sweet	April–May
Muscari moschatum	Olive green	Musk	March–April
Muscari racemosum	Purple-blue	Plum	March–April
Narcissus calcicola	Yellow	Sweet	April
Narcissus canaliculatus	Yellow	Sweet	April
Narcissus jonquilla	Yellow	Sweet	April
Narcissus juncifolius	Yellow	Sweet	April
Narcissus odorus	Yellow	Sweet	March–April
Narcissus poeticus	White	Sweet	May–June
Narcissus pseudo-narcissus	Yellow	Mossy	March–April
Narcissus rupicola	Yellow	Sweet	March–April
Narcissus tazetta	White	Sweet	March–April
Notholirion thomsonianum	Mauve	Sweet	April–May
Northoscordum fragrans	White, mauve	Sweet	May–June
Ornithogalum nutans	Silver grey	Mossy	April–June
Oxalis enneaphylla	Blush White	Almond	May–August
Pamianthe peruviana	White	Sweet	March–April
Pancratium canariense	White	Lily-like	September–October
Pancratium illyricum	White	Lily-like	June–July
Pancratium maritimum	White	Lily-like	August–September
Pancratium sickenbengerii	White	Lily-like	September–October
Pancratium tortuosum	White	Lily-like	January–February
Pancratium verecundum	White	Lily-like	September–October
Polianthes tuberosa	White	Balsamic	All year
Polygonatum odorum	Greenish white	Lily	May–June
Scilla hyacinthoides	Lilac-blue	Balsamic	July–August
Scilla italica	Pale blue	Balsamic	April–May
Scilla odorata	Pale blue	Balsamic	May–June
Scilla pratensis	Lilac-blue	Balsamic	May–June
Sternbergia colchiciflora	Yellow	Sweet	September–October
Tecophilaea cyanocrocus	Pale blue	Sweet	February–March
Trillium cernuum	White	Sweet	April–May
Trillium erectum	Purple	Foetid	May–June
Trillium luteum	Yellow	Lemon	May–June
Tulipa gesneriana	Crimson	Sweet	May
Tulipa persica	Yellow	Sweet	May–June
Tulipa primulina	Yellow	Sweet	May
Tulipa sylvestris	Yellow	Sweet	May
Watsonia marginata	Lilac	Sweet	July–August

Common Names of Bulbous Plants

Aconitum	Monk's hood, wolf's bane	*Haemanthus*	Blood flower Red Cape lily
Agapanthus	Blue African lily	*Hemerocallis*	Day lily
Allium	Flowering garlic	*Hermodactylus*	Snake's head iris
Alstroemeria	Lily of Peru	*Hippeastrum equestre*	Barbados lily
Amaryllis belladonna	Belladonna lily		Equestrian star-flower
Ammocharis	Malagas lily	*Homeria miniata*	Red tulip
Anemone	Windflower	*Homoglossum priorii*	Red Afrikaner
Anthericum liliago	St Bernard's lily	*Hymenocallis*	Spider lily
Asphodelus luteus	Yellow asphodel	*Hypoxis*	Star grass
Asphodelus ramosus	Giant asphodel	*Ixia*	Corn lily
Babiana	Baboon flower	*Ixiolirion*	Blue Altai lily
Belamcanda chinensis	Blackberry lily	*Lachenalia*	Cape cowslip
Bessera elegans	Coral drops		Leopard Lily
Brodiaea coccinea	Californian firecracker	*Leucojum aestivum*	Summer snowflake
	Crimson satin flower	*Leucojum vernum*	Spring snowflake
Brodiaea hyacinthina	Missouri hyacinth	*Lilium candidum*	Madonna lily
Brodiaea icioides	Golden star flower		White lily of the East
	Pretty face	*Lilium cernuum*	Nodding lily
Brodiaea pulchella	Wild hyacinth	*Lilium chalcedonicum*	Scarlet Turk's-cap
Bulbinella hookeri	Maori onion	*Lilium croceum*	Orange lily
Bulbocodium vernum	Spring meadow saffron	*Lilium longiflorum*	Easter lily
Calochortus amabilis	Golden lanterns	*Lilium pardalinum*	Panther lily
Calochortus elegans	Mariposa lily	*Lilium philadelphicum*	American flame lily
Camassia quamash	Quamash		Red lily
Chionodoxa	Glory of the snow	*Lilium regale*	Regal lily
Colchicum autumnale	Meadow saffron	*Lilium superbum*	Swamp lily
Cooperia drummondii	Texas star flower	*Lilium × testaceum*	Nankeen lily
Crocus sativus	Saffron	*Lilium tigrinum*	Tiger lily
Cyclaminus europeum	Sowbread	*Lloydia serotina*	Snowdon lily
Dierama pulcherrima	Wand flower	*Lycoris aurea*	Golden spider lily
Endymion hispanica	Spanish bluebell	*Medeola*	Cucumber root
Endymion non-scriptus	English bluebell	*Merendera montana*	Pyrenees meadow saffron
Eranthis	Winter aconite		
Erythronium dens-canis	Dog's tooth violet	*Muscari*	Grape hyacinth
Erythronium revolutum	Trout lily	*Ornithogalum pyrenaicum*	Bath asparagus
Eucomis bicolor	Pineapple flower		
Fritillaria imperialis	Crown imperial	*Ornithogalum thyrsoides*	Chincherinchee
Fritillaria meleagris	Chequered daffodil Snakeshead daffodil	*Ornithogalum umbellatum*	Star of Bethlehem
Gagea lutea	Yellow Star of Bethlehem	*Polygonatum multiflorum*	Solomon's seal
Galanthus	February fair maids	*Polygonatum odorum*	Angular Solomon's seal
	Snowdrop	*Puschkinia scilloides*	Lebanon squill
Galtonia candicans	Spire lily		Striped squill
Gladiolus	Sword lily	*Sandersonia aurantiaca*	Christmas bells

Scilla amoena	Byzantine squill	*Tigridia pavonia*	Peacock tiger flower
	Star squill	*Trillium cernuum*	Bashful Ben
Scilla cooperi	South African squill		Nodding wood lily
Scilla italica	Italian squill	*Trillium erectum*	Wet dog
Scilla natalensis	Blue squill	*Trillium grandiflorum*	Snow lily
Scilla peruviana	Cuban lily		Wake robin
Scilla sibirica	Siberian squill	*Trillium recurvatum*	Prairie lily
Scilla verna	Spring squill	*Trillium undulatum*	Painted wake robin
Sparaxis	Harlequin flower	*Tropaeolum speciosum*	Chilean flame flower
Sprekelia formosissima	Aztec lily	*Urginea maritima*	Sea onion
	Jacobean lily	*Vallota speciosa*	Scarborough lily
Tigridia	Mexican shell-flower	*Watsonia*	Southern bugle lily
	Tiger flower	*Zephyranthes candida*	Swamp lily

From Sowing Time to Bloom

Species	Time (years)	Species	Time (years)
Achimene	2	*Eucomis*	5 to 6
Acidanthera	3	*Freesia*	9 to 12 months
Agapanthus	5–6	*Fritillaria*	4
Albuca	4–5	*Galanthus*	4
Allium	2	*Galtonia*	5
Alstroemeria	4	*Gladiolus*	4
Amaryllis belladonna	8	*Gloriosa*	2
Anemone	1	*Gloxinia*	2
Anthericum	3	*Griffinia*	5
Antholiza	3	*Habranthus*	3 to 4
Bellamcanda	3 to 4	*Hexaglottis*	4
Bravoa	3	*Hippeastrum*	3
Brodiaea	3 to 4	*Homeria*	3
Brunsvigia	12 to 15	*Hymenocallis*	4
Calochortus	5 to 6	*Iris*	4
Camassia	3 to 4	*Ixia*	2
Cardiocrinum	7 to 8	*Lachenalia*	3 to 4
Chasmanthe	3	*Lapeyrousia*	2
Chionodoxa	2 to 3	*Leucojum*	4 to 5
Clivia	2 to 3	*Lilium*	18 months to 4 years
Colchicum	4 to 5	*Lycoris*	4
Convallaria	2 to 3	*Merendera*	4 to 5
Crinum	3 to 4	*Muscari*	4 to 5
Crocosmia	3	*Nerine*	3 to 4
Crocus	4 to 5	*Nomocharis*	2
Cyclamen	16 to 18 months	*Ornithogalum*	3
Cypella	5 to 6	*Oxalis*	2 to 3
Cyrtanthus	4 to 5	*Ranunculus*	3
Dierama	18 to 20 months	*Romulea*	2 to 3
Dipcadi	2 to 3	*Scilla*	5
Disporum	3 to 4	*Tigridia*	5
Drimia	5	*Trillium*	5 to 6
Endymion	2 to 3	*Tulipa*	4
Eranthis	4	*Watsonia*	3 to 4

Index

Index